THE DAYS GROW SHORT

Also by Ronald Sanders

THE DAYS GROW SHORT

The Life and Music
of Kurt Weill

RONALD SANDERS

Holt, Rinehart and Winston   New York

Library of Congress Cataloging in Publication Data.
Sanders, Ronald.
The days grow short.
Bibliography: p.
Includes index.
1. Weill, Kurt, 1900–1950. 2. Composers—Biography.
I. Title.
ML410.W395S2   782.8'1'0924 [B]   79–17331
ISBN: 0–03–019411–3

FIRST EDITION
Designer: Joy Chu
Printed in the United States of America
1   3   5   7   9   10   8   6   4   2

Grateful acknowledgment is made for use of the following:

Lyrics from "September Song" from the show *Knickerbocker
Holiday* by Kurt Weill & Maxwell Anderson. Copyright 1938
by DeSylva, Brown & Henderson, Inc. Copyright renewed,
assigned to Chappell & Co., Inc. International copyright
secured. ALL RIGHTS RESERVED. Used by permission.

Passages from Maurice Abravanel's article "Maurice Abravanel
Remembers Kurt Weill" from *High Fidelity*, July 1978. Used by
permission.

Lyrics from "A Bird of Passage" from the musical tragedy *Lost
in the Stars* by Kurt Weill & Maxwell Anderson. Copyright
1946 by Chappell & Co., Inc. Copyright renewed. International copyright secured. ALL RIGHTS RESERVED. Used by
permission.

From *In The Twenties: The Diaries of Harry Kessler*. Copyright ©
1971 by Weidenfeld & Nicolson Ltd., London. Reprinted by
permission of Holt, Rinehart and Winston, Publishers.

Wer viel wagt, gewinnt oft viel!
Komm, du schönes Glockenspiel,
Lass die Glöckchen klingen, klingen,
Dass die Ohren ihnen singen!

Who dares much, oft wins a good deal!
Come, you lovely glockenspiel,
Set your bells to ringing, ringing,
Make their ears fill up with singing!

—*The Magic Flute*

CONTENTS

Sixteen pages of illustrations follow page 236.

THE DAYS GROW SHORT

PROLOGUE
In Search of Kurt Weill

But it's a long, long while
From May to December—
And the days grow short
When you reach September . . .

"September Song" from *Knickerbocker Holiday* may be the first Kurt Weill song I ever heard. I was only six when the show opened in the fall of 1938 and, though I grew up in nearby Brooklyn, I was not to see my first Broadway production for another ten years; but, with the help of radio, songs like this seeped through to me all the same. I also had little awareness of composers, however, so for years I did not know who had written "September Song," any more than I knew what show it had appeared in. It was the same with Kurt Weill's "Speak Low," which seeped through to me after the Broadway opening of *One Touch of Venus* in the fall of 1943.

But my sense of things had begun to improve a little by the time two of Weill's shows, *Lady in the Dark* and *Knickerbocker Holiday*, came around as films the following year. Thanks to the screen version, I now knew what show "September Song" belonged to. As for *Lady in the Dark*, it was one of the few movies I missed—its story of a woman getting psychoanalyzed seemed too "sophisticated" for me—but I heard "The Saga of Jenny" being sung everywhere. This somewhat unconventional song had been the show's nearest thing to a conventional hit (indeed, it was the only

1

song in the show that survived the journey to Hollywood intact), and since it was done in the movie by Ginger Rogers, a fan like me knew exactly where it came from. But I still did not know who wrote it, nor that it was by the same composer who did "September Song."

Perhaps the slight foreignness of his name was the reason it resisted my consciousness, just as it apparently resisted that of many others.* These songs were, after all, thoroughly American, even though there was something unique and classy about them. On the other hand, its European sound may have been the very reason why the name began to impress itself upon me toward the end of my high school years, when I was becoming a bit "intellectual," and when Weill's shows were emerging decisively as the intellectual ones of the Broadway musical theater. In 1947 I had been vaguely aware of *Street Scene*, Weill's "Broadway opera" based on the Elmer Rice play of the same name; but the opening of his *Lost in the Stars* in the fall of 1949 and his death the following spring were clear-cut events for me. Alan Paton's *Cry, the Beloved Country*, upon which this musical play was based, already ranked as a classic among my schoolmates, and the fact that Maxwell Anderson had adapted it for the stage gave the play the same status for us, sight unseen—and sight unseen is what it remained to me, for whom an excursion to Broadway still was rare. I heard some of the music, though, and was impressed by a dignity I associated more with opera than with Broadway shows. For this the composer's foreign name seemed right—in fact, I did not yet realize that he was the same man who had done those very "American" shows, *Knickerbocker Holiday*, *Lady in the Dark*, and *One Touch of Venus*.

But though I knew Weill had come from Germany, I did not at that time know anything of *The Threepenny Opera* or the other works he had composed while still there. In fact, I had never even heard of Bertolt Brecht, and though his name subsequently became familiar to me during my college years, I still had not read or seen any of his plays by the time I finished in 1953. It was during the next two years, while I was doing army service in Colorado, that all this began to change for me and for many others. In the spring of 1954, Marc Blitzstein's version of Brecht and Weill's *The Threepenny Opera* opened at the Theatre de Lys in Greenwich Village and did so well that it returned there indefinitely after its first

---

* I still find people pronouncing it "Kurt Weel" when they see it in print. "Wile" would be a correct American pronunciation, or "Vile" for those who prefer to retain the flavor of its German origin.

scheduled short run. It then lasted longer than the war that had destroyed the world from which it came, and by the time I got to see it in the fall of 1961, it was surrounded by something of a legend, which featured Brecht and Weill among the prominent representatives of a sleazy, angry Berlin of pre-Hitler days. Another one of the legend's central figures was Lotte Lenya, Weill's widow, who had been with the Blitzstein revival at the start of its run in the very role of Jenny the prostitute that she had created in Berlin in 1928. She had since done a few significant recordings: in particular, her *Berlin Theatre Songs by Kurt Weill* was something all my friends seemed to have, and eventually I had it, too.

One could say that a vision of the Berlin of the twenties and earliest thirties had now become a fad, and *The Threepenny Opera* was rivaled only by Christopher Isherwood's *Berlin Stories*—particularly as selected and refracted through John Van Druten's stage adaptation, *I Am a Camera*—as a principal source for it. On the most popular level, all the currents seemed to lead to *Cabaret*, first as a Broadway musical with Miss Lenya in a featured role, then as a movie. Among the intellectuals, Brecht was now all the rage, and I for one read him eagerly and thought him to be one of the definitive literary spokesmen for the twentieth century. For me and others, Brecht was what counted, and Weill's distinction rested in having been his apt collaborator for a time. I occasionally remembered the Broadway Weill, but he hardly seemed to matter anymore.

Since then my heart has made a pilgrimage back to old Broadway, but it probably still is the case that in the United States in general, as in the world at large, the German Kurt Weill—or rather, Weill the Brecht collaborator—is now more popular than the American one. This is even more ironic than meets the eye, since in his later years Weill wanted very much to be only an American—so much so that he was generally not inclined to seek revivals of his German works in this country, balked at Brecht's show of interest in renewing the collaboration during World War II, and once wrote a letter of protest to *Life* magazine because he had been referred to on its pages as a "German" composer. And indeed, the audiences who went to his Broadway shows did not do so because he was the composer of *The Threepenny Opera*, which had flopped badly in its first New York appearance in 1933, before Weill himself reached these shores. Many among them probably did not make the connection at all, and Weill apparently was satisfied to have it that way.

To be sure, there is a widespread feeling today, especially in Europe, that Weill's American work is best forgotten. The harshest viewpoint

depicts the Broadway Weill as one long sellout to American commercialism. A gentler version is provided by the German musicologist H. H.
Stuckenschmidt, a friend of Weill's from Berlin days, who writes:

> Weill had decided to write "commercial" music. His songs had lost
> their poisonous bite. Neither *Lady in the Dark*, a psycho-analytical
> play with operetta interludes, nor *One Touch of Venus*, nor the
> American opera *Street Scene* nor the American folk opera *Down in the
> Valley*, written for students, have the sharp attack of the works
> written with Brecht. Weill's new collaborators, famous playwrights
> and social critics like Maxwell Anderson and Moss Hart, experienced
> lyric-writers like Gershwin's brother Ira, could not provide the
> element of acid which would have counteracted the sentimental and
> sugary side in Weill's music. Success was dearly bought by loss of
> quality.

These are words that have to be seriously weighed by even the most
ardent enthusiasts of Weill's American work, among whom I count
myself. Except for the first and last sentences—and even the first has an
element of truth in it—and allowing that Stuckenschmidt means "the
sentimental and sugary side" as something that appears occasionally but
not all the time in Weill's American music, his remarks are, in fact,
incontestable (at least with reference to everything after *Johnny Johnson*,
Weill's first American score, which has some of the old bite to it, just as it
still echoes in places with the Berlin sound). The question is simply
whether the Weill of the Brecht collaboration is the sole criterion to be
held up against the rest of his career. Indeed, the question boils down even
further, since Weill did a few things with Brecht, such as *Der Jasager* ("He
Who Says Yes") and *The Lindbergh Flight*, that have little or none of the
acid to which Stuckenschmidt refers. Should four of his works, then—*The
Threepenny Opera*, *Happy End*, and the two *Mahagonnys*—be made into a
stick with which to beat all Weill's subsequent efforts to do something
different?

For there are even a few more Kurt Weills than the ones I have talked
about so far. From the standpoint of national identity alone, there have
been not only a German and an American Weill, but also briefly a French
one (he lived outside Paris from 1933 to 1935), and even more briefly an
English one (he did a London show in the summer of 1935); and in each
case he managed to write some music that sounds typical of the host
country. He also wrote "Jewish" music—which is not entirely surprising,

since he was the son of a cantor. But the plane of national or ethnic identity is only one of those on which the great variety of his work has manifested itself. His compositions include not only scores spanning all the nuances of musical theater from opera to musical comedy, but concert pieces as well: indeed, there was a time—let us say the summer of 1925—when he was already one of the bright lights of the new generation of German composers but had not presented to the public a single stage work other than a little-noticed ballet for children. Foremost among the compositions he was then known for by a small circle of admirers of avant-garde music were a string quartet, a cycle of songs based on medieval poems, and a violin concerto.

There then followed a series of notable transformations. In another two years, Weill had become known as a composer of one-act operas, which reached a wider audience than his concert pieces did even though they continued to be rather "modern" and free in their tonality. They even were beginning to incorporate jazz idioms, but they still were opera in the strict sense of the term and not the unique distillation, hinted at in that summer of 1927 by the so-called *Little Mahagonny*,* which was to emerge as *The Threepenny Opera* only a year later and achieve enormous popular success. Each of these leaps into new forms and styles—and there were more besides—was made on German soil within just a few years of one another, and each is in its way no less radical than the one made across the Atlantic into a Broadway vein after 1935. And is the transformation from the style of *Lady in the Dark* to that of *Street Scene* any less astonishing? This is a composer who cannot easily be pinned down to any one of his phases.

Indeed, it is tempting to ask: which of all these is the "real" Kurt Weill? There are those who will reply that the only real Weill was a chameleon, who took on with remarkable facility the coloration of wherever and with whomever he happened to be working. They will add that he was simply very lucky to have been colored by Brecht for a time, after which, for obvious reasons, he was never so good again. (It is arguable, by the way, that Brecht also was never so good again.) But, for those who care to listen, there are in fact consistencies of tone and theme in Weill's music that some find almost unique among twentieth-century composers, and that cause almost any fair-sized selection from his work to be unmistakably related to the rest. Furthermore, when one listens to an

---

* This is not the correct title of the work, though it is the one most widely used. See chapter 7.

adequate number of his works in the order in which they were written, the internal lines of development become clear. Like any composer, Weill picked up many sounds from various places along the way, including Bertolt Brecht's guitar, but like the gifted artist he was, he made all of them his own.

Another negative response will associate the "real" Weill with a seemingly unwavering progress into more and more popular—and hence more and more lucrative—styles and forms and see this as the reason for a presumed decline on American soil. But the truth of the matter is that Weill got into relatively "noncommercial" projects just as often as he got into relatively "commercial" ones, in the United States as well as in Germany, because though he wanted to make a living at his art, like Brecht and many other worthy creators besides, he was at all times guided by an artistic ideal as well. To be sure, this ideal included the goal of popularity, but it did so on philosophical as well as practical grounds; and the authors of *The Threepenny Opera* had, in their way, sought to be popular every bit as much as the authors of *Lady in the Dark* had. Weill believed that music had lost much of its vitality in his own time, and that one reason for this was the loss of the kind of spontaneous and down-to-earth relationship between composer and audience that, for example, Mozart had enjoyed. Weill, who revered Mozart, wanted to restore that relationship as best he could, and when he came to America as a refugee from Hitler, he regarded Broadway as the best place to do it: for him this was the proper middle course between what he generally considered to be the lifeless academicism of the opera house and the extreme commercialism of Hollywood.

A Mozart of Broadway? This is a notion that makes no sense at all to those who adhere to some of the conventional distinctions of our time, but Kurt Weill was an artist determined to do away with such distinctions. As he once told an American interviewer: "I have never acknowledged the difference between 'serious' music and 'light' music. There is only good music and bad music." These words come as close as any to summing up the "real" Kurt Weill: they help to explain and bind together the seemingly infinite variety of his works, and also point up the reason that he is perhaps—whether a "great" composer or not—one of the significant artists of this century. This gift from Germany to America was in various ways a great crosser of frontiers.

And now let us have his story.

Two Cornerstones

Tuesday, February 18, 1908, was an important day for Cantor Albert Weill and his family, as it was for the whole Jewish community of Dessau; for it was the occasion, in the glowing words of one local newspaper, of "the ceremonial dedication of its magnificent new synagogue."

The event was a culmination of more than two hundred years of Jewish history in this city of some fifty thousand inhabitants, seat of the small Duchy of Anhalt, that stood about sixty miles southwest of Berlin at the confluence of the rivers Mulde and Elbe. The ruling family here had not always had the most harmonious relations with its Jewish subjects, who had not been admitted to Dessau as a community until 1672; nevertheless, they had often emerged as models for all of German Jewry. Living in their midst from 1686 to his death in 1729, Moses Benjamin Wulff made himself one of the most prominent of the "court Jews" in that era when German princes often placed their financial and even administrative affairs into the hands of wealthy Jewish advisers. And only a few days after Wulff died, Dessau saw the birth of a child who was to become one of the greatest figures in German-Jewish history, Moses Mendelssohn. A friend of Gotthold Ephraim Lessing and esteemed by Immanuel Kant, Mendelssohn was both a philosopher and a seeker of reconciliation between Jewish traditions and the European culture of the Enlightenment, serving as inspiration for the title character of Lessing's play *Nathan the Wise*.

One result of the example Mendelssohn provided for the generation that followed him was the Reform movement in German Judaism, within which his native Dessau proved to be an important center for the moderate approach. It was here that a pamphlet was published in 1818, the *Or Nogah* ("Bright Light") of Eliezer Libermann, in which an attempt was made to reconcile some of the liturgical innovations of the Reform with the requirements of Jewish Law. Certain innovations violated the Law, such as the efforts to change the Sabbath from Saturday to Sunday and to dispense with the wearing of head coverings during services, but others, though they irritated the sensibilities of strict traditionalists, were challenges merely to custom, such as the introduction into the service of organs, choirs, sermons, occasional prayers in German rather than Hebrew, and, in general, an atmosphere of decorum inspired by the Christian churches. Ultimately, most of the Jewish communities of Germany found a middle way between modernization and respect for the Law, and it seems characteristic of Dessau that it should have produced at least one eminent spokesman for this balance. The spirit of the eighteenth century was ever to look down upon this city, and upon its Jews, as if through the eyes of the statue of Moses Mendelssohn that eventually was erected in one of the town squares.

Not that there was anything but a vigorous entry into the centuries that followed. During the nineteenth century, which for the Jews of Germany was a time of struggle and final victory in the quest for complete civil and political equality with other Germans, the Dessau community played its part by reviving in a new and effective form one of its old traditions, that of the court Jew. In 1817, during the Napoleonic era—which had its Jewish counterpart in the rise of the house of Rothschild—a Jewish merchant named J. H. Cohn settled in Dessau and founded a banking firm. It prospered, and Moritz Cohn, the founder's son, rose to become the chief financier of Prince Wilhelm of Prussia. This was a most felicitous alliance, for Wilhelm was not only to become king but also to be crowned German Emperor in 1871, and to reward his financial adviser with the title of Baron Moritz von Cohn. In the meantime, the Jews of the Empire that was coming into being under Wilhelm and his Chancellor, Otto von Bismarck, won complete civil equality by 1869, an event toward which the influence of the future Baron Moritz von Cohn assuredly played its part.

But, ironically, the presence of the Baron does not seem to have been an unmixed blessing for the Jews of Dessau. The Dukes of Anhalt proved to be somewhat resistant to the rights and advancement of Jews in their resident city, both before and after the Emancipation. They had inherited a strong tradition of paternalism from their illustrious ancestor, Leopold Frederick Franz—known fondly for all time as "Father Franz"—who reigned from 1759 to 1817, and this applied to the Jews as to other matters. For a good part of the nineteenth century, the center of Jewish life in Dessau was a school, founded by Father Franz and called the *Franzschule* in his honor, that was supported by the duchy. At times serving in lieu of both synagogue and rabbi, the school, though respected throughout Europe, was a "company union" so to speak, and the threat of more independent Jewish institutions posed by the Emancipation and by the presence of the Baron von Cohn was clearly at variance with the tradition it represented. Indeed, the Empire itself, with which the rising Jewish middle classes of Germany tended to identify, was a threat to the future of small principalities like Anhalt, and the Dukes were uneasy with all of its manifestations. They certainly could not have been happy with a Jewish baron in their midst. The result was a certain instability in Dessau Jewish life even after 1869. In that year, there had been some five hundred Jews living in Dessau among a total population of fifteen thousand—a sizable proportion, and larger than the Catholic population of the city—but by 1895 the figure was the same, even though the general population was expanding rapidly. During this same period, the Jewish community leadership was in a chaotic state: rabbis succeeded one another in rapid succession, and at times the post fell vacant.

Things changed rapidly, however, with the arrival of the new century. The Baron von Cohn died in 1900, and the family banking firm was taken over by his daughter, the Baroness Julie von Cohn-Oppenheim, who had herself married into a wealthy German-Jewish family, and who now became the chief benefactor of the Dessau Jewish community. She provided in the name of her local coreligionists a gentler image than that of her father, at a time when a new generation of provincial regimes like that of Anhalt were learning to live in harmony with a new generation of imperial rule under Wilhelm II. The transformation was completed when the forward-looking, liberal-minded young Frederick II succeeded to the ducal throne of Anhalt in 1903 and soon showed a solicitousness toward the Jewish communities of his duchy that was to characterize the fifteen years of his reign. The Jewish population of Dessau began to grow, and the new stability was manifested in the rabbinate: Dr. Isidor Walter, who became rabbi of the city and of all Anhalt in 1900, was in fact to remain in the post more than three decades.

Unfortunately, the Baroness died in the very year that the new duke came into power, only three years after the death of her father. But even this sad event produced benefits for the Jews of Dessau, for she left a large legacy that provided for the building of a new synagogue. "In view of the fact that the number of Jews in Dessau was growing," wrote the authors of the pamphlet produced for the dedication ceremonies, "and that in particular on the High Holy Days the [old] synagogue was proving to be too small, the general feeling arose that a new house of worship should be erected." The duchy, furthermore, took this opportunity to show its own generosity, and added a small grant to the Baroness Julie von Cohn-Oppenheim Fund.

A site was purchased at the intersection of Stein and Askanische streets, in a residential neighborhood a few minutes from the busy center of town, and the cornerstone was laid in May 1906. Work proceeded rapidly, and by the beginning of 1908 the great, domed, eclectic structure was ready for use. "The exterior architecture can be called Romanesque," explains the commemorative pamphlet with special reference to its cathedrallike windows and porticoes rather than to its indefinable overall shape. "The interior adds Byzantine motifs, and perhaps also ancient Jewish ones, which make the most dazzling impression. . . . The sonorous organ completes the picture. The acoustics are very good in the bright, beautifully modeled sanctuary." Allowing for its faintly Oriental, Jewish-ecclesiastical flavor, the building really was a characteristic monument of the Wilhelminian era, meant to last forever—although it was in fact only to last thirty years, to be destroyed in the Nazi-led riots that began on November 9, 1938, the *Kristallnacht*. It was characteristic of the simultaneous growth of Dessau itself: only seven years before, another of the city's major new buildings, the large town hall, had been dedicated. Emerging into the twentieth century as an important industrial center, primarily for building materials of various sorts, Dessau was already showing the traits that would make it the chosen site of the Bauhaus in the 1920s, and of the Fokker aircraft works in the Hitler period—and hence the target of heavy Allied bombing in World War II.

But something of the old benign provincialism of the eighteenth-century *Kleinstaaterei* at its best was still around to show itself in Dessau at the dedication ceremonies of the new synagogue. "The beginning of the ceremony was set for twelve noon," continues our account. "The participants began to assemble in the new house of worship half an hour earlier." Honored Christian guests from the top ranks of Dessau's business, political, and artistic communities took their places in the front row of benches, and a few minutes before noon "the wonderful house of worship was full. Only a section in the left-hand gallery, nearest to the Holy of Holies, was still unoccupied; this was reserved for the highest-ranking persons, who at last entered the synagogue on the dot of twelve. . . . It was then that His Highness the Duke appeared, followed by Her Ducal Highness the Duchess, Her Highness the Duchess-Mother, Their Highnesses Prince and Princess Edward, His Highness Prince Aribert, and Her Highness Princess Antoinette Anna, among others. Meanwhile the organ, at which the Court Organist Professor Richard Bartmuss sat for this occasion, began a softly played prelude, which led into the first choral selection. At the prayer-leader's stand appeared Cantor Weill, who led the first part of the service singing responsively with the chorus. It was clear that the chorus had been expanded for the occasion; and alongside the sonorous organ, a choir of wind instruments from the Ducal Court Chapel gave added weight and sacred force to the singing and cantillations."

But let us now break into the proceedings and take a closer look at the cantor who stood high before this remarkable assemblage, mingling his own tones with those of some of the finest instrumentalists of a city that also happened to be well known for its musical achievements. The forty-one-year-old Albert Weill was short of stature and not of imposing appearance, but his small, dark, neatly clipped beard and ecclesiastical robe brought out a look of handsome piety in him as he went about the performance of his liturgical functions. Upon closer examination of his wide face, with its heavy-lidded eyes that gave it a slightly Oriental, distinctly Jewish cast, one could have observed that the look of cantorial solemnity was compromised by a slight playfulness in his smile. There was a charm, even a softness, at the center of his dignified look that perhaps revealed something about his life in general. For it must be said that, although he had been one of the two cantors of the Dessau Jewish community since 1898 and, after Rabbi Walter himself, second in charge of its religious school, this may have been a position not quite commensurate with his heritage as a scion of one of Germany's most distinguished rabbinical families.

According to family genealogists, the founder of the Weill line was one Juda, who was born in 1360 in a hamlet not far from Stuttgart called Weil der Stadt, from which he took his name. Nothing more is known about him, but it is clearly established that his son Jacob Weil, who was born in about 1390, was ordained a rabbi in Nuremberg in 1427, and that he added greatly to the distinction of the family line by marrying a descendant of Rabbi Meir of Rothenburg. One of the eminent Talmudic authorities of medieval Germany, Rabbi Meir, born in 1220, had also been a poet and a martyr. When a great quantity of Jewish books was committed to the flames in Paris in about 1242 at the instigation of Pope Gregory IX, Meir composed an elegy that is still chanted in the synagogues; and when he tried to lead a group of persecuted German Jews to Palestine in 1286, he was imprisoned by order of the Emperor, and he died in captivity seven years later. From the time that it mingled its own seed with that of Rabbi Meir, the Weill family, which remained concentrated in the south of Germany (although there also eventually were branches in Holland and France), had rabbis in almost every generation—and priests and ministers as well, since there was one branch that accepted conversion in the seventeenth century.

Albert Weill, who was born in 1867 in Kippenheim in the Grand Duchy of Baden—the fifth and next-to-last child of the merchant Nathan Weill and his wife, the former Jeanette Hochstetter—stemmed from a branch of the family that seemed to be inclined to commerce and to the cantorial calling; but there are signs that he had ambitions as a young man to make contributions worthy of his descent from a line of great rabbis. When he was twenty-six years old and still a bachelor—by then holding a post as cantor in the small town of Eichstätt in Bavaria—he published a volume of his own compositions, which he called in Hebrew and in German, *Kol Avraham: Synagogen-Gesänge für Cantor und Männerchor* ("The Voice of Abraham: Synagogue Songs for Cantor and Male Chorus").

For the better part of a century, the cantors of Germany had, like the rabbis, been seeking legitimate ways to modernize their part of the service. The result was a certain marked tendency toward the German tradition of Lutheran hymn and oratorio. It seems significant that Moses Mendelssohn's grandson Felix, himself a synthesis of Jewish and Lutheran traditions and a composer of numerous sacred oratorios, once did a Psalm setting commissioned by the Reform Temple of Hamburg. By the last decade of the nineteenth century, the chief cantors of the two German-speaking capitals of Europe, Salomon Sulzer of Vienna and Louis Lewandowski of Berlin, had established a style that decidedly repudiated the emotional, often sob-ridden flourishes of the tradition of cantorial singing firmly ensconced in Eastern Europe, in favor of a sound more in harmony with the German-Christian environment. This included the introduction both of organ and of chorus, two elements that were anathema to the synagogues of Eastern Europe, even though the apologists for Reform had done their best to demonstrate that there were no texts that banned them in the body of Jewish Law.

Albert Weill's compositions reflect the careful route of his predecessors in Germany between tradition and modernity; they are, according to an eminent authority on Jewish sacred music, "orthodox and colorless, in the *juste milieu* of the post-Sulzer and post-Lewandowski style." Nevertheless, there are aspects to his book that may well detain us. Particularly interesting is his commitment, in this volume, to the use of the male rather than the mixed chorus, which he justifies in his introduction with these words:

> Worthy of recognition as are the many and varied productions in the realm of song for mixed chorus, and much as the Jewish liturgy has thus far unquestionably gained in ceremony and devotion by the introduction of the mixed chorus into the synagogue, it must nevertheless be conceded that the establishing of such a chorus entails considerable difficulties in many congregations, partly on religious grounds, and partly owing to the particular conditions in each place.
>
> The stability of a mixed chorus is questionable in most cases, as experience has frequently taught; with the result that it is difficult to maintain a good level for the service, and that the cantor's best efforts, to his chagrin, are often in vain.
>
> In the author's view, however, the situation is altered by the introduction of a male chorus. For one thing, this means greater stability in the chorus' membership; for another, there are no misgivings about it among those of more orthodox inclinations. And this type of chorus is at least comparable to the mixed chorus in its solemn, devotion-inspiring character.

A careful formulation, this, striking a nice balance not only between tradition and modernity—true to the spirit of the Dessau congregation to which its author was soon to be called—but also between practical and religious considerations. The main issue surely is the liturgical one: strong traditionalists, though still resistant to the presence of any chorus at all, were at least placated when there were no women in the group standing before the congregation. But the author also makes no effort to conceal his view that, religious sensibility aside, a chorus with no women in it would simply bring the cantor greater peace of mind than one that included them. The implication is that a woman's attendance at rehearsals and services was not as likely to be regular as a man's. Given the strenuous conditions of bourgeois wifehood and motherhood in the Germany of 1893, this probably had some truth to it; but the striking thing is Cantor Weill's readiness to bring it out in a published presentation of his accomplishments as a liturgical composer. This was a man who did not eschew everyday realities, under any circumstances; perhaps he even had scores to settle.

In any case, the book did not make much of a stir: noteworthy is the fact that it was a *mixed* chorus that stood before Cantor Weill on the occasion of the Dessau synagogue dedication in 1908. To make matters worse, he had by then married into a family that, though not of such ancient distinction as his own, was nevertheless now achieving greater eminence in Jewish matters. It was on March 9, 1897, at the age of thirty, that he had married the twenty-five-year-old Emma Ackermann of Wiesloch. The daughter of very pious parents, Emma had a brother who, though only four years older than she, had already made a considerable reputation for himself by the time of her marriage, both in the rabbinical field and in that of cantorial music. Rabbi Aaron Ackermann had published his own volume of synagogue songs in 1892, and in 1896 an essay of his on the history of cantorial singing had appeared as part of a distinguished three-volume collection of studies on Jewish literature. Both works display the possibility of a gap between himself and his future brother-in-law. The songs in his 1892 volume are all for solo voice, and the history, which does not mention Albert Weill, takes a position somewhat opposed to the trend toward choral singing in the German-Jewish liturgy of that day. In general, the Ackermanns seem to have been firmer traditionalists than the Weills, and if an atmosphere of common interest in synagogue music had been part of the attraction between Albert and Emma to begin with, there also evidently were elements in it that were likely to produce tension.

There may well have been something of a contest for a time between the brothers-in-law, but it surely was over by 1908. By then, Aaron Ackermann held the important post of rabbi of the Jewish community in Brandenburg near Berlin, edited a prominent Jewish newspaper, and had published several volumes of history and homiletics in addition to his continuing stream of cantorial studies and compositions. Albert Weill, if less illustrious, was what we have seen him to be, a man not without talent and a place in the world—a place that even occasionally shone with its moments of glory, as on that Sabbath day in February that we have glimpsed. Furthermore, whereas Rabbi Ackermann was childless, Cantor

Weill was the father of four children among whom there were some remarkable qualities. The eldest, Nathan, had been born on January 8, 1898. The others followed in rapid succession: Hans Jakob, born January 14, 1899; Kurt Julian, born March 2, 1900; and then a girl at last, Ruth, born October 6, 1901. These were perhaps already more children than the income of a provincial cantor and Hebrew schoolteacher could bear, and this branch of the new Weill generation thereupon ceased to proliferate. By 1908 all three boys had begun to show considerable talent at the family piano, especially young Kurt; and though this may not have been entirely surprising in the children of a cantor, it was the Ackermann family's claim to being the source of such musicianship that the boys themselves were to endorse more and more as the years went by.

But perhaps our imaginations can summon up a final glimpse of the children at the synagogue dedication ceremony, ages six through ten, lined up alongside their mother on a bench with their feet barely reaching the floor or not at all—for they were all, except for young Hans, well under average height—listening to their father with what may have been one of the last moments of rapturous regard he was to win from them. In particular, we try to imagine how all that music and dramatic ceremony penetrated the eyes and ears of little Kurt, not quite eight years old, who was one day to be a figure of some significance in the music and theater of the century that had entered the world in the same year he did.

Did the young Kurt Weill ever dream of becoming a cantor himself? Very likely—perhaps even in this moment in 1908; his father certainly wanted it for him. But any such idea seems to have vanished completely from the boy's mind before another three years had gone by—during which time, as if by a magical transformation, the theater came to replace the synagogue as the framework within which he underwent his most stirring experiences of music, drama, and spectacle. Nor was the theater of his childhood any less exalted a place than synagogue or church in this city about which a local historian had written in the year of Kurt's birth: "The history of the theatrical and musical life of Dessau is inextricably bound up with that of the princely house of Anhalt." Indeed, the Ducal Court Theater, Dessau's shrine of both opera and drama, stood directly across the Kavalierstrasse from the palace of the ruling family that had built it; and Kurt later recalled of the reigning Duke Frederick II that "every morning between 10 and 11 he drove out of the palace courtyard and across the square, to attend rehearsals of the local theater which presented plays and operas under his patronage."

The Ducal Court Theater was another Dessau institution within which the memory of the eighteenth century lingered amid the emerging gigantism of the Wilhelminian era. Its history began in 1765 with Father Franz, who, having just fought in the Seven Years War alongside Frederick the Great, discovered an interest in music within himself and traveled to Italy to satisfy it. Accompanying him on the journey was a young violinist and composer named Friedrich Wilhelm Rust, the son of a magistrate from the town of Wörlitz, near Dessau. In those days, princely patronage was the foundation upon which good music was built, and after seeing the way it was done in the musical strongholds of the south, Franz and his companion returned home to build such a foundation for themselves. Rust established an ensemble of twelve string players and a few wind instrumentalists at the Court Chapel—the ancestor of the group that performed at the synagogue dedication in February 1908—and added a chorus two years later. Soon he was staging operas as well as oratorios, in an amphitheater that had been built for the purpose in an open field near the palace.

"But in that era of the young Goethe," the local historian adds, "the musical performances were followed soon enough by dramatic ones," and the works of Shakespeare as well as of Goethe and Schiller became regular fare at the amphitheater alongside the operas of Mozart and Ditters von Dittersdorf. Nowadays—outside of Germany, at least—we do not often see opera and spoken drama performed alternately on the same stage, but we should bear in mind that the dividing line between these two art forms never was so clear in Germany, least of all in the days when Goethe himself hoped to see his *Faust* done as an opera, and when the preeminent native operatic form was the *Singspiel* (literally, "singing-play"). A popular form of comic theater that interspersed songs—originally just folk tunes—among the spoken dialogue, the *Singspiel* was, among other things, a means of poking fun at the solemn, highly formalized conventions of Italian opera. As such, one of its direct sources of inspiration was the English ballad opera of the eighteenth century—although it may be significant that the most famous of these, *The Beggar's Opera* of John Gay, had its musical passages transcribed and assembled by a German, Johann Pepusch: apparently, this type of musical theater represented at least one fleeting moment when the German and Anglo-Saxon spirits could come together in a mood of common irreverence during an era dominated by Romance proprieties. Not that the *Singspiel* couldn't attain an exaltation of its own, at least in the hands of a genius; for the greatest of them, Mozart's *The Magic Flute*, is also one of the greatest of all operas.

The Magic Flute was among the works being regularly performed in the amphitheater when, shortly after the death of Friedrich Wilhelm Rust in 1796, Father Franz observed that it was "scarcely adequate space for the performances," in the words of the historian, "and so decided to erect a theater building." To this end, "the old post office in the Kavalierstrasse was bought along with seven adjacent houses on the street behind it (Wallstrasse today), and by the beginning of 1798 it was possible to lay the cornerstone of the new Court Theater. By the end of that year the new house, one of the largest and most beautiful of its day, was given over to its destined purpose." The theater's first *Intendant*, or manager—a post that had been sought by the celebrated playwright August von Kotzebue among others—was Karl August von Lichtenstein, a composer of talent; but after two years its management was taken over directly by Father Franz, who held it through all the shocks of the Napoleonic wars until his death in 1817.

The Ducal Court Theater of Dessau had now been released by its creator to face the nineteenth century on its own, and at first it did well. Under the new Duke Leopold Frederick the post of *Intendant* was revived, and a separate post of music director was created, since the reason Lichtenstein had failed after two years was his inability to handle both the musical and the business affairs of the theater. The latter post was given to Friedrich Schneider, the composer of an oratorio that was then very popular, *Das Weltgericht* ("The Last Judgment"). Schneider founded a music academy in Dessau that became famous throughout Germany and lasted until his death in 1853. The new Duke also rebuilt the theater, decorating it with a portico supported by columns in the neoclassical style, and adding a concert hall upstairs over the main auditorium, at which Paganini gave a recital when it was opened in 1829. The building served as a home for the best concert music, opera, and drama of that bright day when early romanticism mingled with the lingering classical spirit, until disaster finally struck. On March 7, 1855, a fire broke out, and it burned to the ground.

This was the end of an era. Not that the theater remained in ruins for long: the irrepressible Duke Leopold Frederick, now close to the end of the fourth decade of his reign, had it so swiftly rebuilt that it was able to reopen its doors only a little more than a year and a half after the fire, on October 27, 1856. But there was a change in the air, signaled by the more massive look of the rebuilt portico with its giant Corinthian columns jutting out onto the street, and by the work performed on the night of the reopening, Giacomo Meyerbeer's *Robert le Diable*, which was a grand

opera. "With the entry into the new house," our historian proudly
proclaims, "begins the second epoch of the hundred-year history of the
Court Theater, an epoch which not only did not fall short of the first in
artistic successes, but even exceeded it." Certainly the new epoch
exceeded the old in the length and density of its musical evenings, for not
long after Meyerbeer came Wagner. *Tannhäuser* had its first performance
at the Ducal Court Theater on May 20, 1857; in another ten years, the
Wagnerian operas began to be presented there with such frequency that
by the time the composer himself arrived for a visit on March 8, 1872, it
had become something of a shrine for his works, "a North German
Bayreuth," as another of its historians put it.

From the time of Wagner's visit, wrote this second historian in 1914,
"the Court Theater has remained a good Wagnerian one. For years now,
its splendid operatic stage has had performances of the poet-composer's
works in masterful, model presentations. . . . The Duke has dedicated
himself to long and painstaking efforts in behalf of Wagner's art, and as
art's first servant, has striven to have Wagner's requirements carried out to
the very last note. Yet all his rich knowledge of Wagner's genius and of the
wonders of the composer's creations—which restored to opera the highest
poetic and musical unity of the lost art of music-drama—and all his
experience in the field of theater management . . . retire willingly and
discreetly into the background when the first melancholy, troubling notes
of the Prelude to *Tristan and Isolde* sound forth, or when the C major of the
Meistersinger theme seems to bring sunlight into the darkened theater, or
when the Rhinemaidens swim joyously shouting around the rock of
glimmering Rhinegold. . . . The words of the Landgrave Hermann in
Wagner's *Tannhäuser*—'Gracious art, it now becomes reality'—can stand
as the motto for the cultural activities of the Anhalt princes."

Years later, Kurt Weill was to recall for a newspaper interviewer that the
operatic programs at the Ducal Court Theater "were overwhelmingly
Wagner," a composer, he added, toward whom he had "nourished
considerable antipathy" for a long time. The mature composer was
certainly to find his true nature reflected more in the *Singspiel* than in the
Wagnerian music-drama, but it is not likely that he felt this way as a boy,
when many of the greatest living musicians were still largely under
Wagner's spell. To be sure, Cantor Weill, a musical conservative, may not
have wholly approved of the lush, sensual, chromatic, and, worst of all,
anti-Semitic Wagner, but this would surely have been all the more
provocation for Kurt to like him.

There was an easygoing atmosphere in the Weill home, an apartment in the residential complex that had been built alongside the synagogue to house its officials; the informality of relations that prevailed there between parents and children was not unlike that of a typical American family today, but surprising in a German bourgeois household of the early 1900s, especially that of an ecclesiastic. There was perhaps the slightest touch of the bohemian in Cantor Weill—a trait inherited from his mother, Jeanette, who was somewhat musical and artistic—but the underside of this was an inclination on the part of his children, sharpening as they grew older, not to take him too seriously. This was especially true of Kurt, who submitted to his few years of Hebrew and religious studies under Cantor Weill's tutelage just as his brothers and sister did, but who then went on to become the least pious and Jewish-minded among them, even as he emerged as musically the most precocious. Indeed, the more that music became the issue, the more Kurt could assert his independence of his father, whose musical abilities and judgments he grew early to regard as quite inferior to his own. In this respect he was more Ackermann than Weill, despite his relative lack of Jewish piety, and in general very much his mother's son. For if Emma Weill was the stronger of the two parents, the one who most forcefully impressed her influence upon the children, she was especially so with the boy she regarded as her genius. She had seen him as her special one virtually from the moment he was born and it was as much in deference to ambition as to her love for French literature that she had given him his middle name in honor of the hero of *The Red and the Black*. And since she was relatively unmusical amid all the musically gifted men who surrounded her life, Kurt's talent was left by her to develop untrammeled and in a kind of free moral assault upon his father. But in other respects, Emma's dominance was restricting: it was she, for example, who almost invariably disapproved of Kurt's girlfriends. Cantor Weill, on the other hand, seemed to like them all.

By the time Kurt was twelve years old, his life had become entirely centered upon music, mainly within the shadow of the Ducal Court Theater. He had been playing the piano for a number of years, and though his pianism was to become notoriously sloppy in the days when composition would be the chief outlet for his musical energies, it was good enough at this time to attract the attention of Duke Frederick's musical entourage and win him some distinguished assignments. For one thing, he occasionally was hired to be a rehearsal pianist for the opera singers at the Court Theater; for another, he was retained to give lessons to the Duke's youngest daughter, Princess Antoinette Anna. The Duke took a special interest in Kurt's musical development, and granted him and his brothers, who also were gifted in music, free entry to the theater. It has been said that the Duke always willingly showed a special respect for Cantor and Mrs. Weill on account of their three gifted sons: there seems to have been no sign of any resentment in his nature toward whatever demonstrations of special abilities were given by his Jewish subjects. "On occasion," wrote the author of a newspaper interview with Weill many years later, Kurt "was asked to accompany a singer at a palace musicale. After the concert he would be given tea and would visit with the children. He remembers vividly one conversation he had with the nephew of the Duke, a child about his own age, who was very curious about the subjects being taught in the public schools. Weill recited the list of things his class was studying. At first the little aristocrat was swamped by it, but he quickly recovered with, 'I have just learned to make the letter *I*.' " Such incidents do not seem to have harmed young Kurt's status in the palace. If he was very impressed with himself as a gift to the nobility from the humbler world in which he had been reared, a *Wunderkind* bearing melodies to which even those of the loftiest station had to give ear, he was given little reason by those around him to reconsider this estimate. It was an outlook that would serve him well in the years to come.

In Times of Tumult and War

 Kurt Weill began to compose at the age of ten or eleven, and his first effort was in the form with which his ears and eyes had become saturated by then: opera. Years later he was to describe the libretto he used as "an old German play about knights and their ladies." This work has not survived; but what does still exist are copies of some individual songs he had written by the time he was fourteen. One, "*Im Volkston*" ("A Folk-Tune"), based on a poem by Arno Holz, shows the young composer working in a traditional vein, seeking to provide the appropriate musical voice for the poet's pseudo-naïve lament about separation from the beloved. In general, young Kurt seems to have been little attracted yet to the dissonant new tonalities then being sounded in German music, which were later to become influential upon him for a time. But we can see the mature Kurt Weill hinted at here, all the same: for it is significant that he was interested in working in a folk vein at the very beginning of his creative life and that he chose one of the founders of German naturalism as his lyricist, so to speak.

An important event occurred in Kurt's life when he was fifteen. In that year, a little-known but respected composer named Albert Bing was appointed associate musical director of the Dessau Court Theater; this was another manifestation of Duke Frederick's tolerance, since Bing was the first Jew ever to hold a high post there. Bing had studied composition in Berlin with Hans Pfitzner, regarded by 1915, along with Richard

Strauss, as one of the two most eminent living German composers and the foremost defender of the musical values of the nineteenth century against the new trends of the day. Bing evidently was a musical conservative, too, and was therefore an appropriate first teacher of composition for the cantor's son who attracted his attention and whom he invited to become his pupil.

This new relationship brought about subtle changes in Kurt's outlook. He was still the young piano prodigy of the Ducal Court: that very December, for example, he performed at a benefit concert in the Palace recital hall, playing a Chopin Prelude and the Third Nocturne from Liszt's *Liebesträume*. But Albert Bing began to persuade him that he should become a composer rather than a performer. Bing also helped make the world of Kurt's intimate personal associations—as distinguished from the rather formal and distant relationships at the Ducal Court—into a wider one than it had been before. Bing's wife was the sister of Carl Sternheim, then one of the newest and brightest lights of expressionist drama, and her presence meant strong intimations, unprecedented for Kurt, of the living reality of creative art. Furthermore, she was only half Jewish; she and her husband, who had nothing to do with the synagogue, represented a more assimilated and cosmopolitan kind of Jewishness than Kurt had hitherto known, and he was drawn to it. The Bings brought him into touch with the family of Julius Schwabe, a well-to-do Jewish businessman of Dessau who had died a few years before, and whose widow and five daughters were, like the Bings, more inclined to seek their religion in music and literature than in ecclesiastical institutions. Two of the Schwabe girls, Käte and Alice, were close in age to Kurt and his brother Hans, and the brothers became frequent visitors at the elegant villa in which they lived, where they happily whiled away many an afternoon in music.

But more somber tones could virtually be heard in the background of their playing, for the European war was already more than a year old. It was in Germany more than in any other country, perhaps, that the four years from 1914 to 1918 became a violent passage from jubilation to despair. "All my friends hope there will be war," wrote the playwright Ernst Toller some years later, summoning up in the present tense his schoolboy feelings of the fall of 1911, when Germany nearly went to war with France and England over their conflicting claims to influence in Morocco. "The teachers tell us that peace breeds softness, but war a race of heroes. We long for adventure, and think that perhaps we shall escape the last year at school; perhaps we shall all be in uniform tomorrow. What a life that would be!"

These were the feelings of a young man who was to become one of the leaders of the antiwar movement by 1917 and a prominent spokesman of the literary left of his generation in the postwar period. But when the fighting began, there was no difference in zeal between the future members of the left and of the right. Toller, a Jew born in 1893 in Posen, in a region with a large Polish population that was then part of Germany and is part of Poland today, grew up experiencing with great sensitivity the contradictions of race and class in society and was already a budding socialist by 1914. But this did not prevent him from eagerly enlisting when the war broke out, protesting his way into uniform over the doubts of the army medical examiner concerning his fitness for duty. Feelings of fear and patriotic enthusiasm mingled within him as he rode to the Alsatian front, and on his first morning there he awoke before daybreak in excited anticipation. In his memoirs he describes how he "got up and wandered about the village, looking at the blackened walls of the shattered houses, stumbling into the shell holes which pitted the streets. The church door was open, and I went in. The dawn showed grayly through the shivered windows and my heavy boots clattered on the stone paving. A soldier was lying before the altar; when I bent over him I saw that he was dead. His head was broken clean open, and a great steel splinter was wedged between the two halves of the skull, from which the brain spilled in a pulpy mass."

But Toller braced himself, and later that very day he participated, as a member of an artillery battery, in fire upon a French patrol. "The French soldiers scattered, rushed for shelter, but not all of them. Some lay dead or wounded.

"'Direct hit—' cried the subaltern.

"The telephonist cheered.

"I cheered."

The cheer soon turned into a cry of despair at the endless days of torn bodies and seared battlegrounds. Erich Maria Remarque later described, in his *All Quiet on the Western Front*, a transition like Toller's from schoolboy enthusiasm to disillusionment amid the horrors of war. "Kantorek gave us long lectures," the novel's narrator says of his schoolmaster, "until the whole of our class went, under his shepherding, to the District Commandant and volunteered. I can see him now, as he used to glare at us through his spectacles and say in a moving voice: 'Won't you join up, Comrades?'" Later, when Kantorek is called up for active duty at last and appears at the front, the grizzled veterans who had once been his wide-eyed pupils jeer at this man who only now is to learn of the horrors he had urged them into. "I see one of them," the narrator says of a Frenchman shot in a barbed wire entanglement, "his face upturned, fall into a wire cradle. His body collapses, his hands remain suspended as though he were praying. Then his body drops clean away and only his hands with the stumps of his arms, shot off, now hang in the wire."

It was above all the horrors of mutilation that dominated the first works of German antiwar literature. Leonhard Frank's *Der Mensch ist gut* ("Man Is Good"), a collection of sketches published in Zurich in 1917, does not even take place at the front. Consisting mainly of a series of portrayals of those who suffered at home as a result of the war, it ends with a horrifyingly graphic description of wounded and mutilated soldiers in a military hospital. Scenes of this sort, which seemed in a way to be translations into reality of the worst nightmares of expressionism, branded themselves into the imagination of young poets like Bertolt Brecht. A twenty-year-old medical orderly serving just at the end of the war, Brecht later said of those days: "As a boy I was mobilized in the war and placed in a hospital. I dressed wounds, applied iodine, gave enemas, performed blood transfusions. If the doctor ordered me: 'Amputate a leg, Brecht,' I would answer: 'Yes, your excellency,' and cut off the leg. If I was told: 'Make a trepanning,' I opened the man's skull and tinkered with his brains. I saw how they patched people up in order to ship them back to the front as soon as possible."

The revulsion of many like Brecht manifested itself in time as a loathing of that older generation that shipped young men off to a war of its own making. By the fall of 1917, Ernst Toller, wounded and out of the army on a medical discharge, was in Munich, attending lectures at the university and meetings at a nearby castle led by a group of scholars concerned with the effects of the war upon Germany. Describing those high-toned discussions of religious and moral regeneration, he writes: "And so it went on, talk, endless talk, while the battlefields of Europe shuddered beneath the blows of war. We waited, we still waited, for these men to speak the word of deliverance; in vain. Were they deaf and dumb and blind? Was it because they themselves had never lain in a dugout, never heard the despairing cries of the dying, the dumb accusation of a devastated wood; never looked into the desperate eyes of a hunted refugee?" Toller sounds the undertones here of a vengeful anger at his own father, a prosperous businessman who had cried out on his deathbed at his rebellious son. "It's your fault, it's your fault!" and then expired.

Even before the outbreak of the war, the conflict between the bourgeois father and the insubordinate son had begun to emerge as a major theme in German literature, particularly in expressionist drama; after the war, this theme was to take on a new fury.

In political terms the fury had revolutionary implications. They spoke "brave words," Toller wrote ironically of the distinguished scholars whom he heard in those meetings outside Munich; they "laid bare the Reich and exposed its evils" in some cases, but they never got beyond mere anger at the person of Wilhelm II. This only made it clear to Toller what separated his generation from theirs. "We were concerned with more than the sins of the Kaiser," he wrote, "with more than reforming the franchise. We wanted to create a whole new world, believing that to change the existing order would be also to change the hearts of men." In fact, Toller even was able to find gathering in Munich some members of an older generation—but in spirit they were more like older brothers— revolutionary idealists in their forties and fifties like Kurt Eisner and Gustav Landauer, who were eager to create the kind of world to which he aspired. And when revolution began to spread throughout Germany in the fall of 1918, fanned by the prolongation of a war that too many now found intolerable—as had happened in Russia the previous year—Eisner's group seized power in Bavaria on November 7, the anniversary of the Bolshevik uprising, and declared a Government of Workers' and Soldiers' Councils.

But the spiritual fathers were to remain in power a while longer after all, for better or for worse. On November 9, two days after the revolution in Bavaria, the abdication of Wilhelm II was announced and Germany was declared a republic by the leaders of the Social Democratic Party. These stolid parliamentarians were no longer the revolutionary Marxists they had been back in the 1880s when their party had been illegal. Their leader, Friedrich Ebert, though only forty-eight, was conservative enough in his outlook that he accepted the declaration of the republic of which he was soon to be president only with the greatest misgivings. Not at all did he accept revolutionary regimes like the one in Bavaria, or like that threatened by the Spartacists, whose attempted uprising in Berlin in January 1919 ended in its violent suppression and the murder of its leaders, Karl Liebknecht and Rosa Luxemburg. By then, the relatively conservative nature of the republic had established itself. The Eisner regime in Bavaria had been defeated at the polls. Eisner himself was murdered on February 21, 1919, and shortly thereafter Ernst Toller found himself in jail for his revolutionary activities. His time of activism

over, Toller settled down to becoming a playwright and a symbol of the
rebellious young.

During the war Nathan, the eldest son of Cantor Albert Weill, had served
in France as a medical orderly; Hans, the second son, had gone into the
army near the war's end and never saw combat. Kurt had reached military
age eight months before the armistice, but he never served. This probably
was because he was a student, and intended to remain one, at a time when
it still was possible to obtain short deferments for the continuation of
studies. The days were long past when young men like Ernst Toller—and
the gentle Kurt was never much like him in any case—had been eager to
enlist.

Many years later, a newspaper interviewer said that Kurt had been
"pretty nearly supporting his family out of his musical earnings, and when
he violently objected to going to war he got away with it." It is true that
the Weills had fallen upon hard times by 1918, like most Germans; the
Jewish community of Dessau was again, under the impact of the war,
dwindling in size and resources, and Cantor Weill had lost or was about to
lose his post owing to the lack of funds to support it. But it would be hard
to say how young Kurt could have earned them a living with his music at
that moment. There were not likely to be many customers for lessons, not
even from among the Ducal household—which was, by the way, to be
overthrown in the revolution of November. And it was not until the
following year that Kurt was to obtain a job at the former Court Theater.
No, despite the rather dashing picture of himself in 1918 that he provided
for the interviewer, the truth seems to be that Kurt, far from having
avoided military service by being a bulwark against poverty for his family,
was a sharer in its poverty all the more for being at home and not in the
army. Soldiers at least got fed regularly, whereas civilians often went
hungry in 1918, both during and after that terrible "turnip winter"—so
named for the chief staple of many a German's diet at the time. It is said in
family circles that the small, delicately constituted young musician fainted
from hunger that year more than once, and that he greatly welcomed his
opportunities to have dinner as well as music at the Schwabe household,
which remained in far better economic circumstances than his own.

But despite these straits, Kurt was in Berlin by the end of the year.
We know of an initial appearance by him there in April 1918 when,
having just turned eighteen the month before, he came to take the
entrance examination for the state-supported Hochschule für Musik, or
Musical Conservatory. He passed the exam for the fall term, and also

attended some lectures at the University of Berlin while he was at it. Perhaps he even gave a momentary and final thought to the possibility of studying the liberal arts; but Albert Bing and his own talent had persuaded him of his true calling, and in the fall, after evidently spending the summer in Dessau, he was at the Hochschule für Musik.

A full-time music student at last, young Kurt Weill took courses in composition, counterpoint, and conducting. His composition teacher at the Hochschule was Engelbert Humperdinck, the composer of *Hansel and Gretel*, a fact he was to make light of in years to come, but which may really have been significant in his development. Humperdinck was Wagner's most loyal disciple, and if Kurt was now beginning to detest the thick orchestral raptures of Bayreuth, the fact remains that his teacher's most celebrated opera, by dint of being astutely Wagnerian, comes out as a kind of burlesque of that vein. This was assuredly not a conscious irony on Humperdinck's part, but the point may well have come across to young Weill, who was soon to develop an overtly ironic approach to the musical tradition.

But, for the moment at least—and the moment was not to last much longer—Weill was still playing the sedulous disciple to tradition, as he had done with Bing, and as he was now doing with Humperdinck and with his other teachers at the Hochschule as well. His teacher of counterpoint was Friedrich E. Koch, another composer of conservative outlook, about whom it has been written that he "cultivated almost exclusively the large forms; his style was somewhat severe in its elevation; his music followed the Romantic school of Mendelssohn." It was almost as if Cantor Weill had somehow become a teacher of counterpoint. And Kurt learned conducting at the Hochschule with Rudolf Krasselt, one of the better-known conductors and teachers of the day. He evidently had decided that, at least until he could earn enough from his composing to become financially independent, he would make his living as a conductor; this, after all, was the course chosen by Albert Bing, and above all by Gustav Mahler, whom he had come to revere.

In the long run, however, this could not be a year for settling down to studies in the traditional way. Within weeks after the beginning of the term, Berlin became the scene of "one of the most memorable and dreadful days in German history," in the words of Count Harry Kessler, diarist, diplomat, writer, and patron of the arts. That was November 9, 1918, when the Kaiser's abdication was announced and the Social Democrat Philipp Scheidemann interrupted his lunch, stepped out onto the balcony of the Reichstag and proclaimed the German Republic, to

Friedrich Ebert's chagrin; after which Karl Liebknecht proclaimed the socialist republic from the balcony of the abandoned Imperial Palace. We cannot know exactly what Kurt Weill was doing that day, but perhaps at some point he made his way through Berlin streets as Count Kessler describes himself doing on November 9 in his diary: "I passed the barrier on the Potsdamer Platz and walked in the direction of the Palace, from which the sound of isolated shots still came. Leipziger Strasse was deserted, Friedrichstrasse [Berlin's main amusement street] fairly full of its usual *habitués*, Unter den Linden opposite the Opera in darkness. . . . Patrols all around; they challenged and let me through. In front of the Imperial Stables a good deal of splintered masonry. . . . Some cars with armed men rushed over the Schlossbrücke, were stopped, turned around, and sent off. . . . Beyond the Schlossbrücke again a barrier. At both corners of Königstrasse a skulking rabble in small packs which reassembled as often as the pickets broke them up. A sergeant said they were waiting for the chance to pillage; they must be cleared out. Slowly I made my way home."

Also recorded in Kessler's diary is an event, occurring on the night of January 15–16, 1919, that assuredly impressed itself upon young Weill's imagination as it did upon so many of the ardent, progressive-minded members of his generation, among whom he now counted himself: "Liebknecht and Rosa Luxemburg have met with a dreadful and fantastic end. . . . Last night Liebknecht was shot from behind while being taken in a truck through the Tiergarten and, so it is said, trying to escape. Rosa Luxemburg, having been interrogated by officers of the Guards Cavalry Division in the Eden Hotel, was first beaten unconscious by a crowd there and then, on the canal bridge between Kurfürstendamm and Hitzigstrasse, was dragged out of the car in which she was being removed. Allegedly she was killed. Her body has at any rate disappeared." It was found four months later in the canal, and a quiet funeral was held on June 13.

During the course of that year the sweep of events also reached the Hochschule für Musik, where a revolutionary Students' Council was formed and elected Kurt Weill its president. "Having decided that it was up to them to throw out the old-fogey director of the conservatory," according to the above quoted newspaper interviewer, the students "charged Weill with the responsibility of finding a new one." The "old fogey" they got rid of was August Ferdinand Hermann Kretzschmar, a seventy-year-old composer, organist, and musicologist. It was time for a sharp turn into the contemporary, and the replacement suggested by

Weill was the noted pianist and somewhat avant-garde composer Ferruccio Busoni. But in a significant display of the chauvinism that was
managing to survive in spite of everything, the students turned down the
suggestion on ground that Busoni was not a German—this, even though
he had lived in Germany most of his adult life and also could claim
German descent on his mother's side. The matter was not resolved during
the few months that remained to Weill at the Hochschule, but he was to
have his day with Busoni before long all the same.

It is not clear why Kurt left the Hochschule after only a term, which
had been a successful one in many respects. In addition to his stint as
president of the Students' Council, he had completed a major composition
and seen it performed at school: this was a symphonic poem based on
Rainer Maria Rilke's great pseudo-medieval work, *The Lay of the Love and
Death of Cornet Christopher Rilke*—which, incidentally, had been a great
favorite among the more literate German soldiers during the war. Echoing
the more modern tones that had entered the atmosphere of the Hochschule since the revolution, the piece won for its composer a scholarship
from the Felix Mendelssohn Foundation, but he chose to forgo this and
leave school anyway. There was a job waiting for him in Dessau if he
wanted it, and the family economic situation had become so bad that the
help of his prospective earnings was no doubt greatly needed. Perhaps,
also, he was simply eager to get out into the world; the schoolroom
atmosphere was really not for him. Indeed, though he was again to be a
semiprivate pupil for a time, he was, as it turned out, putting all academic
institutions behind him forever when he left the Hochschule that spring
and returned home.

Ferruccio Busoni

The post taken up by Kurt Weill in Dessau was that of *répétiteur*, or coach, with the opera company of the former Court Theater, at the invitation of Albert Bing. It consisted of helping the singers to learn and prepare their roles, accompanying them at the piano during rehearsals, and functioning in general as a musical assistant. This was lively work, and since it was his first assignment as a full-fledged professional musician, the nineteen-year-old Weill enjoyed it thoroughly. No doubt he also recognized that it was not a job for someone with his ambitions to stay in for very long—and, in fact, he was to leave it after only a few months.

His hasty departure may not have been prompted so much by ambition, however, as by the arrival of a new music director shortly after he began there. Hans Knappertsbusch, though only thirty-one, was already well launched on a distinguished conducting career when he came to Dessau. Albert Bing does not seem to have minded having Knapperts-busch appointed over him to a post that was, in any case, still not available to a Jew even in republican Dessau, and he and the new music director became good friends. Young Weill, on the other hand, did not get along with Knappertsbusch. Perhaps the fact that the new conductor was already a prominent Wagnerian made for tensions between him and the budding modernist composer from the outset. There evidently also were personal incompatibilities between them, and one family tradition has it that Weill and Knappertsbusch also became rivals for the affection of the

same young woman. In any case, things came to a head during one
evening's performance when the diminutive *répétiteur*, just as he was about
to prompt the entrance of the tenor, fell through a trapdoor backstage and
was knocked unconscious. The tenor was late for his cue, and Knappertsbusch stormed backstage at the end of the act, in search of his missing
assistant. "He was always so small," he shouted. "Now he's disappeared
completely!"

When a job offer came to Weill in December from distant Westpha-
lia, he and Knappertsbusch were equally delighted; in fact, it was the
conductor who had recommended him for it. The post, a temporary one,
was that of a staff conductor at the Lüdenscheid Civic Opera. Lüdenscheid had a population of only about thirty thousand and its opera house
was a minor one indeed, but being a conductor there, even for only a
season, was better than being a mere *répétiteur* in even so important a
musical center as Dessau: after all, Mahler himself had begun his
conducting career in a minor provincial post, eventually to work his way
from there to the directorship of the Vienna Court Opera. Meanwhile,
there had come to be few if any personal reasons for Kurt to remain in
Dessau, for the Weill family no longer was there. Cantor Weill had by
now obtained the directorship of an orphanage in Leipzig, run by the
B'nai B'rith, and he and Emma were settled there with Kurt's sister, Ruth.
Nathan also was in Leipzig, studying medicine at the university, and
Hans was a business apprentice in Halberstadt. The times still were hard,
but the family situation was more or less stabilized, and Kurt was free to
fend for himself in Lüdenscheid.

"All arrangements were made by telegraph," wrote an interviewer
many years later. "The greenhorn sped to his new job and was only
mildly surprised, on his arrival in the late afternoon, at the instruction that
he was to conduct the local company in a performance of *Martha* that same
evening. His consternation grew a little when he was informed that no
score of the opera was available; the publishers parsimoniously kept such
scores in whirlwind circulation. But he was told not to worry; it would
arrive in time for the performance.

"Waiting for the score, he painfully spent his time trying to
remember what it was all about. Then his most nightmarish apprehen-
sions became a reality. When the score did arrive hardly a page of it was in
its original state. Instead there was a maze of incomprehensible pencil
markings, green denoting 'Hamburg cuts,' red 'Dresden,' blue 'Munich'
and so on. The concertmaster said that the local company used some of
the cuts but not others; he wasn't clear on which.

"The panic which suddenly overtook Weill engulfed him for the whole evening and he is no clearer now about what actually happened during the performance than he was five minutes after the curtain came down. But he is perfectly clear as to why he was put through this torture. The prima donna was in love with the concertmaster, whom she wanted to have installed as conductor. But her husband, the leading tenor, had gotten wind of her plans and had hastily wired for help to his old crony [Knappertsbusch], the director of the Dessau theater. The latter's solution must have been a triple satisfaction to him[self], for it relieved him of Weill, revenged him on Weill and helped out an old friend." But, whatever personal antagonisms may have greeted the young conductor upon his arrival in Lüdenscheid, they seem to have been quickly settled.

The new year began well for Kurt, even if not for Germany in general. Speaking of the national humiliation that was now being suffered at the hands of the Allied Powers, victorious and vindictive, Count Harry Kessler wrote in his diary for January 10, 1920: "Today the Peace Treaty was ratified at Paris; the War is over. A terrible era begins for Europe, like the gathering of clouds before a storm, and it will end in an explosion probably still more terrible than that of the World War." The first rumblings of an angry right were soon heard, and on March 13 the Ehrhardt brigade marched into Berlin, occupied the government buildings without resistance, and declared a new regime under the chancellorship of Wolfgang Kapp. But when the ousted Social Democrats called for a show of national resistance by means of a general strike, a Germany still ready to support the republic responded to the appeal. By the evening of March 17 the leaders of the Kapp Putsch had resigned.

During these trying days for the nation, Kurt Weill was hard at work in Lüdenscheid making his own start in life. This was "where I learned everything I know about the stage," he was to say in later years. And indeed, in this post he learned a good deal, not only about opera but about musical theater in general: his programs ranged from operas that included *The Flying Dutchman* and *Cavalleria Rusticana* to such relative trifles as *Wie einst in Mai* ("Once upon a Time in May") by Walter Kollo, one of the foremost German operetta composers of the day. Helping to run all of this must have been a heady experience for a young man who only turned twenty that March; one of the surviving documents of his life from this period is a letter of recommendation that he wrote for one of his instrumentalists. In such moments he must have thought he might want to remain a conductor all his life. And though he was replaced in this post in

Lüdenscheid at the end of the season, Kurt found a conducting job again that summer, with a men's chorus in Leipzig, where he could again live with his parents.

But Kurt knew that he had to be a composer above all, and he gave his spare moments at Lüdenscheid and Leipzig to developing this craft. Among the many compositions he did during this year are two operas, which unfortunately have not survived. One of them was based on a one-act play, *Ninon de l'Enclos*, by Ernst Hardt. Still only in his early forties at this time, Hardt had long been known in Germany as an ironic reteller of medieval legends: one of his plays, *Tantris der Narr* ("Tantris the Fool"—Tantris, an anagram of Tristan, was one of the names the latter had been known by), was a macabre travesty of *Tristan and Isolde*, and this no doubt contributed to Hardt's appeal for the anti-Wagnerian Weill. *Ninon de l'Enclos*, a pastiche of seventeenth-century French drama, presents in verse the garden intrigues of a Parisian noblewoman who at length learns that her youthful lover is the illegitimate son she had borne at the age of sixteen; when she tells him this, he runs off and stabs himself. Kurt was not yet over his childhood fondness for costume drama filled with violence and romance, although this was now being qualified by a significant element of bitterness and irony.

His other opera was entirely contemporary in subject matter. It was based on Hermann Sudermann's 1908 novel, *Das hohe Lied* (known in English translation as *The Song of Songs*), which describes the struggles of a young woman to make her way in the world. Sudermann, like Arno Holz, was one of the founders of German naturalism, and young Weill's choice of this novel for a subject shows, as had his choice of the Holz poem some six years earlier, his abiding interest in social questions. But obviously of even greater interest to him was the constant inclination of Sudermann's heroine to see her life in musical similes—for her father, who deserted her and her mother when she was a child, had been a music teacher and composer. Various themes from the operatic repertory run through her head at appropriate times; but it is above all her father's unfinished oratorio on the biblical *Song of Songs* that keeps coming back to her, representing a high ideal of poetry and love that she tries in vain to live up to—until she finally gives up and marries a rich man. This presence of a whole dimension that could only be realized by music was bound to be fascinating to Weill, who was to maintain in later years that the only proper libretto for an opera or a musical play was one that was not yet fulfilled until the musical dimension had been added; otherwise, the music was a mere embellishment, and it suffered as a result. Interestingly, this was a doctrine preached by Ferruccio Busoni, with whom Weill was to study the following year.

The Sudermann opera may never have been finished, but what Kurt did produce was an oratorio of his own based on the biblical *Song of Songs*, called *Shulamith*. He had undoubtedly heard his father sing one of the various synagogal melodies to this most sensual of the books of the Bible, which had a natural appeal to a young artist who was "liberated" and yet harbored a continuing fondness for sacred themes. Furthermore, in this piece, as in most of what he had done so far, he showed a turn of mind that was persistently literary, as attached to the word as to music: in this respect he certainly was the scion of cantors. From the beginning, in other words, his most basic inclination as a composer was to write song and musical drama.

But he knew that if he was to develop as a serious composer, he had to write "pure" or abstract music; and so he did this, too, during his busy year in Lüdenscheid and Leipzig. He composed two pieces of chamber music, in this respect showing the bent for smaller ensembles that characterized the composers of his generation: not only was this a way of getting one's works performed more readily, but it also was an assertion that the days of Wagner were over. For some it meant that the days of Schoenberg had begun, but this evidently was not yet the case for Weill, even though his Rilke tone-poem of the previous year had carried echoes of Schoenberg's relatively early and romantic *Pelleas and Melisande*. Rather, the String Quartet in B minor and the Sonata for Cello and Piano composed by Weill that year show their debt to Schubert and Brahms more than to any more modern composer, even though occasional twentieth-century dissonances do get into them. A fragment surviving from one of his operas of this year demonstrates that he was more adventurous when doing vocal and dramatic music; in the vein of "pure" music, however, he was ready, for the moment, to be only a sedulous apprentice to the classics.

This probably also was true of the symphony he began that year, but we shall never know; we only have the completely revised version he was to do of it the following year in a truly contemporary style, under the tutelage of Busoni. For Weill made another crucial decision in the fall of 1920, upon hearing that Busoni had been appointed to an important teaching post in Berlin. Here at last was a chance to study with a master he had long admired. His situation in Leipzig was relatively comfortable, and the life of a composition pupil in Berlin would not be so at all: but was he to go on any longer living with his parents and being a conductor who composed on the side? There could be no doubt about the answer. Kurt applied to become a member of Busoni's master class in Berlin, and was accepted that December.

The life and work of Ferruccio Busoni formed a fabric of striking contradictions. Born in Empoli near Florence in 1866, he was of an old Italian family on his father's side, but his mother was the daughter of a German who had settled in Trieste; and though he eventually married a Swedish woman and settled permanently in Berlin, he went on hoping that he might compose a great Italian opera one day. A child prodigy at the piano, he grew to be recognized as one of the great keyboard virtuosos of his day or any other, but he became contemptuous of this career and sought recognition primarily as a composer. Aspiring mainly to write operas, he became better known as a composer of keyboard works; indeed, he was to become best known in the decades following his death as "Bach-Busoni," the eminent transcriber for piano of the baroque master's works. And though he had been a true offspring of nineteenth-century romanticism in every respect, he nevertheless renounced all his earlier compositions after the turn of the century and tried to write in an utterly contemporary style.

This last decision was a most courageous one, for Busoni belonged to the generation hit hardest by the revolutionary changes that occurred in music during the first ten to fifteen years of this century. For about three hundred years, the tonal system that we associate with the classical tradition in Western music—with its basic patterns of triadic chords, of dominant, subdominant, and tonic, of logical key relationships, and in general, with its treatment of "dissonances" as moments to be swiftly and resolutely passed through on the way to pleasantly harmonious outcomes—had reigned so supreme that it was widely thought of as a set of universal and irrevocable laws, like those of Newtonian physics, with which it was roughly contemporaneous. But just as the old physics had shown signs of breaking down toward the end of the nineteenth century, so also had the old tonality, under the impact of such developments as Wagner's highly chromatic and ambiguous harmonies, the exotic intervals used by Russian composers, including Mussorgsky, and the experiments with scales other than the traditional diatonic one undertaken by Satie and Debussy. Shortly after 1900, as though the change of century had given license for it, a final assault on the crumbling structure was begun by vigorous young men—in particular Arnold Schoenberg, who was born in

1874. By 1909, when he produced his remarkable monodrama, *Erwartung*, Schoenberg had composed a succession of "atonal" works that seemed to thrive on their constant "dissonances" (Schoenberg disapproved of both terms, *atonal* and *dissonance*, as being merely prejudicial rather than truly descriptive) and that proclaimed a dizzying new harmonic freedom for those who were ready to follow.

Gustav Mahler, fourteen years older than Schoenberg, was one who did not care to follow, even though his work often strained at the limits of the traditional system. Indeed, it has seemed to many listeners that Mahler's last works, composed during the very decade in which Schoenberg wrought his tonal revolution, were a set of final, monumental farewells to tonality, in which the composer never completely renounced it but let it virtually dissolve in such places as the concluding chords of *Das Lied von der Erde*, as the rider goes off into eternity. Mahler then died in 1911, at only fifty-one years of age, as though his very being could not survive into the new era. Others of his generation fared better in the face of it. Richard Strauss, four years younger, adventured into a freer tonality during that same first decade of this century with his operas *Salome* and *Elektra*, but then retrenched with the more conservative, occasionally neoclassical style of works of which *Der Rosenkavalier* is an example. Busoni, six years younger than Mahler and only eight years older than Schoenberg, was even eager to embrace the tonal revolution when it came, although he, too, ultimately settled into a position midway between the nineteenth century and the twentieth.

There was, of course, a national aspect to the changes going on. The Russians and the French were making their own radical advances into the twentieth century—Stravinsky leading the way for both—but the stress upon adventures into whole new tonalities was not so great among them as in the German-speaking countries. The Italians seemed, for the moment, almost completely oblivious to the revolution in tonality, and Giacomo Puccini above all fused the legacies of Verdi and Wagner into an operatic style that continued to be unabashedly melodic as well as authentically native. Busoni stood in the middle of these developments as the part-Italian, part-German that he was, somehow evincing just a touch of the Frenchman besides. One of the most intellectual of composers, he was entirely responsive to the changes taking place in German music, but he also felt himself to be rooted in the traditions of his native Italy. Not that he approved of Puccini, whose *Madame Butterfly* he once described as "disreputable" (*unanständig*); indeed, he had frowned upon the entire development of Italian opera after Rossini until he saw Verdi's *Falstaff* in

1893, whereupon he decided there was new hope for the tradition. For him, Italian opera had known its true greatness in the hands of a Rossini, a Pergolesi, or best of all, a Mozart—musically a kind of Italo-German like Busoni himself and the composer he probably revered over all others, including even Bach. Mozartean opera was the quintessence of the kind of naturalness and restraint that Busoni sought all his life, and that had been largely lost since Wagner, whom he detested. On the other hand, Debussy had recovered some of these qualities, and it was from him that Busoni learned many important lessons; to this extent Busoni was, as his pupil Kurt Weill later observed of him, an "Impressionist" among the Germans.

The music Busoni wrote after his Piano Concerto of 1904—itself a remarkable and highly original piece of work but still a product of pure nineteenth-century romanticism—resounds with all the ambiguities of his personality and development. The freer tonality is there, though it is in no way so radical as what he advocates in his 1907 treatise, *Sketch of a New Aesthetic of Music*, which envisions a scale based on intervals of a third of a tone and speaks with enthusiasm of the Dynamophone, an electrical instrument capable of sounding such intervals developed by the American inventor Thaddeus Cahill. Indeed, Busoni's new tonality was always to be far less radical than that of Schoenberg, whose tendencies in these days before the restraining development of the twelve-tone system Busoni came to regard as "anarchy, an arbitrary juxtaposition and superposition of intervals according to whim and taste." There had to be some anchor, Busoni came to realize, and he hovered over one—sometimes with considerable uncertainty—even in the days when he thought he had cut himself loose completely.

The vacillation can be heard in the very work he composed as an announcement of his new style, the Elegies for Piano, which he did in 1907, the same year as his radical treatise. Four of the six original Elegies are explicit reworkings of earlier compositions of his own, another is based on a Bach chorale, and all of them—including a seventh, added two years later upon the death of the composer's mother—echo with themes far more traditional than the avant-garde texture being woven around them. Ever to be Janus-faced, like this work, in his relation to the past and to the future, Busoni brought up his own spontaneous solution to the problem out of his innate contrapuntalism, the product of his Italian origin and his lifelong involvement in the works of Bach. As the years went by, he more and more willingly sought out the most traditional themes to immerse in the free tonalities of his counterpoint, like a fish in a net—at least in his works for the piano—and he even did explicit variations on works by composers including Chopin, Bizet, and Mozart. In this way, he was one of the pioneers of neoclassicism.

But it was above all in opera that Busoni hoped to explore new musical horizons. As he once wrote, "a series of dissonances that is almost unbearable on the pianoforte, is already intelligible in the orchestra, but in the theater it becomes merely a characteristic nuance which is put up with and passes without opposition." In other words, the freer tonality seems to find its most satisfactory fulfillment—and, one is tempted to say, justification—in dramatic declarations by the human voice: a view apparently borne out by the fact that some of Schoenberg's most powerful works, *Erwartung* and *Pierrot Lunaire*, for example, are for the voice, and that among the most widely admired products of his school are Alban Berg's operas, *Wozzeck* and *Lulu*, composed at a later time than we have yet reached in our narrative. And there is another reason that opera and vocal composition in general were important to those who sought to dispense with the old tonality: since the traditional structures whereby "pure" or absolute music was composed, such as sonata-allegro, fugue, variation, and so on, all depended upon the tonal system, larger works no longer were possible—at least until Schoenberg developed the twelve-tone system in the 1920s—unless they were built on a framework of dramatic or literary content. This was why Busoni as well as Schoenberg and his disciples—most notably Anton von Webern—dedicated a part of their energies to the composition of miniatures, forthright statements of musical ideas without development that were typically less than five minutes and often less than a minute long. If opera seemed for a time to be the only viable alternative to the miniature, Busoni even claimed to see an intimate relation between them, asserting that "the opera as a musical composition always consisted in a series of short, concise pieces and that it will never be able to exist in any other form."

Yet despite this overriding interest in opera, Busoni, who ever struggled painfully with his muse, succeeded in writing only four of them in his life, two of them only one-acters. Of the two full-length operas, one of them, *Die Brautwahl* ("The Bridal Choice"), based on a story by E. T. A. Hoffmann, was his very first venture into the operatic form and has been forgotten. The other full-length opera, *Doktor Faust*, is one of the operatic masterworks of the twentieth century, but Busoni had not completed it at the time we now encounter him in this story—indeed, he was never to complete it, and after his death in 1924 the final scene had to be composed by one of his students, Philipp Jarnach. Rather, the two operas he was best known for when Kurt Weill came to him at the end of 1920 were the one-acters, *Turandot*, based on the same Carlo Gozzi play that Puccini used for his own better-known opera of the same name, and *Arlecchino*, a creation entirely Busoni's own. These works both had their premiere on the same day in May 1917, as parts of a double bill, in Zurich, where Busoni had taken refuge from the war along with others from the belligerent countries who wanted to have nothing to do with the catastrophe.

Turandot had originally been written some years before as incidental music for the Gozzi play, and it was worked up into a one-act opera in the spring of 1917 primarily to fill out a program for *Arlecchino*. It is above all *Arlecchino: Ein theatralisches Capriccio in einem Aufzuge* ("Harlequin: A Theatrical Caprice in One Act") that interests us here, not only because it was Busoni's major work prior to *Doktor Faust*, but also because it was the one with the most decisive influence on Kurt Weill. Its witty, almost nonsensical libretto, which is tinged with the incipient Dadaism of wartime Zurich and was written by the composer himself, derives largely from the atmosphere of the *Commedia dell'Arte*, but is in German with only an occasional digression into Italian: this seems almost purposefully to announce the composer's double national identity. Set in eighteenth-century Bergamo, it shows the crafty Arlecchino pursuing his amorous adventures and, in the process, so deceiving a group of pompous, bourgeois characters that they think their town is being invaded by a foreign army: the piece becomes a satire on the war. The music is appropriately capricious and lively, with occasional hints of the more celebrated work that Igor Stravinsky, also in Switzerland, was to compose the following year, *L'Histoire du soldat*. Like that work, and in accordance with Busoni's own theory about opera, *Arlecchino* is "a series of short, concise pieces," monologues, dialogues, and ensembles, in which the different characters express themselves to the audience or at one another in a manner foreshadowing Stravinsky's whimsical instruments. There are no arias as such—which is the fashion of the German opera of that day, though the breaking up of the score into separate set pieces definitely is not—but there are plenty of fragments of aria, mainly intended as operatic parody and often in the form of direct musical quotations.

It is this element of quotation, important in Busoni's work in general, that serves to point up the composer's ambivalence toward tradition. Most of the time, when one or the other character quotes a passage from classic opera or literature—and these, significantly, are the passages that are in Italian—Busoni is making fun of him: it is while Ser Matteo ecstatically reads Dante, for example, that his wife is seduced by Arlecchino behind his back. So much for "culture" in a world destroying itself! But the quotations are all from works like the *Divine Comedy* and Mozart's *Don Giovanni*, which Busoni reveres, so that the mockery really only disguises the anguished query: What, in the realms of morality and tone, are the alternatives to tradition? For if Arlecchino's fatuous opponent, the tenor Leandro, is constantly stopping to sing bits of full-blown opera instead of getting anything done, Arlecchino achieves his own ends without singing a note. The opera's central character, the man of action, is entirely a speaking part.

If this device echoes with a certain despair, however, it is also a piece of careful Busonian craftsmanship in a program to create an operatic style at a pole opposite to the Wagnerian variety—the device of a nonsinging character at the center of the action had been used most notably by Mozart in *The Abduction from the Seraglio*. Busoni was keenly aware of opera as theater, and was perfectly willing to let parts of the drama function without the help of music when they had no need of it. As he once wrote:

> there are "obvious" psychic conditions on the stage, whereof music need take no account. Suppose a theatrical situation in which a convivial company is passing at night and disappears from view, while in the foreground a silent, envenomed duel is in progress. Here the music, by means of continuing song, should keep in mind the jovial company now lost to sight; the acts and feelings of the pair in the foreground may be understood without further commentary, and the music—dramatically speaking—ought not to participate in their action and break the tragic silence.

Opposed to the Wagnerian flood, Busoni felt that there were emotional corners into which music simply could not flow, and should not try to. With characteristic intellectuality, he tried to specify some of the permissible and impermissible moods for the composer. Acceptable were

> dread (Leporello), oppression of soul, invigoration, lassitude (Beethoven's last quartets), decision (Wotan), hesitation, despondency, encouragement, harshness, tenderness, excitement, tranquillization, the feeling of surprise or expectancy, and still others; likewise the inner echo of external occurrences which is bound up in these moods of the soul. But not the moving cause itself of these spiritual affections—not the joy over an avoided danger, not the danger itself,

or the kind of danger which caused the dread; an emotional state, yes, but not the psychic species of this emotion, such as envy, or jealousy; and it is equally futile to attempt the expression, through music, of moral characteristics (vanity, cleverness), or abstract ideas like truth and justice.

Above all, love duets were out of the question for Busoni. He regarded these as "not only shameless but absolutely untrue," and "altogether wrong and fictitious besides being ridiculous."

Busoni's ideals were the formality and restraint of classicism; for him, *The Magic Flute* was the most perfect of all operas. This work was one of those in his mind (though it does not, unlike its Italian contemporaries, have *musical* recitatives) when he made these crucial observations:

> Measurably justified, in my opinion, is the plan of the old opera, which concentrated and musically rounded out the passions aroused by a moving dramatic scene in a piece of set form (the aria). *Word* and stage-play conveyed the dramatic progress of the action, followed more or less meagerly by musical recitative; arrived at the point of rest, music resumed the reins. This is less extrinsic than some would now have us believe.

One might ask at this point why Busoni eschewed the aria in his own operas, but his answer is given in the next sentence:

> On the other hand, it was the ossified form of the "aria" itself which led to inveracity of expression and decadence.

In other words, if a fresh approach to the aria could be found, its restoration to opera would be most desirable. Busoni himself was unable to find such an approach, and so he wrote few arias; it was only after his death that his pupil Kurt Weill was to take up the quest and come up with a solution that threatened the conventions of opera altogether.

Teaching was of the utmost importance to Busoni, who surrounded himself with his piano and composition pupils wherever he went. It was in Switzerland during the war, furthermore, that he established some of his most important teacher-pupil relationships; but this did not prevent him from feeling more and more like an exile there after the war's end. "In the evening visited Busoni," writes Count Harry Kessler for January 20,

1920, when he was in Zurich. "He was in a disagreeably sarcastic mood. Would like to return to Berlin, but puts on airs at every practical suggestion and adopts temperamental Beethoven poses." The image is vivid, if unkind; for Busoni, with his massive head upon a short, sturdy physique, and great mane of brown wavy hair then turning silver, looked something like a Beethoven suddenly become strikingly handsome. But it was the teaching connection that finally brought him a practical suggestion he could accept. One of his former piano pupils, Leo Kestenberg, was appointed to a post in the Prussian Ministry of Education and later in 1920 invited him to return to Berlin and teach a composition class under the auspices of the State Academy of Arts and Sciences. The term did not have to exceed six months a year, and he could teach the class in his home. The offer was irresistible, and by early September Busoni was back in his old apartment on the Victoria Luise Platz in the pleasant Charlottenburg section of Berlin.

Of the five pupils Busoni took on that year for his master class in composition, three had followed him from Switzerland—Luc Balmer, Robert Blum, and Walther Geiser. The remaining two were from Germany, but one of them, Wladimir Vogel, had been born in Russia and had not settled in Germany until the end of the war. Kurt Weill was the only German-born member of the class, a fact that further demonstrates the cosmopolitan aura ever surrounding Busoni's person. In the past his pupils had come from as far away as America, where Busoni himself had sojourned from time to time in his travels as a pianist and where the elder of his two sons had been born.

Perhaps it was to avoid seeming too cosmopolitan that Busoni had accepted Weill, who nevertheless was to become the most cosmopolitan of his pupils. It also was Weill who, a few years later, would be the best able among them to express in words what were the special qualities that Busoni had brought to them:

> After the revolution in Germany we young musicians were filled with new ideals and brimming over with new hopes. But though we recognized the new when we saw it, even when it was not of our own creation, we were unable to find the right form for our own content. We had broken the chains, but we did not know where to go with our new-found freedom. We headed for new horizons and forgot to look back. Suddenly leaping high after years of confinement, we got a case of the bends, and a cramp that lay in our chests like a nightmare—and that we loved anyway, because it represented our freedom.

Then Busoni came to Berlin. We treasured him, because we believed him to have arrived at the particular goal after which we strove. But he really was something different. He didn't have a cramp in his chest; rather, through the suppleness of his clear-seeing spirit and the loftiness of his creative genius he had been able to arrive at a synthesis of all the stylistic modes of the past few decades, at a new art, uncluttered and yet restrained, a "Young Classicism."

The clear air of Busoni's genius seemed to fill the room of his apartment into which his eager pupils gathered themselves every Monday and Thursday afternoon from January through June. "He called us disciples and there were no actual lessons," Weill also wrote, "but he allowed us to breathe his aura, which emanated in every sphere, but eventually always manifested itself in music." Summing it all up, he concluded: "It was a mutual exchange of ideas in the very best sense, with no attempt to force an opinion, no autocracy, and not the slightest sign of envy or malice; and any piece of work that revealed talent and ability was immediately recognized and enthusiastically received." Kurt Weill soon was contributing a steady flow of works to this discussion.

The Young Modernist

Viewing the city to which Busoni had returned in the fall of 1920, his biographer observed that "the first thing that a stranger noticed on revisiting Berlin after the war was its general griminess. There was only one building in Berlin which had had a fresh coat of paint since 1914—the British Embassy. The Friedrichstrasse, once the busiest street in the town, was a chaos of sand and wooden planks; some day there was to be an underground railway beneath it, but in 1920 Berlin was too depressed either to proceed with the railway or to remake the pavement. War had produced poverty and poverty crime. In 1914 . . . honesty could be taken for granted in any German town, at least as regards everyday trifles; in 1920 it was assumed that everything would be stolen if the opportunity was not carefully prevented. . . . On the railways and in the restaurants one was perpetually conscious of the shortage of certain materials—textiles, leather, metal. In Berlin's best hotels the knives and forks were in a disgraceful state; and in the cafés of Amsterdam one was given a little glass rod to stir one's coffee because the Germans who came to Holland stole all the spoons."

When Kurt Weill came to the city at the end of the year, he took a small *Bude* (roughly, "pad"), as one friend later described it, in a pension on the Winterfeldplatz, in western Berlin. Prepared to live the life of a poor student, he was nevertheless not completely without resources, for a prosperous uncle in Mannheim who had no children of his own, Albert

Weill's older brother, Leopold, had offered to provide the musical prodigy of the family with an allowance of fifty marks a month for the duration of his studies. Kurt also wasted no time about getting musical odd jobs, such as playing the piano in cafés, to supplement his income. Conditions were hard, but few suspected how much worse they were to become; the inflation that was to grow so terrible in the ensuing months was still only in its early stages.

But the bohemian life of Berlin did not need prosperity in order to thrive. The popular gathering-places for writers and artists were in action as always, above all the celebrated Romanische Café, at the edge of the fashionable Kurfürstendamm district in western Berlin, just opposite the Kaiser Wilhelm Memorial Church. One of its habitués later described it as "an abortive structure out of the Wilhelminian era, big, with two enormous rooms, one of them ringed by an upper tier, both brilliantly lit until dawn and always filled with noise. Only the terrace was genuinely attractive, especially first thing in the morning, when Literature was still asleep." But the literary crowd was especially interesting for Kurt Weill, who ever was drawn to the word and to cafés like the Romanische.

The literary atmosphere of Berlin in 1920 was that of the old expressionism revived and rekindled by the experience of war and revolution. It was drama—ever a more significant and successfully realized form in Germany than the novel—which above all set the tone, and the most influential drama of the moment was Ernst Toller's *Die Wandlung* ("Transfiguration"), which the author had completed during his first stint as a political prisoner in 1918. The play, which traces the moral history of a young Jewish sculptor—Toller's representation of himself— through unspecified times of war and revolution, moves freely between prose and verse, and between an overcharged naturalism and a kind of proto-surrealism. It opens, for example, with a prologue in a military cemetery, where two skeleton figures, Death-by-War and Death-by-Peace, come together and hold a philosophical conversation. There are several other scenes in the body of the play that are, like this prologue, "on the borderline between reality and unreality," according to the author's stage directions, "to be thought of as scenes watched distantly in a dream." One of them is set like this: "No-man's land. Dark clouds sweep across the face of the moon. To right and left are barbed-wire entanglements in which hang skeletons white with quicklime. The earth is torn up with craters and shellholes." A dialogue ensues among the skeletons, during which some that are legless "pick up their shin-bones and rattle them together." Eventually, all of them begin to dance. In moments like these, Toller has found the points of contact between the kind of imagery of the tortured unconscious that prewar expressionism had thrived on and the real horrors of the war.

Through this maze of strange and terrifying scenes moves the young sculptor Friedrich, usually in his own person, but also sometimes in the form of somebody else who resembles him—for his image comes to represent that of a struggling Everyman of war and revolution. We see him joining the army at the beginning, inspired by the "greatness of the times," then suffering the agonies of battle, and then recovering in an army hospital amid a nightmarish gathering of horribly wounded soldiers. Then we see him after the war, struggling to realize himself as an artist, losing the love of his too-conventional fiancée, discovering the sufferings of the poor until—after another dreamlike scene in which the manhandled workers in a factory seem like the inmates of a medieval prison—he at last appears as an agitator, leading the masses to revolution. Friedrich thus emerges as the representative of a whole generation of idealists; and if his history takes on a special coloration because he, like his creator, is a Jew whose struggles are often part of a quest for acceptance by society, this merely gives dramatic emphasis to the feeling of alienation that many ardent young Germans were undergoing.

Among the many writers Kurt Weill met during his first months in Berlin was a twenty-nine-year-old poet named Johannes R. Becher. One day to rise to high office in the Communist government of East Germany, Becher was already embarking on the kind of post–World War I revolutionary career that had its most celebrated embodiment in Ernst Toller's life and writing. Count Harry Kessler had met him back in the fall of 1919 and had written then in his diary that "Becher does not think much of the workers' revolutionary energy. In Thuringia, where he is in the confidence of the Communist Party hierarchy, there is no thought of an uprising. Indeed, if someone tried it, the Party would do its best to thwart them. The Communist Party [of Germany] is lacking in leaders, in experience, in everything that is essential to a successful revolution. Moreover it is riddled with informers. The workers regard the whole revolution simply as a means of acquiring cars and silk stockings." But despite his disappointment in worldly matters, Becher was then busy cultivating a personal literature of hope, as Kessler observed. "He told me of a play that he now wants to write on the island of Rügen, where he is going: *Workers, Peasants and Soldiers. The Awakening of a People.* The dramatis personae consists first of a single individual spreading his revolutionary ideas, finally of a whole people. At the end the drama is even to include the audience and the action will reach into the stalls."

Becher was ultimately to write two versions of this drama, the second of which was to take on the harder Marxist edge that he would recover for himself by 1924. But his first version, completed shortly after his conversation with Count Kessler, was more quasi-religious than Marxist in its socialist vision, as its amended subtitle indicates: *The Awakening of a People to God*. Written in verse, the work can better be described as a spoken oratorio than as a play; and Becher, who explicitly called for musical effects at various places in the text, undoubtedly hoped that the whole thing might one day be set to music. Kurt Weill was bound to have found the Becher drama attractive. Based on a constant responsive exchange between chorus and various individual voices (representing such characters as the Man, the Woman, the Holy One, the Questioner, the Tyrant, the Mass-Murderer, and so on), it could easily have stirred up the rhythms and intonations of the synagogue lying deep within Cantor Weill's son, even though he was technically no longer religious. Furthermore, the story line, such as it was, had an Old Testament quality, taking as it did a whole nameless people through war and virtual enslavement to liberation and a final march to an unspecified "Promised Land" (*Land der Verheissung*). Finally, the play's Hebraic aura (a product of Becher's pietistically Protestant background) was intensified by the fact that the individual spreading revolutionary ideas in it was a woman specifically described as Jewish—a character doubtless inspired by the memory of Rosa Luxemburg, although differing somewhat from her real-life counterpart in her constant allusions to God. All these elements added up to an ideal synthesis for young Weill, whose claims to having become a freethinker would ever be qualified by a continuing Jewish religiosity in his nature and whose awakening concern for social justice was not capable—whatever he may have imagined in this moment—of hardening into so worldly a creed as Marxism.

Perhaps Weill discussed with Becher the possibility of one day doing the drama as an oratorio; but for the moment, what he did was rewrite his symphony of the previous year along lines laid out by Becher's drama. This became his first major project as Busoni's pupil, but though it was written from April through June of 1921, while the master class was still in session, it was not done under Busoni's close supervision, nor did it have his approval for the most part. No doubt the master found too much murkiness and complexity in the style of this work that really straddled stages in his pupil's development. Inspired in part by Schoenberg's

Kammersymphonie, Opus 9—like that work, it is in a single movement, and makes ample use of harmonic fourths instead of the traditionally sanctioned triads—it contains stretches of atonality throughout; but there is an aspiration to melodiousness constantly seeking to release itself from the rather complicated and jarring harmonic web. Indeed, there are passages that could easily be sung to words—a significant quality in this early effort at "pure" music by a composer who was to say years later in praise of Mozart that there was hardly a passage in his symphonies that could not be sung. Weill was about to make a solid reputation as an instrumental composer for the next few years, but underneath that reputation would always be a turn of mind that was essentially vocal and dramatic.

This can be heard clearly in the symphony he wrote to Becher's poem—which is known today as Kurt Weill's First Symphony—even though it is superficially a "difficult" work. There are even little hints in it of the future *Threepenny Opera,* including the crashing and dissonant opening chords with which the composer suggests a world at war. But the incipient theater composer is revealed less in the hints of works to come than in the structure of the symphony itself, which, without being mere program music, distinctly follows the outlines of Becher's work. Like the drama, it is divided into three parts, following a short introduction: the first is marked *Allegro vivace* with the specification that it be "wild, violent," the second is marked *Andante religioso,* and the last part is designated: "Like a chorale." The journey through these moods is marked by a steadily growing abandonment to the melodic urge: there are places toward the end that seem even to foreshadow Broadway. It also is utterly significant that the work ends in a chorale—a chorale written only for instruments, to be sure, but one that could easily be sung by voices and that carries echoes of the German ecclesiastical tradition going back through Mendelssohn all the way to Bach. The chorale is to play an important role in Weill's work for the rest of his life, and we are seeing here only its first important manifestation. What else can it be but an echo of the synagogue of his childhood and of the quasi-Mendelssohnian music written and sung by Cantor Weill?

Religious themes and the structure of the chorale continued to resound in Kurt's very next works, a Divertimento for small orchestra with male chorus, and a *Sinfonia Sacra,* both composed under Busoni's supervision in 1922. Furthermore, in 1923, after having composed some pieces of a more secular nature, he was to do a *Recordare (Lamentationes*

Jeremiae Prophetae), a work of thoroughly exalted mood, for mixed chorus and boys' choir, also under Busoni.

This sudden onrush of religious preoccupations was certainly in the spirit of the times, but not just for being concerned with God. In Weill's case, it also clearly represented a concern with his father in this moment when he was laying the groundwork for his own life's calling. The concern is particularly evident in the Divertimento, which, despite its strangely inapposite title, is a solemn and grandiose work. It is in four movements, all of which owe something to either Beethoven or Mahler despite their relatively free tonality, but the fourth movement is particularly Beethovenian, for it is choral. The text used here is a religious poem by Jens Peter Jacobsen, the Danish poet who was the author of the text Schoenberg had used for his *Gurrelieder*. It is a prayer to the God of the Old Testament, begging him to temper justice with mercy. The fact that this is sung by a male chorus, and somewhat in the manner of the old-style German chorale—both these traits reflecting predilections of Cantor Albert Weill—suggests that Kurt is approaching his father here.

But in what spirit? The prayer to the God of the Old Testament seems to imply reconciliation, even supplication, before the image of the pious and upright father—a sudden contriteness on the part of the young Berlin bohemian. Yet the musical character of the movement implies other possibilities. For its central theme—not only in the melodic line but in the forcefully rhythmic counterpoint with which the strings accompany it—is reminiscent of a passage in *The Magic Flute*. This occurs at the beginning of the opera's final section, when Tamino stands at the gate of the temple ready to enter and undergo the ordeals of fire and water, and the two armored guards there sing to him a last set of cautions. The melody used here by Mozart is that of an old chorale, *Ach Gott, von Himmel sieh darein* ("O, God, Look Down from Heaven"), and Busoni, who regarded this scene as one of the supreme moments of opera, wrote of it that "drama, morality and action join hands here in order to set this seal of their alliance on the music." These words were written in 1921, the year before Kurt Weill's Divertimento, and Busoni's continuing preoccupation with this scene during this period is shown by his use of it in 1923 as the last of his *Six Short Pieces for the Cultivation of Polyphonic Playing*, the summary piano composition of his career. Busoni's respect for the scene is so profound that his piece recapitulates it virtually note for note and does not introduce any variations until the last page of his score.

Weill's use of material so clearly derived from this scene in a passage relating to the "father" in two senses—the one in heaven and the one back home—may well be an announcement, made consciously or not, of a third "father" relationship in his life: the one with Busoni. But if this is so, then the meaning of Kurt's prayer to God is perhaps different from what it had seemed at first. For if Cantor Weill had once striven, through his treatment of the German chorale, to show his son the way to the Father in heaven, Busoni was now doing a musically superior job of it. By being supplicatory in this particular way, then, to the man who had sired him, Kurt also was finding a way to outdo him even in his own preserve, that of religion itself. It is a touch of the Ackermann spirit coming out again; Rabbi Aaron Ackermann had died ten years before, but Cantor Weill now had somebody else in the family claiming to know more than he himself did about devotional song.

But Kurt's struggles with the shadow of paternal authority were gentle compared to some that were setting the tone for his generation. The theme of the conflict between father and son had taken on violent manifestations in expressionist literature. It was Walter Hasenclever's 1914 play *Der Sohn* ("The Son") that had presented before the public the ultimate conclusion of the conflict: in it, the son points a gun at the father just before the final curtain. In 1922 the German public was to see Arnolt Bronnen's play *Vatermord* ("Parricide"), which had first been drafted in 1913, and in which the son kills the father during a fight that ensues when the latter breaks in upon him in the bedroom, about to be seduced by the mother. And, ominously, this theme, like that of revolution, now was moving from the realm of literature into that of living politics: for the murders by young right-wing thugs of Matthias Erzberger, minister of finance and signer of the Armistice, on August 26, 1921, and of Walter Rathenau, the foreign minister and one of the great statesmen of his time, on June 24, 1922, were only the two most outstanding of what would add up to more than three hundred such political assassinations within the four years that followed the end of the war. They were the symptoms of a deeply troubled Germany, which was now on a rapid plunge into the seemingly bottomless waters of inflation. By the beginning of 1921, the German mark, worth roughly four to the dollar before the war, had fallen to the value of seventy-five per dollar; but the worst was still to come.

Kurt Weill, like many Germans in that moment, soon found barter preferable to money. "It was in Berlin, in May 1922," writes Maurice Abravanel, today conductor of the Utah Symphony, "that I was introduced to Kurt Weill, then twenty-two years old, short, with questioning eyes behind very big glasses. He agreed to teach me harmony and counterpoint, charging half a pound of butter per lesson. He did not expect me to bring butter, but this was the prevailing wage in those days in Berlin, as prices changed almost daily." Maurice de Abravanel, to use what was then still the form of his name—he had been born in Salonika of Sephardic Jewish parents, and had grown up in Lausanne—was only three years younger than his teacher, who was himself still studying with Busoni. But Weill evidently had begun making a good enough reputation to be able to take on a pupil or two of his own. According to Abravanel, "Weill crisscrossed the city in the streetcar to give his lessons," obviously ready to inconvenience himself greatly in order to supplement the small financial aid he was getting from various relatives.

He had also begun to make part of his living as a composer by then. In the fall of 1922 a Russian choreographer named Vladimir Boritch arrived in Berlin with the text of a fairy-tale pantomime for children that he had written. The work was to make its way to the stage of the fashionable Theater am Kurfürstendamm as part of a Saturday afternoon children's series, but it is not clear how Weill got the commission to do the music for it. Busoni may have been responsible, but the young man always had been and ever would be something of a "hustler," and he surely was establishing other good connections for himself at this very time. In any case, the commission was not a particularly important one, but it was a start, and the fact that Weill was to conduct the piece as well meant extra money.

Nor was it in any way compromising that this first professional work of his was to be a ballet for children. Fairy tales, puppet plays, children's stories, and other such exercises in the naïve had become a favorite vein among serious composers in the wake of Stravinsky's achievements. Stravinsky was, as a matter of fact, to become an important influence on Weill, although this illustrious compatriot of Vladimir Boritch was not yet very well known to the young German composer. "Having been exposed to Ernest Ansermet's performances of the music of Stravinsky in Switzerland," Abravanel recalls, "I had the miniature scores of *Firebird*, *Petrouchka*, and *Sacre du printemps* on my rented upright piano. When Weill first saw *Sacre* (Germany had been totally isolated musically), he said I was losing valuable time looking at such 'dreck.' Later, of course, he became an ardent admirer of Stravinsky." Presumably, he had gotten to know these scores somewhat by the fall of 1922, but there also were German examples to be influenced by. Mahler, whom Weill greatly admired, had made splendid excursions into the pseudo-naïve. And now Paul Hindemith, who was rapidly making himself the outstanding musical voice of the new generation—he was five years older than Weill—had done some work in that vein: that very fall he was himself working on the score of a Christmas fairy play, *Tuttifäntchen*, to be presented in Darmstadt in December.

Weill's ballet *Die Zaubernacht* ("The Magic Night") had its premiere performance at three o'clock in the afternoon of November 18, and then was repeated the following two Saturdays, all under the composer's baton. "Busoni, his teacher, went to one performance," according to Abravanel, "and his only comment was that Kurt had *conducted* it well." This reticence about the music Weill had composed for the ballet is perplexing, for it has Busonian touches so far as one can make out today—and this is not as far as one would like, since the score has disappeared, and all that survives are one or two of its songs and a suite Weill later composed from it called *Quodlibet* ("What You Will," a medieval Latin term for a kind of free-style medley). There are a brisk pace and a whimsical bounce to the music that by all means recall *Arlecchino* from time to time, and above all, there is a new simplicity of line that contrasts strikingly with a work like the symphony. No doubt these traits were inspired by the need to be childlike for the occasion, but they were to remain in the composer's future work. In particular, simplification of style was to become one of his overriding aims, and he was to point to this work as the first significant example of it. Since this was a central issue for Busoni, about whom Weill was to say years later that from him "he imbibed the fundamental principle of simplicity," the teacher ought to have been very proud of the pupil. But Busoni, who now was gravely ill and struggling to finish his masterwork, *Doktor Faust*, was perhaps too preoccupied with his own troubles to have enjoyed this afternoon's excursion into his pupil's own magic.

Weill had one more term as Busoni's pupil and was to receive his diploma from the Academy of Arts in December 1923. During this year the crisis of the young German Republic reached a peak. The government was unable to meet its reparations obligations promptly, and on January 11 France took advantage of this excuse to send occupying troops into the Ruhr Valley. This action only added to the atmosphere of financial panic in Germany; in February the value of the mark descended to 48,000 to the dollar and did not stop there. "In the summer of 1923," according to one portrait of the period, "Berliners paid 600 marks to ride the trolley, 1,440 marks for a pint of milk, 100 marks to mail a letter, and 60 marks to make a phone call." Money became a mere absurdity and lives built upon it a constant anguish. The life savings of countless individuals were wiped out in the rush of rising costs, and a week's salary would often become obsolete in the time required to get it to the purchasing counter. By early October it took four hundred million marks to achieve the value of a dollar, and this became more than four trillion in November. On November 9 the thirty-four-year-old Adolf Hitler, with General Erich Ludendorff by his side, led his Nazi followers through the streets of Munich in an attempt to seize power in Bavaria. The "beer-hall putsch" failed and Hitler went to jail, but serious observers knew that this could mean worse things to come.

During this same year Kurt Weill composed his first two important concert pieces, which added greatly to his growing reputation as a young avant-garde composer. The first of these was a String Quartet, Opus 8, which had its premiere before the *Novembergruppe*, an organization of painters, writers, and composers dedicated to finding new art forms for the revolutionary era, of which Weill was now an active member. This new work showed the long way he had come since his String Quartet in B minor three years before. Free in tonality, somewhat expressionist in mood, it declares its kinship with the early quartets of Hindemith, between whose work and Weill's an interplay had begun to show itself since *Die Zaubernacht*. But there are distinct Weillian touches in it: moments that come close to melody in the kind of bittersweet vein that would soon be his trademark and a "choral fantasy" finale, with a fugal texture that bespeaks the composer's training with Busoni in the spirit of the baroque. The whole work, which is in a single movement divided into three main sections, can be played within ten minutes. Kurt dedicated it to his father.

The second important concert work of 1923 was a return to composing for the voice. This was the *Frauentanz* ("Women's Dance"), a cycle of seven songs based on medieval German poems, for soprano accompanied by flute, viola, clarinet, horn, and bassoon. In some ways, this is among Weill's most "difficult" works, tending to complete atonality in places, yet a certain comprehensible center is provided for the listener by the quasi-medieval flavor that is always there. According to one commentator, it "avoids the pitfalls of the Schoenbergian type of intervals" into which so many had fallen, and the deliberate archaism of the musical line seems to be chiefly responsible for this. Another commentator has observed that the work "shows affinities to certain works in archaic style by Hindemith," and one may note that it appeared in the very same year as *Das Marienleben* ("The Life of Mary"), Hindemith's song cycle for soprano and piano to the fifteen-poem cycle of that title by Rainer Maria Rilke. Weill, too, was to do some more songs to Rilke poems, and his *Frauentanz* was to be performed before an enthusiastic audience at the Salzburg Chamber Music Festival in the summer of 1924. People could then begin speaking of him as one of the new lights of German music, along with Hindemith; but his work was already beginning to move in a different direction.

New Turnings

5: The situation in Germany took a turn for the better at the beginning of 1924. The eminent financier Hjalmar Schacht, president of the Reichsbank since December, was guiding the nation's currency back to good health, primarily through the dissemination of a stopgap monetary creation, the *Rentenmark*. The inflation was coming to a halt, and with it, the crisis in Germany's relations with the old Allied powers. The committee led by the American banker Charles G. Dawes, which was to recommend French evacuation of the Ruhr and the restoration of complete economic sovereignty to Germany, held its first meeting in Paris on January 21. Gustav Stresemann, the former conservative nationalist who had become an ardent advocate of cooperation with the Allies, had now, after a stint as chancellor in the fall of 1923, settled into the post of foreign minister and begun to make his influence felt on the improving political climate at home and abroad.

The year began well for Kurt Weill, too. No sooner had his apprenticeship come to an official end, with his graduation from Busoni's master class in December, than he acquired, in January, the first of what was going to be a long and eminent succession of literary collaborators during the course of his career. This was Georg Kaiser, who was in this moment perhaps Germany's most esteemed playwright. Born in 1878, Kaiser had made a slow start as a writer, but during the war, when he was exempt from military service for medical reasons, he wrote several plays that quickly established him as one of the masters of the expressionist mode. The most celebrated of these, *The Burghers of Calais*, a philosophical drama inspired by the Rodin sculpture on that theme, depicts the moral agonies of seven citizens who have offered themselves up as sacrificial victims to a vengeful English king during the Hundred Years War. The king only wants six, and as the other volunteers begin to falter in their resolve, one of them, Eustache de Saint-Pierre, seeks a solution to the problem by taking his own life. In the end, the six survivors are spared, but the king will evidently pay homage to the memory of Eustache, whose last words had been to describe his own sacrifice as a necessary one for the regeneration of his fellow man. This was potent stuff, coming out as it did within months after the outbreak of the war, though perhaps somewhat compromised in retrospect by the fact that its author never had to flirt with self-immolation on the front lines the way so many of his contemporaries did. Another great Kaiser success, *From Morning to Midnight*, written in 1916, was far more cynical in spirit and up-to-date in milieu. It describes the twenty-four-hour odyssey of a bank clerk who, mistakenly believing that a woman has become sexually attracted to him, suddenly absconds with a large sum of money and goes on a spree that wildly contrasts with his hitherto stolid existence. In nightmarish images suggestive of George Grosz paintings, the play passes through an array of sleazy scenes of contemporary urban life in Germany, including a dance hall and a six-day bicycle race, and the hero finally shoots himself, falling with his arms extended like those of Jesus on the cross, in the midst of an electrical short-circuit. Kaiser's depiction of the psychological and techno-logical horrors lurking beneath the surface of humdrum modern life was vintage expressionism.

The violent expressionist style tends to have an operatic character, and Kaiser soon became ambitious to see some of his works actually done to music. His 1914 play *Europa*, a satire on the war and other contempo-rary matters disguised in an ancient Greek setting, was written as a *Singspiel* with music by a friend, the composer and conductor Fritz Stiedry. In 1918 Stiedry suggested that Kaiser rework one of his plays of that year, *Fire in the Opera House*, as an opera libretto, but for some reason Kaiser never did so. It may be that he was still uncertain about what kind of relationship he sought between his work and music, and probably, like most successful writers, he did not want to find himself merely function-ing as someone's librettist. Interestingly, we learn that the premiere production of *Europa* in 1920 was not done with Stiedry's score but with one commissioned by Kaiser from a young composer named Werner R.

Heymann. Kaiser's biographer does not give the reason for this, but it is possible that the playwright feared his work might be overwhelmed by Stiedry's music, which was undoubtedly more "operatic" than Heymann's. In this version the play came across as a *Tanzspiel*, with a heavy stress on Dionysian dancing as a way of satirizing some of the mores of contemporary German youth.

Kaiser had evidently become above all interested in incorporating dance into his works when he went to see one of the performances of *Die Zaubernacht* in late November or early December of 1922. He liked what he saw, and he went up to Kurt Weill afterward to tell him so. This may not have been the very first meeting between the celebrated playwright and the fledgling composer, and in any case it is not likely that Kaiser had gone to the performance entirely on his own initiative. Through a network of professional connections established by Busoni, Weill had become personally acquainted with Fritz Stiedry, and it was probably at Stiedry's suggestion that Kaiser had gone to look over *Die Zaubernacht* and its composer. Kaiser evidently was satisfied that afternoon that young Weill, talented but not overbearing, would be an appropriate collaborator for some kind of dance-drama; but he put aside the idea for the time being.

It was finally in January 1924, more than a year later, that Kaiser got in touch with Weill and, in the composer's words, "volunteered to write a scenario for me of a big, full-length ballet." Unfortunately, there is no way of knowing anything today about the nature of the project. "We went to work together," Weill continues. "In ten weeks almost three-quarters of the work was done. The score of the overture and the first two acts were completed." Then something went wrong with the idea. "There it came to a halt. We had outgrown the material; the silence of these characters troubled us, and we had to break out of the chains of the pantomime: it had to become opera." The moment had arrived, as a result of the seemingly inexorable logic of circumstances—and also, no doubt, of an assiduous application by Weill of the charm and persuasiveness that his various collaborators would come to know well through the years—for Kaiser to overcome his old ambivalence about opera once and for all. Abandoning the ballet, which has since disappeared, "Kaiser took out an old play that he had once previously thought of for an opera, the one-acter *The Protagonist*. Here we had what we were looking for: an unforced, natural interplay of opera and pantomime."

Kaiser had first written *Der Protagonist* in 1920, apparently for the celebrated actor Alexander Moissi, and it had received its premiere performance in Breslau in 1922. Set in Elizabethan England, it readily

appealed to Weill's old fascination with historical drama as subject matter
for opera. Furthermore, it had two pantomime sequences, which made it
possible for the authors presumably to use some leftover material—or at
the very least, some leftover inspiration—from the abandoned ballet. In
short, the choice of material was most appropriate, and young Weill,
assured of seeing his work produced when it bore the name of so
illustrious a collaborator, must have been very eager to get started. But the
next step was not in fact taken so rapidly as his own brief narrative seems
to indicate. Kaiser still had to rework the text as a libretto, and he seems to
have been in no great hurry to do so. No doubt he had other things to
attend to for the moment. Perhaps he still wanted to think the whole thing
over: this, after all, was the very point at which his operatic collaboration
with Fritz Stiedry had quietly come to an end.

Kurt was undoubtedly in anguish, but he was never one to waste any time
when his creative juices were flowing, and after a short trip to Italy in
March he immediately got to work on something else. Having become
acquainted with the violinist Joseph Szigeti, he wanted to compose
something for him, and during April and May turned out a Concerto for
Violin and Wind Orchestra. It proved to be his best piece of purely
instrumental, nontheater music to date, and this is appropriate in the light
of his subsequent career: for, with one isolated exception, induced by
circumstances a number of years later, it was to be his last. Yet even this
piece of "pure" music reveals the theater composer he now was becoming.
The violin in it seems for all the world like a picaresque traveler, a
dissonant Harold in Italy, moving through a variety of adventures and
climes, which are ever sketched out anew by the accompanying chorus of
wind instruments. One music critic has seen the work as "a tonal dialogue
in which the solo instrument has the best 'lines.'" But there are some good
"lines" in the orchestra's part, too. In particular, one section is dominated
by a xylophone, which enters into a whimsical dialogue with the solo
violin and here and there takes over the conversation completely.
    There is much of interest and charm throughout this three-movement
work, composed in "an idiom of dissonant expressionism," as H. H.
Stuckenschmidt puts it, but it is above all the section costarring the
xylophone—one of three parts into which the second movement is
divided—that reveals the essential character of the whole. The entire work
clearly carries echoes, by now familiar in young Weill's music, of Busoni,
Schoenberg, and Hindemith, but its newer intimations of Mahler and
Stravinsky are particularly evident in this section, called *Notturno*

("Nocturne"). The sociologist and musician T. W. Adorno has said of the whole concerto that "there is a strong trace of Stravinsky to be found in the classical, masterly clarity of the sound and in much of the wind writing," but what is Stravinskyan above all is the lowbrow humor of the xylophone, which hints at jazz idioms though it does not quite articulate them. Weill certainly had come to know *L'Histoire du soldat* by now, and one way its influence was to show was in his increasing bent from now on to employ jazz elements in his music. But even before he knew Stravinsky's work, Weill had shown a readiness to incorporate vulgar touches: such moments can be heard in the First Symphony and in the suite from *Die Zaubernacht*. The latter in particular has passages that pay distinct homage to Mahler, and it is clearly from Mahler—in whom the inclination was so obsessive that he had to tell Sigmund Freud about it—that Weill inherited this bent for sudden departures into vulgarity. Was there a common element in their respective personalities that produced this willful commonness in both of them? It is conceivably a Jewish trait, for there really have never been many Jewish musicians who, however exalted the tones they are able to achieve when they want to, do not know the occasional impulse to do some fiddling on the roof—very rarely is there a cantor who does not have within him a streak of the *badkhen*, the traditional wedding-bard of Central and Eastern Europe who fills the ears of bride and guests with a stream of song and story that can move them from tears to laughter in an instant.

We shall have further occasion to consider how many parts *badkhen* Kurt Weill may have inherited, and how many parts cantor, but in the meantime, we cannot help but note the elements of a dialogue between the two sides of the family personality in this xylophone-filled *Notturno*. For, speaking of the concerto as a whole, there is a touch of the cantor-chorus relationship in the responsive dialogue that dominates it, and furthermore it would seem that, in depriving his orchestra of strings, the composer has even shown an impulse toward filial piety: for isn't an all-wind orchestra somehow suggestive of an all-male chorus? In this scheme, then, the xylophone is like a *badkhen*, breaking in upon the cantor's more dignified ceremony with an impish, even taunting countermelody: and isn't the *badkhen* in this case the son, telling the father where he intends to go in the future? For Kurt's music is now about to make a firm departure from the stately solemnity of the previous few years.

The Violin Concerto also was a farewell to Busoni, as it turned out, for Weill's great teacher died on July 27, only a month after it was finished. Although only fifty-eight, Busoni had aged beyond his years, worn out by worry, overwork, and the ravages of the kidney infection that finally took his life. The dimly outlined picture that we have of the relationship between him and the young man who was to become the most famous of his pupils is ambiguous, mingling hints of tension with those of mutual respect, as between father and son. According to Wladimir Vogel, Weill's fellow pupil in the Busoni master class, Kurt "was a modest, rather quiet listener, who greatly respected Busoni and was in turn esteemed by him. Weill's views were much closer to Busoni's than mine were. His compositions in those days very closely conformed to Busoni's aesthetic principles and general outlook." Certainly Busoni's cherished ideal of simplicity became so deeply ingrained in young Weill that it was to remain with him all his life. "Don't be afraid of banality," Weill was to quote Busoni as having said, "after all, there are only twelve tones in the scale!" And one would like to assume that they shared views about music for the stage, particularly since Weill's next few operas were to bear the stamp of Busoni's influence. "Busoni could perceive Weill's talent for the stage even then," Vogel says, but there are signs that he did not greet it with unmitigated joy. Lotte Lenya has written that Busoni once asked him scoffingly, "What do you want to become, a Verdi of the poor?" Presumably, Weill had expressed ideas intimating the kind of popular musical theater he was to develop years later, and according to Lenya he replied, "Is that so bad?"

Wladimir Vogel doubts this story, and though Lenya indeed did not yet know her future husband when he was Busoni's pupil, its existence suggests that in later years Weill continued to recall some kind of clash with his teacher on the matter of opera or theater music. In any case, it seems entirely possible that Busoni never actually encouraged him to write such music, and though this behavior could have been because of nothing more than the teacher's sense of the proper limits of apprenticeship, it could also have had a temperamental factor in it. Young Weill was full of creative energy, perhaps annoyingly so to the aging composer who was struggling to complete his one major operatic effort. The libretto itself of *Doktor Faust*, written by Busoni, shows a certain obsession with the theme of aspirations not fully realized, and with young men rising up to replace the disintegrating old philosopher. When he died with the last scene still unfinished, the job of completing it was done by Philipp Jarnach, who had been his pupil in Switzerland and who had then followed him to Berlin. Busoni had always jokingly referred to Jarnach as his "famulus," which is what the student Wagner had been to Doctor Faust; but though Busoni's opera shows a Wagner suddenly grown ambitious after the old man's demise and eager to be his replacement, it was Weill rather than Jarnach who approximated this development in real life. Years later, explaining to an interviewer his theory that Busoni bore some similarities to Liszt—another great piano virtuoso *cum* composer, who "occupied in the latter half of the nineteenth century a position similar to Busoni's in the twentieth"—Weill was to say: "Just as Liszt started a movement which led to the great music of Wagner and Strauss, so Busoni started a movement which, we think, will lead to the great music of our time." And when the interviewer observed that Liszt had perhaps been more important as a springboard to other composers than as a composer in his own right, Weill replied, "I think that is all very true. And I would say that what Liszt did for Wagner, Busoni did for me." If the slightest germ of this idea expressed by the mature composer had been stirring in the young apprentice—and most likely it was—it could not have made Busoni feel wholly comfortable in his presence.

It was during the summer in which Busoni died that Weill and Georg Kaiser decided to go ahead and do an opera based on *Der Protagonist*. In order to discuss the necessary revisions in the text, they arranged a Sunday meeting at Kaiser's summer home outside Berlin, the Villa Alexander, in Grünheide on the shore of Lake Peetz. Kurt was instructed to get off the train that stopped on the side of the lake opposite the villa, walk to the shore, and wait for someone from the house to come and row him across. When the appointed day arrived, the person to whom Kaiser assigned the task of rowing over and picking up the composer was a young actress and dancer from Vienna who was staying in his house. Her name was Karoline Blamauer, but since she was eventually to become widely known under the stage name that she derived from her nickname of Lenja, we shall call her Lotte Lenya from the start.

Born on October 18, 1898, in Penzing, a working-class district of Vienna, Lotte Lenya had known poverty long before it became the experience of the majority of Germans and Austrians. Her father, Franz Blamauer, was a coachman; her mother, born Johanna Teuschl, was a laundress, and she, according to an interviewer, "was one of four hungry children." But from infancy, it would seem, she had the gift of performing that would be her salvation. "When she was only a baby," our interviewer goes on, "her father would often summon her from the coal bin where she slept and make her dance for him." By the age of six, she danced the czardas in a tiny neighborhood circus, and could do such things as stand on her head or walk a tightrope with an umbrella by the time she was eight. A good student, she managed to get transferred to a school for gifted children in the Hietzing district and eventually to finish secondary school. She then went to Zurich, where she stayed with an aunt and studied ballet and drama at the Civic Theater. By the time the war ended, she was a regular member of the ballet company at the Civic Theater, and was also doing small dramatic roles at the Zurich Playhouse.

In around 1920, Lenya tells us, "I came from Zurich to Berlin with my dramatics teacher. He was the régisseur from the Zurich Schauspiel-haus [Playhouse]. He moved his family to Berlin and I went with them. In Berlin I played with a little theater group, with a very idealistic director." This apparently was Otto Kirchner's Shakespeare Road Company, as it called itself. "We did nothing but Shakespeare, and I played every part possible for me to play." Then, in the fall of 1922, she met Kurt Weill—or rather, did not quite meet him—for the first time. "One day," according to Lenya, "I saw an ad in a theatrical paper for auditions—at the same theater where . . . years later, we would perform *Mahagonny*. They were seeing people for a children's ballet called *Zaubernacht*, and wanted young actors who could sing and dance. The theater was full of mothers and children. They asked me to sing a little song and to dance. Afterwards, someone said, 'Miss Lenya, meet our composer, Mr. Kurt Weill.' I only heard his voice. He was in the pit playing the piano. I never saw him at all." Nor did she get another chance to see him on that occasion, either because she did not get the part, or because—according to one writer's presentation of the story—she walked out in anger when her drama teacher was not hired as the show's régisseur.

It was through her drama teacher that Lenya met Georg Kaiser, presumably to be interviewed for a role. But whatever happened with the role, Kaiser and his wife, Margarethe, evidently took a personal liking to this remarkable girl—this gamine with a face that stood ambiguously between homeliness and some kind of beauty, and with a personality similarly poised between innocence and the toughness that comes from a childhood in the streets. Perhaps even then she had a voice, in speech as later in song, like that of "a disillusioned child singing outside a public house"; certainly this quality was already in her eyes. In any case, the Kaisers grew to like her well enough that when she was having a hard time making ends meet in the summer of 1924, they invited her to stay with them at the Villa Alexander, presumably to help in doing chores around the house. This was her situation, then, one Sunday afternoon that summer when Kaiser, in her words, "asked me to row across the lake and pick up a young composer waiting at the station who wanted Kaiser to write a libretto for him." She said all right, but how would she recognize him?

"All composers look alike," Kaiser replied.

So the young woman set out on her little mission. "There was sun on the waves," she recalls. "At the station I saw a very short young man with a typical musician's hat—the round kind—they don't wear them anymore. Heavy thick glasses. A blue suit and a blue little tie." As she put it on another occasion, "there he was: five feet, three and a half inches tall—an inch taller than I—with his hairline already receding, and thick, thick glasses. That is how I first remember Kurt Weill."

"Are you Herr Weill?" she asked.

"Yes."

"Would you mind entering our transportation?" she went on, pointing to the boat. Their eyes met. They got into the boat and as she began to row, the young man kept staring at her.

"I think we've met," he said.

"Where?"

"You didn't come back for the rehearsal of the ballet."

"Oh—yes."

"I am the composer," he said, as if she hadn't guessed it by now.

As Kaiser went to work on the libretto, the composer found plenty of reason for making return visits that summer, and a romance soon developed between him and the young actress. Kurt apparently was now ready for a deep and viable relationship with a young woman, and if he had not been before, this was not only because of the extremely difficult financial circumstances under which he had been living. The truth is that he had fallen passionately in love two years before, but with a married woman.

Nelly Weill Frank was actually a distant cousin of his, but since she had grown up in Zurich, he had not met her until her appearance at his brother Hans's engagement party in 1922—to which she had come, not because of the Weill connection, but because her husband was a cousin of the bride-to-be, Rita Kisch. There is some reticence about this affair among Kurt's surviving family and friends, but it is evident that the marital status of Nelly Frank was not the only source of anguish for him. She was a wealthy woman, both as the daughter of a prosperous branch of the family and as the wife of a rich man. At the time she met Kurt, she and her husband and two young sons were living in Berlin, and since their wealth was in foreign currency, they were able to surround themselves with an opulence that contrasted painfully with the young composer's situation in a miserable furnished room. But all this, along with the fact that Nelly was three years older than Kurt and far more worldly, did not prevent her from reciprocating his feelings for a time. A romance blossomed, and Kurt and Nelly went together on a trip to Italy in the summer of 1923. On their return to Berlin, Nelly asked her husband for a divorce—not necessarily so she could marry Kurt, but simply to be able to do as she pleased—but he would not grant it. The crisis ended in Nelly's departure with her husband for a brief stay in the United States. Kurt dedicated his *Frauentanz* to her, and his memories as well, no doubt.

But with Lenya now appearing in his life, Kurt soon found himself to be far from the first—as he would be far from the last—lover since Romeo to experience a successful new romance on the rebound from a frustrated old one. There was even a point or two in common between them. Interestingly, both women had come to Kurt by way of Zurich. The fact that she arrived in Berlin from the city where Nelly Frank and Busoni also had lived may well have added a dimension to Lenya's charm. More importantly, both Lenya and Nelly were slightly older than Kurt—and considerably more sophisticated. For a shy young man who had been cherished by a somewhat domineering mother, these were important qualities.

But equally important were the ways in which Lenya was completely unlike either Nelly Frank or Emma Weill, or any other woman Kurt had ever been close to before: for Kurt now needed as much to be free of his mother as he had been to be free of his father. Lenya was not Jewish, a fact that was bound to displease both his parents when they learned of her—all the more so now that both his brothers and his sister were married, and to Jewish spouses. For Kurt, if he married Lenya, would be the only one among his first cousins so far to have a gentile spouse—a situation that suited him perfectly, since he had just arrived that very year at the conclusion that he was no longer interested in the religion of his childhood. Furthermore, Lenya was a number of important things that the Jewish women in Kurt's life were not: an artist, a bohemian of sorts, a daughter of the working classes, and a lifelong fighter in the arena of hardship. What better mate could be asked for by a rebellious, creative young man, sick of the old bourgeois conventions, thirsty for social justice, and very much in need of emotional autonomy at last?

Kurt was also ready in more obvious ways for a new and stable relationship. That summer of 1924 his *Frauentanz* was performed brilliantly at the Salzburg Chamber Music Festival by the well-known soprano Lotte Leonard, and it was very well received—so well, in fact, that it won him a ten-year contract with Universal Edition of Vienna, the foremost publisher in Europe of twentieth-century music. As for his Violin Concerto, Joseph Szigeti did not perform it, but it earned enough of a reputation that it was to be done the following summer in Paris, at a concert of the prestigious International Society for Contemporary Music. There was also the promising new partnership with Georg Kaiser, who seems, furthermore, to have been most eager to promote the new romance between Kurt and Lenya. The composer, as success and a touch of financial improvement began coming his way, was even becoming an attractive young man despite a superficially unprepossessing appearance. An associate his own age described him years later as looking like this at around the end of 1923: a "small, balding young man, squinting at the world through thick, professorial glasses with eager, burning eyes, quiet in his manner, deliberate and always soft-spoken, dressed more like a candidate for a degree in divinity than a young composer in the flamboyant Berlin of 1923, sucking a conservative pipe with the absent-minded absorption of an instructor in higher mathematics." Others were often to talk of what seemed to be "the deep-seated mockery on his lips," an attitude that some took for contemptuousness, but that bespoke the shy intellectual, concealing a romantic and vulnerable interior beneath a cloak of irony. All this was adding up to a special charm, and it suited Lenya, with whom he had settled down into a common apartment before the end of the year.

Composing Opera

In January 1925 Kurt Weill began a sideline career as a music critic for *Der deutsche Rundfunk* ("German Radio"), a weekly journal of broadcasting. This was a significant new source of income, but it also gave him opportunity to show that he was a writer of skill and some wit, who, for example, described the experience of listening to one opera broadcast in April thus:

> Here's how it went: the first act of [Friedrich von] Flotow's *Alessandro Stradella* had unrolled without mishap to the lulled ears of this listener. Stradella had bemoaned his lot, Leonore had joyously proclaimed her willingness to take flight; now they disappear into the crowd, there is a confusion of masked figures as the basses begin to curse—and suddenly there is an interruption. A soft buzzing—ticking—then music again: but wait, that isn't—that's no longer a Venetian carnival of the seventeenth century, it's a London party of 1925! A jazz band, whispering Englishmen, flirting Englishwomen, and then: "I love her in the morning, I love her in the night"—and all the while, those dancing shimmy-steps. But then it's Venice once again, in the broadcasting studio with opera chorus, radio orchestra, and those browbeaten basses.

But Weill also was fully aware of the serious aspects of Marconi's great new toy. "So revolutionary an institution as radio," he wrote later that month, "also demands an entirely new attitude toward art and the economics of art. The irreversible fact is that concert music, as it exists today, no longer has sufficient power for educating society to be able to go on in its present form. But perhaps—perhaps!—a part of its task could be taken up by radio; perhaps the broad masses to whom radio belongs could form the basis for a whole new direction in music."

Weill is demonstrating here that he has become, like his teacher Busoni, an intellectual among musicians; and indeed, in linking the development of music to the surrounding conditions of technology and society, as well as in aspiring to a more democratic relationship between composer and audience, he is evincing an attitude toward art that was widespread among the German intellectuals of his postrevolutionary generation. Furthermore, like that generation, he shows a strong tendency to identify his own inner growth with the general patterns of history. For the skepticism expressed here about the future of concert music is above all a product of his final recognition, after several years as an apprentice, of his true calling as a theater composer.

"Only when I observed that my music contained the tension of scenic action did I turn to the stage," he was to write a short time later, but for him this also was an insight into the general character of music. In the "Operatic Credo" that he prepared for the 1925 Yearbook put out by his music publisher, Universal Edition, he said of his generation:

> The realization that there was nothing more to add to the genre of [post-Wagnerian] music drama, or to be derived from it, made us into fanatics for absolute music. We had to find some way of holding up our century against the preceding one, which we believed to have been too much overlaid with a literary covering, with a kind of artistic materialism. Music had to become once again the sole, self-fulfilling aim of our creative activity. We were sure that an intensification of the musical experience would result from our preoccupation with Bach and the preclassical composers.

Weill noted that, even where an interest in theater music persisted, it tended to manifest itself as ballet—which is to say that the composer simply "enriched the effect of concert music with a set of visual impressions." Apparently there was trouble in perceiving that opera had to be composed "with the same untrammeled unfolding of fantasy as in chamber music." But this does not mean, Weill cautions, that one should simply transfer to opera the elements of absolute music, which would only be a route to cantata or oratorio. It is just the other way around: the dramatic elements of opera can really form the basis of all musical composition. "Mozart taught me that," he proudly asserts, and explains of that master:

> He is no different in opera than in his symphonies or string quartets. He always has the tempo of the stage, and therefore remains an absolute musician even when he lets all Hell break loose over Don Giovanni's head; on the other hand, in the vaulting brios of his symphonies, there are theatrical images throughout.

There is nothing impure about this, for in the last analysis, Weill concludes, "what moves us in the theater is what grips us in all art: heightened experience, the clarified expression of a feeling, humanity."

This was the outlook with which the young composer undertook, in the spring of 1925, to do the music for his opera version of Georg Kaiser's *Der Protagonist*. He finished it at around the time Field Marshal Paul von Hindenburg was elected president of the Republic on April 26. The libretto was about a traveling theatrical troupe in Elizabethan England, which arrives at a country inn and proceeds to set up rehearsals for a performance to be given that evening at the court of the local duke. The duke, it turns out, has foreign guests who would not understand a spoken play in English, so the performance must be a pantomime. In the course of the preparations at the inn that are presided over by the "Protagonist"—in true expressionist fashion, none of the characters has a name—who is both managing director and leading player of the troupe, we learn that he has traveled here with his sister, toward whom he manifests a passion unnatural in its intensity. But unbeknownst to him, the sister has been followed by a "young gentleman," with whom she has already exchanged vows of love. In a brief moment alone with the young man, she agrees to marry him; but she protests that she cannot tell her brother news of the betrothal until he can be caught in a lighthearted mood—as he often is after an exhilarating, comic performance. The occasion seems right for the young lovers, then; for the duke and his guests are in a "merry hunting mood," according to the duke's majordomo, and they would appreciate a light entertainment.

The Protagonist and his company proceed to rehearse a saucy pantomime about a husband, a wife, his mistress, and a bawdy monk. Two corners of an upper gallery are made by the players to represent windows looking out onto the "street" below. We see the jealous wife at one window, the mistress at the other, and the husband dashing back and forth adroitly between the two. The bawdy monk arrives, and the husband sends him to console his wife; but he becomes too ardent in his mission, and the husband finally rushes over and kicks him out into the street. In the end the husband has both wife and mistress to himself all over again.

In the mood of gaiety with which the piece ends, the sister goes to the Protagonist and tells him of her lover. He asks merrily to see the young man, and she goes off to fetch him.

But then everything changes. The majordomo returns with the news that a bishop, a kinsman of the duke, has arrived among the guests, and that a bawdy jest would therefore no longer do for the evening's entertainment. The play must be a serious one. In a clever tour-de-force, the Protagonist begins to rehearse his company in a second pantomime that is, in effect, the same story as the first one, but done in a somber vein and with the promise of a tragic ending. The jealousy and rage of wife and husband are now registered in a serious way, the bawdy monk is now a debauched nobleman, and the offended husband now approaches him at the climactic moment with a dagger. As this scene is enacted, the Protagonist is suddenly seen to be in a mounting fury that is no longer merely of the play, and as he pounds at the door of the "house" in which the wife and her new lover are ensconced, the other actors are thrown into a state of confusion and fright. At that moment the sister arrives, announcing that the man about to enter the room behind her is the one who has been her secret lover. Hearing of this affair as if for the first time, the frenzied Protagonist turns upon her with his dagger and stabs her to death. Her lover arrives in the next moment, and as all gape in horror at what has just occurred, the Protagonist, transported into a state that no longer knows any distinction between art and life, shouts that he must not be arrested until after that evening's performance. For, he says, real and feigned madness have become one and the same: "The bishop and the duke will relish the spectacle!" he cries as the curtain descends.

Weill's score for this opera achieves its greatest individuality in the two pantomime sequences, which represented a chance to do ballet, such as he had originally planned to do with Kaiser, and in which he perhaps still felt a little more confident than in opera. Musically distinct from the rest of the score, they take on special interest not only because they are two separable, self-contained "concert" pieces within what is otherwise a continuous music drama, but also because they were a chance for the composer to represent different levels of reality in musical terms. What

Weill does here is take advantage of a suggestion provided by the original play, in which the comic pantomime is accompanied by a small ensemble sent by the duke and set up in the gallery. Weill has composed music for this ensemble, as well as for the orchestra in the pit. It is the gallery ensemble, consisting of flutes, clarinets, trumpets, and bassoons, that alone plays the first pantomime, in the lively, staccato vein that had characterized *Die Zaubernacht* and some of the comic works of Hindemith: the busy syncopations of this passage at moments even seem to anticipate the jazz flavor of the composer's later works, as the xylophone passage in his Violin Concerto had done. On the other hand, it is the orchestra in the pit, with strings, trombones, horns, bass clarinets, as well as oboes and percussion, that plays the ominous, tragic music of the second panto-mime.

For the rest, the opera is rather Busonian: the very setting and subject matter of the play had suggested *Arlecchino* to some extent. One would listen through this opera in vain for melody of a sort that was to become its composer's specialty in just two or three more years. The emerging inclination toward jazz, hinted at more clearly in the Violin Concerto, has been all but completely suppressed in *Der Protagonist*. It is resolutely free in tonality, and if the pantomime sequences are tinged with a relative melodiousness and a rhythmic vitality that stand out from the whole, the rest of the opera relies simply upon expressiveness for its musical validation. Mainly functional, the music does not so much call attention to itself as intensify the drama. When Maurice Abravanel reviewed its premiere the following year, he said of the opera that, "according to many listeners, one could not even hear the music as such," and explained that "the music does not illustrate the subject matter; it is the subject matter itself." He was reminded of Stravinsky, to whose music he had introduced Weill in the first place, and so was Oskar Bie, one of the eminent music critics of the day, who wrote of *Der Protagonist* that "Weill's musical style is somewhere between the psychological intellectuality of Busoni and the almost graphic brass outlines of Stravinsky." Bie added that he thought Busoni's old pupil had now definitely left the teacher behind.

This certainly was the parting of the ways between the deceased master and the former apprentice. In May 1925, the month after he finished the score of *Der Protagonist*, Weill went to Dresden for the premiere of *Doktor Faust* and showed his new work to Fritz Busch, music director of the Dresden Opera. Busch liked it, and agreed to perform it the following season. On May 21 Busch presented *Doktor Faust*, a splendid, brooding work in a post-impressionist style to which Weill's work was in no way akin. In a sense, both Busoni and Weill had gone their own respective routes since the style of *Arlecchino*, which the pupil would soon be leaving as far behind as the teacher had, arriving at a very different destination.

Three weeks later, on June 11, Weill's Violin Concerto was given its premiere performance in Paris under the baton of Walther Straram with his Orchestre des Concerts, and with Marcel Darrieux as the soloist. It was well received and was soon to become the most widely played of Weill's concert pieces. But the composer himself was not at all ready to rest on the laurels he now was earning in the field of concert music. At the Romanische Café sometime that summer he met a thirty-four-year-old Alsatian poet named Yvan Goll, who had lived in Paris until recently and wrote verse both in French and in German. Goll was a true expressionist of the moment, filled with political radicalism and psychic despair. He had written a poem in German called *The New Orpheus*, which, amid images of the stark, lonely, nightmarish city, tells of a modern bard who arrives in Berlin and sees his "Eurydice" in the crowd at the railway station: she is clearly a prostitute, "with too much rouge on her lips," and when she disappears into the crowd he shoots himself. In September Weill composed to this poem a cantata for soprano, solo violin, and orchestra. It was in his best expressionist vein, with the free tonality of some of his earlier concert pieces and containing hints of parody of popular and traditional themes.

Goll liked it, and he and Weill decided to do a one-act opera together. By January they had completed both libretto and score of *Royal Palace*—which is the opera's very title in German, the fashionably English name of the Italian resort hotel at which it is set. The scene is a terrace of the hotel, with a beautiful lake and landscape in the background, from which comes the tolling of church bells now and then, and the sound of women singing—presumably peasant women, but the effect is as if they were naiads, or "Rhinemaidens" of the post-Wagnerian age. Dejanira enters, followed by three of the men in her life—one is her husband, the others are "Yesterday's Lover" and "Tomorrow's Lover"—as well as by a troop of fawning bellboys who do a brief ballet around her. In the ensuing conversation, Dejanira's three companions express their passion for her, and she expresses her utter boredom with life, while the idyllic scene behind them darkens into night and the voices of the women and of fishermen keep coming over the water. At the end, with the voices singing all around her, Dejanira walks off and drowns herself in the lake.

The score of *Royal Palace* was not among Weill's best works to date, but it was a milestone in his development, for it is the first in which we hear him using distinct jazz motifs. There is a sequence midway through the opera in which the three men take turns in making some very large promises to Dejanira, and each of these is dramatized by stage effects and an extended musical interlude. Among them, the husband offers her "the wealth of the Continent," and the stage darkens while a film projection shows a montage of Dejanira pursuing the high life everywhere—in Nice, on a Pullman to Constantinople, at a ball, at a Russian ballet, on a flight to the North Pole, and so on. This gives the composer free rein to convey the tempo and flavor of the twenties at their frenzied peak, and the interlude is a kind of jazz ballet of the sort that was being done in France by composers like Darius Milhaud—who was to be a friend of Weill's. The opera's finale, in which the various voices from the terrace and from the lake accompany Dejanira's suicide, is sung over a tango accompaniment in the orchestra. The tango, which had made its way from South America in the decade before the war, was a craze of the twenties in Europe as much as in the United States, and it had furthermore won the right to be incorporated into serious music through the example of such works as Stravinsky's *L'Histoire du soldat*, which makes use of ragtime as well. Weill was to make his tangos into something of a trademark.

Royal Palace was not to have its premiere performance for more than a year, but in the meantime there was much of importance to occupy Kurt. The premiere of *Der Protagonist* was set for March, and before that most important of events to date in his professional career, he took the most important step of his personal life: on January 28, 1926, he and Lotte Lenya were married. There is a picture of them taken after the small civil ceremony. They are standing outdoors against a background of trees and an iron picket fence, the bride glowing with her unique radiance and looking like the essence of the twenties in her long checked coat, the groom standing more primly in dark coat, bow tie, hat, and his thick glasses. There is something almost rabbinical about him, though he was now as far as he ever would be from the world of Cantor and Mrs. Albert Weill, who disapproved of this match and were not present. Kurt was taking another important step in the definition of his adult self in his marriage to this intimate companion to whom he dedicated the score of *Der Protagonist*. The theater had indeed become his synagogue, and he no doubt already knew, having just completed *Royal Palace*, that if he was a cantor of the musical stage he was also part *badkhen* there too, just as much as he had proved to be in his Violin Concerto. Perhaps it had even occurred to him by now that he might one day compose theater works in which his bride could sing, even though she was an actress who merely sang on the side and was unable to read a note of music. What did any of the old conventions matter? They were a couple for the Berlin of their day.

The newlyweds, who had been living in a pension out in the Halensee district, still could not afford an apartment, but they found a pleasant pension closer to the center of town. It was in a solid, Wilhelminian-style building on the Louisenplatz, near the Charlottenburg fortress and conveniently close to the Kurfürstendamm theater district. The concierges were Franz Hassforth and his wife, a pair of typical Berliners, stout, earthy, and sardonic in their conversation, who were known to their tenants as "Papa" and "Mama." The Weills moved into two rooms on the third floor, of which one was a parlor-studio. In it Kurt had a huge black piano installed. Lenya has recalled that the rooms "were dominated by paintings of a hideously bloody deer hunt, and the furniture was painted pitch-black. (We called it 'Grieneisen,' after a famous Berlin funeral parlor.)"

The bride no doubt already knew by then what was the lot of a woman who had settled down with a composer wholly dedicated to his music. "Kurt was always at his desk by nine . . . completely absorbed and like a happy child. This was never to change, as a daily routine, except for interruption for rehearsals or out-of-town tryouts." She recalls waiting for him patiently each mealtime down in the dining room. In that period, she has said, "I was not that busy in the theater. I sat at the table, and Weill came down for breakfast, then went back to his music. He came down for lunch and went back to his music. After a few days, I said to him, 'This is a terrible life for me. I see you only at meals.'

"He looked at me through those thick glasses and said, 'But Lenya, you know you come right after my music.' That was my place. Weill was a man who knew only music. Other composers had hobbies: Schoenberg, Gershwin painted. Weill, I think, had music as his hobby." But it was only two months after the marriage that the composer showed what kind of success this dedication could enjoy.

Kurt and Lenya went down to Dresden for the premiere of *Der Protagonist* on Saturday, March 27. Hans and Rita Weill arrived for the performance, too. Their daughter, Hanne, not yet three years old, was with them, and when Kurt and Lenya visited them at their hotel room that afternoon, Lenya asked the little girl, "How are you doing?"—just as if she were addressing a grown-up. "I am very nervous," Hanne replied.

But she was not nearly so nervous as her uncle the composer, who, though he had rented a tuxedo for the occasion, did not show up for the performance that evening at the Saxon State Opera House. Instead, while their opera proceeded under Fritz Busch's baton, Kurt sat with Georg Kaiser in a nearby bar. "After several drinks," according to a writer who interviewed the composer years after the event, "they got into the kind of philosophical discussion that usually accompanies such situations. They had completely forgotten about *Der Protagonist* when the stage manager finally found them. There had been thirty-five curtain calls, and the stage manager, taking charge of Weill, steered him up to the stage and pushed him on for ten more calls." From that night on, Weill was an established composer among a much wider audience than the one that had known and appreciated his concert music. To be sure, there had been some cries of "Pfui!" in the auditorium amid all the applause, mainly from resolute opponents of avant-garde music, and at least one critic thought that, except for the second pantomime, Weill's score was entirely lacking in "creative individuality." But the work soon was given other performances throughout the country, and Weill and Kaiser felt encouraged enough to begin planning a new one-act opera.

Success had its effect upon Kurt's personality: people close to him recognized a new self-confidence and independence of manner, and in particular a new unconcern about what his parents' reactions might be to anything he did. He now plunged eagerly into new projects. Obtaining a commission to write incidental music for a radio production of Christian Dietrich Grabbe's classic play, *Herzog von Gothland*, he worked on this during July and August; the broadcast was done in September. He also went to work on a full-length opera in collaboration with a young music critic named Felix Joachimson. Called *Na und* (roughly, "So What?"), it was a comic portrayal of contemporary Berlin life, as slangy as its title, and full of bits of jazz. Weill evidently had been inspired by his work on *Royal Palace* to try this sort of thing again; besides, the idea of injecting jazz elements into opera was in the air. His music had found its own distinct flavor and tempo, which were quite lively, but had not yet come upon its proper content. Now a possible source was beginning to proclaim itself, however, in the popular music of the day, to which Weill listened as ardently as he did to all music—he was especially fond of his collection of Louis Armstrong records. The realization never was far from him that Mozart and other *Singspiel* composers, as well as Mahler, had been perfectly ready to dip into the most vulgar sources for their melodies.

Weill wrote to his publisher Emil Hertzka, founder and director of

Universal Edition, informing him of the project, and Hertzka invited him
down to Vienna to give a run-through of it at the piano. The young
composer, according to Hans W. Heinsheimer, who was then one of
Hertzka's assistants, soon "was sitting at the depressing upright that had
been installed in Hertzka's office. . . . Weill played the entire opera,
softly singing with a veiled, pleasant, expressive voice, playing the piano
in a dry, matter-of-fact, unflourished manner. Hertzka and I followed
with the libretto." But it did not take them long to realize that they did not
like what they heard. "We did not like the libretto, which was by a
little-known German playwright and musician who had never written a
libretto before, and as we read on we ardently wished he had let it go at
that. We loathed the title of the opera which seemed to reflect the worst
asphalt cynicism of Berlin. . . . The music seemed handicapped and
weighted down by the story and the lyrics. As the composer played on,
one could sense an aura of despair creep into the room."

But Weill, who had already begun to display the kind of utter
professionalism that was to earn the admiration of almost all his colleagues
on two continents, calmly accepted the verdict that was given to him at
the end of his performance. "He listened quietly and with attention" as
the publisher and his assistant explained that the publication of this work
might even be a setback to his career. "Weill closed the score and put it
back in his valise. Hertzka left for his suburban abode and I took Weill
across the street to the *Schwemme* of the Imperial Hotel, a smallish bar and
restaurant where taxi drivers and mail carriers dropped in for a beer
and . . . the juiciest of goulashes. . . . Weill enjoyed his goulash, told
gentle stories during the meal, and spoke of everything but *Na und*. He
mentioned it briefly on the way to the station for the night train to Berlin.
He would be in touch with us. After a few days he informed us that, for
the time being, he had decided to put the opera away." Unfortunately,
after being given one performance at that time by a small group in Berlin,
the score has never been seen again, except for a few fragments.

Weill had much better luck with the next one-acter he did with Kaiser.
Based this time on an original script, *Der Zar lässt sich photographieren* ("The
Tsar Has His Picture Taken") is set in Paris, in the studio of a well-known
and fashionable woman photographer named Angèle. The telephone
rings, and Angèle is informed that the "Tsar"—his country is never
mentioned, and he cannot be identified with any historic figure—is about
to come for a portrait photograph. As she and her two male assistants
excitedly make preparations, the doorbell rings, and in walks a group of

conspirators determined to assassinate the Tsar. Angèle and her two assistants are taken away and replaced by three of the conspirators in disguise. A pistol is fastened to the rear of the camera on its tripod, in such a way that when the rubber ball controlling the shutter is squeezed the gun will go off; the conspirators then cover it with the black cloth that the photographer drapes over her head whenever she takes a picture.

All but the three imposters go off, and soon the Tsar arrives with his entourage. He is a youngish man in ordinary street clothes, who protests that he is above all a human being and wants to be depicted this way. He and the false Angèle are left alone, and soon a flirtatious dialogue between them develops into a romance. She is obviously charmed by the Tsar, but still undeterred from her purpose, she poses him, gets behind the camera, and begins to count: "One . . . Two . . ." Suddenly the Tsar interrupts and says that, just for a whim, he would like to take *her* picture first. He seats her, grabs the ball of the camera, and begins the same count; then she leaps up and stops him, and soon the scene becomes a small ballet as they jockey for position around the camera. Their game grows more affectionate, and finally they are in a passionate embrace.

The Tsar's bodyguard enters and says the police have received word of a conspiracy; a few moments later he reenters and says the police are on their way to the studio. In the little time remaining to them alone, the false Angèle puts a record on the phonograph—it is a tango—and she and the Tsar prepare to make love on a divan in one corner of the room. She asks him to lie down on it with his head covered by a cushion, so he won't see her undressing; and he does so. At that moment the other conspirators return and, seeing the Tsar stretched out on the divan, think the false Angèle has done her job. Then the police arrive and arrest them. The real Angèle, now released, comes in and starts to adjust the camera. The gun goes off—harmlessly, since no one is in the subject's chair—and the shot wakens the Tsar, as if from a dream. He is confused by the apparent change in Angèle, but his entourage readies him for a stately pose, while the photographer and her assistants prepare to take the picture.

This amusing piece—called an "opera buffa" by its authors—is still composed largely in the free-tonal, expressive style of *Der Protagonist*, but distinct touches of the later Weill are beginning to emerge. This is above all evident in the tango sequence, used in a climactic moment as its equivalent had been used in *Royal Palace*, and conveying, as in that opera, a mood of ambivalent eroticism. Another Weill touch is the use, throughout the opera, of an all-male chorus, situated not on stage but in the orchestra, and commenting on every significant development. The very opening chords of the opera are sounded by this chorus: "Der Zar lässt sich photographieren," they sing, and later, when the conspirators break in and announce their plan, the chorus sings, "with a Tsar's blood!" When two plainclothesmen precede the Tsar's arrival and look around the studio, even brushing against the camera, while the false Angèle nervously watches them, the chorus calls out: "There, under the black cloth," but they do not take heed. These asides continue to the very end, and take on an additional dimension of humor by the fact that the chorus is made up entirely of old men in top hats. The *badkhen* in Weill has emerged more clearly than ever in this opera, but we do not hear in it the musical content we associate with his very next works, which had already been sounded to some extent in *Royal Palace* and, undoubtedly, in *Na und*. Weill evidently needed the catalyst of a new collaborator to help him achieve the next transformation in his style. But the need was already being supplied: for he had found an important new collaborator before he even finished composing *Der Zar lässt sich photographieren* in the spring and summer of 1927, and by the time of its premiere in February 1928 the stylistic transformation had already occurred.

Enter Bertolt Brecht

It is possible that Weill and Bertolt Brecht had known one another personally as far back as 1922, when the playwright was still living in Bavaria and making occasional trips to Berlin. One of Brecht's biographers writes that the composer "Nicolas Nabokov has described how he, together with Isadora Duncan, the Russian poet Esenin, Brecht, and Weill, had 'sniggered indecently' at the old-fashioned Russian world presented to them by Stanislavsky's Moscow Art Theater at a performance of *The Three Sisters* in Berlin in 1922 or 1923." Lotte Lenya, on the other hand, says Weill and Brecht did not meet until several years later; and in any case, their acquaintance could not have been more than a casual one until 1927. On March 18 of that year Berlin Radio did a broadcast of Brecht's play, *Mann ist Mann* ("A Man's a Man"), and since it included some musical numbers composed by Edmund Meisel, Weill was provided with an excuse to write about it in *Der deutsche Rundfunk*. He did no fewer than two pieces, one prior to the broadcast, in which he alerted his readers to the forthcoming radio production of "what can be described as the most novel and powerful play of our time," the other his review in the issue of March 27, in which he called the playwright "a poet, a true poet." Brecht became interested in meeting the author of these words, who also was getting to be well known in theater circles for his collaborations with Georg Kaiser and Yvan Goll.

The twenty-nine-year-old Bavarian, a native of Augsburg who had spent some of the formative years of his maturity in Munich and had not settled in Berlin until 1924, had already begun to emerge in the eyes of many as the foremost playwright—and perhaps the foremost poet, as well—of the postwar generation. Ernst Toller had grown silent, at least for the time being, after an early outburst of revolution-minded plays, and Brecht's good friend, the Viennese-born Arnolt Bronnen, had not lived up to the promise of his sensational *Vatermord* ("Parricide"), produced in 1922. At first, Brecht and Bronnen, who once resolved to conquer Berlin together, had seemed very much alike: nicknamed the two "Fasolts" of German literature—the play on their names, made by the Viennese writer Karl Kraus, is a reference to the giant of medieval Teutonic legend and Wagnerian opera—they had written expressionist works of a similar brutality in the early twenties, and Bronnen had even chosen Brecht to be the director of the premiere of *Vatermord* (a choice repudiated, however, by the actors themselves). There was little of Brecht's later left-wing political orientation in his works of this period. His first important play, *Baal*, the sordid adventures of a modern poet loosely modeled on the life of François Villon, and his 1924 free adaptation of Christopher Marlowe, done with Lion Feuchtwanger, *The Life of Edward the Second of England*, are more concerned with raw power and untrammeled sexual expression than with the social revolution of their time. *Drums in the Night* and *In the Jungle of Cities*, produced respectively for the first times in 1922 and 1923, are a little different: the first takes place during the Spartacist uprising, the second seems to be a surrealistic parody of capitalism—but both are politically ambivalent. Bronnen, similarly ambivalent in this period, has told a story of how he and Brecht, out of curiosity, went to see one of Hitler's rallies in Munich on an evening in June 1923. Brecht, he writes, "was of course not blind to the danger that manifested itself in the susceptibilities of the petty bourgeoisie, and the sympathy of the grand bourgeoisie for those work-shirkers' latrine slogans. But then again young Brecht, with the typical Bavarian love of pageantry, delighted in the spectacle, and the mass direction and mass performances of the Hitler-clique."

By the beginning of 1927, the parting of the ways that would soon lead Bronnen into the Nazi party and Brecht to a rather orthodox Marxism had become evident. *Mann ist Mann*, an absurdist morality play about British soldiers in India, is decidedly anti-imperialist and shows its progressive bent in other ways as well. Yet in his personal style the new,

socially conscious Brecht had lost nothing of the Baal-like bullying quality
that he had made into his trademark years before. "Strikingly degenerate
look," Count Harry Kessler was to say of him after their first encounter
late the following year, "almost a criminal physiognomy, black hair and
eyes, dark-skinned, a peculiarly suspicious expression"; though Kessler
conceded that "superficially, at any rate, he has a head on his shoulders
and is not (like Bronnen) unattractive." Though skinny in those days
almost to the point of sickliness, Brecht affected a tough-guy stance,
wearing his soon-famous leather jacket and cap, and a stubble on his chin,
smoking a black cigar, hanging around in bars—where he sang his poems
and accompanied himself on the guitar—going to sports events, befriend-
ing boxers. The swagger was now more that of a man of the people than of
a *poète maudit*, as he demonstrated just before the *Mann ist Mann* radio
production in one of his more notorious flaps. Asked by the journal *Die
Literarische Welt* ("The Literary World") to be judge in a poetry contest,
Brecht announced in the February issue that he found himself unable to
give the award to any of the four hundred young aspirants whose work he
had gone through, finding nothing in it of "practical value." He called the
contestants decadent specimens of contemporary youth "whose acquaintance I should much more profitably have been without. . . . Here we
have them once more, those quiet, gentle, dreamy creatures, the sensitive
section of a used-up bourgeoisie, with whom I do not want to have
anything to do." Brecht then printed a poem that had not been entered in
the contest, but that he considered to be an example of practical value: a
piece of doggerel by the six-day bicycle racer Hannes Küpper in praise of
his world-famous British colleague, Reggie MacNamara.

It was around the beginning of April, then, that Brecht and Weill
either began or renewed their personal acquaintance, at a table in
Schlichter's restaurant on the Lutherstrasse, a favorite hangout of theater
people. Also present were Lenya and some mutual friends of the
composer and the playwright who had brought them together on this
occasion. One tries to imagine what went on then amid Schlichter's
well-known "cold buffet with its famous salads," as described by a Berlin
writer, "and the pictures all around by the owner's brother, the painter
Rudolf Schlichter, which imparted to the otherwise stolid rooms a touch
of artistry and bohemianism." The Augsburg business manager's son and
the Dessau cantor's son, both artistic rebels from their middle-class
backgrounds yet so utterly unlike one another in most ways, must surely
have exchanged compliments and done a good deal of mutual sizing up.

They certainly also recognized what they wanted in each other right away, for "from that point on," Lenya has said, "Kurt and Brecht visited each other quite often and started discussing what they could do together."

At first, they did not have a very clear idea of what they wanted to do and certainly had nothing like *The Threepenny Opera* in mind. Weill, for his part, was a composer-intellectual who, having collaborated on his operas with such writers as Georg Kaiser and Yvan Goll, now wanted nobody but the best to work on his librettos—and many agreed that by 1927 there was no playwright better than Brecht. As for Brecht, he had been a poet before becoming a playwright, had included poems in most of his plays, and wanted to go on doing so; furthermore, in his conception of theater, these poems had to be sung—indeed, he himself had written melodies to many of them. Now there were many points at which Weill's evolving theory of *Zeitoper* ("opera for the times"—a term then popular among German avant-garde composers) and Brecht's evolving theory of "epic theater" were to mesh perfectly in this felicitous moment when they met, but there also were ways in which their respective artistic outlooks were unlikely bedfellows from the beginning. For, if Weill really wanted to do nothing less than *opera* in the long run, Brecht hardly was prepared to settle for the role of mere librettist. But in their first flush of enthusiasm together, as ideas came rushing in on them, they were able to let their potential differences go unnoticed.

The first project on which Weill got to work with Brecht was for the German Chamber Music Festival, which was to take place that summer in Baden-Baden. This annual event, which was moving to new quarters, had taken on European-wide cultural importance. It had been founded six years before at the estate of the Prince von Fürstenberg in Donaueschingen, a picturesque village at the edge of the Black Forest where the two sources of the Danube come together, by a group of young musicians whom the Prince had invited for this purpose. In its first few summers, the festival had specialized in avant-garde music of the purest sort: it was here, for example, that some of Paul Hindemith's earliest chamber works made their debut, played by the Amar Quartet, in which the composer himself was the violist and his brother Rudolf the cellist. Alois Hába's quarter-tone compositions were another feature of the festival in those days. Arnold Schoenberg, when he accepted an invitation to participate in 1924, wrote to the prince in praise of "this enterprise that is reminiscent of the fairest, alas bygone, days of art when a prince stood as a protector before an artist, showing the rabble that art, a matter for princes, is beyond the judgment of common people."

But this was not really the attitude of the postwar generation to the arts in general, and by the mid-twenties new moods, less lofty and more culturally democratic, were making their way into little Donaueschingen from the world at large. Among the bearers of the new ideas were Hindemith's good friend from France, Darius Milhaud, and the ever-young and cosmopolitan Igor Stravinsky. Since the heyday of Debussy and Satie, the French had been keenly aware of the possibilities for genuine merriment that lay in the world's lowbrow musical sources, such as American jazz. Stravinsky had produced masterpieces of contemporary music out of such sources; and Milhaud, who had spent the war years as a diplomat in Brazil and made a trip in 1922 to the United States, where he eagerly visited Harlem, was even more sensitive to such sources than Stravinsky was. In particular his ballets, *Le Boeuf sur le toit* in 1919 and *La Création du monde* in 1923, liberally employed popular motifs that he had brought back from Latin America and from Harlem. The 1920s were becoming in some respects an "American" era in European culture, but in nothing more so than music, and among no other people so strongly as the French, who wore the mantle of Americanization with their own peculiar grace, assimilating it as another Paris fashion.

Now the mantle was being passed on to the squarer German figure, and if Berlin by the late twenties was to become in many respects as "American" as Paris was, a principal recurring occasion for that cultural transfer was the Chamber Music Festival. In particular, as its foremost guiding figure came to be Paul Hindemith—who had played something of the *enfant terrible* of German music for a time and had used jazz forms and motifs in such important early works as his *Suite 1922* for piano—the festival became an occasion for experimentation in such quasi-popular forms as music for films and other games of technology. It was during these summers, furthermore, that Hindemith began to develop his eventually well-known idea of *Gebrauchsmusik*. This untranslatable term—"music for use" is roughly the meaning—represented for Hindemith an artistic goal not far removed from what Brecht had in mind when he extolled the poem about Reggie MacNamara. Influenced by the general new current in German art known as the *Neue Sachlichkeit* (often translated "New Objectivity" but perhaps more aptly "New Matter-of-Factness"), which had arisen in the mid-twenties as a reaction against the unworldly excesses of expressionism, *Gebrauchsmusik* aimed for a relationship with ordinary people that had largely been lost amid the artistic Brahminism of the late nineteenth and early twentieth centuries. In an era of revolution, art had to become as democratic as politics now had become. The movies and the radio were the outstanding media of the new artistic democracy, and perhaps it was a perception of their tremendous psychological impact upon the masses that led some German artists to think, as Brecht and Hindemith did, of the new kind of art as somehow "for use." At any rate, there is a schoolmaster lurking within almost every German intellectual. But certainly the buildings and chairs created by the Bauhaus were art for use, and this school stood at the center of the German artistic conscience.

After the summer of 1926 the composer Heinrich Burkard, who had been the Prince von Fürstenberg's musical director and one of the organizers of the Chamber Music Festival, left the Prince's employ, and the festival was moved to Baden-Baden. Perhaps the Prince had grown dissatisfied with the change in its character; or perhaps the burgeoning annual event simply needed larger quarters. In any case, the program planned for the summer of 1927 was a true manifestation of the new spirit of the festival. Hindemith and the other directors had taken to announcing central themes or formulas for each summer's proceedings, and this time some of the participating composers were asked to produce short one-act operas for chamber ensembles, modest in their dimensions both on the stage and in the orchestra pit, and simple—one might say "useful"—in style. Darius Milhaud received such an invitation, and so did Ernst Toch; Kurt Weill was thus invited, too.

Weill had thought for a time of doing something from one of the classics of world drama—a scene from *King Lear*, perhaps, or from *Antigone*—but his contact with Brecht led to a different idea entirely. As with many moments in the history of the Brecht–Weill partnership, it is now impossible to say which of them came up with the original suggestion: some sources say Brecht, who had begun to envisage a "Mahagonny opera" a few years earlier; others say Weill got the idea after having read Brecht's poems. In any case, the two men chose to do something with a group of poems about a fictitious fool's-paradise of a city called "Mahagonny," which Brecht had included in the *Hauspostille* ("Domestic Breviary"), a volume of his verse published the year before. The "Domestic Breviary" was another example of Brecht's readiness to *épater le bourgeois* at any opportunity, for the first edition of this collection containing many explicit parodies of prayers and mockeries of middle-class proprieties was published to look like a prayer book, with black leather binding and double columns printed on Bible paper.

The five *Mahagonny* poems seem to form a kind of loose narrative sequence, and as such, they are different from most of the other poems in the book: although one of them, about the arrival of God in Mahagonny to send the men there down to Hell—an assignment they refuse, protesting that they have been in Hell all the time—is in keeping with the book's emphasis on mock religious themes. The poems describe various aspects of the life of an imaginary American boomtown that has strong affinities with the Klondike of Jack London and of Charlie Chaplin's *Gold Rush*, a film that had reached Germany in 1926. Men and women come to Mahagonny to be rich and free, and their lives consist of a constant round of fighting, whoring, poker-playing, and whiskey-drinking—indeed, *whiskey* emerges as one of the author's favorite words, especially in the two poems he has written in his own version of the English—or rather, the American—language, the "Alabama Song" and the "Benares Song." Together the poems form a somewhat ambivalent parody of capitalist society, for though the roughneck characters in them are meant as travesties of the bourgeoisie, the would-be roughneck who has created them is clearly fond of their world in many ways. Here, as in other places in his works, Brecht seems to hate nothing so much about the bourgeoisie as their hypocritical airs of respectability, and one suspects that he would almost be ready at times to forgive their acquisitive vices if only they were as earthy in the pursuit of them as the people of Mahagonny are.

A similar ambivalence applies to the "American" setting of the poems. For Brecht in that era, as for most left-wing European intellectuals from that day to this, America was the quintessential capitalist country, a land of unbridled greed—but there also was something exciting about it. "All of us were fascinated by America," Lotte Lenya has said, "as we knew it from books, movies, popular songs, headlines. . . . This was the America of the garish twenties, with its Capones, Texas Guinans, Aimee Semple McPhersons, Ponzis, the Florida boom. . . . Also the disastrous Florida hurricane . . . and a ghastly photograph reproduced in every German newspaper of murderess Ruth Snyder in the electric chair, Hollywood films about the Wild West and the Yukon, Tin Pan Alley songs." It was quite in keeping with this spirit that among the earliest films of one of Germany's most brilliant young film directors, Fritz Lang—himself to be an American one day—was a tale of the adventures of an American from San Francisco (called *Die Spinnen*—"Spiders"—it was made in 1919). Brecht himself maintained a large collection of American newspapers, from which he gleaned material for his writings. England interested him, too, and he never ceased to be both attracted and repelled by the Anglo-American world.

This ambivalence seems also to extend to the word Brecht coined as the name for his gruff never-never land. *Mahagonny* is close enough to the German word for mahogany—*Mahagoni*—to seem to have been derived from it. According to one theory, Brecht coined the word in 1923, the year of Hitler's beer-hall putsch; the poet was still living in Munich part of the time and, dismayed by the sight of storm troopers in the streets, used the term *Mahagonny* to call to mind the "masses of petit-bourgeois, wooden figures in brown shirts." Another theory gives the word an even earlier origin, attributing it to an imaginative overseas chimera in which tropical forests and skyscrapers all came together in Brecht's mind, so that the word evolved by the poet from the one for mahogany became a symbol of America for him. At any rate, even before these poems appeared, he apparently used the word a lot as a conversational catchall for capitalist philistinism, and it eventually represented everything he disliked about the Berlin of that day. Furthermore, it simply had an interesting, somewhat absurdist sound that appealed to Brecht's ear.

It also clearly appealed to the ear of Kurt Weill, who was to make a good deal of musical capital out of the glottal catch between *Ma–* and *–hagonny*. There can be no doubt that Weill had become caught up in a distinctly Brechtian lilt and tone, which showed forth in the music he now composed for the mock cantata he and his new collaborator had formulated out of the five *Mahagonny* poems, reordering them in accordance with a minimal scenario and adding a sixth poem as well. The Brecht of 1927, eager to twit the pretensions of high culture, wanted the theater to be a place of lowbrow fun—after his own peculiar highbrow fashion, of course—in which, he claimed, people should be able to smoke and make conversation just the way they do at sports events. And so Weill wrote what was, with the possible exception of *Na und*, the first of his scores to be entirely permeated by a spirit of low comedy. Such a spirit had manifested itself on occasion in Weill's work before, but there is unquestionably something new in its manifestation here, a quality of coarseness and aggressive audience-needling throughout the piece that is not entirely in keeping with his own gently ironic nature. Now, there is no point in exaggerating the Brechtian component in this and other scores to be produced by the new partnership, as many have wanted to do: Brecht had written music of his own to all five of the original poems, but

Weill had made extensive use of only one of these tunes—that of the "Alabama Song"—and partial use of only one other—that of "God in Mahagonny"—in both cases making them over into something quite a bit more his own. Furthermore, all the purely orchestral interludes between the songs are entirely Weillian, and more distinctly related to earlier compositions of his such as *Die Zaubernacht* than to most of the works he subsequently was to do with Brecht. Yet it must be said that Weill's music is taking an astonishing new turn in this score, and that this can be largely attributed to Brecht's influence.

The most striking new development, and the one that was to mark Weill's work for the rest of his life, was the emphasis upon *song*. "Up to that time," Brecht later wrote of the moment their collaboration began, "Weill had written relatively complicated music of a mainly psychological sort, and when he agreed to set a series of more or less banal *song* texts he was making a courageous break with a prejudice which the solid bulk of serious composers stubbornly held." It is true that Weill had never even included so much as an *aria* in his operas to date, much less a *song* in the sense Brecht intended here, which, according to Weill some years later, "corresponded, I suppose, to the better type American popular song." The Germany of 1927 had popular song composers just as America did, but there were none yet who tried, as George Gershwin was doing in America, to bridge the gap between the worlds of "light" and "serious" music. Not that the idea of incorporating the elements of popular song into "serious" works was without good precedent in German music: Mozart himself had done it in *The Magic Flute*, particularly with Papageno's two arias, *"Der Vogelfänger bin ich ja"* and *"Ein Mädchen oder Weibchen."* Furthermore, Alban Berg's *Wozzeck*, which had had its premiere in December 1925 and which had provided a brilliant demonstration of the operatic possibilities of the Schoenbergian school, contained snatches of song. Both Mozart and Berg unquestionably were inspired, in these cases, by a sheer delight in naïve melody, but a dramatic purpose also was being served, since the songs in these operas were placed as characterizations in the mouths of simple folk. In a sense, these were like the snatches of earthy prose spoken by Shakespeare's common people amid the iambic pentameters of the highborn ladies and gentlemen. But in Germany at any rate, no "serious" composer had yet constructed an entire work around such snatches.

There was, however, a milieu in which composers of all sorts had long been able to try out their songwriting capacities on the side, a place for "slumming," as it were, at least on the part of "serious" musicians.

This was the cabaret, an institution that Berlin had inherited from Paris at around the turn of the century, and for which even so austere an artist as Schoenberg had once written songs. If the cabarets were, on the one hand, outlets for the works of such quality writers of popular songs as Rudolf Nelson, Friedrich Holländer, and Mischa Spoliansky—the German equivalents of men like Jerome Kern and Irving Berlin—they also were places in which one could hear songs of a more highbrow nature, sometimes so because of their musical sophistication, more often so because of their witty, usually satirical lyrics. Our popular American image today of Berlin in the twenties has stressed the sleazy type of cabaret; but there were cabarets of all kinds, ranging from those in which people simply danced and talked to a background of pleasant music to those in which artists and intellectuals gathered to amuse their sensibilities in a more purposeful way. Some of Germany's most vicious political satirists, such as Walter Mehring and Kurt Tucholsky, used the cabaret as one of the major outlets for their works. So also did Brecht, who usually wrote his own melodies and performed them himself, accompanying himself on the guitar. "He was expert on the instrument," the playwright Carl Zuckmayer has written, "and loved complicated chords difficult to finger: C-sharp minor or E-flat major chords. His singing was raw and abrasive, often with the crudity of a street singer or music-hall minstrel. An unmistakable Augsburg intonation underlay it. Sometimes he sang with something approaching beauty; his voice floated along with emotional vibratos, enunciating every syllable with great clarity. When he sang you could say of his voice what [the drama critic] Herbert Ihering had written about the diction of his early works: 'It is brutally sensual and melancholically delicate. There is vulgarity in it, and abysses of sadness, savage wit, and plaintive lyricism.' "

Dreaming always of François Villon, Brecht formulated his own particular attitude toward music while making himself a minstrel of the cabarets and bars, first in Munich and then in Berlin. His biographer Martin Esslin writes that "he hated Beethoven and the sound of violins, but liked Bach and Mozart. But above all he disliked the atmosphere of concerts: the spectacle of frock-coated gentlemen sawing away at their instruments, of polite and educated people gently bored and pretending to be moved." In these respects, his views came quite close to those that had already been evolved by Weill, who also apparently had tried his hand at writing cabaret songs. But in his outlook on music, as on other things, Brecht sought to go beyond limits that relatively moderate men like Weill, however rebellious and imaginative they were, would not be likely to exceed in the long run. In characteristically outrageous fashion, he sought a new word for his own melodic ideal: *Musik* would not do, and so he coined the term *Misuk*. According to Hanns Eisler, who was eventually to become Brecht's collaborator, the playwright's *Misuk* was something "above all popular, and it is best described as reminiscent of the singing of working women in the backyards of tenements on Sunday afternoons." This sounds like a good Marxist ideal, though it rarely, if ever, arranged itself so neatly in practice. At times, Brecht's effort at honest vulgarity seems to have been nothing more than a treatment of the banal with the kind of wise-guy irony that prevailed in the intellectual cabarets: his original musical setting for the "Benares Song" in the *Mahagonny* group, for example, is a sly amalgam of "There Is a Tavern in the Town" and *"Un bel dì"* from Puccini's *Madame Butterfly*. At other times, his *Misuk* seems to have been a strange, Gothic brew of folk motifs as ancient as the Black Forest civilization from which Brecht's forebears had come, something a bit outside the mainstream of Western culture: but if this was the wailing of an ancient peasantry, it was not particularly accessible to the ears of ordinary folk in the twentieth century. In the long run, the cantor's son was to show far greater gifts than Brecht at arousing a wide audience with music—gifts greater than Weill himself so far knew he possessed.

Not that Weill the full-fledged songwriter of only a year later had yet emerged with the utmost clarity in these 1927 *Mahagonny* songs. Of the six, only the "Alabama Song" has the qualities of a conventional song—it is recorded as such by popular singers to this day—and that is the one whose melody was almost entirely provided by Brecht. These largely fragmented pieces are really only parodies of song by a witty avant-gardist who has come to know his Stravinsky well, and who treats his vulgar materials in a way similar to that of *L'Histoire du soldat*—indeed, even the small instrumental ensembles of the two works are similar, except that Weill had human voices to play the lead instead of Stravinsky's scraping violin. Some of the material parodied is purely native: there is a brassy, German beer-hall sound to the opening "Off to Mahagonny!" and the words *"Schöner, grüner"* ("Beautiful, green") in it were an irresistible opportunity for the composer to do a satirical quotation of the music written to the same words in the Bridesmaid's Chorus of Weber's *Der Freischütz*. The two pidgin-English songs are parodies of American-style "jazz" (in the broader, European sense of the term), but the "Alabama Song" has surrealistic overtones in the music as well as in the lyrics, and the "Benares Song" is not so much a song as a hilariously grotesque scene of nonsense dialogue sung to fragmented jazz motifs. The only consistently songlike element throughout the pieces is their underlying structure of recurring stanzas in which the same melodic line is repeated—although the instrumental accompaniment always changes from one stanza to the next.

Nevertheless, despite all these clever evasions of the point, the central principle being played with by composer as well as poet in this work is palpably *song*. This is brought home all the more forcibly by the fact, evident to any listener, that the composer has a distinct flair for melody. The snatches of utterly traditional tune-making in this work are well spread out, but they occur often enough to provide an anchor for the more intellectual, dissonant stretches, and to tease the listener into a more spontaneous enjoyment than the avant-garde framework might otherwise lead him to expect. One can actually go home from it humming bits of melody, as with a popular musical show. This certainly was done with a distinct purpose in mind, by a composer who admired Mozart for his singability, and by a poet who wanted his listeners to have at least a little ordinary fun. But there is something else to it, besides—a quality of melody in a conventional, even in a banal, sense arising suddenly out of the depths of Weill's nature. If its appearance did not astonish the composer yet, it was bound to do so before long.

The authors, wishing to stress the point that they were doing something quite new by introducing song into the fields of cantata and opera—for now they intended to expand this work into an opera right away—developed some new terminology, Brecht-fashion, for what they had created. In the first place, the standard German words for *song* did not seem to them to apply: *Lied* was too redolent of the concert hall and of Schubert and Brahms; *Gesang* was too lofty. Weill and Brecht decided instead to use the English word *song*, which they were later to claim they had introduced into the German language. Using this word as a component, they then coined a second one as a name for the new musical genre they said they were inventing: *Songspiel*, a play on *Singspiel*. To this day, then, though the term *Kleine Mahagonny* ("Little Mahagonny") has often been used for this half-hour-long work, its proper title is the *Mahagonny Songspiel*.

As the authors of the *Songspiel* began to prepare it for production that summer—it was to be staged by Brecht himself with the help of the director Walter Brügmann, and with backdrop projections by Brecht's old friend and colleague Caspar Neher—they hit upon a new idea that was to prove one of the most significant of all. Resolutely regarding this work as a "style study" for the full-length opera he planned to develop with Brecht out of the *Mahagonny* material, Weill had conceived and written it with operatically trained voices in mind. But of the four male and two female voices for which it was scored, not all bore an equal burden of technical difficulties. In particular, the women's parts were easier than the men's, and the "Alabama Song," which was to be done by the two women alone, required only a popular singing technique. Why not give one of those parts, then, to a nonoperatic voice—to a good actress who also could sing? Undoubtedly, this idea came from Brecht; but perhaps it was Weill, agreeing to it, who provided the next suggestion: why not Lotte Lenya?

Weill must have occasionally thought of his wife in connection with his work before this, particularly if he had tried his hand at writing cabaret songs, as he apparently did. She had a good, warm cabaret voice and was quite musical even though she did not read a note; and she had sung in some of her stage roles. Kurt's stage works so far had only been opera in the strictest sense, but his steady movement toward simplification of style and the use of popular motifs must surely have led him by now to consider including nonoperatic voices in them. And if he did so, he certainly had a good stage voice at hand to help him color his musical thinking. As for Brecht, he must have noticed right away the element of "distancing"—of what he was soon to make known as the *Verfremdungseffekt*—that resided in Lenya's murky yet childlike tones: she was truly the child of those working women who sang in the backyards of tenements on Sunday afternoons. If her voice has seemed to many in subsequent years to be the perfect vehicle for some of the Weill music, it has really always been that for the *Brecht*–Weill sound above all.

Lenya has told the story of how Brecht came to her and Kurt at the Pension Hassforth to hear her audition the "Alabama Song." They had awaited his arrival nervously and then heard a commotion downstairs at the front door. Kurt rushed down and found "Papa" Hassforth arguing with Brecht. The God-fearing proprietor had answered the doorbell, taken a look at the disreputable figure standing before him, said, "We're not giving anything," and slammed the door. Kurt explained the situation, then ushered the visitor upstairs, and was soon at the piano accompanying his wife as she sang. Brecht listened, Lenya has said, "with that deep courtesy and patience that I was to learn never failed him with women and actors. 'Not quite so Egyptian,' he said, turning my palms upward, extending my arm outward in direct appeal to the moon of Alabama. 'Now let's really work. . . .' " She had been taught the English words phonetically by another Vienna-born singer and actress, Greta Keller, and though Lenya's pronunciation was very stilted, Brecht could not have cared less: her strange, off-English was precisely in the spirit of what he had written.

The week of the Baden-Baden Festival arrived, and the group of miniature operas to which Weill and Brecht were contributing was scheduled for the evening of July 18. The *Songspiel*, which was the longest piece on the program, was placed at the end. First came an eight-minute-long work by Darius Milhaud, *The Rape of Europa*, then a fairy-tale opera by Ernst Toch, *The Princess and the Pea*. These were followed by Hindemith's sly bagatelle, *Hin und Zurück* ("Forward and Back"), a ten-minute work that starts out as a merely humorous piece of grotesquerie about a quarrel between husband and wife and then turns into a dramatic and musical joke: halfway through, the action and the music suddenly go into reverse, and play back to the beginning. For a while, Brecht had considered outdoing this joke with a much more startling one: he wanted the two women of his *Mahagonny Songspiel* to come out naked. But Weill had not been at all eager to see his wife do this, and the municipal authorities of Baden-Baden, when they eventually got wind of the idea, had wasted no time about vetoing it.

Despite this act of censorship, however, the *Songspiel*, when it was performed for the festival audience, proved to be more startling than its predecessors on the program in almost every respect, including its conscientious lowbrowism. To the astonishment of the spectators, the stagehands set up a small boxing ring, and then the singers took up their positions in it by climbing through the ropes. Though dressed more or less for an evening out, the men in bowlers and the women more rakishly in straw hats, they adopted the attitudes of tough characters, with the names Jessie—this was Lenya—Bessie, Charlie, Billy, Bobby, and Jimmy. On the rear wall appeared the first of Caspar Neher's projections, which were to be a series of raw, expressionistic depictions of scenes of violence and greed. The first raucous chords were struck up by the small ensemble of violins, clarinets, trumpets, saxophone, trombone, percussion, and piano, conducted by Ernst Mehlich, and then, after the instrumental prologue, the men were "Off to Mahagonny"; they soon were followed by the women, seeking "the way to the next whiskey bar" as they sang the "Alabama Song." Lenya stood in the middle of the ring, as one observer recalls, and did her solo "in a hoarse voice with lascivious inflections." By the time the life of Mahagonny had been depicted in full, there was some commotion in the audience, and before the epilogue was over people were on their feet, either cheering, booing, or whistling. The singers, by now in shirt sleeves, responded by pulling out small whistles and blowing back at the audience; Brecht came out and blew one, too. The performers also were carrying placards with provocative slogans, and Lenya was waving one that said: "*Für Weill*."

The performers did not know right away what the mood of the spectators really had been. Afterward Lenya left the theater and went to the hotel bar at which most people were gathering and "found a frenzied discussion in progress. Suddenly I felt a slap on the back, accompanied by a booming laugh: 'Is here no telephone?' " This was one of the more delightful bits of barbarous English in the "Benares Song." The backslapper turned out to be Otto Klemperer, the distinguished conductor of the Kroll Opera in Berlin. "With that," Lenya goes on, "the whole room was singing the 'Benares Song,' and I knew that the battle was won." Kurt also received compliments, many of them from composers impressed by the combination of sophistication and simplicity in his style. Some could not help remarking: "But that Alabama song; it's written in the key of G!" To everyone's astonishment, however, the touch of conventional tonality was acceptable in the kind of piece Weill and Brecht had created, in which the spirit of modernity had been satisfied to some extent by the replacement of dissonance with insolence.

Not that the audience that night had been universally enthusiastic. Among them had been the young American composer Aaron Copland, the same age as Weill, who wrote a short time later:

> The chamber opera which aroused most discussion [at the festival] was Kurt Weill's *Mahagonny* (accent on the third syllable, please!). A pupil of Busoni's, Weill is the new *enfant terrible* of Germany. But it is not so easy to be an *enfant terrible* as it used to be and nothing is more painful than the spectacle of a composer trying too hard to be revolutionary. Weill, in writing *Mahagonny*, cannot escape the accusation. It is termed a "songspiel" and is, in effect, a series of pseudo-popular songs in the jazz manner. . . . Weill is not without musical gifts but these are too often sacrificed for the sake of a questionable dramatic effectiveness.

Yet, in the last analysis, dramatic effectiveness had been the point. It was a novel dramatic idea that had called the tune, and with this had come a novel combination of musical ones. In the context, even touches of banality were allowed; for banality, along with melody itself—both banished for a time from the "serious" musical stage—was now being welcomed back by a newfound sense of humor.

The Birth of
The Threepenny Opera

 "In Berlin's memory the twenties live as the Golden Age," wrote one of the city's historians three decades later. "Something of its luster is reflected upon anyone who had the good fortune to live in Berlin in those days. 'So you, too, are a twenties person?' is one of the forms of greeting between old Berliners who come across one another in their Diaspora, far from their city. And even as the 'twenties people' become fewer and begin to disappear, the legend of the Golden Years glitters all the more. Under its glow the memory of the Kapp putsch, which was the curtain-raiser, fades out, as does that of the unemployment crisis with which it all ended. The inflation lasted through 1923, and by 1929 the end was signalled with the great American Stock Market crash. Strictly speaking, Berlin only had five carefree years. But never was the city greater, richer, more colorful or dazzling than it was then, never had it belonged to its children more than in this brief moment."

For some the glow was a tawdry one. "All values were changed, and not only material ones," wrote the Viennese author Stefan Zweig of Berlin in the twenties; "the laws of the State were flouted, no tradition, no moral code was respected, Berlin was transformed into the Babylon of the world. Bars, amusement parks, honky-tonks sprang up like mushrooms. What we had seen in Austria proved to be just a mild and shy prologue to this witches' sabbath; for the Germans introduced all their vehemence and methodical organization into the perversion. Along the entire Kurfürstendamm powdered and rouged young men sauntered and they were not all professionals; every high school boy wanted to earn some money and in the dimly lit bars one might see government officials and men of the world of finance tenderly courting drunken sailors without any shame. Even the Rome of Suetonius had never known such orgies as the pervert balls of Berlin, where hundreds of men costumed as women and hundreds of women as men danced under the benevolent eyes of the police. In the collapse of all values a kind of madness gained hold particularly in the bourgeois circles which until then had been unshakeable in their probity. Young girls bragged proudly of their perversion, to be sixteen and still under suspicion of virginity would have been considered a disgrace in any school of Berlin at that time, every girl wanted to be able to tell of her adventures and the more exotic, the better."

Zweig the novelist probed beneath the surface of this behavior, saying that "the most revolting thing about this pathetic eroticism was its spuriousness. At bottom the orgiastic period which broke out in Germany simultaneously with the inflation was nothing more than feverish imitation; one could see that these girls of the decent middle class families much rather would have worn their hair in a simple arrangement than in a sleek man's haircut, that they would much rather have eaten apple tarts with whipped cream than drink strong liquor; everywhere it was unmistakable that this over-excitation was unbearable for the people, this being stretched daily on the rack of inflation, and that the whole nation, tired of war, actually only longed for order, quiet, and a little security and bourgeois life. And, secretly it hated the republic, not because it suppressed this wild freedom, but on the contrary, because it held the reins too loosely." The worst excesses had passed with the inflation, but the Berlin of sleazy excitement remained along with that of more golden glories by 1927 and 1928, which perhaps were the best of the city's five carefree years.

A good part of the significant creativity of those years took place in the theater, which Germans continued to love with the special passion they had inherited from the time of Lessing, Schiller, and Goethe. But it was not the playwrights who were particularly brilliant in the twenties; rather, the excitement was provided by outstanding actors and directors. For one thing, this was still the era of Max Reinhardt. Born in Austria in 1873, Reinhardt—who, both as a Viennese and as a Jew, was a characteristic type of Berliner in the arts during the first decades of this century—had come to Berlin in his twenties and won the post of chief producer at the Deutsches Theater by 1905. He had soon made his mark with uniquely spectacular productions, mainly of classics by the Germans, the Greeks, Shakespeare, and others. He staged the medieval morality play *Everyman* on the steps of Salzburg Cathedral, and his production of the *Eighth Miracle of the Virgin Mary* (widely known just as *The Miracle*) by Karl Gustav Vollmoeller, a contemporary, was played before an audience of ten thousand in London in 1911. After a sojourn in Vienna in the early twenties, Reinhardt came back to Berlin in 1925 and took over the Grosses Schauspielhaus, the city's most grandiose theater, which had been built in 1919 on the site of a circus arena.

Reinhardt's enormous crowd scenes were considered vulgar by many, especially among the postwar generation. Some of these found their ideal in the work of Leopold Jessner, who emerged in the early twenties as something of a counterforce to Reinhardt, seeking utter simplicity in his productions. Perhaps the most expressionist of directors, Jessner became especially known for his use of the staircase, often placed on stage without any justification in realistic terms, as a spatially rhythmic platform upon which the dramatic line could be played as a virtual melody.

But the most daring of the new directors of the twenties was Erwin Piscator, who had begun his career in 1919 as the guiding force of an enterprise called the Proletarian Theater. Piscator hoped that, in the postwar, postrevolutionary era, theater would not only reach out to the working masses but also become a place in which revolutionary ideas would be generated. In 1924, for example, he staged a politically provocative revue to support the Communist Party's campaign in the Reichstag elections. Another political revue, called *In Spite of Everything*, traced the history of revolution in the twentieth century down to the murders of Karl Liebknecht and Rosa Luxemburg, using newsreel footage as part of the staging. In this and in other ways, Piscator developed some of the techniques of what he and Brecht began calling "epic theater" at around the same time.

When Piscator moved into the comfortable Theater am Nollendorfplatz in 1927 and established a company there, he engaged a team of writers that included Brecht and Ernst Toller. Little had been heard from Toller since his succession of fervently revolutionary plays in the early twenties, but Piscator initiated the new company in September 1927 with a production of his *Hoppla! Wir leben* (roughly, "Let's Go Now! We're Alive"). Using film projections between scenes to convey the larger historical context, the play is a series of scenes depicting various unnamed modern cities that resemble Berlin, gathering places of greed, venality, and corruption. Toller's protagonist is a man somewhat like himself, Karl Thomas, who has been seen in the prologue participating in a thwarted revolutionary attempt in 1919, and who steps forth in the play's main action after eight years of confinement in a lunatic asylum. The madness that Thomas sees all around him reaches its climax when one of his former revolutionary comrades, now prime minister of the republic and a betrayer of the old ideals, is murdered by a young fanatic who considers him too left-wing. At length, Thomas is arrested and taken to prison; there he commits suicide in his cell.

This play caused a stir, but Piscator created even more excitement in January 1928 with his production of *The Good Soldier Schweik*. This dramatization of Jaroslav Hašek's great novel had originally been done by two of the late author's colleagues from Prague, Max Brod and Hans Reimann, but Piscator, dissatisfied with their version, had given it over for revisions to three members of his playwriting team, Leo Lania, Felix Gasbarra, and Bertolt Brecht. The character of Schweik, the maddeningly compliant but spiritually invincible peasant in uniform, as shrewd as he was coarse, took a powerful hold on Brecht's imagination, and the result was an exciting piece of epic theater, filled with films, puppets, masks, and a treadmill. The performance of the leading role by Max Pallenberg, one of Germany's most celebrated comedians, was found by many to be unforgettable. But the greatest sensation of the play was provided by the satirical artist George Grosz, who did the background projections and included among them a picture of Jesus on the cross wearing a gas mask. Like Brecht, Grosz had the ruthless irreverence of a disillusioned German pietist. When the sketch for this projection was published in a volume of drawings, with the caption *Maul halten und weiterdienen* ("Shut your trap and keep on serving"), Grosz and the publisher were put on trial for blasphemy; but, arguing that these words were those of the artist as an ironic commentator on Christian hypocrisy rather than something imputed to Jesus, they finally were acquitted.

In the meantime, Brecht was engaged in his own activities as well as those of the Piscator group. The same month as the *Schweik* premiere also saw the first Berlin production of his *Mann ist Mann*, at the Volksbühne Theater. After that, he began settling down to work on an envisioned sequel of sorts to *In the Jungle of Cities*, another parody of capitalism set in the Chicago stockyards, to be called *Joe Fleischhacker* (the last name means "butcher"). But then, in March or April of 1928, an event occurred that

was to give rise to the pivotal work of his career, and of Kurt Weill's as
well.

Ernst-Josef Aufricht, twenty-nine years old, had already been known to
some theater people around Berlin and Dresden as an actor of little talent;
but now, armed with a substantial cash gift from his wealthy father in
Silesia, he was embarking on a new career as a producer. Having just
leased the Theater am Schiffbauerdamm, a relic of nineteenth-century
rococo hidden away on the north bank of the Spree a short distance from
Max Reinhardt's Grosses Schauspielhaus, he and his associates were
looking for a play with which to make their debut that September. At first
they had thought of doing an established work. Erich Engel, the highly
successful young director who had agreed to stage Aufricht's first
production, suggested Frank Wedekind's turn-of-the-century classic,
Spring's Awakening; but Aufricht decided against it, maintaining that this
was the sort of thing Reinhardt did. Then they looked at Karl Kraus's
brilliant but lengthy antiwar drama, *The Last Days of Mankind*, and
concluded that it was unproducible: although, in the process, Aufricht
became close enough to Kraus that he hired the latter's young friend and
literary executor, Heinrich Fischer, as *Dramaturg*, or production assistant.
Finally they began seeking a new play and contacted a number of younger
writers, including Ernst Toller and Lion Feuchtwanger, but none of them
had anything ready.

Aufricht tells in his memoirs how one day, in desperation, he went to
lunch at Schlichter's, determined to find a playwright at this favorite
hangout of theater people, where Brecht had met Weill a year earlier.
Brecht was there now, sitting alone, and Aufricht, accompanied by
someone who knew the playwright—either Engel or Fischer, or both—
was introduced to him for the first time. It is hard to believe that this
meeting took place as casually as it appears in Aufricht's description,
particularly since Engel had been the director of some of Brecht's works.
In any case, the would-be producer and his companions sat down with
Brecht, and they soon were discussing possible business together. Brecht
described a play he was working on, probably *Joe Fleischhacker*, but
Aufricht was not interested; undoubtedly this struck him as something
that would not have enough popular appeal. With dramatic emphasis, he
waved to the waiter and asked for the check.

"All right, then," said Brecht, according to Aufricht's account, "I
have something else I've been doing on the side. You can have six of its

seven scenes to read tomorrow. It's a reworking of John Gay's *The Beggar's Opera*. I've given it the title *Gesindel* ['Rabble']." Brecht then proceeded to describe John Gay's work, which had first been produced in London in 1728, just two hundred years before, and had enjoyed a successful revival in that city from 1920 to 1924.

It is hard to say precisely what Brecht had in hand to show Aufricht at this early stage, although there is evidence to suggest it was something quite a bit closer to Gay than *The Threepenny Opera* finally turned out to be. On the other hand, it is not hard to see why a man like Brecht had become fascinated by Gay's "Newgate Pastoral," with its thieves, scoundrels, and whores playing out a mockery of high-flown romance and adventure. Evidently the play had been spotted for him by Elisabeth Hauptmann, his indispensable collaborator, who had been sent to him as an editorial assistant in 1924 by his publisher, Kiepenheuer, and who had then stayed on with him even after his contract with them fell through. Hauptmann knew English well, and she kept a file of "Anglo-Saxon" works for Brecht's benefit, some of which she translated into German from time to time. Her interest in *The Beggar's Opera* was no doubt helped along by the fact that it simply was in the air after the great success of its London revival: Paul Hindemith, for example, had been asked by his publishers in 1925 if he wanted to do a modern musical version of it.

Aufricht listened to Brecht's description, and was convinced that the idea "smelled of theater." The next morning Fischer went to Brecht's studio on the Spichernstrasse to pick up the manuscript, and Aufricht waited for him at the apartment of his in-laws on nearby Meinekestrasse. It was a rainy day, so that by the time Fischer returned to Aufricht with the typewritten play, the pages were soaked through and some of the letters had run. But this did not prevent Aufricht from being greatly impressed by "the dry wit and impudence" of the piece as he and Fischer read through it, and by the time they had finished they knew they wanted it. They phoned Brecht and told him the news. He then informed them for the first time that he planned to write the piece with new music by Kurt Weill.

It would seem that Brecht had actually discussed *The Beggar's Opera* with Weill before this, and had even spoken to some producers about the idea. But no one had been interested, and Brecht and Weill had turned to things they considered more important in any case. It is quite possible that one reason producers had not been interested was the involvement of Weill, who had done avant-garde concert works and operas, but never anything for the commercial theater. Aufricht, too, was bothered when Brecht told him of it, and to satisfy his curiosity about this composer whom he had more or less hired but whose work he did not know, he went to see a performance of *Der Protagonist* and *Der Zar lässt sich photographieren*—which, in the few weeks after the premiere of the latter in February, were on their way to becoming a standard operatic double bill. The experience did not make Aufricht any less uneasy, however, and when he hired the popular dance band conductor Theo Mackeben to be music director for the Brecht version of *The Beggar's Opera*, he asked him to prepare an arrangement of the original score, compiled for Gay by Johann Pepusch out of traditional melodies, just in case Weill's contribution did not work out.

Since the performance of the *Mahagonny Songspiel* the previous summer, Weill's main energies had been concentrated on the full-length opera that he and Brecht planned to work up from that material; but he had found the time to do other things besides. Using as his text a Brecht poem, *Vom Tod im Wald* ("Death in the Forest"), which had appeared first in *Baal* and then in the *Hauspostille*, he had written a concert song that was performed by the bass Heinrich Hermanns with the Berlin Philharmonic on November 23, 1927. This solemn, powerful work, free in tonality and form, was a clear demonstration only a few months after the *Songspiel* that even his collaboration with Brecht had not turned Weill completely away from the more "elevated" style of some of his earlier compositions.

On the other hand, the contacts he made through Brecht were now bringing him to try doing songs in a more unabashedly popular style than he had ever used before. One of Brecht's colleagues on the Piscator team, Leo Lania, had written a satirical play about machinations in the international oil trade, called *Konjunktur* (roughly, "A Favorable Turn on the Market"), and another member of the team, Felix Gasbarra, had produced an ironic song lyric for one of its scenes. Called *Die Muschel von Margate* ("The Mussel of Margate"), it describes how a picturesque little stand selling mussels at an English seaside resort is eventually replaced by an oil refinery. As with the *Mahagonny* songs, its jarring sounds are right there in the words, so that when Weill took on the task of composing the music for it, there was little more he could contribute in the way of dissonance. Rather, he found an additional element of irony by making the song a melodious fox-trot, which sounded more like the Broadway that lay in his future than anything he had yet written. The song proved to be a striking demonstration of the resources of popular melody hitherto hidden inside this young avant-gardist, and it seems appropriately symbolic that on April 24, 1928, only two weeks after the opening of *Konjunktur*, Weill met George and Ira Gershwin, who were passing through Berlin on a European junket.

The occasion was an informal get-together between the Gershwins and a few German composers, to whom the American visitors explained the workings of the music publishing business in their own country. Did Weill have any inkling that he himself would one day be a member of the American Society of Composers, Authors and Publishers (ASCAP), with which the Gershwins dealt in their talk? Certainly he was interested in America as a subject, and—though the Gershwins had an interpreter—evidently knew by now a fair amount of the language in which he and his colleagues were being addressed. This knowledge came not only from his school days, but from his many contacts with American culture that streamed through Berlin in those days. Undoubtedly, he had heard Paul Whiteman's band performing the *Rhapsody in Blue* and other Gershwin works when it came to Berlin in 1926. He also probably had seen Duke Ellington's revue, *Chocolate Kiddies*, when it played there in the summer of 1925. As for Josephine Baker, whose dancing was then the rage of Berlin, Weill had even almost done some music for her, and probably still intended to.

That project had been initiated by Count Harry Kessler, who had described his first meeting with Josephine Baker, on February 13, 1926, in terms that add fitly to our portrait of Berlin in that era. "At one o'clock [in the morning]," Kessler writes, "a telephone call from Max Reinhardt. He was at [Karl Gustav] Vollmoeller's and they wanted me to come over because Josephine Baker was there and the fun was starting. So I drove to Vollmoeller's harem on the Pariser Platz. Reinhardt and Huldschinsky were surrounded by half a dozen naked girls, Miss Baker was also naked except for a pink muslin apron, and the little Landshoff girl (a niece of [the publisher] Sammy Fischer) was dressed up as a boy in a dinner-jacket. Miss Baker was dancing a solo with brilliant artistic mimicry and purity of style, like an ancient Egyptian or other archaic figure performing an intricate series of movements without ever losing the basic pattern. This is how their dancers must have danced for Solomon and Tutankhamen. Apparently she does this for hours on end, without tiring and continually inventing new figures like a child, a happy child, at play. She never even gets hot, her skin remains fresh, cool, dry. A bewitching creature, but almost quite unerotic. Watching her inspires as little sexual excitement as does the sight of a beautiful beast of prey. The naked girls lay or skipped about among the four or five men in dinner-jackets. The Landshoff girl, really looking like a dazzlingly handsome boy, jazzed with Miss Baker to gramophone tunes.

"Vollmoeller had in mind a ballet for her, a story about a *cocotte*, and was proposing to finish it this very night and put it in Reinhardt's hands. By this time Miss Baker and the Landshoff girl were lying in each other's arms, like a rosy pair of lovers, between us males who stood around. I said I would write a dumb show for them on the theme of the *Song of Solomon*, with Miss Baker as the Shulamite and the Landshoff girl as Solomon or the Shulamite's young lover. Miss Baker would be dressed (or not dressed) on the lines of Oriental Antiquity while Solomon would be in a dinner-jacket, the whole thing an entirely arbitrary fantasy of ancient and modern set to music, half jazz and half Oriental, to be composed perhaps by Richard Strauss."

Max Reinhardt liked the idea, and it was arranged that he and several others come to dinner at Kessler's home a few days later, to discuss it further. At the dinner Kessler outlined the first scene. "My plot is how Solomon, handsome, young, and royal (I have Serge Lifar in mind), buys a dancer (the Shulamite, Miss Baker), has her brought before him, naked, and showers his robes, his jewels, his entire riches upon her. But the more gifts he lavishes, the more she eludes him. From day to day he grows more naked and the Dancer less perceptible to him. Finally, when it is the King who is altogether bare, the Dancer utterly vanishes from his sight in a tulip-shaped cloud, first golden in color and composed of all the jewels and stuffs of which he had stripped himself to adorn her, then turning black. At the end of the scene, in the semi-gloom, there enters the young Lover, wearing a dinner-jacket, and . . . For the present, I told them, I would keep the continuation to myself." Reinhardt and Vollmoeller found this scene so dramatic that they thought the ballet should end right there; Josephine Baker was so enthusiastic about what she had heard that she burst into a spontaneous dance around Kessler's Maillol statue.

Kessler's diary has little more to offer on the subject of the ballet until November 1927, nearly two years after the above scenes. By then, Richard Strauss had obviously proved to be unavailable to do another *Salome* for Kessler, and someone apparently had recommended the young composer of the *Mahagonny Songspiel* instead. The idea was in some ways an appropriate one for Weill, whose interest in the *Song of Songs* went back a number of years, and for whom the idea of combining jazz and Oriental or Hebraic themes challenged various elements in his nature. "Kurt Weill arrived at half past seven," Kessler's diary reads for November 14, "and we talked about the ballet project. He would like to do it, he says, but he has meanwhile accepted a commission from his publisher to compose a big opera [the full-length *Mahagonny*] and has already received an advance for it. He must therefore ask the publisher whether he will give him leave, so to speak, for two or three months for the ballet. He proposes that this music should be mainly *sung* from behind the scenes, using only a very few instruments—flute, saxophone." Then Kessler told Weill about his encounters in Barcelona with the Catalan folk dances called *sardanas*, and played some samples of them on the phonograph. Weill "listened attentively and declared this music, which he had never heard before, to be very remarkable. Finally we took our leave, agreeing that he would visit me in Weimar."

The project never materialized, but we can perceive in the story some of the musical ideas that must have been taking shape in Weill's mind at this time. He was absorbing, with characteristic omnivorousness, the various exoticisms in the air, whether they came from the Iberian peasantry, from some idea of the Orient, or from American Blacks. No doubt he was familiar with what his colleague from Vienna, Ernst Krenek, who was exactly his own age, had done with American jazz themes in his opera, *Jonny spielt auf* ("Johnny Strikes Up"), which had been premiered the previous February. The zany Dadaistic libretto of this opera, written by the composer himself, is about the escapades of a German composer, an Italian violin virtuoso, and a Black American jazz musician, as well as the women in their lives. One of the central elements of the plot is the theft of the Italian's violin by Johnny, the Black American, who, after a series of chases through European hotel rooms, is seen in the finale perched atop a giant globe, playing his jazz leitmotiv on the violin as all the surviving main characters head for the New World. Krenek, who was eventually to settle in the United States himself, seems to be saying something about where the future lies, in this finale and in the numerous jazz quotations interspersed throughout the opera—which is otherwise a typical, free-tonal, European avant-garde piece of the twenties. "A sketch extended to an evening's entertainment," Count Kessler called it, "with good, bad, and indifferent all mixed up together. Not very original, musically, but talented." Weill undoubtedly knew he could do better. The jazz passages in Krenek's opera were pure imitations, pasted onto the structure, whereas Weill had already shown in the *Mahagonny Songspiel* that he could draw from jazz and create a sound of his own, as Gershwin had done.

Within a few weeks after his meeting with Gershwin, Weill was hard at work on the John Gay adaptation, which its authors soon were calling *Die Luder-Oper*, a rough translation from Gay, instead of the harsher *Gesindel*—mainly, no doubt, because the idea of presenting the play as a parody opera was now at the forefront of their thoughts. By now, it had become Weill's firmly established method to work with his collaborators on the librettos, not as coauthor, but as intimate adviser and editor—he had done this with Yvan Goll and with Kaiser on *Der Zar*, and now he was doing it with Brecht. He therefore was ready to go along when Brecht, uneasy at one of the rare deadlines of his career, decided that he could do the job better with a change of scene. Someone suggested Le Lavandou on the French Riviera, and before the end of May Brecht was down there with the actress Helene Weigel, soon to be his wife after his divorce in November from the actress Marianne Zoff, and with their three-year-old son, Stefan. Following along in Brecht's entourage were Kurt and Lenya—who, like Helene Weigel, was to have a part in the play—as well as Elisabeth Hauptmann and Erich Engel. The Brechts stayed in a house they had rented near the beach, the Weills—and presumably, Hauptmann and Engel as well—in a pension nearby. The authors worked night and day, interrupting their labors only for occasional quick swims. Lenya later recalled watching "Brecht wading out, pants rolled up, cap on head, stogy in mouth." She never saw him completely immersed and thought that perhaps he was "slightly water-shy." Kurt, on the other hand, was an avid swimmer on this occasion, as he had been all his life.

By the beginning of July the Weills had returned to Berlin by train, and Brecht had gone to the Ammersee in his native Bavaria, one of his favorite country spots, to continue working on the text. Important changes and additions were still to be made, but the work was sufficiently shaped that Weill could go home and begin composing some of the music. By now it was clear—and it probably had been from the start—that Weill would compose more or less in the popular ballad style used by Pepusch, and not in an operatic style, except parodically now and then. On the other hand, though there now was a lively tradition of musical comedy in Berlin, he did not want to write in that style either, except to make fun of it. It was to be his first complete score in a relatively popular vein, and the prospect no doubt made him uneasy.

Sometime that July he was visited by his old friend H. H. Stuckenschmidt, who noticed some freshly covered musical manuscript sheets on top of the piano. "I'm working on something there that could be successful," Weill told him with a smile, but Stuckenschmidt noted that his eyes were melancholy behind his thick glasses. At around the same time Wladimir Vogel, Kurt's colleague from the Busoni master class, dropped in and saw similar music sheets strewn all over the room. When he asked what was doing, Weill replied casually, "Oh, a summer theater wants to put on a play by Brecht, and asked me to write a few musical numbers and interludes—some kind of theater music." Vogel had the impression that his friend did not attach much importance to it all and was eager to change the subject, so they did. These two recollections imply that Weill was not overly enthusiastic about the purely musical side of the project, but that he was at least occasionally convinced, as in the Stuckenschmidt account, that it would have commercial value. Indeed, money must have been the main reason he was willing to drop work temporarily on the *Mahagonny* opera in order to turn out what he and Brecht both still regarded as something of a potboiler.

By the end of July Brecht was back in town with some new scenes and several additional songs. The opening was scheduled for August 31, and rehearsals began on the first day of that month. But Weill's music still had to prove itself as far as the producer was concerned, and that day the composer and his wife showed up at the door of Aufricht's office.

"I want to play my music for you tomorrow," Weill said, "and I have one more request: I would like my wife to play Jenny, one of the prostitutes."

Aufricht was taken aback. He had never even heard of Lotte Lenya before, much less seen her perform. But he was struck by something in the way she looked and moved. "Good," he said, deciding he would at least give her a try.

"Weill is also going to compose a song for me," Lenya added, still standing in the doorway.

Aufricht found himself thinking that her shamelessness was quite becoming, and also wondering how "little Weill" had gotten such an attractive wife for himself. The next day, a piano was rolled out from the property room onto the stage, and Aufricht, along with Theo Mackeben, Heinrich Fischer, and another *Dramaturg* on the staff named Robert Vambery, sat down in the auditorium to listen. "The gentle little man with the glasses," Aufricht relates, "began to play and to sing in a soft, metallic voice that expressed precisely what he wanted. I think we were not sure how to respond at first, but then Vambery came over and whispered into my ear: 'The music is as likely as the play to be a great success.' The more Weill played, the more my prejudices faded away. In spite of its strangeness, this music had something naïve about it, but also refined and exciting, that touched me." Mackeben put aside his own music and began to assemble the small jazz band required for Weill's songs.

This matter was settled, then, but the problems of the production were only just beginning. From the outset there were difficulties with the cast. The leading roles of Macheath and Polly had been given, respectively, to Harald Paulsen, a musical comedy star, and Carola Neher (no relation to Caspar), with whom Brecht had once been in love. "She was the ideal realization of the part," Aufricht writes of her, "a swamp blossom under the moon of Soho. Her flat, even-featured face with a cat's nose could just as easily be merry as be sad. Aside from Lotte Lenya, she was the best woman interpreter of Brechtian lyrics and of songs by Weill." But her participation was soon in question. She was married to the well-known poet, born Alfred Henschke in 1891, who called himself Klabund—a name constructed out of the first syllable of *Klabautermann* (a ship's hobgoblin) and the last syllable of *Vagabund* ("vagabond"). A type of *poète maudit* who cultivated a working-class image for himself, sang in cabarets, and became a Communist in the early twenties, Klabund had been an important influence on Brecht's development. But now he was in Davos, Switzerland, dying of consumption; and only three or four days after rehearsals began, his wife was by his bedside. "We wrote letters, sent telegrams," Aufricht relates, "and got no answer. When she finally got to a telephone, she said in a low voice that Klabund was in agony, but that I must not give the part to anyone else. We continued exchanging phone calls twice a day." On August 14 Klabund died.

Carola Neher returned to Berlin and finally began rehearsing. No doubt she noticed immediately that many cuts had been made in her part, as in everyone else's, during her absence, but at first she said nothing. The time soon arrived for the first complete run-through of the play. "It was an evening rehearsal," Aufricht goes on, "and we wanted to do it without any interruptions. Not surprisingly, however, there soon were interruptions, and on the stage a chaos of discussions between actors, author, and director, of changes in the text, of positions being shifted, of cries and sudden silences—when suddenly Neher declared that she would not go on, because her part was too small. Brecht immediately broke in:

"'I'll take care of that—please, lower the curtain!'

"He had a small table brought onto the stage, at which he and Neher sat down together, and he began to write. The exhausted actors waited patiently in the auditorium, and I gave them a pep talk. At five in the morning their patience gave out. They wanted either to rehearse the last scene, which still was lacking, or go home and go to bed. I went up to the stage, where Brecht was eagerly reading line after line, and Neher was merrily vetoing every one of them. When I suggested that they continue their work in my office, she stood up, flung the manuscript at my feet and said: 'Play that crap yourself!' She walked out of the theater. It was a week before opening night, and we first had to cast the female lead."

They quickly found a music-hall actress named Roma Bahn: "this graceful woman, with blue eyes and blonde hair, was tart and unsentimental; in four days she learned the unusual music and the difficult text, and on opening night she was flawless." But there were other problems in the meantime. Brecht's wife, Helene Weigel, was to play the role of Mrs. Coaxer, the brothel madame, and had even developed the idea of doing it as a woman without legs, pushing herself about on a wheeled platform. She came down with an attack of appendicitis, however, and John Gay's Mrs. Coaxer was cut out of the Brecht version entirely as a result. There was a momentary stir when the actor originally chosen to play Peachum—according to one account, it was the young Peter Lorre, then at the beginning of his career—got sick and had to be replaced; Erich Ponto, a star of the Dresden Theater, was quickly obtained for the role. Later on, he too almost walked out because of the cuts in his part, but Aufricht, his old colleague from Dresden, persuaded him to stay. Trouble also came from Rosa Valetti, one of Berlin's outstanding cabaret singers, who had been cast in the part of Mrs. Peachum. A large woman with, as Aufricht puts it, "furrowed face, vulgar voice, and the sassy Berlin manner," she seemed perfect for the coarse-grained wife of the boss of the beggars. Her principal song, "The Ballad of Sexual Need," was appropriately raw, but one day she astonished everyone by stopping short in the middle of it and refusing to sing "those filthy words." This unlikely outburst of priggishness was treated with respect—even though Valetti's husband and manager, liking neither Aufricht nor the play's prospects, had signed her up for a cabaret engagement beginning one day after the opening—and the song was cut from the show.

Another song, "Lucy's Aria," had to be cut because Kate Kühl, who had been cast in the role, could not handle this difficult piece of operatic parody. In general, the actors had trouble with the music; but on the other hand, one of the best songs in the score—and eventually to be its most famous—got written because of the eagerness of one of the actors to flaunt himself. Harald Paulsen, carried away with his developing Macheath character, had obtained the services of a prominent Berlin tailor and outfitted himself in accordance with his own conception of the vaguely late-Victorian milieu that had been chosen for the play. He sported a "double-breasted lounging jacket cut in the turn-of-the-century style, tight trousers with suspenders, patent-leather shoes with white spats, a thin sword-cane in his hand, a bowler on his head." To this he had added a huge bow tie of bright blue-colored silk. This caused an uproar: authors, director, producers all objected to the dandified appearance of their gangland boss, while Paulsen, growing hoarse in the quarrel, insisted he would sooner give up the role than his bow tie. Then Brecht had an idea, which he confided to Aufricht in the privacy of the latter's office.

"Let's let him be sweet and charming," Brecht said. "In the meantime, Weill and I will introduce him with a *Moritat*, which will sing of the grisly and sinister deeds performed by this man in the bright blue bow tie."

A *Moritat*—the word is formed from *Mord* ("murder") and *Tat* ("deed")—is a traditional type of ballad about legendary criminals that used to be sung at German street fairs. The idea was a natural one for the Gothic streak in Brecht's nature, and it took him only one night to write his poem about the evildoings of Mackie Messer (best known in English as "Mack the Knife"), which is what the Germanized Macheath was now being called. Weill immediately caught the spirit of the song and also took only one night to write the music for it. There are various theories about the origin of this haunting melody. Some say that Brecht had the basic theme in his head along with the words, and that he either hummed, strummed, plunked, or whistled it for his colleague, who then went home and expanded upon it: this version of the story seems to have originated with Brecht himself. On the other hand, Weill told an American colleague years later that it was while riding home on the streetcar that the remarkable combination of third, fifth, and sixth notes of the scale came to him, as if out of the Berlin traffic. Today the melody seems to represent to us the very atmosphere of Berlin in that era, which was in the process of being defined in part by the creative combination of Brecht and Weill. We must simply grant them a mutual influence so interpenetrating that the two parts can no longer be clearly distinguished from one another. At any rate, the new song was enthusiastically received, and Harald Paulsen himself wanted to do it, as Mackie introducing his own evil deeds to the audience. But Paulsen's voice was too pleasant, and the show's creators decided to give the song to the more surrealistic instrument of the massive

Kurt Gerron, who was playing the corrupt police chief Tiger Brown—Brecht's variant of Gay's Lockit. The new role of the streetsinger was created, supplied with a Bacigalupo barrel organ according to Weill's prescription, and Gerron doubled in it along with the role of Tiger Brown: another Brechtian *Verfremdungseffekt*.

Amid all this tumult, Lotte Lenya moved quietly, stoically accepting setbacks and gradually consolidating her strength. Her role of Spelunken-Jenny ("Jenny of the Dives"—that is, of low-down joints—which was Brecht's perhaps willful mistranslation of Gay's "Jenny Diver") was not as important as it has subsequently become as a result of her artistic and promotional gifts. The "Pirate Jenny" song, telling of the sinister ship with eight sails that comes into the harbor, has been so much a trademark of hers in our own day that many will be surprised to learn that it was not written for the part of Jenny the prostitute, but for Polly Peachum. In other words, Brecht wanted Carola Neher to sing it; but even after she left the cast it remained Polly's song, sung by her at the wedding party in the stable, and it was performed by Roma Bahn. The only two songs originally slated for Lenya as Spelunken-Jenny were the "Tango Ballad," the duet with Macheath that ends with her dancing him into the arms of the police, and the "Solomon Song," a historical meditation on the disillusionments of fame and power, sung to a hurdy-gurdy accompaniment. The tango proved to be one of the rousing moments in the show, and Lenya says that when Aufricht—who had admitted her to the cast on only a three-day trial period—first saw her do it with Paulsen, he became utterly convinced of her talents. But it probably was the "Solomon Song" that Lenya had in mind when she told Aufricht on the first day of rehearsals that Weill was going to write something for her. Nevertheless, she did not get to sing it on opening night, for in the very last hours before curtain time it was cut when the show seemed to be running too long. Nor was this the end to her setbacks; for on the programs to be distributed on opening night her name was inadvertently omitted.

The many conflicts and disasters that occurred during rehearsals, the uncertain status of the producer in the Berlin theater world, and the unusual character of the play—with its peculiar combination of straight theater and song, of opera, jazz, and cabaret—all led to growing rumors around town that the project was doomed to failure. During rehearsals the auditorium was regularly inhabited by friends, admirers, or mere colleagues of Brecht's, from whom advice and criticism were always forthcoming, and some of whom urged that the show be closed before it was too late. Fritz Kortner, one of the eminent young actors of the day, was of this opinion; at any rate, he felt that if the show was to go on, certain things should be cut. One of the things he objected to the most was the chorale that Weill had written for the finale; arguing that it sounded like Bach and that there was no place for Bach in a play like this, he momentarily even persuaded Aufricht and Erich Engel that he was right. But Weill, who had an ally on this point in Caspar Neher—who was doing backdrops and projections for this show as he had done for the *Mahagonny Songspiel*—and probably in Brecht as well, held fast, and the chorale finale stayed in.

On the other hand, some of the colleagues who showed up during rehearsals offered moral support. Karl Kraus, Heinrich Fischer's mentor and a writer respected by all, even offered a second stanza to the "Jealousy Duet" sung by Lucy and Polly in front of Mackie's cell, and Brecht gladly accepted it. The best supporting gesture of all came from Lion Feuchtwanger, the novelist and playwright who had collaborated with Brecht on his adaptation of *Edward the Second*, and, before that, had been one of the principal voices in the literary establishment to help spread his reputation. Feuchtwanger suggested that the play be called *Die Dreigroschenoper*: this would preserve the lowdown implications and stress upon opera of Gay's title while serving notice that Brecht and Weill had turned out something new. This, then, was the name that went up on the marquee.

"I rang the bell as a signal to begin," writes Aufricht, who was sitting in his box that opening night. "Then came the overture in the form of a fugue, and the audience was filled with consternation. The curtain went up, several members of the cast were standing around a barrel organ, and the actor Gerron, dressed as the street singer, began to crank and to sing, 'And the shark-fish, he has big teeth . . .', but the barrel organ didn't make a sound, because someone had forgotten to set it. In the second stanza the orchestra came to the rescue. The Peachums marched past, dragging along their daughter Polly. The shadowy figure of Macheath, with his bright blue bow tie, sword-cane tucked under his arm, hat tilted on his head, stepped out and crossed the stage with light, pantherlike steps, followed by the longing gaze of the prostitutes, with Lenya at their head, who ended the scene saying in her sharp voice: 'That was Mack the Knife!' The audience gaped in astonishment, but no one applauded." Few people had known what to expect, and the strange combination formed by the overture and the prologue had not helped to clarify matters.

Nor did the first scene of Act One, set in Peachum's outfitting shop for beggars, improve the situation. "Erich Ponto, in his precise and suggestive way, explained the difficulties of his trade, which aimed at getting people into the unnatural state of being ready to give money away. One could feel the letdown. The audience sat on its hands. Heinrich Fischer was sitting next to me and I noticed that his knees were shaking. Then came the wedding scene. None of the funny lines got a laugh; the audience just froze." Polly sang the remarkable "Pirate Jenny" song, but this drew no notable response. But then suddenly, as Macheath and Tiger Brown sang their raucous "Cannon Song" about the old army days in India, the breakthrough occurred. The audience came vividly to life. "Clapping, shouting, stamping their feet, they demanded an encore. Before the performance I had forbidden any repeating of songs because I considered that to be unserious. But they wouldn't let the actors continue, and seeing from my box that nothing could be done, I gave the signal for an encore. From this moment on, every line, every note, was a success."

Troubles were not quite at an end, however. During the break at the end of the first act, Aufricht, flushed with a sense of impending victory, headed backstage and suddenly could not believe his ears. Weill was shouting furiously—quiet Kurt Weill, who alone had remained unruffled through all the hysteria of actors, writer, director, and producer in the month of rehearsals. "Pigsty!" he bellowed, "this is a pigsty! My wife won't go on! I won't allow it!" He had discovered the omission of her name from the program. "For the first and last time in his whole theater career," Lenya writes, "Kurt completely lost control—though not out of consideration for his own interest." She remained calm as she had been throughout and helped Aufricht to quiet her husband, assuring him that "billing or no billing, nothing could keep me from going on." Aufricht promised that the programs would be corrected and newspapers informed of the error, and Lenya, according to one of her accounts, told Kurt: "They'll know who I am tomorrow."

This proved to be true to some extent. In the course of his rave review of the production the following day, Alfred Kerr—the most eminent of Berlin's theater critics, who wrote for the prestigious *Berliner Tageblatt*—said of the prostitutes: "Four actresses took these parts—and one of them seems to come from Munich." (Kerr had caught Lenya's South German accent, but he had not placed her far enough south.) "She was very, very good. The quality of her voice reminds one of Carola Neher. And her articulation was particularly good." Aufricht's correction to the program had obviously not reached Kerr's desk, but the hitherto unknown Lenya certainly was on the way.

As for the play, its great success was signaled by the fact that Kerr—aesthetically and politically a bit of a conservative, and one of Brecht's most resolute detractors—had liked it, at least for the time being. As for Herbert Ihering of the *Berliner Börsen-Courier*, Kerr's rival and Brecht's most enthusiastic supporter, he found the play not merely excellent but a pathway to new artistic horizons. It "proclaims a new world, in which the frontiers of tragedy and humor are eradicated," he wrote. "Brecht has torn language, and Weill music, from their isolation. Once more we listen to speech on the stage that is neither literary nor shopworn, and music that no longer works with threadbare harmonies and rhythms." There was as much excitement in the musical as in the theatrical world about what Weill had done in *The Threepenny Opera*, although the praise was not universal. Arnold Schoenberg, who had liked Weill's one-act operas, would ask his friends mockingly: "What has he done? He's given us back three-quarter time!"

But the main thing was the response of the audiences—of that wider public that Brecht and Weill both had sought—as the play settled down to a long run. Count Harry Kessler, who went to see it four weeks after the opening, wrote in his diary: "A fascinating production, with rudimentary staging in the Piscator manner and proletarian emphasis (apache style). Weill's music is catchy and expressive and the players (Harald Paulsen, Rosa Valetti, and so on) are excellent. It is the show of the season, always sold out: 'You must see it!' "

On *The Threepenny Opera*

In *The Beggar's Opera* John Gay ridiculed pompous conventions on two levels. On the level of the story itself, Peachum is a parody of bourgeois proprieties; for he is stuffy and self-important, but he is by profession a fence, and when his daughter, Polly, marries the bandit captain, Macheath, he is scandalized that she should be marrying at all. He and his wife then use all their illicit influence around London—with Lockit, the warden of Newgate prison, and with the prostitutes, among others—to have Macheath arrested and sentenced to death. "Through the whole piece," we are told by the Beggar who has introduced it, "you may observe such a similitude of manners in high and low life, that it is difficult to determine whether (in the fashionable vices) the fine gentlemen imitate the gentlemen of the road, or the gentlemen of the road the fine gentlemen." But throughout, the unwarranted airs of respectability assumed by the Peachums suffer by the contrast with the dashing Macheath's honest knavery.

On the level of form, the play is a parody of the Handelian operas then fashionable in London. The actors keep bursting into song, but the melodies are those of simple, traditional English ballads; the only musically "operatic" moment comes when, with pointed irony, a chorus of thieves is made to sing the March from Handel's *Rinaldo*. In the introduction the Beggar tells the Player that "I have introduced the similes that are in all your celebrated operas," but adds: "I hope I may be forgiven, that I have not made my opera throughout unnatural, like those in vogue; for I have no recitative: Excepting this, as I have consented to have neither Prologue nor Epilogue, it must be allowed an opera in all its forms." A bit of unnaturalness is brought in at the end, however, when Macheath is about to be hanged. The Player interrupts the action protesting that "the catastrophe is manifestly wrong, for an opera must end happily." To which the Beggar replies: "Your objection, sir, is very just; and is easily removed. For you must allow, that in this kind of drama, 'tis no matter how absurdly things are brought about." And he sends the rabble to cry a reprieve.

Brecht and Weill placed themselves squarely on Gay's foundation when they developed their own version of his material. Their play works on the same two levels as Gay's does, mocking the conventions of bourgeois society in the story and those of bourgeois art in the form and music. The basic plot outline of *The Threepenny Opera* is the same as that of *The Beggar's Opera*, ending in the same absurd reprieve of the hero. Some stretches of dialogue in the Brecht version are virtually identical with their counterparts in Gay, and Weill's score uses one tune intact from the Pepusch original—that of Peachum's "Morning Chorale" at the beginning.

Yet in the end the adapters had created something very much their own. Brecht, not unexpectedly, made his satire on the bourgeoisie more pointed than Gay's. Peachum is now no longer a fence but boss of the London beggars and proprietor of an establishment that supplies them with the pitiable guises needed to make people feel sorry for them and give them money: wealth based on the public's willingness to be taken for a ride is more like that of modern capitalism than the wealth of Gay's Peachum had been. Brecht's Mackie is a satirized petit bourgeois, but he is, in the tradition of Gay's Macheath and the men of Mahagonny, a rather dashing rogue; Brecht once said of him that he was better than most of his class because he was not a coward. Even more distinctly Brechtian than these characterizations, however, are the song texts in this play, which remain unique even though some of them turned out to have been borrowed liberally in places from a German translation of François Villon. And the music of the songs has a jangling vitality that remains fresh to this day.

The special quality of the music presents itself immediately in the overture; although Aufricht had some reason to be a bit dismayed at it, for this fugue echoes as much with the Weill of the past as with the one now about to reveal himself. It even has affinities with the First Symphony, though it contrasts strikingly with that work by its greater confidence and simplicity of form. Above all, what heralds the new Weill is the "jazz-band" orchestration: an overture played by saxophones, trumpets, trombones, timpani, banjo, and harmonium, with no conventional strings at all, is certainly making fun of the word *opera* in the title. Nevertheless, we are being warned here that the concept of opera also should not be forgotten in the course of what ensues.

And what immediately ensues then takes us as far from conventional opera as we can go. The "Moritat of Mack the Knife" is, indeed, fairly unique in the whole history of musical theater: there is hardly anything else like this vaguely medieval streetsong, telling in mysterious strains of its hero's dark deeds. We have seen that it was a last-minute inspiration in the course of creating the play, a song that was not part of the original plan—yet from this point on in the score, and for all posterity since that moment, it is the song that serves to define the entire work. This was a fateful development, for both Weill and Brecht had begun with a different conception of what they were up to, and this song now came to represent a destiny pulling them in a new direction. It was in some ways a triumph of Brecht over Weill, for the song, whatever the particular history of its gestation, is decidedly Brechtian and obviously remained one of the playwright's favorites among his own creations—as is suggested by the fact that he was to record himself singing it a few years later. It was a point at which Weill had to separate himself most radically from whatever he had been in the past. But it now also was a signpost to his future, and it would remain one of the melodies most clearly typifying the Weill style of the years to come. The pure melodist that had been lying within this young avant-garde composer all the time had now stepped forward unequivocally.

The play itself now begins, and Peachum is seen in his shop singing his "Morning Chorale," as in *The Beggar's Opera*. The melody—which, as we have seen, is reproduced by Weill exactly from Pepusch—is that of a pious-sounding hymn, and Peachum delivers his text in the style of a sermon. Gay's words are cynical, telling us what a world of rogues and charlatans this is, and Brecht's German broadly paraphrases them, adding an element of angry pietism. Gay's original, with its unforced earthiness, is much the superior. Peachum is to deliver pseudo-pious little sermons throughout *The Threepenny Opera*, and the music in them will often be Weill's variations on this original theme.

A dialogue ensues between Peachum and Filch, as in John Gay, except that it has been completely transformed: Filch, Peachum's aide in the original, is now a would-be beggar who, in the course of a vivid demonstration by Peachum of the shop's resources, is outfitted for his new profession. Then Mrs. Peachum enters and, as in Gay, expresses her fear that their daughter has taken up with Macheath. Polly has been out all night, but they speculate that she has perhaps been with someone else, and sing their "*Anstatt-dass*" ("Instead of") duet, which mocks the aspirations of young lovers. This crisp little song, written in a march tempo, has blues elements in it and is the first of the play's several numbers that echo the sounds of the music hall; but it has quietly operatic aspirations as well, which can be noticed particularly in the contrapuntal accompaniments provided by trumpet and saxophone. The bit of highbrowism is allowed, however, because the counterpoint is a jest: the dotted eighths and sixteenths march along as if on tiptoe, like sneaky parents spying on the young couple on the porch swing.

The next scene, the wedding celebration of Mack and Polly in a stable "deep in the heart of Soho," is Brecht's creation out of whole cloth, with no counterpart in Gay. The members of the gang have set up for the occasion with stolen furniture and food, and the lowbrow comedy of the scene is punctuated by their "Wedding Song for Poorer Folk" about the shotgun marriage of Bill Lawgen and Mary Syer. Their words and music come in slow, deliberate monosyllables, like the stage speech of illiterate tough guys, and keep culminating in the cry of "Hoch, hoch, hoch" (the German equivalent of "Three cheers," regularly shouted at weddings), spoken without musical content in surly and mocking tones.

The bride herself then performs for the company, and this is the correct place in the play's text for the "Pirate Jenny" song, even though a subsequent performance tradition has tended to give it to Jenny the prostitute and to place it in another scene. In the original context, Polly attributes the song's sentiments to a girl she once saw washing glasses in a cheap Soho dive. Angered by a jeering clientele, the girl sings of how one day a pirate ship, "with eight sails and fifty cannons," will appear in the harbor and demolish the entire town except for the shabby hotel in which she lives. Then a hundred pirates will come off the ship, take prisoners everywhere, and ask the girl which ones are to be killed. She will say, "All of them!" and when the heads begin to roll she'll cry: "Hoppla!" At last, the ship will sail away with her on it.

The music of this song, accompanied by piano and banjo as well as wind and percussion instruments, is as terrifyingly beautiful as the text. Each stanza is sung in a rapid, breathless patter that at once conveys the girl's anger, excitement, and simplicity of mind; then it breaks into the starkly contrasting refrain, in which the girl with slow, awe-filled tones invokes the image of the ship, sung over dark, sustained chords and piano arpeggios in the accompaniment. Some observers have noticed that, in its overall conception, the text of this song is a burlesque of Senta's ballad in *The Flying Dutchman*, with its vision of a redeeming lover who will come mysteriously from over the sea. Weill in no way imitates Wagner here, but in the refrain he demonstrates his skill at creating a quasi-Wagnerian atmosphere of mystery and lofty expectation, translated into neurotic twentieth-century terms.

Brecht has, of course, made his own Senta into an angry proletarian, who expects her redeeming lover to avenge her on all of society. The song has been seen as a vision of socialist revolution, and the Marxist critic Ernst Bloch once characterized Jenny's cry of "Hoppla!" when the heads roll as "apocalyptic." But there is a strange ambiguity about this vision, something perhaps even more quasi-fascist than socialist in a fantasy of revenge upon an unjust society that is based on brutality, destruction, and a lone personal triumph. The Brecht of 1928 has not yet become the more or less orthodox Marxist of only a year or two later, and there is something still rather irresponsible in his two-fisted wise-guy leftism of this moment. Perhaps he and his friend Bronnen had not yet fully defined the ways in which they were becoming different from one another. In any case, Brecht was only showing some of the more sinister symptoms of the kind of antibourgeois bohemianism in vogue at this moment in Germany. There was an unresolved mixture of elements in it, proto-fascist and proto-socialist at the same time, that seems in retrospect to foreshadow the impending disaster of German society.

This problem becomes even more evident in the play's very next song. Mackie's old friend, the corrupt police chief, Tiger Brown—who is Brecht's updated version of Gay's Lockit for the age of imperialism—comes to the wedding, and the two men proceed to recall their days together in the British army in India. Brecht, who had been reading Kipling—and who had even included some songs based on Kipling in an early draft of his John Gay adaptation—had already dealt with themes of this sort in *Mann ist Mann*, but evidently there still were ideas left over from it. The result was the "Cannon Song," which, we may recall, was the number that finally awakened the first night audience. Its music certainly is rousing—a kind of old-school pep song done as a savage and very noisy jazz dance (it is marked "Foxtrot-Tempo"), brassy and heavy-footed in the German manner. The words are recollections of the time when Mackie and Brown were the kind of whiskey-drinking roughnecks who populate Mahagonny, now reappearing as imperialist brutes in uniform. Their lives were filled with cannons and looting in those days, and when they encountered a colored man they ground him into "Beefsteak Tartar." The song by all means satirizes these British soldiers, but it also is great fun, and Brecht's old fondness for men of this sort emerges once again. Their raucous pleasures seem appealing—but among these pleasures are the expressions of a violent racism. The enthusiasm of the audience for a song like this did not bode particularly well for the German future.

The scene in the stable approaches its end as all the wedding guests leave, and Mackie and Polly settle down to spend the night there together. Alone, the couple sings a love duet—part of it in "Boston-Tempo"—that is a very good example of the kind of bittersweet flavor the Brecht–Weill combination was uniquely able to achieve. From start to finish, the words make fun of romantic love and marriage: they begin with the very phrases about the moon over Soho and beating hearts that the Peachums had sneered at in their *"Anstatt-dass"* song, go on to catalogue all the bridal favors that either were not to be found at this wedding or had been stolen, and end noting that love is something that might not even last. Yet there is something touching about the lyric; by taking an ironic stance toward a number of old-fashioned romantic images that would be embarrassing to a sophisticated Berliner of the 1920s, Brecht has made them work again. This kind of tough-minded ironic distance from sentiments is a key element in Brecht: laughing at sentiments is a face-saving way of indulging in them. But in this song, as in some others that Weill and Brecht did together, the music, relying for safety upon the ironic distance of the words, indulges more frankly in the sentiments. The melody, even with its mildly satirical instrumental accompaniment, remains sweet and at times even sugary. Weill must have written it with his best mocking smile on his face the whole time; and he must also have astounded himself—as he certainly did others—that he could bring it off so well. Did he at all suspect that melody of this sort would form a large component of his works many years later?

Scene three begins with Polly's return home and her announcement to her parents that she is married. She explains her choice of husband by singing the "Barbara Song," in which the narrator tells how a succession of nice young men with clean collars and good manners simply had not been for her, whereas she gave her heart right away to an ill-mannered cad. Another characteristic piece of Brecht–Weill bittersweet, the song has

certain affinities with Polly's other ballad-monologue, "Pirate Jenny."
Like that one, it is made up of a succession of stanzas in a breathless,
almost childlike patter rhythm, each of which breaks into a repeated
refrain that is broader and more melodious: but if the refrain in "Pirate
Jenny" was mysterious and slightly operatic, the one in this song (which
has strong echoes of the Russian "Dark Eyes," *Ochi Chorniye*) is worldly,
and has a wistful metallic romanticism about it, like a slow melody on a
nightclub saxophone. Indeed, this is the song that bears, more than any
other in *The Threepenny Opera*, the stamp of the dance cabaret of that
period: one can easily imagine it being sung by a Marlene Dietrich or a
Greta Keller before an elegant gathering of night-outers; and it often was.

The Peachums vow that they will have Macheath arrested, even
though Tiger Brown is his good friend, and the scene ends with them and
Polly singing the "First Threepenny Finale," which brings Act One to a
close. The verbal content of this number is a dialogue between parents
and daughter, the latter protesting that all she wants is a little happiness
with a man—is this asking too much? In his best sermonizing manner,
Peachum says yes; and repeats over and over again throughout the
number that, though it would be nice for human beings to be good to one
another, present circumstances—*die Verhältnisse*—won't permit it. Musically this number, violent and energetic, is a triumphant combination of
vaudeville and opera—still more the former, but with Weill's insistent
parody of the latter making itself heard. There are moments reminiscent
of some of the Gilbert and Sullivan patter ensembles, but the beat is
harsher and more satanic, in the Berlin manner of the twenties.

Act Two begins with Polly coming to Mackie in the stable to warn
him that he is going to be arrested; Mackie, preparing to leave town,
appoints Polly temporary leader of the gang in his stead. They take leave
of one another with a music-box waltz melody that echoes and varies their
earlier love duet. Then there is an interlude in which Mrs. Peachum,
knowing that Macheath is likely to dally in the brothel at Turnbridge
despite his eagerness to escape, promises money to the prostitute Jenny if
she will turn him over to the police. Mrs. Peachum thereupon sings her
"Ballad of Sexual Need," which was cut from the Berlin opening, as we
have seen. This tribute to the urge that calls upon men whatever their
estate is a pure piece of Berlin satirical cabaret, right down to its simplistic
accordion style melody in three-quarter time, which could just as easily
have accompanied the words of a children's song.

In scene five, sure enough, we see Mackie in the brothel, and soon he
does his "Tango Ballad" with Jenny. The two ex-lovers dance and sing of

the time when he was her pimp and they lived together in a whorehouse. A vintage piece of Brechtian bittersweet, the lyric is quite rough in its content yet ultimately sentimental: they are an attractive pair, in their way. The final piece of ironic distancing comes when Jenny ends the number by dancing Mackie into the arms of the waiting police, whom she had sneaked into the room. The music is the most memorable of what was now becoming a whole succession of Kurt Weill tangos. By now he had developed a kind of trademark with them, whereby they persistently functioned as an ambivalently erotic expression, the sound of an illicit love that stands on the borderline of disaffection or betrayal. It is passionate, destructive, and also a little comic—an appropriate assemblage of moods for the tango in an era that partly defined itself through the films of Rudolph Valentino.

Mackie is brought to his prison cage, and Tiger Brown is there to apologize for not having prevented the arrest. Left alone, Mackie then sings his "Ballad of the Good Life," which says that, when all is said and done, comfort and plenty are what count. This lyric, like the one for the tango, is among four or five in *The Threepenny Opera* that were based on K. L. Ammer's German translations of François Villon, and borrow some lines from them. Like the words, the music has a roguish flavor: it is marked "Shimmy Tempo," and could easily be sung on a vaudeville stage. Then Lucy Brown enters, another of Mackie's former mistresses, apparently pregnant by him, angry at having been betrayed, yet still completely susceptible to him—this is Brecht's counterpart to Lucy Lockit, and she is the daughter of Tiger Brown, this play's equivalent to Lockit. Mackie tries to calm her down, but then, to his chagrin, Polly comes on and the two women sing their "Jealousy Duet" in front of Mackie's cell. This is a parody of opera, two stanzas—the second of them by Karl Kraus—in each of which the alternating shrieks of the women at one another end in an ultrasweet chorus about "Mackie and me" that they sing together in perfect harmony. Polly soon leaves, dragged off by her mother, and Mackie persuades Lucy to help him escape, which she does.

Act Two now ends with the "Second Threepenny Finale," sung as an unconnected interlude before the curtain by Mackie and Mrs. Peachum (it is only subsequent versions that make this a duet by Mackie and Jenny), with chorus. "What keeps a man alive?" they ask, and then deliver their sermon—the bitterest lyric in the entire play, and the one in which Brecht most clearly takes his political position. Men live by preying upon one another, and there is no such thing as morality until the matter of feeding one's face is settled first. The song is something of an assault upon the audience, delivered in a tone of hostility that Brecht was to use again, notably in the full-length *Mahagonny*, but that is rare in the generally playful *Threepenny Opera*. Weill's music for it is appropriately stark, punctuated by booming trombone and trumpets answering one another in a broad, violent strophe and antistrophe. The least operatic of the score's three finales, this number sounds like a nightmarish version of a Salvation Army hymn, a choral preachment turned into an antibourgeois black mass.

At the beginning of Act Three, Peachum is shown persuading Tiger Brown to arrest Mackie again, using the threat of disrupting the Queen's coronation with a swarm of beggars and paupers. In the course of this scene Peachum sings a song "On the Inadequacy of Human Striving," in which he observes that men are never sly enough, bad enough, or deviously undemanding enough to make out in this world. This bit of cynicism is another one of Peachum's sermons, but it is not delivered in his usual lugubrious manner; rather, it is one of the most high-spirited moments in the play and the score. The raffish melody is pure Berlin music hall, a sort of Teutonic "Every Day Is Ladies' Day with Me" that almost calls out for straw hat and cane but is heavier than its English counterpart. There is a recording of Brecht singing this song with all the gruff relish of a Bavarian butcher drinking beer and watching a six-day bicycle race. It is true *Misuk*, grossly banal—and enchanting.

The next number, cut from the Berlin opening, is an interlude in which Jenny steps out before the curtain and sings the "Solomon Song," a ballad that tells of the sorrows and downfalls of various men and women of high estate, from Solomon and Caesar to Macheath. Sung to a hurdy-gurdy like the "Moritat of Mack the Knife," it also has the flavor of a street ballad, but it is in fact a conventionally melodious waltz: the wheezing accompaniment is what makes it sound exotic—and appealingly low-down in the *Threepenny* way. This score constantly rescues the banal with an element of tawdrification, especially in the instrumental accompaniments.

There then follows a scene that was cut from the original Berlin production and has rarely been performed since; for it was meant to include "Lucy's Aria," a protestation of her jealousy of Polly that was the most ambitious and difficult parody of opera in the whole score and that, as we have seen, the actress playing Lucy could not perform. In it, Lucy and Polly tensely confront one another and end up friends; Lucy even confesses that her apparent pregnancy is really a bit of stuffing in her dress. The scene ends with the news that Macheath has been caught again, once again betrayed by the prostitutes, and next we see him in his cell. In the course of the ensuing scene he sings two songs, both of them based on Villon: the "Cry from the Grave" and the "Ballad in Which Macheath Asks Everyone to Forgive Him." The first is an agitated, haunting outburst of anger at his fate, sung in rapid patter against a repeated tom-tom beat. The second transforms the feeling of the first into a philosophical mood of reconciliation, its conversational flow moving more slowly and deliberately. It is akin musically to the "Cry from the Grave," but now it also shows kinship with some of Peachum's sermonic melodies, especially those in the "First Threepenny Finale." But its melodic structure is ultimately more ambitious than those, and it breaks into a savage refrain that at one point echoes the opening of Weill's First Symphony. Then, accompanied by solemn processional music, Macheath is led to the gallows.

The noose is around Mackie's neck when Peachum steps forth and gives the equivalent to the Beggar's final announcement in the Gay version: since this is opera, there will be a happy ending. The orchestra now imitates the hoofbeats of the horse upon which the Queen's messenger is riding with word of Macheath's pardon, as the chorus cries in elevated tones: "Hark! Who comes?" When the messenger arrives—it turns out to be Tiger Brown—and announces that Macheath not only has been pardoned, but has been awarded a title, a castle, and an annual income of ten thousand pounds, the scene is full of musical reminiscences of *The Magic Flute*. Other operalike snatches are heard as Mackie and Polly sound the notes of their joy and the Peachums sing a few more lines stressing that life is not really like this; then everyone joins in the chorale that climaxes this "Third Threepenny Finale," the most "operatic" of the three.

The importance for Weill of the operatic element in this score was made clear by him in a succession of magazine articles that he published both before and after the play's successful opening. "Opera," he wrote somewhat portentously in a composers' symposium that had appeared the previous October, "will be one of the essential factors in that development, observable in all fields, whereby the coming liquidation of the merely sociable arts is manifesting itself." Written in the flush of that summer's success with the *Mahagonny Songspiel*, this is somewhat Brechtian language, indicating that the two collaborators had found a happy fusion of their ideas for the moment. Brecht, of course, despised opera of the traditional sort as much as he did any art form that seemed to be only for the stuffy and well-to-do; it was for him the paragon of what he called "culinary" music, meant to be consumed like a luxurious meal. And now Weill, too, recently involved in the idea of *Gebrauchsmusik* and long imbued with the Busonian ideal of a vigorous, earthy relationship between opera composer and audience in the manner of Mozart and the Italian masters, had become scornful of much of the post-Wagnerian tradition on sociological as well as aesthetic grounds. In this politically and artistically democratic age, the old quasi-aristocratic social base would not do: opera had to step out of its "splendid isolation"—as Weill wrote, using the English words—and reach a wider audience. In particular, the artificial modern distinction between opera and theater had to be eliminated.

In October 1927 the revolutionary new sort of opera that Weill meant to write was still the full-length version of *Mahagonny*. But though he apparently at first regarded *The Threepenny Opera* as a mere diversion, it is evident that he took an increasingly serious view of it as time went on. If it was primarily a new form of theater for Brecht, Weill had come to see it as a new form of opera by the time of its successful opening. He soon had plenty of opportunity to express this view in print, among other places in the music supplement of the prominent intellectual journal *Anbruch*, which asked him to explain his conception of *The Threepenny Opera*. "What we wanted to create," he wrote in an article that appeared in the January 1929 issue, "was the most archetypal form of opera. With every work of musical theater the question emerges anew: How is music—how, above all, is song in general—possible in the theater?" These are Busonian questions, now colored by a Brechtian skepticism concerning traditional art forms: men and women do not burst into song in everyday life, so what are their grounds for doing so in a play? Weill goes on to give his answer, with reference to *The Threepenny Opera*:

> Here, for once this question is resolved in the most fundamental way. I had a realistic text, and so I had to juxtapose onto it music that responded to its every possibility for a realistic formulation. This meant that the text had either to be worked up in such a way as to require that music be part of it, or to be brought purposely to various points at which it simply had to be sung. Then it came to us that this play was an opportunity to set forth the very idea of "opera" as the theme of an evening in the theater. Right at the beginning of the play it is explained to the audience: "This evening you are about to see an

opera for beggars. Because this opera was conceived so ostentatiously
that only beggars could have thought it up, it is called *The Threepenny
Opera.*"

In other words, if the play itself was more or less realistic, the
framework enclosing it was to be, like the proscenium itself, a clearly
proclaimed artifact. Just as Gay said, in effect, here is an opera as
Newgate would do it, so Brecht and Weill were giving us an opera as
various beggars and roughnecks would present it. The two collaborators
thereby established a vehicle that enabled both of them to show off their
particular talents to best advantage. For Brecht, the stress upon the
artificial element made the conception into epic theater, and for Weill, it
provided a chance to realize the old dream of doing a kind of updated
Singspiel, made up of popular melodic motifs, which were justified by the
conscientiously lowbrow atmosphere of the play.

This was the formula that brought out of Weill hitherto hidden
resources for various kinds of popular-style melody; and it also was the
one that brought out the conditions for a new route to opera. If the three
Threepenny finales—and in particular the last one, with its tribute to
Mozart and its conclusion in a chorale, ever an important element in
Weill's music—were so crucial to the composer's conception, it was
because they constituted the signposts for this route. The only significant
pieces in the play involving more than two singers, and not precisely
"songs" like most of the others, these three finales were a route through
operatic parody back to opera itself, in Weill's view. For, as he goes on to
say in the *Anbruch* article:

> the last *Threepenny* finale is in no way a parody; but rather, the idea of
> "opera" here becomes the explicit resolution of the conflict, and it is
> thus brought in as an element illustrating the action. It therefore had
> to be presented in its purest, most archetypal form.

As with Brecht—and as with Busoni, too—the element of ironic
distancing has made many things possible once again, including traditional, even banal, art forms and sentiments.

It is doubtful whether Brecht ever thought of the "Third Threepenny
Finale" as anything but parody, but surely he would have agreed that it
was the point at which the play became opera. It was funny because opera
was what he, like Gay, was gladly making fun of, and he did not share

Weill's craving to find a way back to some legitimate form of it. He could not have cared less than he did about opera's future, and he was content to have worked out some new kind of musical theater. Posterity tends to agree with his view of *The Threepenny Opera*, and to pay tribute to Weill for his part in it; but Weill did not see things quite that way in the moment of creation. Not that he was unable to perceive that his score, seeking to eliminate the boundaries between opera and theater, had stepped forth into a wider and more nebulous category than that of opera pure and simple. He concludes his *Anbruch* article with these observations:

> This return to a primal operatic form brought with it a far-reaching simplification of the musical language. It was necessary to write a kind of music that could be sung by actors—that is, by musical laymen. But what seemed at first to be a limitation proved in the course of the work to be an enormous enrichment. It was above all the shaping of a comprehensible, easily perceived melodic line that made possible what was achieved in *The Threepenny Opera*, the creation of a new genre of musical theater.

Ultimately, the creation of new forms and concepts of musical theater rather than opera was to be Weill's central artistic aim (although the operatic ideal was never to be abandoned by him completely). Indeed, the very next full-length work he and Brecht were to mount on a stage would be a piece of musical theater even less operatic than *The Threepenny Opera*. But with that exception, Weill's main interest as long as he remained in Germany was to be opera. This was to be so much the case that, though the ideals of simplification and melodic accessibility that he had evolved primarily with Brecht would always remain with him, the emphasis upon *song* would not: there also were other ways of doing what he now sought to do. Indeed, for all his skill at song, he was to try hard at times to eschew it, and was occasionally to succeed even for the length of an entire work.

One artistic issue on which Brecht and Weill seem to have been in perfect theoretical harmony just after the success of *The Threepenny Opera* was that of "epic theater," a cause that they considered themselves to have advanced immeasurably. It is a matter of learned debate whether Brecht or Erwin Piscator had done more to evolve this conception of a form of drama that, repudiating all sentimental involvement in the action, sought to place the spectator at an emotional distance from which he could ponder the larger historical and sociological context. We have seen, with reference to such productions as *The Good Soldier Schweik* and Ernst Toller's *Hoppla! Wir leben*, how Piscator used such nonnaturalistic devices as cinematic projections and treadmills to create the desired "epic" atmosphere: Brecht carried on this tradition in *The Threepenny Opera* by employing Caspar Neher's highly artificial sets, backdrops, and projections. Epic theater also stressed an artificial acting style, one that was closer to the cabaret than to the naturalistic theater, and that found particular fulfillment in moments of recitation—or of singing, such as *The Threepenny Opera* amply provided. Years later, Brecht appended to the published edition of this play some "Hints for Actors," in which he gives significant advice about doing the songs:

> When an actor sings he undergoes a change of function. Nothing is more revolting than when the actor pretends not to notice that he has left the level of plain speech and started to sing. The three levels—plain speech, heightened speech and singing—must always remain distinct, and in no case should heightened speech represent an intensification of plain speech, or singing of heightened speech. In no case therefore should singing take place where words are prevented by excess of feeling. The actor must not only sing but show a man singing. His aim is not so much to bring out the emotional content of his song (has one the right to offer others a dish that one has already eaten oneself?) but to show gestures that are so to speak the habits and usage of the body.

Singing is presented here as another manifestation of what Brecht came to call "gestic" or "gestural" theater (depending on how one likes to translate his neologism *Gestus*). In Brechtian drama the *Gestus* came to be some form of distinct artifact—it could be, for example, an outlandish trick of makeup, even a mask—whereby the essential meaning of a character or a situation is underlined in some resolutely simplistic, even cartoonlike way. But vivid as the *Gestus* was to be, it was not to be emotive, or conducive to any attitude but reflection. Now, it is not hard to see the ways in which the Brechtian *Gestus* not only readily entails the use of certain kinds of music, but even coincides perfectly with some of Weill's—and Busoni's—earlier ideas of how music should be used on the stage. In fact, the meeting of views on this point is so harmonious at around the time of *The Threepenny Opera*, that one cannot be certain whether the idea originated with Brecht or with Weill. It is entirely possible that not only the gestic conception of music, but the idea of *Gestus* itself, originated with the composer. In one sense, it is simply an updating of the ideas of the *Singspiel*, not to mention those of Busoni's *Arlecchino*. If the concept of the *Gestus* meant the fulfillment of epic theater to Brecht, to Weill it also meant the return to a style of opera that had become completely obscured under the flood of Wagnerian music-drama.

Weill was having it both ways when he wrote for the symposium published in October 1927 that the new type of musical theater he advocated, "as it answers to the naïve attitude of the new listeners, conduces to an epic fulfillment of the musical stage work, which for the first time makes it possible for us to give an absolutely musical, concertlike presentation without having to forsake the laws of the stage." He is paying his dues here to the Brecht–Weill vision of an epic theater for a new, relatively uncultivated mass audience, but he also is rejoicing in the Busoni–Weill aspiration to eliminate Wagnerian excesses and restore a concertlike purity to the opera stage. For what was the *Gestus*, speaking in musical terms, other than a miniature concert presentation within a dramatic context? It was a moment within which the spoken action came to a halt and was replaced by a separate and completely self-contained musical number to provide a new dimension for the play's meaning. Weill may have left the concert hall behind, finding it too arid and exalted a place for what he wanted to do, but this does not mean that he was unready to realize its best possibilities in the livelier and more popular arena of the theater. If he had done the *Mahagonny Songspiel* as a concert piece tending to become theater, he now had in *The Threepenny Opera* a theater piece that, in its musical passages, tended to become a concert.

A most important difference between gestic music and concert music, however—and the reason that had above all brought the literary-minded Weill into the theater—is that gestic music is ever provided with explicit, verbalizable reasons for the shapes it takes on. We hear the voice of the man who had always been a theater composer at heart—just as he considered his beloved Mozart to be—in these lines from an article, "On the Gestic Character of Music," that he published in the journal *Die Musik* in March 1929:

How are the gestic elements of music shaped? They express themselves, first of all, in a rhythmic fixing of the text. Music has the capacity to take note of the accents of language, of the distribution of long and short syllables and, above all, of the pauses; so it is thereby able to rule out the worst sources of errors in the staging of the text. But one can rhythmically interpret a sentence in the most varied ways, and even the self-same *Gestus* can be expressed in various rhythms; the important thing is only that the right *Gestus* be brought out. . . . The melody, too, carries within itself the *Gestus* of the action being represented, but since the stage action has already been established rhythmically, it remains for the formal melodic and harmonic structure to be fit into a much more distinct playing space than would be the case in a purely descriptive kind of music, or in a kind that constantly runs alongside the action. The rhythmic fixing of the text is therefore no more restricting a fetter for the opera composer than, for example, the formal schema of the fugue, the sonata, or the rondo had been for the classical masters.

For the moment, then, it was an excellent marriage between composer and playwright. Brecht's idea that drama and music were not to be emotive but only conducive to thought, also appealed to Weill for the time being. Like Busoni, he had so far written music that was primarily intellectual and unemotional, and like Busoni he was to violate this ideal before very long—indeed, he had already done so in places in *The Threepenny Opera*. But then again, Brecht was not always perfectly true to the ideal, either. In the meantime, it was the results that counted, and *The Threepenny Opera* was being celebrated by the *cognoscenti* and the masses alike, making its authors rich as well as honored.

But if the Weill of *The Threepenny Opera* seemed, to the German audiences that flocked to the play, to share in the Brechtian traits of insolence, intellectuality, and bittersweet irony that so many of them admired, and if they came thereby to extol him as the *dernier cri* of musical modernity, there nevertheless were a few who thought they perceived something else beneath the surface. Arnold Schoenberg was sure that he heard affinities with Franz Lehár; and this is what Count Harry Kessler wrote in his diary for December 29, 1928:

At lunch talked to Diaghilev, Lifar and others about my ballet. Diaghilev is still against using Weill for the music. "*Il faudra vous trouver un musicien.*" Weill, in his view, simply follows in Donizetti's footsteps, but camouflages the fact by inserting the appropriate number of discords at the right moment.

Had he lived to hear the Broadway Weill of a few years later, Diaghilev would no doubt have reiterated this remark without the qualification about the discords. Was this Cantor Weill's son after all, beneath all that Berlin sass? Cantor and Mrs. Weill did not like *The Threepenny Opera* when they saw it, but they were hearing what the majority, rather than Diaghilev, heard. His was an amazing insight, in its way, whether one agrees with the animus or not; but few were sharing it at the end of 1928.

1929

With *The Threepenny Opera* moving into a larger theater for a long run, a Universal Edition piano score of it doing well, and Lenya in sudden demand for other stage roles besides Jenny, the Weills saw that their financial straits had ended. They looked for better quarters than the Pension Hassforth and eventually found an apartment in an elegant new residential complex on Bayernallee, behind the Reichskanzlerplatz. They also bought a car. "I have never seen a man enjoy his first automobile—a Graham-Page—more than Kurt Weill," according to Hans W. Heinsheimer, by then head of Universal Edition's opera department, "and I will not forget the exuberant, relaxed, boyish pleasure with which he drove the car, with Lenya and me, and a lovely lady of my choice from Vienna over the mountains toward Italy. A short stretch of the pre-Autobahn horrors of the road was in splendid condition, and as he gave the American car all it had, Weill improvised a childishly primitive doggerel, singing with his famous veiled voice:

> *Ja, so ein Strässchen*
> *Ja, das macht Spässchen . . .*

("Such a little street is a laugh . . .")

Lenya and Weill were now frequent visitors at Brecht's attic studio, where the playwright held group work sessions that were becoming well known in Berlin literary circles. "To get to his studio apartment," according to one of Brecht's associates of those days, "you had to climb five flights, balance your way over a sort of catwalk, open a massive iron door, and pass along a broad corridor. From the large windows you could look down upon Berlin. This meant that Brecht always had under his eye the roofs of the German capital, which he planned to conquer. . . . On a long table pushed to the window stood a typewriter, open and ready for work, and many files containing material, mainly newspaper cuttings from the old and particularly the new world. When a visitor appeared Brecht regarded this as an event which helped in his work. He read to the visitor a particularly tricky passage, either trying out the quality of the work on him, or testing it with him. Sitting down right away at the machine, he typed the new version. Brecht gathered round him young people, collaborators. They collected material, discussed his plans with him, made suggestions, changes, improvements."

The room often was filled with people, but when Weill came, either alone or with Lenya, the other visitors usually would leave—with the exception of Elisabeth Hauptmann, if she was there. Lenya has recalled the intensity with which Kurt used to concentrate during those sessions with Brecht, "his face like a young seminarist's behind the thick glasses. His precise answers were made in a quiet, deep voice that held a slight hint of mockery—from shyness, not arrogance, as some people mistakenly thought. . . . Sometimes Brecht impressed on Kurt his own ideas for a song, picking out chords on his guitar. Kurt noted these ideas with his grave little smile and invariably said yes, he would try to work them in when he got back to Hassforth's." These exchanges always took place within an atmosphere of the utmost mutual respect, though never of warm friendship.

At the beginning of 1929 the two collaborators were back at work on the full-length *Mahagonny* opera, but in the meantime, Weill had had occasion to produce two other results of their partnership on his own. Both were composed in the fall of 1928 and were performed in the first half of the following year. The first of them to be performed was a suite from *The Threepenny Opera*, which Weill named *Kleine Dreigroschenmusik*, perhaps taking a hint from Mozart. This had been commissioned by Otto Klemperer, whose enthusiasm for the *Mahagonny Songspiel* was more than matched by what he felt for *The Threepenny Opera*, which he saw "about ten times," according to Aufricht. Klemperer conducted it on February 8 at his own Kroll Opera in Berlin, on the occasion of a benefit ball.

Orchestral suites put together from larger stage works were a tradition extending from Mozart to Stravinsky; they could either be straightforward condensations of the larger works, or efforts to explore the new possibilities provided by the concert format. Although Weill used virtually the same jazz-type instrumental ensemble for the suite as he had used in the original, he chose the latter course to some extent, rearranging the order of the numbers, trying out interesting thematic juxtapositions within some of them and occasionally creating new accompaniment figures for the principal melodies. In general, full enjoyment of the piece seems to require a prior knowledge of the full-length dramatic original, but there unquestionably are ways in which it works as "pure" music: one sees clearly, for example, the relationship between the overture and the chorale finale. The suite is above all a reminder that Kurt Weill, even when he wrote a collection of very good individual songs, was at all times a composer of *scores*.

Also in the immediate wake of *The Threepenny Opera* came a commission from Frankfurt Radio, and Weill responded by composing a cantata based on several poems Brecht had already written. In its original form, *The Berlin Requiem* consisted of seven pieces for male voices and small band, all on texts that deal with death or the dead. As Weill said of the work—which has a solemn and rather inspirational character, with little of the usual Brechtian irony—"it makes an attempt to express what the big-city dweller of our time has to say before the presence of death." But this was not a subject matter chosen merely for reasons of artistic mood, for it was meant to commemorate the tenth anniversary of the end of the war and of the Spartacist revolt. Not only do two of the pieces deal with the "Unknown Soldier," but two others are about Rosa Luxemburg—and though the original versions of the latter had not mentioned her by name, Brecht even prepared an alternate text for one of them dealing specifically with *"Rote Rosa"* ("Red Rosa"). This unexpected orientation of the material made the radio authorities uncomfortable, and performance of the piece was postponed several times before it was finally broadcast, without the new "Red Rosa" text, on May 22, 1929.

Weill had taken on this task with special relish, for he still believed in the artistically revolutionary possibilities of radio, and still wrote music criticism for *Der deutsche Rundfunk*. As he wrote in an article for the May 17 issue, dealing with the forthcoming broadcast of his cantata, "radio presents the serious musician of our day with the task of creating, for the first time, works that are accessible to the widest possible range of listeners. The form and content of these radio compositions must therefore be such as to interest a broad mass of people from all walks of life; and the musical means of expression must not provide the uncultivated listener with any difficulties."

This is good Brecht–Weill talk, but it must be said that *The Berlin Requiem*, however starkly simplified its harmonies, is not the model of easy accessibility that *The Threepenny Opera* had been. Except for "The Drowned Maiden"—one of the Rosa Luxemburg songs—there is little in it of the quasi-popular style that had made such a hit the previous summer at the Theater am Schiffbauerdamm. Weill had still not put to rest some of the lofty aspirations of younger days, and what this work does is revive some of the quasi-religious, elegiac qualities of his early student compositions—indeed, like those, it seems almost to have been a spiritual confrontation with Cantor Weill, a demonstration that the insolent perpetrator of *The Threepenny Opera* still is capable of sounding notes of high solemnity. But it also goes beyond appeasement and answers the father with the angry, godless religiosity of a generation that knows no saints but those who died on the barricades or in the trenches. Some of the sounds are quite large, such as the vast and solemn chords that open the introductory section, "*Grosser Dankchoral*" ("Great Thanksgiving Chorale"). On the other hand, there are quiet passages of recitative, mainly in the two "Unknown Soldier" pieces, that are done in the old Weillian operatic manner of expressive declamation. They were among the most powerful passages Weill had ever composed; but they were not likely to keep the mass audience from fidgeting with the dial.

By the summer, Weill and Brecht had completed the *Mahagonny* opera and begun work on a new musical play for Aufricht; but radio was the intended medium for the work that they next brought before the public. This was an entry for the 1929 Baden-Baden Chamber Music Festival—a piece for which Weill was, for once, not Brecht's sole musical collaborator, but co-composer with Paul Hindemith. It was in fact one of two works that Brecht had done with Hindemith for that summer's festival. Hindemith, whose publishers had suggested to him a collaboration with Brecht as far back as 1925, had become friendly with the playwright at the 1927 festival, when the *Mahagonny Songspiel* was presented. He clearly had felt the impact of the Brecht–Weill phenomenon, as is suggested by his opera, *Neues vom Tage* ("News of the Day"), which had its premiere that June of 1929 at the Kroll Opera under Klemperer's baton. Its librettist was Marcellus Schiffer, the well-known lyricist of cabaret and light musical theater who had done *Hin und Zurück* with Hindemith for the 1927 festival, and its plot—a satire on modern urban life about a couple getting divorced and being besieged by the publicity media in the process—included a cabaret sequence that was an intentional parody of Brecht and Weill. This sort of thing was now the highbrow fashion, and besides, Hindemith had been an *enfant terrible* and a literary composer long before Weill had even been heard of. Hindemith may have felt a twinge of competitiveness where Weill was concerned, and this could have been why he was now ready to try his own hand at working with Brecht.

Hindemith, who now was teaching at the Hochschule für Musik in Berlin—where Weill had studied—had become fascinated with the didactic possibilities of his art and had proposed as a theme for this year's festival the *Lehrstück* ("Didactic Play"), an extension of the idea of *Gebrauchsmusik* into the libretto itself. Brecht was invited and eventually wrote not one, but two *Lehrstücke*. There had long been a didactic element in his work, but this, as a result of his steadily growing Marxism, of his repudiation of mere "culinary" art, and of his desire to bring moral ideas to a wide audience, now sought a more distinct formulation than before. He was, in fact, as eager to move away from the style of *The Threepenny Opera* as Weill was. But in his case—now that the work on the *Mahagonny* opera had been completed, not without tension between the two collaborators—this eagerness entailed an interest in possibly finding a new partner for musical plays. One of the evenings at the festival was to be devoted to *Lehrstücke* for radio, and for this Brecht wrote *Der Lindberghflug* ("The Lindbergh Flight"),* a presentation of Charles A. Lindbergh's great exploit of 1927 as an achievement of moral significance for mankind. This evidently was the first of Brecht's two festival pieces to be written, for the other one, now known as *Das Badener Lehrstück vom Einverständnis* ("The Baden Didactic Play on Acquiescence"), and also about flying, seems to be a sequel to it. The first was written with both Weill and Hindemith as collaborators, the second with Hindemith alone. This was one of several signs that Brecht was entertaining the possibility of a regular collaboration with Hindemith; but the outcome was to be most disappointing.

The Lindbergh piece, performed at the festival on July 25, was essentially a cantata for soloists—Lindbergh himself, and such varied antagonists as Fog, Snowstorm, and Sleep, singing in personified voices—with chorus and orchestra. Written in a conscientiously naïve, epic theater style, it is divided into fifteen sections, such as: "Invitation to

---

*   Brecht subsequently renamed this work *Der Ozeanflug* and made changes in the text, primarily to eliminate the flyer's identity. The description here is based on the Brecht–Weill score edition published in 1930.

the American flyer to fly over the ocean," "Presentation of the flyer Charles Lindbergh," "The City of New York asks the ship [if it has sighted the plane]," "In the night came a snowstorm," "Sleep," "During the whole flight all the American newspapers speak incessantly of Lindbergh's luck," and so on. Lindbergh's introduction of himself is resolutely matter-of-fact: without literary flourishes he tells the audience his name, age, ancestry, and nationality, then proceeds to give an itemized list of the equipment he is carrying. This is a most extreme form of literary *Neue Sachlichkeit*. The scenes were set to music alternately by Weill and Hindemith.

Brecht became more surrealistic in the *Lehrstück* on acquiescence that he did entirely with Hindemith, which was presented at the festival three days later. This took up where the Lindbergh one left off, flying as it were from sunlight into darkness. Four men who have tried to fly across the ocean have crashed somewhere and now ask mankind to help them stay alive. "Does man help man?" becomes the theme of an epic discussion, and a series of scenes shows that man's inhumanity to man is more likely the rule, a reality in which the flyers must acquiesce before there can be any hope of changing the world. In one scene—this was *not* a radio play but a vivid stage presentation—a giant clown, played by an actor wearing stilts and other props, comes out and complains that his various limbs are hurting him; two other clowns show their human sympathy by proceeding to saw them off, one by one. When this was done, a wave of disgust swept through the audience. Gerhart Hauptmann, the elder statesman of German drama, who was present that evening, got up and stormed out of the theater.

Upset by the scandal this piece caused, Hindemith subsequently gave instructions in his published version of the score that the clowns' scene—which was almost entirely dialogue without music, anyway—did not have to be performed. Brecht not only objected to this, but insisted on making revisions in the play that would have required changes in the score. Hindemith demurred, and in the debate that ensued the work was withdrawn from circulation. The composer now wanted to have nothing more to do with Brecht, with whom he had begun planning an opera, and he repudiated his contribution to the Lindbergh piece as well. As a result, a new version of the radio cantata was prepared, with Kurt Weill doing the whole score instead of only half of it.

The final version of the Lindbergh work seems more significant in terms of Weill's development than successful in its own right. It once again moves away from song—of which Weill was having his fill in other pieces he was working on—and reverts to the expressive, declamatory line of his operas and parts of *The Berlin Requiem*—but with important new features. As a result of his recent involvement in song, Weill, taking advantage of the episodic character of the play, perceived it musically as a series of enclosed numbers, each one a fully realized miniature on its own. This was, of course, a fulfillment of Busoni's ideal of opera, which had known its most successful manifestation in the eighteenth-century formula of aria and ensemble framed by spoken dialogue or recitative. A play with songs, as *The Threepenny Opera* had been, was a most convenient modern way of reworking this principle; but such a recent work as Alban Berg's *Wozzeck*, which had developed entire scenes on traditional concert-music structures like sonata-allegro and passacaglia, had shown that a more complex approach was possible. Weill saw that the tightness of song structure could be imposed upon a whole scene of drama—just as, conversely, a whole line of dramatic development could be contained within a song: the two forms were, roughly, to be understood as expansions or compressions of one another, in musical terms. It was along these new lines that he had just composed his full-length *Mahagonny* opera.

Each of the fifteen scenes of the Lindbergh cantata, then, is a fully rounded musical composition, with a beginning, a middle, and an end. The structure of each is broader, freer, and less obvious than song, but not so complex as in Alban Berg's specimens of revived traditionalism. In most of them, the essential unifying element is some recurring figure, vigorous and highly rhythmical, that appears as a rule in the instrumental accompaniment but sometimes in the sung part as well. Weill's use of recurring rhythmic figures ultimately comes from the Busoni of *Arlecchino*, and it is to be found at various places in his early operas, but it is now emerging as a trademark and a central element of the structure. It will have this function in forthcoming works as well; but here in the Lindbergh piece, it seems especially suggestive of the plane's motor—of the technological dimension of modern life, which Weill now felt was significantly echoed in much of the music he was writing—even though there is no attempt at mere imitation. Indeed, little is done in the music to make one see or feel the flight; and though this was undoubtedly a purposeful *Verfremdungseffekt*, the result, if honorable, is in the end unsatisfying. "It is noteworthy," wrote the musicologist and critic Alfred Einstein of the Weill final version of the piece when it was conducted by Otto Klemperer in Berlin, a few months after the festival, "that the strong impression made at Baden-Baden does not register again; it has all become a bit sober, almost to the point of dullness. Inspiration is lacking—the heroic, the appeal to fantasy. The 'flight essence' is missing." Einstein recognizes the point when he concludes that "in the last analysis the performance of the work is not so important as the fact that it was composed," for he sees its significance on the path to a new kind of music. But the excessive sobriety of the piece was fair warning that the team of Brecht and Weill was not out to have fun anymore—not, at any rate, if they could help it.

A last bit of fun had been extracted from them in the same spring and summer of 1929 that had seen the emergence of the Lindbergh piece. After the successful opening of *The Threepenny Opera*, Ernst-Josef Aufricht had persuaded Brecht and Weill to try doing something similar for the following season. In the middle of May 1929, just a few weeks after the completion of the *Mahagonny* opera, they had even headed once again to the south of France in their separate cars, planning to work there on the new play. But Brecht had cracked up his Steyr on the way, and he and Weill had returned to Berlin to develop the text and music of their comedy about gangsters and Salvation Army workers in Chicago, which they had decided to call *Happy End* (its exact title in German). By the end of July, Aufricht was ready to begin rehearsals, hoping to open on the first anniversary of *The Threepenny Opera*. He had assembled the same production team as that of the earlier play: Erich Engel was to direct, Caspar Neher to do the sets, and Theo Mackeben to conduct the orchestra. As for the cast, Carola Neher, now eager to participate, had the lead feminine role of the Salvation Army lieutenant; the massive Heinrich George, one of Germany's foremost actors, was to play the gangster Bill; and the young Peter Lorre was to play one of his first in a long succession of roles as sinister Orientals, Dr. Nakamura—a characteristic specimen of Brecht's still somewhat questionable racial outlook in that period. Everything was ready to go; but there were troubles again, this time caused entirely by the playwright.

After the *Mahagonny* opera and their experiments with the *Lehrstück* idea, neither Brecht nor Weill had found himself eager to return to the *Threepenny* genre; but Aufricht's moral claims upon them and the lure of further financial success had been very great. Weill had been able to bring the matter off and even explore some new ideas for the genre, but Brecht was having great trouble seeing it through. The idea of doing a play merely for fun and profit and not for some higher moral and sociological purpose had become completely distasteful to him. When rehearsals were due to begin, he was still in his Bavarian summer retreat at Ammersee, and had not yet turned in his third act. Aufricht felt that he could not proceed without it and wondered what to do.

Weill, used to dealing with Brecht by now, came up with the suggestion that Aufricht send him a telegram saying that the play had been cancelled and that Aufricht had gone away for a vacation. "Get out of town tomorrow," Kurt went on, "and take Lenya with you. Brecht will think the telegram is a ruse, and he'll call me from Augsburg. He'll learn from me that you've gone to the country with Lenya."

Aufricht went up to Warnemünde with his wife and Lenya, and waited there two days. At last, word came from the theater that Brecht was there and wanted to see him immediately. "We drove back as fast as we could," Aufricht writes, "Lenya and I taking turns at the wheel every hour." As it turned out, Brecht had still not written a third act, but evidently he satisfied everyone that it was forthcoming, and rehearsals began. However, the effects of problems he was creating had already begun to show themselves. At Ammersee he had fashioned a whole new character for the unfinished third act, the woman gangster chief called "The Fly," and he wanted his wife, Helene Weigel, to play the role. Apparently this was to satisfy not only familial requirements but also a whole new Marxist orientation that he hoped to work into the text; but in the process he had taken some material from the lead role of Bill to give to "The Fly." This was more than Heinrich George would tolerate, and he resigned from the cast; to replace him Aufricht quickly obtained young Oscar Homolka, then just beginning his career. Brecht was not finished having difficulties with the actors, however. Many of them were justifiably tense when general run-throughs began and there was still no third act, but it was the enormous Kurt Gerron, who had doubled in the roles of Tiger Brown and the streetsinger in the original cast of *The Threepenny Opera* and was now playing the gangster Sam, who finally exploded. In the middle of a rehearsal that had gone well into the night he suddenly stopped, strode to the footlights, and yelled out to Brecht that he was tired of functioning like some kind of extra in the third act and wanted his lines.

Brecht roared back at him. "You fat-ass clown, you abortion! If you ever lose any weight, you'll be out of work!"

"And you should have written a play," Gerron shouted in return, "instead of shitting all over the stage!"

"I want that man disciplined immediately!" Brecht said. "Otherwise I'm walking out."

Aufricht writes that he could barely keep from laughing, and it was

Heinrich Fischer who had to come to the rescue, saying that nobody was going to get disciplined at four-thirty in the morning. Rehearsals went on, Gerron stayed in the cast, and the play survived, even though Brecht never did produce a complete third act. Erich Engel even resigned over this issue for a time, during which Brecht directed the play, but he finally agreed to return and help assemble a third act out of whatever materials were available. By opening night Brecht was ready to wash his hands completely of the enterprise.

His attitude was made clear by the peculiar credits on the *Happy End* program. For he had by now refused to have his name appear as the author of the play—although Weill, putting his foot down for once, had at least persuaded Brecht to keep his name in as coauthor of the songs. The play was designated a German adaptation by Elisabeth Hauptmann of "a magazine story by Dorothy Lane," which ostensibly had appeared in something called the "*J & L Weekly*, St. Louis." All this has proved to be something of a mystery, since neither the author nor the magazine has otherwise ever been heard of, from that day to this—nor was Brecht himself ever to be enlightening on the subject, since he was to banish *Happy End* from his collected works. And the mystery is compounded by the plot, for this comedy about a Salvation Army lass trying to save the souls of a group of gangsters and getting romantically involved with one of them in the process does strongly resemble an American short story: "The Idyll of Sarah Brown," by Damon Runyon, which was to become the source for the 1950 Broadway musical, *Guys and Dolls*. But the Runyon story was not to appear in print until 1932, three years after the opening of *Happy End*. Perhaps, as some have suggested, the two works do go back to some common American source, which was disguised by Brecht and Hauptmann under the false names "Dorothy Lane" and "*J & L Weekly*" to avoid accusations of copyright infringement—an issue on which Brecht had already experienced trouble. But another possible explanation is that both Damon Runyon and Elisabeth Hauptmann—who was indeed responsible for suggesting the Salvation Army to Brecht as a subject— were inspired by George Bernard Shaw's *Major Barbara*, which they reworked in terms of a common inclination toward a gangster milieu. It seems significant that Brecht, once he had put *Happy End* out of the way, was to develop his Salvation Army material into another play, *Saint Joan of the Stockyards*, that was frankly derived from Shaw.

All of Brecht's ambivalence about this project came to a head during the opening-night performance itself. The first two acts went well, and during the second intermission people could be heard proclaiming that this would be another hit like *The Threepenny Opera*. But there still remained the hurdle of the thrown-together third act, in which the mysterious ringleader, "The Fly," appears at last, discovers one of the Salvation Army officers to be her long-lost husband, and proposes that their two organizations join forces in a world so corrupt that there is no difference between those who beg for money and those who steal it—a familiar *Threepenny* conclusion, though with perhaps a greater touch of impiety to the context. The curtain went up, and the plot staggered toward its conclusion. Aufricht, standing in the wings and tensely counting the minutes that remained, listened to the coughing and rustling of the audience and thought that its disappointment was audible. Then to his surprise, as the finale was about to begin, Helene Weigel as "The Fly" made a sudden move toward the audience and said:

"What's a jimmy alongside a stock certificate? What's robbing a bank alongside founding one?"

These words apparently were in the script but Aufricht claims that she added "other vulgar-Marxist provocations," and Lenya, who was in the audience, has said that she even read from a pamphlet. At any rate, she spoke words that were as unrehearsed as her sudden speech-making stance evidently had been, and the audience was as shocked as her collaborators were. "The audience, hitherto bored," writes Aufricht, "had been brutally aroused from its lethargy and now called tumultuously for the curtain to be brought down." As it happened, the play's creators had prepared their most provocative piece of *épater le bourgeois* for this very moment, and down came, not the curtain, but two stained-glass church windows to the opening chords of the scathing mock hymn, "Hosanna Rockefeller." But it could not be heard amid the tumult. No one knows to this day whether Weigel had done her impromptu routine on her own initiative or by an arrangement made in advance with her husband, but in any case it was the resentment of the Brechts at this whole bourgeois undertaking that had thereby expressed itself. The attitude had succeeded, by various means, in making the show a flop, and in the aftermath Berlin paid little attention to the fact that Weill had written some of his best songs for it.

Weill had been doing some other songwriting that year. For one thing, he did a cabaret-type number called "Berlin in Light"—referring not to the light of the sun, but to the sophisticated glare of the city's lights—a piece of German turn-of-the-century style sentimentality that sounds a bit like Lehár. Also, continuing to write incidental music for plays, he did a song for Lion Feuchtwanger's *Die Petroleuminseln* ("The Oil Islands"), another one of the sardonic pieces on the international oil trade that the Brecht circle had been turning out. Like the one Weill had done the previous year for Lania's *Konjunktur*, his song for the Feuchtwanger play, "The Song of the Brown Islands"—brown being the color into which the land had been turned by the oil-drilling—was an exercise in musical banality, and thus once again an ironic counterpoint to the bitter lyrics. Also a fox-trot, this one had an interesting blues line in the opening bars of each stanza that bore strong affinities with Philip Braham's 1921 London hit, "Limehouse Blues." Once again, Weill was giving a striking demonstration of what a very good popular songwriter he could be when he wanted to be: but, for now, he wanted to be that only under the special conditions of irony that his lyricists were establishing.

This was the case also in some of the music of *Happy End*, which contains even more exercises in banality than there had been in *The Threepenny Opera*, mainly in its several satirical Salvation Army songs. The opportunity to parody Salvation Army music was irresistible in this show—one can just see Weill lingering long and often at street corners to listen to the Army's bands—and at least seven of the thirteen numbers do so. Three of these are marches, a vein in which Weill had shown skill as far back as *Die Zaubernacht*, and which now emerges with a sardonic brilliance. Yet they could also be played or sung, without words or with different ones, in a straightforward, unironic manner, and they would work equally well, albeit for a more innocent consciousness than they were intended for. This is especially true of the heroine's marching leitmotiv, "Dear God's Little Lieutenant," which is a much gentler relative of the "Second Threepenny Finale," and which is in pure melodic terms a rousing piece of *Gebrauchsmusik*.

Of the four other Salvation Army songs, two are hymns: one of them, "Don't Be Afraid," would sound as good in a revivalist church as it does in the mocking Brechtian context, and the other, "Hosanna Rockefeller," also has a valid if overly strident hymn melody until it breaks, with heavy-handed absurdism, into a raucous jazz refrain. But it is the two remaining Salvation Army songs that provide the most significant examples of Weill's growing tendency, as a songwriter, to have it both ways—to serve up a parody by juxtaposing a perfectly conventional melody with an ironic text. "In Youth's Golden Glimmer" and "The Song of the Liquor Dealer" are both ballads in that tearful nineteenth-century vein, peculiarly American it would seem at first glance, that was somehow able to make itself equally at home in a pew or alongside a spittoon. The first sounds like a barbershop quartet number, the second—which is a mock conversion tale akin to the one told in "Sit Down, You're Rockin' the Boat" in *Guys and Dolls*, though musically quite different—sounds like a barroom ballad, heavy with beer, or like a street-corner revival song, heavy with trombones.

The true significance of these two songs in the Kurt Weill canon, however, was not to emerge for some years to come. For the composer was to use both melodies again, one of them twice. Both reappear in his Broadway years, the first indeed as a barbershop quartet (in *One Touch of Venus*), the second as a purely instrumental motif related to the theme song of a simple, small-town American boy (in *Johnny Johnson*). But the barbershop melody had already had an earlier reincarnation in Paris, when Weill put it to French lyrics and thereby made it sound like the kind of sobbing number one would regard as typical of a *chanteuse* of the era. In their Broadway reincarnations, these two melodies were used with an ironic smile, as in Berlin, but one so much gentler than the Brechtian variety as to represent a cultural transformation even more radical than that implied by a change of language and nationality. In the Paris reincarnation, even the smile was gone, but the tearful melody worked all the same.

In other words, licensed by Brecht's bitterly ironic frame of reference, Weill had made his way once again, in these *Happy End* songs, to the vein of sentimentality lying within himself. And if this vein was now being brought to light by contact with "American" themes, it was because the specimens of American culture that Weill encountered, from popular music recordings to Charlie Chaplin films, were pervaded by that peculiar combination of humor and sentimentality that seemed to thrive in the New World. That the whole thing turned into a glimpse into the future is an irony of fate much larger than any that Brecht or Weill could have conceived.

For the most part, the six songs in *Happy End* that are not Salvation Army parodies are in a very different vein: these are the offerings to whoever, like Aufricht, wanted a re-echoing of *The Threepenny Opera*, though they fill that request a bit less than first meets the ear. In particular, three of them, the "Bilbao Song," the "Sailors' Song," and "Surabaya Johnny," have become as famous as some of the *Threepenny* songs and sound like a continuation of them. "Surabaya Johnny," in fact, begins its refrain with the same melodic phrase as that which opens "The Moritat of Mack the Knife"—though in a different key, to be sure—and this establishes a perhaps intentional connection, since the Johnny to whom the abused girlfriend is singing her lament seems to be a world-roaming version of Macheath. In content and dramatic context, it is the equivalent of the "Barbara Song": both are parables sung by a hitherto innocent girl who has fallen in love with a scoundrel, poetically describing her lot, and both were intended for Carola Neher. Both are ideal cabaret songs, though "Surabaya Johnny" is far torchier and was to become, even more than the other, a particular favorite of Marlene Dietrich's. Together they represent a kind of hard-boiled boulevard sentimentalism that had once been a trademark of Brecht's, but that he was renouncing by the summer of 1929; and it is no surprise to learn that "Surabaya Johnny" was one of several lyrics in *Happy End* that had actually been written a few years earlier (in 1925, for Brecht's revision of Feuchtwanger's play, *Calcutta, May 4*, in which it was sung to music composed by F. Bruinier).

But "Surabaya Johnny" ultimately breaks out of the *Threepenny* mold, as do the "Bilbao Song" and the "Sailors' Song." All three are lengthy dramatic monologues that use the elements of song—and of jazz—to create not simply some new variant of song, as in *The Threepenny Opera*, but a new kind of aria. Not that Weill was trying to write music that was operatic—he had done plenty of that in the just completed *Mahagonny*—though, it must be said, these songs are far more challenging to actors' voices than are any of the *Threepenny* songs except for the rarely sung "Lucy's Aria." Rather, he was trying, in the Busonian tradition, to explore the dramatic possibilities of musical set pieces—or, to put it another way, he was restoring the trappings of song to the kind of thing he had been doing in the Lindbergh cantata. Like the segments of that work, each of the three major *Happy End* songs is an entire miniature drama unto itself: Bill sings to the cronies in his Chicago saloon of the good old days when he had an establishment in Bilbao; Lieutenant Lillian, suddenly a bit drunk, sings for Bill a raucous ballad of the sailors' life; and then, falling in love with Bill, she sings to him the monologue of a girl who has been kicked around by her rat of a lover in Burma and India, who curses him and is crazy about him in spite of everything. Unlike the Lindbergh sections, each of these numbers presents itself as a song, with stanzas and refrains. But the stanzas—with the exception of those in "Surabaya Johnny"—tend to be irregular in structure and inordinately long for the song form, and the refrains—with the exception of those in the "Sailors' Song"—are almost anti-refrains, fragmented in character, and broken up by passages of pure speech. In the "Bilbao Song" Bill keeps forgetting the words of the song they sang in the good old days, so that part of the refrain regularly consists of his moanings over this fact, spoken to the piano's ragging accompaniment. "Surabaya Johnny" also breaks into speech whenever it reaches the heights of its emotional intensity. By contrast, the "Ah, the sea is blue, so blue" refrain of the "Sailors' Song" is conventional in shape and melodiousness, but nothing else in the song is: its stanzas are the longest and most irregularly constructed of all, and it contains the longest passage in any of the songs of words spoken without melody. This song, by the way, is a tango, though the fact—as in the tango in Stravinsky's *L'Histoire du soldat*—is not always obvious, and it is significant that, though there is nothing erotic about the content of the song, its context in the play suggests the kind of ambivalent eroticism that had traditionally made the dramatic occasions for Weill's tangos.

Other songs in *Happy End* are more distinctly *Threepenny* encores. "The Song of the Tough Nut" is another piece of the merry Brechtian cynicism of 1928, telling you that you can't be soft if you want to make the big time, and sung more or less in the music-hall style of "The Ballad of the Inadequacy of Human Striving," though much jazzier, a soft-shoe on heavy Berlin feet. "The Song of Mandalay," another chip from Brecht's India worktable, is a relative of the "Cannon Song," only this time the boys have gone to Mother Goddam's whorehouse and it is musically even more violent than its predecessor: Kurt Gerron could certainly make himself noticed singing this one. In general, *Happy End*'s songs seem more strident, more overdone, and angrier than those of *The Threepenny Opera*. The two authors were straining at the leash; the more carefree mood of 1928 had passed.

Indeed, the halcyon days of the twenties were coming rapidly and dramatically to an end. On October 3 Gustav Stresemann died, and with him Germany—and the world—lost the statesman who, single-handedly, had been doing the most to restore peace among the nations. "What I fear, as a result of Stresemann's death," Harry Kessler wrote, "are very grave political consequences at home . . . and the facilitation of efforts to establish a dictatorship." Yet the worst fomenter of such consequences was still to come: for just three weeks later, on Thursday, October 24, the New York stock market underwent the first shocks of its historic collapse, precipitating the worldwide depression that was to have effects in Germany more dire than in any other country.

The *Mahagonny* Opera

Although the full-length *Mahagonny* opera had been completed by the end of April 1929, it was not to have its premiere until the following March. There were various reasons for the delay. For one thing, Dr. Emil Hertzka, director of Universal Edition, who had harbored misgivings about the project from the beginning, urged Weill and Brecht to make some modifications in the opera's frank handling of sexual matters, and they complied. For another, in the emerging economic crisis, opera and theater managers were less ready than they once had been to take risks at the box office. Weill had hoped for a premiere at the Kroll Opera in Berlin, with his longtime supporter Otto Klemperer conducting; but the Kroll had become wary of avant-garde operas since its performances of Hindemith's *Neues vom Tage* in June, for which the audiences had been small, and by the end of the year it was in serious financial trouble. Also, the political climate was steadily darkening, and staid opera companies were not eager to challenge their audiences with the increasingly provocative Brecht. Berlin theater managers were another matter, but Weill, at least, was not yet ready to do the reworking of his score that would have been necessary to make it appropriate for the ordinary musical stage. It was an opera, and he wanted to see it produced as such.

Finally, a contract was obtained with the Leipzig Opera, whose music director, Gustav Brecher, had a history that predisposed him to look with favor upon a new work of unusual character by Kurt Weill. In

145

the course of his long career he had been associated with both Mahler and Busoni, and he was a determined champion of the younger composers. It was, in fact, Brecher who had given the premiere performance of *Der Zar lässt sich photographieren*, at Leipzig, on February 18, 1928. *Aufstieg und Fall der Stadt Mahagonny* ("The Rise and Fall of the City of Mahagonny") was now scheduled to open there two years and almost a month later, on March 9, 1930, just a week after its composer's thirtieth birthday. The production was to be staged by Walter Brügmann, who had done both *Der Zar* and the *Mahagonny Songspiel*, as well as Krenek's *Jonny spielt auf*. Caspar Neher would once again do the sets.

As the date of the premiere approached, further troubles arose in the preparation of the work. By this time the temperamental, artistic, and political differences always implicitly existing between Brecht and Weill had clearly emerged. Indeed, though Germany was to see one more major work by them that summer, it had already been completed, and the partnership was really at an end. Brecht had no more patience with Weill's operatic aspirations, and if he had always been inclined to look upon the bourgeois Dr. Hertzka with some contempt, this feeling certainly had been helped along by the latter's request for bowdlerizations. He did not intend to be Weill's librettist, even though this is precisely what Weill wanted him to be; indeed, Brecht had already begun working with another avant-garde composer, Hanns Eisler, who, though a former pupil of Schoenberg's, was perfectly willing to play that role of songwriter to Brecht's plays into which Weill had never neatly fit. Furthermore, as the brother of a prominent figure in the German Communist Party, Gerhardt Eisler, this new collaborator was much closer to Brecht's political outlook than Weill had been.

The political content of the *Mahagonny* opera was among the problems still being ironed out just before the Leipzig production. In the finale, as the city of Mahagonny goes up in flames, members of the cast sing and march about the stage carrying placards; but whereas Brecht wanted these placards to be of a specifically political nature, satirically expressing the bourgeois outlook on various social questions, Weill wanted them to have a more general character. In general, if Brecht saw the play as a parable of capitalism, Weill became less and less inclined to take this view of it and preferred looking upon it as a parable of human greed. By this time, Weill was clearly moving away from the bitterness of the original conception.

In this connection, he was to make some significant remarks a few years later to an American newspaper interviewer, who had asked him about Caspar Neher's *Mahagonny* projections. What the interviewer had seen were drawings from the 1927 *Songspiel* production, and he had found them frightening. When he asked if these meant that the work was "sardonic" in nature, Weill replied that these applied only to the early version of *Mahagonny* and went on to stress: "I am not sardonic in the least. The *Mahagonny* of 1927 was a mere sketch, differing completely from the opera of the same name, given its premiere at Leipzig in 1930. The early sketch reflected the effects of the horror of war, which we had witnessed, and which we wanted to throw off in a cynical manner. This was only a passing phase. This first *Mahagonny* was merely an attempt to invent a new style for use in the larger work, in which the atrocities referred to were eliminated. Bert Brecht, the librettist of *Mahagonny*, and I had a moral idea as the background of that opera, namely, that a city given over to pleasure must perish, which is hardly sardonic."

The political content of the placards was modified for the Leipzig production—though not enough, as it was to turn out. Meanwhile, in the weeks before the premiere, another question arose concerning the "American" aspect of the libretto. The *Mahagonny* poems and libretto had been, along with such works as *In the Jungle of Cities*, *Happy End*, and others, expressions of Brecht's peculiar vision of America. A somewhat surrealistic conception of the United States can be found in German literature at least as far back as Karl May's "westerns" of the late nineteenth century, in which the German cowboy Old Shatterhand appears among Indians and white bandits like Siegfried among gods and Nibelungen, all in the midst of a landscape no more concrete than a Schopenhauer concept. In Franz Kafka's *Amerika*, concretion becomes a sword instead of a torch in the hand of the Statue of Liberty. The American hero of Fritz Lang's 1919 film *Die Spinnen* ("Spiders")—an extension of the world of boys' adventure literature onto the screen—bears the unlikely name of Kay Hoog (the first name rhymes with "pie") and spends some of his time chasing villains in an underground city beneath San Francisco's Chinatown. To this tradition Brecht added the products both of his socialist outlook and of his own uniquely modern-Gothic imagination. Upton Sinclair and Sinclair Lewis provided him with materials for an image of the United States as the homeland of unadulterated capitalism, but this image was compounded by elements of murkier origin. In the 1920s Brecht's America was a sinister though fascinating never-never land of the western ocean, where different races mingled and brawled, whored and drank, and passed as easily from Chicago to Benares, Bilbao, or Mandalay as one did from Berlin to

Munich or Hamburg. It is not at all surprising that the Widow Begbick, herself a blend of Mother Goddam and Texas Guinan, should turn up in America founding her city of Mahagonny after having last been seen in the India of *A Man's a Man:* these are adjacent locations in the Brechtian landscape.

Weill's view of America seems always to have been less harsh and more realistic than Brecht's. Music has always been one of the principal routes along which European artists and intellectuals, put off at first by the image of rampant money-grubbing, are able to make their way over this obstacle into some appreciation of American civilization. Weill loved the music of Louis Armstrong and of George Gershwin, and this appreciation helped make his feeling for the United States somewhat benign. Another factor conditioning his attitude toward America may have been his Jewish origins. In the postwar era, the United States had clearly emerged as the country of the world that offered the fewest obstacles for Jews in the realization of social equality and freedom from opprobrium. Weill, who had even met such a uniquely *American* Jewish phenomenon as George Gershwin, must have been fully appreciative of this fact, even long before he knew that the United States was going to be his own home one day.

At any rate, as the time for the Leipzig production of *Mahagonny* drew near, Weill decided that the opera's sardonic treatment of America was not to his taste. Not that anything could have been done either to change the setting or to modify the satirical content; both were part of the work's essential fabric. But Weill thought that the "American" aspect could at least be played down, and Mahagonny be depicted as a place that could exist anywhere in the world. Among other things, he suggested that the "American" names hitherto borne by the characters—Jimmy Mahoney, Jack O'Brien, Bill, Joe, and the like—be replaced by German ones, which would be more culturally anonymous. He even proposed some names, such as Heinrich for Joe, Jakob Schmidt for Jack O'Brien, and—oddly drawing upon his mother's family name—Johann Ackermann for Jimmy Mahoney. At his request Universal Edition placed these alternative names on the frontispiece of the published score of the opera,* along with this caution, also demanded by the composer:

---

* Different names—including various alternative versions—were used in different productions, and to this day the names of characters in various editions of *Mahagonny* are a chaos as a result.

Any approximation of wild West and cowboy romanticism, and any echoing of a typically American milieu, are to be avoided.

These strictures were easily observed for the production by Caspar Neher, who was no realist anyway. As for the music, there was very little in it that could be taken for American pastiche.

In spite of all the modifications in the politics of *Mahagonny*, the mood in which the Leipzig public greeted its arrival was mainly political. The unemployment crisis had given the Nazis a new strength that was soon to show itself at the polls, and Brecht and Weill were among the artists they reviled. Only that winter, while visiting Brecht in Augsburg to work on revisions of the *Mahagonny* text, Kurt had looked in upon a Brown Shirt rally—Bavaria was the preeminent Nazi stronghold—and had been astonished to hear his name mentioned along with those of Albert Einstein and Thomas Mann as among the "dire forces" threatening the country. Momentarily fearing for his safety, Kurt had then realized that no one recognized him, and he had quietly slipped away. Now in Leipzig, where the Nazis had also gained some strength, Brown Shirts were demonstrating in front of the opera house on the day of the scheduled *Mahagonny* premiere. Brecht did not show up, but the Weills did; this, after all, was the city where Kurt once had lived and where his parents still lived. That evening, Kurt went ahead to the opera house to help take charge backstage, and Lenya and the elder Weills—by now fairly well reconciled to each other—arrived later to take their seats out front. Wholly absorbed in the performance at first, Lenya noticed only after a while that there was "something strange and ugly" in the mood of the audience.

"Even at the beginning of the evening, storm signals were in the air," the critic Alfred Polgar later wrote of the occasion. "A tension, a crackling disquiet, an audible unfolding of discontent. The various moods, including some unanticipated ones, sent up small bubbles, as if they were simmering over a fire that was slowly bringing them to a boil. There was a strong scent of an antipathy that had been brought into the theater and was awaiting its moment." The Nazis had undoubtedly helped to create this atmosphere; indeed, it is possible that they had even bought blocks of seats to plant themselves among the spectators and help stir up the demonstration that finally broke out during the finale, as the singers marched about the stage with placards saying things like: "For the Natural Disorder of Things," "For Higher Prices," "For the War of All against

All," "For the Just Distribution of Unworldly Goods," "For the Unjust Distribution of Worldly Goods," and so on.

Suddenly, according to Polgar, "war cries echoed through the auditorium. In places hand-to-hand fighting broke out. Hissing, applause that sounded grimly like faces being slapped . . . all were pitted against one another. . . . A worthy gentleman with the face of a boiled lobster took out his keys to wage a heroic struggle against the epic theater. Four of the keys hung down on their long chain . . . while this non-appreciator held a fifth one pressed against his lower lip. He then caused streams of air to pass over the hole at its end at an extremely high rate of vibration. The noise thus produced had an implacable quality: it cut right through your stomach. Nor did his spouse desert him in this hour of trial; a large, round woman, she was the Valkyries riding all over again, with a bun and a blue dress with yellow flounces. This lady had put two fat fingers into her mouth; she closed her eyes, blew up her cheeks, and produced a whistle louder than the key had made." "It was a scarlet occasion," wrote another observer, "of free fights, wild defiances, female fainting fits and shrieks of *'Pfui, Teufel, Schluss!'* from the custodians of righteousness." By the end of the performance, Lenya recalls, "the riot had spread to the stage, panicky spectators were trying to claw their way out, and only the arrival of a large police force, finally, cleared the theater."

Further performances had been scheduled, and the citizenry of Leipzig, shocked at the news of this outburst, wondered if they should not be canceled. The city council held a meeting the very next day to deliberate this question and at length decided to let them go on, with precautionary measures. At the very next performance, policemen lined the walls of the theater and the house lights were kept on; the evening went by without mishap. Meanwhile, performances had been scheduled in other cities, and there was concern about audience reactions in them. Only three days after the Leipzig premiere, *Mahagonny* was done in Cassel under the baton of Weill's old friend Maurice Abravanel; but by then the authors had made further changes in Act Three and had produced a version that, in Weill's words, "the Pope himself could no longer take exception to. It is made clear that the final demonstrations are in no wise 'Communistic'—it is simply that Mahagonny, like Sodom and Gomorrah, falls on account of the crimes, the licentiousness and the general confusion of its inhabitants." The Cassel performance went peacefully enough, and there were other performances later that year; but opera companies had become even more hesitant to take on *Mahagonny* than they were before the Leipzig opening. In Oldenburg, where another performance had been scheduled for that fall, it was canceled at the behest of a Nazi-led faction in the town council. The political climate was rapidly darkening: at the end of March, Chancellor Heinrich Brüning had formed a right-wing government without any Social Democrats in it, which was to stay in power more than two years and rule the country, by invoking the constitutional provision for special measures in times of emergency, as a virtual dictatorship.

Opera audiences tend to be more stolid than those that go to the theater, especially in provincial towns, so it is not really surprising that the good burghers of Leipzig should have been no more tolerant at the *Mahagonny* premiere than the sophisticates of Berlin had been at that of *Happy End*. To be sure, there is no political provocation in *Mahagonny* so explicit as "The Fly's" little closing speech. But, this and other brief moments aside, *The Rise and Fall of the City of Mahagonny* was, taken as a whole, more of an assault upon the German bourgeois audience of its day than were any of the preceding works of Brecht and Weill. Today the antibourgeois elements of *Mahagonny* look like those of a period piece, but they are relentless and lightened by very little of the merriment that pervades *The Threepenny Opera* or *Happy End*—or, for that matter, the *Mahagonny Songspiel*, which provides the full-length opera with most of its relatively few moments of comic relief. For, though the six *Songspiel* numbers are in it, and it has other moments as well that bear affinities with those other works, the full-length *Mahagonny* is something quite different from all of them. There have been notions to the contrary in subsequent years, but it really is *opera* in every sense of the word: two and a half hours of continuous recitative, arioso, aria, and ensemble broken only by two intermissions—a considerable challenge to any audience, and so much the more to a bourgeois one that must submit to an evening of *épatement* at the same time.

The listener does not have to wait long to discover the true musical nature of *The Rise and Fall of the City of Mahagonny*: for the opening scene—in which the truck occupied by the Widow Begbick and her two cronies, Fatty and Trinity-Moses, stalls in an American desert—begins with a fuguelike orchestral prelude and a recitative that are more reminiscent of Weill's early one-act operas than of anything else he had done with Brecht. Since the three fleeing charlatans are near the Florida "gold coast," they decide to found on that spot a "City of Nets"—this, Widow Begbick tells us, is the meaning of the word *Mahagonny*—in which to ensnare prospectors eager for pleasure, and an establishment called the

Hotel zum Reichen Manne ("Rich Man's Hotel") in the more anticapitalist version of the text, the *Hier-darfst-du Schenke* ("Do-What-You-Want-Here Inn") in the more conciliatory version. At the end of the recitative the Widow and the two men break into the trio, "But This Whole Mahagonny," which was the finale number in the *Songspiel*—and the very fact that this, the most solemn song of that earlier group, is now being placed first is a signal as to the altered nature of the new *Mahagonny*.

A few more legacies from the *Songspiel* follow: in scene two the women arrive in the new city singing the "Alabama Song," and in scene four the men come in doing their "Off to Mahagonny" number with the little parody quotation from *Der Freischütz*. But from then on, the score makes a radical departure into opera, though this has become disguised in scene five by a subsequent tradition. In that scene Widow Begbick urges the men to pick out their favorites from among the prostitutes. She tries to push Jenny* onto Jack O'Brien (or Jakob Schmidt), asking fifty dollars for her, but O'Brien offers only thirty. Jenny tells him he should think this over in her briefly autobiographical "Havana Song," which has become well known more recently in a version sung by Lotte Lenya: "*Ach, bedenken Sie, Herr Jakob Schmidt.*" But this was not the music originally composed by Weill, which was a neoclassical arioso for an operatic soprano voice. *Mahagonny* was to be done later in a Berlin theater version, as we shall see, and among the changes Weill was to make for this was a new version of the "Havana Song" that could be sung by Lenya. This is the version that has become familiar today, and though it is different from anything in either *The Threepenny Opera* or *Happy End*, it nevertheless has more of the flavor of those works than of opera. It has thus contributed to a widespread misapprehension of the true nature of the full-length *Mahagonny*. On the other hand, there can be no mistaking the character of scenes six, seven, and eight—dealing with the romance between Jenny and Jimmy Mahoney (we shall call him that, among his various names), with economic crisis in Mahagonny, and with Jimmy's abortive attempt to leave the city—which are made up of pure recitative, arioso, and operatic ensemble, and in which even the spoken lines have an orchestral accompaniment.

Scene nine reverts to musical parody—but of a more ambitious and

---

*   The character called Jessie in the *Songspiel* had now been given the same name as the prostitute of *The Threepenny Opera*. Weill obviously had grown fond of it, for he was to use it again in later years: more than one Jenny can be found in his American works.

sophisticated sort than Weill had hitherto composed. The men are sitting around smoking and drinking while a pianist on stage plays a tinny and outrageously ornamented rendition of "The Maiden's Prayer," a sentimental popular song of the nineteenth century that was well known to German audiences in the 1920s. During this performance Jack O'Brien dreamily says, "That is immortal art." Jimmy Mahoney then sings a sentimental song of his own in three-quarter time, which is an operetta-like variation upon "The Maiden's Prayer," and in which he recalls the good old days when he and the boys felled trees in Alaska. He wonders why he has come to Mahagonny, where no one does anything, and the number becomes an ensemble of all those present. Jimmy grows angrier and his music more agitated, and it looks as if he is again about to leave town when a cry goes up: a hurricane is approaching Mahagonny.

The next three scenes are devoted to the hurricane, which never reaches Mahagonny, and which is represented in the action only by the music and by pseudo-meteorological projections onto a screen. The principal hurricane music, a swiftly marching counterpoint in which the lines keep echoing one another, carries recollections of the opera's prelude and is a vintage example of the Weill instrumental style of this period: the feeling of mechanical, repetitious movement is there, as in the Lindbergh cantata, and there is again no effort actually to imitate what is being represented. But the most remarkable moment in the hurricane sequence comes when a group of the men of Mahagonny are heard singing in the distance: *"Haltet euch aufrecht, fürchtet euch nicht"* ("Stand tall, don't be afraid"). For the music here is a close imitation of the chorale sung by the two temple guards in the finale of *The Magic Flute*—a sequence that, as we have seen, was of great importance both to Weill and to his teacher Busoni and that Weill had already made use of in his music. In verbal content this moment in *Mahagonny* is the most straightforwardly solemn of the whole opera, completely free of Brecht's usual sardonicism, and the exalted, chorale-type music seems most appropriate. But Weill also seems to be up to something else, to have taken advantage of this opportunity to do something quite personal. It is as if he had anticipated that opening in the city where his parents lived and had decided to send a message to his father, saying that religious exaltation was still possible for him even amid all this nasty Berlin irony; in any case, it was a message to himself.

But the hurricane sequence also contains moments that are highly Brechtian—its message is that no storm can be as terrible as human beings are to one another—and it is significant that the end of scene eleven, which is the finale of Act One,* brings out the one song written expressly for the *Mahagonny* opera that sounds as if it could have been part of *The Threepenny Opera*: "*Denn wie man sich bettet, so liegt man*" ("For, as you make your bed, so you must lie in it"). Sung by Jimmy (it is later to be reprised by Jenny), it reminds us again of how the world is—that you're either going to kick or be kicked, and that it might as well be the former. This is another— indeed, it is one of the most outstanding—of the many cases in which Weill, satisfied that the text is jarring enough, has ironically set it to the most melodious of tunes: but for the somewhat strident orchestration, one could sing it to the words of a love song. The presence of this song has helped to further the impression that the *Mahagonny* opera is something other than what Weill intended it to be; but his intentions return to the fore in the very last bars of the Act One finale, as we briefly hear the distant men's chorus once again, singing their Mozart-like chorale.

Act Two, after the passing of the hurricane in its first scene, is devoted to a succession of scenes showing the men of Mahagonny engaging in pleasures even more unbridled now that a moment of national danger has come and gone—presumably, like the people of Berlin after the war. A chorus sung repeatedly by the men throughout the act reminds us that foremost among these pleasures are *Fressen* ("eating," but like a pig), the *Liebesakt* (the "love-act," bowdlerized into just *Liebe* at Dr. Hertzka's behest), *Boxen* ("boxing"), and *Saufen* ("boozing"). The *Fressen* scene shows Jack O'Brien literally eating himself to death, to the accompaniment of corny Hawaiian-style music played onstage by a zither and a bandonion. Next is a whorehouse scene, musically one of the most brilliant in the opera, in which the men sing a "Mandalay" theme akin to the "Cannon Song" in *The Threepenny Opera* and to the "Mandalay Song" in *Happy End*—it even shares some phrases with the latter—but quite different from both. It is a slow fox-trot, sung to a steady, jazzy beat played by a small ensemble, that in places has very much the feeling of a tango, though technically it is not one: this is a classic Weillian tango situation, but the music is not at all a conventional song. Weill was justly proud of this scene, but though he and Brecht had been persuaded by Emil Hertzka to tone it down in a number of ways, the opera directors in Leipzig, Cassel, and elsewhere still considered it too raw to be done on their stages at all. Instead, a whole new scene stressing *Liebe* rather than the *Liebesakt* was written in at this point, a lyrical "Crane Duet" between Jimmy and

---

* This is according to the score version; Brecht's own final text version of *The Rise and Fall of the City of Mahagonny* is divided only by scenes and has no division into acts.

Jenny—in which they implicitly compare themselves and their love to the wild birds flying by—that is verbally and musically very fine in its own right. The result has been a certain confusion for recent opera directors, who have rightly reinstated the original scene, but who also rightly wish to do the "Crane Duet," though it is hard to fit the latter in properly.

In the boxing scene Joe is killed in the ring by Trinity-Moses; and in the big drinking scene that follows—in which a variety of musical motifs is used, including "Whoever Stayed in Mahagonny" from the *Songspiel* and another nineteenth-century popular song, "Stormy the Night"—Jimmy Mahoney treats everyone to a round and then cannot pay the bill. Inability to pay is the one capital crime in Mahagonny, and Jimmy is arrested; a final appeal is made to Bill and to Jenny, but neither the friend nor the mistress is willing to help him, and Jenny underscores her point by singing a reprise of *"Denn wie man sich bettet."* Scene seventeen, which ends Act Two or begins Act Three, depending on the version one consults, shows Jimmy alone in his cell dreading the arrival of day: Brecht apparently meant this as a parody of Florestan's dungeon solo in *Fidelio*, though Weill's music does nothing to fulfill this intention.

Scene eighteen shows Jimmy's trial, at the end of which he is condemned to death. This is followed, in Weill's score, by a scene in which Jenny, Widow Begbick, and other residents of Mahagonny are shown sitting around a bar and singing of the better life in Benares that they have read about; but though the "Benares Song" was perhaps the most popular number in the *Songspiel*, nothing could illustrate more dramatically than its presence here how far Brecht and Weill had come from their 1927 conception. It presumably demonstrates how much Mahagonny had declined by now, no longer having either whiskey or telephones, but it is dramaturgically untenable at this point—or any other—and Brecht has justifiably dropped it from his own final text version. Musically, however, it remains irresistible. Nor is the "God in Mahagonny" sequence, which follows soon after in both the score and text versions, really any better integrated into the libretto. Jimmy, having exchanged farewell kisses with Jenny and sung a final Weillian chorale— "Don't Let Yourself Be Misled"—accompanied by a chorus, prepares himself for his end by asking about God; and Begbick replies to the question by suddenly having Jenny and the men put on a "play" about "God in Mahagonny," in which Trinity-Moses takes the part of God. The song is a must, but its inclusion here makes little dramatic sense. Indeed, its main point, that Mahagonny has been hell all the time, has already been made in the hurricane sequence, albeit in a slightly different form.

Jimmy is put to death in the electric chair—this is another "American" touch that Weill resisted, but it remained in the text anyway—and the final sequence ensues, with Mahagonny going up in flames and the persons of the drama marching about the stage with their placards. Some of the opera's musical numbers are reprised, but all the strains ultimately lead into the stark sermon "Cannot Help a Dead Man," which had been used in an early version of the *Berlin Requiem* but had since been inserted here instead. It is characterized by a blasting, aggressive hostility similar to that of the "Second Threepenny Finale," and is bound to leave an audience in a state of agitation, whether benign or aggressive. With this age-of-anxiety *Götterdämmerung*, the opera comes to an end.

"There are good things everywhere in the score, only it is not everywhere good," was the judgment on the *Mahagonny* opera to be made many years later by Igor Stravinsky, who had liked the *Songspiel* better. There can be no doubt that the radical expansion of the original conception had created problems, though perhaps more so in the text than in the music, for Brecht's full-length play is overly static: Stravinsky's remark could apply just as well to the text as to the score. There certainly were not the makings of popular success in this work, not even in the modified version of it that was to open in Berlin for a theater run at the end of 1931.

Nevertheless, if *Mahagonny* was not entirely pleasing to the bourgeoisie, it did cause some excitement among intellectuals. Theodor W. Adorno, eminent young Marxist theoretician, professor of philosophy, future director of the Frankfurt Institute for Social Research, and himself a composer and music critic, had come to regard the Brecht–Weill works as a kind of mirror of the age, a truly contemporary art of the utmost significance; and *Mahagonny* was, in his view, the most significant of them all. In it, he wrote for the journal *Der Scheinwerfer* ("The Searchlight") shortly after the opera's premiere, "the bourgeois world is presented as already moribund in its moment of twilight, and it is demolished in scandal as its past catches up with it." The Marxist dialectic itself was being played out on the stage, and the music, in Adorno's view, carried out this intention perfectly, conveying "shock from the first note to the last, functioning as the objectification of the fallen bourgeois world suddenly manifesting itself. The music restores the utterly misunderstood *Threepenny Opera* to its rightful place as a milestone between the early *Mahagonny Songspiel* and this final outcome, and shows how little this really is a matter of intelligible melodies, easy amusement, and raucous vitality; it shows how these qualities, which are unquestionably present in Weill's

music, are only means for introducing the terrors of a perceived
demonology into the human consciousness." Adorno sees Weill's use of
the fragments of conventional melody and harmony—from popular
sentimental tunes to music-hall songs to jazz—as a dialectical reworking of
the rubble of bourgeois culture into something "utterly of the present."

Adorno was only adding new dimensions to the viewpoint on their
work taken by Brecht and Weill themselves, who by all means saw what
they had done in dialectical terms. Brecht, too, insisted that the
conventional elements in *Mahagonny* were precisely the most revolutionary
ones, transmuted by an ironic or dialectical framework. "Why is
Mahagonny an opera?" he asks in a set of notes that he wrote to accompany
the published edition of the text. "Because its basic attitude is that of an
opera: that is to say .culinary. Does *Mahagonny* adopt a hedonistic
approach? It does. Is *Mahagonny* an experience? It is an experience.
For—*Mahagonny* is a piece of fun." But these culinary pleasures end up,
through a kind of dialectical transformation of elements, by serving
another purpose than mere aesthetic consumption. "As for the content of
this opera, *its content is pleasure*. Fun, in other words, not only as form but
as object. At least, enjoyment was meant to be the object of the inquiry
even if the inquiry was intended to be an object of enjoyment. Enjoyment
appears here in its current historical role: as a commodity." It is the old
Brechtian method of having it both ways: the pleasures you see being
indulged are wicked bourgeois ones, presented as object lessons, but
meanwhile you might be enjoying yourself as you watch.

Weill did not miss his opportunity to ride with his *Mahagonny* score
on the dialectical bandwagon so much in fashion among German
intellectuals at this time. In an article published the very month of the
Leipzig premiere he wrote:

> The content of this opera is the history of a city, its emergence, its
> first crises, then the crucial turning point in its development, its most
> scintillating time, and then its downfall. It is a series of "moral
> pictures of our time" projected onto a broad plane. This content can
> be expressed in the purest form of epic theater, which is also the
> purest form of musical theater. It is a succession of twenty-one
> distinct musical forms. Each of these forms is an enclosed scene, and
> each is set out in narrative form by a title card. The music is thus no
> longer an element for the developing of the drama; rather it is placed
> therein as a way of expanding upon the circumstances. The text is so
> laid out that, from the beginning, it presents an arraying of situations

one against the other, and this is given a dramatic form in its musically characterized, dynamic action.

It is as if the teachings of Busoni had become blended with those of Karl Marx—or at any rate, with those of the Frankfurt School, for Weill's "arraying of situations one against the other" was the most up-to-date of Marxist aesthetics. In this sense too, a true Brecht–Weill synthesis had been achieved; but like all moments of dialectical equilibrium, it was inevitably to be transcended.

Even on the left, *Mahagonny* had not been unanimously welcomed. Some felt, with good reason, that it had been inapposite to use workers as the vehicles for this display of capitalist misbehavior. Kurt Tucholsky, writing in the prominent left-wing journal *Die Weltbühne*, attacked the play for its negative viewpoint and thought it was without true contemporary relevance. "Life is not like that," he wrote, "not even in the Klondike of yesteryear, certainly not in the America of today, and the relevance of it all to the Germany of 1930 is highly tenuous. This is stylized Bavaria." Quite true; and if Kurt Weill was, to begin with, not very much at home amid the language and commitments of Marxism, this strange Brechtian landscape was someplace very far away indeed. He had performed wonders there, but now it was time to start trekking back.

School Opera:
Der Jasager

Weill and Brecht had done one last work together before the Leipzig premiere of *Mahagonny*. After the Lindbergh cantata they had been invited to contribute another *Lehrstück* to the annual Chamber Music Festival, which was to move in the summer of 1930 from Baden-Baden to Berlin. They chose to do an adaptation of a fifteenth-century Japanese tragedy that Elisabeth Hauptmann had found in Arthur Waley's 1921 collection of English translations, *The Nō-Plays of Japan.* "Oriental" parables had become a favorite literary genre in Germany: Karl May had set some of his novels in the Far East as well as in the American West; Alfred Döblin, one of the foremost German novelists of the postwar years, had written a novel called *The Three Leaps of Wang-lun*; Fritz Lang had set one of the sequences of his four-part film *Destiny* in a highly stylized and artificial China; and Brecht's mentor Klabund had written a play, *The Chalk Circle*, that was based on an old Chinese legend that Brecht himself would one day turn into a play with only a slightly different title. There is a strange ambivalence in all this German orientalism of the time, for its image of Chinese or Japanese was often far from flattering. But the Orient also represented a popular ideal of wisdom: and in Brecht especially, one can trace a steady progress from a virtually racist view of the Oriental into a highly respectful one of him as the hero of various parables. In the case of the *Lehrstück* he adapted with Weill from the Arthur Waley translation, he did not retain an explicitly Japanese setting, but the flavor of an Oriental parable remains there nonetheless.

Taniko ("The Hurling into the Valley") by Zenchiku is a very short, one-act play that begins with a monologue by a teacher who runs a school at a temple and who is about to lead a group of the older students on a religious pilgrimage into the mountains (the Waley translation, which we follow here, does not give any place names). He has a pupil, a young boy, whose father is dead, and he goes to the boy's home to take leave of him and his mother. There he learns that the mother is ill and that the boy, who has been absent from school a long time, has been home taking care of her. The teacher pays his respects, and when he tells of his forthcoming journey the mother, remarking that it will be very dangerous, asks if he intends to take her son along. The teacher replies that it is no journey for a child. But when he leaves the mother's room, the boy follows him and asks to be allowed to come along, so that he may pray for his mother's recovery. The teacher goes back to consult with the mother, and though she protests, the boy remains adamant, saying: "I must climb this difficult path and pray for your health in this life." The mother and the teacher, moved by the depth of his piety, both finally give their consent.

The second of the play's two parts takes place in the mountains. The pilgrims have reached the first hut, and they stop to rest. The boy takes the teacher aside and says he does not feel well. The teacher tries to make light of this and tells the boy to rest, but the other pilgrims sense that there is something wrong. When they ask about the boy the teacher tells them he is only tired, but perceiving that things are worse than that they invoke an ancient custom "that those who fail should be cast down" and ask that the boy be thrown into the valley. The teacher starts to protest, but recognizing the awful might of the custom, goes to the boy to tell him of it, saying he would gladly change places with him if only that were possible. The boy understands and says that he knew his choice to come on the journey could even cost him his life; his only regrets are for his mother. The pilgrims then gather together and, "sighing for the sad ways of the world and the bitter ordinances of it," throw the boy to his death.

It is clear that this fifteenth-century Japanese play is about imperatives as relentless as those of God or Fate depicted in the *Book of Job* or *Oedipus*. Such imperatives are not readily acceptable to the liberal rationality of modern Europeans, but the 1920s and 1930s were a time when the humanistic attitudes of the nineteenth century were being severely questioned, above all in Germany. What did the Great War, the Russian Revolution, the ravages first of inflation and now of the

Depression say to the hopes that had been harbored by men of goodwill in previous generations? History seemed to be demolishing the claims of the individual will, and many European artists and intellectuals were making ready to renounce the old, apparently outmoded liberalism and submit to the new master. Brecht now was one of these, and the theme of *Einverständnis*—of submission, acquiescence, consent, as it can be variously translated into English—had been preoccupying him since his 1929 *Lehrstück* on that theme with Hindemith. The question of *Einverständnis* stood at the very center of his newfound Marxist beliefs: how ready is one to yield to a will outside one's own when it represents a larger social and historic claim than one's private interests?

Brecht perceived the theme of *Einverständnis* in the Zenchiku play, and there proved to be very little that he had to do to bring it out in Elisabeth Hauptmann's translation of the Waley text: indeed, about 75 percent of the Brecht libretto that Weill set to music is the Hauptmann translation, unaltered. Aside from the additions and changes made to bring out the central theme, some others were made to translate the play's moral context into terms meaningful to twentieth-century Europeans. In Brecht's version, the journey into the mountains becomes a scientific expedition instead of a religious pilgrimage: "For in the city on the other side of the mountains there are great savants," the teacher tells the mother; and she adds that she has heard there are great physicians among them. The boy, then, decides he wants to join the expedition in order to obtain medicine and advice with which to cure his mother's illness. When the mother and the teacher agree to let him go along, they now are moved by the depth, not of his piety, but of his *Einverständnis*—for, as the chorus has told us in Brecht's prologue, some people acquiesce in what is false, such as the incurability of the mother's illness, and not to do so is as wise as to acquiesce in what is true.

But the substitution of science for religion introduces some problems into the play's moral balance: for now that we are in so rational a universe, how do we admit so primitive a custom as the one ultimately requiring that the boy be cast into the valley? Brecht's solution is to make the other pilgrims—now presented as three students—the spokesmen of the primitive, while the boy and the teacher are rational moderns. Furthermore, primitive beliefs are reinforced by a touch of practicality, for when the students invoke the ancient custom against the boy, they now add that the most difficult part of the climb is coming up and that they could not carry anyone through it. When the teacher accepts their demands, he adds a Brechtian amendment to the custom: it also holds, he tells them, that the sick man may be asked whether he would have the party turn back for his sake instead of be thrown into the valley.

For a moment, then, it seems that the boy now has a choice, between a survival that would be antisocial and a death for the cause: this would be a liberal's view of the confrontation between the requirements of the individual and those of a collective movement. But things turn out to be not so simple. For one thing, when the teacher leaves the students to go and present the situation to the boy, they agree among themselves to cast the boy into the valley no matter what he decides. For another, when the teacher explains the custom to the boy, he adds something that he had not told the students. According to the custom, he says, when the sick person is asked if the party should turn back for his sake, that person replies: "You shall not turn back." There is no choice, after all, but only the illusion of one: we have moved from the possibility of freely willed submission to a higher good into a realm of pure totalitarianism. The boy of course replies, "You shall not turn back," and when the teacher asks if he is willing to accept the traditional consequences, he replies simply, "Yes." The drama pivots around this single word, the boy's ultimate expression of *Einverständnis*, and it became the source of the title Brecht and Weill gave the work: *Der Jasager* ("The Yes-Sayer"). The boy makes one last request, that his pack be taken and filled with medicine for his mother, and he is taken away as the chorus describes his fate.

Weill made *Der Jasager* into a two-act miniature opera about forty minutes in length. Since the piece had a child in the central role, he and Brecht took the *Lehrstück* genre a step further with it and wrote what they called a "school opera"—one, in other words, that could be produced in schools and performed entirely by students. This was in the vein of *Sing- und Spielmusik* ("Music to Sing and Play") that had already been developed by Hindemith as an extension of the *Gebrauchsmusik* idea; some called it *Gemeinschaftsmusik* ("communal music"). Hindemith also was preparing a children's opera for that summer's festival; *Wir bauen eine Stadt* ("Let's Build a City") was even worked up by him with the advice of children. Simplicity was the main requirement for works of this sort. At around this time, Weill was asked by the *Berliner Tageblatt* to write what he would say about his approach to music were he standing before an audience of twelve-year-olds, and in his reply he said: "I have just played some music by Wagner and his followers. You have seen that this music consists of so many notes that I was unable to play them all. I am sure that you would have liked to join in and sing along but this proved impossible. You also noticed that during the music you felt sleepy and somewhat intoxicated, as though you were under the influence of alcohol or drugs. You do not wish to go to sleep. You wish to hear music that can be understood without explanation. You probably wonder why your parents attend concerts. It is a mere matter of habit to them. Nowadays, there are matters of much greater interest to all; and if music cannot serve the interests of all, its existence is no longer justified."

Der Jasager also carries out this ideal on the level of performance. It calls for the simplest possible means of presentation: a minimum of props on stage, and a small orchestra that can vary according to what is available (the only stringent requirement being that *no* violas be used). The vocalists called for are: a boy soprano (or a soprano to play the boy), an alto for the mother's role, a bass for the teacher's role, three male voices for the students, and a chorus of mixed voices to provide the ongoing commentary. As for the music itself, it is written in a style that could be handled by the most minimally competent instrumentalists and vocalists. The range is accessible, the pace is deliberate and unhurried, the intervals, harmonies, and rhythms all of a sort that would not cause amateur musicians any loss of sleep during rehearsal periods.

One may well wonder if the music of *Der Jasager* is so accessible to the ears of uncultivated listeners, however; for there are no songs or arias in it. The technique is much like that of the Lindbergh cantata. Like that piece, it is divided into separate sections—the teacher going to the boy's house, the teacher and the mother together, the teacher and the boy together, and so on—that are enclosed dramatic pieces, and the vocal lines within them are expressive recitative, interspersed with ensembles and choruses. Also, as in the Lindbergh cantata, the orchestration is very often based on vigorously repeating accompaniment figures, though the flavor of them now is different. Far from seeming musical echoes of the machine age, these figures create an atmosphere suggestive of ancient and primitive ritual, which is added to when the sound is fused with children's voices. The overall effect is of a primal outburst, as in Stravinsky's *Les Noces*, though it is far less ferocious: the opening chorus in particular, Brecht's little sermon about the importance of learning *Einverständnis*, has the benign quality of our Western image of Oriental sages.

Indeed, the similarities between *The Lindbergh Flight* and *Der Jasager* in the end only serve to point up the latter's superiority: it is one of Weill's finest scores and was, in fact, later to be his favorite of all the works he did in Germany. The starkly simple vocal lines of *Der Jasager* are more symmetrically structured than those of the Lindbergh cantata and make

careful use of an important innovation: they are usually full of repeating
figures, like the instrumental accompaniment, so that a line of dialogue,
consisting of phrase after phrase sung to the same small group of notes,
often seems to be intoned as in a religious ceremony. They are
occasionally based on pentatonic scales, which have an exotic and folkish
character. The atmosphere of primitive ritual is thus reinforced in the
vocal drama itself. But the effect is not just the coolly gratifying one that
would be provided by a highly stylized, pseudo-Japanese print; for these
lines are riddled with a now irrepressible Weillian melodiousness, and
they are in places powerfully emotive. In the climactic scene, the teacher
sings each of his two final questions to the boy—a repeated B that at last
dips to an A near the end of the phrase and resolves itself through the B
again to the C—canonically with the orchestra in a mighty fortissimo. To
each of the questions the boy sings a soft, plaintive reply that is
unaccompanied and that has been preceded only by a sad, quiet phrase on
the piano. His first reply, "*Ihr sollt nicht umkehren*" ("You shall not turn
back"), dwells on the *nicht*, the same B intoned by the teacher, but an
octave higher, as vulnerable as the other is awesome. His second reply,
the simple *Ja*, is also on the B, and it is frailty itself, a little mountain
flower standing before the howling winds of destiny. Then the teacher
and the students begin to intone, "*Er hat ja gesagt*" ("He said yes"), over
and over in the lilt and melody of a funeral lament, and one can easily be
moved to tears. Sentiment has once again made its way by means of the
music into the Brecht–Weill epic theater style and created a counterpoise
to the *Verfremdungseffekt;* but this time it is not merely the sentiment of
song but something more taboo: it is the sentiment of music-drama. *Gestus*
and schoolroom simplicity have found their own sort of Wagnerism.
Brecht could not have been very pleased about this.

Der Jasager was performed as part of the Chamber Music Festival on June
23, 1930, two days after *Wir bauen eine Stadt*, at the Central Institute for
Education and Teaching in Berlin. Kurt Drabek conducted the student
singers and instrumentalists, but Brecht and Weill had both personally
supervised the rehearsals. The music had a powerful effect upon all those
who cared to listen to it. As one of the student performers, a member of
the chorus, wrote in a magazine article that appeared later that year:

> The attitude toward the music of *Der Jasager* among our chorus of
> young people was positive almost without any reservations. . . . It
> was a heart-rending experience, a real and gripping experience, for us

to feel our way through this music from the beginning; it astounded me at the first hearing. How can this be explained?

It has to do with the fact that this music has captured the atmosphere in which we live. It resounds with rhythms and melodies that normally lie deep within us, untouched. . . . This music is simple, clear, and without excessive pathos. It is uncomplicated, but not in any way crude.

The reactions to Brecht's libretto were not so good, however. On the political left in particular, there were critics who found its message to be questionable. One article, written by Frank Warschauer for *Die Welt-bühne*, seems to have been especially galling to Brecht. Entitled "Nein dem Jasager!" ("A No to the Yes-Sayer!"), it said in part: "In this tendentious fable, it is taught as an essential bit of life-wisdom: do not comport yourself in a human and rational way, my child, but do one thing above all else—obey! Heed convention without trying to find out why, however spiritually off the mark it may be! When it makes the demand, do not seek help, but let yourself be thrown immediately into the abyss. Do not think about the ethical shortcomings of it all! One cannot help but observe that this yes-sayer strikingly calls to mind the yes-sayers during the war." This last point must have cut to the quick. Warschauer concluded by saying that the music of the piece was very good, but that this belonged to the realm of aesthetic judgment, which was not his concern: "Here it must be stated as far more important: that this school opera artfully breathes into the souls of young people a view of life that contains all the evil ingredients, well diffused but highly effective, of reactionary thinking based on senseless authority."

What was no doubt especially irksome about this for Brecht was the fact that he had already grown impatient, some months before, with the possibilities for expressing his point presented by this particular Oriental fable. Indeed, that spring he had gone on, with the help of Slatan Dudow, another member of his literary circle, to write a whole new Oriental fable with music by Hanns Eisler. *Die Massnahme* ("The Measures Taken") is set in modern China and deals with the decision of a group of Communist agitators from Moscow to put to death a romantic young Chinese revolutionary who is supposed to be working for them, but whose unthinking ardor constantly thwarts their purposes. The whole thing is done in the manner of a dramatized school lesson: at the beginning, the "Control Chorus," representing the conscience of the party, asks the four agitators to act out what they have done and why they have done it, and in each of the ensuing scenes—showing the young revolutionary committing his various errors—they take turns playing his role. In the climactic scene, the young man is persuaded that, for the good of the revolution, he must be shot and buried in a lime pit so that he will disappear without a trace: *Einverständnis* here becomes a preview of the Moscow trials of only a few years hence! As a *Lehrstück*, the play had been submitted along with *Der Jasager* as an entry in the Berlin Chamber Music Festival; but though it is one of Brecht's finest pieces of craftsmanship, and remarkably prophetic no matter what its conscious intentions, the festival committee saw it as the outright bit of agitprop that it is and indicated some readiness to censor it for being too political. Brecht and Eisler refused to submit to censorship, and the piece was withdrawn.

Hanns Eisler must have been especially annoyed at missing this opportunity to show the music world that he could be a better Brechtian than Weill was. In an appendix to *Die Massnahme*, explaining some of his musical effects, he tells why the song sung by a gross capitalist at one point is done as jazz. "The brutality, stupidity, arrogance, and self-loathing of this type cannot be 'shaped' in any other musical form. . . . In other words, one must know how to differentiate between jazz as a technical means and the repulsive fare that the pleasure industry makes out of it." There is an implied criticism here of Weill, many of whose jazz passages were written above all for the pleasure of it. Brecht now clearly wanted a greater austerity of style than that of *The Threepenny Opera*, but otherwise he preferred the old song technique to what he and Weill had since developed. But whereas Weill was now resolutely pursuing the path of opera, Eisler was ready to try out new developments of the song form with Brecht.

Die Massnahme was to be performed that December in Berlin by the Greater Berlin Workers' Choir; but meanwhile Brecht was not satisfied to leave things the way they were with *Der Jasager*. It was performed in various schools that fall, and reactions to it continued to echo that of Frank Warschauer. The crucial moment came with a production of it at the Karl Marx School in the Berlin working-class district of Neukölln, when Brecht asked the teachers to discuss it in their classes afterward, and to submit reports on the students' reactions. The great majority of the students concluded that the boy should not have been killed, or that he at any rate should not have submitted so readily. A class of ten-year-olds offered the collective opinion: "It would have been nicer if he had said, I want to think it over, and if a dialogue among the young people had then taken place." Another very young group said that the students should have taken the boy along with ropes, in spite of the difficulties. A class of eleven-year-olds thought the boy should have been given some "Bio-Malt," an energy-giver of the day; and one group of fourteen-year-olds who did accept the premises regarded the whole drama as a demonstration of what a terrible thing superstition is—a view somewhat opposite to the point. The older students came up with objections that were more sophisticated, and sometimes more Marxist. "Why isn't the whole society overthrown, and its sick members saved instead of killed?" asked a class of eighteen-year-olds, who went on to observe: "The motivation of the action is not convincing enough." And an evening class of twenty-year-olds put the matter in terms redolent of a university drama class: "The question is to prove whether the advantage gained is so great that the sacrificial death of the boy is necessary."

Brecht responded to all this by writing two new versions of the play. In one of them, the mother's illness is turned into a matter of universal social concern: she is the victim of a plague that is ravaging the whole city. The scientific expedition now is not merely for the enlightenment of society, but has the same urgency for everyone as it has for the boy in particular; medicine and medical advice are needed by all. Under these circumstances, there are imperatives enough that Brecht felt he could eliminate the ancient custom, the element of superstition. The problem now is that the expedition simply cannot be delayed, that the coming ascent is far too precipitous to allow for dragging someone along without a disastrous loss of time; and so the boy must be—not thrown to his death, but left behind. The boy is still given the right to decide whether the whole group should turn back for his sake, and he says they should not; but when the teacher then asks if he is ready to accept the consequences, he replies not with the simple "Yes" of old, but with an "I want to think it over." He pauses briefly to think it over, and then says, *"Ja, ich bin einverstanden"* ("Yes, I acquiesce."); but, protesting only that he is afraid to die a slow death alone in the wilderness, he asks that he be thrown into the valley. The students balk at this, but the teacher persuades them to agree, and the boy is cast over the precipice as before. But poetry is beginning to be thrown over the side as well.

This second version was still called *Der Jasager*; but Brecht's third version of the play reversed the climactic response and was called *Der Neinsager* ("The No-Sayer"). In this version, as in the original one, there is no plague and the expedition is simply for the purposes of research. Once again, it is only the boy who has an urgent mission, that of finding medicine and advice for his sick mother's sake. The only significant change from the original in the first act comes when the teacher asks the boy if he would acquiesce, be *einverstanden*, in "anything that might befall him during the journey," and he replies with a simple "Yes"—the only one in this version, as it turns out. In the second act, primitive tradition is back in the saddle: the students once again invoke the "great custom" against the sick boy's life. This time, however, when the teacher asks the boy if he acquiesces in the custom, he replies: "No. I do not acquiesce." ("*Nein. Ich bin nicht einverstanden.*") The teacher and the students are stunned, and they remind him of his answer to the teacher's question in the first act; to which the boy replies that his answer had been "false, but your question was falser." After all, as we know from the earliest version, *Einverständnis* is the capacity for saying no to the false as well as yes to the true. The boy then enters upon a discussion of logical and moral questions, which demonstrates that a new custom is required. (Presumably, the one that did away with the young revolutionary in *Die Massnahme* would do.) The students finally agree that the boy's answer "is rational, even though not heroic," and arm in arm they all march back home.

Tragedy has now been completely replaced by a seminar, and though we have no explicit reply on record to all these changes by Kurt Weill, we can get the picture well enough from the fact that he never wrote any other musical version than the first one. By this time Brecht was proclaiming that instruction, not art, was his chief concern, and though a practitioner of *Gebrauchsmusik* was able to acquiesce in this for a time, the hitherto imperceptible gap between art and didacticism had suddenly widened into a chasm. Indeed, for sheer poetry, no text of this play had been better than the original *Taniko* by Zenchiku, and the poetic virtue of Brecht's first *Jasager* text had lain primarily in its closeness to that original. For the rest, the beauty of the opera created out of it was in the music, which captures some of the primitive power in a story still relatively unmarred by twentieth-century moral casuistries. But beauty, it would seem, was of little concern to Brecht right now, least of all when Weill was involved. Evidently not satisfied that the partnership was at an end, he seems to have been determined to run roughshod over Weill's good efforts for him as well: he had done so with *Happy End* the previous year, and now was doing so again, not only with *Der Jasager*, but with no less established a work than *The Threepenny Opera*, which was about to be made into a film.

The *Threepenny* Trial and Film

 It was in May of 1930 that Weill and Brecht had signed a contract for a film version of *The Threepenny Opera.* Throughout the 1920s, the German cinema had been one of the liveliest in the world, its studios in the suburbs of Berlin turning out works that, at their best, were as much the international criterion of film art as those being made in Hollywood were of film entertainment. Indeed, there had long been a certain interplay between Berlin and Hollywood: not only had some of Germany's best actors and directors done stints in American movies—these were the beginnings of what was to become a large-scale exodus after Hitler's rise to power—but America had sometimes reciprocated. In 1928 G. W. Pabst, one of Germany's outstanding film directors, had done a screen version of Frank Wedekind's two classic "Lulu" plays, *Earth Spirit* and *Pandora's Box,* combined into a single script under the latter title; and the starring role—after several native Germans had been considered for it, including the young and as yet little-known Marlene Dietrich—had been given to the American actress Louise Brooks. In the days of silent films, foreign accents were no problem.

The advent of sound films gave rise to new international combinations. By 1930 an upstart company named Tobis (an acronym of Ton-Bild-Syndikat) had bought up all the German, Danish, and Swiss patents on sound film and formed a monopoly in combination with the two largest German electricity trusts. An ad hoc producing company was then formed in partnership with Nero Films, an established organization that had been the producer of Pabst's *Pandora's Box*. Its owner was an enterprising young American named Seymour Nebenzahl: a large American presence in the ownership of the German film industry had been one of the legacies of the Dawes plan. For his first venture into sound film, Nebenzahl obtained backing from Warner Brothers, the American developers of talkies, and the result was the largest pool of funds for a single project in the history of the German cinema.

The *Threepenny Opera* was an obvious choice for Nebenzahl; it was, in the words of the man who was to be the film's editor, "a very hot property at the time: it had come out as a big theatrical hit; in fact it was almost phenomenal how much it influenced a complete generation. . . . When *Dreigroschenoper* came out, every girl in the country wanted [her boyfriend] to be like Mackie. Apparently, the ideal man was the pimp. Warner Brothers thought that this was a big hit and they bought the rights for *Dreigroschenoper* from Kurt Weill, who had written the music, and Bert Brecht, who had written the play." Furthermore, the play was beginning to find an audience outside Germany as well. A Paris production was already in the offing; it was to open that October at the Théâtre Montparnasse and obtain such fans as Jean-Paul Sartre and Simone de Beauvoir. "We knew nothing about Brecht," de Beauvoir writes in her memoirs, "but the way in which he presented Mack the Knife's adventures delighted us. . . . Sartre knew all Kurt Weill's songs by heart, and often afterward we would quote the catch phrase about meat first and morality afterward." At an early stage in the evolution of the film project, in fact, Nebenzahl and his associates decided to do a French version in addition to the German one: each scene of *L'Opéra de Quat' Sous* would be filmed with the French cast right after the filming of the German scene, and on the same set.

The film company's contract with Brecht and Weill gave them a total of 40,000 marks for the screen rights and stipulated further payment for whatever work they did on the adaptation—for both authors had insisted upon artistic control of the material down to the film's final cut. They had been granted the right to participate in the adaptation, a condition that was soon to prove a great source of trouble; for, if filmmakers are notoriously ruthless toward their source materials, Brecht was a man who required not only that he be in control of any situation in which he got involved, but also that he be able to push it around a little. Leo Lania, the author of *Konjunktur* and Brecht's old associate on the Piscator playwriting team, had been hired as one of the screenwriters for the project—along with Ladislaus Vajda, who had done the screenplay for *Pandora's Box*—evidently with the idea that Lania would be the go-between bearing into the professional film circles the ideas of Brecht, whose only previous experience in cinema had been a disastrous collaboration with Arnolt Bronnen back in 1922, called *The Isle of Tears*. But G. W. Pabst had been hired as the director of the *Threepenny* film, and he was not a man to play artistic second fiddle to anyone.

The potential clash of temperaments began to manifest itself within two months after the contract was signed. In July 1930 Brecht was once again in Le Lavandou, working with Elisabeth Hauptmann and another longtime associate, Emil Burri, on two new plays—including *Saint Joan of the Stockyards*, his own conclusion to the unhappy interlude of *Happy End*. Pabst and Lania went down to see him there and discuss their various ideas for the *Threepenny* film. It soon became clear that Pabst and Brecht had developed views on the project that were utterly irreconcilable. The problem, however, was not the traditional one that the director wanted to make changes unacceptable to the original author; on the contrary, in this case it was the original author who wanted to make changes that the director could not accept. Brecht had written *Die Massnahme* by now, and he was no longer willing to present to the world anything under his name that did not have clear-cut Marxist significance. The *Threepenny Opera* of Schiffbauerdamm fame was too politically ambiguous for the Brecht of 1930, who now proposed wholesale revisions in the story to make it ideologically more satisfactory. Pabst, along with the producers, understandably wanted to make some recognizable version of the stage hit of 1928, so that Brecht's proposals were hardly welcomed by him. But when he brought the bad news back to Nebenzahl, they agreed to let Brecht submit a story treatment, giving him an August 3 deadline.

When the time came, Brecht met the deadline by calling the story in to Lania on the telephone, a fact that did not help endear him with the already apprehensive producers. Upon reading the treatment he presented, they found their fears to be fully justified. Written in collaboration with Slatan Dudow and Caspar Neher, the story even had a new title, *Die Beule* (freely translated as "The Lump on the Head"). Peachum now heads a begging trust, and Mackie's gang has 120 members: they are competing magnates and behave in every way like rich capitalists. Mackie's wedding with Polly is now a fancy social occasion, attended by dukes, lords, a general, and a magistrate. A war has been going on between the gang and the beggars, and in the process a beggar named Sam receives a bruise on his head that becomes a symbol of the conflict between them. As a retaliation against the police for their collaboration with Mackie, Peachum does not merely threaten to unleash his beggars on the Queen's coronation—but actually does so. Tiger Brown has an apocalyptic dream, in which he sees great masses of the London poor emerging from underneath a Thames bridge and overrunning the city. In fear he uses the prostitute Jenny to help him arrest Mackie in a car chase. But Polly and the gang have in the meantime taken over the directorship of a bank, and they use their funds to bail Mackie out of prison. Peachum, who has now become afraid of the potentially revolutionary rabble he has unleashed, placates the crowd that had been expecting Mackie's execution by handing Sam over to them instead. Sam is hanged, and Mackie and Peachum settle down as bourgeois guardians of law and order.

Upon reading this, the producers decided to get rid of Brecht. They offered him full payment for his story treatment if he would agree to remove himself from further work on the film; but they did not know their man. Not only did Brecht refuse to be bought off, but he brought legal action against the film company for violating the contract. This is the point at which Kurt Weill reenters the picture. Although Weill was ostensibly the musical consultant for the film, a lot of the preparation of his material was actually in the hands of Theo Mackeben, the music director for this production as he had been for the stage version. There no doubt were technical considerations that were not yet within the competence of Weill, who was entirely inexperienced in the infant medium of sound film. But the material was further removed from Weill's hands by the evident fact that the makers of the film, though they well knew which of the original *Threepenny* songs were indispensable for its popularity, had decided at an early stage that they wanted to do a drama with music rather than a musical: in this, at least, they saw eye to eye with Brecht. Weill's operatic structure, with its three *Threepenny* finales, was doubtless doomed from the very beginning, along with part of the score. Furthermore, the requirements of cinematic construction soon were moving the songs that did survive into a different order than they had followed in the original score.

Weill certainly must have been unhappy about the eliminating and reordering of musical numbers, but he learned to accept this, and it was not the reason that he joined in with Brecht, as he did, in a common suit against the film company that fall. Rather, he did so because, in a few minor places, the filmmakers were trying to insert passages of music that he did not write—presumably the work of Theo Mackeben. The film's editor, John Oser, already quoted above, put it rather testily when he said in an interview given years later: "Kurt Weill went into the act too, and they sued Warner Brothers and Nero Films for not having followed the music exactly. I remember that there was one trumpet fanfare when the beggars start their march which was not officially composed by Weill."

The problem may indeed have been no more serious than this where the music was concerned, but in any case Weill's claim was a more reasonable one than Brecht's. Collaborators no longer, the two authors of *The Threepenny Opera* were now emerging as strange bedfellows. Not only were they demanding two very different things from the film producers, but Brecht was actually making demands that threatened to do far more damage to Weill's artistic conception than anything the producers were doing. The scenario of *Die Beule* made few specifications about the use of songs along the way—indeed, the only ones it did make were either for new verses to the *Moritat*, or for some completely new songs—and though this was not *necessarily* an exclusion of most of Weill's score, there obviously were many places in which his old music simply would not have fit in. Once again, in other words, Brecht was seeking to revise a previously existing Brecht–Weill work in a way that entirely ignored the integrity of the music.

The remarkable thing, then, about Weill's combined suit with Brecht was not that he was seeking redress for a mere trumpet fanfare or two, but that he was willing to abet Brecht's crusade to turn both music and words of their *Threepenny Opera* of 1928 into a pile of rubble. Why did he do this? It may be that he had not seen the text of *Die Beule* and did not know how far Brecht planned to go from the original conception. Weill must surely have seen Brecht's suit as a claim for a just redress of artistic grievances against the screenwriters for whatever changes *they* were making without the authors' consent. Perhaps he was being a little naïve under the circumstances; or perhaps he recognized that, though there were good tactical reasons for presenting his case together with Brecht's, in the long run his was the stronger of the two.

By the time the hearings began in October, German politics had made another stumble in the direction of the abyss. On September 14 general elections to the Reichstag had been held, and nearly six and a half million of the roughly thirty-five million voters had given their support to the Nazi Party. Before this, the party that had failed to seize power in the Hitler putsch of 1923 and had then sought to rise by means of the electoral process instead, had held only 12 seats in the Reichstag; now it had 107, forming the second largest bloc after the Social Democrats with their 143 seats. A similar turn to extremism had also occurred on the left, for the Communists won 77 seats, an increase of 23 over the number they had held in the previous Reichstag. Feeling the ravages of Depression and unemployment, the German public was now beginning to seek extreme solutions. The old political decorum gave way to rowdyism, not only in the Reichstag but on the streets, where Nazis and Communists frequently engaged in hand-to-hand fighting.

The court assembled on Friday, October 17, in the gloomy Berlin Amtsgericht, and the room was filled to overflowing with spectators ranging from members of the press to fashionable members of Berlin high society, eager to see the famous Brecht put on a performance. "Brecht's friends and his Nazi enemies were all present in force," one spectator, the film historian Lotte H. Eisner, has written, "though the latter did not quite know which leg to stand on; while detesting Brecht, the friends of Arnolt Bronnen could not entirely support a producer [Nebenzahl] who was both Jewish and American." But for the most part the Berlin literary intelligentsia knew where it stood, for Brecht was presenting his case before the public as a plea for the integrity of a work of art—a plea really closer to the spirit of Weill's case than to that of Brecht's own. "In the present instance, he declared," Eisner goes on, "he was in no way defending his copyright, his literary property, but—and this is very significant as to Brecht's attitude towards his audiences—*the property of the spectator*, who had the right to demand that a work be transmitted intact and according to the author's intentions." Did the spectators realize that Brecht's intentions were in fact to do something very different from the *Threepenny Opera* that they knew and loved? But Brecht stood with Weill firmly on the issue of integrity, for their suit took the form of a plea for an injunction that the producers cease all work on the film forthwith, and they promised to return all money they had received from it so far. This was an obvious ploy, for the actual filming had already begun, and the film company was not likely to renege now on its investment of 800,000 marks.

If one of Brecht's intentions in the rather ambiguous case he was making had been to create a piece of living theater, he succeeded admirably in this. The audience for it was so large that on the second day, Monday, October 20, the hearings were moved to more spacious quarters. On that day, according to Lotte Eisner, "the discussions were particularly vehement. On several occasions the presiding judge had to call for silence among the rival parties, the public, and even the press, threatening to

clear the court. Journalists from all over the country tirelessly took notes."
In a climactic moment the film company's lawyers challenged Brecht's
own attitude toward literary properties by raising the issue of his
abundant use of K. L. Ammer's German translations of Villon poems in
some of the *Threepenny* songs. This had been turned into a *cause célèbre* the
previous year by Brecht's old rival, Alfred Kerr, the drama critic of the
Berliner Tageblatt, who had repented of his initial fondness for *The
Threepenny Opera* upon discovering this bit of literary exploitation. But
Brecht had delivered a public apology for it, had been defended against
Kerr's attacks by some outstanding members of the literary elite, and had
eventually even written a preface for a new edition of Ammer's Villon
translations, which rose in sales as a result; he therefore was able to deal
scornfully and successfully with this courtroom maneuver. Finally,
however, the "counsel for the producer Nebenzahl angered Brecht with
insinuations and, after briskly riposting without being called upon to
speak, Brecht swept out of the courthouse leaving his lawyers to carry on
with the proceedings." Another touch of theater came by dint of the fact
that the members of the court, though not the public, had been given a
command performance of *The Threepenny Opera* on the Sunday before the
second day of the hearings; as for the general public, it would also be given
its chance to see the play again, for in response to the notoriety of the case
the Theater am Schiffbauerdamm scheduled a revival for November.

During the hearings the judge ruled that Brecht's and Weill's
common suit should be split into separate actions. The result, when the
verdict finally was delivered on November 4, was that Weill won his case
but Brecht lost his. "Brecht's plea was rejected," according to Lotte
Eisner, "on the grounds that he had not fulfilled the requirements of his
contract, considering that he had broken off all discussion during the work
in common and voluntarily ended his collaboration in the script." This
was a technicality, and it was not even entirely true, since Brecht had put
in some appearances on the set when the filming began, and he had made
his influence clearly reflected in the final script. In any case, he did not
even come off badly in the settlement. The film company bought him off
with a payment of 16,000 marks and an agreement that film rights to *The
Threepenny Opera* would revert to him after only two years. Furthermore,
he had obtained a moral victory with his own public, which he further
exploited by publishing a long essay called "The *Threepenny* Trial: A
Sociological Experiment," in which he developed his theories about the
contradictions between cinema as an art and cinema as a capitalist

enterprise. And, having gained some practical film experience at last, he was to go ahead the following year and make a film of his own with the support of Communist organizations: *Kuhle Wampe*, depicting the life of the unemployed workers of Berlin, directed by Slatan Dudow, with music by Hanns Eisler. Eventually, he would even get to develop some of the ideas in *Die Beule*—and take them further still from the original conception—in his one book-length work of fiction, *The Threepenny Novel* of 1934.

"Weill," Lotte Eisner concludes with some condescension, "always more pliable and rather inclined to make a few concessions, had more luck: having continued working until Nero Films themselves had dismissed him at the same time as Brecht, he won his case." He had indeed won, but it is not necessarily true that he had more luck than Brecht in this matter. Having made only modest demands, he was granted them all: not a single musical phrase was used in the film that was not written by Kurt Weill. But, on the other hand, his score had been abandoned in favor of a mere anthology, miscellaneously ordered, of its better-known songs. Brecht, to be sure, had been forced to let other people write the screenplay from his material, but aside from that very traditional concession on the part of an author to the screen adapters, he really obtained more satisfaction in the end than Weill did.

For, in spite of everything, the final cut of the film was remarkably close to some of the basic elements of *Die Beule*. The big pseudo-capitalist gang war is not there, but the film does end with the march of the beggars that disrupts the coronation, and with Mackie's becoming president of a bank founded by Polly and the gang. Leo Lania had obviously paid some attention to the desires of his old friend and associate Brecht while working on the screenplay; but it was probably not he alone who was responsible for this turn in the direction of *Die Beule*. After dismissing Brecht as a collaborator on the screenplay, the producers had hired as a replacement for him Béla Balázs, a Hungarian-born playwright of Marxist convictions who also had worked with the Piscator collective. The drama critic Herbert Ihering, Brecht's ardent supporter, was later to accuse Balázs of having betrayed the left-wing cause by taking this assignment, but Balázs would insist that his participation had saved the project for the cause; and it would seem that his presence was indeed another reason that the final screenplay came closer to Brecht's new ideas than even the original shooting script had done. Brecht was not even to be so very dissatisfied with the result when the film had its premiere in February

1931, although he thought it had all been done "in far too prettified a form."

The differences between the shooting script and the final cut of the film of *The Threepenny Opera* clearly show a transformation from an idea closer to the 1928 stage version to one closer to *Die Beule;* but this was not the only significant transformation that occurred. For in the same evolution from shooting script to final cut, the part of Jenny the prostitute was changed from the interesting minor one that it had been to one that would make Lotte Lenya an international star. Up to this time Lenya had been enjoying a good career as a featured player in the wake of the 1928 *Threepenny Opera*—but not precisely stardom. At the beginning of 1929 she had left her role of Jenny to do a succession of performances, mainly in repertory with the Berlin State Theater, but also in productions that succeeded the original run of *The Threepenny Opera* at the Theater am Schiffbauerdamm, where Aufricht still presided and continued to take pride in having discovered her. One of the latter productions was a play, *The Pioneers of Ingolstadt*, by Marieluise Fleisser, a woman with whom Brecht had been intimately involved, and Brecht himself directed it. At the Berlin Volksbühne, another repertory theater, Lenya had worked with Peter Lorre in a production of Frank Wedekind's classic, *Spring's Awakening*, and at the same theater did a blackface part in a fantasy about Harlem that was mistakenly called *Das Lied von Hoboken*: this play had incidental music by Kurt Weill that has unfortunately been lost.

Most of Lenya's roles during this period were not singing parts, and she was not thought of primarily as a musical performer. Nor was she indelibly associated with the role of Jenny, for though there were occasions when she had returned to the stage run of *The Threepenny Opera*, she had done so at least once in the role of Lucy. Moreover, she does not seem, at any time prior to the making of the film, to have publicly performed the song so intimately associated with her in subsequent years, "Pirate Jenny"—which, we may recall, was Polly's song in the original script and score, not Spelunken-Jenny's.

In the original shooting script of the film there had been no change on this latter point: Polly—to be played by Carola Neher at last—was to sing "Pirate Jenny" in the wedding scene (which was finally set in a dockside warehouse instead of a stable). Jenny's only song, as in the 1928 stage production, was to be her tango, at the end of which she would again dance her former lover into the waiting arms of the police. But by the time of the film's final cut, Jenny had changed character somewhat—she had, in fact, become part Lucy, who was eliminated from the film. In the completed version Jenny repents of having taken Mrs. Peachum's bribe just as the police arrive at the brothel, and instead of betraying Mackie she creates a diversion which enables him to make his escape; later, after he has been caught anyway, she helps him to escape from his cell as Lucy had done in the original stage version. But just as there now is no betrayal in the brothel scene, there also is no tango, which had found its dramatic logic in the old ironic conclusion. (A few bars of the tango music are heard being played on the brothel piano at the beginning of the scene, but that is all.) The result was that Jenny would have had no song at all if she had not been given "Pirate Jenny," which was switched to the brothel scene, evidently to replace the tango. For the wedding scene, Polly now was given the "Barbara Song" instead, which she normally would have sung later. These switches were to have historic reverberations; for if the world little remembers Carola Neher's performance of the "Barbara Song," it has rarely forgotten Lenya's "Pirate Jenny"—a performance which has enjoyed the additional advantage of having been recorded several times, beginning with the album of *Threepenny Opera* selections that was cut in December 1930, immediately after the film's completion. Indeed, Lenya has since made it so much Spelunken-Jenny's song that even subsequent productions in which she has not played have given it to Jenny in the brothel scene, even while retaining the tango as well.

There are several possible reasons for this change in the song's assignment, and perhaps all of them contributed to the final outcome. One prominent reason would be the requirements of cinematic economy: the shooting script had far too many scenes in it for a viable film, and so a good deal of cutting and compression became necessary. Under the circumstances it was easy to dispense with the character of Lucy, who even by the night of *The Threepenny Opera*'s opening in 1928 had been reduced to a pitiful remnant of her former identity in John Gay and in Brecht's and Weill's earlier script and score versions. But since the new version of the script, under Brecht's influence, eliminated the old device of the Queen's messenger pardoning Mackie at the end—and in fact had Mackie jailed only once, not twice as in the play—it was convenient to retain Lucy's function of helping him to escape. Perhaps the fact that Lenya had once played Lucy gave the screenwriters the idea of transferring that function to Jenny. The result was to make the character more sympathetic, so that when the idea occurred to them of sending Mackie to jail only once, it then made sense not to have Jenny betray him in the first place. The next logical step would have been to eliminate the tango.

There could have been other grounds for eliminating the tango, however. For one thing, the style of the film was more naturalistic than that of the play—partly because of the sociological trend of Brecht's new treatment of the material, partly because sound film (though by no means silent film, especially in the hands of German directors) tends to gravitate toward the naturalistic more readily than theater does, and partly because G. W. Pabst and the producers undoubtedly wanted it that way. Such an approach was bound to eschew all but the most indispensable of those moments in which music and song took a direct part in the action, as in the tango and other numbers that were cut from the film. The musical numbers in the film tend to be dramatically justifiable asides—such as those of the streetsinger, who functions as the film's occasional scene-setter and is seen doing the *Moritat* and various other snatches of song at significant moments throughout, or the "Barbara Song," which Polly introduces by telling the wedding guests that she is going to sing to them. Some of the tunes are played in the pub to which Mackie takes Polly and her mother early in the film. Even "Pirate Jenny" seems to justify itself in naturalistic terms by being presented as Jenny's meditation, sung when she is standing off by herself, as if music were the medium whereby her thoughts could be made audible to the film's viewers. But it is notable that the film's musical economies have clustered in particular around Mackie—played by Rudolf Forster, an outstanding star of German stage and screen but evidently no singer—in such a way that he is required to sing as little as possible, and almost never by himself. The tango may well have been too much for him. As a final point concerning the widespread reduction of the musical component in the film, we might note that this was what Brecht wanted and was evidently another of the things he got from a team of screenwriters who were in the end more compliant with his wishes than he gave them credit for being.

The foregoing points tend to account for the elimination of the tango, then, but they do not explain why the character of Jenny, by way of compensation, was given "Pirate Jenny" to sing and not some other song—or, for that matter, why she had to be compensated at all. Did Weill make his anger felt once again, as he had done that night in 1928 when he learned that his wife's name had been left out of the program, in a moment when it seemed she would have nothing to sing in the film? Or perhaps Brecht had favored giving Lenya the "Pirate Jenny" song; for he had always liked her, and he may furthermore have been stirred as a poet by the new tragic depths the song gave to the now sympathetic Jenny character, singer and song bearing the same personal name. But, on the other hand, Brecht was more than casually fond of Carola Neher, who lost a good song as a result of the switch. Indeed, there may well have been some artistic rivalry between Lenya and Carola Neher: it is striking that, on the December 1930 recording of *The Threepenny Opera*, not only does Neher not participate at all, but Lenya sings *both* the "Barbara Song" and "Pirate Jenny," as well as a few other things besides. In just the last few months of 1930 Lenya's star had risen dramatically, and to some extent it had done so at Carola Neher's expense.

Probably Neher was partly paying the price of her original display of temperament and insouciance over the Polly role back in 1928. It also is conceivable that the French cast of the simultaneously filmed *L'Opéra de Quat'Sous* was a factor in some of these changes in characterization and musical assignments. The French Polly was played by Florelle, a well-known musical comedy performer whose champagne voice may have been considered inappropriate for the harshness of "Pirate Jenny." On the other hand, the song was well suited to the French Jenny, Margo Lion, whose stylized manner and low, almost sinister voice had made her a star in the cabarets of Berlin, the city in which she had made her home several years before with the successful lyricist and sometime Hindemith collaborator Marcellus Schiffer.

There could have been still other factors influencing these changes, but surely the most crucial one is the figure standing at the center of them all, Lotte Lenya herself, gifted, ambitious, and ever a tough combatant in the game of life, who had once again taken full advantage of an opportunity when it presented itself. The first peak in her ascent to fame had been achieved with the beginning of the Brecht–Weill partnership, and now the second and higher peak was being reached as that partnership was coming to an end. In a sense, she was setting her seal upon it as having been a three-way partnership after all, at least in its most celebrated moments; and now she was joining her tones with theirs in singing what was tantamount to a swan song for the Berlin of the twenties, the Berlin for which Lenya, Weill, and Brecht would forever be among the foremost representatives.

Goodbye to Berlin

Although Weill had been sorely tried in his relationship with Brecht during recent months, it had not yet reached the point of hostility at the beginning of 1931. On February 6, thirteen days before the world premiere of the film of *The Threepenny Opera*, Brecht's *Mann ist Mann* had its first Berlin opening, at the State Theater, and the music for this new production had been composed by Weill. In all likelihood Weill had done the music at least a year earlier, at a time when he and Brecht were still working together; but Brecht, who directed this production himself—its cast included his wife, Helene Weigel, in the role of the Widow Begbick, as well as Peter Lorre, who had just completed work in his now-historic role of the child-murderer in Fritz Lang's *M*—evidently did not feel impelled to dispense with Weill's music. The two old *Threepenny* collaborators even found themselves vacationing together for a time that year: for in May and June, when Brecht made another of his working trips down to Le Lavandou, accompanied again by Elisabeth Hauptmann and Emil Burri, he found Weill and Lenya staying there.

It was the fact that their successes kept coming back to them—an irresistible source of irritation, to say the least—that turned what might have been a quiet parting of the ways into a vehement antagonism. That fall Ernst-Josef Aufricht decided to try doing a Berlin theater run of *The Rise and Fall of the City of Mahagonny*. Like many Berlin theater producers in the early 1930s, Aufricht had fallen upon hard times and had in fact just given up the Theater am Schiffbauerdamm. He was now running a modest producing enterprise, with the assistance of his old *Dramaturg* Robert Vambery; Heinrich Fischer had gone to Munich. One day the well-known cabaret singer Trude Hesterberg, who was starring in a popularized version of Donizetti's *Daughter of the Regiment* that Aufricht had produced, had suggested to him that he do a run of *Mahagonny* with her in the role of Begbick. Evidently the idea from the outset was that it be a modified theater version of the opera, the sort of thing that Aufricht had made into something of a specialty during the past two years. Hesterberg was even able to come up with financing for it, for she had recently become romantically involved with a banker, Fritz Schönherr, whom she was soon to marry, and he proved to be quite ready to support the project.

Aufricht obtained one of Berlin's leading houses, the Theater am Kurfürstendamm, for the production and hired Caspar Neher to be its codirector with Brecht as well as designer. He engaged the original Mackie Messer, Harald Paulsen, to play the role of Jimmy Mahoney, and Lotte Lenya to do Jenny, whereby she would once again sing the "Alabama Song" that she had introduced to the world more than four years before. Trude Hesterberg would of course do Begbick, but outside these three principals—attractive drawing cards for the theater audience—the roles would once again be done by opera singers. Weill was persuaded to make substantial cuts for this theater version, and other modifications besides: as we have seen, he rewrote one entire song, the "Havana Song," to accommodate it to Lenya's vocal limitations and particular virtues. But he certainly resisted any overall efforts to turn the work into simply another *Threepenny Opera*, and he had been able to shore up his position by seeing to it that no less a musician than Alexander von Zemlinsky, a serious and respected composer who had been a major influence upon the musical development of his brother-in-law, Arnold Schoenberg, was hired as music director for the production—this had decidedly not been a job for Theo Mackeben, even though Aufricht had wanted him for a while.

But the call for revisions inevitably brought out the underlying tensions between the two authors of the work. "During the rehearsals of *Mahagonny*," Aufricht writes, "Brecht and Weill finally split up completely. . . . Brecht fought for the priority of the word, Weill for that of the music. Their lawyers would come into the theater and make threats at one another. Once Brecht knocked a camera right out of the hands of a press photographer who had taken a picture of him standing with Weill.

"'I'm going to put on full war-paint and throw that phoney Richard Strauss right down the stairs!' Brecht yelled after Weill as the latter walked away."

In spite of these problems, the production, which opened on December 31, was reasonably successful for that time, enjoying a run of more than fifty performances. But there was no longer any possibility that Weill and Brecht could work together—not at least, until time and circumstances had inflicted whole new imperatives upon them. Indeed, in the summer and fall of 1931 Weill had produced a whole new major work with a new partner—his first without Brecht in more than four years. It was a full-length opera and in many ways a repudiation of the more popular among the styles he had developed with Brecht—almost nothing of the composer of *The Threepenny Opera* and *Happy End* can readily be heard in it—but it bore earmarks of the Brecht legacy all the same. This above all shows itself in the librettist with whom Weill chose to do the work: for, rather surprisingly, it was Caspar Neher. Though Neher was to do other writing for the stage in years to come, there is no evidence of any literary aspirations on his part before this. But on the personal side, he was a long-time bridge between Brecht and Weill—"friendly with both Antipodes," Aufricht writes of him—about whom we may recall that he had been a supporter of Weill's particular musical aspirations as far back as the 1928 rehearsals of *The Threepenny Opera*, when he defended the continued inclusion of the final chorale against the opinions of other friends of Brecht.

Nevertheless, he was not an experienced writer, and the libretto he turned out for his opera with Weill, *Die Bürgschaft* ("The Pledge"), was an odd piece of pseudo-Brechtian dramaturgy. It was based on a parable written by the eighteenth-century German essayist and historian, Johann Gottfried von Herder, called "The African Verdict," in which Alexander the Great visits a gold-rich province of Africa and watches a civil judgment delivered by its king. Of two citizens who have come before him, one has sold the other a sack of grain, in which some gold turns out to have lain hidden. Both parties are righteous men: the one who bought the grain wants to return the gold to its original owner, while the one who sold it insists that everything in the sack—including the gold—belongs to the buyer. The king finds the solution to the problem when he learns that one of the men, the buyer, has a daughter and the other has a son: he rules that the two children are to marry, and that they are to be given the gold as a wedding present. The tyrannical Alexander is astonished at this humane decision, and he informs the king that if such a case had come up in his own country, the two men would have been beheaded and their money confiscated by the state.

Influenced by the rising threat of Nazism, Neher created out of this material an operatic never-never land called Urb, where men behave in a similar spirit of justice and altruism until the forces of tyranny take over. The Prologue establishes the terms of the friendship between the opera's two principals, Johann Mattes, a cattle farmer, and David Orth, a grain dealer. Mattes has gambled away all his money, and as three creditors arrive to take away all his belongings, he rushes off to his friend Orth for help. Mattes's wife, Anna, barely holds the creditors off, until her husband at last returns with Orth, who pledges surety (*Bürgschaft*) for his friend's debts. Mattes is saved; and during the course of this action the chorus has informed us, not only that we have seen the relationship between the two men being defined, but also that, in general, men never change of their own accord—it is only circumstances that alter their conduct. This latter point, reiterated throughout the opera, is as close to some kind of Marxism as this libretto ever gets; but the theme of "circumstances"—of *Verhältnisse*—also has a Brechtian ring to it, reminiscent of the "First Threepenny Finale."

Act One begins six years later, and now we get a reworking of the Herder parable. Mattes buys two sacks of grain at Orth's store. When he leaves, we learn in a dialogue between Orth and his son Jacob, not only that there is a lot of money tucked away in one of the sacks, but that Orth had been fully aware of the fact. Orth explains his behavior simply by saying that Mattes needed the money, and he also expresses his belief that when some new supply ships arrive his friend will repay the debt. Mattes makes his way home safely past three highwaymen—sung by the same tenor, baritone, and bass who had played the three creditors in the Prologue—who let him go by when they see that he only has two sacks of grain. It is not until he gets home that he finds the money, and, assuming that Orth was not aware of its presence in the sack, he decides he will say nothing of it, even after the new supply ships arrive. But three extortionists—played by the same three menacing singers as before—have somehow learned of the money, and when he refuses to pay them, they run off to tell Orth the truth. The chorus then describes a race to Orth's house between Mattes and the extortionists. Mattes arrives before the extortionists can say anything. He tells his friend the truth, but when he offers to give the money back, Orth refuses it, and they decide to settle the matter before a judge. The act ends with the chorus reminding us of the point that men never change of their own accord, that only circumstances alter their conduct.

Act Two begins in the judge's chambers, where the case is presented and the judge decides as the king did in Herder's parable. But circumstances are in flux, and no sooner has the public left the court than the judge is confronted by the envoy of a neighboring "Great Power," who announces that Urb is soon to be taken over by it. When the Commissar of the Great Power arrives, he looks over the judge's records, and demands that the case of Mattes and Orth be reviewed: the spirit of Alexander the Great has taken over. The two men are arrested and the money is confiscated. The act ends with Anna Mattes's discovery that her daughter Luisa has disappeared from home.

At the beginning of Act Three six more years have passed, and Mattes and Orth, having returned to business after serving their jail sentences, now are rich men. The chorus reminds us of a now-familiar point about men and circumstances. And these are troubled times, as we now are shown in a general history of Urb, presented by the chorus in the manner of a cantata somewhat reminiscent of Johannes R. Becher's *Awakening of a People*. The people of the city pass in succession through the four "Gates" of War, Inflation, Famine, and Sickness, each of which is presented in a full choral piece. Interspersed among these are scenes showing the principals giving way to greed—for, if circumstances have made Mattes rich, they have made Orth selfish—and to despair; Anna Mattes, ever singing a lament for her lost daughter, dies of a broken heart even as we catch a glimpse of Luisa leading a life of dissipation in the city's dives. The opera reaches its climax when the hungry mob discovers that Mattes has cheated them, and they pursue him to Orth's house, where he flees in search of help once again. But the world is no longer the secure one in which Orth had once been able to show benevolence, and now he refuses to help Mattes. They fight, and when Mattes collapses, Orth turns him over to the mob in order to placate them, and they mortally wound him. When the dying Mattes asks Orth—who had protested just before the betrayal that neither they nor their friendship had really changed (we do not need to be reminded once again what *has* changed)—why he has done this, Orth sings a final soliloquy to the effect that, from the beginning, everything has really only taken place according to "one law": that of money and power.

Weill did the best he could with this dismal material, and in places that was very good indeed. The score is an attempt to return to the Busoni–Weill tradition of Kurt's early one-act operas, now redefined by the composer's artistic experience and growth in the works with Brecht: in particular, *Die Bürgschaft* bears strong affinities with *Der Jasager* in many places. Urb is hardly defined as African, or as anything else; but it is decidedly an exotic, non-European place, and the slightly Oriental, "parable" flavor of the *Jasager* music—along with such devices as the rhythmic, repeating phrases, in both the orchestra and the vocal line—is transferred to it. Distinctly Busonian traits are found in the expressive musical line of the monologues and the dialogues, free in tonality but ever on the borderline of melody and often crossing it, and in the witty counterpoints of the ensembles sung by the three sinister men (they are really always *mock*-sinister) in their various incarnations throughout the opera. These ensembles often have affinities with some of the ones in the *Mahagonny* opera. Also Busonian is the fact that there are no full-fledged songs and few arias, but rather a series of scenes that are fully developed musical units—in this case, the units are conceived as orchestral pieces with the voices playing the role of contributing instruments, as in Berg's *Wozzeck*. But the whole thing is done with a simplicity of idiom that is uniquely Weill's.

There also are various passages that bear his exclusive trademark. In several places there are march tempos—most notably where the Great Power comes marching in—that provide further demonstrations of his remarkable gift in this truly *Gebrauchsmusik* vein: they are mocking and rousing at the same time. Anna Mattes's lament for her daughter, sung at various points throughout to remind us of the humanity that is being left behind in the march of circumstances, is a haunting lullaby constructed out of only four notes by the unmistakable melodist of Berlin and, later, of Broadway. Ernst Bloch thought it had "a touch of a Jewish Verdi to it . . . a southern quality," but "darkened and Jewish" and "without sentimentality": and there can be no doubt that Anna is something like an idealized vision of the Jewish mother—an Emma Weill, perhaps, lamenting the disappearance of her child into the fleshpots of Berlin. As for the scene in which we glimpse Luisa Mattes amid the fleshpots, submitting with zombielike resignation to being picked up in a dance hall, the music is another Weill tango, true to the character of the situation.

But most striking and emphatically Weillian of all the elements of this work are the choral passages, particularly those in the "Four Gates" cantata during the last act, which is so distinct that it seems to stand forth as a separate work. These passages, the most brilliant and moving in the opera, form a link between Weill's earliest mature efforts and his last—between the "Lamentations of Jeremiah" and *Lost in the Stars*—and show his persistent desire, despite his mastery of so many other veins of very different character, to return to the mood of sacred chorale that was crucial in the shaping of his sensibility from childhood. In recent works, most notably *The Threepenny Opera* and *Happy End*, it was the *badkhen* in him that had presented itself with a touch of genius; but the cantor in him still sought expression as well, and was now coming forth and showing equal gifts.

Indeed, when *Die Bürgschaft* opened on March 10, 1932, at the Civic Opera House in Berlin, conducted by Fritz Stiedry, some observers sensed the presence of a pious sensibility in the music as well as in the libretto that, from a modishly left-wing viewpoint, could only be described as a display of bourgeois sentimentality (in America more recently the term would be *middlebrowism*). Brecht's friends in particular were amused by it—the fact that both authors were former Brecht collaborators only added to the fun—and Hanns Eisler, evoking a popular magazine for the bourgeois home, the name of which would be translated into English as "Arbor" or "Bower," spoke of the opera as a piece of *Avant-Gartenlaube*. As H. H. Stuckenschmidt has written of it: "The rough, hard-drinking and whoring Americanism of *Mahagonny* had become domesticated." If Neher's libretto seemed to the Brechtians to be a piece of petit bourgeois philosophy cloaked in pseudo-Marxian terms, they saw the music to be a fulfillment of this in its utter decorousness and lack of the old Brecht–Weill stridency and music-hall vulgarity.

Nevertheless, left-wing critics hesitated to come down too hard upon the opera in the face of current political events. For it was only three days after the premiere that Germany had its first presidential election in seven years, and the results were ominous. Though the incumbent Hindenburg won a plurality with more than eighteen and a half million votes, he did not win a majority, and Hitler had come in second with over eleven million. A runoff election had to be held, and in an atmosphere in which a Hindenburg—once thought of as a disaster by anyone politically to the left of center—now stood as a bulwark of the Republic, the gently progressive intentions of *Die Bürgschaft* could not be scorned either. In the second election of April 10 Hindenburg won a majority, but by a margin over Hitler of only six million out of the thirty-six million votes cast—a slim margin, considering that the future of civilization itself was being decided upon. On April 25 Count Harry Kessler had lunch in Frankfurt with a friend, Heinz Simon, and they had a searching conversation that he summed up in his diary. Simon "declared himself to be more or less at a loss what to make of the outcome of the elections. The German nation, he added, will always remain a riddle to him, with its depth of feeling and delicacy, as evinced in its poetry and medieval works of art, going hand in hand with barbarity. For my part, I said, I have through the years come to recognize two characteristics as being absolutely and inalterably basic to all Germans, but especially the younger generation, whether they belong to left or right, the Communists, the Nazis, the Social Democrats or the middle class: escape into metaphysics, into some sort of 'faith,' and the desire for discipline, for standing to attention and receiving orders or issuing them. The German, because of some feeling or other of insecurity, is through and through a militarist and through and through an escapist into some kind of beyond or Utopia, and the awful part is that he mixes them together!—Simon's young nephew, who is a fifth former in a secondary school here, told me that all his classmates are without exception Nazis."

In the arts there had been some last-ditch efforts over the past year to protest against the tide of reaction. Ernst Toller continued turning out plays with unabated idealism. In 1930 he had collaborated with Hermann Kesten on an "American" play, *Mary Baker Eddy*, which was a disguised diatribe against authoritarianism; then he had written a play the following year about the sailors' revolt at Kiel that had started the 1918 German revolution. Even the more commercial type of play that he wrote in 1932, *The Blind Goddess*, which was about a murder trial and the railroading of an innocent couple, was turned into an indictment of Germany's legal system and its society in general. But Toller had lost his youthful fury, and was no longer taken seriously even by the left. One of the great hits of 1931, first on stage and then on the screen, had been Carl Zuckmayer's comedy, *The Captain of Köpenick*, based on a real-life incident. A Berlin down-and-outer named Wilhelm Voigt, unable to obtain a much-needed passport, had in desperation bought a secondhand army captain's uniform and, merely by wearing it, had succeeded in commandeering a platoon of soldiers and using them in a takeover of the Köpenick town hall, just outside Berlin. The papers Voigt wanted had turned out not to be there anyway, but the incident alone had proved to be a significant commentary on German militarism for people with a sense of humor, and Zuckmayer's treatment of it combined humor with an appropriately matter-of-fact style.

The cinema in particular became an entrenchment against militarism, authoritarianism, and blind nationalism in the early 1930s: G. W. Pabst, who had done the most devastating of antiwar films, *Westfront 1918*, just before working on *The Threepenny Opera*, then created a moving appeal for Franco-German understanding just after it, *Comradeship*, which depicted a mine disaster that had actually once occurred on the border of the two countries and in which the two sides had collaborated in the rescue. No two works of art ever scored more severely against authoritarian schoolmasters and schoolmistresses than Josef von Sternberg's *The Blue Angel* in 1930 and Leontine Sagan's *Mädchen in Uniform* in 1931. But the Nazis gave a vivid demonstration that cinema, too, was a losing battle when, by creating disturbances in the theaters where it showed, they succeeded in closing down the American film version of Remarque's *All Quiet on the Western Front* in December 1930. Soon they were to take over the cinema and put some of its best artists—provided they were not too anti-Nazi and not Jewish—to work for them: strangely enough, even Fritz Lang, who was half-Jewish and whose last film made in Weimar Germany, *The Testament of Dr. Mabuse*, contained an anti-Nazi message between the lines and, in fact, did not get to open, was asked by Goebbels in early 1933 if he wanted to work for the party. Lang thought better of it and fled the country.

Kurt Weill continued to make contributions to the drama of protest in the summer and fall of 1932, when unemployment in Germany had gone over the six-million mark and when the political situation had become a rapid succession of crises: in July alone, Franz von Papen, who had become chancellor after Brüning's resignation, put the government of Prussia under the rule of martial law, and a Reichstag election was held in which the Nazis gained a peak of 230 seats, by far the largest bloc though still just short of a majority. At around this time, a group of writers and musicians contributed their various talents to a "Red Revue," a sort of political cabaret for the stage, which was entitled *Wir sind ja sooo zufrieden . . .* ("We're So *Very* Satisfied"). Brecht and Hanns Eisler took part in this, and Weill did a song for it with the poet Günther Weisenborn called "The Blind Maiden," which was sung by Lenya.

The passion to make political statements on the stage also was reflected in a work Weill now embarked upon in collaboration with his old partner Georg Kaiser. There does not seem ever to have been a real estrangement between Weill and Kaiser, though there certainly must have been hard feelings for a time. Kaiser could still have thought of himself as Germany's leading playwright at the moment when Weill went to work with the rising young Brecht; but while the team that created *The Threepenny Opera* reached the heights of fame and fortune, Kaiser became a bit passé. He even was inspired to try his hand again at musical theater and in 1929 turned out a sophisticated comedy about a group of Germans who sail to America in the course of their romantic entanglements: called *Zwei Krawatten* ("Two Neckties"), it has some of the atmosphere of the kind of movies Fred Astaire would make with Ginger Rogers a few years later. Kaiser would no doubt have liked Weill to do the songs, but he did well enough in getting the popular cabaret and musical comedy composer Mischa Spoliansky instead; the cast also was good, featuring the well-loved singing star Hans Albers and the as yet little-known Marlene Dietrich, and the play did well.

It was a time for seriousness again when Kaiser and Weill got back together in 1932, although not a time for returning to opera as far as they were concerned. *Der Silbersee: Ein Wintermärchen in drei Akten* ("The Silver Lake," subtitled: "A Winter's Tale in Three Acts") was an effort to do a play with music in the tradition of *The Threepenny Opera*, but with the relative decorum of standard opera: there are humorous moments in it, but it is basically a straight drama interspersed with "serious" musical numbers. Its style is on a borderline somewhere between realism and fantasy, and it takes place in a country that, though clearly a mythicized representation of Germany, is never identified. The fable is a strange one, filled with homoerotic undertones beneath its "social" message. A group of unemployed youths who live in a colony of moss huts in the forest goes to the city to rob a store; in the getaway, Severin, their leader, is shot down by a policeman named Olim. As Severin recovers in a prison hospital, Olim repents of his deed, and when he suddenly wins a large sum of money in a lottery, he decides to retire from the police force and devote himself to Severin's welfare. He buys a castle, and the two men try to live an idyllic life there until the housekeeper, Frau von Luber, an embittered, déclassée member of the nobility, conspires with a Baron Laur to cheat them of the property. Olim and Severin rush into the forest in despair, intending to drown themselves in the Silver Lake, but when they reach it they find it frozen over, even though the winter has ended. They then recall the words of Frau von Luber's niece Fennimore, an idealistic girl who had worked in the castle as a maid, to the effect that the Silver Lake will support anyone who decides that he must go on further. Urged on by the voice of Fennimore, singing as if from the horizon, the two men disappear over the glistening surface.

Reason disappeared over that surface, too; although if Kaiser meant the Silver Lake to represent the Atlantic Ocean—and he probably did not—he certainly had found a prophetic metaphor for the only viable solution to social and political problems that the Olims and Severins of Germany would find in years to come. In some ways the play seems to be an unconscious representation of the disintegration of German liberalism, a quality only emphasized by the fact that virtually every one of its musical numbers and asides is a piece of explicit social commentary: the unemployed youth at the beginning bury an effigy of Hunger in an elaborate and bitter ceremony; two salesgirls at the store about to be robbed reflect in a duet about the machinations of their bosses and the false scarcities that are created to keep prices up; when Frau von Luber and Baron Laur cook up their schemes, they sing a set of Brechtian observations about the nasty things one has to do to stay on top in *Schlaraffenland* ("the land of Cockaigne," the fool's paradise of medieval tradition); and, in the play's crowning moment, Fennimore entertains her employers at dinner with "The Ballad of Caesar's Death," a pointed—and once again, utterly Brechtian—historical lesson about the downfall of tyrants.

Weill, ever a musician guided by his literary sources, composed for this irresolute text a score that is correspondingly uneven both in quality and in style. At times he writes in the vein of straight opera—most notably in the mock-burial scene at the beginning and again in the finale—and at times in the vein of *The Threepenny Opera*, though sometimes misguidedly: why, for example, does the lottery agent sing his good news to Olim in the form of a tango? As we have seen, Weill had established his tangos as a leitmotiv of ambivalent eroticism throughout his works to date, and the use of one here seems particularly irrelevant and inane. One has the feeling, here and elsewhere, that Weill felt called upon—perhaps by Kaiser himself, perhaps by the producers in the wake of such commercial-ly unsuccessful Weill works as *Die Bürgschaft*—to reach into his bag of *Threepenny* tricks for materials with which to arouse the audience, whether he could handle them with artistic conviction or not. And "The Ballad of Caesar's Death," written in the heat of powerful political events and feelings, is the only one of the unadulteratedly *Threepenny*-type songs in this score that really comes off.

But there are other songs that merely approach the *Threepenny* style and then glance off it into something new—most notably the salesgirls' duet, which is an enchanting and not overly sardonic waltz, and "Fennimore's Song," which Frau von Luber's niece sings alone on stage at the very beginning of the second act, introducing herself to the audience as she is about to enter the castle. Both these songs are applications of the old Weill–Brecht formula of writing sweet music to bitter texts, but the sweet music has changed since the days of *The Threepenny Opera* and *Happy End*. Weill is returning to song here for the first time in three years, and he has developed fresh melodic resources in the interim. There is a new mellowness in these songs, and an air of sincerity as against the almost disdainful crackle of the early works with Brecht: Weill has distinctly given up the effort to be the wise-guy Berlin intellectual of the twenties. "Fennimore's Song" in particular seems, in retrospect, to have more in common with Weill's future works than with anything he had done in the past—except that there is a single, brief moment in *The Lindbergh Flight*, in which the flier remembers his home in Missouri, when the music seems to foreshadow it. There is nostalgia in Fennimore's melody, and though what she dreams of in the song is simply a life in which she wouldn't have to be anyone's poor relative, the nostalgia of the music is somehow suggestive of *place*. Furthermore—as in the Lindbergh passage and in related passages to come—the place suggested has the flavor of a rural American idyll. Is Weill having some prescience of what lies in store for him over his own Silver Lake?

For the very circumstances under which the play opened, on February 18, 1933, made it clear that retreat would probably soon be necessary. Less than three weeks earlier, on January 30, Hindenburg had finally yielded to the pressure of popular feelings and incessant political maneuverings and appointed Hitler chancellor of the German Republic—a republic that had thereupon destroyed itself by purely constitutional means. "I was astounded," Harry Kessler, whose days in Germany also now were numbered, wrote in his diary for that day. "I did not anticipate this turn of events, and so quickly at that. Downstairs our Nazi concierge inaugurated exuberant celebrations. . . . Tonight Berlin is in a really festive mood. SA and SS troops as well as uniformed Stahlhelm units are marching through the streets while spectators crowd the pavements. In and around the Kaiserhof [Hotel] there was a proper to-do, with SS drawn up in double line outside the main door and inside the hall. When we left . . . some secondary celebrities (Hitler himself was in the Chancellery) were taking the salute, Fascist style, at an endless SA goose-stepping parade."

Der Silbersee, which opened simultaneously in several cities—though Berlin was not one of them—was bound to meet with Nazi disapproval, above all for "The Ballad of Caesar's Death." Kaiser and Weill went together to the opening in Leipzig, where *Mahagonny* had almost been closed down by a riot three years before and where Kurt's parents still were living. That evening went surprisingly well; but in Magdeburg, where *Der Silbersee* also opened, Nazi demonstrators disrupted the performance and succeeded in having the play closed down. Soon, the theaters showing it in other cities followed suit. When the official Nazi organ, the *Völkischer Beobachter*, published its review of the Leipzig performance a few days after the opening, it had a few words to say about the composer:

> As is well known, from Kurt Weill comes the music for Bert Brecht's *Dreigroschenoper* and the opera *Aufstieg und Fall der Stadt Mahagonny*, which incurred an unmistakably negative response in Leipzig in March, 1930. An "artist" who has devoted himself to such subjects, who for such dissolute and abortive texts, thought mistakenly to be art, has written "music" that suits them perfectly—such a composer must be approached with the greatest suspicion, all the more so when he, as a Jew, takes the liberty of using a German opera stage for his *unvölkisch* purposes! The music of *Der Silbersee* demonstrates that such suspicion is well grounded.

The reviewer adds the tidbit that "Herr Weill, it is reported, dismissed several of the women singers, because their presence in the chorus made it sound 'too beautiful and too healthy' to him." He now was truly, in Nazi language, a *Kulturbolschewist* ("Culture-Bolshevik").

It would take a few more years for decisive proof to emerge that there was no future left for Jews in Germany; but by now it was clear enough that life there was becoming untenable for a Jewish artist who had collaborated with a man like Brecht. When the Reichstag building suddenly and mysteriously went up in flames on February 27, whereupon Hitler blamed the Communists and Hindenburg issued a set of emergency decrees suspending many constitutional liberties, Brecht promptly read the handwriting on the wall and drove with his family to Prague the next day, to become one of the first of a stream of artistic exiles. But Weill hung on a little longer. This is almost inexplicable, except for the fact that he had work in Berlin, and work was ever his opiate in the midst of whatever might befall him.

For one thing, Weill had a commission to write a symphony and had begun it—but this, of course, could be done anywhere and would in fact

be completed in exile. More significantly, he was working on a film. Hans
Fallada's *Little Man, What Now?*—a highly successful novel about the lives
of ordinary people in the Depression—had been bought by Europa Film,
which hired Caspar Neher to do the sets and Weill to do the music; this
would have been his first original sound track. The company had even
lured Berthold Viertel—who had been one of the important young stage
directors of Berlin in the early twenties—back to Berlin to write and direct
the film, even though he had lived and worked in Hollywood for several
years and was a Jew. Viertel arrived for work the very next day after
Hitler's appointment as chancellor, and though he immediately found
himself having to share his directorship and salary with a newly hired
"Aryan" as a result, he stayed on until the Reichstag fire; then he resigned.
Weill may have stayed with the film a little longer, but he also did not
finish it; in another month he would be an exile, too.

There is some mystery surrounding Weill's personal life at this point.
Although Lotte Lenya has never intimated anything to this effect in the
many public statements she has made about her life, some people who
were close to her and Kurt have asserted that an estrangement grew
between them at around this time. There certainly is a widespread
impression that, at least from this time on, they were not always to be
exclusively devoted to one another. Indeed, for Kurt there never in his
adult life had been any devotion greater than that which he harbored for
his work, nor would there ever be. His zeal for work was bound to be
exasperating to anyone living close to him, and certainly to Lenya, a true
actress and liberated woman of her generation, who was far more
fun-loving and restless than he in her personal comportment. And if she
was beginning, as some say she was, to manifest occasional romantic
interests outside her marriage, Kurt was doing so, too. But Lenya was less
likely than Kurt was to repress and idealize her feelings.

The record of their whereabouts during 1932 is ambiguous concerning the state of their personal relations. Lenya spent part of the year in
Russia, working on a film being made under the direction of Erwin
Piscator from Anna Seghers's novel *The Revolt of the Fishermen of Santa
Barbara*. But in December she and Kurt were both in Paris, for a
performance of a double bill consisting of *Der Jasager* and a revised version
of the *Mahagonny Songspiel*, in which she sang her original role. Kurt then
went back to Berlin, but it is not clear whether Lenya did.

On March 21, 1933, Weill received word from a friend that he was
about to be arrested by the Gestapo; he promptly packed a few of his

belongings and drove in his car to the French border. According to the recollection of friends of what he told them some years later, he then left his car on the German side and continued on foot, in order to make his way surreptitiously past the German border authorities. This was an arduous and dangerous task, but he accomplished it successfully and then went on to Paris. The accounts are conflicting, however, about whether Lenya was with him on this journey. The only thing that can be said with certainty is that a new life had now begun in France both for Lenya and for Weill; and that, whatever gap may have recently emerged between them, it was now to be closed by the force of overwhelming new circumstances.

Paris Interlude

The December 1932 concert of the *Mahagonny Songspiel* and *Der Jasager* had been given in Paris under the auspices of a chamber music society called La Sérénade, which counted some of France's leading composers—including Weill's friend Darius Milhaud—among its guiding lights and which obtained financial support from such prominent patrons of the arts as the Vicomtesse Marie-Laure de Noailles, who had been born in Germany. In accordance with Weill's wishes the program was conducted by his former pupil Maurice Abravanel, who had worked with him on a revision of the *Mahagonny Songspiel*—based on the full-length opera version—for this occasion. "This new *Mahagonny*," Abravanel writes, "was an incredible success both at the Vicomtesse de Noailles's salon and at the Salle Gaveau the next day."

"I was lecturing in Holland at the time the concert was given," Darius Milhaud recalls in his memoirs, "and in the train that was bringing us back to Paris, I told [my wife] Madeleine that we should no doubt find that the city had been taken by storm. Little did I know then how true this was, for the delirious enthusiasm aroused by these two works lasted for several days. The Montparnasse set used the concert as a pretext for political diatribes; it saw in it an expression of the moral bankruptcy and pessimism of our times. Smart society was as carried away as if it had been the first performance of a Bach *Passion*, in mentioning which I am merely repeating what was said to me by one of my friends, a lady somewhat infected by the captivating snobbishness that enabled the Sérénade to keep going." But the performance by no means appealed exclusively to dilettantes. "Stravinsky expressed his admiration for it," Abravanel goes on with reference to the *Mahagonny* piece, "preferring it to the three-act version. He said it had a much higher density. Later, when we were approached to take a touring company to Spain and possibly to Italy, Stravinsky wanted *L'Histoire du soldat* as a companion piece. An ideal bill, he called it."

In other words Weill, though he arrived in Paris on March 23 bedraggled and virtually penniless, was not without an audience there as a foundation upon which to rebuild his fortunes. Furthermore, he had the concerned attention of such patrons as the Vicomtesse de Noailles and the American-born Princesse Edmond de Polignac, heiress to the Singer fortune and one of the world's foremost supporters of modern music, who had already given him a stipend while he was still in Germany to begin work on a new symphony. He could also count on the activities of the now rapidly growing colony of German expatriates in Paris, some of whom had considerable means and a strong desire to keep German culture alive in exile. Count Harry Kessler, who had left Germany only about two weeks before Weill did, but who had spent a good part of his life in France and was perfectly at home both in the country and in its language, was already deeply engaged in such activities. His diary for April 23 describes a visit to a Mme. Homberg. "Discussed the outlook for establishing a German-speaking theater in Paris. Agreed on a plan to arrange for [Otto] Klemperer to come to Paris and conduct a German opera season at the Théâtre des Champs-Élysées: Weill's *Silbersee* and Berg's *Wozzeck*. Her advice was to have Mme. Charles de Noailles (*née* Bischoffsheim) as head of the initiating committee." Weill, who did not take easily to the French language, at least was surrounded by people eager to make him feel at home. Indeed, according to one source, he was provided with living quarters in the large town house owned by Madame de Noailles and her husband. Furthermore, he had Maurice Abravanel, whose mother tongue was French and who had decided to stay on in Paris and try his fortunes there after the December Brecht–Weill concert.

Abravanel had found work as a conductor with a new dance company, Les Ballets 1933, formed by the brilliant young Russian choreographer, George Balanchine, who had worked with Diaghilev. This proved to be the source of Weill's first important commission in Paris. A wealthy Englishman, Edward James, had been looking for a ballet company that could serve as a home for his wife, a Viennese dancer and mime named Tilly Losch; for this service he would provide a generous subvention. The choice fell upon Balanchine, who once had choreographed for Miss Losch and who now undertook to design one of his company's six new ballets specifically for her. Weill, who knew Tilly Losch, an old friend of Lenya's, and Boris Kochno, Balanchine's collaborator and a friend of Count Harry Kessler, was asked to do the music for it.

Weill accepted and then apparently decided on his own initiative to invite Brecht, who was at that moment in Switzerland, to come and do the scenario. During his first days in Paris, Weill had no doubt heard many praises of his works with Brecht—the only works of his that were widely known there—and frequent expressions of the wish that the collaboration be revived. Why not try reviving it, then, in spite of everything? Weill had a nature that was both gentle and practical. A new work with Brecht seemed like a certain route to a financial success that both of them urgently needed in this moment—for they had left most of their assets behind them in Germany.

As for Brecht, when he received Weill's invitation, he evidently saw this as an opportunity not only to make some money quickly but also to sound out his prospects in Paris—for he had not yet decided where he wanted to settle with his family. Setting himself up in a small hotel room on the Left Bank, he held court for a time almost as if it were Berlin. To Ernst-Josef Aufricht, who also had shown up in Paris, he proposed a "Theater of Judgment," which would stage trials of prominent Nazis in juxtaposition with trials of various counterparts throughout history: for example, Goering would be tried for burning the Reichstag, alongside Nero for burning Rome. But Brecht got into an argument with Walter Steinthal, the prominent Berlin journalist who was to be another partner in the enterprise, and that was the end of it.

Brecht made it clear to Weill that he did not think much of ballet as an art form, and he proposed an idea for a piece that could be sung as well as danced. Weill respected the word as much as Brecht did, and so he agreed. *Die sieben Todsünden der Kleinbürger* ("The Seven Deadly Sins of the Petits Bourgeois"), to give the piece they wrote its full name, was built around the adventures of two "sisters," Anna I, who narrates the story, and Anna II, who pantomimes and dances it—and who really are, we are told, two different representations of the same person. The two Annas start out from their native Louisiana—for we are once again in one of Brecht's surreal American landscapes—and go to various cities, where they make their way up in the world through a succession of sleazy occupations, such as kept mistress and cabaret dancer. Seven scenes—there also are a Prologue and an Epilogue—depict the classic "sins" of Sloth, Pride, Anger, Gluttony, Lust, Avarice, and Envy; but Brecht, who regards these merely as the demons of petit bourgeois morality, does not take a conventional view of them. Anna I, who is the speaking and singing voice of the lower-middle-class conscience, has nothing against the various sleazy occupations that we watch her sister pursue; on the contrary, she heartily endorses all the trades and methods through which they accumulate their fortune. The "sins" occur only when the dancing Anna II, endowed with a more spontaneous human nature than her scheming alter ego of a sister, lapses into occasional normal displays of laziness, pride, anger, and so on, that interfere with her progress in the world. But the good little bourgeois Anna I, occasionally abetted by the singing voices of the family back home, keeps chiding the earthy Anna II and bringing her back onto the straight and narrow path of rotten self-advancement. At the end, bourgeois "virtue" triumphs, and the two girls go back to Louisiana, to the solid house that their family has been able to build from the money they have earned.

If Weill had bristled at Brecht's satirical Americas before this, he was not very likely to appreciate one at a time when emigration to the United States had no doubt become a distinct possibility in his own mind. But his answer to Brecht was to assemble some of the sounds of a different kind of imaginary America than the one characterized by the two *Mahagonnys*—or by the text of *The Seven Deadly Sins*, for that matter.

To be sure, much of the sardonic Brecht–Weill sound is still there, and enough familiar echoes of their earlier works to satisfy those who seek in this ballet the continuity of the *Threepenny* tradition. As a recent Brechtian biographer has intoned, in almost hypnotic repetition of a formula: "The music of *The Seven Deadly Sins* bore to the melodies favored by the bourgeois world a relation analogous to the method used by Brecht, the intention of which was to cast doubt on the prevailing view of morality and transform it. With as much virtuosity as in *The Threepenny Opera* and *Rise and Fall of the Town of Mahagonny*, Weill again denounced the musical forms he repudiated by paraphrasing them ironically." We have heard T. W. Adorno using words to this effect as far back as 1930. And Weill has even found levels of irony that were not present in those earlier works, especially in the passages that include the voices of Anna's family back

home, who call out their petit bourgeois homilies and build their new
house in stages as the daughter's earnings come in: Weill has composed
these passages for four male voices—two brothers, a father, and the
mother who, in an early adumbration of the theater of the absurd, is sung
by a bass—and he has used in them some of the humorous canonic and
contrapuntal ideas he had developed for the three sinister men in *Die
Bürgschaft*.

But much of the time in this ballet, Weill has quietly pulled away into
a mellower tone than he had ever used with Brecht, a tone akin to that
which can be heard through a large part of *Der Silbersee*. It is as if Weill has
once again taken a glimpse over the ice of that Silver Lake toward some
Promised Land lying in his own future and has already become nostalgic
about it. In particular, there is a loping orchestral refrain, a lilt of jazzlike
sentimentality, that occurs whenever Anna I invokes the idyllic image of
her home back on the Mississippi—particularly in the Prologue and the
Epilogue—and that has strong affinities with the melody of "Fennimore's
Song." This refrain expresses a love for an American landscape that the
composer has yet to see.

Nevertheless, the practical task at hand was to stress the revived
elements of an old winning combination, and the image of *The Seven Deadly
Sins*, despite its vagrant undertones, was Threepennyized as much as
possible. Caspar Neher was summoned from Berlin to do the sets, and, to
complete the reconstitution of the old partnership, Lotte Lenya was
chosen to sing the part of Anna I. It clearly had not been part of Kurt's
original plan to have her doing the role, for he composed it in a soprano
range that was too high for Lenya: and even when the score was
subsequently published, the passages that he had rewritten for Lenya's
range appeared as an appendix and not as part of the main text. The
addition of Lenya's voice into the combination completed the illusion of a
fully reconstituted Brecht–Weill sound, just as it provided the illusion to a
wide public that the celebrated three-way partnership had not in various
ways fallen apart. The idea of calling her in may not have originated with
Kurt. Tilly Losch and Edward James both were eager to have her. Brecht,
who had always been fond of Lenya, no doubt supported them in
this—and, as Maurice Abravanel has recently said, summing up this
whole set of developments, "Kurt was forgiving with Brecht, as he was
with Lenya."

Yet the disparities in the conception seem to have shown through to
the public all the same when the ballet was given its premiere at the

Théâtre des Champs-Élysées on the evening of June 7, 1933, under the baton of Maurice Abravanel and with Balanchine's choreography. The reviews were respectful but only lukewarm; H. H. Stuckenschmidt has said that the production "enjoyed only literary success." Brecht wrote to his wife, who was now in Denmark, that "the ballet went quite nicely, but really [was] not so significant." According to one historian of the occasion, the Paris audience, traditionally the world's greatest ballet lovers—but perhaps not so much of ballets infused with Marxist meanings—found the piece "disagreeable." Serge Lifar, another of the great Russian exponents of ballet working in Paris, is quoted by Count Harry Kessler as saying of Les Ballets 1933 in general and *The Seven Deadly Sins* in particular, "*C'est de la pourriture de ballet.*" Kessler adds: "Weill's ballet has been a disappointment to most people here." A few days later, on Saturday evening, June 17, Kessler went to the Théâtre des Champs-Élysées to see for himself. "I thought the music attractive and individualistic," he wrote afterward in his diary, "though not much different from *Dreigroschenoper*. Lotte Lenya, whose voice has only small range but considerable appeal, sang (in German) Brecht's ballads and Tilly Losch danced and mimed both gracefully and fascinatingly." But, having noted once again the ballet's "bad reception both from the press and the public, despite Weill's popularity here," he goes on to observe: "Obviously too much has been expected of Weill, snobbery dictating that he should be put right away on the same level as Wagner and Richard Strauss." No doubt the Vicomtesse de Noailles had been using words to that effect.

Later that summer an English-language version of the ballet, translated by Edward James himself under the title *Anna-Anna*, was done at the Savoy Theatre in London, and this met with a better reception than the Paris production had. Kurt wrote to Hans and Rita Weill that it was "the great success of the season and furthermore Lenya was a great hit," but this was a somewhat euphoric view of the matter. *The Dancing Times* bemoaned what it saw as an abandonment of "the Latinity of style from which ballet has culled so much beauty" and opined that the work had nothing in it "to clarify or elucidate the heavy darkness of the Germano-American text." Reactions like this could well be taken as a sign that the Brecht–Weill combination had strained beyond its proper moment; and, as if to remind the public of the long distance that had been traveled since better days, a performance of the *Mahagonny Songspiel*, with Lenya in her original role, also was done at the Savoy at this time. Brecht had needed no more reminding: having given up on Paris shortly after the ballet's premiere at the Théâtre des Champs-Élysées, he bought a house on the Danish island of Fyn, and settled there with his family before the end of the year.

All the events and activities of the preceding six months had put Weill under a nervous strain that took its toll toward the end of July in an outburst of psoriasis, a painful skin disease from which he had suffered all his life and which usually struck in periods of anxiety. This, indeed, was the way his body paid its price from time to time for the ironic calm he usually maintained during even the most frantic moments of assembling a production. It was time to take it easy for a little while, and as soon as he got back to Paris from London he went on a vacation, spending a few weeks of unhurried travel in Italy.

But meanwhile, the experience of working together on *The Seven Deadly Sins* seems to have brought about an improvement in relations between Kurt and Lenya. They now had been in London together and had made contacts in the theater world there that were encouraging to both of them. The euphoria of renewed professional activity together in other European capitals outside Germany had evidently led them to consider a reconciliation. "A good Jew always forgives his wife," Kurt said to Maurice Abravanel at around this time. This was perhaps the reason that he began looking for new quarters after he got back to Paris at the end of the summer: the home of Madame de Noailles would hardly have been an appropriate place for him and Lenya to be in together.

Kurt looked at first for an apartment in Paris, but one day the rental agent took him out to the grounds of what had been Madame du Barry's château, in the suburb of Louveciennes, and showed him a former servants' cottage. The idea of living in nearly countrylike surroundings outside the city, though conveniently close to it, suddenly captured his imagination, and he rented the house. This is where he was to live for the remainder of his time in France, and where Lenya would be living with him before long at least, though it is not clear whether they actually moved into it together.

Weill now went to work on the symphony that had been commissioned by the Princesse de Polignac and that he had begun just before leaving Germany. Aside from the *Threepenny* Suite, derived from one of his theater scores, this was to be his first large piece of "pure" concert music, without singing, since 1924. In all likelihood the main reason for his decision to undertake it was simply that a great patron had expressed a desire to have a Weill symphony—it should be remembered that the work of 1920–21 known as the First Symphony today was then still unpublished and unknown to the public—and that she had offered him money for it. He probably was not as eager to return to absolute music at this time as he was to return to opera, which he regarded as his true calling. As for the concert hall, his feelings about it probably were not very different from the way they had been in his mildly Marxian mood of the late twenties, although the fact that some of his best recent successes had been there may have given him a more benign view of it.

That very fall he enjoyed another success in a Paris concert hall; but the triumph was flavored with the wormwood of questions of the moment that went beyond music. Maurice Abravanel tells the story. "In the fall of 1933, I was to conduct the Orchestre de Paris in two concerts, and the manager insisted that I perform something by Weill, whose name would guarantee a very large attendance. I begged Kurt to write something or at least let me use anything he had composed, and he said: 'Look, I had a big success with *Mahagonny*, but already, at the *Seven Deadly Sins* performances, there are protests. Don't play anything of mine right now. People are jealous, and it doesn't do you any good.' I offered new works by Krenek and Hindemith, but the manager persisted—nothing would do except Weill. Finally, Kurt gave in, and I programmed three songs from *Silbersee*, for which Madeleine Grey, at the peak of her fame for doing the *Songs of the Auvergne* by Canteloube, was engaged; Madeleine Milhaud translated the songs into French.

"I will never forget that performance at the Salle Pleyel. Great applause after each song and, at the end, a real triumph, with shouts of '*bis*.' But to my ears, louder than all that was a voice yelling, 'Vive Hitler!' Grey, bless her soul, focused on the cheers, and she prompted me to go back onstage. Again there were bravos, but this time they were clearly overshadowed by Florent Schmitt's and his friends' insults. Kurt came backstage with an infinitely sad look. 'Did I need that?' he said.

"There was nothing I could say. I wandered through the streets, missing one commuter train after another. I was staying then with my parents in a suburb and finally caught the 5 A.M. train, after seeing all the bales of morning papers in the station with big front-page headlines about the incident. I slept about two hours, then Kurt was on the phone, and I went back to town to have coffee with him. He was very sad. Obviously we would have to go elsewhere."

Weill had encountered some of the ugly feelings that were to explode that very fall with the Stavisky case. Serge Stavisky, a Russian Jew, was accused of fraudulent financial dealings and found dead one day in

December, an apparent suicide. Since his complicated affairs seem to have reached into the highest government circles, there was a widespread belief that he had, in fact, been murdered; in any case, the incident became oil on the flames of right-wing anger against the republic and against Jews. In January there was a succession of demonstrations in the streets of Paris, and on February 6, 1934, a mob led by quasi-fascist groups tried to storm the Palais Bourbon. The police opened fire, wounding some three hundred people and killing eleven. In the ensuing political crisis, Premier Édouard Daladier was forced to resign. A mood of anti-Semitism became part of the general atmosphere of anger and disarray.

It may have been dismay at events such as these that caused Weill to take as long as he did to compose his symphony. He did not finish his sketch of it until December, and the full score was not ready until February: since there is no evidence that he was working on anything else during this period—other than some scattered "single" songs of the Paris cabaret variety, which were easy for him—his progress must be counted as untypically slow.

Also slow was the progress of the symphony, once written, toward obtaining a public hearing. It was of course promptly performed in the drawing room of the Princesse de Polignac, but it did not find a regular concert engagement right away. Finally Maurice Abravanel, visiting his native Switzerland, stopped in Zurich to see Bruno Walter, who now was making his home there, and talked about his friend's symphony. Walter suggested that Weill come see him about it anytime he was in Zurich. Kurt never needed too much of an excuse to be in Zurich in any case, since his brother Hans had recently settled there with his family. Furthermore, that summer, as it happened, he was invited to Max Reinhardt's home outside Salzburg to discuss an important project, so that a stop in Zurich on the way back to Paris would have been called for in any case. He went to see Walter, who agreed to conduct the symphony in a guest appearance with the Concertgebouw Orchestra of Amsterdam that October.

Weill went to Amsterdam shortly before the scheduled October 11 premiere to watch rehearsals as well as be present for the concert itself; in an excited letter to Lenya he praised the rehearsals and also expressed his dismay at the latest setback in French politics—the assassination of Louis Barthou, the French foreign minister, along with the visiting King Alexander of Yugoslavia, in Marseilles on October 9. The premiere performance itself was well received by the audience. The work ought to have been an audience-pleaser, for it was as accessible a piece of music as a twentieth-century symphony can be. Though its idiom is distinctly modern and free in tonality, this "Symphonic Fantasy" or Nocturne Symphonique, as Weill alternately called it, has the flavor of a medley of theater tunes. The composer of *The Threepenny Opera*, *Mahagonny*, and *Die Bürgschaft* had simply applied the style he knew best to the symphonic form. Not that this sort of thing was without precedent: Stravinsky had done a virtual medley of songs in his *Symphony of Psalms* in 1930, albeit with human voices, which Weill did not use for this work. In general, a new tunefulness was entering the concert hall at that time, perhaps in reaction against the sour notes of social and political disaster that were everywhere in the air: just that year, Hindemith, still in Germany but in growing discomfort there, had completed a thoroughly romantic symphonic adaptation from his as yet uncompleted opera *Mathis der Mahler*. Nevertheless, the critics in Amsterdam were somewhat perplexed at what Weill was doing. The Belgian critic Henri Monnet—who thought the symphony had not only a "Berlin dialect" but also "from time to time, an accent coming from somewhere else, perhaps out of the Semitic"—agreed that the work was pleasing for the audience, but ruminated: "If the audience is right about this, I ask myself, then what pleasure can it go on finding in concerts? Works like this put the question in an especially significant light, for one may well ask whether they mean a revival of the concert hall or its death-knell." Weill was no doubt asking himself the same question.

Monnet had put the matter as though standing at a crossroads in the history of music; at any rate, this was a crossroads in Weill's career. For a moment he had ventured along the road of a new kind of symphonic writing and had simply produced echoes of the musical theater. Now he was to step back and take the road of musical theater again, but along a turning he had never followed before. Almost from the first moment he made his home in Paris, Weill had begun to think of the comparison between himself and another composer who had been born in Germany the son of a Jewish cantor, and who had come to Paris and taken it by storm: Jacques Offenbach. Even in his early days as an apprentice composer in Berlin, he had been passionately interested in Offenbach and had admired his use of music as a means of satirizing society. If he had, in the late twenties, occasionally thought of himself as an Offenbach of Berlin, this notion would not have been too extremely wide of the mark. Maurice Abravanel says that when Weill first arrived in France, André Gide and Jean Cocteau and other writers wanted to work with him, and that Weill's comment had been: "All right. They won't accept me as a serious composer. Maybe I can be a new Offenbach." This would have meant becoming a Berlin Weill all over again in Paris.

As it turned out, however, nothing of importance materialized with either Gide or Cocteau—were they discouraged by the cool reception accorded *The Seven Deadly Sins?*—and when the opportunity finally arose at the end of 1934 for Weill to do a Paris boulevard musical, the material he worked with could hardly have been considered Offenbachian. Jacques Deval—who subsequently went on to achieve international fame with his romantic comedy about Russian émigrés in Paris, *Tovarich*—had written a sentimental novel with only mildly satirical undertones called *Marie Galante*. Set in the port city of Panama, it tells the story of Marie, a girl from Bordeaux who had been shanghaied a few years before by a cargo captain hoping to have her as his shipboard mistress, and who had resisted him and then been abandoned by him in South America. Marie has made her way up to Panama and, dreaming that she will earn enough one day to pay her passage back home, has become a prostitute. She is befriended by an older man, Tokujiro Tsamatsui, a cosmopolitan Japanese merchant of the city, who turns out to be involved in espionage activities—primarily, it would seem, on behalf of the Americans in the Canal Zone. He promises her enough money for her ticket back to France if she will perform a few simple undercover assignments; and she does—until one day she is shot and killed. The tale ends as Tsamatsui sadly places her coffin onto a ship that will bring her back to Bordeaux at last.

Deval was to make something of an industry out of this novel: in another year, it was to become a Hollywood movie starring Helen Morgan, but without music. The Paris stage version that he prepared was to feature Florelle in the role of Marie. Florelle had played Polly in the French film version of *The Threepenny Opera*, so she was perhaps the go-between who had brought Weill together with Deval to do this show. It had ten scenes, seven of which featured musical numbers. The score presented Weill with opportunities to rework some old veins: there is a mildly satirical "Panamanian Army March" in it, as well as a mildly sleazy fox-trot number for the dance cabaret where Marie hangs out; and, as we have seen, one of the *Marie Galante* melodies was lifted out of *Happy End*. There also was an exciting new opportunity to do something "American," for a group of Black sailors at the bar sings a spiritual. But for the most part, Weill's task was to be as sentimentally French as possible—to convey the echoes of Marie's nostalgia with no irony whatsoever. This was indeed a new turning: for, though he had already composed individual songs of a "straight" and sentimental character for the cabarets of Berlin and Paris, this was the first time he was doing it for a whole show.

The amazing thing—amazing, not in retrospect, but solely in the light of what Weill had done so far—was that he did it so well. Not only are the show's four "French" songs good pieces of sentimental musical theater, they also seem as French as can be, pure specimens of Paris cabaret melody demonstrating once and for all that Weill had a remarkably adaptable ear. And yet one of them, "*Les Filles de Bordeaux*," simply uses the tune of "In Youth's Golden Glimmer" from *Happy End*, a song originally written to satirize one kind of American sentimentality for Berlin ears. The common element in these two versions is the sentimentality: with the French text, the satire disappears, and the song somehow becomes "typically" French in the process. If the creation of new, French-sounding melodies was a display of Weill's good ear, the ability to pick an old one of his that would lend itself to the French sound was an equally striking display of this gift.

But it was stirringly displayed by one song above the rest. Marie's broadly melodious expression of hope that a ship will come one day to take her back to Bordeaux, "*J'attends un navire*," is one of the loveliest songs Weill was ever to write—one can hear the ocean waves in it—and so at home in France that it was later to become a theme song used by the Resistance. It bears, by the way, a significant relation to the "Pirate-Jenny" song. Like that one, it is the monologue of a needy woman who is literally waiting for her ship to come in, but now the bitter vengefulness is gone. The new song is still filled with sadness, even with gentle touches of anger, but the Berlin rasp has been replaced by the sob of the Paris *chanteuse*, and it is bravely sweet and affirmative in the end. This was not the last time Weill was to return to the theme of the woman waiting for her ship; and its next occurrence, like its previous ones, would seem to plot yet another significant point in the graph of his emotional outlook and artistic development.

Marie Galante opened at the Théâtre de Paris on December 22, 1934, and though its run was rather short, it was well enough received that Weill felt encouraged to pursue the vein of light musical theater. To be sure, he had grander ideas—there was the project with Max Reinhardt, and he was thinking of writing a ballet about the world of Toulouse-Lautrec—but for the moment the main thing was to make a living. At around this time Robert Vambery, Aufricht's old Berlin associate, came to Paris with the text of a satirical play called *Der Kuhhandel* ("The Cow Deal"), which he had written in Germany but could not hope to get produced there with

Hitler in power. Set on a fictitious island off the coast of South America, it deals with a young couple whose only worldly asset is a cow, and with their efforts to get married in the face of a would-be militaristic regime that levies an armaments tax and distrains the cow. All ends happily, so that this political satire also was a potential piece of musical comedy. Vambery persuaded Weill to write music for it, and an arrangement to produce it was made with the same Savoy Theatre in London that had put on *Anna-Anna* and the *Songspiel* in the summer of 1933.

The English adaptation, called *A Kingdom for a Cow*, was done by Reginald Arkell and Desmond Carter—and Carter, who had written lyrics for George Gershwin as well as some other prominent theater composers, did the words for the Weill songs. One of them, "Two Hearts," uses the music of "*Le Roi d'Aquitaine*" from *Marie Galante*, but another, "As Long as I Love," is as English as "*J'attends un navire*" had been French and could have been written by Noël Coward. The play was not well received, however, when it opened on June 28, 1935; the *Times* critic wrote: "It is not stated whether [Kurt Weill's] recent departure from Germany was occasioned by his partiality for politically tendentious satirical texts like this one or for the kind of music he writes, but the music would be the German authorities' most valid justification."

This response must have been especially disappointing because of the fact that Weill felt more at home in the English language than in French and perhaps hoped for a moment that he might be able to transfer his activities from Paris to London. But this was not to be. Rather, as it turned out, his destiny lay in that giant of the English-speaking world farther west across the Atlantic—and, in fact, the machinery was already under way for the enterprise that would bring him and Lenya to the United States before the end of the year.

The Road to New York

The initiatives that finally resulted in Kurt Weill's passage across the Atlantic began in distant Chicago—Brecht's city of demon capitalists—with a man who, though the European-born son of a Jewish cantor as Weill was, would have seemed in most respects a most unlikely person to play a crucial role in the composer's life. Meyer Weisgal, born in Poland in 1895, had come to the United States with his family as a boy and grown up in Chicago and New York. His life became in some ways the classic success story of the rising Jewish immigrant—but with one significant variation: he was a passionately committed Zionist and made his career as a hard worker in this field at a time when most American Jews were still rather indifferent to this cause. After working his way through the Columbia School of Journalism, he had edited a succession of Zionist publications and had risen to the position of national secretary of the Zionist Organization of America just in the moment when this branch was becoming of vital importance to the world movement. Zionism needed money, and Weisgal, whose exuberance and drive became legendary, began to exhibit a spectacular gift for fund-raising that would make Chaim Weizmann, the movement's world leader, eternally grateful to him.

In the 1930s Weisgal had become involved in theater—or theatrical spectacle, at any rate—as a way of serving the cause that dominated his life. It had all begun in 1931 at the Chicago Opera House, with a fund-raising spectacle depicting the triumph of the Maccabees that he had organized for Hanukkah. Fascinated by this kind of project—there was always a theatrical element in Weisgal's character, featured above all in a gift for salty Yiddish storytelling—he then produced a much larger spectacle for the Chicago World's Fair of 1933: called *The Romance of a People*, it was a survey of Jewish history made up primarily of dramatized selections from the Old Testament. It had a musical score composed by Isaac Van Grove, the young director of the Chicago Civic Opera. The show was well received, and it subsequently went on tour, sojourning for several weeks in New York among other places.

All this was happening at the time of Hitler's rise to power in Germany, which Weisgal contemplated not only with dismay but with a Zionist's sense of history: for he saw it as significant that the greatest Jewish community in the world was now being turned—like Spanish Jewry and so many others before it—into a community of outcasts, some of whom were already going into exile. He also took special note of the fact that some of the greatest Jewish artists and intellectuals of the era were already among the refugees. Part preacher and part impresario, he felt an urge, not only to appeal to their talents as a moral weapon against Hitler, but also to try to awaken in them a better consciousness of a heritage they had by and large tended to ignore. As Weisgal tells the story: "While I was working in Chicago on *The Romance* I read an item in the paper that Max Reinhardt had to flee Germany. In one of my inspired moments I sent off a cable: 'To Max Reinhardt, Europe. IF HITLER DOESN'T WANT YOU I'LL TAKE YOU.' " The telegram went on to ask Reinhardt if he would come and take over *The Romance of a People*, reworking and restaging it in his celebrated style. Reinhardt apparently never received the message, but the idea stayed with Weisgal. Indeed, it grew and took on a new form: now he dreamed of "a Reinhardt-directed spectacle on a theme resembling *The Romance*, as a sort of answer to Hitler; but unlike *The Romance* it was to be the project of some of the greatest artists of our time."

By November 1933 Weisgal was in Paris, and he immediately set about trying to see Reinhardt, who was then doing a production of *Die Fledermaus* at the Théâtre Pigalle. It was not easy to get past the great director's entourage, and for nearly two weeks, Weisgal later was to tell an interviewer, "I bumped my head against the stone walls of the Théâtre Pigalle." But then he obtained the good offices of a prominent gentile Zionist, Pierre van Paassen, who was Paris correspondent of the *Toronto Star* and who knew Reinhardt personally. Weisgal got to see him at last, and in his own, Yiddish-based version of the German language proceeded to explain his idea. "I talked and talked for hours. Now, Reinhardt is a very polite person, and all he said to me was, 'Ja, ja, that is most interesting.' I couldn't tell whether he was really listening or not."

But he was, and soon he had suggestions of his own to make. He proposed that the writer of the drama be the celebrated Viennese novelist Franz Werfel. Weisgal must have paused for a moment over this, since Werfel, whose wife had been Gustav Mahler's widow, had very nearly followed the route of that Jewish-born composer into conversion to Catholicism. But on the other hand, the rise of Hitler to power had made Werfel reluctant to take the final step; so that now he was an outstanding example of that phenomenon, observed with such interest by Weisgal, of artists who were suddenly becoming Jews again in spite of themselves. Reinhardt then recommended that the music for the production be written by Kurt Weill. To Weisgal, this was almost as shocking a suggestion as Werfel had been. He did not yet know that Weill was a cantor's son like himself, and he was under the impression that Brecht's former collaborator was "some sort of Communist," which, for a middle-class Zionist, was almost as much of an apostasy as conversion to Catholicism would have been.

In spite of his reservations, Weisgal was ready to accept Reinhardt's suggestions. Reinhardt agreed to contact the writer and the composer, and he and Weisgal set a tentative date for a meeting of the four of them the following summer at Schloss Leopoldskron, Reinhardt's estate in the mountains near Salzburg. Weisgal then returned home and proceeded to contribute to the enterprise his own outstanding talent for raising money. It was to be a large spectacle, of course, and to be done in New York: Reinhardt's first idea was to do it under a tent in Central Park. But no one yet dreamed how expensive it would turn out to be, or how much time was to pass before it would finally open.

Weill was already settled into the house at Louveciennes when Reinhardt presented Weisgal's idea to him. It had several features that readily appealed to him. In the first place, it held out the prospect of more money than he had earned in several years, at a time when his finances were only just beginning to recover from the shock of exile. Moreover, the theme of Jewish exile and wandering that the play was going to stress not only echoed significantly with his present life situation, as Weisgal had meant it to do, but also caused his really strong Jewish roots to come alive for the first time in years. In fact, one of the first things he did after speaking with Reinhardt about the project was to sit down and compose "a melody that he thought would express the swan song of Moses, denied entry to the

Promised Land." The image of Moses on Mount Pisgah, weary after leading his people through the wilderness for forty years and now glimpsing his goal at last, is a striking one for Kurt to have become preoccupied with at this moment. Was this his conception of his own lot? Not that he ever for a moment considered the Promised Land of Moses and of Zionism to be the goal that he longed for, even though several members of his immediate family were soon to end up there and had no doubt already given it a good deal of thought; but he certainly was beginning to see Paris as only his Pisgah. Here, then, was another very appealing aspect of Weisgal's project: it held out the prospect of at least making a visit to the United States, which Kurt could then examine closely to see if it should indeed be the final goal of his wanderings.

In July 1934, just prior to the scheduled meeting with Weisgal, Reinhardt summoned Weill and Werfel to a preliminary get-together in Venice, where he had a residence and where he had just put on a production of *The Merchant of Venice* in the streets of that city itself. Between walks on the Strand and swims in the Adriatic, they discussed their various conceptions of the proposed biblical spectacle, and it soon emerged that Werfel, among the several scenes he had sketched out, had also done a treatment of Moses on Pisgah. He and Weill immediately compared notes, to see how well their words and music meshed. The outcome of the story, as told in an American press release more than a year later, may well have been as exaggerated as the distance given: "Both, inspired two thousand miles apart—words and music—matched to perfection the first time they were tried." This would have been a more perfect match than Weill and Werfel were themselves; but at any rate, all the relationships involved proved at least to be viable ones for the duration of the project.

Soon after that, the three men reassembled at Reinhardt's Austrian castle to meet with Weisgal. The latter has described it as "a strange and ominous setting: three of the best-known un-Jewish Jewish artists, gathered in the former residence of the Archbishop of Salzburg, in actual physical view of Berchtesgaden, Hitler's mountain chalet across the border in Bavaria, pledged themselves to give high dramatic expression to the significance of the people they had forgotten about till Hitler came to power." Weisgal took advantage of the opportunity to take his own measure of the artists Reinhardt had obtained and to explain matters to them in his own way. "I spent a whole night talking with Werfel in the garden and explaining to him, as well as I could, that this was a *Jewish* play—that and nothing else. It was our history, the history of his and my people, that had to be portrayed—not some alien or abstract concept. Remote as he was from Judaism, there was enough of the poet in Werfel to grasp at the idea even through my barbarous German."

Weisgal had felt he had to sell his point to Werfel, but when it came to the composer for the projected work, he discovered that "Kurt Weill was a quite different kettle of fish. Like myself, he was the son of a *chazan*, the descendant of a long line of rabbis; but unlike me he had shaken himself free of Jewish life." Not so very free, however, and Weisgal soon realized he had discovered in Kurt a man whose art he could trust even by his own special standards. "Our discussions revolved round the play and the music," Weisgal writes, "and from the beginning there was a dispute between Werfel and Weill as to whether it was going to be a musical drama or a drama with music." This was a familiar enough conflict to Weill, but it was new to Weisgal, who gradually realized that a musical drama was what he wanted. Not that he disliked the way the text was turning out. Werfel read aloud some of the scenes he had roughly sketched out. "I cried," Weisgal later told an interviewer. "Weill cried. Werfel cried. Finally, Reinhardt cried. Then I knew we had something." But Weisgal was always to be attracted more to the musical side of the project, just as he was attracted more to Weill than to Werfel: some spontaneous inner harmony had been sounded between the two sons of cantors.

A contract was drawn up at the end of the meeting, which stated that the parties involved "undertake to devise, write and compose a musical biblical morality play to express the spiritual origin, the earliest mythical history and the eternal destiny of the Jewish people to whom they belong." The next move was Werfel's, and in the ensuing months he wrote the text of *Der Weg der Verheissung* ("The Road of Promise"), which was eventually to be known—in the English translation by Ludwig Lewisohn used for the New York production—as *The Eternal Road*. Werfel's play—which, in its overall thrust, has remarkable affinities with Johannes R. Becher's *Awakening of a People*—is essentially a succession of scenes from the Old Testament, moving from Abraham through the Prophets and stressing the perpetual wanderings of the Jewish people, ultimately toward the goal of the Promised Land of Israel. Its principal dramatic device is to center the story upon a synagogue congregation in more or less modern times. The Jewish community depicted is about to be expelled from the land in which it is living—no names or dates are given, so that the pointed reference to current history becomes transformed into a generalized view of a classic situation—and in order to console themselves at their fate the congregants proceed to read passages from the

Bible, each of which is then enacted dramatically as the synagogue scene fades into darkness. At the end the entire congregation takes to the eternal road, or road of promise, just as Abraham, Moses, and others depicted in the pageant have done from the beginning. For the most part, Werfel wrote the synagogue scenes in prose and the biblical scenes in verse.

Until he got Werfel's completed text, Weill prepared for his work on *The Eternal Road* by doing some research. He began by jotting down on manuscript paper every Hebrew melody that his memory could summon up from childhood. "With about 200 songs," he later told an American interviewer, "which I had written in several days' memory seeking, I began work at the Bibliothèque Nationale to trace their sources as far as possible. Many I discovered had been written in the eighteenth and nineteenth centuries, some borrowed from the most surprising sources— from opera, 'hit-songs' of the time, street tunes, concert music, symphonies. Those I dismissed, retaining only the traditional music. With that as my guide, I attempted to create music that would communicate naturally and inevitably the stories of the Old Testament." This ritual of purification was surely another way that Kurt had found of settling moral accounts with his father. Suddenly he was virtually putting on the robes of the cantor himself, and in doing so he took the opportunity to reject most of his father's musical vocabulary as not pure, not truly Jewish, at all.

Not that he resorted exclusively to Jewish themes when he began composing the score, after receiving Werfel's text, in the summer of 1935. Since most of the play takes place in biblical times, and most "Jewish" melodies belong to the era of the synagogue, only that part of the action set in the synagogue was given explicitly Jewish music by him. Otherwise, as another American interviewer was to put it, "it is Mr. Weill's conviction that the Old Testament, of which the play is a résumé, is primarily a great human document belonging in its appeal, not to any particular era, but to all time. For this reason, he considers 'local color' of small importance and feels justified in employing a contemporary style." Elsewhere this interviewer stresses that "modernism will be rampant in the tonal investiture given the spectacle by Kurt Weill, the modernist German opera composer."

These last remarks are perplexing because the completed score of *The Eternal Road* shows a style somewhat removed from rampant modernism. Indeed, there are many touches of banality in it. Musically, the entire work is in a carefully neutral style, "contemporary" only in the sense that the composer has so simplified and popularized the tradition of nineteenth-century oratorio that it now represents little of a challenge, either to untrained singers or to uncultivated audiences. Weill no doubt knew what he was doing. The decision had been made early on that this would be a "popular oratorio"; it would be performed by actors rather than singers and accessible to a broad public—and, after all, hadn't he done this sort of thing before? But the mocking, aggressively lowbrow approach of *The Threepenny Opera* had been something far removed from the conscientious pietism of *The Eternal Road*. For a German avant-gardist of the twenties and thirties, it was much safer to use popular conventions in order to sneer at them than to draw them to oneself in a tearful embrace. It is as if Weill had suddenly decided to do a reworking of "The Maiden's Prayer" with a straight face and was now ready to nod in solemn agreement with any Jack O'Brien who might want to call it "immortal art."

Not that *The Eternal Road* is without its moments of considerable power. It is full of choral passages, and choral music—not least of all in a sacred vein—was always an area of strength for Weill. The chorus of angels with which the play's first biblical section is opened has a truly exalted quality. Furthermore, the musical dynamics of the work—the dramatic interplay of speech, recitative, chorus, orchestra with the ongoing action—are a display of theatrical craftsmanship that often is breathtaking. On this level the work is decidedly akin to *Die Bürgschaft*— and one hardly need add that the script, based on the Bible, is a far better one. But the melodic and harmonic sophistication of Weill's last German opera is decidedly lacking in *The Eternal Road*.

It would be easy to conclude that Weill composed so simplistically in this case because he recognized a situation in which popular pieties and the spirit of rallying to a cause were likely to take precedence over artistic values. This may have been part of it, but chances are that there was a large element of sincerity in his work on *The Eternal Road*. It is noteworthy that at least one of the songs in the score, describing God's fateful promise to Abraham, was dedicated by Kurt to his father. This song was written at just around the time when the Nuremberg Laws were passed by the Nazi regime, depriving German Jews of citizenship and setting them aside as a race with whom sexual intermingling by non-Jews was prohibited. Kurt's sister, Ruth, and her husband, Leon Sohn, who was employed by the Zionist movement, had already settled in Palestine with their daughter, and Cantor Weill and his wife were soon to follow them there. In such circumstances the streak of pietism that had always lain beneath

Kurt's ironic personal and artistic style was inevitably brought to the surface. He had, after all, composed such solemn, quasi-religious works as the Divertimento and the "Lamentations of Jeremiah" in his apprentice days, and he was now reverting to that mood. The difference, however, was that where he had once been a passionate young modernist of the concert hall, he was now an established composer for the theater. Banality was part of his stock in trade: but banality as part of a wicked comic strip was of a different import from the banality of a synagogue pamphlet. The effort at high-minded decorum had put the *badkhen* in retreat and shown Kurt to be his father's son, after all—at least for the time being.

The long expected opportunity for Weill to follow *The Eternal Road* to New York came in the summer of 1935. Max Reinhardt had been in the United States most of the past year, mainly working on *A Midsummer Night's Dream*, of which he gave a typically spectacular production in the Hollywood Bowl and which he then made into a Warner Brothers movie. In New York he had done some preliminary work on *The Eternal Road* with Weisgal and the celebrated industrial designer Norman Bel Geddes, who had designed a production of *The Miracle* for Reinhardt some years before and whom they had engaged for this production. New York did not have a Hollywood Bowl, and, after Reinhardt's vision of a tent in Central Park had been rejected, the three men had hoped briefly for the old Hippodrome on Sixth Avenue; but that was not available because a major musical, Billy Rose's *Jumbo*, with book by Ben Hecht and Charles MacArthur and songs by Rodgers and Hart, as well as a cast that included an elephant, was scheduled to open there in the fall. Finally the choice had fallen upon the Manhattan Opera House, on Thirty-fourth Street just west of Eighth Avenue, and Bel Geddes had gone to work rebuilding the inside of the theater for the planned mammoth production.

Reinhardt was back in Salzburg in August, when he held another meeting there with Werfel and Weill. But the play was to open in December, and it was time for the artists to begin coordinating their activities at the site of the production itself. All three of them made plans to go to New York soon, but because the musical and acoustical problems entailed by the redesigning of the stage required the composer's presence most urgently of all, it was decided that Weill would be the first of them to sail. Indeed, by the end of August, Weisgal was in Europe, first to confer with his three artists at Schloss Leopoldskron once again, then to follow Weill to Paris and personally escort him to New York.

By this time Kurt and Lenya were back together in the house at

Louveciennes, and Kurt had decided—apparently not without soul-searching—that he could not go to America without her. Whether love had actually revived between them is hard to say; but what they had rediscovered was a need for one another that could survive the ravages of all other emotions—and that was in fact to last the rest of their lives. Kurt had never been able to bear being alone—even when working, he usually preferred knowing that there was someone in the next room—and he certainly could not face the prospect of being by himself on a new continent. What better person was there to have with him on this new adventure, then, than the woman with whom he had intimately shared the most important moments of his life so far? As for Lenya, whatever her other feelings may have been, prominent among them must have been the realization that her destiny was somehow inextricably bound up with Kurt's. Just that spring, when she performed in an operetta in Zurich, Kurt had given her a chance to show herself off to best advantage by writing an additional song for her to sing.

Kurt, Lenya, and Weisgal sailed on the S.S. *Majestic* and descended the gangplank at New York on September 10, 1935. The newly arrived couple then found themselves being put up in style at the St. Moritz on Central Park South. They were right in the heart of the landscape of skyscrapers that was known from films and photographs the world over and that had filled the Berlin imagination, too, having achieved there its most radical translation into expressionist imagery by means of Fritz Lang's futuristic fantasy of 1926, *Metropolis*. That unique skyline of brick and concrete—to be engulfed by the present one of metal and glass only in the decades following World War II—had just achieved the fullness of its classic profile; for Rockefeller Center, the last of the major structures of the prewar era, was now having the finishing touches put upon it. The Empire State Building was already a few years old. In general, New York in 1935 was showing a vitality that bespoke the beginnings of recovery from the worst depths of the Depression. This was also true of the country in general, where the effects of President Franklin D. Roosevelt's New Deal were now being felt: that barometer of the nation's economy, Detroit, was to report a sale of more than 2.7 million automobiles for the year, which was two and a half times the number sold in 1932.

Kurt and Lenya excitedly made their way around the city that seemed in some ways utterly familiar to them for all the times they had seen it in movies. They were especially excited by elevators, which still were rare in Berlin and Paris. They went to movies and the theater. They also headed, like so many European jazz-lovers before them, in the direction of what they took to be New York's celebrated Negro quarter. But the American blackface play they had worked on together in Berlin had been mistakenly called *Das Lied von Hoboken*, and so they made their way onto the Hoboken ferry. Only after they arrived in New Jersey did they learn that Harlem, in uptown Manhattan, was what they were after.

In all these wanderings language proved to be little of a problem, because Kurt had a musician's ear for languages and had always known some English anyway. A story Meyer Weisgal liked to tell was of himself, during the transatlantic voyage that September, waking up seasick one morning and then getting together with Kurt, who remarked, "Mr. Weisgal, you are not good-looking." Weisgal's utterly engaging homeliness was already one of his legendary qualities, but he was ready to remark that this was no time to remind him of it, until he realized Kurt had meant to tell him he did not look well. But this was a minor problem and did not last long. Within a few months after his arrival, Kurt was speaking a very fluent and reasonably correct English—and colloquially American despite his heavy German accent. Lenya had more trouble learning the new language.

Weill wasted no time making contacts in the world of the Broadway musical theater, where his name was well known. For one thing, *The Threepenny Opera* had played on Broadway in an English translation in the spring of 1933, and though it had bewildered critics and audiences alike and closed in less than two weeks, professionals had greatly admired the music. For another thing, the *Threepenny* film and, above all, the record album that Lenya and other cast members had made at the end of 1930, were highly appreciated in knowledgeable circles. One of the first parties Kurt and Lenya attended in New York was at George Gershwin's apartment on Riverside Drive. Kurt was thus renewing an old acquaintanceship; Ira Gershwin was there, too, and in a moment of conviviality, Kurt startled him by saying that he hoped to collaborate with him someday. George contributed his own share to the startling remarks when he told his two German guests that he was very fond of the recording of *The Threepenny Opera*, which he played often, but that he had never liked the "squitchadickeh voice" of the leading lady. George evidently had forgotten that the lady with the squeaky voice was one of the people he was now speaking to. Later on, when he knew better, he would try to put his feeling in friendlier terms and say he thought Lenya sounded like a hillbilly singer; but this probably was no more pleasing to her than the original remark had been.

It was the Gershwins who provided Kurt with one of the most

exciting and significant moments of those first euphoric weeks in New York. Ira took him to see a rehearsal of *Porgy and Bess*, which was to open October 10 at the Alvin Theatre on West Fifty-second Street. As they stood in back of the theater watching and listening, Kurt became filled with wonderment. To his ear, the insolent jazz sounds of the twenties were taking on new meanings in this music and yielding to a lyricism worthy of the finest elements in the European operatic tradition. And yet it all remained so fresh, so American. Filled with emotion, Kurt leaned over to Ira and said:

"It's a great country where music like that can be written—and played."

The man Kurt Weill had arrived in America some days earlier, and now the artist had arrived, too, and he would never be the same.

Taking on Broadway:
Johnny Johnson

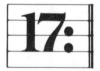 Weill no doubt was already certain that he wanted to settle in the United States, as many of his fellow German exiles had done by now, even though he had not yet given up his house at Louveciennes. But in the first two or three months after his arrival he retained the air of a visiting émigré rather than that of an immigrant. The difference is crucial in this country: an émigré is a distinguished bearer of Old World culture and class, while an immigrant is a poor foreigner who has flung himself upon the mercy of the great American scramble for dollars and a place in the sun. Many an émigré is really an immigrant in disguise, and Weill was one of them: but the disguise was still working, for example, on December 19, 1935, when Weill gave another one of a whole succession of newspaper interviews he had given since his arrival, this one with a reporter from the *New York World-Telegram* who signed himself "R.C.B."

The article, which appeared the next day, began: "At 35 years of age, Kurt Weill, one of the interesting modernist composers, has secured a particular niche of his own in contemporary music. . . . America with a keen and anxious ear has heard the transoceanic rumblings and as a consequence Mr. Weill is now on a visit to this country in the interest of his incidental music to Franz Werfel's play *The Eternal Road*, which Max Reinhardt is preparing for production at the Manhattan Opera House. Only last Tuesday evening he was the guest of honor at a reception and musicale given by the League of Composers." On that occasion, a concert of excerpts from his operas and musical theater pieces had been given, with Lenya singing numbers from *The Threepenny Opera, Mahagonny*, and *Marie Galante*; but perhaps just as significant as the honor thus accorded Weill is the fact that much of that audience of distinguished musicians and connoisseurs had gone home at the intermission. As for *The Eternal Road*, it had originally been scheduled to open the evening after the "R.C.B." interview, but it had by now been postponed two or three times, to late January, because of the enormous alterations Norman Bel Geddes was making in the Manhattan Opera House. There were signs that the opening might have to be delayed even longer, which would mean a delay in much-needed income for the composer as well as many others involved in Meyer Weisgal's pageant.

Nevertheless, Kurt remained the unruffled émigré for the *World-Telegram* reporter. "The impressions received upon being admitted by the composer to his apartment at the St. Moritz were of affable courtesy and an indefinable feeling that he is easy to get along with. Of average height and build"—this, by the way, for a man who was slightly under five feet four inches, but who also gave others the impression of being a bit taller than he was—"he has dark eyes—he wears glasses—thinning dark hair and an oval, smooth-shaven face. Dispensing with fancy preliminaries, his visitor asked him about jazz." And Weill, dispensing also with fancy preliminaries, proceeded to reply in careful, correct English.

"American jazz has influenced modern music undoubtedly," he said. "Rhythmic and harmonic freedom, simplicity of melodic material, directness—saying things as they are—these are the contributions of jazz." The composer paused to light his pipe, then continued. "I do not mean the jazz of today, but the jazz of the time of the *St. Louis Blues* and other pieces of that period. Today it is much more complicated, and it has been influenced in turn by Debussy, Rimsky-Korsakov, and so on." Then, after an apparent moment of reflection, he went on emphatically: "I wish to make it clear that modern composers did not go to jazz to borrow its idiom. It was not the actual taking of material. It was an influence you did not feel." Weill was certainly speaking for himself with these words, though not necessarily for others.

At that moment the telephone rang in the next room, and the composer answered it. After a brief exchange he was back with the interviewer, and back into his flow of ideas. "In all times," he went on, "the dance has had an effect on music. It was so with Bach, Chopin, Beethoven, Schumann and others. They took the popular dance music of their or other days and lifted it into the region of art."

The interviewer remarked that some have considered Weill the creator of a kind of European jazz; Kurt did not seem at all displeased. "I consider myself a theater composer," he said, relighting his pipe. After a brief discussion of the works he had done with Brecht, the conversation then turned to George Gershwin's *Porgy and Bess*, which had confused the critics with its combination of idioms from Broadway, opera, and Negro folk music and had so frightened the public with its operatic form that it was obviously going to close soon. Weill expressed his ardent admiration for the composer and for the work, and said: "Audiences and critics are impatient with musical talents. It takes time to develop a creative style. I find it so in myself.

"For instance, I write absolute music in order to—how can I say it?—control my own style. You must turn away from your own habitual way occasionally. So then I write symphonic works. Last year Bruno Walter played my latest symphonic composition, 'Nocturne Symphonique.' He plays it everywhere." Weill evidently was eager, for the sake of his American audience, to place himself in the same category as George Gershwin—another composer who did both "light" music and concert works, both song and opera. "My style is melodious," he went on, stressing an aspect of it that he would have played down only two or three years earlier. "People say they can recognize my music when they hear only three measures of it. I believe in the simplification of music. If someone has something to say, it is not important what means he uses so long as he knows how to use them."

These last words in particular, though they were redolent of the old Weill, were really an assertion of a new readiness to take on the American milieu. Not all of those among his old colleagues who were touching upon American soil felt quite the same way. Brecht was in New York at this very moment, having arrived from his home in Denmark at the end of October to supervise a production of his play, *The Mother*, based on Maxim Gorky's novel and with music by Hanns Eisler. The production, which had opened at the Civic Repertory Theatre on November 19, was being put on by the Theatre Union, a left-wing group that obtained some support from the Communist Party; but in spite of seeming political affinities, Brecht had become engaged in fierce conflicts with the producers over matters such as the English adaptation of the text, the cuts made in it, and the actors' interpretations of the roles. He and Eisler, also in New York, wrote a memorandum saying that the Theatre Union "behaved no differently from any Broadway theater that treats a play simply as merchandise or the raw material for salable merchandise." The play was a box-office disaster, and an angry Brecht, who occasionally got together with Weill in the meantime, was to sail back to Europe on December 29.

At the very end of his interview "R.C.B." reminded Weill of his émigré status once again by asking him what he thought about the present situation of music in Germany. Kurt replied: "Lots of the best talents have left Germany, and I hear nothing from the pens of those who remained. I don't think they can be dead." But it was a world that was dying as far as he was concerned.

By the end of January 1936 the opening of *The Eternal Road* had been postponed again, and members of the cast had begun to rebel against the situation. The regulations of Actors' Equity specified that actors had to be paid after six weeks of rehearsals, and that deadline had long passed; furthermore, as the date of the opening became more and more uncertain, some of the players began thinking of giving up *The Eternal Road* for new commitments. Early in February Equity called off rehearsals, the actors were paid, and the opening was indefinitely postponed. Weisgal found himself with a debt of nearly a quarter of a million dollars and "not much else to show for it but a huge gaping hole in the Manhattan Opera House." He was determined to go on, but for the moment all the other participants in the project had to find something else to do. Reinhardt went back to Hollywood and did a revival of his Hollywood Bowl production of *A Midsummer Night's Dream*, a tie-in with the film, which had just opened in October; later he went on tour with it, and Weisgal went along to supervise the details and forget for a moment about the tortuous difficulties of *The Eternal Road* (reporters were already quite aware of the ironic relation between the play's title and its production history). Bel Geddes left the big hole he had dug and went to work on the Broadway production of Sidney Kingsley's *Dead End*. Werfel went back to Vienna. Weill and Lenya left the St. Moritz and found more modest quarters at the Hotel Park Crescent on Riverside Drive and Eighty-seventh Street, an area where the accents of German refugees would fill the air in years to come.

Kurt was now an immigrant in need of work, more or less like any other, and he wasted no time in looking for it. If his distinguished background was not necessarily bringing him financial security right now, it was at least providing him with valuable contacts. At around this time, a chance arose for him to go to Hollywood, probably through Max Reinhardt's intervention, but he still hoped to stay in New York and go on doing some kind of musical theater. The question was: What kind? He obviously was not a Broadway composer in the sense that Richard Rodgers or the George Gershwin of *Girl Crazy* were—not yet, at least; and the failure of *Porgy and Bess* seemed to have put a damper on works of a higher seriousness. Perhaps he could have tided himself over by teaching courses at the New School for Social Research, as Hanns Eisler was doing, along with growing numbers of German exiles in other fields; but the academy had never been for him. Also, if worst came to worst, he could always go back to Paris. His lease on the house at Louveciennes was to terminate on June 1, but he was thinking of renewing it and at least spending the summer there.

Then at a party he met Harold Clurman, one of the young directors of the Group Theatre, which had come into being a few years before as a splinter that broke off from New York's foremost producing organization, the Theatre Guild. Clurman and Lee Strasberg, budding actors and directors by trade but quasi-religious reformers of the theater by calling, had joined forces with Cheryl Crawford, a young Theatre Guild staff member, in an effort to realize their own high hopes for American drama. This "bizarre trio, two Old Testament prophets and a WASP *shiksa*," as Cheryl Crawford has put it, managed to obtain the blessings of the Theatre Guild, as well as the rights to a play that the Guild had bought, Paul Green's *The House of Connelly*. Green was a Southern liberal writer whose play about the struggles of a Negro ex-slave to improve his lot, *In Abraham's Bosom*, had won the Pulitzer Prize for 1927. *The House of Connelly* also was about the South, depicting the decline of the old plantation class in the early years of the twentieth century. Strasberg directed the Group production of it, which opened with Theatre Guild support on September 28, 1931, and was a great success. The Group Theatre went on to become a well-knit troupe of some of the finest young actors and directors in the American theater, and took on an image that seemed to typify the politically as well as artistically radical mood of the thirties. "During the period of the Group Theatre's personal depression," Brooks Atkinson writes, "most of the actors lived in a ten-room tenement in West 57th Street, for which they paid $50 a month. Meals came out of a common fund; two of the actresses did the marketing, and a few of the men did the cooking. It was like a metropolitan kibbutz." One member of this "kibbutz," Clifford Odets, suddenly achieved fame in January 1935 as the author of *Waiting for Lefty*, a red-hot theatrical happening about unions, strikes, and visions of social revolution. *Awake and Sing*—Odets's naturalistic drama about a Bronx Jewish family during the Depression—followed a month later, and the fame and success of the Group Theatre thereby reached its height.

Clurman was impressed at meeting the composer of *The Threepenny Opera*. As much an intellectual as a man of the theater, he was familiar with the cultural scene in Europe, where he had spent some time as a student; he also was a good friend of Aaron Copland's and knew a lot about music. Weill, for his part, had heard of the Group while still in Europe, and he still felt the pull of radical theater. No doubt his conversation with Clurman turned quickly to the idea of doing a musical play; the Group had never done a musical before and was not necessarily eager to, but a Kurt Weill work would be something else again.

In the ensuing days, Clurman introduced Weill to various of his colleagues, and the idea was bruited about. Lee Strasberg and his wife, Paula Miller, a Group actress, gave a dinner party at which Weill presented some general thoughts on the subject. According to a newspaper account written some months later, "He told Strasberg of two general themes—one comic, one tragic." Years later Cheryl Crawford was to write that Weill wanted to try "a very American subject." This must have seemed a rash proposal for someone just arrived in the country. On the other hand, he also proposed a musical version of *The Good Soldier Schweik*, but Strasberg thought this was "too European."

Gradually, the idea emerged that the desirable thing to try would be some kind of Americanized *Schweik*. There evidently was uncertainty about the next step, however. Although the Group had often been involved in the planning and writing of plays, they had never really commissioned one from the ground up, with the theme stated in advance. This, of course, was the way Weill preferred doing things. Now, in the case of *Schweik*, there of course was the book by Jaroslav Hašek, from which a playwright could make his adaptation; but there also was the dramatized version, partly written by Brecht, that Erwin Piscator had presented in Berlin in 1928. Apparently deciding they would try to do something with the latter, the Group directors got hold of a copy and prepared an English translation.

Then the picture took a different shape one day early in April when Harold Clurman dropped in on an old Group colleague who was teaching at the University of North Carolina. "On a visit to Chapel Hill to discuss a play about college life that Paul Green had submitted to us," Clurman writes, "I learned something about Paul's past that he had never before mentioned. He had fought overseas in the last war and had an intimate

acquaintance with the American soldier of that day. I mentioned Kurt
Weill's suggestion, particularly since Paul was fascinated with the element
of music in the theatre." Actually, there are indications that Green had
been discussed by the Group directors in this connection even before
Clurman's trip. A man of solid character and high ideals, Green had been
developing in his native North Carolina a kind of regional theater that he
liked to call "symphonic drama"—presentations of the history and folklore
of whites and Blacks alike that made use of music and dance as well as the
spoken word. But deeply American as he was, Green was not completely
alien to the German background of Kurt Weill and the Piscator *Schweik*,
for he had gone to Germany on a fellowship in the late twenties and had
even seen *The Threepenny Opera* there. He was a natural choice in some
ways, and he proved to be interested in the idea outlined by Clurman.

"When I returned to New York," Clurman goes on, "I advised
Cheryl Crawford and Weill that Paul would be the right man for the
proposed musical play." By this time Cheryl Crawford, a great lover of
The Threepenny Opera and of good popular music in general, had become
the foremost enthusiast among the three directors about the prospect of
doing a Weill work. She immediately got in touch with Green and sent
him a copy of the translation of the Piscator *Schweik*. Green proved ready
for the time being to drop his college play, which was having problems,
and to devote himself immediately to the new project. The prospect of
Green's participation evidently caused Clurman and Strasberg to put
aside some of the doubts they had been having, and since a good new play
was still lacking with which to open the Group's season in the fall, all eyes
were now turned upon this one as a possibility. There was not a moment
to lose. Weill also was eager to get started on what promised to be his first
American work, and by the beginning of May he and Cheryl Crawford
were on their way down to Chapel Hill.

They traveled separately: Cheryl Crawford went with a friend by
car, and Kurt was brought by Group members to Pennsylvania Station
and put onto the train. His first sally into the American heartlands was
being made all alone. Paul Green was always to remember this event
vividly. He waited at the station for the appointed train, but Weill did not
get off it when it arrived, and Green finally returned home in bewilder-
ment. At last the telephone rang. It was Weill, calling from a remote
farmhouse, to which he had wandered after getting off mistakenly at a
siding that had not been used as a passenger stop for years. Green
ascertained the spot, got into his car, and drove to it. The early North
Carolina summer had already struck, and he found his prospective

collaborator waiting outside in the hot sun, forlorn, bareheaded, and wearing a baggy suit that, as it turned out, was to be his sole attire all the rest of the summer. Green sensed that this was a man in some financial need but also admired his courage as he got into the car quietly and without complaint.

Cheryl Crawford soon was there—she and Weill stayed in rooms at the Carolina Inn, just off the university campus—and the three of them got to work. Developing the character of their American Schweik, whom they would take through the trenches with the American Expeditionary Force, they rummaged through German sources for thematic ideas and American ones for local and period flavor. "In our search," Cheryl Crawford writes, "we discussed *The Good Soldier Schweik*, Buechner's *Wozzeck* and *The Captain of Koepenick* for general inspiration." The outcome of their efforts also suggests that they took a close look at Ernst Toller's plays, especially *Transfiguration* and *Hoppla! Wir leben*. But in any case, they soon left the *Schweik* of both Jaroslav Hašek and Erwin Piscator far behind, though that basic idea remained. "We spent days at the local library reading newspaper articles about the period and even *Dere Mable*, a popular novel of letters from a private soldier. At night we talked, and soon a rough scenario began to evolve."

After about a week Weill and Cheryl Crawford returned to New York with their scenario, and Green began working on a finished draft of the play. The plan was that Green would send completed portions to New York every week or so, and Weill in turn would write back comments and suggestions in addition to making the first sketches of his score. Kurt began sorting out his plans for the next few months. Since it looked as though the play could be ready for summer rehearsals, he decided not to renew his lease at Louveciennes, but instead made plans for a little working vacation with Lenya and Cheryl Crawford at Virginia Beach, where they could keep in close contact with Green and perhaps even see him. Things were not destined to go so smoothly, however. Clurman and Strasberg read the scenario that was brought back from Chapel Hill, and they were utterly dissatisfied. The play did not seem to them to be taking feasible shape, and they began seeking out other scripts to consider for their first offering in the fall.

This could have thrown the project into disarray, but Cheryl Crawford handled the situation with astute diplomacy. Convinced that a few pages of finished text and some Weill music would put the whole matter in a different light, she seems to have said nothing at first about the dissension in her letters to Green; she merely urged him to start sending passages to Weill as soon as possible. Going to Virginia Beach by herself at the end of May—evidently Kurt and Lenya were not sure what they wanted to do with themselves at this very confusing moment—she even wrote to Green from there that everyone who had seen the scenario was very enthusiastic. This was at any rate true of the Group *actors*, some of whom gathered at around this time to hear Weill describe the play to them and perform at the piano some of the music he had written for it. Indeed, their response was so enthusiastic that Strasberg and Clurman began to be interested in the project again.

By the beginning of the summer both a Clifford Odets script and one by John Howard Lawson had been considered by the Group and turned down, so that there once again seemed to be no alternative to the American *Schweik* as a candidate for the fall opening. Cheryl Crawford triumphantly gathered her composer and her playwright to finish their work in a truly Group-like communal arrangement. It was an established practice of the Group Theatre to stay at a resort each summer, earning their keep by giving performances and at the same time getting fresh air and rehearsal space for their projects. This year they put up at Pine Brook, an adult summer camp near Trumbull, Connecticut; and Cheryl Crawford, Paul Green, Kurt Weill, and Lotte Lenya took cottages there about a mile away from the others. Kurt, who had eagerly been doing research into American local color for weeks, "worked at his piano below my bedroom," according to Cheryl Crawford's recollection, "so the songs were drilled into my head day and night. We called the script *Johnny Johnson* after our hero, an ordinary simple soldier who hated war and tried to stop it. The story was told in terms of vaudeville, fantasy and poetry."

Rehearsals had started by the beginning of September, but there still were unresolved problems. The script was not even finished; Green had gone back to Chapel Hill at the beginning of August and had been sending song lyrics from there to Weill, who frantically composed music to them as they arrived. "As the script had only just begun to be presentable," Clurman writes, "backing for the play had not yet been secured. It was to be our most expensive production"—for, among other things, thirteen elaborate sets were being designed for it by Donald Oenslager.

Worst of all, however, were the problems within the organization itself. The fact was that the Group, already past its peak, was having artistic, financial, political, and temperamental difficulties. Among the actors, a demoralizing atmosphere had been created by the fact that Hollywood was making attractive offers—and that a few had already yielded to this temptation, considered by some of the others to be virtually from the devil. This atmosphere had been further exacerbated by dabbling in radical politics and flirtations with the Communist Party on the part of some of the actors. As for the directors, these three powerful personalities were beginning to be at odds with one another. They recently had undergone some crises in their relations with one another, and now a new one arose over the question of which of them should direct *Johnny Johnson*. Cheryl Crawford was not in the running because she was functioning as its producer and had enough to do in that capacity; besides, of the three, she had been the least successful as an actual stage director and was not really interested in that line of work. She seems to have favored Strasberg as director from the start, but Strasberg may still have had too many doubts about the project. In any case the assignment devolved upon Clurman, who had enjoyed great success the previous year as the director of *Awake and Sing*.

But Clurman, who was very busy in his capacity as managing director of the Group, wondered if he could do the job. He seems to have wanted it and not wanted it at the same time, while Strasberg and in particular Cheryl Crawford became more and more doubtful about his suitability to direct the Group's first musical and in many ways its most difficult production to date. In the atmosphere of growing uncertainty, Clurman asked Weill one day whom he would like to see directing the play, and the composer replied, "*You*, of course"; but Clurman sensed that he really wanted Strasberg. Resisting the inevitable a moment longer, Clurman at one point proposed two of the Group's actors as possible candidates for the assignment: his wife Stella Adler, who was in fact to direct a revival of *Johnny Johnson* some two decades later, and Elia Kazan, one day to be among the most honored directors in the United States; but they were turned down by the others as being too inexperienced. Clurman finally stepped down one day and Strasberg took over the direction of the play, but the changeover was made in a climate of acrimony from which their relations never were to recover, and which did not bode well for the health of *Johnny Johnson* either.

There also was some unease in the orchestra pit, which was mainly—and untypically—Weill's fault, a sign of his extreme nervousness at the preparation of his first American play. The job of music director had been given to Lehman Engel, a twenty-six-year-old composer and conductor who, through his friendship with Aaron Copland, had become known to Clurman and other members of the Group. Engel was eventually to become one of Broadway's most sought-after conductors, but this was his first Broadway show and Weill, who approved of this choice of music director, nevertheless remained nervous about him. The circumstances of their first meeting had not helped matters any. Kurt and Lenya had gone to visit the show's prospective conductor at his Greenwich Village bachelor apartment one afternoon, and Engel, who "did not know that Mrs. Weill was Lotte Lenya," had committed a gaffe. "In my desperate need to make conversation I spoke of The Threepenny Opera with sincere enthusiasm but added that the female singer on a recording I had was terrible! The Weills smiled indulgently and said that I must have the French recording. No, I persisted, I had the German one. It was then that I found out that the singer was Lotte Lenya, my guest!" Engel goes on to explain in his autobiography that he had not yet learned to understand that kind of singing, and that he was to become deeply appreciative of Lenya's performances in later years; but whatever explanation he may have offered in that moment of embarrassment, the fact that he had conducted the first American performance of Der Jasager—three years earlier, at the Neighborhood Playhouse of the Henry Street Settlement, with the Group's Sanford Meisner as its stage director—was very much in his favor from the composer's viewpoint.

Still, during rehearsals, Weill hardly let the young conductor out of his sight. Engel was never to forget the many times that the composer stood right behind him calling out tempos: "Faster, faster!" he would cry in his German accent, and then, "No, slower!" Engel was made so nervous that, on the last night of rehearsals, Strasberg was to make a special point of going to him and saying: "Stop thinking of what somebody has told you about the music. It is yours now. Give a performance!" Weill's unusually tense state of mind also impressed itself upon Morris Stonzek, a good friend of Engel's who had obtained through him the job of orchestra contractor for the show—the man who obtains the musicians and forms an important liaison between them, the composer, and the arranger—in this case the latter two being the same person. Stonzek was to recall years later that he had hired a very good rehearsal pianist who, evidently after a hard week, happened to be rather tired on the day of the show's first run-through. After it was over, Weill took Stonzek aside and said:

"I think we should get another pianist. He's not interested in my music."

"Why do you say that?" Stonzek asked.

"He yawned."

Stonzek was so exasperated at this that he thought of quitting the show, but Engel persuaded him to stay on. The pianist was not fired and everything worked out all right. Stonzek, who was to work with Weill on every one of his shows from then on with the exception of *The Eternal Road*, was never to see him behaving so touchily again.

On the production side, money was raised, and things seemed to go better during rehearsals for as long as they were held, under a temporary arrangement, at a small theater called the Belmont. "Here the production seemed charming," Clurman writes: "informal, unpretentious and sweet. But no house was available to us now except the Forty-fourth Street Theatre, one of the largest on Broadway. I knew the large house would be a disadvantage; it proved to be disastrous. Our actors' voices sounded so small they were occasionally inaudible; Donald Oenslager's sets, which had been designed larger than I anticipated, now appeared monstrous; the performances now looked amateurish." The large theater brought out one difficulty in particular from which the show was never fully to recover— that of the singing. Weill had made it clear from the outset that he meant to write music for actors with untrained voices, as he had done for *The Threepenny Opera;* but the Group Theatre cast seems to have had special disabilities as far as his songs were concerned. He had begun coaching and drilling them at Pine Brook, during the summer, but their musical performances were, with one or two exceptions, never to be wholly satisfactory. When Paul Green first heard them, he had felt that they should give up full-throated singing and try for a kind of recitative style—the sort of thing Rex Harrison was to bring off so successfully in *My Fair Lady* twenty years later. But he could not convince anyone of this course.

The first previews, held at the beginning of November, went badly. Clurman describes them as "the most distressing experiences I have ever gone through in the theatre. . . . After the first five minutes of the first preview half the audience left. By the end of the performance there were no more than twenty people in the auditorium." Eddie Dowling, the owner of the theater, thought that the production should be dropped; friends of the Group sent in letters urging the same thing. "In a way," Clurman goes on, "I did not understand what had happened or what was happening. I felt as if everything was giving way underneath me—not only the production, but six years of work." Nevertheless, belief in the play persisted, and rehearsals and revisions went on. "At such times," Clurman reflects, "everyone becomes superstitious, 'expert,' confused, and weary all at the same moment. The director, especially when he is as sensitive a person as Strasberg, becomes a veritable sacrifice. Many of the musical numbers were cut—in a smaller theatre they need not have been—but what becomes most damaged in the process of saving a production in jeopardy is people's psyches. At one point during a midnight conference Strasberg shouted: 'I know more about acting than any of you,' and made feverishly irrelevant and disparaging references to the script and the music. As usual under such circumstances, everyone was patient and brave; but sanity and clarity never returned."

Yet it seems to have been above all Strasberg's will that held things together, and in a few days there was a marked improvement. It was with fairly hopeful spirits in spite of everything that the show's creators and cast went into opening night on November 19, 1936.

One of the problems Lee Strasberg never quite resolved concerning *Johnny Johnson* was, in effect, the one pertaining to many Kurt Weill efforts: was this a musical or a play with music? Strasberg, who eventually thought of it as a "musical play"—and, as such, the first in the history of the American theater—was to admit years later that he had treated it more as "play" than as "musical" and that he had given it too naturalistic a bent as a result. But the fact remained that, to anyone who was prepared to listen, Kurt Weill was providing what would prove to be one of the most significant scores he ever wrote, a milestone between Germany and the United States that seems consciously intended to tell the world both where he was coming from and where he was going.

This purpose is made dramatically clear by the overture, which, after a few opening chords, suddenly breaks into a familiar theme: it is "The Song of the Liquor Dealer" from *Happy End*. We have already noted that this melody was intended as a piece of imitation Americana the first time it was written. But the spirit had then been one of parody, in the fiercely ironic Brechtian vein; whereas the recapitulation of it now, though not without humor—Johnny Johnson is a comic character as well as a mildly sentimental hero—has taken on a new mellowness in the treatment, a serene acceptance. When the theme first appears in the overture, it seems to be a signature—Kurt Weill, formerly of Berlin, proclaims his presence to the American audience—but later, during the play itself, it makes a few brief appearances until at last it fades away and yields up to the main theme, "Johnny's Song," which is musically related to it (and which had, in fact, been composed as a melody by itself in Berlin). "The Song of the Liquor Dealer" thereby becomes, in this context, more than just a signature: it is a bridge from Germany to Johnny Johnson's America.

The play begins on an open field outside a small town, where the mayor presides over a ceremony at which a monument to peace, carved by the town's young tombstone-maker Johnny Johnson, is about to be unveiled. (Much of this opening ceremony is done as a rhythmically spoken recitative over a musical background; and since this scene, in fact, had undergone some late-stage revisions, it would seem that here, at least, Paul Green's recommendation concerning how to perform the songs was put into practice.) But the date is April 6, 1917, and even the praises of peace, pompous and agitated, have strangely jingoistic undertones. Minny Belle, beloved by Johnny, steps forward to sing a "Democracy March" about Washington, Lincoln, and Woodrow Wilson that lays some stress on warfare and carnage, and her Grandpa Joe sings—or recites—a musical reminiscence of the fierce fighting he took part in at Chickamauga Hill during the Civil War. A few moments later word arrives that war has been declared—the lanky, barefoot boy on a bicycle who brings this news is accompanied by parody music reminiscent of that of the "Glorious Messenger" in *The Threepenny Opera*'s last finale—and the whole atmosphere does not so much change as find its true content. Minny Belle and her friends immediately sing a new version of the "Democracy March," with the words "War, War, War" intoned in place of the former "Peace, Peace, Peace"—this music, by the way, is another vintage Kurt Weill march, which, though performed satirically here, could serve quite well at an Independence Day parade. Johnny expresses his doubt about war, while Minny Belle and the young mineral-water bottler, Anguish Howington, who is Johnny's chief rival for her love, display patriotic enthusiasm. Left alone and bewildered at the end of the scene, Johnny pulls the drawstring of the cover on his now forgotten monument and exposes the word "Peace" forlornly inscribed on it.

Johnny continues to court Minny Belle at her home, where he is not well received. Minny Belle's widowed mother, Aggie, whom we see singing sadly about her lot in life to the rhythm of her sewing machine, does not like the simplehearted young tombstone-maker and much prefers the craven Anguish Howington, who she knows will make good in the world. When Johnny is alone with Minny Belle, they recall an old love song they had seen in a book, and as Minny Belle sings it—here Weill does a nice pastiche of sentimental nineteenth-century Americana, a result of his researches—Johnny almost believes she is in love with him. But she remains largely cold to him until, reading in the newspaper that his beloved Wilson has pronounced this "a war to end war," he decides to enlist in such a cause. Meanwhile, Aggie plots with Anguish Howington their course for getting Anguish medically disqualified from military service.

After a brief interlude of parody military music, Johnny goes to enlist. We meet the town recruiting officer—a vain young man clearly inspired by the captain whom Wozzeck shaves in the Büchner play and the Berg opera—reading a cheap magazine and singing aloud to his colleagues a sleazy love story from its pages: his song is a tango, and this seems once again to be a signature on the part of the composer from Berlin. The song is occasionally drowned out by the strains of the "Democracy March," being sung by the crowds out in the street: Weill is having fun here with two sides of his own identity. Johnny is examined and at first rejected, because his highly individualistic ways of answering the questions on the absurd army intelligence test persuade the examiners that he is some kind of imbecile. But when he gets into a brawl with a gigantic soldier at the recruiting office and knocks him down easily, they decide to take him.

The next scene shows an imaginatively conceived New York harbor, with ships passing in the night and an illuminated Statue of Liberty in the background. Johnny, in uniform, is seen on the deck of a troopship heading for Europe, and as he gazes in wonderment at the Statue, he recites a soliloquy to it over a musical background—an American offspring of Busoni's Arlecchino, he does not actually *sing* until the end of the play—in which he swears to comport himself honorably in this war to end wars. He goes to sleep on the deck and then, in strange, dark tones, the Statue of Liberty sings back to him: she is just a thing of stone, she says, without a heart, and yet while her million-year sleep goes on, men foolishly persist in dying in her name. It is a simple irony, but the music goes deep. It has a primal quality that reminds one—in general feeling, though not in musical content—of the passage in *Siegfried* when Erda rises from the depths and sings to Wotan of her lot. This is as Wagnerian a moment as one can find in the music of Kurt Weill, although by the end of the "Song of the Goddess" his trademark distinctly returns: for her final refrain is that of a "single" he had written back in Paris, with lyrics by Roger Fernay, called "Youkali." In that song Youkali is the land of our dreams and desires, but the refrain tells us with great lyricism and longing that it doesn't exist; and now, to the same melody, the Statue is telling us something quite similar. The melody is so beautiful, however, that for a moment one thinks one is in that better world all the same.

The next scene is like a piece of German expressionism; it could be straight out of Ernst Toller's *Transfiguration*, which this play parallels in some ways, including in its transitions back and forth between naturalistic and surrealistic effects. We see a battlefield in France, with the dark silhouettes of burnt trees and the twisted figures of passing soldiers. A column of wounded Frenchmen marches slowly by, and they sing of their pain: "*Nous sommes blessés.*" This haunting and powerful song, which hurls a few more challenges at the borders of tonality than most of the other numbers in *Johnny Johnson*, has a Russian feeling and bears affinities with some of the moments in the score Prokofiev was to compose two years later for the film *Alexander Nevsky*. It is accompanied in the orchestra by a strange, almost dancelike lilt that suggests the limping of the soldiers. As the grim column passes on, Johnny suddenly appears, fresh and optimistic on his way to battle, and calls out Pershing's famous—and probably apocryphal—remark: "Lafayette, we are here!"

In the trenches, Johnny is annoyingly brave and eager to volunteer for every mission. Some of the national and local types in the trenches are parodied: the British soldiers, sitting unperturbed over their afternoon tea, sing a "Tea Song," and a soldier from Texas sings a reminiscence of the Rio Grande that is Weill's broad parody of the songs from cowboy movies. Then the soldiers go to sleep and suddenly, after Johnny briefly dreams of Minny Belle singing the old love song to him, three great cannons push up into view from beyond the trench and lower and aim themselves straight out toward the audience, over the heads of the sleeping soldiers. This is a purely surrealistic effect, for out of the mouths of the cannons comes a weird lullaby—music that contains some of the most avant-garde harmonies of the score, yet constructed around a melody that is purposely, ironically sweet. The cannons sing of the deadly use that will be made of them the next day, mourning in passing the better uses to which their metal might have been put. The next morning Johnny volunteers to go out and get a sniper who has been causing trouble.

We now see a shell-battered churchyard, with a large hollow wooden statue of Christ in the center. As Johnny crawls onstage in the grass, the orchestra commemorates the battered statue with the "Music of the Stricken Redeemer," a pure string ensemble that is really a brief chamber music interlude. While Johnny hides, the German sniper appears and sneaks inside the statue through a trapdoor in its rear; then, through a hole in its breast, he pushes the muzzle of his rifle until it "comes to rest on the outstretched hand of the Redeemer." Johnny leaps up, throws a lasso around the statue and captures the sniper. But the frightened German soldier turns out to be only sixteen years old, and he and Johnny strike up a friendship. Johnny hands him some clippings of Woodrow Wilson speeches and lets him go back to spread these messages of peace among his comrades. At that moment Captain Valentine—the vain recruiting officer and tango-singer—arrives and tries to shoot the retreating German soldier; Johnny prevents him from hitting his target, but in the scuffle he is nipped on the behind by a sudden volley of German fire. With this embarrassing wound he is sent to the hospital.

Johnny wakes up in a hospital ward—we are again reminded of Toller's play—and a pretty French nurse is by his bedside. Her song, "Mon Ami, My Friend," which sounds musically like another bit of French pastiche left over from Weill's workbench at Louveciennes, offers Johnny a little more than medical comfort, but he is still dreaming of Minny Belle and he resists her advances: surely this scene is poking a little fun at *A Farewell to Arms*. Some laughing gas is brought into the ward to combat Johnny's dour mood, but he refuses it; when he sees its enlivening effect on a lugubrious woman of charity after it goes off in her face, however, he remarks that it's a "pity they don't use laughing gas in the war instead of poison gas" and gets an idea. When everyone leaves, he takes a cylinder of his new secret weapon and sneaks out of the hospital.

The scene changes to a meeting of the Allied High Command. The generals and ministers planning the next great offensive are presented in a farcical manner, speaking forth their arguments "with puppet pomp and solemn precision." The music turns into a comic march that resembles the "Parade of the Wooden Soldiers." Then Johnny enters—having used his cylinder effectively on all the guards—makes a speech for peace before the shocked gathering, and lets loose his laughing gas. For a few moments the officers and statesmen are transformed: they laugh, they are loving, they sing and dance and declare that they want peace. Johnny gets them to sign a cease-fire proclamation. Armed with this, and by now wearing a general's cap and overcoat, he runs off to spread the news just as the effects of the gas begin to wear off among his victims.

Johnny gets to the trenches in his general's disguise—here the story makes a bow to *The Captain of Köpenick*—and orders the cessation of hostilities. A celebration ensues, and the German soldiers come over from the opposite trenches and join in. But officers soon arrive from the High Command and order the resumption of the war, and the German soldiers rush back to their own trenches in a shower of bullets. Then, as the chaplains from the German and American sides are heard reciting, in their respective languages, the prayer "In Times of Tumult and War," we get a series of tableaux of battle before our eyes, scenes of cruelty, agony, and

Clockwise, from top left: *Kurt Weill's paternal grandparents,
Nathan and Jeanette Hochstetter Weill of Kippenheim; and his
parents, Cantor Albert and Emma Ackermann Weill.*   JULIE SONDER

Above: *Kurt Weill at around fifteen years of age with young Peter
Bing, the son of Albert Bing, his first composition teacher.*   ALICE BING

Above: *Ferruccio Busoni (center) in 1922, surrounded by four members of his master class in composition—(from left) Kurt Weill, Walther Geiser, Luc Balmer, and Wladimir Vogel.*   H. H. STUCKENSCHMIDT

Left: *Georg Kaiser.*   WIDE WORLD PHOTOS

Right: Bertolt Brecht in around 1928.

Below: At a rehearsal of the Mahagonny Songspiel, *with the boxing ring set up and a Caspar Neher projection in the rear. Kurt Weill is standing at the far left, with Neher and Paul Hindemith immediately to the right of him. Bertolt Brecht is standing at the far right, and of the two women sitting in the ring, Lotte Lenya is the one on the left. This is one of very few photographs showing Brecht and Weill together.*

Above: *Lotte Lenya as Jennie and Rudolf Forster as Mackie in the G. W. Pabst film of* The Threepenny Opera, *1931.*   MUSEUM OF
MODERN ART

Left: *The last scene of* The Threepenny Opera, *at the Theater am Schiffbauerdamm, Berlin, 1928. From the left: Erich Ponto as Peachum, Roma Bahn as Polly, Harald Paulsen as Mackie Messer, and Kurt Gerron as Tiger Brown.*   ULLSTEIN BILDERDIENST

Right: *Meyer Weisgal and Max Reinhardt plan* The Eternal Road. THEATRE AND MUSIC COLLECTION, MUSEUM OF THE CITY OF NEW YORK

Below: *A cartoon by B. F. Dolbin in the* New York Post, *January 8, 1937, just before the opening of* The Eternal Road. *Depicted are Franz Werfel and Kurt Weill at the top, Norman Bel Geddes, Max Reinhardt, and Meyer Weisgal at the bottom.* REPRINTED FROM THE NEW YORK POST

LAUNCHING "THE ETERNAL ROAD"

Bottom: *The three Group Theatre directors at Dover Furnace, New York, in the summer of 1932. From the left: Harold Clurman, Cheryl Crawford, and Lee Strasberg.* HAROLD CLURMAN

Top: *Paul Green*.   PAUL GREEN

Bottom: *The cannon scene in* Johnny Johnson. *Russell Collins, as Johnny, is lying in the foreground, center*.   LIBRARY AND MUSEUM OF THE PERFORMING ARTS, LINCOLN CENTER

Opposite top: *The last scene from* Knickerbocker Holiday. *Walter Huston, as Peter Stuyvesant, is ordering the town councillors to hang Brom Broeck, played by Richard Kollmar. Tina Tienhoven, played by Jeanne Madden, can be seen between Brom and Stuyvesant*.   THEATRE AND MUSIC COLLECTION, MUSEUM OF THE CITY OF NEW YORK

Opposite bottom: *A scene from* Knickerbocker Holiday. *Walter Huston as Peter Stuyvesant and Jeanne Madden as Tina Tienhoven are at the center, with the Dutch maidens on either side of them*.   THEATRE AND MUSIC COLLECTION, MUSEUM OF THE CITY OF NEW YORK

Above: *Moss Hart (left) and Ira Gershwin join Oscar Levant (right) and others for a bite at Lindy's during rehearsals of* Lady in the Dark.   CULVER PICTURES

Opposite top: Lady in the Dark: *Liza Elliott's office at* Allure *magazine. From the left are Margaret Dale as Maggie Grant, Danny Kaye as Russell Paxton, Evelyn Wyckoff as Miss Foster, Macdonald Carey as Charley Johnson, Victor Mature as Randy Curtis, and Gertrude Lawrence as Liza.*   THEATRE AND MUSIC COLLECTION, MUSEUM OF THE CITY OF NEW YORK

Opposite bottom: *The "Circus Dream" from* Lady in the Dark. *Gertrude Lawrence and Victor Mature are at the far left; Danny Kaye is at the far right, and Bert Lytell is standing just below him.*   VANDAMM COLLECTION

Right: *Ogden Nash (left) and S. J. Perelman working on* One Touch of Venus. CULVER PICTURES

Below: *Kurt Weill at the piano rehearsing the principals of* One Touch of Venus—*(from left) Mary Martin, John Boles, Paula Laurence, and Kenny Baker.* CULVER PICTURES

Above: *Mary Martin singing "That's Him."*
VANDAMM COLLECTION

Right: *Maurice Abravanel in 1945.*
CULVER PICTURES

Kurt Weill at Brook House around 1946, with Woolly lying in the rear. ASCAP

Right: *The three creators of* Street Scene—*(from left) Kurt Weill, Elmer Rice, and Langston Hughes.* CULVER PICTURES

Below: Street Scene: *Brian Sullivan as Sam Kaplan and Anne Jeffreys as Rose Maurrant.* THEATRE AND MUSIC COLLECTION, MUSEUM OF THE CITY OF NEW YORK

Left: *Kurt Weill (left) and Alan Jay Lerner at work on* Love Life. CULVER PICTURES

Below: *The "Green-Up Time" sequence in* Love Life. *Nanette Fabray is at the center, Ray Middleton is standing in the doorway to the left.* THEATRE AND MUSIC COLLECTION, MUSEUM OF THE CITY OF NEW YORK

Left: *From the left, Maxwell Anderson, Rouben Mamoulian, and Kurt Weill at a rehearsal of* Lost in the Stars. CULVER PICTURES

Below: *Inez Matthews as Irina and Todd Duncan as Stephen Kumalo in* Lost in the Stars. THEATRE AND MUSIC COLLECTION, MUSEUM OF THE CITY OF NEW YORK

Top: *Brook House, the Weill home in New City, New York, as it looks today.* PHOTO BY BEVERLY SANDERS

Above: *Kurt Weill's grave at Mount Repose cemetery, Haverstraw, New York.* PHOTO BY BEVERLY SANDERS

death, shown in various flashes of light as the orchestra sounds terrifying
chords. Weill also makes ironic use of a Hammond organ for the prayer in
this sequence so redolent of the spirit of German expressionism and
antiwar drama. At the end of the sequence Johnny is arrested, and we
then see him on the deck of a troopship again, this time returning to New
York harbor; a military prisoner, Johnny does not even look at the Statue
now. He is sent to a state mental hospital, which is presided over by a
parody figure of a psychiatrist—he sings an ironic ballad about his
profession—who may well be more insane than any of his charges. The
doctor has summoned Minny Belle—who, in a characteristic display of
callousness, arrives with Anguish Howington and furthermore asks
Johnny why he is back when the war is not over yet—but it is only to
inform her of the decision of the army "psychological experts" that Johnny
must stay in the hospital. She cries, but she goes off with Anguish, who
comments that "an asylum is where he belongs."

The next scene shows Johnny, still in the hospital ten years later, as
the organizer of a kind of mock United States Senate among the patients,
debating an idea resembling that of the League of Nations. At their
meeting, the desire for peace is ardently expressed, and the implication is
that the participants are really saner than anyone in the bellicose world
outside: this idea, borrowed in part from Toller's *Hoppla! Wir leben*, has
had one of its most notable recent reappearances in Philippe de Broca's
popular film *King of Hearts*. The scene provides Weill with the opportunity
to do two pastiches of nineteenth-century American church hymns, sung
by the members of Johnny's earnest debating society. Anguish
Howington, now a wealthy benefactor of the hospital, visits this scene of
his charities, and when Johnny buttonholes him and asks about Minny
Belle, Anguish coldly informs him that "Miss Tompkins did me the honor
some years ago of accepting my hand in marriage."

Johnny is at last released from the hospital, and he reluctantly goes
forth into the world. He becomes a street hawker, selling toys from a tray
hung around his neck. We see him one evening encountering the young
son of Anguish and Minny Belle—she stands off in the distance, and we
are not sure whether she recognizes Johnny—and, when the boy expresses
disappointment at the fact that he does not have any toy soldiers to sell,
Johnny tries to discourage his childish military ideals. There are rumors of
another war in the offing, and Johnny, left alone again, hears the
"Democracy March" being played in the distance. He is deeply saddened
by it all; but then he stirs himself up in a Chaplin-like gesture of
reaffirmation and goes off singing "Johnny's Song" for the first time: a

wistful reflection on Johnny's undying hope for mankind, it is one of
Weill's most beautiful songs. Musically, the entire score has built up to it,
and it completes the synthesis of European and American sounds that has
been suggested by the action and shifting locales of the play itself, as well
as by the composer's experience.

"Opening night was the greatest shock of all," Harold Clurman writes at
the end of his account of *Johnny Johnson*'s agonies of preparation. "The
performance went smoothly, and the audience appeared wildly enthusiastic. It looked as if our disgrace had been converted into a hit." Suggesting
a certain general surprise at the way the stage business worked without
mishap, Cheryl Crawford writes: "The three huge cannons pushed out to
the audience over the top of the trenches on time, singing sweetly to the
sleeping soldiers. The large Statue of Liberty appeared promptly to sing a
lovely song to Johnny as he stood on board a troop ship leaving for France.
The audience's response to the show was excellent, and the three
directors, barely able to stand, were, as Lee would say, 'flabbergasted.'"
Eddie Dowling, who had recommended the closing of the show only four
days earlier, could not believe his eyes at the improvement. But it should
be pointed out that, in addition to the well-known talents of the authors,
the director, and the set designer, the production had in its favor some of
the finest acting talents of the time. Although Russell Collins and Phoebe
Brand, who played Johnny and Minny Belle, are less well known today,
they were accompanied by players whose names have since become
celebrated: Jules (later John) Garfield as the youthful German sniper;
Morris Carnovsky as the somewhat mad psychiatrist (whose performance
of the "Psychiatry Song" was considered widely to have been the best
singing of the evening); Luther Adler as a general of the High Command;
Elia Kazan as a Jewish soldier in the trenches (who, according to one
critic, duplicated "the rhythms of the Descent from the Cross" while
sleeping during the cannons' song); Lee J. Cobb as the medical examiner at
the recruiting office; Sanford Meisner as the vain Captain Valentine;
Robert Lewis as the mayor; Albert Van Dekker (later known in the
movies without the *Van*) as a corporal in the trenches; Roman Bohnen as
Grandpa Joe; Paul Mann as the German chaplain; and so on. Members of
the audience who went in expecting a conventional musical may have been
perplexed by what they saw and heard, but they could not have been
unmoved.

    But the morning after the opening, as Clurman puts it, "brought still
another shock. The press seemed very bad." Clurman stresses the *seemed*

because the reviewers were really quite respectful, but their reservations were so pronounced as to be severely damaging to the play's commercial prospects. Brooks Atkinson wrote in *The New York Times* that the play was "part fantasy, part musical satire, part symbolic poetry in the common interests of peace; and also, one is compelled to add, part good and part bad, since new forms cannot be created overnight. There are many interludes in Mr. Green's work when both the satire and the idealism wither away to restless emptiness. Although Mr. Green is an honest and exultant poet, he is not a virtuoso theatre man." Thus ends Atkinson's first paragraph; his second one begins: "Having given the Broadway flaneur fair warning in that last sentence, this column proposes from this point on to celebrate a sincere and generally exalting attempt to put on the stage an imaginative portrait of recent history." The rest of the review is an appreciation of a work of obvious high quality, whatever its flaws; but the damage had been done—and other reviews did the same.

In *The New Yorker* the following week, Robert Benchley, who had even seen one of the disastrous early rehearsals, made an effort to come to the rescue:

> Since *Johnny Johnson* is the first imaginative and exciting entry in a season of old, dead-tired waxworks, I think it ought to be given a break or two. My God, if we don't grab onto something really big when it comes along, even if it does have its flaws, the theatre may go right on as it has started this year. . . . At times the humor goes fairly pre-school, as in the laughing gas scene at the Council of the High Command, but for the most part it is real, double-play satire which reaches its high point in an entirely adventitious scene in which Johnny Johnson confounds a psychiatrist merely by being sane. This scene is beautifully played by Morris Carnovsky as the head of the mental retreat, with Russell Collins, as the hero, carrying on in the same forthright, honest manner which serves him so well through the entire piece.

But Benchley did not save the day, and *Johnny Johnson* was to close late in January after sixty-eight performances.

When asked by one of his colleagues how he felt about the fate of his first American work, Weill replied: "How many plays that have survived were hits in their day?" He was quite ready to go on.

The First Sally into Hollywood

 *The Eternal Road* finally opened on January 7, 1937, more than a year after the date originally planned. Its cost had risen to nearly half a million dollars, but Meyer Weisgal had obtained the additional funds from various ardent supporters of Jewish causes. Much of the original cast had been rehired, but there were some inevitable changes. Young Sidney Lumet, in later years to be known as a film director, was to have played little Isaac being taken to the sacrifice; but during the long delay, as Weisgal writes, "his voice changed and he sprouted hair on his upper lip." Lumet was moved to the synagogue sequences, and Dickie van Patten played young Isaac instead. Sam Jaffe was originally to have played Abraham, but the role was no longer available by the time he returned to the cast, and he too was moved to the synagogue; there, in the role of "the Adversary," the bitter opponent of all of the congregation's highest ideals, he was so good that many viewers feared he was throwing the play's spiritual message off balance. Lotte Lenya went on in the role of Moses' sister, Miriam, for which she had been hired back in the fall of 1935.

The production's history of troubles continued down to the last minute: on the afternoon of the scheduled opening, fire department inspectors arrived and, finding many violations in the enormous set, decided the show could not go on. Weisgal made frantic efforts to reach Mayor Fiorello LaGuardia, who finally arrived in person. LaGuardia saw that there indeed were violations, but recognizing the implications of the investment at stake, solved the problem by assigning to the theater that night a detail of firemen with extinguishers in their hands. The required improvements would have to be made the very next day.

Weisgal has described the long-awaited moment. "I got to the theatre about ten minutes before the opening. The air was vibrant with expectation, the more so as the packed audience had no idea what to expect. We had no curtain; all the effects were based on lighting—$60,000 worth of it. When the first lights went on dimly they revealed only the small synagogue, and the Jews, men, women and children, huddled together in fear—nothing more. Then the *chazan* . . . began to chant 'And God said to Abraham. . . .' Slowly the stage began to light up, revealing the depth and height of five broad ascending tiers, and finally, at the top, the choir—one hundred singers in the robes of angels, a heavenly host. The audience caught its breath and one could hear a collective 'A–ah.' I knew the play was made."

The "eternal road" or "road of promise" itself was there before one's eyes, winding upward and backward in stages from the pit of the theater to the proscenium vault, seeming to disappear into Heaven. "Here is a drama," Bosley Crowther wrote in *The New York Times* a few days later, "which is actually played upon a man-made mountainside—the whole erected upon what was formerly the conventional stage of a large opera house and upon which 200 performers can mass without difficult crowding." The biblical pageant was played on various parts of this road, which was wide enough to admit the whole cast in some places, and so narrow in others that it allowed only single individuals to pass; while the little synagogue was far below in an area that had once contained the orchestra pit and the first few rows of seats. From that point to the rear of the stage the theater had been completely rebuilt. The play, Crowther continued, "is so vast and so unorthodox in its construction that there is no room in the wings for the usual operating facilities. The huge switchboard is down in the basement, far removed from sight or sound of the set. . . . And the many ramps and apertures by which the actors enter and exit are so variously scattered and masked that the proper cueing of traffic through them would seem impossible." The whole thing was run by two stage managers in control booths, who telephoned cues to the various backstage areas throughout the performance.

As for the instrumental accompaniment, the original plan had been to record all of it by a special new RCA process, since there was no room in this setup for a conventional orchestra. Maurice Abravanel, who had recently arrived in New York, was to remember years later that Weill was "happy as a child" about this. "Think of it," he said to Abravanel. "No worries with those musicians who play wrong notes." But the American Federation of Musicians had intervened, and Weisgal had been forced to hire a live orchestra of sixteen instrumentalists, to be used in conjunction with the recorded score. This group, conducted by Isaac Van Grove, was stationed in a soundproof room high up on the left side of the auditorium, from where the occasional effects that it supplied were piped onto the stage, just as the recorded accompaniment was. Abravanel found the whole "canned music" effect rather unsatisfactory; but for less trained ears, this fault was overcome by the power of the musical effects onstage, especially those provided by the chorus.

The Eternal Road was well received, by audience and critics alike. Brooks Atkinson wrote: "Let it be said at once that the ten postponements are understood and forgiven. Out of the heroic stories of old Jewish history Max Reinhardt and his many assistants have evoked a glorious pageant of great power and beauty. Call it pageant, if you will, or call it opera, spectacle, fantasy or profound religious teaching, for it is all of these things in equal measure." Atkinson was particularly impressed with the music, which, he was to write years later, "was the most moving part of The Eternal Road. The composer of the raffish Threepenny Opera endowed The Eternal Road with religious exaltation."

By the middle of January, then, Weill had two shows running in New York, and Lenya was playing in one of them; but their financial worries were far from over. Johnny Johnson was clearly about to close; and though The Eternal Road was playing to good houses, it was still running up a deficit because of the enormous costs, so that its prospects for a long run were not good. Meanwhile, Kurt and Lenya wanted a satisfactory place to live: since the previous summer in Connecticut they had been sharing an apartment at Beekman Place with Cheryl Crawford and the actress Dorothy Patten, but even though it had two entirely separate wings and a splendid view of the East River, the arrangement obviously would not do for very long. Furthermore, Kurt's parents had just emigrated to Palestine, where cantors were by no means in short supply, and they were now in need of financial support from their children.

Weill hoped to do more collaborations with Paul Green, with whom he had developed a warm friendship in spite of a small unpleasantness shortly after the Johnny Johnson opening. Weill and Cheryl Crawford, convinced that "Johnny's Song" could be a hit as a sheet-music single, but dissatisfied with its lyric (as Green himself also was), had gone ahead and published it under the title "To Love You and to Lose You" with words by Edward Heyman. It was no hit anyway; and the gentle-natured Green overcame his annoyance soon enough that he and Weill were discussing a new idea by January.

Meanwhile, Kurt finally succumbed to the irresistible lure of Hollywood. In some ways Hollywood was becoming one of the world's foremost refuges for exiled Central European artists, many of whom, in great demand there, found its salaries and the Southern California climate to be far more persuasive reasons for settling in the United States than anything the Eastern cities could provide. Reinhardt was already there, along with a growing number of great names from the theater worlds of Berlin and Vienna—as well as a few that would only now become famous. Even some who were not interested in playing the Hollywood game were attracted by its atmosphere: Thomas and Heinrich Mann were to live there, and Arnold Schoenberg, making his home at Berkeley as a professor, would occasionally pass through. Musicians seemed especially fond of it: Igor Stravinsky was soon to settle down there; Hanns Eisler was already doing stints with the studios; and as for Erich Wolfgang Korngold, once a promising young composer of operas and concert music in Vienna, he had settled down at Warner Brothers after Reinhardt had brought him there to arrange Mendelssohn's music for *A Midsummer Night's Dream* and was soon to be a creator of symphonic accompaniments to various adventures of Errol Flynn. Weill was not eager to do sound-track scores, but Hollywood was a kind of home away from home, and a very lucrative one at that. He had even tried his hand at some sketches for a sound-track score the previous spring, while still in New York, when a producer had proposed that he do music for a film version of Richard Hughes's novel *A High Wind in Jamaica*; but this project did not get off the ground.

What specifically drew him to Hollywood at the end of January was his involvement in something of an emigration on the part of the Group Theatre. The Group was in disarray; but Walter Wanger, one of the outstanding independent Hollywood producers, had made an arrangement with it whereby he had the use of a number of its actors for a time. He also put Cheryl Crawford and Harold Clurman on his payroll; Lee Strasberg did not take part in this. While Cheryl Crawford remained in charge of the New York office, Clurman went to Hollywood, where he was to assist in the making of a film for which Clifford Odets was then writing the script. Weill was engaged to compose the score, but this was not his only prospective business in Hollywood. There was a possibility that Wanger would do a film of *Johnny Johnson*, with Burgess Meredith in the title role. Furthermore, the Los Angeles chapter of the Federal Theatre Project—which was the WPA activity in the performing arts—was planning a production of *Johnny Johnson* that spring, and Weill wanted to be on hand to supervise it.

Settling in at the Hollywood Roosevelt Hotel after the three-day train ride, Weill wasted no time in making contacts in the film capital. He sought out Max Reinhardt and discussed with him the new idea involving Paul Green, which Reinhardt had adumbrated sometime over the previous year. One of Reinhardt's traditional mainstays had been his production of the medieval *Everyman*, done in town squares and amphitheaters all over Europe and America. Now, looking for something to compensate for the box-office disaster that the film of *A Midsummer Night's Dream* had turned out to be, Reinhardt wanted to do an American *Everyman*, with a text by Paul Green and music by Kurt Weill. Green even had hopes of doing it as an all-Black production: this was an idea in the air, for the Federal Theatre Project in Chicago was planning to do an all-Black *Johnny Johnson* that spring—although, as it turned out, this was never to come off. In this first Hollywood get-together with Weill, Reinhardt also held out the hope that their American *Everyman* could be done as a film; when Weill got back to the hotel, he eagerly sat down and wrote Green a letter about this. In the long run the project was simply to fall by the wayside, like Reinhardt himself.

Two other people Weill sought out very soon after his arrival in Hollywood were George and Ira Gershwin, who had been living there since the previous summer to work on *Shall We Dance* with Fred Astaire and Ginger Rogers, and then on other films. George, a bachelor, along with Ira and his wife had rented a large Spanish-style house on North Roxbury Drive in Beverly Hills, where they held a regular Saturday night gathering for friends and colleagues. Among the frequent guests were such fine songwriters as Harold Arlen and Arthur Schwartz, as well as outstanding lyricists, including E. Y. "Yip" Harburg. Weill met Harburg at these gatherings, and he also met Bella and Samuel Spewack, the husband-and-wife writing team whose satirical play about Hollywood, *Boy Meets Girl*, was then still running on Broadway well over a year after its opening. Before long the chemistry of this particular combination of personalities had produced an idea for a play, to be written by the Spewacks and with songs by Harburg and Weill.

The story, of which the Spewacks soon prepared a treatment, concerned a Jewish theatrical troupe that, in better days, had regularly toured Germany giving musical comedies that they themselves had written. At the beginning of the play they have fled Nazi Germany and are on their way to the United States; they are first seen aboard ship trying to rehearse and prepare their favorite show for its new American career. But since they had been forced to leave the score behind in their hurried escape from Germany, they have to rely on memory to reconstitute the music. Most of it comes back quickly, but the waltz that always climaxed the show resists their recollections. In the end they put on their show in America, and the waltz gradually emerges through the course of it, coming out fully defined at last in the finale.

By the beginning of May this project had made such progress that it was submitted to the eminent producer Max Gordon back in New York, apparently in the hope that it might even have a fall opening. Weill had already begun writing some of the music, even though Harburg had not done many lyrics—a procedure that, though standard on Broadway, was most unusual for Kurt. Even in his "lighter" works, he had always worked in the manner of an opera composer, creating his music only after every word of the libretto was on paper—the libretto already, of course, containing the implications of his musical thought because he would always have collaborated on it. Broadway composers, on the other hand, though they usually developed their ideas in close contact with their lyricists, generally composed their melodies first and let the lyricists fit in the words later. It may be that Weill worked this way in the present instance—and he was rarely to do it again—because it was the way Harburg was used to doing things. The result was that the composer of the "popular oratorio" *The Eternal Road* and of the still slightly German *Johnny Johnson* was suddenly—way out in Hollywood—behaving more like a Broadway composer than he ever had before. The music for this show, never to be completed, apparently has not survived, so there is no way of judging to what extent Weill was approaching a Broadway sound in it. At least the musical ideas were still fairly unconventional: one of the songs, as Harburg was to recall many years later, was a letter from a member of the troupe to the "Aryan" occupant of his apartment back in Germany, asking how all the old things—the books, pictures, furniture, and so on—were doing. Certainly the play dealt with matters that bore far more than the usual relationship to the composer's sensibility.

Weill had by this time bought a second-hand Oldsmobile and settled into a rented cottage on Whitley Terrace in Hollywood itself. At first, according to a letter he sent Norman Bel Geddes at the end of February,

he had found Los Angeles "pretty dull"; but, as he then observed, it had
rained a lot since his arrival, and only the California sunshine could
compensate for what struck him as an "ugly city." No doubt the
acquisition of a car and the onset of spring weather changed this initial
impression, for he was to consider Los Angeles pleasant enough in years
to come. As for the studios, they fascinated him from the outset, even
though he remained skeptical of their artistic outlook and wrote to Cheryl
Crawford that they hated "any kind of enthusiasm." Amazed at how
much expertise there was in each separate department, he considered the
whole thing to be "a strange mixture of organization and confusion."
Judging the film capital as a whole in a letter to another friend, he wrote:
"It is the craziest place in the world and I have never seen so many worried
and unhappy people together."

But meanwhile, the projects he had come for were not materializing.
There was to be no *Johnny Johnson* film; and as for the one Clifford Odets
had been writing for Walter Wanger back in January, it had run into
complications. The original idea had been to do an adaptation of Ilya
Ehrenburg's novel *The Love of Jeanne Ney*, which had already been made
into a very fine German film by G. W. Pabst in 1927. The story, full of
the ambivalences of Ehrenburg's own peculiar history and personality,
sets the love affair of a French girl and a young Soviet agent against a
background of intrigues mainly in Paris; but there also are early scenes of
the Russian Revolution and Civil War that Pabst had made excellent use
of in his film. Wanger no doubt expected a similar epic scope from his own
film, which was to be directed by Lewis Milestone, who had done the
screen version of *All Quiet on the Western Front*. Its star was to be
Madeleine Carroll.

Working on the script together, Odets and Milestone—who often
found Kurt Weill at their side, making suggestions—soon had decided
that they wanted to update the background of the story from the Russian
Revolution to the Spanish Civil War. The conflict in Spain was almost a
year old and had already grown into an engagement between the
European-wide forces of fascism and communism. The Republic had
suffered major setbacks by now, and as men and women of various
politically progressive persuasions the world over made Spain the focus of
their concerns, Hollywood—teeming with exiles from European upheav-
als and with a morally ardent younger generation of American-born
writers and artists—became a prominent center of pro-Loyalist feeling in
America. Odets and Milestone came to envision their film—which they

had first renamed *Castles in Spain* and which they now proposed to call *The River Is Blue*—as one of the very first from Hollywood to deal with the Spanish struggle.

But progress on the film was delayed that spring, and Odets and Milestone lost interest in the project. They resigned, and at Clurman's suggestion, Wanger called in John Howard Lawson, whose play *Success Story* had been one of the Group Theatre's outstanding productions and who had already worked in Hollywood, though he was now in New York. Lawson, who had been an organizer of the Screen Writers Guild, and who was to become widely known a decade later as one of the "Hollywood Ten," felt deeply committed to the Spanish Republican cause and gave himself wholeheartedly to the project. At his suggestion the Paris locale of the story was abandoned and Spain was made the scene of its entire action, so that the film, as Lawson hoped, "would be a real documentary about the Spanish struggle."

Work proceeded slowly, however, on the film that was eventually to be called *Blockade*, and Weill was growing impatient as summer arrived. He still regarded Broadway as the place where he could do the kind of things he hoped to do in America, and his thoughts had been turning to there more and more during his months in Hollywood. The project with the Spewacks and Harburg was still in the works, and though Max Gordon had not yet made a firm decision about it, hopes were still high that it could open in the fall. There also was still the American *Everyman* that Weill was doing with Paul Green: the Federal Theatre Project was interested in producing it, and Weill wanted to get back to work with Green on the story. Other ideas were fermenting as well. There was the possibility of a project with Marc Connelly, author of *The Green Pastures*. And sometime during the spring Weill had contacted the Theatre Guild back in New York saying he would like to do a musical version of Ferenc Molnár's *Liliom*: as some people, at least, understood his proposal, the work would be "along the lines of *The Threepenny Opera*." Only three years before, Fritz Lang, then still in Paris before moving on to Hollywood, had done a film version of *Liliom* with Charles Boyer in the title role. Molnár himself had evidently been satisfied to see his work as a film; but when Weill's suggestion was conveyed to him, he turned it down, saying he was not interested in having the play done as a musical. Eight years later, when the Theatre Guild proposed the idea to Richard Rodgers and Oscar Hammerstein II, Molnár was to have a change of heart, and *Carousel* came into being.

Weill finally got back to New York at the end of June. The completion of
Blockade was still a while off, and though he had begun to discuss a new
film project with Fritz Lang, the work on that was not to begin until the
fall. Meanwhile, *The Eternal Road* had just closed and it was time for Kurt
and Lenya to devote some of their energies to getting their affairs in order.
Having now definitely decided that the United States was to be their
permanent home, they proceeded to apply for citizenship and made a
short trip to Canada in August for the purpose of reentering on an
immigrant visa. They returned to New York and, at the beginning of
September, rented a duplex apartment with a roof garden and terrace in
an attractive town house on East Sixty-second Street.

One other event occurred during the summer, a tragic one, that was
to be of significance in Weill's life. It was around the time Kurt left
Hollywood that George Gershwin, long suffering from symptoms of
nervousness and irritability that had been considered purely neurotic and
for which he had consulted psychoanalysts, began to complain of
headaches and dizziness. These were still thought by both physicians and
friends to be neurotic symptoms until, on July 9, the thirty-eight-year-old
composer fell into a coma. He was rushed to a hospital, and only then was
it discovered that he had been suffering from a brain tumor; he died on the
morning of July 11. Gershwin's body was flown back to New York for
burial.

It was time now to get to work in earnest on the new play with Paul
Green. Something had delayed the project with the Spewacks and
Harburg, and so it looked as though—of the various possibilities in the
air—this one with Green would be the very next Weill show to open. The
Federal Theatre was still interested in it and began to envision an opening
date early in 1938; by this time, Max Reinhardt no longer was involved in
it. There was much to do, and during the summer and fall Weill made two
trips to Chapel Hill, one at around the beginning of August and another
for a full week in early October; there also were many exchanges of letters
between the two collaborators during this period, Weill constantly making
suggestions for the story line.

At first the idea had been to do a broad pageant freely derived from
Everyman and set in the American South during the Revolution. But now
the *Everyman* concept was all but disappearing, and the idea of a pageant
of early American history was becoming predominant. Weill and Green
began to formulate a work to be done in the manner of *The Eternal Road*,
showing in scenes widely spread apart the birth of the American colonies,
the Revolution, and the making of the Constitution. Weill was becoming

passionately American, and this feeling was manifesting itself not only in a love of the history and folklore of his newly adopted country, but also in a resurgence of the quasi-religious pietism that had marked some of his earliest efforts as a composer and had most recently been brought out in his "popular oratorio" on the theme of Jewish exile. He, at any rate, had arrived in his Promised Land, even if Moses had not; and, like many a European artist coming to these shores, his first impulse was to reach out in a wide Whitmanesque embrace.

After a time, however, Weill and Green decided that they could get better results if they restricted their material and did more of a play than a spectacle. By the fall they were concentrating their sights on Boston during the Revolution and thought they would make Samuel Adams the focus of the play. Then the good idea came—in the tradition of Sir Walter Scott—of putting Sam Adams and the other real historical personalities into the background and making a fictitious Everyman named Jonathan Smith, "a kind of Johnny Johnson of 1776" as Kurt put it, into the play's protagonist. *The Common Glory*, as they were calling it, began to take shape: by mid-November Green had done a rough draft of the first few scenes, and Weill was beginning to write the music for them.

Still inclined to keep as many irons in the fire as possible, however, Weill became involved in another project at just around this time. Charles Alan, who had been Reinhardt's assistant director for *The Eternal Road*, had come up with the machinery whereby another of Weill's visions of Americana could hope to become a reality. He and Weill wanted to produce a show called *The Ballad of Davy Crockett*, with a script by Hoffman R. Hays, and in order to do so they formed an *ad hoc* producing company with Burgess Meredith, who was to play the lead, and the eminent set designer Robert Edmond Jones. The project was financed by the singer and actress Libby Holman, and an opening was envisioned for the spring. They also looked over Albert Bein's play *Heavenly Express* as possible material for a musical show with a score by Weill and with Meredith playing the lead.

Weill was now frantically at work on his various projects, and as if things were not hectic enough, in December he began receiving telephone calls and wires reminding him that it was time to report back in Hollywood for work on the Fritz Lang film. Holding it off as long as he could, he finally departed with Lenya for the West Coast on December 13. His hopes were that this job could be finished in about four weeks, after which he would return to New York and resume his commitments there. In the meantime he did not cease to communicate with Green from the oceanside cottage he and Lenya rented in Santa Monica, writing extensive comments on his collaborator's developing draft of *The Common Glory* and sketching out his own music for it.

Fritz Lang was making his third American film. So far he had managed in Hollywood to uphold his dignity as one of Germany's foremost directors and make only films of social significance. *Fury*, with Spencer Tracy and Sylvia Sidney, dealt with the passion for revenge of a man who had been falsely accused of a crime and nearly lynched as a result; *You Only Live Once*, with Sylvia Sidney and Henry Fonda, was about an ex-convict trying to go straight and unable to do so because of the stigma of his criminal record. The present film idea, *You and Me*, was a comedy which devolved upon Lang primarily because its star, Sylvia Sidney, wanted him again as her director; but it had elements in common with his two previous Hollywood films, and there were moments in the script when Lang even thought he could apply some ideas going back to his Berlin days.

The main scene of the story's action is the Morris Department Store in New York, where a large number of ex-convicts are employed because the owner considers such a policy to be his own particular form of charity. The ex-cons are grateful, but their loyalty is put to the test by a crook who turns up and threatens to expose their various histories to the world if they don't collaborate with him in a robbery of the store. Many are won over, but Joe Dennis—to be played by George Raft—the one among them upon whom the success of the job would really depend, remains incorruptible. Meanwhile, Joe falls in love with Helen (this is Sylvia Sidney's role), who also works in the store—and who also, in fact, is an ex-convict, although she does not inform Joe of the fact, despite his candor to her about his own background. They get married, and when Joe finally learns the truth about her, he is so disillusioned that he decides to throw in his lot with the planned robbery. But Helen gets wind of it, and, on the night they break into the store, the astonished conspirators find her there awaiting them, along with Mr. Morris and the police. To their further astonishment, Morris takes their guns and leaves with the police, telling them he expects them to listen to Helen and then show up for work as usual the next morning. With blackboard and chalk, Helen then gives a lecture on the subject of "crime does not pay," with literal realism. Doing some quick arithmetic, she demonstrates that the $35,000 they were planning to steal would in fact, once all the payoffs were made and the money divided up, bring each of them a return of only $133.33! They are easily persuaded that honest work is more profitable; and Joe and Helen soon decide to live happily ever after.

Lang saw in this material the opportunity to do a kind of Brechtian *Lehrstück* with music by Weill. Since the final cut of the film has only two musical sequences by him—which was all he finished before being overwhelmed by his impatience to return to New York—we can only guess at the full nature of the film Lang had in mind. The first Weill sequence is in the montage that opens the film, which gives various views of the abundant goods in the Morris Department Store while an off-camera voice sings "You Can't Get Something for Nothing"; the song and the sequence end as the camera pans in on a would-be shoplifter. Weill's number is mainly a patter song—with words by Sam Coslow— which, though musically undistinguished, is effective in the context. His next song is better, but it is less well integrated into the action. Joe and Helen, not yet fully aware that they are in love with one another, are spending what is ostensibly their last evening together before Joe goes to California to start a new life. They go to a dance hall and hear a torch singer, Carol Paige, do a song about the man that got away called "The Right Guy for Me." This will eventually persuade Joe and Helen to stay together and get married; but while the song is being sung, the camera illustrates its story with a pantomime dramatic sequence, showing smoky waterfront bars and a dashing sea captain with a parrot perched on his shoulder who seems for all the world like Surabaya Johnny gone to Hollywood. We are getting an illustrated *Happy End* right in the middle of *You and Me*, and the two dramas do not mesh.

Lang had envisioned at least one more musical sequence. The ex-convicts are gathered in a cellar, planning their robbery and waiting to hear if Joe will come and join them. Suddenly they start reminiscing about their days in prison, and as one of them taps the table with his finger, then another with a spoon—apparently evoking the ways they used to communicate with one another by tapping on the cell walls—they begin a strange, spoken chant over this rhythmic accompaniment. This is how the scene is done in the film's final cut; the whole thing makes no sense at all without music.

But by this time Weill had given up. He and Lenya stayed in Santa Monica until early February while he worked on this film. Then they returned to New York for various reasons; but Kurt went back to Hollywood alone in April to finish the job, as he thought. This was not his only reason for the second return to Hollywood in April; for *Blockade* was nearing completion and he still intended to do the score for that. But

Hollywood was notorious in those days for keeping creative artists—
notably writers and composers—waiting long periods of time with
nothing to do, albeit at salaries that very much eased the pain. Weill could
not bear the pain, however, especially since his stay in New York during
late February and March, while bringing disappointment about the
prospects of an opening for *The Common Glory* that season, had also
brought into being the most exciting project since his arrival in America.
By the third week of May, with both *Blockade* and *You and Me* still awaiting
completion, he could bear it no longer, got into his Oldsmobile, and
headed back to New York.

Back to Old New York:
Knickerbocker Holiday

In 1938 the figure of Maxwell Anderson was one of those that loomed largest on the Broadway scene. A midwesterner who had made an early career in journalism, he had suddenly achieved fame in 1924 at the age of thirty-five as coauthor, with Laurence Stallings, of *What Price Glory*, a robust drama about men at the front in the World War. After two more efforts with Stallings, both of them unsuccessful, he proceeded to write plays on his own, and by the end of the decade these were appearing on Broadway at the rate of about one a year and usually doing quite well. Not contented with mere box-office success, however, Anderson, a man of vaulting literary ambitions, had turned increasingly to the writing of drama in verse, first on historical themes—as with *Elizabeth the Queen* and *Mary of Scotland*—and then at last on a contemporary one with *Winterset*, which was based on the Sacco–Vanzetti case. In *High Tor*, which won the New York Drama Critics' Circle Award for the 1936/37 season—*Johnny Johnson* came in second—Anderson achieved a fusion of styles and materials, combining historical and contemporary characters by means of a naturalistic approach that veered over into fantasy, and moving freely between verse and prose. The style of the play seems almost to call out for music, but Anderson had yet to write a musical of any sort.

Anderson had been occasionally associated with the Group Theatre: many of his friends were in it, he had been among its financial supporters when it began, and it had produced one of his plays, *Night over Taos*, in

1932. He had even submitted *Winterset* to the Group, who had rejected it; Harold Clurman, for one, has said that "I could not make myself comfortable in its atmosphere of an 'Elizabethan' East Side!" It was at a party probably given by members of the Group, then, that Anderson first met Kurt Weill sometime in late 1935 or early 1936. Anderson was no doubt familiar with *The Threepenny Opera*, but at this moment most of the recognition was the other way around: Weill was filled with admiration for the man who had written *What Price Glory*—which had been done in Germany by Reinhardt—and the screenplay of *All Quiet on the Western Front*. According to the kind of legend press agents love to weave, he wasted no time in saying to Anderson: "I'd like to write a play with you."

Anderson apparently made a polite reply. In New York, until quite recently at any rate, the musical theater was not considered a place in which serious playwrights could work; Berlin had been far more daring on this issue, as on many others. There had been exceptions, but not necessarily persuasive ones: the Gertrude Stein–Virgil Thomson *Four Saints in Three Acts* of 1934 was perhaps too exceptional, and *Porgy and Bess* must have caused many a dramatist to wonder if he was willing to be as overwhelmed by the music as DuBose Heyward's work had been. But *Johnny Johnson* proved to be something else again; it certainly was as much a play as a musical play. Maxwell Anderson, when he saw it that fall of 1936, realized that this was the sort of thing he could do, and he and Weill began to discuss possible ideas whenever they saw one another.

Nothing clicked, however, until the beginning of April 1938, when Weill was back from his second trip to Hollywood and getting ready for his third, still working on *You and Me* and ostensibly on *Blockade* and increasingly unhappy with the prospect. Kurt and Lenya were spending a weekend at the home of Anderson and his wife in the countryside near New City, a few miles north of New York and in close proximity to High Tor, the mountain overlooking the Hudson Valley upon which Anderson had set his recent play of that name. In the play the lives of the contemporary characters at the center of the action are intruded upon by characters from the area's seventeenth-century Dutch past. Increasingly fascinated by local history, Anderson—again, according to a press agent's account—now suddenly turned to Weill and said:

"Kurt, do you think we can make a musical comedy out of Washington Irving's *Knickerbocker History of New York*?"

Weill thought so. In the first place, he was in a mood to be agreeable to almost any suggestion Anderson might have made. All his New York projects were falling through. The Federal Theatre Project was having financial and political troubles—indeed, it was not to survive much longer—and clearly could not produce *The Common Glory* this season. The Davy Crockett play had also been deferred, owing to dissatisfaction among the producers about the way Hoffman R. Hays's script had turned out so far. Something also had gone wrong in the project with the Spewacks and Harburg, for Harold Arlen was now being mentioned along with Weill as the possible composer for it; and in fact it was soon to be shelved altogether. In other words, Anderson's proposal presented Weill with his only prospect for an immediate rescue from Hollywood— and to make it more enticing, it was coming from the man who was perhaps Broadway's "hottest" playwright of the moment.

But there also were attractions in the subject matter. Weill was now passionately fond of American history and folklore, and this would be his one chance to work that vein in view of the demise of *The Common Glory* and the Davy Crockett project. Furthermore, Irving's New Amsterdam was a kind of historical American milieu in which he, the German immigrant, could feel particularly at home. One wonders if Anderson and Weill began immediately, that weekend in April, to discuss the comic Dutch burghers who would form an essential element in the play—and whose vaudeville accents would come close enough to Weill's German-American speech that he and Anderson must often have realized they were doing a parody of it. Weill was perfectly capable of self-mockery, particularly where his German background was concerned. Moreover, the German musical tradition provided a nice source of inspiration for this kind of material: Albert Lortzing's comic opera of 1837, *Zar und Zimmermann* ("Tsar and Carpenter")—little known in the United States, but a perennial favorite in Germany and long beloved by Weill—was dominated by the comic figure of a seventeenth-century Dutch burgomas-ter. Weill was to use some German and mock-German musical ideas in his score, and for the moment even thought he would do research to discover seventeenth-century musical sources somehow relevant to New Amster-dam and evocative of its character.

When Weill set out again for Hollywood later that month, Ander-son's parting words to him were, according to the press agent's account: "If the idea works out, I'll have the book ready upon your return." But this implies a lesser degree of involvement in the creating of the libretto than was usual for Weill—and than in fact was the case here. Weill's letters to Anderson from Hollywood show that the essentials of the plot had already been worked out by them before his departure and that the composer was still involving himself in the development of the script even at a distance, as he had done with Paul Green. They had decided right away that the action would be set during the governorship of Peter Stuyvesant and would weave some kind of love story around a young man who rebels against Stuyvesant's tyrannical methods and the corrupt manipulations of a rich town councillor. In a letter typed on the train to California, Weill presents a conception of the play as being about three "fathers" in conflict with one another: the rebellious young man is the father of all those who live in America because they see it as "the land of the free"; the corrupt town councillor is the father of all crooks who try to profit by the country's freedom; and Stuyvesant is "the father of all ambitious governments who try to help the country but cannot get along without the help of the crooks." As far as Weill was concerned, any resemblances to the present were entirely intentional.

This also was true of Anderson, for whom the Dutch-American setting of the play had a special political resonance: for he saw his Stuyvesant as a satire on Franklin Delano Roosevelt. There was more than a touch of the old-fashioned Populist in Anderson, the son of a small-town preacher; long a proponent of individual liberties against the encroachments of big government, he was perfectly capable of being a liberal or even a radical on certain issues, such as the case of the two anarchists Sacco and Vanzetti. But the New Deal, in spite of its concern with that common man who often was the focus of Anderson's sympathies as well, had increasingly aroused his ire; and now he was going to deliver it his playwright's *coup de grâce*. He was writing a comedy, to be sure—*The Mikado* was serving as his model for it, just as *Henry IV, Part I* had served for *What Price Glory*—but he meant its political message quite seriously. He had certainly discussed it in these terms with Weill, who must have been perplexed at seeing Roosevelt, whom he had revered from abroad, now being depicted as a tyrant. Perhaps Weill was satisfied that the real villain of the piece as thus far conceived was the rich councillor, and that the Stuyvesant character—who even was slated to discover the error of his ways in the end, but too late—was merely misguided. He did not foresee that, in subsequent drafts, the wicked councillor Tienhoven was going to be turned into an ineffectual booby. Nevertheless, one cannot help but suspect that, in his eagerness to do a play with Anderson, Weill was going against his own better judgment on this issue.

Anderson's colleagues in the newly formed Playwrights Company were another matter, however. That very spring, a group of the most distinguished playwrights on Broadway—Anderson, Robert E. Sherwood, Elmer Rice, Sidney Howard, and S. N. Behrman—had gathered together and created their own producing company, and they now were preparing to make the Weill–Anderson musical one of their first offerings. One of the procedures of the Playwrights Producing Company from the outset was to take a seminar approach to each other's works in progress— to read various drafts and be forthcoming with comments and suggestions right down to the opening-night curtain. It was around the beginning of June, shortly after Weill's return from the West Coast, that the other members of the company were given copies of Anderson's rough draft to read. It must have come to them as something of a shock. "The rest of us were strongly pro-Roosevelt," as Elmer Rice has put it—Sherwood, after all, was even to work for Roosevelt one day and eventually be his biographer—"and though, of course, we had no control over Anderson's script, we did succeed, mainly by cajolery, in getting him to delete some of the more pointed references to the New Deal." This was the first stage in a shifting of emphases from which the dramatic balance of the play never was really to recover.

The next stage came about under the influence of Joshua Logan, who, at twenty-nine, was one of the brightest new lights on Broadway and who had been obtained to direct the production of what was now being called *Knickerbocker Holiday*. Logan had seen *What Price Glory* at the age of fifteen and had regarded it as one of the great experiences of his life; he also knew *The Threepenny Opera*, and so he felt flattered at being called in to do a Weill–Anderson musical. But some of the psychological advantages were really on his side. That spring he had directed Rodgers and Hart's *I Married an Angel*, and it had been a hit. He was now, in other words, an established figure in the Broadway musical theater; whereas Anderson, working on his first musical, was unsure of what he was doing, and Weill was still groping for the formula that would make him as successful on Broadway as he had been in Berlin.

Logan has recalled his first meeting with the play's authors, which took place at Anderson's house in New City. Weill was there, and so was Lenya, who "was to help Kurt sing the score for me." Kurt and Lenya were renting a summer house in New City, and by this time much though not all of the music had been written. "Kurt sat at the piano," Logan writes, "staring at his manuscript paper through the two hunks of thick glass he used for spectacles. He was a little musical juggernaut. Nothing stopped him once he launched into a song. He caterwauled the melody in a toneless tenor with an accent so thick it hurt him as much as it did us. Lenya just smiled her pearly bear-trap smile. Kurt banged insistently on the keyboard to emphasize the bass rhythms."

Logan listened through and decided he wanted to do the show. The material was very different from the Rodgers and Hart variety he had just become accustomed to, but he admired Weill's music and found Anderson's lyrics to be "poetic and funny." When he announced his decision, "there was a small celebration consisting of clasped hands and squeezed shoulders. I was amazed by how much my approval meant to them." Of course, he had not yet seen the script; and when he did, he only then perceived the scope of the problems he had taken on. In the draft he read, he found that "the old fat Dutch burghers were pure Weber and Fields and the boy and the girl were pure coy. It wasn't until the new governor, peg-legged Peter Stuyvesant, entered, flashing his silver-encrusted stump of a leg, that things began to crackle. He was obviously a dictator and less obviously, a satire of Roosevelt. I hesitated to tell Max what I thought."

But Anderson was eager for advice at this point, and Logan gave it. Stuyvesant now had to become not only less of a Roosevelt satire but also a more prominent character in the action. This idea entailed a further shifting of the play's balances, to which another development occurring around this time also contributed. When Anderson first created the role of Brom Broeck, the freedom-loving young hero, he had thought that it might be taken by Burgess Meredith, who had played the lead in *Winterset*, *High Tor*, and the most recent Anderson play, *The Star-Wagon*, and who lately had also been involved in some of Kurt Weill's activities. In May, when Meredith saw the first half of the first draft of *Knickerbocker Holiday*, he had said that he wanted the part. He was much in demand at this time, however, and by the beginning of summer he had decided upon other commitments. The result was that the Brom Broeck character began to lose weight just at the moment when Stuyvesant, with Logan's help, began to gain it.

"We knew that we needed a great star for Stuyvesant," Logan goes on, "and also that it was a comparatively small part which made attracting a big star difficult." At that point somebody suggested Walter Huston, then at the height of his fame after having done both the stage and the screen versions of Sinclair Lewis's *Dodsworth*. Logan had his doubts that Huston would be interested; only the previous fall he had tried to get him for the lead role in Paul Osborn's *On Borrowed Time*, and Huston, after showing the script to the producer Max Gordon for advice, had decided to turn it down. The play had gone on to be Logan's first big hit. This recollection, according to Logan, caused Weill to say eagerly:

"Call him, Josh, call him now. Maybe he's sorry now that it's such a big hit. Only tell him not to send ours to Max Gordon."

Logan called Walter Huston, who was with his wife in their mountain retreat at Lake Arrowhead, California, and described the role. Huston was interested; he had started his career as a vaudeville song-and-dance man, but at fifty-four years of age he had yet to perform in a musical. Furthermore, he was intrigued by the challenge of doing a role on a peg leg. Logan promptly flew to California and soon found himself sitting in view of the San Jacinto Mountains and the Lake, reading and singing *Knickerbocker Holiday* to Walter and Nan Huston.

"Clickety-clack, clickety-clack, swish!" he began, according to Huston's recollection, and was promptly interrupted.

"Did you say this was a play by *Maxwell Anderson*?" Huston asked incredulously.

"Yes, with music by Kurt Weill. This is the opening chorus of the Dutch maidens."

Logan resumed, and he noticed by the time he reached the end that the Hustons were making "enthusiastic sounds."

"He's an old scoundrel," Huston said.

Logan felt a tightening in his stomach, but he said nothing.

"Oh, I like the nasty part, except that the character's pretty skimpy."

"It can be longer," Logan replied.

"Not longer, just better. It's too one-note, too cool-headed. Couldn't this old bastard make love to that pretty young girl a bit? Not win her, just give her a squeeze or tickle her under the chin, and she could even consider him for a fraction of a second when she hears his song."

"Song?"

"Sure—something nice I could sing to her. I like the other songs, 'The Scars' particularly, but I mean something, you know, a moment for the old son of a bitch to be charming."

"No problem, Walter," Logan said, "you'll have the song you want. I guarantee it."

Logan returned to New York with the news, and Weill promptly took up his new assignment by sending a telegram to Huston: "What is the range of your voice?" Huston wired back: "I have no range. Appearing tonight on Bing Crosby program. Will sing a song for you." That night, Weill and Anderson sat by the radio in the latter's home and listened to Huston as he rasped pleasantly on coast-to-coast radio.

When he had finished, Weill said: "Let's write a sentimental, romantic song for him."

In an hour Anderson had turned out the lyrics for the "September Song," and Weill wrote the music for it the same evening. Once again, as with the "Moritat of Mackie Messer," Weill had written what was to be the show's most famous song as a virtual afterthought. The next day Logan arrived in New City, and the three of them placed a call to Huston in Lake Arrowhead. First Weill played and sang the song in front of the telephone, then Logan reprised it without accompaniment, stressing the lyrics.

He finished, and after a pause Huston said: "Yes, yes, yes, yes, yes—play me the tune again."

They did, and then, to everyone's astonishment, Huston sang the whole song back to them.

The cycle was complete: Maxwell Anderson's political satire was now a comedy about a charming old codger named Stuyvesant, whose dances and capers on a peg leg—worn on his knee, while his lower leg was strapped to his thigh underneath billowing pantaloons—would amaze and delight all audiences, and whose wistful song about love in the autumn of life was to become one of the great moments in the history of the American musical theater. Under the circumstances Stuyvesant's gestures at tyranny were not to seem too menacing, and Brom Broeck's pleas for liberty—from the mouth of the charming but hardly overpowering young actor Richard Kollmar—were to sound lightweight indeed. But buried somewhere in all this was Anderson's original, and now badly battered, political message. "I still have a clear picture of Max at the end of the first run-through," writes John F. Wharton, chief counsel for the Playwrights Company; "he stood shaking his head and saying, 'My, my, we certainly do go to pieces in the last act.' He was right; we did. The script had been twisted too far."

If Walter Huston's irresistible performance was one guarantee that the show would do well in spite of its faults, another was provided four nights before its scheduled New York opening, after tryouts in Boston and Hartford. For a performance was given in Washington, D.C., on the evening of October 15, at the National Theater, and in the audience was the object of Anderson's ironies, President Franklin D. Roosevelt himself.

This provided very favorable publicity for the show, since Roosevelt had gone to the theater only once before since his first inauguration in 1933, and for the same reason—to see his friend Walter Huston perform, in that case as Dodsworth in the stage version of the Sinclair Lewis novel. Whether Roosevelt also had heard that he himself was the object of the play's satire, and had come to see this with his own eyes, is something he was never to reveal.

As the president entered his box that evening, the orchestra struck up "The Star-Spangled Banner" and Roosevelt rose to his feet from his wheelchair. Logan thought he looked like a "caped statue of victory" standing there. When the music ended, the audience applauded the president until he sat down. Then the curtain went up.

"Of course the play went to hell that night," Logan recalls, "for the entire audience turned compulsively to FDR's box at each funny line to see if he was laughing. Since he howled at each joke, they didn't have time to follow suit, so they turned silently back to the stage. To a blind man, it must have seemed like an empty auditorium except for one crazy, laughing fool." One joke that Roosevelt particularly enjoyed was Brom Broeck's definition of democracy as "when you're governed by amateurs." Another one he was not to forget was a topical reference: for this year of grave international developments, which had begun with the *Anschluss*, had just culminated the previous month in the Czech crisis and the infamous Munich agreement. During the crisis Roosevelt had sent an appeal to Hitler; and Anderson had taken the opportunity to satirize this by having one of the comic councillors—the one named Roosevelt, based on the president's New Amsterdam ancestor—say in response to a threat of war with the Yankee settlers in Connecticut: "Maybe ve send dem a letter—maybe dey go vay." Evidently Anderson, deprived of some of his Stuyvesant barbs, had decided that he could at least draw a little Roosevelt blood through the character of that name.

Roosevelt did not say anything about this particular joke until later that evening, at a White House reception to which some of the show's creators, staff, and players were invited. Kurt Weill undoubtedly was there, now drinking dizzying draughts from the cup of his American experience; Maxwell Anderson was not. The president put his guests at their ease by shouting out their individual drink orders and then began to proclaim in speech-making decibels how much he had enjoyed the show—except for one line.

"That 'letter' thing wasn't funny," he said, according to Logan's account. "In the first place, it was a *telegram* I sent to Hitler and I sent it personally. The important thing about that was the fact that that bastard's secretary didn't throw it into a wastebasket, but rather put it on top of the important mail to be answered. If it hadn't come from a *powerful* United States it would never even have gotten onto that desk. We've simply *got* to stay powerful enough to stay out of the wastebasket."

Someone asked if war was inevitable, and Roosevelt said that it was—it was only a question of time. The surviving fragments of Anderson's anti–New Deal satire, and the question of whether the president had seen the thrust of it all and not just this isolated dig, began to seem trivial indeed. In the ensuing conversation Roosevelt urged Logan to put some further warnings against fascism into the play. It is not clear whether this was actually done, but by the time the play opened in New York, many observers were to see in it as much a lighthearted warning against fascist dictators as a satire on the New Deal. Maxwell Anderson was to feel impelled, a few weeks after the opening, to publish an article in *The New York Times* explaining the *American* significance of his message in *Knickerbocker Holiday*; but few people seem to have cared.

The framing device for the musical play that opened at the Ethel Barrymore Theatre on October 19 is offered by the character of the young Washington Irving, whom we meet—as played by Ray Middleton—in his study getting started on the composition of his *Knickerbocker History of New York*. In a charming patter song against an orchestral accompaniment, he invokes the village of New Amsterdam in 1647, introducing the various characters as they appear: the town crier who has nothing to report; the Dutch maidens mopping their stairways to the "clickety-clack" of their pails; the comic scoundrels who comprise the town council—they alone among the play's principals speaking in vaudeville-Dutch accents— entering to a march that sounds straight out of *The Mikado*; and finally the young lovers, Brom Broeck and Tina Tienhoven (played by Jeanne Madden), daughter of the chief councillor who, unbeknownst to her, has pledged her as a bride to the imminently arriving new governor, Peter Stuyvesant, a widower.

Much of the first act revolves around the absurd notion arrived at by the councillors that the gala occasion with which they plan to welcome the new governor must include a hanging. For their victim they choose Brom, who has recently had an argument with the chief councillor, Tienhoven, his beloved's father, and struck him on the head. Brom is indeed someone for them to dislike, for as he tells Tina in a tender scene with her—which culminates in the fine duet "It Never Was You"—after a recent experience of living among the Indians he finds himself no longer able to take orders. This becomes a central theme of the play and the subject of one of its principal songs, "How Can You Tell an American?"; for Brom's independence and anti-authoritarianism show him to be the first true American of New Amsterdam. Brom is caught and summarily sentenced, but he quickly shows his American shrewdness by begging of the sluggish-minded councillors that they hang him in the traditional way, around the neck, rather than in the modern way, around the waist—which, says Brom, is horrible because the victim dies slowly. Naturally, the councillors string him up by the waist, and he sways unharmed in the air as Peter Stuyvesant arrives in the harbor and enters upon the scene—accompanied by a Weill parody of an old Prussian march, with a hobble in it for the governor's peg leg.

Once the situation has been explained to him, Stuyvesant orders that Brom be cut down and pardoned for his cleverness. At the same time the new governor warns the assembled townspeople that he will brook no insubordination—which he can smell when it's in the air, he adds, sniffing ominously in Brom's direction. After a succession of musical numbers, Stuyvesant is left alone with Tina, whom he wants to marry immediately. When she asks for more time to think it over, Stuyvesant protests that one has no time at his age, and he sings the "September Song." From this point on, it is impossible for the audience not to love this aging but indefatigable charmer, no matter how outrageous he becomes, and so the play's political satire ceases to have any effect at all.

Brom reenters and demonstrates his insubordination by objecting to the imminent marriage, and Stuyvesant has him put in jail. Act One ends with the assembled townspeople singing a reprise of a song they had done shortly after Stuyvesant's entrance, "All Hail, the Political Honeymoon," a rousing near-relative of the "Democracy March" from *Johnny Johnson*.

Act Two opens with Brom in jail and Tina coming in secret to protest her love for him. The next day, in a succession of numbers strongly reminiscent of Gilbert and Sullivan, the New Amsterdam army does some maneuvers and the wedding of Tina and Stuyvesant is prepared; Stuyvesant tries to justify the virtues of age and experience in a vaudeville number, "The Scars," which comes close to the spirit of *The Threepenny Opera*. But the proceedings are interrupted when Indians attack the village: their coming is heralded by a witty musical anachronism, "The Algonquins from Harlem," a sort of rain dance as it might have sounded at the Cotton Club. In the melee Brom escapes from jail and enters into battle, ultimately saving Stuyvesant from capture. At one point, when one of the Dutchmen is mistakenly thought to have been killed in battle, the chorus sings a "Dirge for a Soldier" that is clearly an Americanized cousin of some of the pieces in the *Berlin Requiem*. At the end, Stuyvesant is going to hang Brom in spite of everything, but Washington Irving himself intervenes and tells the governor that posterity would take a better view of him if he would temper justice with mercy. Stuyvesant thereupon pardons Brom—we are in the world of the "Third Threepenny Finale"— and furthermore, recognizing true love when he sees it, renounces Tina so she and Brom can get married. The curtain goes down to a reprise of "How Can You Tell an American?"

Kurt Weill's score for *Knickerbocker Holiday*—which was conducted by his old friend and former pupil Maurice Abravanel, now in the United States and trying out his skills on Broadway after two unhappy seasons with the Metropolitan Opera—is best understood if one tries, for a moment, to consider what it looked like prior to the writing of the "September Song." Early in the game Weill realized that it was no use trying to do the musical evocation of the time and the place that he had originally envisioned; as he later commented: "I don't think there was much music in New Amsterdam except Dutch folk music." Instead, what he and Anderson evolved was a combination of vaudeville and operetta, and this is reflected in the music. The vaudeville part is full of the spirit of the composer of *The Threepenny Opera*—or, at any rate, of the somewhat gentler ironist who had done *Die Bürgschaft* and *Der Silbersee*, now returning to a *Threepenny* approach. "The One Indispensable Man," a mock tribute to Councillor Tienhoven in his role as "the pay-off man," sung by Stuyvesant and Tienhoven himself, is close in spirit to the *Threepenny* ballad "On the Inadequacy of Human Striving"; but it is introduced by a melodic theme closely akin to Anna Mattes's lament for her daughter in *Die Bürgschaft*, its sadness now turned ironic. The council's evocation of "Our Ancient Liberties" is a comic "*Valse lente*" very similar to the waltz sung by the two shopgirls in *Der Silbersee*.

In its operetta aspects, the score is more derivative of other composers. Several numbers are deliberate pastiches of Gilbert and Sullivan, some of it very good indeed; other songs seem to draw upon Sigmund Romberg—and even upon Noël Coward, in the case of "Will You Remember Me?" which is a parody, since this duet between the two young lovers is performed when Brom seems about to be hanged, and it is full of deadpan gallows humor. The most Rombergian of the songs is Brom and Tina's duet "It Never Was You," but this is arguably better than Romberg and contains distinct Weill touches—such as a highly unusual break (the song only hints at the standard Broadway thirty-two-bar formula, but eschews it) containing one melodic passage that is sustained for not fewer than twelve bars: the effect almost suggests Berlioz. "It Never Was You," by the way, was the song originally envisioned as the show's possible hit "single," but it was then overshadowed by the "September Song"; also, to the listener of later years, it suffers by the fact that the aforementioned long melodic break in it contains echoes—or foreshadowings—of the song "Lost in the Stars," which Weill and Anderson were to write only a short time later, even though the musical play of that title and containing it was not to be written until 1949.

"It Never Was You" has a Broadway sound, as do a few of the other songs—most notably "How Can You Tell an American?" which borrows some musical ideas from the title song of the 1930 Gershwin political satire *Strike Up the Band*, and Brom's piece of down-in-the-dumps optimism, "There's Nowhere To Go But Up!" But there are twenty-eight musical numbers in *Knickerbocker Holiday*, and very few of them live up to the comment made in subsequent years that this was the show in which Weill had suddenly "gone Broadway." It shares the eclecticism of *Johnny Johnson*—including some similar efforts at pastiche Americana, such as the "Ballad of the Robbers," sung by Washington Irving at the beginning of Act Two, and Stuyvesant's apology for the virtues of "Sitting in Jail," sung right after it, both in the vein of folksingers' jailhouse blues; and, as in *Johnny Johnson*, there are a few deliberate uses of the idiom of the audience being addressed. But it was far from Weill's intention to write a conventional Broadway show, and the results show it. Essentially, what he has done in this score is a parody of a whole range of styles, presented in the atmosphere of a satirical play—a work, in other words, entirely in the tradition of *The Threepenny Opera*. One reason for the difference between the two works—aside from the fact that Anderson simply was not a Brecht—is that the German-born and -bred composer of 1928 had been able to pour all that sly eclecticism into a firm stylistic container, whereas the German immigrant composer has not yet formulated his American container (*Johnny Johnson* had still used the German one, somewhat leaky by then).

What has above all given the *Knickerbocker Holiday* score a "Broadway" image for many is the "September Song." This is ironic, not only because the song was an afterthought, but also because it really was untypical of Broadway in its day, whatever it has come to seem since then. Like "Johnny's Song," it is really German-American and is in fact closely akin to "Surabaya Johnny." Arriving from very different tonal frameworks—as from very different cultural frames of reference—"September Song" and "Surabaya Johnny" nevertheless land from time to time on passages that are musically close to one another, so that the two songs seem almost to function in a purposive interplay. Certainly they both are about the passing of love's better days. But, once again reaching back, as with "Johnny's Song," to the preconceived Americana of *Happy End* for some thematic material to use on American soil, Weill has found a mellower tone. If "going Broadway" means renouncing the old Brechtian bitterness, then Weill certainly has done that; but he had already done it in Berlin, with *Die Bürgschaft* and *Der Silbersee*.

Anderson and Weill, at any rate, must have known they were playing with German themes in this song, as they were in the comic Dutch accents of the councillors. Surely they recognized that the "long, long while" of the refrain (*Langeweile* in German) was a punning rejoinder to the "short while" that was the composer's name; this must have been great fun. How could they have known then that Kurt Weill would, in fact, never go the whole distance from May to December, but die in the September of his life?

Looking for a Niche

20: *Knickerbocker Holiday* had opened four days after the Playwrights Company's very first offering, Robert E. Sherwood's *Abe Lincoln in Illinois*, and this fact caused Richard Watts, Jr., theater critic of the *New York Herald Tribune*, to write:

> In their second production, the associated playwrights are still contemplating the problems of democracy. Since it is the most vital matter in the world today, it is only right that our most important dramatists should be pondering it, and we should be especially grateful when their contemplations can result in an *Abe Lincoln in Illinois*. The second play, however, takes as its central character old Peter Stuyvesant, and, with all best wishes for the prosperity of *Knickerbocker Holiday*, I cannot help feeling that the new offering of the Playwrights Company is as inferior to the earlier one as Peter Stuyvesant was to Abraham Lincoln. Kurt Weill's score is admirable, the production is colorful and charming, and the players, headed by the ever-welcome Walter Huston, are excellent, but it seems to me that most of Mr. Anderson's work is both ponderous and heavy-handed, a particularly unfortunate defect in a musical comedy.

This was the general tenor of the reviews; but the Broadway audiences, attracted by Anderson's reputation, Huston's performance, and the fact that President Roosevelt had attended a preview, at first flocked for seats in such numbers that the production was moved to a larger theater in February. Then, suddenly, the mixed response took effect, the attendance became smaller, and the show closed and took to the road at the beginning of April. "Although *Knickerbocker Holiday* closed its Broadway run without entirely paying off its original nut," *Variety* wrote with characteristic professional lingo, "the Maxwell Anderson–Kurt Weill musical rates as a financial success. Show had earned back all but about $7,000 of its original $52,000 cost and was still operating at a profit when it was taken on tour." It soon got into the black and was rated by the Playwrights Company as a "mild success."

"September Song" also gradually took hold on the general public and turned into a source of income for its creators that would flow uninterrupted for the rest of their lives. Weill was becoming established on Broadway, although he was still far from enjoying the kind of attention being lavished on such songwriters as Cole Porter, whose *Leave It to Me!*—which is what finally had attracted Bella and Samuel Spewack away from their project with Weill—opened three weeks after *Knickerbocker Holiday*; or Richard Rodgers, whose new musical with Lorenz Hart, *The Boys from Syracuse*, also opened in November; or Jerome Kern, who, though settled in Hollywood, was to make a return to Broadway the following fall, collaborating with Oscar Hammerstein II on *Very Warm for May*. Indeed, though he was eventually to write music more similar to theirs than anything he had done so far, Weill was essentially different from them in remaining a *composer* in the fullest sense of the word, even when doing musical comedy. From the very beginning of his Broadway career, with *Johnny Johnson*, Weill drew the admiration of his collaborators by being the sole arranger and orchestrator of his own scores: that this was part of the opera composer's task went without saying, but it was most unusual for Broadway songwriters. In a sense, Weill's closest musical kinsman in New York was the thirty-three-year-old Marc Blitzstein, who had studied with Arnold Schoenberg in Berlin and greatly admired *The Threepenny Opera* when he saw it there. Blitzstein's politically and socially oriented "play in music," *The Cradle Will Rock*, largely influenced by *The Threepenny Opera*, had been performed in New York two evenings in June 1937—another work initiated by the ill-fated Federal Theatre Project. But there was one crucial difference between Weill and Blitzstein, not yet fully in evidence but clearly adumbrated by the "September Song": unlike Blitzstein, Weill could write a Broadway hit song just as good as any ever written by Porter, Rodgers, Kern, and the others.

The Weills were beginning to make a decent living—the previous
spring Lenya had done a six-week singing engagement at a New York
supper club, Le Ruban Bleu. They celebrated the New Year with a short
vacation in Florida and, looking for some more permanent living situation,
they rented a farmhouse in the woods near Suffern, New York, in the
early months of 1939. At first, they retained the Manhattan duplex as
well, but they gave it up before the end of the year. As in Paris, Kurt
wanted to live in rural surroundings just a short ride away from the center
of a metropolis. But another reason for living in Suffern was the proximity
to Maxwell Anderson's home in New City. Anderson, a large bearlike
figure of a man whose personal presence was as commanding as his role in
American drama, was the central figure of a sort of backwoods Greenwich
Village that had grown up in Rockland County, where the painter Henry
Varnum Poor and the actor Burgess Meredith, among other gifted friends
of Anderson, were living in close proximity to him and to one another.
The Weills were now being drawn into this orbit.

The two authors of *Knickerbocker Holiday*, who were beginning to
form a strong friendship, were at work on a new play. This time the idea
came from a historical novella, *Eneas Africanus*, by Harry Stillwell
Edwards, the editor for many years of the *Macon Telegraph* in Georgia,
who had died only a few months before. Edwards's book tells, in an
epistolary form, the story of Eneas, a slave in the family of Major George
E. Tommey, which has temporarily evacuated its home at the time of
General Sherman's march to the sea. Eneas has been sent out with an old
horse and a wagon in which the family silver is hidden under a load of hay;
but when the danger passes, he is unable to find his way back home.
Misled by a series of confusions concerning place names, Eneas wanders
through much of the South with his cargo, covering more than three
thousand miles in the course of the next eight years. His lot in life
improves considerably in the meantime: he marries, has several children,
and becomes the owner of a champion racehorse—foaled by his flea-bitten
mare, who turns out to have had "illicit" relations with a prize stallion
back at the Tommey plantation—which earns a small fortune for him in
competitions. But Eneas, who does not even realize that he is no longer a
slave, remains faithful to the Tommey family and ultimately returns to
them with the silver. The story has a certain charm, but it is marred by an
attitude of chuckling condescension that does not seem to have troubled
Maxwell Anderson. He and Weill envisioned, on the basis of it, a
theatrical panorama of the Reconstruction South that would even include
a minstrel show in which Eneas becomes involved during his

wanderings—Kurt looked forward with relish to doing this bit of Americana.

Anderson saw the prospective play as a study of the relationship between freedom and responsibility, and this was how he put it in a letter he wrote to Paul Robeson in March 1939, asking him if he would take the lead role. Robeson, however, recognized the innate condescension in the story—Anderson had sent him a copy of Edwards's novel, as well as an account of what he planned to do with the material—and refused the part. This was discouraging to Anderson, who still lacked confidence in the field of musical drama and had wanted the assurance of a major star, as he had obtained for *Knickerbocker Holiday*; and so he went to work on a nonmusical play, *Key Largo*, instead. He and Weill did not completely abandon *Eneas Africanus*, however, and their interest was to revive later that spring when they made contact with Bill Robinson, who, though known primarily as a dancer, was ready to take on the role. But Robinson was then starring in *The Hot Mikado*, one of the two all-Black reworkings of Gilbert and Sullivan running on Broadway that season—and he would not be available for a while at least.

Meanwhile, Kurt had found work with the greatest "off-Broadway" theatrical production of the moment: the New York World's Fair. One of the largest pavilions at the fair was built by the Eastern Presidents' Conference, an *ad hoc* organization created by twenty-seven railroad companies having terminals in the eastern United States, to display the might of what was still America's predominant form of overland transportation. As part of the exhibit a writer named Edward Hungerford, who had done similar works for the Chicago World's Fair and other expositions, created a historical pageant, called *Railroads on Parade*, that required music—and massive production facilities as well, since trains were its starring players. It is not clear who among those connected with this pageant thought of making contact with some of the people responsible for *The Eternal Road*, but the idea was a sensible one, since they were a group well experienced in theatrical gigantism. Charles Alan, who had been Reinhardt's assistant producer, was engaged to direct *Railroads on Parade*, and Harry Horner, another of Reinhardt's assistants for *The Eternal Road*, was hired to do the scenery and costumes. To complete the transfer from dusty biblical path to shining rails, Isaac Van Grove was engaged to conduct, and Kurt Weill—Charles Alan's associate in their own producing enterprise—was taken on as the composer. Others from *The Eternal Road* were nearby: Meyer Weisgal, still adhering to the route to

Zion, was in charge of the Palestine pavilion at the fair; and Norman Bel Geddes was creating the vast General Motors Futurama, spending money far beyond the point at which Weisgal had given up on him in fright—but "fortunately for Bel Geddes," as Weisgal has written, "General Motors could afford him."

Railroads on Parade was one of the shows previewed on the night before the fair's official opening on April 30, 1939. With a cast of some two hundred persons, and locomotives—either the actual ones or full-scale replicas thereof—ranging in vintage from 1829 to the present, the outdoor pageant presented various scenes in the history of American railroading, including the famous "wedding of the rails" for the first transcontinental track in 1869. "The pageant has loads of charm," wrote the composer Elliott Carter in a survey of World's Fair music published shortly after the opening, "with real steaming and smoking locomotives playing the prima-donnas' roles. When the famous halves of the Union Pacific meet, the iron horses sing little songs with toots between phrases." These are the good cousins of *Johnny Johnson*'s cannons. "Weill," he continued, "has appropriately used all kinds of American tunes, including one of my favorites, *Fifteen Years on the Erie Canal*, with fine taste, intelligence, and showmanship. All this is played and sung by an orchestra of twenty-six and a chorus of eighteen who are below stage; the music is piped up and amplified to sound above the locomotives' roar." Here, at last, was a chance to do some of the Americana that Weill had been longing for; and, if the occasion did not call for him to produce the most serious of scores, he must nonetheless have been struck by the fact that he had now created a piece of *Gebrauchsmusik* truer to that ideal than anything he or most of his contemporaries had done in Germany. Indeed, the World's Fair had also attracted Hanns Eisler, to do the same sort of thing for a film at the Petroleum exhibit—presumably without any evident Brechtian ironies; and composers of the quality of Aaron Copland, William Grant Still, and Vittorio Giannini had also produced scores for the fair's exhibits.

At the end of May Maxwell Anderson, having finished the first draft of *Key Largo*, went with his wife to California, where the Pasadena Playhouse was presenting eight of his plays for its festival that summer. Weill and Lenya set out by car on June 6 and joined them in Malibu, where they were staying. Between frequent swims in the ocean the two collaborators made such progress on *Ulysses Africanus*, as they soon would be calling it, that they thought it might be ready for production in the fall, depending on Bill Robinson's availability. It is around this time that they wrote the song "Lost in the Stars," which was meant for this show. But

The Hot Mikado went on the road, and *Ulysses Africanus* had to wait. By the end of August, the Weills and the Andersons were back in New York.

Weill no doubt was greatly disappointed to be approaching the fall with no prospect of a major opening before him; but his personal feelings must also have felt themselves drowned in the onrush of world events that September, as World War II broke out in Europe. His immediate family, at least, was safe: his parents had been living in Palestine for two years, settled in the coastal town of Nahariya, where there was a large German-speaking community; his brother Nathan and his sister, Ruth, and their families, also were in Palestine; and his brother Hans—ever the closest member of the family in Kurt's affections—had come to America the previous year and settled with his wife, Rita, and daughter, Hanne, in New York. But these transplantations were all the more a sign that the old life was going up in smoke, like the synagogues of Dessau and elsewhere in the wake of the *Kristallnacht* the previous fall.

Among Weill's old Berlin circle in particular, there had been persecutions, suicides, and violent deaths that seemed to sum up the history of the times. Carl von Ossietzky, editor of *Die Weltbühne*, which had so often reviewed the works of Weill and Brecht, had been arrested by the Gestapo in February 1933 and was still a prisoner when he was awarded the Nobel Peace Prize in 1936; he had finally been released in broken health to die in a Berlin hospital in 1938. Kurt Tucholsky, one of *Die Weltbühne*'s most brilliant contributors, also was dead, a suicide in Sweden in 1935. Ernst Toller hanged himself in a New York apartment that very fall of 1939: "The twelfth hour has passed," he had said to his American friends. Brecht was now in Sweden, but some of his friends and associates who had gone to the Soviet Union had become martyrs to their convictions. Carola Neher, who had gone there with Erwin Piscator to make *The Revolt of the Fishermen of Santa Barbara*—on which Lenya had briefly worked—and stayed there with him to try to form a German theater in exile, had been arrested in 1936 and sent to a forced labor camp, where she died a short time later. (Piscator, abroad at the time of the roundup, was eventually to make his way to the United States.) Even the peaceful deaths seemed to have a special significance. Dr. Emil Hertzka, director of Universal Edition in Vienna, had died in 1932, at around the time Weill's contract with him expired, and none of Weill's music had been published by that house since then. As for Count Harry Kessler, who had been witness to a world coming to an end, he then died with it himself, in France on December 4, 1937, at the age of sixty-nine, quietly and forgotten.

Unlike many others, Kurt had succeeded not merely in reaching the United States but in becoming an American spiritually as well, and this was a time to rejoice in the fact. Indeed, the very next work he completed with Maxwell Anderson, a radio cantata called *The Ballad of Magna Carta*, was just such a celebration—and really was a piece of Americana despite its title. The well-known radio writer Norman Corwin was presiding over a regular Sunday afternoon program called *Pursuit of Happiness*, and that November he had brought about a significant moment of American cultural history by presenting Paul Robeson in a performance of the *Ballad for Americans*, a piece that Earl Robinson and John Latouche had written for the Federal Theatre Project the year before. Corwin wanted a follow-up and got Anderson and Weill to do a piece in a similar vein for broadcast in February. In their text Anderson and Weill were to make it quite clear that, in choosing Magna Carta as their subject, they were celebrating American liberties.

Using a narrator who alternates freely between speaking and singing—for the February 4 broadcast this assignment was taken by Burgess Meredith—the piece sets its scene in 1215 and describes the oppressions of King John of England: significantly for the times, his persecutions of Jews are mentioned among his wrongdoings. Then the narration weaves freely in and out of various dramatized scenes, culminating in the confrontation between John and the rebellious nobles at Runnymede and in his signing of the historic document; the actors also alternate between speaking and singing. At the end the chorus jubilantly sings the theme of the fifteen-minute drama, that "Resistance unto tyrants is obedience to God"—a point Anderson's text has underscored with some veiled references to Roosevelt as well as the obvious ones to Hitler.

The music Weill wrote for this piece, which ranges from the kind of broad Americana sound that characterizes the *Ballad for Americans* to the tones of English folksongs, is among the freest he had ever composed. "It's a ballad like the old Scottish ones, set to music," he told an interviewer just before the broadcast, "but between the stanzas there are prose passages, sometimes spoken, sometimes in recitative. Even the spoken parts, though, are in rhythm, so that the whole thing has a definite pattern." But the published score of the piece in fact instructs the performers to make their speech patterns as free and as natural as possible once they have mastered the overall rhythms. The result is something really quite different from the German Weill—from *The Lindbergh Flight*, for example, or from *Der Jasager*, to which this work is in some ways related. The old formula of rigidly enclosed units is all but gone entirely, and the music now flows from scene to scene, as well as in a freer interplay than ever before with lines spoken and sung, and with the dramatic action. It is as if Weill is expressing a newfound American freedom in the very texture of his music—and this freedom is decidedly an American phenomenon for him, for we had first begun to hear it in parts of *Johnny Johnson*. One thing this trait means is an at least partial renunciation of the Brechtian *Verfremdungseffekt* (not to mention the Busonian equivalent), for it represents an infiltration of emotional fervor and even of a frank sentimentality into Weill's music. His art is certainly being influenced by his state of mind; though we might also point to influences in his environment that have helped to produce this freedom—such as the *Ballad for Americans* and, above all, the movies. For this technique of music accompanying action and occasionally flowing into it is a phenomenon of sound films, an art form that had had a very strong influence upon Weill by this time, as upon many other artists.

Weill told his interviewer that he and Anderson hoped to follow up this work with a whole series of "ballad histories," as they called them, "one about the Boston Tea Party, another about the Emancipation Proclamation, and so on. I think we've worked out a very interesting form," he continued. "Radio has limitations, of course, but it also has possibilities offered by no other medium. We've tried to make the most of them." Here, certainly, is a Weill we have already met in Germany. Indeed, Weill goes on in this interview with William G. King of the *New York Sun* to develop anew some of his ideas about cultural democracy and the role of music, this time stated with the relatively free flow of his American style and without the confinement of Marxian concepts. After a brief discussion of the old ideal of *Gebrauchsmusik* he observes: "I'm convinced that many modern composers have a feeling of superiority toward their audiences. Schoenberg, for example, has said he is writing for a time fifty years after his death. But the great 'classic' composers wrote for their contemporary audiences. They wanted those who heard their music to understand it, and they did. As for myself, I write for today. I don't give a damn about writing for posterity." This last remark, often repeated in the years to come, was to become well known among Weill's friends, and it was taken by many of them to mean that he did not care what posterity would think of him; but that is clearly not its meaning here.

"And I do not feel," Weill went on, warming up to his theme, "that I compromise my integrity as a musician by working for the theater, the radio, the motion pictures or any other medium which can reach the public which wants to listen to music." And then he made another remark that was to become well known and that we have already encountered: "I have never acknowledged the difference between 'serious' music and 'light' music. There is only good music and bad music." Finally, the import of all this is summed up by these observations made elsewhere in the interview: "You hear a lot of talk about the 'American opera' that's going to come along some day. It's my opinion that we can and will develop a musical-dramatic form in this country, but I don't think it will be called 'opera,' or that it will grow out of the opera which has become a thing separate from the commercial theater, dependent upon other means than box-office appeal for its continuance. It will develop from and remain a part of the American theater—'Broadway' theater, if you like. More than anything else, I want to have a part in that development." In later years Weill was to find himself a little more attached to the word *opera* than he was in this moment, but in every other respect this was an ideal to which he would remain unflinchingly true to the day of his death.

To prove his point Weill was at this moment showing his willingness to write incidental music for even the straight dramatic efforts of the Playwrights Company, with which he now had a close though informal relationship. In the summer he had done some music for a play by Sidney Howard, a modern retelling of the Faust story called *Madam, Will You Walk*, which was to have starred George M. Cohan. But in August, while working on his revisions, Howard had died in a freak accident on his farm in the Berkshires: he had cranked up his tractor while it was in gear, and it crushed him against the wall of the barn. The task of finishing the play was taken on by Robert E. Sherwood, but Howard's widow resisted many of the changes he thought necessary, and the resulting script was so weak when the play opened for a Baltimore tryout in November that Cohan walked out after a few performances. The play never made it to Broadway. In the fall Weill composed incidental music entirely for novachord for Elmer Rice's romantic comedy set in Manhattan, *Two on an Island*, which starred Betty Field and Luther Adler. He also started to work on incidental music for a play by S. N. Behrman. Later in 1940 he was to do music for Anderson's play based on an incident in the life of Jesus, *Journey to Jerusalem*. But by then he was deeply involved in his next major work for the musical theater, the one that would bring him to the height of American fame and fortune at last.

Success on Broadway:
Lady in the Dark

It was at a party given in New York by Walter Huston in November 1939, after the national tour of *Knickerbocker Holiday*, that Weill was first introduced to Moss Hart. Up to that time Hart had still been primarily involved in his celebrated series of collaborations with George S. Kaufman; *The Man Who Came to Dinner* had just opened that fall. But he also had done some successful scripts on his own, all of them musicals; and though the story goes that he and the composer of *Knickerbocker Holiday* exchanged nothing more than greetings and a few mutual compliments on this occasion, chances are that Weill's eager eye was already fixing itself upon another potential collaborator.

Hart's name then came up a few days later in a conversation Weill was having with the stage director Hassard Short, a specialist in musicals. By this time several of Weill's projects had fallen into abeyance. With Bill Robinson temporarily unavailable, Maxwell Anderson had lost interest in *Ulysses Africanus*, and was at work on other things. Hoffman R. Hays's script for the Davy Crockett project was still full of problems and that, too, had been shelved. There were hopes of getting back to work with Paul Green on *The Common Glory*, but Green for the moment was very busy with regional theater projects, and besides, this idea did not seem too commercial. Weill's financial situation was still shaky, and, since Lenya was having trouble finding work in America, a good deal depended on his getting involved in something lucrative. He evidently was now thinking more in terms of the Broadway box office than ever before, and this was why he had gotten together with Short. Someone had just sent him a script called *The Funnies* as a possibility for a musical show; the idea was rather conventional musical comedy stuff, but Kurt was fond of American comic strips and wanted to have Short's opinion about whether this was something they might do together.

Short liked the idea but thought it needed a lot of rewriting. Weill suggested Moss Hart as someone who might be able to do the job. Now, Short had staged a number of Hart musicals, including two with songs by Irving Berlin, *Face the Music* and *As Thousands Cheer*, in 1932 and 1933, and one with songs by Cole Porter, *Jubilee*, in 1935. He recalled that there even had been a number called "The Funnies" in *As Thousands Cheer*. He thought, then, that Hart would be perfect for the job, provided he was willing to do it. Weill and Short got in touch with him, and he asked to see the script. In another few days Hart called Weill, and they arranged to meet for lunch.

Sitting at their table in an elegant little restaurant called the Hapsburg, Weill and Hart took the measure of one another. Hart had been going through a long psychoanalysis with Dr. Gregory Zilboorg, who also had analyzed George Gershwin and other prominent show business figures, and one result was an urgent need on his part to end the collaboration with Kaufman and have a career on his own. With *The Man Who Came to Dinner* just out of the way, he was searching for the right material with which to do this. As for Weill, he was at something of a crossroads in his American career. He needed a hit and was willing to be a little less austere than before in his artistic aims in order to get one; yet he still did not want to compromise his integrity as a serious theater composer. In a sense, Hart was exactly the right partner for him at this moment: he was primarily an entertainer rather than a pursuer of lofty themes like Anderson, but his comedies with Kaufman, at their best, were entertainment lifted onto the level of art.

Hart made it clear from the outset that he was not interested in the script at hand. He did not want to work on somebody else's idea; and furthermore, he was fed up with the kind of conventional musical comedy at which it intimated. "I refuse to waste any more time," he said according to a press agent's account, "wracking my brain to provide a good excuse for the boy and girl to burst into a love duet." He could not have put it better as far as Weill was concerned: these words were spoken as if by a Busoni come to Broadway. Weill said that he, too, was not really interested in doing conventional musical comedy—but the problem, he went on, was that in America it was hard to get serious playwrights to do things for the musical theater the way they had done in Germany. This was most diplomatic. By the end of the afternoon Hart knew that he wanted to do a play with Weill; but though they were in warm agreement concerning principles, they had not yet come up with a concrete idea.

This was not long in emerging, however. Hart got back in touch with Weill only a week or so later. Many people who knew Hart in this period have observed that psychoanalysis had become a favorite preoccupation of his, not only as a method to deal privately with his emotional health but also as an obsessive subject of conversation. And so it had now occurred to him to do a play about psychoanalysis—Brooks Atkinson was to remark jokingly after its successful opening that this was one way of getting back all the money Hart had given to Dr. Zilboorg. But the idea seemed to have genuine musical possibilities. "Why not show someone in the process of being psychoanalyzed and dramatize the dreams?" as the program for the resulting production was to put it. "And what more natural than that the dreams be conveyed by music and lyrics so that the plane of reality and that of the dreams would be distinct?"

The idea of doing dream sequences that would be completely self-contained musical compositions was well suited to Weill's artistic aspirations. Furthermore, the playing with various levels of fantasy and reality was a vein he had not explored since the days of *Der Protagonist* and *Royal Palace*. Indeed, he must have sensed from the outset that this project would be something of a return to expressionist techniques—except that now the mood was to be comic and in a Broadway idiom. Allowing for these differences, the heroine of the new play was to have a certain kinship with Dejanira of *Royal Palace*, even down to the fact of having three suitors. And one more important link between the idea proposed by Hart and those early expressionist operas must also have occurred to Weill: like them, it was to be totally unpolitical. Even *Marie Galante* had played with political themes, and *The Lindbergh Flight* and *Der Jasager* were disguised tracts; in other words, this was to be his first major theater work in a dozen years effectively devoid of any political content. But this was in some ways a response to the war; Weill was far from the only serious person at the end of 1939 who felt that, with the great issues now being decided by generals and statesmen, artists were not evading their responsibilities if they provided their troubled fellow men with a little diversion—with "escape" entertainment, as it came to be called.

And so the process of Weill's "going Broadway" more than ever before was under way, and its next step came with the question: since

Hart was not a lyricist, who would do the words for the musical sequences? Perhaps it was Weill rather than Hart who suggested Ira Gershwin; at any rate, he was bound to be enthusiastic at the idea. Weill had long hoped to work with him, and now that the composer of *Die Bürgschaft* and *Johnny Johnson* was about to do something a bit frothy, it was appropriate that he join forces with the man who had run the gamut with his brother from *Funny Face* to *Porgy and Bess*. But the suggestion was problematical. Since his brother's death, Ira Gershwin, who was now settled permanently in Beverly Hills, had only completed the scores of the two more films he and George had been working on—*A Damsel in Distress* and *The Goldwyn Follies*—and had done nothing more in the intervening two years. Many people thought he had retired, though he was only forty-three years old. And even if he had not, would he be willing to work in New York again?

Hart wasted no time about finding the answer. It was on New Year's Day of 1940, according to Benjamin Welles in *The New York Times*, that "the call of the theater broke in once more on Ira Gershwin. Through the lazy round of afternoon tennis games and evening poker parties with a few intimate friends in Beverly Hills came the tinkling of a long-distance phone. Moss Hart on the wire in New York. He was writing a new show about a brilliant editor of a fashion magazine, a woman admired and envied yet unhappy and alone. The action would revolve around her psychoanalysis. Kurt Weill had agreed to do the score. They both wanted him for the lyrics. Would he consider it?

"Gershwin didn't consider it. He said yes, and hung up. Then he thought about the blissful, sun-drenched ease of Beverly Hills. He feared that his wife might not take too kindly to the winds and stone chasms of New York in the fall. But as the days passed he knew he was going back to work and when Moss Hart arrived later in Hollywood to confer on the filming of *The Man Who Came to Dinner* the deal was set. Ira Gershwin was ready for the wars." Weill was working on *The Ballad of Magna Carta* and would then have to write new music for the revised production of *Railroads on Parade* being prepared for the reopening of the New York World's Fair that April 30; but then he would be ready to give all his time to the new project. And so it was arranged that Gershwin would come to New York in May to begin working on the three-way collaboration.

Meanwhile, Hart had been making enough progress in his rough draft of *I Am Listening*, as the play was now being called, that he could begin showing it to potential candidates for the starring role. Indeed, early in the year, he thought he had found his star in Katharine Cornell, who at that moment was demonstrating once again her right to be considered one of the great ladies of the American stage in a highly successful tour, with Laurence Olivier as her costar, of S. N. Behrman's *No Time for Comedy*, produced by the Playwrights Company. Weill, whose friends at the Playwrights Company may have been influential in arousing her interest in his new project, must have been especially excited at the prospect of getting her to perform her first singing role. But what he had in mind was more than incidental music for a straight drama, whereas this apparently was what she at first thought it would be. In time, as the musically ambitious character of the dream sequences began to be more evident, Katharine Cornell decided that the part was not for her.

"Then on a Sunday night," as Hart later related, "I went to a rehearsal of a British war relief party for which George Kaufman and I were to do an act, and Gertrude Lawrence, among others, was there to rehearse her bit." In recent years Gertrude Lawrence had been giving more and more of her time to straight dramatic parts—one of the triumphs of her career had been her performance opposite her good friend Noël Coward in his 1930 play, *Private Lives*—but she was still well remembered as a star of musical comedy, one of the few from England who were as popular in America as they were at home. Moss Hart was reminded of this fact once again as he watched her perform that evening. "After the rehearsal finished," Hart's account continues, "I asked Gertie to come and have a snack with me at the back room of the Plaza, and as we drank our beer I asked her point-blank if she wanted to hear my new play. She was charming and, from even the little I told her, it seemed nothing could be more exciting than the prospect of playing Liza Elliott. She was, as a matter of fact, searching wildly about for a play for the new season and would give me an answer immediately."

But, as it turned out, her final decision had to be deferred two weeks because, according to Hart, her astrologer had told her to "do nothing until April 7." The playwright had no choice but to retire to his farm in Bucks County, Pennsylvania, "cursing Gertie's astrologer all the way," and spend the next two weeks working quietly on the script. Then, on the morning of April 6, he received a telephone call from his hoped-for star. She asked if the play was finished and he said yes—which was true enough of the spoken parts, though the dream sequences had not even been begun.

"Wonderful, darling," she replied, "it's all working out beautifully, because I've just had a cable from Noël and he arrives tomorrow morning. Isn't that wonderful?"

Hart said yes it was, but what did Noël have to do with it.

"But don't you see, darling," she explained, "it all works out! My astrologer said to do nothing until April 7 and I never do anything without Noël's advice and here he is arriving on the very day! You must read the play to Noël and if he says 'yes' I'll do it. It's all working out beautifully. Bless you, darling!"

The next day Hart reluctantly called Noël Coward, whom he and Kaufman had just amiably caricatured as Beverly Carlton in *The Man Who Came to Dinner*. He was in New York on a war mission. "Noël, as always, was unpredictable, infuriating and a tower of strength. He made no secret of the fiendish delight he took of the spot I had maneuvered myself into, but he agreed, busy as he was, to hear the play the next afternoon. It was a nervous lunch we had at my house [in New York] the next day, and as we went upstairs to begin the reading you could have bought all of Freud and psychoanalysis from me at a very nominal sum."

But Coward liked the play. "Gertie ought to pay you to play it," he said, and they went to the theater where she was finishing her matinee performance of Samson Raphaelson's *Skylark* to tell her the news. "Bless you, darlings," she said when she heard it, and then Hart went with Coward to bring the word to the Lunts. Eventually the two men reached the hotel where Coward was staying.

"Uncle Moss," he said as he took his leave, "now your troubles are really beginning."

"But Gertie said 'yes,' didn't she?" Hart insisted.

"That's just the point, my boy. Gertie said 'yes!'" And he turned and disappeared through the doors.

It was to take Hart three more months to get her to actually sign a contract; but the coportrayer of Sheridan Whiteside and his circle was no doubt used to this sort of thing. For Kurt Weill, this world he was about to enter was rather different from any of the ones he had known before.

Ira Gershwin arrived in mid-May and the three collaborators went to work, spending twelve to sixteen hours a day at it, spreading themselves out in various places. They even went to Hart's Bucks County house now and then, as Gershwin has recalled: "The food was excellent, the guestrooms cozy; there were a large swimming pool and thousands of trees and any amount of huge and overwhelmingly friendly, woolly dogs; there was even that rarity for those days (1940), a TV set; but the show was ever on our minds and mostly we were at it, discussing the score in progress and what lay ahead."

At this point the script called for four dream sequences, each of them, as Weill conceived it, "little one-act operas" in the American musical-comedy idiom. In the first one, Liza Elliott—who, though she edits a fashion magazine, is quite austere in her personal style—dreams of herself as a dazzlingly glamorous creature, beset by admirers ranging from college students and headwaiters to Aldous Huxley, Igor Stravinsky, and the president of the United States. In the second, which occurs after her longtime lover has said he is going to divorce his wife, various fantasies of marriage alternate with her recollections of elementary and high school days. The third was to be a minstrel show that would gradually transform itself into a trial at which she sings her own defense. The fourth, coming after Liza has received a marriage proposal from the movie star Randy Curtis, was to be her fantasy of the life she would lead in Hollywood: "an enormous ranch in the San Fernando Valley," as Ira Gershwin has described it, "with a palatial home furnished from the Hearst Collection, butlers galore, private golf course, Chinese cooks, fifty-thousand-barrel gushers on the property, &c." The script also called for one song to be sung outside these wholly musical sequences: "My Ship," the childhood song that Liza keeps trying to remember and that recurs in snatches as a leitmotiv through all the dreams, is sung by her in her final session with the analyst, which is otherwise nonmusical and in which she is "cured." The song is also briefly reprised at the very end of the play.

Before the summer was over, however, a major change had been arrived at. Ira Gershwin writes: "The third musical dream sequence . . . a mixture of Court Trial and Minstrel Show, was practically completed when it was decided that minstrel costume and background weren't novel enough." Weill, no doubt eager to try out his minstrel show ideas left over from the frustrated *Ulysses Africanus*, must have been brokenhearted at this decision. "Agreeing that a circus setting seemed preferable—there could be more riotous color and regalia—we changed the opening, the jury patters, and most of the recitatives, from an environment of burnt cork and sanded floor to putty nose and tanbark." One song, however, was salvaged from the minstrel show—for the time being, at least—and inserted into the circus scene: this was Liza's defense, cast in the form of "a six- or seven-minute pseudo-metaphysical dissertation based on the signs of the Zodiac and their influences, all pretty fatalistic; in short, she'd done what she did because she couldn't help doing whatever she did do." No doubt this had been inspired by Gertrude Lawrence's passion for astrology, but Weill and Gershwin had become deeply involved in the song they created. "We were quite proud of this bizarre and *Three Penny Opera*-like effort and felt it could be the play's musical highlight."

This was the way things stood with *Lady in the Dark*, as the show was now being called at Gertrude Lawrence's request, when Gershwin returned to California at the end of August. But the phase of creation at the hands of three lone artists now was over, and the amassed forces of production were moving in. A meeting, attended by Hart and Weill, was held at the New York office of the show's prospective producer, Sam H. Harris, during which Hassard Short, who was to stage the production, and Max Reinhardt's old assistant Harry Horner, who was to design it, presented their plan. There were to be four revolving stages and a cinematic fluidity of movement from one fabulous set to another, depicting the various levels of reality and fantasy, such as had never been seen before on a Broadway stage; and the cost would be an estimated $125,000. When Hart heard this figure, he turned to Weill and remarked that *this* was the outcome of a "nice little lunch" at the Hapsburg the previous fall; to which Kurt replied: "We should have had lunch at Child's."

Costs had to be trimmed, and the first thing to go was the "Hollywood Dream," which did not really advance the dramatic action and also threatened to make the show some fifteen or twenty minutes too long. Weill at first refused to consider this cut, since it meant sacrificing not merely a song but an entire musical sequence. But when Hart and Short suggested some corresponding cuts in the nonmusical part of the play, he saw the dramatic logic of it all and capitulated—though he still hoped to salvage some of the material and place it in the second musical sequence, the "Wedding Dream." He also claimed the right to withhold a final decision on the matter until they had consulted with Ira Gershwin; but in fact the step was already irrevocable.

This was not to be the end of Weill's and Gershwin's frustrations, however; for the next thing to fall victim to production values was the "Zodiac Song." The underlying question did not really apply to this song in particular: Hart and Short simply felt that the show in general was lacking a funny, rousing number for its star—that she had plenty of charming, sentimental stuff to sing, but not one real showstopper. Since the circus sequence was to be the climactic one, it was obvious that such a number should occur there; but so far, all Liza had in it was the "Zodiac Song," which Hart and Short thought to be rather more contemplative than funny—indeed, when Sam Harris spoke to Gershwin about it by long-distance telephone, he gave the impression that the song was thought of as "dour and oppressive." What Hart, Short, and Harris wanted was a little more of the kind of sophisticated humor at which Gershwin was considered a master. Weill could not see their argument; he tried playing the song one day for Maxwell Anderson, Elmer Rice, and their wives, and they "laughed long and loud" at it. Even when he gave in and agreed that Gertrude Lawrence might need a new, more rousing number in the circus sequence, he hoped that the "Zodiac Song" might be retained in it as well. But, craftsman that he was, he must have known in his heart of hearts that once the new song was written the old one would become redundant.

Ira Gershwin telephoned Weill after hearing from Sam Harris. Kurt was a man whose professionalism always remained intact even when his artistic nature felt battered. "His feeling was, right or wrong, we owed them a go at it, since, generally, everything else we'd done had been found so acceptable"—*everything else*, meaning, by now, two sequences out of their original four. "So, a few days later," Gershwin goes on, "I was again in New York. At one conference Moss had a suggestion that we do a number about a woman who couldn't make up her mind. That sounded possible; and after a week or so of experimenting with style, format, and complete change of melodic mood from the Zodiac song, we started 'Jenny,' and finished Liza's new defense about ten days later." The final song, "The Saga of Jenny," was about a woman whose afflictions were all because she *would* make up her mind, always and with too much resolve. Once again, as with *The Threepenny Opera* and *Knickerbocker Holiday*, Weill had written the show's hit song on demand late in the game, as a virtual afterthought—although, unlike its two predecessors in this respect, this song was not among the best he had written, nor was it even one of the best in the show of which it was a part. The removal of the "Zodiac Song"—for this, of course, is what ensued—left an emotional and artistic gap that was not so easily filled.

It is likely that "The Saga of Jenny" was not the only song in the final version of the "Circus Dream" to have been inserted late and on demand. By a brilliant stroke of casting, the role of Russell Paxton, the fey and loquacious fashion photographer, had been given to the rising young comedian Danny Kaye. He was not yet widely known, but his talents clearly were well understood by the creators of the show, and it was probably after he was hired that the decision was made to give him a virtuoso patter song. Ira Gershwin dipped into his bag of tricks for this and came up with a piece of light verse he had published in the old humorous weekly *Life* in 1924. The final result, also appearing in the circus sequence, was "Tschaikowsky," in which the singer recites the names of forty-nine Russian composers at a speed that would defy most tongues not belonging to Danny Kaye.

After the closing of *Skylark* in New York, Gertrude Lawrence had done a summer revival of *Private Lives* for British War Relief and then spent the early fall touring the United States in the Raphaelson play. The tour was to end November 16, and only after that date and a brief rest for the star could rehearsals of *Lady in the Dark* begin in earnest. Meanwhile, all the principal roles had been cast except that of Randy Curtis, the "beautiful hunk of man" from the movies. Buster Crabbe had been considered, among others, as well as Leif Erickson from the Group Theatre, but so far none had proved wholly satisfactory. Then, Ira Gershwin writes, "about a week before rehearsals were to start, a friend of mine, Gene Solow, just in from California, popped in to see me at the Essex House. When I told him of our casting problem, he said that a likely prospect, Victor Mature, had been on the plane with him, but he didn't know where Victor was to stay." After calling several hotels, they tried the front desk of the one they were in and got Mature just as he was checking in. Furthermore, he was interested in the role, though, as it turned out, he had been coming to New York to try out for the leading role in a Group Theatre production, that of Irwin Shaw's *Retreat to Pleasure*. When Mature signed with *Lady in the Dark* instead, a few tense days ensued during which Harold Clurman—the lone member of the original directorate still with the Group—hinted at possible legal action. The matter finally was settled quietly and amicably, but there must have been a few embarrassing moments for Weill, torn between old and new loyalties. The irony was that Mature, though he was in other respects a perfect Randy Curtis, proved unable to sing his principal song, the rather chromatic "This Is New" in the "Wedding Dream." Randy and Liza were each to have sung a chorus of it to the other; instead, Gertrude Lawrence ended up singing both choruses.

The big problem remaining unresolved throughout rehearsals, however, was that of Gertrude Lawrence's crucial number in the "Circus Dream." She was singing "The Saga of Jenny," as Ira Gershwin put it, "most acceptably," but not in such a way as to persuade him or Weill that the "Zodiac Song" would not have been better. To make matters more problematical, Danny Kaye's "Tschaikowsky," which preceded Gertrude

Lawrence's "Jenny" by less than a minute, was doing so well that it threatened to upstage her. This is the way things stood when the show opened for tryouts in Boston on New Year's Eve. Ira Gershwin describes the scene: "We were playing to a packed house, and the show was holding the audience tensely. It was working out. I was among the standees at the back of the house; next to me was one of the Sam Harris staff. In the circus scene when Danny Kaye completed the last note of 'Tschaikowsky,' thunderous applause rocked the theater for at least a solid minute. The staff member clutched my arm, muttered: 'Christ, we've lost our star!' couldn't take it, and rushed for the lobby. Obviously he felt that nothing could top Danny's rendition, that 'Jenny' couldn't compete with it, and that either Miss Lawrence would leave the show or that Danny Kaye would have to be cut down to size.

"But he should have waited. The next few lines of dialogue weren't heard because of the continuing applause. Then, as Danny deferred to Miss Lawrence, it ended; and 'Jenny' began. She hadn't been singing more than a few lines when I realized an interpretation we'd never seen at rehearsal was materializing. Not only were there new nuances and approaches, but on top of this she 'bumped' it and 'ground' it, to the complete devastation of the audience. At the conclusion, there was an ovation which lasted twice as long as that for 'Tschaikowsky.' 'Tschaikowsky' had shown us the emergence of a new star in Danny Kaye. But 'Jenny' revealed to us that we didn't have to worry about losing our brighter-than-ever star."

The new "musical play," as its authors called it, opened in New York on January 23, 1941, at the Alvin Theatre—where *Porgy and Bess* had opened in the fall of 1935, shortly after Kurt Weill's arrival in America. Now he was Ira Gershwin's collaborator, and this opening at the Alvin seemed in some ways to dramatize the fact that he had completed a cycle of transformation into an American composer.

Lady in the Dark is the story of Liza Elliott, editor of the successful fashion magazine *Allure*, who in her late thirties has reached a crisis in her hitherto settled life. For a number of years she has been the mistress of the magazine's publisher, Kendall Nesbitt, a married man, but her possible doubts about this relationship seem to be part of the general emotional turmoil that has brought her to a psychoanalyst in the opening scene. Another sign of the turmoil, as she tells the analyst, was a fit of rage on her part at a staff conference the day before, which had ended with her throwing a paperweight at Charley Johnson, the advertising manager.

Her analysis then begins, and as she describes a recent dream—the "Glamour Dream"—it takes place in all its lavishness before our eyes. After the session is ended, we follow the next few days in Liza's life, in alternating scenes at the magazine and at the psychiatrist's office. Kendall Nesbitt announces that his wife will divorce him at last—a development that provokes Liza to have her "Wedding Dream" while lying alone on a couch in her office. The movie star Randy Curtis comes to the magazine to pose for some pictures and falls in love with her. She continues her ongoing quarrel with Charley Johnson, who announces that he is going to quit, but who meanwhile wants her decision on a circus tie-up he has planned as a theme for the entire Easter issue. She cannot make up her mind and instead dreams of a circus looking exactly like Charley's proposed cover, which constitutes itself into a court trying her for her indecisiveness. But by the end of the play and of her analysis—all of which takes place, miraculously, in only a little over a week—Liza has discovered who is the man for her and what kind of woman she wants to be. She wants to be submissive rather than bossy, after all, and the insubordinate Charley Johnson is given clear evidence by the final curtain that he is soon to be not only her husband but also coeditor of *Allure*.

About half the play's length is taken up by the three musical dream sequences. The first one presents Liza, severely dressed in her waking life, as a glamorous woman bedecked in blue—we are to learn during her analysis that, in childhood, her mother had told her she would never be able to wear blue. In her lavish apartment, which takes up the seventeenth to twenty-second floors, she is serenaded ("Oh, Fabulous One") by a group of admiring men in "faultless evening clothes." She receives telegrams and letters from her legions of admirers ("Huxley"): Huxley and Stravinsky want to dedicate works to her, Epstein wants her to pose for him, thousands of students look forward to her appearance at the Yale–Harvard regatta, and so on. Then she goes out in her chauffeur-driven blue Duesenberg (with blue license plates and a blue Picasso in the car), heading for a nightclub, but on the way she stops in Columbus Circle and makes a speech on a blue soapbox advocating a philosophy of living it up ("One Life to Live"). At the nightclub she is toasted by all those present, who sing her praises as the "Girl of the Moment." Then a marine arrives with the announcement that the president of the United States wants Liza's portrait to appear on the new two-cent stamp and proceeds to paint her picture. But the dream ends darkly: for when she is shown the portrait she sees, not the glamorous Liza of the dream, but the severe one of reality, and the crowd of admirers around her suddenly becomes a jeering one. The dream ends, and the next scene, at Liza's office, shows us some of its significance in relation to her everyday life: her photographer, Russell Paxton, is the image of the man who had been the chauffeur in her dream; Kendall Nesbitt, her lover, had appeared as the headwaiter in the nightclub; and Charley Johnson, her abrasive advertising manager, had been the marine who painted the revealing portrait.

But the nuances and ambiguities of the dream have above all been dramatized by the music, which flows uninterrupted through the entire sequence like a stream of consciousness. Taken as the unified composition that it is—as a "little one-act opera"—the "Glamour Dream" is among Weill's finest achievements. One can easily be deceived about its qualities because it is unabashedly constructed out of Broadway and Hollywood musical idioms. "Oh, Fabulous One" and "Girl of the Moment," as well as a glamour theme that is constantly reiterated by the orchestra though never sung as a complete song, are traditional sorts of Weill parody, utilizing the flavor of dozens of melodies that have often accompanied the doings of elegant women in Art Deco boudoirs and their admirers in top hats and tails; and, like other such Weill parodies, they happen to do quite well if one wants to take them straight. But the real intention behind them is underscored not only by Ira Gershwin's humorous treatment of the material—at one point *glamorous* is rhymed with what is posed as its opposite, *Hammacher Schlammorous*, and this sums up the spirit of the whole—but also by Weill's virtuoso development and variation formulas, which make these banal-seeming melodies into components of a sophisticated musical composition as well as a constant commentary upon the dream's changing moods. While Liza poses for her portrait, for example, "Girl of the Moment" is reprised by the chorus as "an oratorio with Bach-like harmonies," which is designated in the score as a "Larghetto religioso"; then, when everyone sees the revealing likeness, it is again reprised as a wildly agitated rumba. Similarly, the glamour theme, which, when first sounded, ripples like a negligee worn on a terrace in summer, undergoes different variations and becomes a fox-trot upon Liza's entrance into the nightclub.

In other words, Weill has constructed a kind of dramatic symphony—a comic one, to be sure—which is in constant development in the orchestra as the voices of the stage performers relate to it in various ways, moving from spoken to sung recitative, to arioso, to song, and to full choral passages. In a way, this composition is a synthesis of two of his most cherished ideals, one European, the other American: for in its free flow—the freest of anything he has written so far, including *The Ballad of Magna Carta*, which has passages that foreshadow it in some ways—it is a realization of musical aspirations that have grown in him on American soil; but in the unique context of *Lady in the Dark*, it also happens to fulfill his old Berlin ideal of a completely enclosed number.

The "Wedding Dream," occurring after Liza has met Randy Curtis and has furthermore been told by Kendall Nesbitt that he plans to get a divorce, begins with images and echoes of her school days: we hear a chorus singing the "Mapleton High School Song"—another utterly convincing Weill pastiche—and childish voices reciting a French lesson and singing "*Au clair de la lune*." All this sweetness is constantly challenged, however, by a disturbing bolero melody that seems to come from the deepest recesses of Liza's consciousness. It becomes especially pronounced when a chorus of voices announces that the Mapleton High School girl, Liza Elliott, is now about to marry Kendall Nesbitt. Kendall comes for her, and they prepare to select a ring from a tray brought in by a salesman—who happens to be Charley Johnson. After some hesitation Liza points to one of the rings, and Charley gives her a small golden dagger instead.

Then both men disappear, and Randy Curtis is spotlighted. He sings to her his love song, "This Is New"—or, at any rate, she sings it to him, since Victor Mature had to give up trying, as we have seen. Liza dances as the song is reprised and suddenly begins to hum the same snatch of melody—"My Ship"—with which she has begun both dream sequences so far, unable to go beyond a certain point. She stops again in vexation, and as the bolero theme returns, the chorus asks her why she is so unhappy on her wedding day. She is suddenly impelled to remember a school play called *The Princess of Pure Delight* in which she was to have been the princess, but wasn't—she forgets why—and proceeds to tell the story of it in a childlike fairy-tale song. After this an eerie wedding scene occurs, in which Kendall Nesbitt is the groom, Charley Johnson the minister, and Randy Curtis a choral leader. The various voices—including those of the chorus—enter into an interplay of musical themes, and the bolero gradually emerges in the orchestra, until, as the stage directions read: "It all becomes a bizarre combination of oratorio and mysterious and ominous movement winding up in a cacophonous musical nightmare."

This second dream sequence is not as rich as the first, and, though it shares some of the best qualities of the "Glamour Dream," Weill was never completely satisfied with it, regarding it as "a little slow, dragging and humorless." This was why he hoped to pep it up with elements from the discarded "Hollywood Dream," adding on some livelier visions of marriage with Randy to the passage in which he appears singing "This Is New"—but there proved to be no time available for this material. Presumably, Weill would have been happier with this sequence if it had contained at least one candidate for hit-song status, such as he and Ira Gershwin considered "One Life to Live" to be—though Gertrude Lawrence herself never liked it. Actually, as individual songs go, "This Is New" is really the best one in the entire score; but it was much too sophisticated musically ever to become a hit, and it is cloaked in some of the lugubriousness that characterizes the whole wedding sequence.

As for "The Princess of Pure Delight," it was too cute, too much of a novelty number, ever to be a candidate for a hit. It was, by the way, a *tour de force* on several levels. Since it tells the old story of a king ready to marry his daughter to the suitor who can solve a certain riddle, it is an echo of the *Turandot* tale that Busoni had once set to music, and thereby a tribute by Weill to his old teacher. Moreover, since the princess in the story has four suitors, three of them princes and the fourth, the one who wins her, a minstrel, her history is a bit like what Liza's will turn out to be. As for the content of the riddle, it is the old conundrum asking what word of five letters is always spelled wrong—the answer, of course, being "W–R–O–N–G." Ira Gershwin was proud of this, though it is a bit creaky; he was justified in his pride, however, at having made the king's chief sorcerer ask for a twenty-gulden fee for proposing the riddle: at various places in the play, there is mention of the twenty dollars Liza pays her analyst for each session.

The third dream, the circus, is musically the most simplistic of the three even though it is the most elaborate *mise-en-scène*. Left alone in her office with Charley Johnson's proposed circus cover, Liza is suddenly transported into that very scene, the most breathtaking one of the production. Clowns, tumblers, and other circus performers come on singing "The Greatest Show on Earth," another piece of cleverly conventional Weill pastiche. After a brief "Dance of the Tumblers," the ringmaster, who is the photographer Russell Paxton, announces that this is really a courtroom in which Liza Elliott is being brought to trial for her inability to make up her mind—about the Easter cover, about Kendall Nesbitt, and about the kind of woman she wants to be. Charley Johnson, appearing as a trapeze artist, takes the role of prosecuting attorney; Randy Curtis, bareback rider, is her defense lawyer; Kendall Nesbitt, lion tamer, is brought on as the first witness for the prosecution. The jury is introduced from among the performers, and they, to remind us of the Gilbert and Sullivan atmosphere being established, sing a snatch of "My Object All Sublime" from *The Mikado*—after which Ira Gershwin proves unable to overcome the temptation to rhyme "irrelevant" with "Gilbert and Sellivant."

The trial proceeds until the judge, ringmaster Russell Paxton, asks who was the composer of one snatch of melody just heard; when told "Tschaikowsky," he replies ardently that he loves Russian composers and proceeds to sing his song rattling off the names of forty-nine of them. Ira Gershwin has written that Danny Kaye used to get through the list in thirty-nine seconds—but adds that one night in Madrid, years later, he was clocked at thirty-one. The trial is resumed, and the defendant is asked if there is any good reason why she cannot make up her mind. Liza replies that there is and sings "The Saga of Jenny," about a woman who always *would* make up her mind, and whose life was a series of disasters as a result. As the song ends, prosecuting attorney Charley Johnson takes up a copy of the circus cover and shows it to the jury, who begin to read it like a sheet of music, humming a snatch of the old "My Ship" melody. This drives Liza into a panic, and the scene ends in a frenzied whirl of circus music as Charley accuses her of being "afraid to compete as a woman" and the jury exhorts her over and over again to make up her mind.

The "Circus Dream" is a prime illustration of the ironies of Broadway success: for though it was the smash-hit production sequence of the play and contained the two songs that nobody forgot, it is musically inferior to the other dream sequences by a considerable margin. "Tschaikowsky" was nothing more than a specialty number for Danny Kaye, and the music—a humorously frenzied "Allegro barbaro" that opens with a brief musical quotation from the composer for whom the song was named—is simply adequate to the purpose, no more nor less than it should be. "The Saga of Jenny" has a slight *Threepenny* flavor—Ira Gershwin calls it "a sort of blues bordello"—with a nice hot-licks trumpet in the accompaniment, but it is a bit too drab for the many verses that are sung to it. Ira Gershwin's lines are often funny, but they are permeated by a gallows humor that does not sit well on him in the long run—the lyricist of *Girl Crazy* cannot so easily become a Bertolt Brecht. Aside from these two songs and the "Dance of the Tumblers," however, there is little of any musical interest going on in this sequence at all: the various snatches merely function as connectives and are not developed. We are witnessing the result of the punishing process by which a Broadway show is turned out: for by this point, Weill, having had two entire sequences taken from him and being pressed for a whole new one, obviously was tired. Down to the last minute, not only was he writing and rewriting songs, as all Broadway composers do, but creating and reworking whole orchestrated compositions, as none of them did but Weill. Under the circumstances it is a wonder that the circus sequence is as much fun as it still happens to be.

In a final session with her analyst Liza goes back to a series of scenes from her childhood and adolescence that, with one exception, are not sung, though they help illuminate some of the things that have been going on both in her dreams and in her life. We learn—Moss Hart's lesson in Freudianism proves to be rather simplistic, after all—that Liza had a beautiful mother but was herself considered homely by her parents. She is "afraid to compete as a woman" because she is afraid to compete with her mother—even though her mother died when Liza was a child—and she gets back at her by trying to teach other women to be beautiful. In the school play, it turns out, she didn't play the princess because the boy who was to play opposite her thought she was homely, and she had quit in humiliation. Only once, at a high school dance, was there a moment when she seemed about to triumph over the memory of her mother; a boy almost forsook the prettiest girl in the class in her favor, but then he callously changed his mind. This was the moment, according to the analyst, after which Liza "withdrew as a woman."

But it is during that moment—and again, at the very end of the play, when she realizes she is in love with Charley Johnson—that Liza remembers in full the "My Ship" song, which her father used to sing with her when she was a child and which has been haunting her all the time. At various moments during the dream sequences, the snatches of it have seemed even menacing, but now it emerges, when she sings it in full, as a sweet and idyllic vision of love. The song Weill wrote for this purpose—his first theater song to be cast in the thirty-two-bar convention of American popular songs, and one of the very few for which he composed the melody before the lyrics were written—is almost perilously sweet, but as such it serves its purpose admirably. It seems, furthermore, to be a conscious culmination of its composer's own ship-comes-in cycle. We have seen the hopeful connecting link formed by "*J'attends un navire*" in *Marie Galante*; but now the cycle of aspirations, like the cycle of emigration that corresponds to it, has been completed from the dark vessel of "Pirate

Jenny" to this bright American one with sails made of silk and decks trimmed with gold.

George S. Kaufman saw another aspect of the journey and its fulfillment when he sent Weill a congratulatory telegram after the opening night performance; it read: "Your ship has sails that are made of gold, relax." *Lady in the Dark*, enthusiastically received by critics and audience, was about to become one of the biggest hits Broadway had ever known.

A Composer in Wartime

 If *Lady in the Dark* was Weill's great American break-through to worldly success, it also was a signal for some music critics to express grave reservations about what was happening to the composer of *The Threepenny Opera*. On February 23, 1941, a month after the show's opening, the *New York Herald Tribune* carried a severe attack by Virgil Thomson, whose own *Four Saints in Three Acts* had appeared on Broadway in 1934. Thomson had always been ambivalent about Weill. Reviewing *The Seven Deadly Sins* from Paris in 1933, he had remarked that Weill did for Berlin what Gustave Charpentier, the composer of *Louise*, did for Paris, and concluded that:

> Weill is not a Great Composer any more than Charpentier is. He has a warm heart and a first-class prosodic gift. The rest is moving enough, perhaps too moving. It smells of Hollywood. It is hokum like *Louise*, sincere hokum. If it really touches you, you go all to pieces inside. If not, it is still something anyway, though not so much.

But, cautioning his readers to remember that "the line between hokum and real stuff is far from sharp," he had delivered as his final words: "Let him who has never wept at the movies throw the first stone at Weill's tearful but elegant ditties about the Berlin ghetto."

In *Lady in the Dark*, however, the thin line once separating the Berlin Charpentier from complete hokum had been crossed as far as Thomson was concerned. Outside of "The Saga of Jenny," all the music in the score seemed to him "monotonous, heavy, ponderously German. It reminds one of Berlinese jazz from the early 1920's, of reviews called 'Die Schokoladen Kiddies,' of sentimental ditties called 'Ein kleiner Slow-Fox mit Mary.'" In retrospect, the old Berlin Weill now seemed a little better to Thomson:

> Weill's finest creative period, that of his collaboration with the poet Brecht, is characterized by satirical writing both melodically and harmonically. In parodying cheap sentiment to the utmost he achieved a touching humanity. His characters expressed their self-pity in such corny terms that we ended by pitying them their corn.

And whatever faults Thomson may once have found in that corn, the overriding point for him now was:

> Those sentimental days are gone and Mr. Weill seems ever since to have avoided working with major poets as he has avoided all contact with what our Leftist friends used to call 'social significance.' His music has suffered on both counts, it seems to me. It is just as banal as before; but its banality expresses nothing. Nothing, that is, beyond the fact that Mr. Weill seems to have a great facility for writing banal music and the shamelessness to emphasize its banality with the most emphatically banal instrumentation.

The very last remark must have hurt the most because it was only under the pressure of producers that Weill had succumbed to orchestrating for conventional Broadway ensembles; but, as for putting the instruments of those ensembles to the parodic uses he had made of them in *The Threepenny Opera* and other works with Brecht, this was something he had ceased wanting to do even in Germany, as far back as 1931. Weill never made a public response to Thomson's remarks, though they bothered him enough that he wrote about them in a letter to Ira Gershwin, who was back in California, on March 8. He thought that the remark about having "avoided working with major poets" was "a rather bold statement" and could only conclude, in his still occasionally shaky syntax: "Well, I am used to this kind of attacks from the part of jealous composers. In some form or another it happens every time I do a new show." But clearly Thomson had wounded him.

The moment was full of its consolations, however; for, as he writes in the same letter: "it is lots of fun to have a smash hit." There were twenty to a hundred standees at every performance, a new phenomenon on Broadway, and no fewer than two record albums of the show's principal songs had been made—not only one featuring Gertrude Lawrence, but another by Hildegarde, which had been produced first and was selling better. By the time another month had gone by, there were no fewer than seventeen different records of various *Lady in the Dark* songs, including a Danny Kaye album in which his disc of "Tschaikowsky" was already an offering to American cultural history. Sheet music sales also were very high. And best of all, movie rights to *Lady in the Dark* had been sold to Paramount, one of the original investors in the show, for $283,000, the highest price Hollywood had ever paid for a property of any kind.

Kurt and Lenya wasted no time about settling into their new prosperity. A friend recalls that, just before the premiere of *Lady in the Dark*, Lenya had gone to Klein's to get her gown for the occasion, and Moss Hart had remarked disapprovingly about this, saying she was not taking the proper measure of their forthcoming success. After the opening the same friend recalls going with Kurt to an exclusive midtown shop to help him get the first good suit, of tweed and beige, that he had ever owned in America. The Weills also bought a new Buick convertible. Ernst-Josef Aufricht, recently arrived in America and ensconced on the Upper West Side of Manhattan, was to recall Weill's driving to the door in this car on his first visit. Together they rode to the Alvin to see *Lady in the Dark*, and Aufricht, who had been a rich man in Europe and was now nearly destitute, was overwhelmed with the feeling that the shoe was now on the other foot. On the trip back to his apartment he asked Weill for a loan, and his rich American friend promised to send a check the following day. It turned out to be for $100, and Aufricht thought this a bit stingy until his and Weill's old associate Robert Vambery, who had been in New York a while longer, explained that in America people don't lend money on a person-to-person basis as readily as they did in Europe. Americans went in for public charities, Vambery said, but individuals here were expected to earn their own way as best they could. For Aufricht, the whole incident seems to have become one of many reasons for never wholly liking America or the American Kurt Weill.

Most important of all, the Weills found a new and permanent home for themselves. On South Mountain Road in New City, the actor Rollo Peters had remodeled a late-eighteenth-century farmhouse and put it up for sale. "Brook House," as it was called, was made of wood and stone and trimmed with hand-hewn planks and beams; it also had fourteen acres surrounding it and, running by the windows, the trout-filled brook that gave it its name. For Kurt it was that ideal rural spot within a short ride of the city; and not the least important of its aspects was the fact that it was right down the road from the home of Maxwell Anderson, who had no doubt been the one to bring this property to his attention. Weill and Anderson had not yet resumed their collaboration, but their friendship had blossomed in the meantime. Anderson was just the sort of strong creative personality to which Kurt had always been susceptible, and which he had always needed for the sustenance of his own creativity and emotional stability. Furthermore, the community of writers, artists, and actors that lived in New City and tended to gravitate toward Anderson was a rare and irresistible cultural bounty on American soil. As for Lenya, she had developed a warm friendship with Anderson's wife, Gertrude, known as "Mab" to all her intimates. The Weills bought the house in April and moved in at the beginning of June, Lenya in particular occupying herself with the dizzying round of tasks to be accomplished when one takes on a new house. They also were soon to have a cook, but for the moment the one other member of the household was a woolly sheep dog that Moss Hart had contributed as a gift from his own brood: "Woolly," as they called him—"Voolly," as it sounded to the ears of most visitors—soon became Kurt's beloved companion.

Success did not mean any letup in work for Kurt, however. For one thing, *Lady in the Dark* was in constant need of attention. Weill went to the Alvin about twice a week to deal with any problems the singers and instrumentalists were having, and to help prepare understudies when they suddenly had to take over lead roles—as happened for a while in April, for example, when Victor Mature was laid up with appendicitis.

A large share of the problems, however, came from the temperamental star of the show. In January and February Gertrude Lawrence kept postponing her contracted recording session with RCA Victor until she heard that Hildegarde had done a *Lady in the Dark* album for Decca. Then she rushed to it; but her anger at this turn of events remained so strong that she subsequently refused to lend her signature to a limited edition of the play's text that was to have been signed by herself, Moss Hart, Ira Gershwin, and Kurt Weill, and so the volume was never published. Weill liked her recording but thought her voice sounded "a little shaky" in it, and he seems to have liked Hildegarde's recording equally well. Later that spring Gertrude Lawrence began making known her dislike of "One Life to Live"—which perplexed Weill, since she was getting her second biggest ovation in the show for it. Nevertheless, he was ready to comply with her desire to have a new song in its place; but Ira Gershwin, in distant California, was not. Then, as the summer approached, she insisted that the show be closed for three months while she visited England. The producers' dismay at the prospect of this long recess was compounded by their fear that, under wartime conditions, she would not be able to return. As it turned out, she spent the summer in Massachusetts, but the long break provoked some of the lead players to leave the cast—including Danny Kaye, now very much in demand, who took the starring role in Cole Porter's *Let's Face It!* Consequently, in the fall Weill had a whole new group of singers to train.

In spite of all this, he was ever on the alert for some new show to do. Moss Hart, elated at the success of *Lady in the Dark*, seemed eager to do something else with Weill and Gershwin, but he insisted that it had to follow the formula of the present "musical play" and could not be a conventional musical; the result was that, between his inability to come up with an appropriate idea and Gershwin's reluctance to come east for another long sojourn so soon after the previous one, no sequel developed. Meanwhile, Kurt was approached with proposals by William Saroyan, Philip Barry, Paul Osborn, and John Latouche—with whom he considered doing a musical play on Billy Sunday—but none of these was to get anywhere. A new possibility came up with Maxwell Anderson, but this, too, went by the boards. There also were ideas involving other works of the Playwrights Company. Having done incidental music in 1939 for the late Sidney Howard's *Madam, Will You Walk*, which had closed out of town, Weill was now considering a whole musical based on it. Moreover, S. N. Behrman was back at work on a play for the Lunts, *The Pirate*, that he and Weill had started working on as a musical two years before and then put aside; they now talked again of doing it as a musical play—as "a kind of *Three Penny Opera*," in Weill's words. (As it eventually turned out, *The Pirate*, which was done as a straight play with the Lunts on Broadway in the fall of 1942, was not to appear as a musical until it became a movie in 1947, with a score by Cole Porter.) Weill even heard again around this time from his old collaborator Georg Kaiser, who proposed making a musical play out of Melville's *Billy Budd*. He also tried going back to pure music, even starting a symphony; but he gave up, writing to Gershwin: "It seems too silly just to write music in a time like this." For Weill an era of emergency meant all the more that he had to compose works he knew would be widely heard and enjoyed.

He also continued trying to arouse Ira Gershwin to another project, even without the participation of Moss Hart. Exchanging letters from coast to coast, they discussed the possibility of doing a musical version of Molnár's *The Play's the Thing*, to be adapted by Bella and Samuel Spewack. Another possibility arose in relation to Gabriel Pascal, the Hungarian-born British director who had succeeded in making George Bernard Shaw's *Pygmalion* into a romantic film with the playwright's cooperation. Weill had met Pascal in New York and had talked with him of getting the rights to do musicalizations of some Shaw works, including *Pygmalion*, and to do a proposed RKO musical film of *Arms and the Man*, with Cary Grant and Ginger Rogers. Kurt hoped Gershwin would be the lyricist for these projects; but they never materialized. Other ideas were discussed between the composer and the lyricist, including the possibility of doing some songs for Greta Garbo—who had expressed interest in doing the film version of *Lady in the Dark*—in her next movie; they also discussed the project that eventually was to materialize, without Gershwin's participation, as *One Touch of Venus*.

It was one month after disaster had struck on December 7, 1941, that Gershwin finally explained why he had been reluctant about all these projects. As he saw it, the country now was facing a crisis at least equivalent to that of the Great Depression ten years before—when he had also had a smash hit: *Of Thee I Sing*, with music by his brother, and a book by George S. Kaufman and Morrie Ryskind that won the Pulitzer Prize. "I felt then," he wrote, "that it was a tough period for any new show unless it was so extraordinary that it could overcome the prevailing gloom." But, not heeding his own feelings, he and his brother had gone on to do a couple of flops, including a sequel to *Of Thee I Sing*, *Let 'Em Eat Cake*. Not wanting to repeat that mistake, Gershwin now urged Weill to wait until something turned up that really *had* to be done. The advice had some point to it, but it also was far better suited to Gershwin's current mood of repose than it was to Weill's unflaggingly restless spirit.

Still, America's entry into the war had dampened Weill's creative ardor, as it did that of many people. It was a time for getting involved in the collective effort—but what was to be done by a forty-one-year-old composer who was not particularly robust and not yet an American citizen? He could at least give his talent to the cause. Indeed, in the fall, he had written music for a Madison Square Garden pageant put on by Fight for Freedom, an organization dedicated to promoting America's entry into the war—which was a cause favored by most German refugees, Weill included, whatever their political persuasion. The drama, called *It's Fun to Be Free*, was written by the team that had created *The Front Page* back in 1928, Ben Hecht and Charles MacArthur—MacArthur and his wife, Helen Hayes, lived in Nyack, New York, not far from the Weills in New City, and since Burgess Meredith was in the cast of the pageant, chances are that Kurt had become involved in it through the contacts made around his new home. The drama made a sweeping journey through American history, from the Revolution and the Declaration of Independence to the Gettysburg Address and finally to the present, and gave Weill a chance to try out some of his Americana ideas left over from *The Common Glory*; he could even use some spillover from *The Eternal Road*, since one scene, showing the patriotic participation of Haym Salomon and other Jews in the American Revolution, was set in a Colonial synagogue.

Weill found opportunity to do some other bits of patriotic Americana in the ensuing months. For radio he did a musical setting of the "Song of the Free," a Whitmanesque poem by Archibald MacLeish. In April he went to Chicago to supervise an RCA Victor recording by Helen Hayes, in which she recited various patriotic verses—including the words of songs, like "The Star-Spangled Banner" and "The Battle Hymn of the Republic"—to a musical background he composed, mainly by developing the melodic themes of the songs used. Among the poems she recited were some by Walt Whitman—an old favorite of Kurt's, as of many Europeans discovering America—and he was subsequently inspired to write three concert-style songs to Whitman poems. These settings to "Oh Captain! My Captain!" "Beat! Beat! Drums!" and "Dirge for Two Veterans"— midway in style between German *Lieder* and the best type of American theater songs—are among the most beautiful of the shorter works composed by Weill in America.

But he wanted an ongoing patriotic enterprise to which to devote himself, and this came into being during the early months of 1942. At the beginning of the year, the actress Aline MacMahon had combined forces with Moss Hart and others to do a study of the ENSA (Entertainments National Service Association), the British government-sponsored enter-prise for providing entertainment both to servicemen and to factory workers, and see if an American equivalent could be founded, at least to function in defense plants. The American Theatre Wing was persuaded to donate $10,000 for the venture, and the group prepared a program to try out during factory lunch breaks. It was at this point, in March, that Moss

Hart asked Weill if he would participate in the project. He was delighted to do so and soon found himself working as the regular production manager of *Lunch Time Follies*, as it came to be called, touring the East Coast—there also eventually was a West Coast branch—and helping to cram variety shows into whatever small spaces could be found amid the machinery of war production and into the half hour that was allotted for lunch. Sitting on girders and munching sandwiches, the workers would watch comedians, singers, and lines of chorus girls, usually performing on such themes as parodies of the Axis leaders and singing songs like Harold Rome's "Gee, But It's Cold in Russia."

The work was purely voluntary, and the enterprise was rather humble in content and in its relation to the great struggle going on in the world; but Weill found it one of the thrilling experiences of his life. For him the whole thing "had the spontaneity, the unfeigned popular touch and immediate contact between audience and performers that one experiences when a travelling circus arrives in a small town." He saw it as something of a return to the earthy atmosphere that theater must have had in ancient Greece, in China, or in the Middle Ages when the mystery plays were performed, and he never ceased to feel the excitement of communion with ordinary people whenever the lunch whistle blew and signaled that the entertainment was to begin. Here, then, organizing the productions and writing songs like "Inventory"—a rousing paean to the defense worker—he found as rich a fulfillment as any he had known of the artistic revolution envisioned with Brecht back in 1927. All the old notions of what constituted art had been challenged then; and so, too, were they being challenged now.

Ironically, as if fate wanted to test the differences between those old revolutionary days and these new ones for Weill, Brecht now made a reappearance in his life. Leaving Denmark at the outbreak of the war in 1939, Brecht had sojourned briefly in Sweden and then in Finland before traveling across the Soviet Union and sailing from Vladivostok to Los Angeles in the summer of 1941. Lion Feuchtwanger and the many other old friends of Brecht's who were in Hollywood had persuaded him to stay there and try his luck, and he was now living with his wife and children in Santa Monica. It was from here at around the end of March 1942, that Brecht wrote to Weill asking for his consent to an all-Black production of *The Threepenny Opera* that someone had proposed to do in Los Angeles. Concerning Weill's response, the only evidence we have is a cryptic entry in Brecht's journals saying that he "created difficulties." This might seem to imply that Weill objected to an all-Black production of one of his works; but in the light of his personality and career such a conclusion would be absurd. Weill may have resisted this project, just as he did not seek any revivals of his German works on American soil, because he wanted to become entirely identified as an American composer and did not care to test his reputation, for better or for worse, by the products of his old career. Another factor, undoubtedly, was his status as an applicant for citizenship: *The Threepenny Opera* had been politically controversial, and this was no time to create such problems for himself.

Brecht, according to an entry in his journal, then asked Theodor W. Adorno—once among the outstanding advocates of the Brecht–Weill theater works and now conducting the affairs of the exiled Frankfurt Institute for Social Research from Los Angeles—to write Weill a letter in an effort to win his consent to the production of *The Threepenny Opera*. Weill answered him, according to Brecht, "with a nasty letter full of attacks on me and a hymn of praise for Broadway." Brecht writes that Weill had written his letter in English, saying: "It's easier for me and I like it better." Weill's defense of Broadway and his career there was probably in response to some challenge he felt, with or without justification, to have been hurled at him. But it is hard to make out the nature of his attack on Brecht; it is not likely to have been worse than many things Brecht had said about him through the years, and, in any case, it was not so serious as to keep Brecht, when he visited New York a year later, from getting in touch with him to discuss a possible new collaboration.

By that time Weill had given another demonstration of his eagerness to dedicate his art to the struggle in Europe by composing the music for Ben Hecht's Madison Square Garden pageant, *We Will Never Die*. The news of the deaths of hundreds of thousands of Jews under the Nazi occupation was now reaching the United States, and Hecht conceived of the project in the hope that it would arouse some kind of action against the slaughter. Produced by Billy Rose, directed by Moss Hart, and starring Paul Muni, Edward G. Robinson, Luther Adler, and other actors, the pageant was given two successive performances on the evening of March 9, before audiences of twenty thousand each time. Presented as a kind of vast memorial service, it was divided into three parts: "The Roll Call" was a recitation of the great Jewish names in the arts and sciences from ancient times to the present; "Jews in the War" dramatized some of the contributions of American-Jewish war heroes; and "Remember Us" presented some reports of the present slaughter. The large chorus was made up of two hundred rabbis—twenty of whom were refugees from the Nazi-led ghettos—and two hundred cantors: here again was Weill's tribute to the world of his origins, now going down in flames.

It was war propaganda work that brought Weill and Brecht together again in the spring of 1943. Their go-between was Ernst-Josef Aufricht, who now was producing a German-language radio series for the Voice of America called *The Schultzes of Yorkville*, the saga of a refugee family in New York and their various politically relevant adventures. For one of these broadcasts Aufricht had persuaded Weill to do a musical setting of Brecht's antiwar poem, "And What Did the Soldier's Wife Get?" It was sung by Lotte Lenya, who soon after recorded it for the Office of War Information, with which Weill was now associated, doing the score of a U.S. Army training film. Taking advantage of the mood created by these activities, Aufricht proposed, while Brecht was in New York, that he and Weill collaborate on a new musical version of *The Good Soldier Schweik*. Both proved to be interested. For one thing, neither had ever gotten Schweik completely out of his system—in Weill's case, as we have seen, *Johnny Johnson* had turned out to be something quite different. But there were other reasons for their readiness in this moment to consider reviving the collaboration. Brecht had sold only one scenario in Hollywood and was eager to make inroads into the American theater, where Weill's reputation now counted for a great deal. As for Weill, despite his Broadway successes and hymns of praise for it all, he was genuinely concerned that he may have been drifting in a direction away from his most serious aspirations. Indeed, he proved ready to discuss not only the *Schweik* project with Brecht but also a possible musical version of a play Brecht had written in Sweden and Finland and now showed to Weill, *The Good Woman of Setzuan*.

Brecht went back to California and immediately got to work on *Schweik*. Suspecting that one reason Weill was interested in both this and the *Setzuan* play was a desire on his part to have some roles for Lenya, Brecht created one character, that of the landlady, Kopecka, specifically with her in mind. But the script he sent back to New York after some six weeks of work proved satisfactory neither to Aufricht nor to Weill. "Brecht had copied down page after page of dialogue from the book," Aufricht writes, "and contrived a conclusion: Schweik meets Hitler on the snow-covered fields of Russia and gets into conversation with him." It would seem that both he and Weill considered the play—which Brecht went on to finish with Hanns Eisler as *Schweik in the Second World War*—to be unworkable for artistic reasons, or for box-office reasons if one prefers. But Brecht's biographer, Klaus Völker, suggests that Weill also opposed the play on political grounds.

This is unverifiable, although it is quite possible that in August 1943, when he repudiated the *Schweik* script, Weill at least momentarily eschewed any association with Brecht. For it was on August 27, that same month, that he was sworn in as an American citizen—another well-known German-speaking artistic exile, Otto Preminger, was sworn in by his side—and, according to Maurice Abravanel, Weill was asked: "If we were fighting Russia, would you take up arms against her?" This question shook him up considerably, according to Abravanel, who takes it for granted—and therefore, presumably, Weill did so, too—that the reason he was asked it was his old association with Brecht. It is now known that the FBI was keeping a file on the playwright, and that Brecht was aware of the fact. This would certainly have made Weill uneasy. That April Victor Samrock, general manager of the Playwrights Company, had received a form letter along with a questionnaire from the Department of Justice concerning Weill's application for citizenship, which, in the language of the letter, was to be handled with "great care" since "the petitioner is a citizen or subject of a country with which the United States is now at war." Samrock had already sworn to the petitioner's loyalty.

If, then, there was indeed a moment of fainthearted behavior on Weill's part where Brecht was concerned, it was surely out of fear for his citizenship. And becoming an American citizen was the most important event in Weill's life since his departure from Nazi Germany ten years before. "It's strange," he is said to have remarked after receiving his final papers, "our family goes back to 1329 in Freiburg* and I lived in different parts of Germany till I was thirty-three. Yet I never felt the oneness with my native country that I do with the United States; the moment I landed here I felt as though I'd come home." This seems to have been quite sincere; he was often to remark that there was no spot back in Germany he had ever loved so much as he did the drugstore in New City, where he was always filled with admiration at the containers brimming with one of his favorite American discoveries, ice cream. A volunteer plane-spotter with Maxwell Anderson, he was always ready to be summoned to the

---

* This goes back even further than the published family genealogies do. Weill may have been referring to a tradition that begins with the *father* of Juda Weil der Stadt, the family's official founder.

tower some three miles from his home to do this patriotic duty and was thoroughly amused when he once telephoned a report to a nearby air force base and heard the reply: "Sounds as if the Germans have arrived already." But despite his accent, Abravanel points out, "Kurt was so enthusiastically American that it would infuriate him if anybody would start speaking German to him." Maybe Brecht's voice had simply been more of the past than he could bear in this moment of consummation in his love affair with America.

Broadway Sophistication:
One Touch of Venus

 By the time of his swearing-in as an American citizen, Weill was completely absorbed in the preparation of his next major Broadway production. It was in November of 1941 that Irene Sharaff, who had designed the costumes for *Lady in the Dark*, had brought to his attention the novella that was ultimately to give rise to *One Touch of Venus*. Written in the 1890s by the English humorist Thomas Anstey Guthrie, who signed himself "F. Anstey," *The Tinted Venus* was a highly imaginative reworking of that same Pygmalion legend that George Bernard Shaw was going to use very differently just a few years later. A young London barber, Leander Tweddle, engaged to a girl of slightly higher social status, goes without her to a garden party one evening and, on a whim, tries out the ring he is planning to give her on the finger of a statue of Venus along the path. This brings the statue to life, and for the rest of the story poor Leander, who wants only to make his way respectably in the world, is plagued by the presence of this creature not easily explained to fiancée and friends. There are hints of an amorous attachment between Leander and Venus, but in the end he wants only to get the ring off her finger and let her revert to statuedom; this he does, then marries his Matilda and lives happily ever after.

Most of the story's humor lies in the contrast between the unflaggingly noble manner of Venus and the petty concerns of the young twerp to whom she has attached herself; and this surely was why Weill thought it provided, as he wrote to Ira Gershwin, "a first-rate idea for a very entertaining and yet original kind of 'opera comique' on the Offenbach line." It is significant in this connection that, about a year later, Weill very nearly was to become involved in a revival of Offenbach's *La Belle Hélène* that the singer Grace Moore wanted to do and for which she wanted him to write additional music. Clearly, his initial conception of the Venus musical included some bits of Offenbachian Greek burlesque; but this element was to disappear completely in the long run.

Ira Gershwin remained indifferent to the *Venus* idea, as he did to the many others Weill proposed to him at this time. But then, early in 1942, Kurt found himself back in touch with Cheryl Crawford, who had become an independent producer since the breakup of the old Group Theatre directorate. After some initial setbacks on Broadway, she had been running a year-round theater of the summer stock variety in Maplewood, New Jersey, and in the course of two years there had rediscovered a fact first brought to her attention in *Johnny Johnson* days: she was especially good at producing musicals. Indeed, at this very moment, her production of a revised *Porgy and Bess*—for this version the sung recitatives were eliminated, and the work was recast as something more like a musical than an opera—was so successful that it was heading for Broadway, where it would become established as an American classic at last. Eager now to try another Broadway musical, she got back in touch with Weill, who thereupon presented the *Venus* idea to her, which she liked. Its appeal for her, as she has written, was that "it could involve the world as we see it and as the goddess sees it and allow us to compare the two views, which would of course be quite different. I thought it could have social bearing and also be amusing." Seeking an author of the book for the show, she got in touch with Arthur Kober, whose "*Having Wonderful Time*," which stole Jules (John) Garfield from the cast of *Johnny Johnson* and made him into a star, had been one of the hits of 1937. Kober was interested at first, and it was still hoped that Ira Gershwin could be brought into the collaboration; but neither of these worked out. By the summer Cheryl Crawford had engaged Bella Spewack, without her husband as collaborator this time, to do the book and had come up with the novel idea of getting Ogden Nash, the celebrated writer of light verse, to do the lyrics.

When Crawford and Weill saw Bella Spewack's first rough pages of *One Man's Venus*, as it was then being called, they decided that the role of the goddess was a natural one for Marlene Dietrich. Though the setting of the story had no doubt already been changed to New York by now, the script evidently still laid stress on Venus's exotic and dignified character. This was in keeping with the image that Marlene Dietrich had developed since going to Hollywood, and Kurt, who knew her from Berlin days, got in touch with her about the idea. She showed enough interest that, by the end of September, Weill and Crawford were in Hollywood to discuss the matter with her in person. They found her interested but evasive—and often ready to interrupt conversation and end the evening by performing on her favorite new toy, a musical saw, with which she would accompany herself while singing various songs, including Weill's "Surabaya Johnny." Kurt took advantage of his stay in Hollywood to visit Ira Gershwin and other old friends and to give a talk to the Hollywood Writers Mobilization on the need for material for *Lunch Time Follies*. But in October he and Cheryl Crawford had to return to New York with nothing more than the hope that Marlene Dietrich was still interested—and with the promise that she would be there in a few weeks, when they could discuss the matter further.

Once she had arrived in New York, Marlene Dietrich made frequent visits to the Metropolitan Museum of Art to study various statues and paintings of Venus and was even persuaded to demonstrate how her voice sounded on the stage of the empty Forty-sixth Street Theatre; but she remained uncommitted and was about to return to Hollywood that way until Cheryl Crawford, according to her own account, caught her under the influence of a strong headache pill and got her to sign a contract. But these were not auspicious circumstances, especially since no more than half the show had been written by now. Indeed, trouble developed over the script almost immediately thereafter. Weill and Bella Spewack proved to be a not overly compatible team, and the work developed slowly and unevenly in their hands; until finally, at around the beginning of February 1943, the playwright came up with a completed draft that was immediately found unsatisfactory by Weill and everyone else involved. Bella Spewack was thereupon dismissed from the project, and Ogden Nash persuaded his friend S. J. Perelman, the well-known humorist and scriptwriter for Marx Brothers movies, to come in and replace her. In a short time an entirely new script had been turned out, with an earthier, sexier Venus than Thomas Anstey Guthrie had ever imagined—and also, as it turned out, with no Marlene Dietrich to perform it. For when she saw the new version, she called it "too sexy and profane," and protested that, as the mother of a nineteen-year-old daughter, she could no longer display herself on a stage the way she once did.

If, then, there had been a star but no play at the beginning of winter, by spring's end there was a play but no star. For a while some of the other actresses considered for the role were still in the image of an exotic Venus: Ilona Massey was briefly mentioned for the part, and at the beginning of the summer Vera Zorina was very nearly engaged. Born in Berlin, Zorina, who had been married to George Balanchine for a time, was by now the world's most successful ballerina-turned-popular-star, a hit both on Broadway and in Hollywood. But a conflict developed, according to Cheryl Crawford, because by this time Agnes de Mille, fresh from her success with *Oklahoma!* that spring, had been engaged as choreographer for the show. Zorina, after consulting about the matter with George Balanchine, decided she did not want to work with Agnes de Mille and did not take the part. Weill, who was to write two ballets for the show anyway, was no doubt disappointed at this loss of an opportunity to do more. At one point in the star search, Venus's accent changed from Central European to Anglo-Saxon, and Gertrude Lawrence and Leonora Corbett, another British musical comedy star, were approached; an at least slightly exotic lady was still wanted. But they both turned it down, and by the beginning of August the role was given to Mary Martin, who would make it as American as apple pie.

"I couldn't believe it," Mary Martin writes in her memoirs. "Me in a part for Dietrich? And Venus?" In fact, her name had come up that spring as a candidate for the role and had been rejected—doubtless, not only because its image at that time was still the exotic one, but also because she did not seem to be a big enough star for it. She had risen to sudden fame on Broadway in 1938, singing "My Heart Belongs to Daddy" in an otherwise small role in the Cole Porter–Bella and Samuel Spewack musical *Leave It to Me!*; but then she had gone to Hollywood and made a few movies that were not particularly successful. That spring she had tried to return to Broadway, but her show had closed in Boston. After months of anxious searching, however, the creators of the *Venus* show were now ready to give it a whirl with this good singer and lively performer. She at first had her own doubts about her suitability for the part, but the matter seems to have become settled early on both sides by a kind of marriage between the woman and a song. Mary Martin remembers going with her husband to a Manhattan apartment—probably Cheryl Crawford's—on a hot night in August to hear Kurt Weill play some of the music from the show. "All my life," she writes, "I will remember that man singing Venus' lovely number, 'That's Him,' with a kind of quavery, German sound . . . 'Ummmmmmmmnnnnnnhhh, that's him . . .' I longed to sing that song, but I still could not see myself as Venus." Her husband,

Richard Halliday, took her to the Metropolitan Museum to show her all the different ways Venus could look and promised her she would play the part wearing the most beautiful clothes in the world.

To assure her of this, Halliday won the ear of the celebrated couturier Mainbocher, who at the beginning of the war had returned to his native United States from a successful career in Paris. At first Irene Sharaff had been asked to do the costumes for the show in recognition of her having suggested the *Venus* idea in the first place. But she was in Hollywood, and apparently did not reply to Cheryl Crawford's letter. Mainbocher was doubtful about doing something for the theater for the first time in his life, but he was persuaded to reserve his final decision until he had heard Mary Martin sing the part. They all met again at the same apartment as before, where Kurt Weill arrived to accompany his Venus at the piano. "As Kurt played the introduction to 'That's Him,' " Mary Martin recalls, "I picked up a little chair and carried it over right in front of Main. I sat on it sideways and sang 'That's Him' right smack into those kind brown eyes."

When she had finished, Mainbocher said: "I will do your clothes for the show if you will promise me one thing. Promise me you'll always sing this song that way. Take a chair down to the footlights, sing across the orchestra to the audience as if it were just one person."

And that is precisely how she sang the song, clad in her Mainbocher negligee—one of the fourteen costumes with which he provided her—on opening night at the Imperial Theatre, October 7, 1943, and in all of the 566 performances that were to follow.

Whereas Thomas Anstey Guthrie's Venus had been a kind of stone guest, grayish of color and marmoreal in texture, Mary Martin's was very much a creature of flesh and blood during her sojourn in this world. One of her characteristic lines—which Mary Martin blushingly hesitated to deliver until she heard the laugh it got at the first Boston tryout—was: "Love isn't the dying moan of a distant violin—it's the triumphant twang of a bedspring." Anstey's prim Victorians would never have dreamed of saying such things. Indeed, from the first moment that the ungainly barber Rodney Hatch—played by Hollywood's own Nanki-Poo, Kenny Baker—slips the ring on Venus's finger at an art museum and brings her to life in a roll of thunder, there is no doubt about what she wants from him.

Much of the comedy in the ensuing scenes, as Venus pursues Rodney around the city, is based on the contrast between her frank, earthy amorousness and the nervous, essentially pleasure-denying conventions of

modern urban life. Rodney is caught up in his commitments to a fiancée
and a future mother-in-law who are the bane of his life even before
marriage; the millionaire art collector, Whitelaw Savory, who has bought
the statue of Venus because it resembles a girl he once loved, is caught up
in a romanticism that apparently keeps him from taking love as it is; and
the crowds on the New York City streets are caught up in their frenzied
rush. Even after Venus has triumphed and won a joyous night with
Rodney at a deluxe hotel—this is when she sings "That's Him"—the
lucky young man can only dream, in his song "Wooden Wedding," of a
suburban marriage with Venus just as conventional as the one he would
have had with his now jilted fiancée. In the end she has to depart from a
world like this: a final ballet sequence shows her as a humdrum housewife
in Ozone Heights, until she is suddenly snatched away to Olympus by the
messengers of the gods.

At the beginning of the Boston tryouts this was the way the show
ended; but, though this conclusion made the play's satirical point, it left
the audiences unsatisfied. Something had to be done for the forlorn
barber, and Agnes de Mille finally came up with the solution. A new
scene was added after Venus's disappearance into the clouds: we are back
in the art museum, and Rodney is gazing unhappily at the statue, asking
why she has left him. He sings a reprise of the show's principal love duet,
"Speak Low," and at that moment a girl enters, looking for the art class.
She looks exactly like Venus, but "her clothes are simple, and she has an
attractive, awkward grace; she might be Venus's country cousin." Gaping
in astonishment, Rodney asks her where she comes from, and she says
Ozone Heights. He asks her if she likes it there, and she says she wouldn't
think of living anywhere else. "My name is Rodney Hatch," he says, and
she starts to reply, "Mine is—," but he interrupts her: "You don't have to
tell me. I know." And they go off arm in arm, as the orchestra plays
"Speak Low" and the curtain descends. It was a perfect Broadway ending;
and Venus's country cousin was to prove so appealing to Oscar
Hammerstein II, for example, that the moment he saw her enter,
according to Mary Martin, "he wanted to write a part for the innocent,
eager little girl in the white-piqué blouse, pink polka-dot skirt, and
matching rolled-brim hat. He wrote it, too—Nellie Forbush in *South
Pacific* was a descendant of Venus."

Musically speaking, the result of all these transformations was that
Kurt Weill's would-be "opera comique" in the Offenbachian vein had
ended up as a piece of pure Broadway, largely in the vein of Cole Porter.
"Apparently he can turn out one success after another with a sure hand,"

wrote Elliott Carter, with mingled admiration and dismay, of the composer of *One Touch of Venus*. "Weill, who orchestrates and arranges his own work, whose flair for discovering and using the stylistic earmarks of popular music is remarkable, has finally made himself at home in America. Where in pre-Hitler days his music underlined the bold and disillusioned bitterness of economic injustice, now, reflecting his new environment and the New York audiences to which he appeals, his social scene has shrunk to the bedroom and he has become the composer of 'sophisticated' scores. . . . Even the orchestration with its numerous piano solos in boogie-woogie and other jazz styles constantly recalls night-club atmosphere." Carter could hear only occasional traces of *The Threepenny Opera* and *Mahagonny* and thought the music less "ingenious" and "striking" than that of *Johnny Johnson*. "But in the atmosphere of Broadway," he concluded, "where so much music is unconvincing and dead, Weill's workmanlike care and his refined sense of style make up for whatever spontaneity and freshness his music lacks."

Actually, in a sense Weill was doing in *One Touch of Venus* the same thing he had done in *The Threepenny Opera*—parodying popular music. The crucial difference is that the parody in the *Venus* songs is, like the satire in the play's text, a good deal gentler than that in *The Threepenny Opera*. One could say it is so gentle as to play right into the hands of the audience; but on the other hand, Brecht in his harshness also pleased *his* audiences. Brecht and Weill succeeded in having it both ways just as much as Nash, Perelman, and Weill did; but if in one case, satire was a boxer's smashing blow to the jaw, and in the other, a mild poke in the ribs, this was in part a result of the difference in atmosphere between pre-Hitler Berlin and wartime New York. Berlin on the brink of disaster was capable of a kind of frenzied excitement; New York as a refuge from disaster could often be bland. An object lesson in the difference between the two is conveniently provided by Weill at one significant point in his *Venus* score. This occurs when the millionaire Savory, looking for his missing statue, arrives with two of his men at Rodney's barbershop; pretending for the moment to be customers, they join the proprietor in singing a barbershop quartet, "The Trouble with Women," the verse of which has the same melody as "In Youth's Golden Glimmer" from *Happy End*. Now, parody was the intention in both cases, and fun was, too; but the fun of the *Happy End* version had been darkened by anger, whereas the fun of the *Venus* barbershop quartet is that of a group of American college boys doing an 1890s nostalgia turn. The difference is perhaps summed up by the presence of Whitelaw Savory, who—as a collector who specializes in modern art—is a much gentler satirical treatment of the Rockefellers than Weill had participated in with the "Hosanna Rockefeller" of *Happy End*.

The point at which parody and satire all work best to create a delightful song in its own right is in "That's Him," Mary Martin's showpiece of the evening. Basically a humorous torch song—a breezily Olympian "Man I Love" or a tongue-in-cheek "My Bill"—it takes on a Cole Porter flavor in its conversational lilt and smart, wisecracking references to things ranging from the "Rhapsody in Blue" to Antoine the hairdresser. The basic humor lies in the fact that Venus is rapturously in love with a simple barber, and the song manages to convey both her rapture and the comic absurdity of the situation. But the main thing about it is that, whatever its parodic and satirical intentions, it is simply a delightful song in the Broadway vein; witty and romantic at the same time, it is as good as any equivalent by Cole Porter.

For the truth of the matter is that *One Touch of Venus*, the most completely "Broadway" of Kurt Weill's scores, is a first-rate Broadway musical. One's response to its music depends on how one feels about the Broadway musical comedy tradition, and about Kurt Weill's readiness to line himself up with it at least this one time. But, within the boundaries of that tradition, Weill made some memorable contributions to it in *One Touch of Venus*. "Foolish Heart" is a fine romantic waltz reminiscent of turn-of-the-century operetta. And "Speak Low," with its long, sinuous, haunting melodic line—the hit of the show and widely thought of as another "Begin the Beguine"—remains to this day one of the great American popular songs.

Weill's own passions as an artist were perhaps most aroused by the two ballet sequences he wrote for the show. The first one, placing the serene goddess amid the frantic lunch-hour crowds at Radio City, from which she plucks out a boy and girl and brings them together, is constructed musically out of the interplay of two of Venus's songs—"I'm a Stranger Here Myself," a kind of urban-anomie blues, and the romantic "Speak Low" for the young couple. The second ballet, in which Venus is transported from Ozone Heights back to Olympus, is constructed on themes all its own and is a more sophisticated composition. Originally it had contained a whole bacchanal section that, as Cheryl Crawford writes, Weill thought to be "the finest piece of orchestral music he had ever written. Agnes [de Mille] thought it the best thing he'd done since *Threepenny Opera*, but she went on to point out, 'He cut the bacchanal to pieces and the dance went with it. He was ruthless about such things; he wanted a success. He was predominantly a theatre man.' " This was the way others remembered him, too, disclaiming high artistic pretensions and protesting that he wanted to be simply a good theater composer, a professional. And there was, indeed, no more consummate a professional than he. But did this mean the artist in him was completely satisfied?

Last Efforts with Ira Gershwin

By the time *One Touch of Venus* had established itself as Kurt Weill's second big hit in a row, something of a legend had begun to grow up about Broadway's most unusual composer. Ogden Nash wrote in *The New York Times* that "after working some six months with Kurt Weill, I still don't know where the music comes from. He has a piano, but he does not sit at it picking out melodies with one finger; he uses it for laying his pipe on before going out to chunk pebbles at the trout in the brook that runs past his window. He does not pace the floor in a brown study humming tum-ti-tum, tum-ti-tum until suddenly he claps his brow and his face is transfigured with ecstasy as another ballad is born. Nor is he ever to be found curled up in his favorite armchair poring over a dog-eared copy of Tchaikovsky. He simply puts in a full day at the OWI, gets on the Weehawken ferry, rides for an hour in a non-air-conditioned smoking car, gets home, goes to his desk and writes 'That's Him.' " Others noted Weill's propensity for composing while he had the radio on full blast—playing, not music, but anything else that would create a wall of sound around him and shut out the world. He also enjoyed hearing voices in the house when he worked—particularly when one of them was Lenya's, his favorite voice of all.

But it was noted by many that this apparent ease of creativity was replaced by furious hard work once a show was actually being prepared, particularly since Weill alone of current Broadway composers did his own orchestrations. "You sleep about two hours a night for the four weeks that it takes," Weill told a *Life* magazine interviewer right after the *Venus* opening, "but it's fun. Not until the rehearsals get under way can you start your orchestrating, since until you know who the singers are going to be you can't tell what key to put each number in." He admitted Wagner didn't go about it just that way. "American musical comedy, however, is different. It is distinctly a tailor-made job." But he hastened to add that "even Offenbach had a particular soprano in mind for most of his operettas." In other words, Weill was still applying the standards of a classic European composer to himself in spite of everything. The results were, as the *Life* interviewer observed about the *Venus* score, "a smooth, even, fascinating job to one whose ears are attuned to such details; the composer lays great stress on the attention he has given to the proper leading of all the voices. The professional orchestrator, he tells you, thinks in chords and merely assigns each instrument or choir a place in the harmony, often with awkward melodic results, as far as the inner parts are concerned." The *Venus* score, on the other hand, "has what musicians call texture." Some of Weill's colleagues felt he was all but killing himself working this way—sometimes entire orchestrations had to be changed at the last minute, amid all the other hectic demands of rehearsals and tryouts—but he could not imagine doing otherwise. It was his trademark; furthermore, there had been times in the past, before the big hits, as there would be times in the future, when the additional income provided by the orchestrator's fee was much needed by him.

But in these years when his cup was running over—Weill was not the only person beset by the irony of success in the very time when his old European home was suffering untold agonies—another significant source of income was provided by Hollywood. By the time *One Touch of Venus* opened, two of the shows he had worked on—not only *Lady in the Dark* but also *Knickerbocker Holiday*—had been sold to the movies, and *Venus* was soon to follow. Under the circumstances Hollywood became more attractive to him than it once had been, and he found himself becoming, as one interviewer was to put it, a kind of "creative commuter" between Broadway and Hollywood, "who uses his whim for a timetable." Early in the summer of 1943 Kurt spent two weeks in Hollywood, in connection with his work on the film versions of *Lady in the Dark* and *Knickerbocker Holiday*; and then he went again in November to finish this work—during which time he also started on an original film project with Ira Gershwin. Weill and Gershwin had remained in constant contact by letter and were still discussing various ideas for another show together, but in the meantime Gershwin had become involved in movies again: he did lyrics for the 1943 pro-Russia propaganda film, *North Star*, which had music by Aaron Copland and a script by Lillian Hellman, and again for the Jerome Kern musical that was to be released in 1944, *Cover Girl*, starring Gene Kelly and Rita Hayworth. The movie Weill and Gershwin worked on from November 1943 through February 1944, to be released the following year, was *Where Do We Go from Here?*, a Morrie Ryskind screenplay produced by William Perlberg for Twentieth Century Fox, directed by Gregory Ratoff and featuring Fred MacMurray, Joan Leslie, and June Haver in the cast.

For the most part the final products of these efforts were not to be too distinguished artistically. *Lady in the Dark*, directed by Mitchell Leisen and starring Ginger Rogers as Liza Elliott, emerged from the Hollywood production line and entered the theaters at the end of February with very little of Weill's score left in it. Among his songs only "The Saga of Jenny" had remained intact; and of the three dreams, only the circus sequence followed with reasonable fidelity the lines originally conceived. Snatches of "My Ship" were hummed by Ginger Rogers in great perturbation throughout the film, but it was never sung in its entirety. Other passages of Weill music were also heard in fragments, either in the dream sequences or as backgrounds to the action on the sound track: "This Is New" could be heard being played by a nightclub band. For the rest, new songs were written for the film by studio composers.

The film of *Knickerbocker Holiday*, released in April, was only a little less unkind to the original Weill score than that of *Lady in the Dark* had been, but it was a worse movie. Nelson Eddy was woefully miscast in the role of Brom Broeck, particularly since he was not even given "It Never Was You" to sing; equally miscast was Charles Coburn in the role of Peter Stuyvesant, particularly since he *was* given the "September Song." "Failing the material to suit his voice," wrote Otis L. Guernsey, Jr., in the *New York Herald Tribune*, "Mr. Eddy, who plays Brom Broeck, is just a little ridiculous as an early champion of democracy parading around in bloomers, the seventeenth-century version of what the well-dressed New York Dutchman should wear. . . . The Stuyvesant role, that of a political finagler with a good heart, was the best part in the original, but it has had all the vitality boiled out of it; and sad to say, Mr. Coburn just hasn't got the voice for the September song, even aided by sound track's amplifier." Once again, the services of studio composers were used to write songs in place of Weill ones that were discarded.

Weill was distressed at what had happened to the scores of these first two screen adaptations of his Broadway works, and, remembering also the unhappy experience of the filming of *The Threepenny Opera*, he was determined to try to prevent such things from occurring again. This was among the reasons he had hired the services of a New York theatrical agent, Leah Salisbury, to represent him in all matters relating to *One Touch of Venus*. Miss Salisbury's principal assignment was to get him a good film contract for this show—one that would protect his artistic as well as his financial rights.

As for *Where Do We Go from Here?*, though it was really just a trifle—a true wartime "escape" comedy—it at least provided Weill with the one chance to see a score of his go into a film more or less intact and entirely unembellished by other people's music. Furthermore, he and Gershwin had a great deal of fun making it, "and for the first time," as he wrote Leah Salisbury from Hollywood, "I have turned out a job here which I can be proud of." This, and a salary of $2,500 a week while working on the film had begun to make Hollywood seem very attractive indeed. Weill even looked upon *Where Do We Go from Here?* hopefully as a dress rehearsal for possible cinematic efforts of a more serious nature; for, as he was to tell an interviewer after the film's release, it "was frankly an experiment with an opera form, in which the music and lyrics are integrated with the story, advancing it rather than retarding it as is the case with most musical films." Stressing that he was not of the opinion, widespread among Hollywood filmmakers, that screen music had to be accounted for or explained, he went on to say: "It isn't necessary for someone to walk over to a piano in order to show he is going to sing. The opera form is just a convention, and ninety-nine out of a hundred people in the theater wouldn't notice, and wouldn't care if they did, whether the music is introduced by story cues or not. That's what we tried to do in *Where Do We Go from Here?* Ira Gershwin and I simply put the whole thing into musical form—we let the action sing for itself."

It was crucial what kind of story was used for this purpose, Weill pointed out, and it is significant that once again—as had often been the case in the past—he used one that moved freely between reality and fantasy. The film opens with Bill Morgan (Fred MacMurray), judged 4–F by the military medical examiners, doing his bit for the war effort by collecting scrap metal and washing dishes at a USO canteen and wondering how he will ever get into uniform. A genie, inhabitant of a lamp Bill discovers while rummaging for scrap metal, promises to come to the rescue by granting him three wishes. Bill of course wishes to be in the army and the genie complies—but, unfortunately, centuries of repose have thrown off his time sense, and Bill finds himself transported into Washington's army at Valley Forge. After some adventures there, Bill desperately asks for the navy, and he finds himself on Columbus's flagship about to discover America. Subsequently he buys Manhattan Island and finds himself in the world of *Knickerbocker Holiday*. At last, the genie gets things right and Bill is transported by magic carpet into the modern American army. All ends well for him romantically, too: for the two girls in his life, one nice (Joan Leslie) and the other naughty (June Haver), have reappeared, in likenesses at any rate, throughout his adventures; and this being the wholesome America of wartime, niceness has triumphed.

Although there is music in the "realistic" parts of the film—including a very nice specimen of the Jerome Kern type of love ballad, "All at Once"—it is the fantasy sequences that provide, in the manner of *Lady in the Dark*, the opportunities for long musical interludes. At Valley Forge the Hessian soldiers gathered in a tavern sing the "Song of the Rhineland," a thoroughly Ira Gershwin-esque, pun-filled spoof of the typical operetta drinking song. The lyrics for this, by the way, show another instance of Kurt Weill's good-hearted willingness to participate in a ridiculing of German accents. But the musical, as well as the comic, heart of the film is the Christopher Columbus sequence, for which Weill and Gershwin created a whole mock operetta some twelve minutes long in the final cut—the longest nondancing musical sequence that had ever been used in a Hollywood film. Bill finds himself in the middle of the mutiny of Columbus's sailors, who are in despair of ever seeing land again; this is all done "operatically." But Bill of course knows they are about to hit the jackpot of world discovery, and he sings them an aria telling, quite anachronistically—e.g., that a city in Ohio will be named after the explorer, and so on—of the splendors of the land they are about to discover. This persuades the sailors to go on, although, in a final passage, cut from the movie, Columbus wants to turn back when he learns from Bill that his discovery is going to be named after "that second-rate explorer Amerigo Vespucci." At the end land is sighted, and all is well.

"With that kind of material," Weill told his interviewer, "we felt we could afford to have fun. . . . We had good singers, too, men like Carlos Ramirez [as the leader of the mutineers] and Fortunio Bonanova [as Columbus], but we also had MacMurray, and thanks to the mechanical wonders of the microphone we were able to make his voice come out like an opera singer's." This led the "creative commuter" between Broadway and Hollywood to offer a few reflections. "That's the great advantage of the movies over the stage. One of the difficulties in casting a stage musical is to find actors who can sing or singers who can act. It's very hard to get a combination of the two. But in pictures you can take actors who don't need to know anything more than how to carry a tune and the mike will do the rest. Like these aviators, our movie actors can sing by instrument." Movies, in spite of everything, were presenting a whole new set of possibilities to Weill's imagination.

But the theater was where his heart still was, and by the summer of 1944 he and Ira Gershwin had come up with an idea that revived their collaboration for Broadway at last. During the previous two years, their exchanges of letters had increasingly included the name of Gershwin's friend Edwin Justus Mayer, one of the most popular Broadway play-wrights of the 1920s, who had since settled down in Hollywood as a writer of movie scripts. Indeed, in the fall of 1942, Weill, Gershwin, and Mayer had even reached the point of drawing up a contract for a musical play about Nell Gwynne, the actress who became mistress to King Charles II of England; it was to have been done by the same group, presided over by Grace Moore, that had wanted to do *La Belle Hélène* with emendations by Weill. That project was abandoned, however, and in the spring of 1943 the three of them considered doing a play about Cinderella after her marriage to the Prince, in which she turns out to be a termagant; but it soon was recognized that this one-gag idea, good for a sketch, could hardly fill up a whole evening.

Finally, in February 1944, a group of people approached Weill in New York with the idea of doing a musical version of Mayer's 1924 play *The Firebrand*. A comic romance about the adventures of Benvenuto Cellini, *The Firebrand*, a great hit of its day, had had it both ways by making audiences laugh at the secondary characters but thrill at the exploits of the hero, dashingly played by Joseph Schildkraut. Weill was at first "very unenthusiastic" about the idea, but when asked if he would be interested if Ira Gershwin consented to do the lyrics, he said yes. As it happened, Gershwin had even done a song—with music by Russell Bennett and Maurice Nitke—for the 1924 production, and he now proved quite ready to try the first full score of his career for a costume drama, which would enable him to "do a lot of things in form that I'd hesitate to experiment with if the show were placed in modern times." Thereupon Weill, who saw the projected work "more as a light opera than a musical comedy," thought that it might prove to be a good offering to the international market at the end of the war.

And so the team of Weill, Gershwin, and Mayer, having found the subject of their long sought-after costume musical in their own backyard, contracted with the producer Max Gordon in the spring to do a version of *The Firebrand*. Actually, this was not to be the first such effort. In 1928 the producers Horace Liveright and Otto Kahn had wanted to do a musical of the Mayer play and had engaged Sigmund Romberg and Oscar Hammerstein II to write it. But then Romberg and Hammerstein withdrew, and it was the little-known team of Eugene Berton and Isabel Leighton who did the music and lyrics for *The Dagger and the Rose*, which opened and closed in Atlantic City before reaching Broadway. Even by the time Weill and Gershwin got hold of the Mayer play, there were other people interested in doing a musical version of it. A producer named Paul Feigay had announced in October 1943 his intention of doing such a show, claiming that he had obtained Vernon Duke and John Latouche to do the songs. It was possibly Feigay or someone associated with him who had first approached Weill with the idea in February; at that time he wrote to Gershwin that the book for the prospective show was being worked on by "Elisabeth Layton and a Hungarian by the name of Szold"—is the first of these two names Weill's carelessly registered version of Isabel Leighton, the lyricist for *The Dagger and the Rose*? In any case, when Max Gordon took up the property and engaged the team of Mayer, Gershwin, and Weill to do it, Mayer denied he had ever given Feigay the rights, despite the latter's claim to the contrary, and the matter ended there.

These were not particularly auspicious beginnings, however; and a certain inauspiciousness seemed to dog the play during its entire period of gestation. Originally scheduled to open in November, it did not do so until March 1945. Undergoing a little more than the usual number of changes in title, it started out as *It Happened in Florence*, then became *Make Way for Love*, and then *Much Ado About Love* until the very eve of the New York opening; it finally arrived on Broadway as *The Firebrand of Florence*. During the Boston tryouts Broadway's most eminent play-doctor, George S. Kaufman, was called in to apply his medicine. Furthermore, the production had come to be conceived on a lavish scale, with the result that it sat heavily upon the action, and the director John Murray Anderson had great trouble getting it to move. This is what had happened to the "intelligent, intimate operetta" Weill had envisioned at the outset.

There also were problems in the casting. Unquestionably there had been ambitious ideas at first about the casting of the Cellini role: someone connected with the production has intimated that Ezio Pinza had at least momentarily been thought of as a possibility—he might thereby have begun his Broadway career four years earlier than he actually did. But the part was finally given to Earl Wrightson, a young man with a pleasant baritone of the operetta variety but not as strong a personality as may have been hoped for at first. The role of Cellini's beloved Angela was given to Beverly Tyler, who also was not a star personality. There was greater strength in the casting of the comic secondary roles of the Duke and the Duchess, but there were problems there, too. Duke Alessandro the Wise was originally to have been played by Walter Slezak, a fine character actor of emphatically Central European cast. The son of Leo Slezak, an international opera star, the younger Slezak was himself a very good singer. But he withdrew, and the role fell upon Melville Cooper, a delightful comedian in the British farcical tradition but representing a very different image of the role. This change, according to Lotte Lenya, who played the Duchess, was what threw her own performance out of kilter.

This not only was Lenya's first role in one of her husband's musicals since *The Eternal Road* in 1937; it also was only her second appearance on a Broadway stage since that time. In 1941 she had played the secondary role of a saucy Austrian maidservant in Maxwell Anderson's *Candle in the Wind*, starring Helen Hayes, and had toured in this for several months the following year; but otherwise, her career as an actress had fallen into eclipse virtually from the moment of her arrival in the United States in 1935. One problem had been her severe difficulties with the English language, but even that occasional role for which a strong foreign accent was appropriate did not fall her way: in the preparation of *Johnny Johnson*, both Kurt and Paul Green had wanted her for the role of the French nurse in the hospital, but it had gone to Lee Strasberg's wife, Paula Miller. Kurt never ceased to be troubled by Lenya's artistic inactivity. "After each success we would walk near his home," Maurice Abravanel writes, "and I would say, 'Now Kurt, you write an opera.' And he would say, 'First I must write something for Lenya.' " It is very likely that one of the reasons he overcame his initial reservations about *The Firebrand* was that he saw a possible role for her in the Duchess.

But this concern for his wife's career merely proved disastrous in the end, for her and for everyone concerned. "My style would never ever jell with Melville Cooper's," she was to tell an interviewer years later; and there are rumors of a serious antagonism that arose between Lenya and Cooper during rehearsals and performances. When the tryouts opened in Boston, where so many repairs and changes were to be made, the reviewer for the *Boston Post* expressed great hopes for the show once it had been overhauled but offered this severe reservation: "Unfortunately, one of the principals is not suited to her role. Lotte Lenya, as the Duchess of Florence in this legend of Benvenuto Cellini, is hardly up to the comedy and the songs which have been given her. Her ability is not in question, nor her personal charm. But someone else should be playing the Duchess, for the sake of all concerned." In essence, this was to be overwhelmingly the judgment of the Broadway critics and audiences. As Weill's friend Billy Rose was to write in his syndicated column about two years later:

> The script called for a sexy duchess, someone with the full-blown charms of Irene Bordoni or Vivienne Segal. Kurt handed this plum to the sensitive Lotte.
>
> It was the first time he had been able to feature her in one of his American shows. . . . Kurt thought it was about time his talented wife got her chance. It's my guess their up-and-down years together had something to do with this casting. When you've lived through Brownshirts marching Unter den Linden, a couple of skinny seasons in Paris, and the agonizing job of adapting your talent to the Broadway tempo, you don't figure to be too analytical when a part comes up you think your wife can play.

The play that opened on March 22, 1945, at the Alvin Theatre—where *Lady in the Dark* had made its smash-hit debut a little over four years earlier—actually contained some of the most ambitious music Weill had ever written for the Broadway stage. This was particularly true of the opening scene, set in a public square in Florence, where Cellini is about to be hanged until—in the *Threepenny* and *Knickerbocker* tradition—he is pardoned by the Duke, who has commissioned a statue from the celebrated sculptor and goldsmith and wants to see it finished. More than fifteen minutes of continuous music, this scene depicted all the dynamics of life in Florence on the day of a hanging, with street vendors, church bells, choruses of chauvinistic citizens, and of course a romantic farewell ballad from the condemned hero, "There'll Be Life, Love, and Laughter." Essentially, the musical idea underlying this sequence was the same as that for the dream sequences in *Lady in the Dark*—to do a continuous and thoroughly developed composition based on original popular-style themes. But whereas the themes in, say, the "Glamour Dream" had been parodies and pastiches of Broadway and Hollywood cocktail sophistication, those of the opening scene in *The Firebrand of Florence* were pure operetta, with almost no parody at all.

This was, to be sure, an appropriate foretaste of things to come. For, as the play's two acts unfolded the ensuing adventures of Cellini—saving his neck from his enemies while pursuing Angela, who also is being pursued by the Duke on the sneak from the Duchess, who is in turn more interested in Cellini than in her husband—almost all the songs proved to be in an idiom of Broadway-ized operetta, as if Weill were trying to show that he could also be a latter-day Lehár when that was what he felt like being. Indeed, some of it was very nice operetta: "There'll Be Life, Love, and Laughter," for example, was good enough to provide a hint or two for Frederick Loewe when he and Alan Jay Lerner composed "It's Almost Like Being in Love" for their 1947 hit, *Brigadoon*. But the only song in the score that is truly distinguished—and the only one that has a distinctly Weillian flavor—is the Duchess's entrance number, "Sing Me Not a Ballad," which, according to Ira Gershwin, had originated in "a rather bizarre melody" Weill had written for the Duchess's page to announce her arrival. "When we had to face the writing of a solo song for the Duchess," Gershwin continues, "Kurt wondered what sort of melodic mood should be striven for. The page's little sing-song had echoed many times in my mind, and I suggested that its first line of ascending notes seemed a theme that could be developed into a refrain. Kurt thought this a good idea and, using the six notes of the first line, evolved this full and distinctive melody." And thus Kurt had made a final offering to his wife in the form of the best song in the score; but it succeeded in saving neither her performance nor the show, which closed after forty-three performances, the worst flop of Weill's American career.

What had gone wrong? There was widespread agreement that Lenya's performance, coy to an extreme and striving too hard to fill a role that did not fit her, was one major source of the trouble; but this wasn't all. The production seemed oversized to most people who saw it, too stiff and ponderous for its slight leading players and even slighter material. For, in the long run, the chief problem was the text. George Jean Nathan, in justification of Weill's relatively weak score, observed that "when the book is as sour as that of *The Firebrand of Florence*, it would require the services of Lehár, Eysler, Kálmán, and Victor Herbert operating in combination and at the top of their form" to make the play a success. But Mayer's original play had been a trifle to begin with, a hit for the tastes of a certain day and no other, and it had brought down the level not only of Weill's work but of Gershwin's as well. Envisioning a comic operetta,

Gershwin had seen it as, among other things, an opportunity to exercise his passion for puns, spoonerisms, and other wordplay to an extreme that became tiresome. This fit of self-indulgence helped bring about the undoing of *The Firebrand of Florence*, and though Ira Gershwin was to make one more stab at Broadway in the wake of this disaster, the collaboration between himself and Kurt Weill was never again to be revived.

Broadway Opera:
Street Scene

"Here in America is the best audience in the world to write music for," Weill told a reporter in Hollywood on June 3, 1945, not quite a month after the end of the war in Europe, not quite two after the sudden death of President Franklin D. Roosevelt. "They are remarkably quick to catch what you are trying to put over. They laugh when the music is meant to be funny. I find I can switch them over from laughter to tenderness or any other kind of response in a few bars." Marveling at how vividly young Americans responded to their favorite instrumentalists, he noted that in Europe "young people liked music deeply but they listened to it in a kind of dumb rapture. The average youngster over there didn't have any appreciation for orchestration and they didn't know one instrument from another. They were fed on classical music and they accepted what was given them. But here the great instrumentalists like Benny Goodman and Harry James and Gene Krupa are gods. The young people can tell the minute they hear a recording what band is playing. The younger generation here may not know or care anything about so-called classical music but it would be an easy step for them if they wanted to take it." Weill now wanted nothing more in the world than to help them do so, and above all to achieve this by bringing his music from the popular forms he had mastered into some truly "classical" American style of his own.

As always, he wanted to do this by writing music for dramatic contexts—for the theater as always, where he felt increasingly the desire to try an American opera at last, but also for radio and for movies. Hollywood had become fairly attractive to him in recent years, in spite of its mistreatment of his *Lady in the Dark* and *Knickerbocker Holiday* scores—he liked the friends he had there, he liked the money it offered, and the pleasant experience of *Where Do We Go from Here?* had stimulated in him a genuine interest in the possibilities of the film form. Indeed, though the main reason he was in Hollywood now was to work on the film score of *One Touch of Venus*, which had been sold to Mary Pickford Productions, another thing he was doing was discussing with the director George Cukor the possibility of an original musical film by him and Maxwell Anderson, who also was there at this time. What they proposed was a movie based on the autobiography of Joseph Jefferson, the nineteenth-century American actor who had become celebrated for his performance of Rip Van Winkle in Dion Boucicault's dramatization. Cukor seems to have been interested, and Weill was quite enthusiastic about an idea that presented such good possibilities for fantasy and Americana all at once; but by the fall Anderson, still doubtful about his ability to do musicals, had withdrawn and involved himself in other projects instead. He and Weill also had begun to revise *Ulysses Africanus* at around this time, because Paul Robeson was suddenly prepared to show some interest in it; but that also fell by the wayside.

Weill looked into various other possibilities back in New York when he returned there that summer, the *Venus* film project having become indefinitely delayed. But the fact was that, for the first time since the fall of 1939, he found himself going into a new season without a show either in preparation or running and in need of attention. In some ways this simply was an accident of professional circumstances: Ira Gershwin and Maxwell Anderson were the two people he most wanted to work with these days, and both had suddenly made themselves unavailable. Ogden Nash and S. J. Perelman had presented a new idea to him that spring, but he had turned it down, saying that what they needed for it was a "very hot jazz composer." But surely the effect of current history on Weill's state of mind also had something to do with the situation. The war with Japan had now ended, too, in two enormous blasts that heralded a terrifying new era. And full knowledge of the consequences of the war in Europe was now reaching American ears: Berlin and other cities were piles of rubble, millions were dead, Jews in particular the victims of unimaginable slaughter; and tens of thousands of Jews were among the homeless who

were filling the Displaced Persons camps. It was a time when a man of
Weill's background was likely to feel a special gladness at being an
American and a special guilt at being a Jewish survivor.

He soon had opportunity to give vent artistically to each of these
feelings in turn. A chance to realize his old dream of a full-fledged piece of
Americana came at around this time out of an idea developed by Olin
Downes, the music critic for *The New York Times*, and a businessman
named Charles McArthur. McArthur wanted to underwrite a quality
musical program for radio, and he had asked Downes to help him
formulate an idea and be host for the show. What they proposed was a
series of short operas based on American folk music. The moment seemed
ripe for such an idea: serious composers like Aaron Copland and Roy
Harris had been utilizing American folk themes in their ballet and concert
works for several years, but there still was little in the way of opera
constructed on this basis. Nevertheless, Downes and McArthur had
trouble finding composers who were interested. Then the orchestra
contractor Morris Stonzek suggested that they try his old friend and
collaborator Kurt Weill. This surprised them at first; they thought their
idea was something only native American composers could carry out. But
Weill had been tinkering with American folk themes on and off for the
past ten years, and when they approached him they soon found he was
indeed someone they wanted.

The task now was to find a librettist with whom to work out and
develop a subject. Weill wanted Paul Green, but he proved unavailable,
and once again it was Morris Stonzek who came to the rescue. He had
recently worked with Lehman Engel, fresh out of the navy, on a Russian
War Relief show at the Mecca Temple (now the New York City Center),
and one of the contributors to it had been an interesting young playwright
named Arnold Sundgaard. Stonzek got in touch with him, and he proved
most eager for the opportunity to work with Kurt Weill; he also came up
quickly with an idea, based on the song "Down in the Valley," that Weill
liked.

The two collaborators went to work, and in a few weeks they had
produced a simple tale based on the story themes of "Down in the Valley"
and several other folk songs, which were also developed musically and
woven into the fabric of the piece. Written for narrator, soloists, chorus,
and orchestra, it was a free-flowing little musical drama somewhat in the
manner of *The Ballad of Magna Carta*. "We then cast the opera," Weill was
to explain a few years later, "and made what in radio circles is known as an
audition, a recording of which, in turn, was submitted to prospective

sponsors." This was necessary because McArthur could not afford to underwrite the show entirely on his own. "We found these sponsors frightened by the idea that they might be accused of submitting an opera to the public. It seemed that our project for radio advertisers was somewhat ahead of its time." The whole thing was shelved as a result; but it was destined to reemerge before long.

Weill's chance to do a Jewish work also arose at around the time the war was coming to an end. A New York cantor, David J. Putterman of the Park Avenue Synagogue, had conceived the idea two years earlier of commissioning liturgical pieces from various American composers, for use in his Friday evening services. He now got in touch with Weill, who welcomed the opportunity to do such a piece; it would be a chance, he told the cantor, to clear his conscience with respect to his father. Putterman went to see him at the offices of the Playwrights Company on Fifth Avenue, where he had a desk, and they decided that Weill would do a *Kiddush*, a Friday night blessing over the Sabbath meal. Weill did not get to the task right away, but by the beginning of the following year he was at it. When he finished the composition he dedicated it to his father and datelined it: "Purim 1946. Brook House." He did not accept payment for it.

Weill's *Kiddush* was sung by Cantor Putterman, accompanied by organ and mixed chorus, at the Park Avenue Synagogue on Friday evening, May 10, 1946. The piece, only a little more than five minutes in length, is a remarkable synthesis of elements in its composer's sensibility. The passages sung by the cantor alone have a traditional Jewish sound, with just the slightest hint of an American blues to them. The passages sung responsively by the chorus are almost pure Broadway, not only reminiscent of some of the choral passages in *The Ballad of Magna Carta* and *Down in the Valley* but also clearly heralding the choral work of Weill's next major scores. This relationship of challenge and response between cantor and chorus seems once again to revive the old quarrel in Kurt's nature, between what we have called the cantor and the *badkhen* in him. But something new has happened to the *badkhen*, represented here by the chorus: he is chastened, he weeps, he hopes, he is pious and sentimental. The old mockery is gone, and the playful elements that had once served this purpose are now aligned for the discovery of a new kind of seriousness. The chorus sings back to the cantor like his child, who, having found its own voice entirely, can now speak to him of its own purposes, but on new terms.

Weill also now had an opportunity to do a work of urgent Jewish significance for the theater. In the wake of the war the plight of the Jewish survivors in Europe and the status of Palestine, still under the British Mandate, had emerged jointly as one of the burning questions of the day. Aware of the tensions with the Arab community being created by Jewish immigration into Palestine, the British had established a strict quota for Jewish entry—in 1939, at the very moment when Jews were beginning to pour out of Europe searching for places of refuge. Now in the wake of the Holocaust thousands of ragged survivors of the slaughter were arriving at the coast of Palestine in overcrowded ships, most of them to be turned back or sent to British internment camps elsewhere, while only a lucky few were smuggled in. World Jewish opinion, especially in the United States—now the home of the largest Jewish community in the world— became fiercely anti-British, and there were some who talked of getting the Mandate out of Palestine by force.

Ben Hecht was one of the latter. The popular author of *The Front Page* and other plays and film scripts, as well as several novels and short stories, was the sort of man who could not become identified with a cause without getting aroused to an extreme. Once indifferent to his Jewish background, Hecht had begun to be acutely aware of it by the time World War II broke out in Europe, and from then on he was a Jewish nationalist of an uncommonly belligerent sort. It was on this basis that he was prominent in the Fight for Freedom, which agitated for American entry into the war until this occurred in December 1941; and it was on this basis that he became, not just a Zionist, but an ardent supporter of the Irgun Tzva'i Leumi, the terrorist organization of Palestinian Jews that performed its own acts of war against the British, reaching a climax on July 22, 1946, when it blew up a wing of the King David Hotel in Jerusalem.

Weill, who had worked with Hecht on the Fight for Freedom pageant *It's Fun to Be Free*, in the fall of 1941, and on the Jewish pageant *We Will Never Die*, in the winter of 1943, was strongly drawn to him, as he often was to this type of personality: Brecht had been Weill's Ben Hecht for his very different political mood of 1928. Weill and Hecht had often got together to discuss what they could do about the plight of the Jews in Europe and in Palestine; and by the summer of 1946 they had come up with a new idea for a pageant, one that could be formulated this time as a regular drama for the theater. The proceeds of *A Flag Is Born* were to go to the American League for a Free Palestine. Some of the finest talents in the American theater, Jews and non-Jews alike, rallied to the project, willing to work at the Equity minimum and even in some cases turn their salaries back in to the cause: Luther Adler directed it, and the leading roles were played by Paul Muni, Celia Adler (the half-sister of Luther and Stella), and the then little-known Marlon Brando. The radio news announcer Quentin Reynolds, well known not only for his work during the war but for the pro-Jewish broadcasts he had been making from Palestine, took the role of narrator.

A *Flag Is Born* opened at the Alvin Theatre on September 5, 1946. The drama weaving together the elements of the pageant was a quasi-surrealistic one. Tevya and Zelda, husband and wife, two elderly survivors of the Holocaust, are on their way to Palestine on foot and they pause to rest in a graveyard. It is Friday night, and Tevya begins the Sabbath prayers; this leads to visions of a succession of figures from the Bible, who speak and sing such passages as the Twenty-third Psalm and the Song of Songs and who enter into discussions with Tevya about Jewish destiny. Finally, Tevya imagines himself before a world tribunal—the United Nations is vaguely hinted at—and makes a speech for a Jewish Palestine that begins as a quiet appeal and turns into a roaring challenge. This was the moment in the play that led Howard Barnes to remark in the *New York Herald Tribune* that it as good as declares war on England. The last part of the drama focuses on young David, an angry survivor of the Holocaust whom Tevya and Zelda have encountered in the graveyard and who at first wants to kill himself in his despair. But he, too, sees visions: they are of the future, however, rather than of the past, and consist of Jewish resistance fighters in Palestine beckoning to him. Tevya and Zelda die, and at the end of the play David takes the old man's prayer shawl, affixes to it a Star of David he has taken from one of the gravestones, and holds it aloft as a flag with which he marches off to Palestine.

Of the music for A *Flag Is Born*, Brooks Atkinson commented that Weill "has written a beautiful theater score"; but, though appropriately moving, it was no more distinguished than the play itself. Emotions were running high, however, and this drama served them well enough that it played to standees at every performance and won pledges for contributions far exceeding the box-office receipts. *A Flag Is Born* ran for the entire season, with Luther Adler eventually replacing Paul Muni in the role of Tevya; then it went on tour with Jacob Ben-Ami, a star of the Yiddish theater, playing the lead. Weill had found an effective outlet for his conscience, even if not for his highest artistic aspirations, in doing this work. But now the time had arrived for him to bring his concern with

social questions into play with his fullest creative abilities; for he was at
work on an American opera at last.

Weill had long had a close relationship with the Playwrights Company,
and in June 1946, on a trip to Hollywood, he even entered into discussions
about a possible film production tie-in for the group, speaking as its more
or less official representative. He had a desk at the company's offices on
Fifth Avenue, where he sometimes worked. Under such circumstances it
seems natural that he should have been elected a full member of the
company, as he was later that summer. The only reason this had taken so
long to happen was that the company had been adhering to a policy of not
expanding beyond its original membership in spite of the death of Sidney
Howard in 1939; but by the beginning of 1946 a controversy had arisen
between S. N. Behrman and the other members, leading to his resignation
that summer. Weill was promptly elected to replace him.

Among the significant relationships Weill had developed with the
members of the Playwrights Company, other than with Maxwell Anderson, was one with Elmer Rice, for whose *Two on an Island* he had
composed incidental music back in 1939. Actually, Weill had been
introduced to Rice in 1936, during rehearsals of *Johnny Johnson*. He had
immediately thought of *Street Scene*, Rice's Pulitzer Prize-winning play of
1929, which he had seen in Europe; he "had thought of it many times as a
perfect vehicle for a musical play," he was to write later in *The New York
Times*. "It was a simple story of everyday life in a big city, a story of love
and passion and greed and death. I saw great musical possibilities in its
theatrical device—life in a tenement house between one evening and the
next afternoon. And it seemed like a great challenge to me to find the
inherent poetry in these people and to blend my music with the stark
realism of the play."

Weill was not the first composer to have noticed the musical qualities
inherent in *Street Scene*: Deems Taylor, for example, had wanted to do a
version for the Metropolitan Opera, but Rice had been unable to accept
his request for a libretto considerably different from the play. Other
composers approached Rice as well, but he, according to Weill, "thought
it was too early for a show of that type." Then at last, Weill goes on, "on a
hot summer day in 1945, as we were leaving a Dramatists Guild meeting
together, we started talking about *Street Scene* again and decided that now
was the time to do it. The Broadway musical scene had changed quite a lot
in the ten years since we had first discussed the plan. Broadway
composers had become more 'book conscious.' Opera was now a popular

entertainment; the public had become interested in singing. Before the second drink arrived (we were planted in a cool bar by this time), Elmer and I had made up our minds to go ahead with *Street Scene*. We decided to do it as a musical version of the play, to cast it entirely with singers, so that the emotional climaxes could be expressed in music, and to use spoken dialogue to further the realistic action."

Actually, Weill is being a bit disingenuous in this article written just before the Broadway opening of the work. In the first place, there are indications that Maxwell Anderson also was part of the early discussions of this project; Rice, after all, was not a poet, and lyrics would be needed for a musical version of his play. But chances are that Anderson also was prepared to do the entire adaptation, since Rice had long been less than tractable about making changes in his Pulitzer Prize–winning text—and was in fact to remain so. This undoubtedly led to a clash of personalities, however, and Anderson bowed out of the project completely after a few weeks. And in the second place, what Weill was now setting about to create out of Rice's play was not just "a dramatic musical," as the producers chose to call it, but an opera, albeit one making extensive use of the Broadway idiom. There was still some fear, however, that the Broadway audience would be frightened by the term *opera*, so guarded language was being used. As for his decision to use whole passages of spoken dialogue—something George Gershwin had not done in his Broadway opera, *Porgy and Bess*—Weill was not making a mere concession to Broadway tastes but adhering to the traditions of the German *Singspiel*, which, as Beethoven's *Fidelio* demonstrates, was as capable of serious drama as it was of comedy. Weill was later to explain the passages of spoken dialogue to an interviewer in this way: "I address myself to Americans and I don't think they want 'Do you want another cup of coffee?' to be sung."

The final text of the Weill opera, prepared in collaboration with Rice, was to adhere rather closely to the original play; but nevertheless a lyricist was needed. According to Rice's memoirs, it was he who suggested asking the eminent Black poet Langston Hughes if he would take the assignment; others have said it was Weill's idea. In any case, though neither of them knew him personally, Hughes accepted, and in time a strong working relationship grew up among the three of them. They began by gathering for meetings at Weill's home in New City to make a preliminary reconnaissance of the proposed operatic terrain. "First we said," Weill was to tell an interviewer, "what do we take out? Then we decided what the big musical moments would be, and after that we went through it in detail and decided the contents of the numbers." But according to John F. Wharton, lawyer for the Playwrights Company, Elmer Rice did not yield easily to cuts, changes, and insertions in his original. "The others tried ceaselessly to point out that in a musicalization one used music rather than dialogue to achieve certain effects. Elmer was not easily convinced; he began to recount, again and again, how certain scenes had gripped the audience in 1929." The final results suggest that he was eventually brought into line on all the essentials; but the text itself was not the only area in which he provided difficulties. Owing to an apparent nervous condition suffered at this time by his wife, the actress Betty Field, Rice found that he could not readily leave her alone in their house in Greenwich, Connecticut. At first he proposed that he withdraw from the project, but then it was decided that Hughes and Weill would stay and work at his guest cottage, where he had a piano installed. Finally, on the eve of rehearsals, he fell ill and had to be hospitalized for several weeks.

Weill and Hughes had some interesting experiences working together. They had wanted a blues number, and Rice had created a Negro janitor for this purpose—apparently with the intention of replacing the Swedish janitor of the original entirely; but in the end the latter was retained as well, so that the humble apartment house of the opera enjoys the unlikely luxury of two full-time maintenance men! Hughes wrote a poem for the new janitor, "I Got a Marble and a Star," and, in order to find the right musical idiom for it, he took Weill to various Harlem nightclubs. The resulting song, Hughes observed, was "composed in a national American Negro idiom; but a German, or someone else, could sing it without sounding strange or out of place." Similarly, he and Weill roamed together through the streets of New York, often for hours at a time, to watch children at play; for they had decided to open Act Two with a whole "Children's Game" sequence. For the active and verbal content of the game in the opera, Rice and Hughes put their American-born heads together and got lively results; then, according to Hughes, "Weill took the verses we wrote and shaped a piece out of it so faithful to reality that many people assumed it was an authentic children's game." It was experiences like this that led Hughes to regard Weill as a truly universal artist, who could with equal justice be claimed by Germany as a German, by France as a Frenchman, by America as an American, "and by me as a Negro." When an interviewer later asked Weill how he was able to capture an American milieu so well in *Street Scene*, he replied: "First, I could see the country from the outside, so I had more respect for it.

Second, my whole musical background is very closely related to American jazz. That's why the Nazis attacked me so."

On the production side, however, things did not go so smoothly. The opera was clearly going to require a large cast and orchestra, and Rice and Weill had felt at the beginning that the Playwrights Company did not have the resources to handle it. Consequently, they had approached Richard Rodgers and Oscar Hammerstein II, who were now producing other shows besides their own. Rodgers and Hammerstein were interested; but the Playwrights Company was scandalized upon hearing of the prospective deal from which it was being excluded, and tried to save the situation by proposing a coproduction. Rodgers and Hammerstein would not hear of this, however, and the upshot was that the Playwrights obtained Dwight Deere Wiman, a well-known producer who had in fact rejected the original *Street Scene* back in the 1920s, to go in on a coproduction with themselves. The Playwrights were producing the opera after all, but apparently not without misgivings.

John F. Wharton, whose account of *Street Scene* in his memoirs betrays an unhappiness with it on his part from the outset, writes that "trouble began when definitive casting became essential. We needed a young star, someone who could at least approximate what Mary Martin was when she entered the Broadway scene with 'My Heart Belongs to Daddy.' There was no such young star. It seems unbelievable, but it is true that the era of Berlin, Kern, Gershwin, Porter, Rodgers, and others brought forth only a handful of real stars; of all the girls who played the lead in *Oklahoma!* not one became a star of first magnitude. Anne Jeffreys, who finally was our choice, was proficient and lovely to look at, but she lacked that peculiar 'star quality.' " What Wharton neglects to mention is that Anne Jeffreys, a featured Hollywood actress, was a trained singer who had performed on the operatic stage; for this sort of background, rather than that of the conventional musical comedy star, was what Weill's new work required. Indeed, for the two crucial roles of Frank and Anna Maurrant—Anne Jeffreys was to play their daughter, Rose—the production obtained the bass Norman Cordon, a regular with the Metropolitan Opera, and the soprano Polyna Stoska, of the New York City Center Opera Company (later to become the New York City Opera).

Wharton found that other performers cast in the production also seemed to be wanting in "star quality." "One character in the play," he writes, "is a young man evidently modeled on what Elmer conceived himself to be at that age. It was a difficult part. . . . Weill found a young man of whom he felt so sure that we signed him before production began. As soon as he appeared on a rehearsal stage, everyone (including Kurt) wanted to replace him." Eventually, the role of young Sam Kaplan was given to Joseph Sullivan, an opera singer who had recently played Gaylord Ravenal in a revival of *Show Boat* and who was to open in *Street Scene* as Brian Sullivan because there already was someone else with his own name in the Actors' Equity register.

The glum attitude Wharton manifests toward *Street Scene* even when writing about it many years later evidently was that of the Playwrights Company in general, which might not have taken on the project at all but for embarrassment at the prospect of a Rodgers and Hammerstein production of it. Of the production team, only Dwight Deere Wiman seems to have appreciated the full significance of the new *Street Scene*. He favored calling it an "opera," for example, but was obviously outvoted by those who wanted to bill it as some kind of musical. "Wiman," writes Wharton, "was perhaps the only Broadway producer who could appreciate fully Kurt's genius."

Weill's genius was not fully appreciated by the audiences in Philadelphia, either, when *Street Scene* opened there at the Shubert Theatre for a tryout in the fall of 1946. Wharton writes that the musical numbers received only "minimal applause," and that Weill came to him afterward and said: "I can reorchestrate any of those songs so that it will surely get a big hand, but it won't be *solid* applause. So why do it?" Wharton may have wondered why not; but Maurice Abravanel, on the other hand, conducting *Street Scene* as he had done every one of his old friend's shows starting with *Knickerbocker Holiday*, treated every note of the score "as though it were Bach." Abravanel, who had even tried, without success, to get Weill and the Metropolitan Opera interested in one another when he conducted there, knew that he was taking part in a significant chapter in American musical history. But it is not as if Weill, who had worked longer and more painstakingly on *Street Scene* than on any of his previous American works, had renounced his old Broadway professionalism either: Charles Friedman, who staged the production, was to speak with admiration of the composer's willingness to make cuts in the score when the flow of the action seemed to require it.

But the three-week tryout in Philadelphia, in spite of all efforts to save the situation, was, as Rice put it, "cataclysmic. The reviews were tepid, the attendance pitiable. Night after night we played to an audience of a few hundred scattered in the vastness of the Shubert Theatre. We had one packed house—on New Year's Eve, when of course every play sells out. Wiman, to lighten the gloom, invited us all to a champagne supper, where we tried to be merry. At one point Wiman's sister said, 'I loved the show so much, I'd like to see it again at the matinee. Do you think I could get a ticket?' There was a moment of silence; then Forrest Haring, Wiman's business manager, leaned across the table and with perfect timing said, 'Could you use a couple of hundred seats?' Our laughter was not gay." Wiman and the Playwrights Company made arrangements to cut their expected losses and with great trepidation opened *Street Scene* in New York at the Adelphi Theatre on January 9, 1947.

It would be hard to guess the moment when a perceptive listener on that opening night may have begun to realize he was hearing something more like an opera than a musical; but he would surely have noticed, as the orchestra struck up the opening measures, that he was hearing an introduction much like the one in *Porgy and Bess*. Like that one, the *Street Scene* introduction is based on a repeating, driving pattern of groups of sixteenth notes—a thoroughly Weillian pattern from his earliest days, as we have seen, but now articulated with a fully realized American jazz intonation that proclaims its kinship with Gershwin, except that it appropriately has more of a "big city" sound than its equivalent in *Porgy and Bess*. Also as in Gershwin's introduction, the one in *Street Scene* every so often pits contrapuntally against these agitated sixteenths a broader, syncopated jazz theme in quarters and eighths. Furthermore, the parallels between the two "Broadway operas" continue into their opening scenes: for just as the Gershwin introduction leads into the opening ensemble and the singing of "Summertime," so also does the Weill one lead into the group of people on the New York stoop singing "Ain't It Awful, the Heat?" which is musically close to Gershwin's curtain-raiser about the same season. Indeed, as the curtain went up on Jo Mielziner's single set for the *Street Scene* opera, "the exterior of a 'walk-up' apartment house in a mean quarter of New York," one could easily have looked upon it as a New York equivalent, biracial and ethnically varied in its inhabitants, of the Catfish Row depicted in *Porgy and Bess*. As if to emphasize this kinship, the next number after the curtain-raiser in *Street Scene* is "I Got a Marble and a Star," the blues sung by Henry Davis, the Black janitor.

But once this kinship has been established, *Street Scene* departs from *Porgy and Bess* onto its own course, remaining similar to Gershwin's work only in that it, too, clearly becomes opera while retaining the idioms of jazz and of Broadway all the while. The operatic aspirations of Weill's work have by now been hinted at, not only in the opening ensemble, but also in the third number, "Get a Load of That," in which the three gossipy ladies of the front stoop sing their reactions to an affair they know Anna Maurrant, of their building, is having with a Mr. Sankey from down the street. The harmonies and rhythms of this patter trio are quite sophisticated, but one can easily be deceived concerning its true nature because of its content: can such lowdown sidewalk chatter really be opera? Weill's sly assertion that it can be is his final answer to Wagner; these humble New York types are his Brechtian beggars in a culturally translated form. Indeed, he even shows a specifically *Threepenny*-like intention in the next number, "When a Woman Has a Baby," an arietta sung by Mr. Buchanan, whose wife upstairs is about to give birth and who protests it's all just as hard for him as it is for her: for this is a little piece of operatic parody, especially when the ladies on the stoop begin to punctuate his musical phrases with an absurdly lofty obbligato.

There can be no doubt about Weill's grand-operatic intentions a few moments later, however, when Anna Maurrant, after a brief scene with her abusive husband, sings of her disappointed youthful aspirations for love and tenderness in the aria "Somehow I Never Could Believe." This was bound to come as a shock to any listener who may still have thought he had come to a Broadway musical, just as it is likely to surprise any listener to this day who knows other Kurt Weill works and not *Street Scene*. For it is not only the most conventional aria in the nineteenth-century operatic tradition that he ever wrote; it also sounds to many ears almost like pure Puccini. With characteristic catholicity, Weill had long admired Puccini, even back in his days as an apprentice to Busoni—who, we may recall, had regarded *Madame Butterfly* as "disreputable." Weill may have vacillated now and then in his feelings about Puccini's music itself, but he had always honored Puccini on the same principle whereby he unreservedly admired Verdi: these were the honest, almost instinctual protagonists of a native melodic tradition, enjoying the same spontaneous relationship with their audiences for which he revered Mozart. And by now, the American Weill was readier than he had ever been to adopt sentimental modes when his art seemed to require it. What better model was there than Puccini, then, of an opera composer who could be sentimental and utterly modern at the same time? Furthermore, he was the composer whose sounds were the most familiar "operatic" ones to New Yorkers better acquainted with musical comedy than with opera, the very people Weill was reaching out to now.

Not that Anna Maurrant's aria does not contain passages other than Puccinian: it is full of stretches that are jazz and of others that are unmistakably Weill. And though there still are many listeners for whom the overall idiom, as a *Variety* reviewer put it about the *Street Scene* score as a whole, "smacks something of a tired and discouraged Puccini," the combination of elements is unique, and the whole thing is quite moving no matter what sources it has drawn upon. Harold Rome has observed with respect to Weill that "a good composer seeks what is right," without worrying whether he is always being utterly original from one passage to the next; and this is what Weill always did. In the dramatic context of *Street Scene*, Anna Maurrant's aria is more than right; it is the path that leads the listeners up to a peak of powerful emotional intensity from which they rarely depart from that moment on.

The mounting drama is underscored in the next few moments as Mr. Sankey walks by on his way to the drugstore and Anna Maurrant, pretending to look for her young son, Willie, hastens off after her lover. This provides occasion for the ladies on the stoop to sing a reprise of their gossipy "Get a Load of That," now grown more ominous, though its vein is still humorous enough to herald a momentary return to a lighter mood. What follows is a stretch of pure comic relief: one of the neighbors in the building, Lippo Fiorentino, an Italian immigrant violin teacher, comes home carrying a handful of ice-cream cones; as he passes them around, everyone joins into the "Ice Cream Sextet," at once a broad parody of Italian opera and Weill's heartfelt tribute to his favorite American sweet. Then the dark tones are resumed as Frank Maurrant, who has come home before his wife returns, gets into an argument with one of the neighbors about how to raise children and sings his aria, "Let Things Be Like They Always Was." But the mood changes again, to merriment and, if not precisely to comedy this time, then to musical comedy; for the number that ensues sounds so much like Rodgers and Hammerstein as almost to seem a deliberate parody of them. Indeed, "Wrapped in a Ribbon and Tied in a Bow," sung by a group of girls coming home from their high school graduation and triumphantly holding aloft the diplomas that the song's title commemorates, was originally going to turn into a full-scale block party; but, as the director Charles Friedman later told the press, "it was too much musical comedy, so it was cut to the bone for simplicity. All this meant that some excellent music of Kurt Weill's had to go. But it gave us a show."

By this time we have met Sam Kaplan, the sensitive student who is Elmer Rice's vision of himself as a young man, and as all the neighbors go inside to their respective apartments, he is left alone to sing his arioso lament, part blues, part opera, "Lonely House." One of the principal pieces in the score, it has a rambling melody that could almost pass for musical comedy, except that it is more difficult than meets the ear. Sam goes inside, and along comes young Rose Maurrant, the daughter of Frank and Anna; she is escorted by Harry Easter, her supervisor at the real estate office where she works, who is now showing a more than professional interest in her. A smoothy, Easter tells her he can get her into show business and sings "Wouldn't You Like to Be on Broadway?"— another light jazz piece that is more difficult than it sounds and that sums up the character of the singer and the situation at hand as well as anything in operatic literature does. Rose turns down his offer, singing "What Good Would the Moon Be," a cavatina that joins hands with "Wrapped in a Ribbon and Tied in a Bow" as one of the two most "Broadway"-sounding numbers in the score—except that it is somewhat more chromatic than its typical musical-comedy equivalent and is furthermore so touching that one is no longer likely to care what genre of musical theater it belongs to. By now, we have followed Weill in his exploration of the line between opera and musical comedy to the point where the line no longer seems to exist; which is exactly where he wants us to be. As if to prove that the distinction no longer matters, the next number, "Moon-faced, Starry-eyed," sung by a fast young couple who arrive after Easter has departed and Rose has gone offstage, is a rousing piece of 1940s jive that ends with the couple doing a wild jitterbug.

The first act ends in one of the opera's high points, "Remember That I Care," a duet sung on the stoop by Sam Kaplan and Rose Maurrant, the two young dreamers of the building, who are so fond of one another that for a moment they almost believe they are in love. This duet also has moments melodically and harmonically reminiscent of Puccini, but these and other elements integrate into a powerful piece that seems to become utterly American when Sam and Rose begin to quote from Walt Whitman's "When Lilacs Last in the Dooryard Bloom'd." Weill, who passionately loved the lilacs that bloomed every spring in front of his own Brook House, provides here a splendid fulfillment of his adopted Americanisms and Whitmanisms—a deeper one, by the way, than had been achieved only a year before by his old colleague Paul Hindemith, also now an American citizen, in his own musical treatment of this poem, *A Requiem for Those We Love*. Composed as a lament for the death of Franklin Delano Roosevelt, Hindemith's setting of the whole poem for chorus and orchestra is an attempt, characteristic of European lovers of Whitman, to grasp the work in all its spaciousness, with the result that it is overlong and faltering. Weill, on the other hand, has taken just a corner of the poem, and viewed it from a certain angle—the poignant one of two young people in a New York slum longing for a pastoral America they have never known. This above all is what the duet is about, just as it really is what Whitman is about to most Americans in the twentieth century. Weill has grasped a truth about the poem that goes beyond the text itself, and the result is a moment of great operatic emotion. Busoni's strictures have been left behind here—although this still is no orthodox love duet that Weill has written.

Act Two, set the following day, begins with various sounds suggestive of early morning in New York and then launches into the children's games: the melodies sung here are typical of American children's songs, but the section is interestingly introduced by an orchestral allegro vivace reminiscent of the accompaniment to the children's tormenting of the idiot in *Boris Godunov*. The opera's atmosphere of foreboding then returns in a trio, "There'll Be Trouble," sung by Frank, Anna, and Rose Maurrant; which is followed, after Frank goes off to an out-of-town assignment on his job, by a duet in which Rose warns her mother that the neighbors are talking about her and Mr. Sankey. Anna, over whose head there now hangs an atmosphere of impending disaster, sings a song to her brat of a son, Willie, "A Boy Like You," which poignantly sums up her persistent longing for better things in the face of all the facts to the contrary that overwhelm her life. Soon Rose and Sam are again alone on the stoop, and they fan their own hopes of a better life in "We'll Go Away Together," a breathless duet that carries echoes of the earlier one. Their ardor is extinguished, however, when Harry Easter comes along, offering to escort Rose to their boss's funeral, to which she had been planning to go by herself; they go off together, leaving Sam alone on the stoop.

The scene is now set for tragedy. Sankey comes by during a moment when Sam has briefly disappeared inside and the stoop is empty of people; Anna Maurrant beckons to him from her window, and he goes up just as Sam reappears and quietly perceives what is happening. Several more vignettes illustrative of the life in and around the house occur, and then Frank Maurrant suddenly enters, having decided not to go to his out-of-town assignment after all. Sam, sensing the oncoming disaster, tries to block his way; but Maurrant, his suspicions now aroused, flings the young man aside and dashes into the house. Sam frantically calls up to Anna Maurrant's window, but in a moment screams are heard from there, followed by two shots, then another. A crowd gathers, but Maurrant, brandishing his gun, comes down and makes a getaway before the police arrive. By the time Rose reappears, ironically, from the funeral she has attended, the bodies of Sankey and her mother are being brought down by ambulance attendants. The entire ensemble is now onstage, and they proceed to sing one of the most powerful choral pieces Weill ever wrote, "The Woman Who Lived up There." At the same time Sam Kaplan sings a solo lament that weaves through the choral passages in a way reminiscent of a cantor singing responsively at a service: at this moment, Weill as well as Rice seems to have found a way of identifying himself with the young Jewish protagonist of the drama. This musical rendering of the special pathos of urban life in America is made complete by the sound of the street hawker crying "Strawberries" in the distance.

Then there is an orchestral interlude, and the second scene of Act Two begins with a moment of quasi-Shakespearean comic relief. Two nursemaids enter, wheeling carriages with two infants of the upper classes inside them, and pull out a tabloid carrying the news of the murder. Pointing to the newspaper and to the broken window upstairs, they proceed to sing a sardonic lullaby intermingling their whispers of "sleep" and "hush" to the babies with a lurid description of the crime. Before long they are even singing to the babies some of the dirt about their own parents. It is noteworthy that, though Elmer Rice collaborated with Langston Hughes on the lyrics of several of the opera's numbers, this "Lullaby" is the only one in which Hughes did not participate at all and which was written entirely by Rice. Its sardonicism was not for the largely sweet-natured Hughes.

After this the drama is brought to its conclusion: Maurrant, caught hiding in a nearby cellar, is brought on in handcuffs to be confronted by his daughter. The crowd has gathered again, and Maurrant sings his apologia, "I Loved Her, Too," accompanied by Rose and the ensemble in another choral number—the second of the two in the opera, both sung in these climactic moments of the second act. The effect is of individual tragedy turned into the tragedy of an entire community: *Street Scene* becomes here one of the few genuinely successful operas dealing with social questions. Maurrant then is taken away, and Rose and Sam sing a duet musically and verbally recalling their earlier ones, so full of dreams that have since become quashed by terrible reality. Rose intends to go away somewhere, and the still rather childish Sam wants to go with her; but she firmly though tenderly repudiates him. She leaves, Sam rushes brokenhearted into the house, and at last no one is left on the stoop but the gossipy ladies of the first act, who sing a reprise of "Ain't It Awful, the Heat?" as the curtain falls.

Street Scene is unique among Kurt Weill's works not only because it is the one full-fledged opera he wrote on American soil, but also because, as such, it is quite different from any of the ones he did in Germany. Its score is a complete realization of the new freedom of form and sentiment that he had discovered upon coming to the United States. In a set of notes he subsequently wrote for a recording of selections from *Street Scene*, he described this opera as a fulfillment of two old dreams—one, of writing an American opera, which he had harbored since coming to this country, and the other, going all the way back to Germany in the twenties, of doing "a special brand of musical theatre which would completely integrate drama and music, spoken word, song and movement." He then spoke of various of his works as stages in the full realization of this ideal. "In the *Threepenny Opera*, which was my first musical play, we deliberately stopped the action during the songs which were written to illustrate the 'philosophy,' the inner meaning of the play. *Mahagonny* was a sort of 'dramatic review,' using elements of the theatre from slapstick to opera. *The Silver Lake* was a serious musical which mixed realism and fantasy and used actors together with a singing chorus and a symphonic orchestra. But not until fifteen years later, not until *Street Scene*, did I achieve a real blending of drama and music, in which the singing continues naturally where the speaking stops and the spoken word as well as the dramatic action are embedded in overall musical structure." The old *Threepenny* question ("How is music—how, above all, is song in general—possible in the theater?") no longer had to be asked: now music could simply flow naturally, through the fabric Weill had woven out of his American experience. The days of American jazz parody, conceived and executed on German soil, had been left far behind; for Weill had achieved an American idiom all his own, developed primarily on Broadway and frankly rejoicing in its sounds.

Promised Lands

To the surprise of everyone involved, not only were the reviews of *Street Scene* excellent but the box office was, too, at first. To Olin Downes, Weill, whose contention had been that the Metropolitan Opera House was a fine museum but no place for new opera, had now offered convincing proof of this. "This piece," Downes wrote, "is as idiomatic American, direct and unacademic in its approach to the musico-dramatic problem as the artificial and unrooted opera, also of native authorship, given the week previous at the Metropolitan was not." He was referring to an opera by Bernard Rogers, with a libretto by the radio writer Norman Corwin, called *The Warrior*. Downes could not hold back a certain patriotic enthusiasm at the "extraordinary evolution" he perceived in Weill:

> We recall his satirical piece, *Mahagonny*, heard at a modern music festival in Baden-Baden in the 1920s. It was the work of one of the bold, bad musical intellectuals of the advanced European group of the day. A war has intervened, and experiences too, since that time, including Mr. Weill's arrival here . . . and his acquirement in fact and spirit of American citizenship. In view of what he has done: the complete discarding of the aesthetic snobbery of earlier days; the evolution, in the art of a pupil of Ferruccio Busoni, from the sophistications of the (professed) avant-garde to the plain, direct emotional expression which he has sought and so largely attained in

this score—from these precedents and evolutions of attitude as well as style and technique—we are given to wonder whether it is not the very artist coming here from a European social and cultural background who will be quickest to perceive in its full significance an aspect of American life; and feel it as those who always have been in its vicinity might not, and, in communicating it, take a historic step in the direction of genuine American music-drama.

These ideas were very much in the air, particularly since another American opera composer of European origin also was achieving fame at this time; indeed, Gian Carlo Menotti, like Bernard Rogers, had seen his work reach the stage of the Metropolitan Opera. Friends of Weill's noticed that the Menotti phenomenon made a deep impression on him and troubled him concerning the precise nature of his own reputation.

This question took on greater significance after the initial euphoria over *Street Scene* passed and box-office returns began to sag. *Finian's Rainbow* had opened the very next night after *Street Scene*, and two months later came *Brigadoon*, both smash hits: these were a far cry from "Broadway opera," though they were very fine musicals—the first with lyrics by a near-collaborator of Weill's, E. Y. Harburg; the second produced by Cheryl Crawford and with lyrics by a future collaborator of his, Alan Jay Lerner—and they decidedly were what the Broadway audiences wanted. As *Street Scene* clearly began heading toward an early demise, tensions mounted among its creators: when Dwight Deere Wiman sought to reawaken public interest by means of a heavy advertising campaign, Weill, Rice, and Hughes reacted strongly against this as constituting an admission of defeat. It was an established understanding on Broadway that hit shows did not have to advertise after their first week.

For Weill, tension reached a height on March 1, the day before his forty-seventh birthday, with the sudden death from a blood clot of his brother Hans, at only forty-eight years of age. Among Kurt's whole immediate family—two brothers, a sister, and their parents—Hans, who alone among them so far had joined him in settling in the United States, had been the one he loved the most. Indeed, taken in its entirety, this was perhaps the warmest relationship of his life; and now it was over. Coming on top of everything else, the blow was too much for Kurt, and he suffered a nervous breakdown.

It was, in general, a time for taking stock. Kurt himself, though he had not suffered any serious illnesses in his adult life, had never been in robust health. All his life he had been afflicted by outbreaks of psoriasis, a skin condition that often produced a rash when he was undergoing great tension. And tension—buried beneath a mild exterior, pushed back and rarely given vent to in the fashion of so many "temperamental artists"— was of the very essence of his nature. The trait had yet to show any symptoms more troubling; but this was, in any case, a moment to sense the presence of mortality.

Kurt had not seen his parents since his departure from Germany fourteen years before. Albert Weill had turned eighty in January; his wife, Emma, was seventy-five. Kurt, along with his brothers, had loyally been sending them money through the years—Cantor Weill had never found regular employment in Palestine, having arrived there at the age of sixty-eight—but he had remained distant from them emotionally as well as physically. Indeed, before the war, Kurt's feeling of estrangement from his parents had been aggravated by their emigration to Palestine, for he had been rather vehemently anti-Zionist in those days. Kurt was a classic kind of ambivalent Jew most of his life, fluctuating between a genuine pride in his background, even a persistently Jewish-tinted religiosity of a very personal sort, and an impatience that often expressed itself in the only half-joking wish that all Jews would marry gentiles and thereby put an end to the whole question. But the war and the Holocaust had caused him, as it caused many others, to feel his Jewish roots with unwonted strength, and now, along with Ben Hecht and so many of his friends and colleagues, he ardently wished for an independent Jewish Palestine. These feelings, along with the death of his brother, made him want to visit his parents upon recovering from his collapse.

Kurt set out alone on May 6, first taking the S.S. *Mauretania* to England. Retracing the route of his emigration for the first time, he thought the six-day steamship passage to be "medieval" and decided he would fly when he returned home. Spending two days in London, he found it "very grim" and still lacking in amenities two years after the war's end. But he managed to enjoy himself all the same, having dinner out with Burgess Meredith and his wife, Paulette Goddard, going to the theater, discussing possible London productions of *Lady in the Dark*, *One Touch of Venus*, and *Street Scene*, as well as a possible original film opera for Alexander Korda. He admired the English spirit; but he did not feel the same about the French when he went on to Paris, which he found "as corrupt as a Balkan city." Nevertheless, he was charmed at revisiting this city where he once had lived and decided he would pass through again on his return. Here, too, he discussed possible productions of his works.

After a sojourn in Switzerland, he flew to Palestine on May 20 and made the trip up to Nahariya accompanied by Meyer Weisgal, who was there doing Zionist work in this year of crisis, when the UN had begun to take over responsibility in the country from the British. Kurt and Weisgal met the elder Weills strolling on the beach; Weisgal was struck by the resemblance between father and son.

Kurt stayed in Nahariya, where his remaining brother, Nathan, also was living, with his family, and practicing medicine as a specialist in X-ray diagnosis. Nathan made Kurt submit to his first medical examination in a long time and found he had the same high blood pressure condition from which Hans had suffered and which had led to his final illness. Kurt's condition was not so grave, but it was nevertheless another reminder of mortality for him; and though the initial shock of the discovery soon was to pass, he would never quite get over the feeling from this moment on that time was running out on him.

Otherwise, his stay was genuinely pleasant and refreshing for him. "Palestine is like fresh air after Europe," he wrote from Nahariya to Maxwell and Mab Anderson. "One sees happy faces everywhere, youth, hope, and the general theme is construction." He saw his sister, Ruth, and her family in Haifa, visited agricultural settlements, swam in Lake Tiberias, and had dinner with Nathan in the home of an Arab effendi, who was one of his brother's clients. Kurt was fascinated by the interplay of different civilizations in the country, and especially by the Oriental element. In Jerusalem he was publicly received as an important spokesman for both music and theater in America, meeting members of the Palestine Philharmonic Orchestra and of the Habimah Players. A reporter for the *Palestine Post* (now the *Jerusalem Post*), the city's English-language daily, asked him to "compare attempts in the United States and Palestine to create original music. He said that Jewish music had made further progress toward a style of its own than American music and that he thought that in style Palestine music had a labor spirit." He promised to write a piece for broadcasting over Palestine Jewish radio. Habimah, the oldest Hebrew-speaking dramatic troupe, invited him to its productions of *Oedipus*, *The Dybbuk*, and *The Golem*, and he promised to see what he could do about arranging an American tour for the company.

Leaving Palestine after a stay of about two weeks, Kurt passed through Europe again, spending a night in Rome, a day in Geneva, two days in Paris, and then a weekend in the English countryside. This time he noticed that the English were quite bitter about American criticism of their role in Palestine, and in particular about "Ben Hecht's silly one-man campaign" against the British Empire; but he found them somehow to be "beyond anger." He loved the flight home, marveling at the fact that it took only seven hours to cross the Atlantic and discovering upon his arrival in New York "some of the same emotion as arriving here 12 years ago." As he wrote shortly afterward in a letter to Anderson, who was in California, the trip only served to confirm his love for America, of which he had been reminded anytime he saw on his trip a manifestation of the "decency" he had come to regard as the outstanding trait of his adopted country. As for Lenya, who awaited him at home, Kurt's trip had been good for her, too, in a way. "One forgets in times," she had written to Mab Anderson while Kurt was still in Palestine, "how much one has become a part of the person one loves—and to be left alone for a while gives you time to reassemble your feelings and thoughts and then you know again and sure, that you wouldn't like to live without him."

As soon as he was back home, Weill began looking around for a new project. *Street Scene* had closed in May after 148 performances, and he was ready to put opera aside for the time being and aim again for a less difficult, though nonetheless serious, piece of musical theater. For a moment he and Maxwell Anderson talked of getting started on something new, but this did not materialize just yet. William Saroyan proposed a collaboration that evidently did not interest him. Meanwhile, always browsing through current literature for ideas, Weill came across a novel just published that year, *Aurora Dawn*, a first, highly successful work of fiction by the young Herman Wouk. He thought this might form the basis for a musical. As it turned out, Charles Friedman, the director of *Street Scene*, knew Wouk from having done entertainment work with him at a summer resort in the Berkshires, and he was able to bring Weill and the novelist together. In the ensuing weeks, Weill and Wouk—who had worked for a time as a writer for the Fred Allen radio show—developed a treatment for a possible musical play based on Wouk's novel about the world of radio. When it came time for the next step, however, Wouk wanted to finish his second novel, then well advanced, before getting involved in a Broadway production. Weill, for his part, had by then been approached once again by Cheryl Crawford, fresh from her success as the producer of *Brigadoon*. There had been a bit of a falling out between that show's librettist, Alan Jay Lerner, and its composer, Frederick Loewe, and she proposed that Lerner and Weill get together and do a show. This was no problem, since they already were neighbors in New City and both part of Anderson's circle there. They were agreeable to the idea, and the project with Lerner became Weill's next one.

Lerner had an idea well suited to Weill's passion for Americana. In a succession of scenes ranging from the first years of the American Republic to the present, he wanted to trace the history of a single marriage, treating that century and a half as though it were only a few years in the life of the couple. By means of this device the play could take a view of what had happened to this country since its beginnings by focusing specifically on what had happened to marriage in America—Lerner, as it turned out, had a rather glum view of both. Furthermore, the idea provided opportunity for musical treatment of a wide variety of American periods and styles. Indeed, as the two collaborators got to work that August, the image their play took on as a kind of succession of Currier and Ives prints suggested that they emphasize its artificial and proscenium aspects, and so it began to evolve as a "vaudeville." This provided a device for yet another dimension of Americana. Now, not only was each scene in the life of the couple to be done in a different musical style, suggestive of the period being treated, but each would be introduced by a different vaudeville "act"—a minstrel show, a magician, a soft shoe dance, and so on—covering a variety of American theatrical forms. Filled with enthusiasm at the developing material, Lerner and Weill had completed several scenes and eleven songs by September; but then the project became delayed in the search for a star to play the wife.

Weill now felt more American than ever. The previous February he had written an annoyed letter to *Life* magazine, which had very favorably reviewed *Street Scene* but called him a "German composer" in the process. "I do not consider myself a 'German composer,'" he wrote. "The Nazis obviously did not consider me as such either, and I left their country (an arrangement which suited both me and my rulers admirably) in 1933." He concluded by pointing out not only that he was an American citizen, but that he had written exclusively for the American stage since his arrival in this country, listing the titles of his Broadway shows to bring home the message. Indeed, one of the striking things about the list—which did not include *The Eternal Road*, written mainly in Europe—was that, with the solitary exception of *The Firebrand of Florence*, every title on it was American in subject matter. And now, after his first visit to Europe in twelve years and a sojourn in the Promised Land of his parents—as well as of one of his brothers, his sister, their families, and hundreds of thousands of other Jews—he was more immersed in Americana than ever, writing not only the Lerner show but also a revised and expanded version of *Down in the Valley*. He had been proud to learn that in Europe, after a twelve-year Nazi ban, *The Threepenny Opera* and his other German works were becoming popular again; and as for the new State of Israel created by UN vote that November, he was excited enough about it to compose, for a dinner honoring Chaim Weizmann in New York, an orchestration of *Hatikvah* that would soon be performed by the Boston Symphony Orchestra. But despite these various feelings, he was quite satisfied that his German past was far behind him, and he no more regarded Israel as the final goal of his wanderings than did some five million other American Jews, who also took pride in it and gave it support but were perfectly happy to be where they were. As he had told an interviewer back in 1944, if he were to be removed to somewhere "like off the earth," he would not be homesick for any spot but "the drugstore in New City."

This was a feeling now being tested among many of Weill's old colleagues and near-colleagues from Germany. In particular, those who had remained involved in radical politics—and this had been widely the case in Hollywood—found the growing American cold war mood to be oppressive. Furthermore, opportunities began to beckon from a gradually recovering Germany, eager to revive some of the cultural greatness that had been quashed and dispersed by Hitler. A small return migration got under way: some, like Thomas Mann and Paul Hindemith, were to settle in the years to come for the cultural way-station of German Switzerland rather than a complete return; others, like Ernst-Josef Aufricht, Fritz Kortner, and T. W. Adorno were to resume their careers in Germany itself. It was, of course, the House Committee on Un-American Activities that provided many with a special incentive to return to Europe: Hanns Eisler was simply deported. Bertolt Brecht was summoned to appear before the committee in Washington on October 30, 1947, as one of nineteen "unfriendly" witnesses named in its hearings in Hollywood earlier that month. Of the eleven "unfriendly" witnesses actually called to the stand, all but Brecht eventually went to jail and came to be known as the "Hollywood Ten."

Brecht, in a performance that some have considered to be the most definitive of his versions of *The Good Soldier Schweik*, told the committee that he neither was now nor had ever been a member of the Communist Party, managed to confuse all his listeners concerning the political intentions of *Die Massnahme*, and ultimately drew compliments from Chairman J. Parnell Thomas: "He is doing all right. He is doing much better than many other witnesses you have brought here." And, having done that, he left for Europe the next day, never to return to the United States. Some who knew Brecht have considered it possible that he might have stayed in America, in spite of everything, had he been able to obtain better acceptance here for his work. As it was, by the fall of 1947 he had seen only one scenario of his produced as a film in America—the anti-Nazi *Hangmen Also Die*, which had dropped his name from the screen credits—and had not penetrated to Broadway at all. Yet at the time of his departure he and Weill had not given up a commitment, made by contract three years before, to do a musical version of *The Good Woman of Setzuan* together. For Weill, *that* would have been something of a return to his German past, and it is possible that he was no longer prepared to make it anyway, by the fall of 1947. In any case, Brecht's departure clinched the matter: the German Weill was no more.

It was at around this time that Fritz Busch's son, Hans, who was teaching music at the University of Indiana, asked Weill for a musical-dramatic work that could be performed by the students. Fondly remembering his old Berlin "school opera" *Der Jasager*, Weill cast about for a subject on which to do an American equivalent and suddenly realized that *Down in the Valley* would be ideal for this purpose. He got back in touch with Arnold Sundgaard, and they went to work revising their old radio opera. "We changed the original radio piece into a musico-dramatic form, about twice as long as the original, with new scenes, new lyrics, and new music, and a brand-new orchestration for the special requirements of school orchestras."

The final version of *Down in the Valley* was similar to *Der Jasager* in length, in simplicity—concerning both the means of production and the musical demands made upon performers—and even occasionally in quality; but there the similarities end. *Down in the Valley*, constructed out of the melodic and story material of several American folk songs, is not only native in sound and content; it is also stylistically a prime specimen of the American Weill, free-flowing in form and unabashedly emotive and sentimental in expression. Narrator, chorus, and soloists interplay with the orchestra to tell this story set in an idealized rural America. After an introduction—essentially a setting of the folk song "Down in the Valley"—that is sung by narrator and chorus, we encounter Brack Weaver in the Birmingham jail, about to be executed for murder. It is obvious from the start that he is a nice young man who has met an undeserved fate; and it is only because no letters have arrived from his beloved Jennie Parsons that he suddenly makes an escape, determined to see her in his last hours. Jennie has been prevented from getting in touch with him by her father, and when Brack comes to her sitting on her porch that night, they exchange vows of undying love—this passage is based primarily on the song "The Lonesome Dove."

The two lovers then recall their unhappy history, and the whole middle section of the piece is devoted to a flashback. Jennie and Brack had met at a prayer meeting, which is evoked to the strains of the spiritual "The Little Black Train." After the meeting Brack asks her to go with him to a dance that Saturday night, which he celebrates with a rendition of "Hop Up, My Ladies"; Jennie accepts. But when she gets home she finds her father sitting on the porch with the sinister Thomas Bouché, who is interested in her and whose financial dealings have made her father beholden to him. Bouché wants to take her to the same Saturday night dance—he sings a reprise of "Hop Up, My Ladies" as if it were being danced by a lame nonagenarian—and when she refuses him, her father warns her not to go to the dance with anyone else. She goes with Brack anyway—the square dance is depicted by the chorus clapping its hands and singing "Sourwood Mountain"—and just as they are exchanging vows of love, Thomas Bouché, angry and drunk, strides in with a knife in his hand. The two men fight, and Bouché is killed by his own knife. The narrator and chorus remind us that this is the reason Brack Weaver has been sentenced to death. We return to the present, and Brack, satisfied that Jennie will love him forever, takes leave of her and turns himself back into custody; the chorus and the principals then join in a final rendition of the title song, which, on the line "Angels in heaven know I love you," seems to soar heavenward.

The piece is characterized by a conscientious seeking out of a naïve style, at moments too much so perhaps; and, it must be said that, in the case of the libretto, simplicity occasionally turns into simplemindedness. There are places, both in the text and in the music, that sound more like the rural America of Rodgers and Hammerstein than any more authentic version thereof; and now and then the orchestra indulges in a flourish that could serve perfectly well as background to a soap opera. Yet, on the whole, *Down in the Valley* is a highly successful work, moving and lyrical, and in its best moments a kind of American-rural counterpart to *Street Scene*. In its feeling for the possibilities of traditional American folk melodies, it is entirely as rich as equivalent works by Aaron Copland and Roy Harris. It also happens to be, in retrospect, peculiarly evocative of the late 1940s in this country, of the tone of the folklore revival that took place here in the wake of World War II. The mood then was generous and full of hope even in its inauthenticities, and the same can be said for Weill's *Down in the Valley*.

The work was scheduled for performance in Bloomington, Indiana, on July 15, 1948, and Kurt and Lenya arrived there a few days early. Weill busied himself with the details of the production; Wolfgang Roth, a scenic designer who had worked with him in Berlin and was doing this production at his invitation, was impressed at his display of a knowledge and creativity in theatrical matters that seemed equal to his musical abilities—the result of a lifetime of working in the theater with some of the major playwrights of the era. As for Lenya, she thoroughly enjoyed this opportunity to see an American campus up close; she later wrote glowingly, in a letter to Mab Anderson in California, of the atmosphere of youth and learning, adding characteristically of the students that "they seem to be so protected from the outside world. For the time they are there, anyway." *Down in the Valley* was performed before an audience of more than four thousand and was enthusiastically received.

Kurt and Lenya got onto the train the next day and rode homeward filled with a sense of well-being—from which they were suddenly jolted by a sight that met their eyes at a siding in Dayton, Ohio, where they stopped for half an hour. Standing there between rows of milk cans and piles of automobile tires were some of the coffins of American soldiers that were still being brought home from overseas battlefields three years after the war's end. It was a grim reminder to the Weills of the terrible times through which their life's personal struggles had been carried out; and Lenya, who wrote about the incident to Mab Anderson, was particularly dismayed at the indignity that was being visited upon these dead men.

Upon returning to New York City, Weill immediately went back to work on his show with Alan Jay Lerner. When they had first begun working on *A Dish for the Gods*, as it was called during its inception, they had envisioned Gertrude Lawrence in the lead role. She seems to have wavered in her feelings about it, however, and by the fall of 1947 they had started looking for another star. Cheryl Crawford then thought Mary Martin might be ideal for the show, "so I made arrangements for Alan, Kurt and me to play it for her one November Sunday in 1947, in Chicago. Unfortunately, the one song that really sent her was called 'Susan's Dream,' a lovely number for a black woman to be done in one of the interludes. The words were very touching, but it was impossible to conceive of them being sung by a white woman. Mary decided against the show." The star search continued through the winter, and by February Ginger Rogers's name had come up, but she did not take the role either. In April there still was no star, and an additional problem arose in the matter of a director. Until then, the show was to have been staged by Robert Lewis, a former Group Theatre actor—he played the Mayor in the opening scene of *Johnny Johnson*—who had since become a director and had done *Brigadoon* for Cheryl Crawford. But a conflict of personalities arose, whereupon Lewis withdrew from the Weill–Lerner project and Elia Kazan was taken on as director.

It was not until the summer of 1948, by which time the show was being called *Love Life*, that the central role of Susan Cooper was filled—by Nanette Fabray, who had just enjoyed success as the star of another American period-musical, *High Button Shoes*. Cast opposite her in the role of Samuel Cooper was Ray Middleton, who had played Washington Irving in *Knickerbocker Holiday* ten years before and who had recently won attention playing Buffalo Bill to Ethel Merman's Annie Oakley in Irving Berlin's *Annie Get Your Gun*. Michael Kidd was engaged to do the choreography and Boris Aronson to design the sets. *Love Life* finally opened on October 7 at the Forty-sixth Street Theatre.

The show's opening scene is the first of the "vaudeville" acts; in it a magician performs with the assistance of Sam and Susan Cooper, levitating the husband and sawing the wife in half. The disarray into which he places them is seen as symbolic of their lives at the present moment and of a marriage that, we are told, was "almost gone" fifty years ago and "beginning to slip" fifty years before that; one hundred fifty years ago, on the other hand, they "had it." The next scene shows us those perfect days in rural Connecticut in 1791. The Coopers and their friends are living the Yankee eighteenth-century idyll, running their farm, doing everything with their own hands, and selling Sam's homemade furniture to supplement their income; the scene is climaxed with Sam's singing of the Broadway-lyrical "Here I'll Stay." But the imminent downfall of this way of life is proclaimed in the vaudeville act that follows, in which eight men do "an old-time soft shoe" number called "Progress." The lyrics tell of how there once was a time when love was all that mattered, but how economic progress has since intervened to make human beings into the nervous, loveless creatures they now are. The next scene shows this beginning to happen: it is 1821, and we see the Cooper farm again, but now the meadows and hills in the background are obscured by rising factories. Sam is going to close his shop and start a factory, to the sadness of his wife and children, who will no longer have him nearby all day and home for lunch. But this scene is climaxed by one last outburst of bucolic enthusiasm, when the Coopers and their friends sing and dance "Green-Up Time," the show's most rousing number.

The ensuing vaudeville song, "Economics," a follow-up in spirit to "Progress," is sung in ragtime by a quartet of Black men and women. One of the women was then to have stepped forward and sung "Susan's Dream," a blues song about a woman's vision of a better life that turns out to be pretty much the same as the life she was leading. This was the song Mary Martin couldn't have—but neither could anyone else, as it turned out, for "Susan's Dream" unfortunately was cut from the show. In the next scene, set in 1857, Sam is a railroad magnate too busy to take time out for making the new child Susan would like to have. Then, after three children do a waltz-clog to a song about "Mother," the Coopers are seen at home in the 1890s: this time, it is Susan who is becoming too busy for domestic idylls, for she is involved in the women's suffrage movement. The next vaudeville act consists of a ventriloquist and his dummy doing a reprise of "Economics," after which the Coopers are seen on a shipboard cruise in the 1920s, Susan flirting with another man, Sam with another woman: this scene is done in the style of a typical musical comedy of the period. With this, the first act ends.

The second act opens as a group performs a madrigal—a form of pastiche George Gershwin had tried at least twice—with joking lyrics about drunkenness and neurosis. Then we see the Coopers in a present-day New York apartment, undergoing all the agonies of modern neurosis, Oedipal jealousy, careerism, tension, and marital infidelity; the scene ends with Susan singing forlornly, "Is It Him or Is It Me?" After a brief interlude showing Sam playing cards with the boys in a locker room of a Turkish bath, the Coopers' divorce is depicted in terms of a full-scale ballet sequence. This is followed by the largest production number of all, a minstrel show in which various characters come on and sing their different sardonic, selfish, or confused versions of what love is all about. One of the songs, "Madame Zuzu," appeals to astrology for the answers—this, along with the general character of the sequence, suggests a certain inspiration derived from the abandoned "Minstrel Dream" of *Lady in the Dark*, with its "Zodiac Song." The show ends in one last glimpse of Susan and Sam as tightrope performers, falteringly but hopefully making their way toward one another in spite of everything.

Alan Jay Lerner has written of the premiere of *Love Life* that "the audience stood up and cheered at the end and the press was very mixed indeed." Brooks Atkinson, though he liked Kurt Weill's music as always, thought that the play was "joyless—a general gripe masquerading as entertainment." There were many clever ideas in the script, but they certainly were marred throughout by a peculiar kind of special pleading, as well as by an unwarranted intellectual pretentiousness. At that time and in years to come, Lerner had an occasional propensity for playing fantastic historical games, with often questionable results. Cheryl Crawford, who concedes that the *Love Life* script had major shortcomings, notes also how it affected Weill's music. "Because Kurt's score served the style of the writing," she observes, "it didn't have the warmth of his best ballads."

Indeed, the show's principal ballad, "Here I'll Stay," was colorless, as were many of the other songs. "Progress" and "Economics" were delightful pieces of pastiche, but too much so—too derivative to stand out as achievements on their own. Only two songs, "Green-Up Time" and "Susan's Dream," were both original and fully up to Weill's standards— and the latter was, as we have seen, cut from the show before opening night. Kurt's hope of doing his first piece of old-fashioned Americana for Broadway at last had resulted in one of the least artistically successful scores he had ever written. And commercially the play's "respectable" run, as Cheryl Crawford puts it, of 252 performances, did not justify this. If there was a possibility that time was running out on him, then how could he go on spending it this way?

Musical Tragedy:
Lost in the Stars

 The movie version of *One Touch of Venus*, made by Universal Pictures after Mary Pickford Productions had finally given up on it, was released three weeks after the opening of *Love Life*, and it was another disappointment for Weill. The Hollywood mill had finally transformed it into a largely non-musical comedy in which his melodies could, for the most part, only be heard in the background. Weill's disgust at this outcome caused a strain not only in his professional relations with Leah Salisbury, but in his personal relations with Ogden Nash and S. J. Perelman as well. Nevertheless, the money and the creative prospects offered by Hollywood continued to attract him, and he was there again shortly after the film's release, staying at the Hotel Bel-Air in Los Angeles. One thing he was looking for on this trip was a film contract for *Love Life*, which was never to materialize; he also was still discussing the possibilities of a tie-in between some film producer and the Playwrights Company. But at the end of November he was back east, and was attending the Baltimore tryouts of Maxwell Anderson's latest play, *Anne of the Thousand Days*, which starred Rex Harrison as Henry VIII and Joyce Redman as Anne Boleyn.

By this time the Andersons and the Weills had become intimate friends in addition to already having been neighbors, most of whose leisure time at home—as well as some of their work time—was spent with one another. The network of friends on and around South Mountain Road in New City was something like an extended family, at the center of which stood not only the Weills and the Andersons but also the painter Henry Varnum Poor and his wife, the novelist Bessie Breuer, the cartoonist and creator of *Terry and the Pirates* Milton Caniff and his wife, Bunny, Burgess Meredith, Bill Mauldin, Marion Hargrove, and other well-known people of talent. Life among them consisted of an easygoing but constant round of dropping in, of lunches, dinners, card games, or gatherings before that new toy, the television set—in July 1948 Kurt and Lenya watched the Republican convention at the Caniffs', and it was then they decided to buy a set for themselves. When the Weills spent time with other friends outside this circle, they usually did so by having them as weekend guests at Brook House.

In the case of Kurt and Maxwell Anderson, this intimacy extended to their work: even when they were not discussing possibilities to try together, they were discussing each other's separate projects and offering mutual advice. The Weills had become particularly involved in the gestation of *Anne of the Thousand Days*; when Anderson had still been searching for actors to play it, Lenya at one point urged that the role of Anne Boleyn be given to Jean Simmons, whom she had just seen as Ophelia in Laurence Olivier's film of *Hamlet*. Indeed, when the play opened in New York on December 8, Kurt was at the theater as the personal representative of the author, who found himself emotionally unable to attend. Joshua Logan tells a significant story in this connection. Logan had seen the Philadelphia tryouts of the play, and when asked for critical comments he had said there were too many scenes switching back to Anne in her cell in the Tower of London, from which the main action had begun as a flashback. Anderson had taken some literary pride in the soliloquies of which these scenes were made up and was not pleased at Logan's suggestion that they be cut; the experience of sacrificing the intellectual aspirations of one of his scripts to Logan's tough-minded stagecraft was a grimly familiar one to him. Nevertheless, at the New York opening Logan discovered to his surprise that the cuts he recommended had been made and was gratified to see that the play, which became a hit, was much improved as a result. After the final curtain and a brief strained conversation with Anderson by telephone, Logan went backstage to congratulate Weill, the author's "proxy" for the evening. He was startled by the dark look he received.

"Max and I," said Weill in an emotional voice, "don't believe in the boom-boom-boom school of theatre the way you do, Josh."

"What's the boom-boom-boom school, Kurt?" inquired Logan.

"We believe an audience doesn't have to sit forward in their seats the whole evening. Once in a while they like to sit back and relax."

Logan felt a rage welling up inside and held it back. "If you've got them leaning forward," he said hoarsely, "don't ever let them sit back and relax. Keep them leaning toward you, hold them there, tie them there. I never heard of the boom-boom-boom school of theatre before you said it, but I believe in it now. If it means never bore an audience, then I say boom-boom-boom forever! And as for those soliloquies—" But he was pulled away before things could get worse.

There is a special irony in this story, because the man Weill was confronting with this demonstration of loyalty was living testimony to the fact that he and Anderson had thus far turned out only a single theater work together, and that had been ten years before. Why had so much time gone by? Weill had in fact been unflagging in the effort to get Anderson to do another play with him. In 1945 they had discussed doing the operatic version of *Street Scene* together, as we have seen; and in 1947 they had discussed a story idea about a man who travels on a spaceship to a planet that, because of a time fault occurring in the journey, turns out to be Earth a few thousand years in the future—a gimmick later used in the film *Planet of the Apes*. But Weill and Anderson wisely perceived that this idea, apparently suggested to them by the Playwrights Company, was not suited to their particular talents. In general, the experience of *Knickerbocker Holiday* had done little to overcome Anderson's doubts about being a librettist for musicals, and so far only *Ulysses Africanus* had really engaged him. This perennial diffidence might well have tried the patience of someone less devoted to Anderson than Weill was; but Kurt went on needing the emotional anchoring with which the playwright's strong personality provided him.

It was earlier that year that Anderson had finally come up with the idea for a musical collaboration he really wanted to do. The germ of it had been planted aboard the S.S. *Mauretania*, on which he and his wife were returning from a trip to Greece in December 1947. Also on board were Dr. Everett Clinchy, president of the National Conference of Christians and Jews, with his wife, and Oscar and Dorothy Hammerstein. The three couples formed a group for the voyage, and out of their conversations came the idea of trying to organize meetings of playwrights, directors, and producers to discuss ways in which the American theater might deal with some of the problems facing mankind in the postwar era. In the course of these conversations, Dorothy Hammerstein mentioned a book to be published by Scribners in February, of which she had read an advance copy: Alan Paton's *Cry, the Beloved Country*. Paton's novel about Blacks in South Africa, as described by Dorothy Hammerstein, struck Anderson as possible material for a play that might require a musical component, and upon his return to New City he discussed it with Weill even before either of them had read it.

In the ensuing weeks Hammerstein called the meetings envisioned on shipboard, which were attended not only by himself and Anderson, but also by Kurt Weill, Robert E. Sherwood, Elmer Rice, Howard Lindsay, Russel Crouse, and Elia Kazan, among others. Arnold Toynbee was guest speaker at one of them, and he said: "There is nothing that can save us except brotherhood. Brotherhood, amity, tolerance, understanding—understanding that crosses all the boundaries—this is the great need." Anderson took these words to heart, and they evidently were still reverberating within him at the beginning of March when he finally sat down and read the copy of *Cry, the Beloved Country* that Dorothy Hammerstein had lent him. This proved to be the kind of story about brotherhood he had been looking for, and, after showing the book to Weill, he wrote a letter to its author asking for permission to do a dramatization of it.

Paton's novel is written in a highly charged lyrical style that no doubt struck Anderson right away with its quasi-musical properties; but it was also for structural reasons that he conceived of a dramatization requiring music. As he wrote to Paton, he thought that "to keep the plot and the dialogue in the form you gave them would only be possible if a chorus—a sort of Greek chorus—were used to tie together the great number of scenes, and to comment on the action as you comment in the philosophic and descriptive passages." The idea of writing dramatic music for a Greek-style chorus appealed to one of Weill's oldest dreams as a composer for the theater, and he entered into this project with great enthusiasm. But as he and Anderson conceived the play at first, there was to be no music other than that which would be sung by the chorus. The main individual roles would only be spoken. Indeed, if Anderson and Weill had any dramaturgical model out of the Broadway repertory in mind at this time, it was not so much that of any musical work as that of Marc Connelly's *The Green Pastures*, in which the Hall Johnson Choir had sung spirituals as an integral part of the action but had not commented upon it in the manner of a Greek chorus. Connelly's play was so much in the minds of Anderson and Weill that for a time they even sought the man who had played Adam in it, Daniel L. Haynes—who was now an African Methodist minister in Kingston, New York—to take on the lead role of Stephen Kumalo in their dramatization of *Cry, the Beloved Country.*

In the summer and fall of 1948 Weill and Anderson both had other projects to occupy them; but *Love Life* opened in October and *Anne of the Thousand Days* in December, and right after that they went to work on the new play. By the end of February, they had finished a draft of both the text and the score; a few individual songs had now made their way into the script alongside the choruses. A fall production was planned by the Playwrights Company.

During March and early April the search took place for a suitable director. Several were tried, but Weill's heart became set on Rouben Mamoulian, who had done *Porgy and Bess* and *Oklahoma!* and whom he had wanted for *Street Scene.* Mamoulian had been tied up with another project at that time, and he claimed to be now, too, when Anderson and Weill got in touch with him one day in the middle of April; but he agreed to have lunch with them all the same. Mamoulian did not yet know what their play was about; but as it happened, he and his wife had just been on a trip to Haiti, where they had found their interest in racial questions aroused. This, then, was what he began the conversation with as he sat down to lunch with Weill and Anderson in the Oak Room of the Plaza Hotel. As he spoke, he noticed them breaking frequently into smiles and significant looks at one another, and when he finally asked them why, they explained that what he was talking about was the subject of their play. Then they described it to him, and he agreed to look at their rough draft. He was given a copy on April 21, and, as Anderson was later to write, "on April 23 he said to us, as I remember it: 'Well, I don't know what will come of this, but it's what I want to do. I can't turn it down.'" Mamoulian asked the Theatre Guild if it would delay his other project, Morton Gould's musical, *Arms and the Girl.*

The next thing the three men did was to rent a New York hotel room with a piano in it, where Weill sat down and played the entire score as it then was constituted. As we have seen, the musical component of the play had already grown larger than it was in the original conception; but Mamoulian, after listening to it, decided that it was still not large enough. Explaining how he thought the music and the action could be more fully integrated, he even suggested specific places at which songs could be inserted. As he spoke, Weill smiled and kept nodding eagerly, but he noticed that Anderson sat "like a stone statue." When he had finished, Anderson got up and walked solemnly over to him: "He was six-foot-three," Mamoulian has recalled, "and I thought he was going to hit me." But instead Anderson said to him: "We must have you. Everything you've suggested we'll try to do." The next day he called up the Theatre Guild and got an agreement to a delay in Mamoulian's commitment there.

If the play was now turning into a bit more of a successor to *Porgy and Bess* than had originally been intended, the fact was that Weill and Anderson had already conceived of a full-fledged musical about Blacks some years before. Anderson was later to write, as if the whole thing had been inevitable from the outset, that the subject of *Cry, the Beloved Country* "fitted exactly into the scheme for a musical tragedy* which Kurt Weill and I had hoped for some years to be able to write." And as Weill later told an interviewer, he and Anderson once had "tried to do a musical play about racial problems. We had to lay it aside finally, but the desire to do such a play stayed with us." In other words, they had come back once again to *Ulysses Africanus*. In its last reincarnation in 1945, this play had once again been thought of as a vehicle for Paul Robeson, but he had become unavailable for a second time as well. After that, it could not have taken very long for Robeson's increasingly radical political stance of those years to have alienated Maxwell Anderson, a fervent anti-Communist. It may be, then, that Robeson had become so integrally a part of Anderson's conception of *Ulysses Africanus* that the play had to be abandoned by him along with the star. But now the essential elements of that play had found a new identity; and in fact, by the time the job was done, at least three of its songs were to have made their way into the new "musical tragedy"— one of which, "Lost in the Stars," was to provide the work with its title.

There were some respects in which *Cry, the Beloved Country* was indeed akin to the play Anderson had evolved out of the novella by Harry Stillwell Edwards: it had a similar theme of the growth of responsibility at the center, and it was similarly a white liberal's sympathetic treatment of the plight of the Black man—both containing, in fact, an unconscious hint of condescension. Robeson had noticed this about the *Ulysses Africanus* material, and others have noticed it about Paton's book, albeit that it is a passionately well-meaning work by a man of truly noble character. Anderson, in his dramatization of it, was to carry the condescension in *Cry, the Beloved Country* a few steps further, and in the process bring out an even greater drawback inherent in the choice he had made: for why, after

---

*   The term *musical tragedy*, which Anderson and Weill used for *Lost in the Stars* and which they evidently were also willing to apply loosely to *Ulysses Africanus*, despite its benign nature and happy ending, was meant primarily as a contrast to the prevailing term *musical comedy*.

all, did he have to turn to South Africa for material on a problem that was just as much an American one? Perhaps the answer to that question lies in a remark Weill was to make the following year, to the effect that this story had "a rare quality of lack of violent hate, which makes it not particularly suitable for a drama but ideal for a musical play." No doubt Weill was thinking of, among other things, Richard Wright's *Native Son*, which his old collaborator Paul Green had turned, with Wright's help, into a very fine play back in 1941. *Native Son* could conceivably work as an opera, but probably not as a musical play, for the reason Weill gives; in any case, however, it was not material for a play by Maxwell Anderson, who was far less able than Paul Green was to gaze upon grim truths. *Cry, the Beloved Country* had for Anderson the double advantage of being gentler than works like *Native Son* and further away from home.

The major problem now was that of finding a good singing actor to fill the lead role of the Black preacher, Stephen Kumalo. In this matter the dream of Paul Robeson could only have died hard. In 1939 Anderson had protested to Robeson that "although there may be other people who could act the part, I don't know of anybody who could both act and sing it and the script might be wasted completely if you were not available." Ten years later Anderson described his search for an actor to play Kumalo in these words: "There are many good Negro actors. There are many good Negro singers. But when we looked for a great Negro actor who was also a great singer and who could play the part of a minister over fifty—it seemed there wasn't one in that category." There didn't seem to be one besides Paul Robeson, at any rate. "Rouben went to California in June to continue the search," Anderson's account goes on. "Kurt and I remained in New York, holding daily auditions. We saw several hundred applicants and found possibilities for other parts, but not for Stephen."

Interestingly enough, another of the major roles—that of James Jarvis, the white planter who ultimately befriends Kumalo—was given to the English actor Leslie Banks, who had befriended Paul Robeson on screen more than a decade earlier in the title role of the English film *Sanders of the River*. Anderson continues: "Rouben returned from California, luring George Jenkins with him to design our sets, but reporting that there was no Stephen in Hollywood. 'As a matter of fact,' he added, 'I'm more and more inclined to the belief that Stephen Kumalo is in Australia under contract to the Taft Brothers.' I asked him who the Taft Brothers were. 'They manage concert artists down under,' Rouben answered. 'Todd Duncan is singing for them out there now. He did Porgy for me, and he could do Stephen. There's nobody else.' " And so another link with *Porgy and Bess* was established, by the engaging of the man who had played the lead role then to play the lead role now. To add to those links, Warren Coleman, who had played Crown in the original *Porgy and Bess*, was cast in the role of Stephen Kumalo's brother, John.

But in spite of this expansion of the musical content, the show was still being budgeted like a play. There were to be no big production numbers, the size of the orchestra was kept down to only twelve instrumentalists, and the services of a musical director who would not be expensive were sought. Weill could not in any case rely on obtaining his old friend Maurice Abravanel, who had been invited the previous year to go to Salt Lake City and organize a Utah Symphony Orchestra; *Love Life* had been the first Weill show since *Johnny Johnson* and *The Eternal Road* to be conducted by someone other than Abravanel. At first Weill had wanted the man who had conducted *Johnny Johnson*, Lehman Engel, to do *Lost in the Stars*; but by this time Engel was very much in demand, and the Playwrights considered him too expensive. Finally, Maurice Levine, musical director of the YMHA on Lexington Avenue at 92nd Street, who had done a concert production of *Street Scene* that Weill had liked, was hired for the job.

During the rehearsals Mamoulian continued to involve himself in the changing content of the play, particularly its score. He proposed not only additions but also cuts from time to time. Indeed, he remembers having proposed a cut in the music on the very first day of rehearsals, which Weill made without protest. Then, on the second day, he proposed another one, and again the composer silently complied. On the third day, as he recalls, he took his seat in the empty theater and suddenly saw Weill coming down the aisle toward him, gleefully rubbing his hands. "Well, Rouben," he said, "what do we cut today?" The joke was typical of him, just as was the fact that it concealed strong feelings; for Kurt was bringing to bear on this project hopes and creative energies greater than any he had called upon since *Street Scene* almost three years before—greater indeed than almost any in his entire career.

When *Lost in the Stars* opened at the Music Box Theatre on October 30, 1949, many listeners were surprised at how little African-sounding music there was in the score. This was the result of a deliberate decision Weill had made at an early stage, after having listened to recordings of Zulu music. He had thought it too exotic for his purposes. "It's not harmony and it's not melody," he later told an interviewer, "and it relies on a great many quarter tones. But, you see, I wasn't trying to reproduce the native music of Africa any more than Maxwell Anderson was trying to provide with words a local-color picture of life there. I'm attempting to get to the heart of the public, and my public wouldn't feel anything if I gave them African chimes." He also used very little music having a distinctly American-Negro sound. "Mr. Weill wanted to avoid the tom-tom beat familiar to Americans through many jazz compositions," the interviewer tells us, "as well as to avoid the style of the Negro spirituals of our South. 'Yet there must be tom-toms in the score at times,' he said. 'Also, American spirituals are closer to African music than many people realize.' " The result is a score that hints at all these traditions in turn and some others besides, but that in the end emerges with a sound all its own.

Lost in the Stars really consists of two scores, one superimposed upon the other; the bottom layer is that of the chorus intended, more or less in the Greek tradition, to accompany the original, otherwise nonsinging play, and the upper is that of the song score inspired by and partly derived from *Ulysses Africanus*. Weill once said that of the eighteen distinct musical numbers making up *Lost in the Stars*, some six or eight are songs. These are the upper layer; and it might be added that, whereas the songs are what tend to arouse the most attention and controversy, it is the other numbers, primarily the bottom layer of choral and recitative, that provide the main strength and true character of the work. This is demonstrated, after a brief orchestral introduction, in the very opening number, "The Hills of Ixopo." Sung by the Black chorus leader, a baritone, with the humming accompaniment of the chorus itself, this recitative consists, with only small cuts and variations, of the text of the famous opening chapter of *Cry, the Beloved Country*. The description of the green hills and desolate valleys in which the story begins is sung mainly in a pentatonic scale, so that the effect is primitive, even slightly Oriental; the rituallike repetition of phrases and notes suggests a litany. We are in a world akin to that of *Der Jasager*, though the sadness is far more demonstrative.

In the first scene of the play, as in the second chapter of the book, the Reverend Stephen Kumalo is shown at home with his wife in the village of Ndotsheni, receiving a letter that summons him to Johannesburg. The letter is about his sister, Gertrude, who, as it turns out, has become a prostitute in the big city. But Kumalo's decision to go there is provoked mainly by the desire to find out about his son, Absalom, who also has gone to Johannesburg and has not been heard from in almost a year. Grace Kumalo expresses the belief that their son has come to no good; but Stephen chides her and sings his hopeful song, "Thousands of Miles," asserting that "the pathways of the heart" can conquer any distance, physical or spiritual, that comes between parent and child. Like all Stephen Kumalo's songs, it has a broad, open melodiousness, rather like many traditional songs of the American West: it is closely akin to "Home on the Range" or "We'll Hit the Trail of the Lone Prairie." To emphasize a sweep that covers the vastness of frontiers—South African in the context but also suggestive of American parallels—the instrumental accompaniment is based on a regular beat that is purposefully imitative of a railroad train, one of the basic rhythmic metaphors in all Weill's music. The contrast between the diatonic openness of this song, so optimistic in its reach, and the pentatonic lamentation that has preceded it forms one of the thematic principles of this score and of the drama it conveys. In other words, here as well as elsewhere, the two layers of the score relate to one another successively in a kind of counterpoint.

The two elements come together in the next scene, as Kumalo goes to the station to wait for the train to Johannesburg. The Black members of the chorus come on now as part of the action—for this musical drama has been done in the same fluid style as that of *Down in the Valley* or *The Ballad of Magna Carta* (both having originated, significantly, as works for radio), in which the various scenes and character groupings are constructed in an almost makeshift way, simple and easily movable. The number sung by the leader and the chorus, who are seeing off a fellow Zulu going to work in the mines, tells that white men go to Johannesburg and eventually return, but a Black man never comes back. It echoes the rhythm of train wheels that we have heard in the accompaniment of "Thousands of Miles," but now much more agitated and in the main melody; indeed, in a reprise at the end of the scene, the chorus actually sings a "clink clink clickety" and a "woo woo" in imitation of the arriving train. And in other respects, too, the trainlike elements reminding us of "Thousands of Miles" serve now to emphasize the contrast with that number. The leader and the chorus have really brought us back to the spirit of their opening number; like that one, this is a lamentation filled with ritualistic repetitions—though the pentatonic sounds of the hills and valleys have now been replaced by the diatonic dissonances of the railroad, just as the mournful serenity of the earlier number has given way to a wild, locomotivelike frenzy. The melody sung here, by the way, is one of the few in the score to carry a distinctively South African sound; it is rather like the folk songs that were being sung around this time by Josef Marais and Miranda.

The narrative content of this scene is entirely Maxwell Anderson's invention, not to be found in the novel. Also at the station are James

Jarvis, the wealthy white planter who lives in the green hills above Ndotsheni, his son, Arthur Jarvis, a lawyer and crusader for Black rights on a visit from Johannesburg, and Arthur's young son, Edward. Arthur sees Stephen Kumalo and goes over to greet him, to the chagrin of the elder Jarvis. Since Arthur—as in the novel—is soon to be shot dead by Stephen Kumalo's son, Absalom, this scene serves to underscore the irony of the ensuing situation. Indeed, it does so to the point of crudeness. And at the same time it neatly avoids a question it has raised by ending before Stephen Kumalo and Arthur and Edward Jarvis all get onto the train. For they could not have sat down together without provoking a riot; but we are spared seeing them get into separate cars, for this would have undone the point made so feebly by the scene in the first place.

The next scene, which is entirely without music, shows Stephen Kumalo with his sister's young son, Alex, already in tow—he will take the boy back to Ndotsheni and raise him there—entering the tobacco shop of his brother, John. A reworking and compression of several elements in the novel, this scene depicts John Kumalo as a worldly cynic who sneers at his pious elder brother and as a somewhat half-baked political crusader who exploits his poor Black followers for personal gain. This is a legitimate formulation of the character in the novel—indeed, the fact that this is the only type of Black crusader Paton portrays in detail is one of the novel's shortcomings—but the dramaturgical compression and the shedding of the rich background of sociological detail to be found in the original give Anderson's portrayal of John Kumalo a distorted shape. This man has charm, but he is essentially a caricature of wickedness, whose legitimate questions about his brother's total acceptance of the white man's criteria in an unjust society thereby lose force. To a later generation, Stephen Kumalo, fine a man as he is, seems just a bit too accepting; but Maxwell Anderson did not see it this way, and to underscore his own view, he succeeded in making Stephen's dissenting brother even more worthless a scoundrel than he is in the original novel.

John gives Stephen an address in Shantytown at which he might be able to find Absalom, and we follow the *umfundisi*,—Zulu for *parson*—as he makes his way through squalid streets and inquires of various people regarding his son's whereabouts. In his wanderings he is now and then accompanied by the chorus, this time outside the action; here their melodies are suggestive both of lamentation and of the rhythm of the railroad, not precisely echoing the earlier equivalents but musically derived from them. When Kumalo returns with young Alex to the wretched quarters they have found for themselves, he begins to describe the home back in Ndotsheni to which they soon will go and sings, "There's a Little Gray House," one of the songs taken from *Ulysses Africanus*. In melody and mood this song is a close relative of "Thousands of Miles," another expression of Kumalo's optimism and redolent of an open landscape that sounds Western American; more idyllic, however, than its predecessor in the score, it is not accompanied by an agitated railroad beat but by an almost jazzlike lilt. It also is framed and occasionally punctuated by a choral accompaniment.

In the next scene, another that is not to be found in the novel, we meet Absalom Kumalo before his father does. It takes place in a dive in Shantytown, where Linda, a sexy Black singer, is entertaining the company with a rendition of "Who'll Buy My Juicy Rutabagas?"—which is not about selling vegetables at all, even though it is melodically akin to the songs of the street hawkers in *Porgy and Bess*: the sleazy instrumental accompaniment is what joins Linda's gestures in conveying the double entendre. Absalom is shown joining in with Matthew Kumalo—John's son—and another young man as they plot an armed burglary. Irina, the girl who is bearing Absalom's child, comes in and pleads with him not to steal, but to no avail. Irina is then seen alone in her hut in Shantytown, where Stephen Kumalo arrives looking for Absalom. Stephen at first angrily confronts her with the fact of her easy virtue but soon evinces compassion for her, and when he leaves they agree to help one another. Alone again, Irina sings a soliloquy about Absalom, "Trouble Man," which had originally been composed as "Lover Man" for the score of *Ulysses Africanus*. This lament is a blues in spirit if not in actual musical content. Its relentless, throbbing beat, dissolving now and then in a kind of lyrical exhaustion, seems vaguely German; indeed, it is closely akin to "Surabaya Johnny," though starker and less attractive.

Scene eight, which also is a wholly new construct out of various elements in the novel, begins the climactic sequence of the play's first act. Enacted entirely to a musical accompaniment—one that is highly agitated and filled with intimations of terror from the outset—this scene shows Absalom and his two companions attempting to rob the home of Arthur Jarvis, who suddenly appears and whom Absalom shoots down in fright. The chorus then comes on as groups of white and Black residents of Johannesburg gathering, much the way the crowd does after the murder in *Street Scene*, to sing in horrified tones, "Murder in Parkwold!" After an intervening scene showing James Jarvis at his dead son's house ruminating on the irony of the fact "that an advocate of Negro equality should have been killed by a Negro," the "Murder in Parkwold!" chorus is reprised to form a bridge into the most powerful passage in the score, "It Is Fear!"—sung strophically by the white and Black choruses as if hurling challenges at one another. All the agitated rhythms and dissonances heretofore sounded now mount to a frenzied pitch: terror, anger, human intolerance, and confusion are all in this music, which is a direct descendant of the choral passages—depicting War, Inflation, Famine, and Sickness—that dominate the last act of *Die Bürgschaft*. Weill was almost always at his best in choral music; and a deep-lying, enigmatic bitterness that always lay concealed in his nature and burst forth only now and then has manifested itself in these choral passages toward the end of Act One of *Lost in the Stars* to produce some of the most frighteningly powerful music he ever wrote.

This serves to emphasize the unassailable solidity of Stephen Kumalo's spirit, which is manifested in his next song, "Lost in the Stars," sung after he has found his son, Absalom, at last—in a prison cell, accused of a murder that he did indeed commit. The show's title song—originally written, as we have seen, for *Ulysses Africanus* and Paul Robeson—fits into the succession of open-spirited melodies that have characterized Stephen throughout, with an appropriate new note of doubtfulness and near-despair injected into it; but the most skillful musical craftsmanship has nevertheless not completely concealed the signs of its origins in another epoch and frame of reference. It is a thoroughly beautiful song, but clearly an offspring of the Black showstopper tradition on Broadway that had reached its height in Vincent Youmans's "Without a Song" and Jerome Kern's "Ol' Man River." Paul Robeson sang only some of these, but all of them sound as though they had been written with his voice resounding in the composer's inner ear. "Lost in the Stars" happens to be one of the very best of them, for it has a distinct Weill intonation, an almost foreign undercurrent that makes it unique—and that also, incidentally, makes it seem quite appropriate for the never-never land, not quite African, not quite American, that Anderson and Weill have created in this play. But, belonging as it does to the musical vocabulary of an earlier Weill—we have noticed its passing affinity with "It Never Was You"—it has a texture that does not mesh perfectly with that of the rest of the score.

Act Two begins with the leader and chorus singing "The Wild Justice," a reflection on the continuity between primitive and modern forms of retribution that recaptures the dark mood of some of the earlier choruses. We then see Stephen and John Kumalo in the latter's shop again, discussing the forthcoming trial of their sons. It turns out that, whereas

Matthew Kumalo and the third accomplice are going to lie in court, Absalom, who alone fired the shot that killed Arthur Jarvis, plans to confess his guilt. Stephen reflects upon this situation in a soliloquy, "O Tixo, Tixo, Help Me!" (*Tixo* is a native African word for "Great Spirit" or "God"), which shows signs of having been influenced by Boris Godunov's soliloquies in the Mussorgsky opera; he concludes that the loss of Absalom's life would be better than the loss of his soul. Stephen still hopes that there will be mercy for his son, however; but this hope dims when he goes to see James Jarvis, still sojourning at his dead son's home, and Jarvis sternly warns him that justice must be done. In the next scene Stephen visits Irina, who agrees to marry Absalom no matter what the verdict will be; she sings "Stay Well," a strangely beautiful love soliloquy that seems, both musically and verbally, to be a kind of free but purposeful counterpoise to "Trouble Man."

At the trial Matthew and the other accomplice lie and they go free, and Absalom tells the truth and is sentenced to death. This is a compressed version of what happens in Paton's novel, and this sequence is indeed the one that raises the most serious questions about *Cry, the Beloved Country*. One need only compare the behavior from the murder onward of Absalom Kumalo with that of his counterpart Bigger Thomas, in Richard Wright's *Native Son*, to see a significant difference in attitudes taken on similar questions by these two novels, one written by a white, the other by a Black. Richard Wright's novel does not defend murder by any means, but it recognizes the ways in which Bigger Thomas's spirit achieves a peculiar transcendence, a true breaking of the chains imposed upon it, by dint of his having murdered a white girl. He goes to his death defiantly, unlike Absalom Kumalo, who, like his father, sees in the end only that he has broken the law and must pay for it. Whereas Bigger Thomas is a seething reality whose act of murder we experience and understand in all its horror, Absalom Kumalo is so much a pawn in a sociological construct that we end by asking, even in defiance of the book's obvious intentions: Why did the author, if he meant so well, write a novel depicting a Black murderer instead of a white one? Asking such a question, moreover, one is sneakingly inclined for a moment to appreciate the machinations of John Kumalo and his son and feel less than endeared to Stephen and Absalom; but there is, of course, no hint of such an attitude in Anderson's play.

Stephen's final visit to Absalom in his cell, in which he performs the marriage of his son and Irina, is framed by the chorus's singing of one of the finest numbers in the score, "Cry, the Beloved Country." This number is built mainly on a pentatonic scale like the opening chorus of the play and is closely related to it in both musical and verbal content. In the next scene Stephen has brought his young nephew, Alex, back to Ndotsheni. Alex sings a song about a "Big Black Mole"—a metaphor for a Black miner—which is a close imitation of various Anglo-American folk songs on the subject of mining, such as "Drill Ye Tarriers, Drill" and "Dark as a Dungeon." The song is both extraneous to the drama and below the general quality of the score, and its inclusion can only be explained by the need to fill out the upper layer of the score by letting one more of the principals, besides Stephen and Irina, have a song. It seems also to have been meant as a showpiece for the talents of young Herbert Coleman, who played the role. The scene goes on, significantly, to show Arthur Jarvis's young son, Edward, now living on his grandfather's farm, playing with Alex. Jarvis enters and shows his disapproval; but then he overhears Stephen Kumalo inside the church telling his congregants that, because of everything that has happened, he is resigning from his pulpit at Ndotsheni. The parishioners protest and join with the chorus in singing "A Bird of Passage," a quasi-religious hymn about the fleetingness of life that has distinct musical affinities with "O Little Town of Bethlehem." This appealing andante religioso was written some three years before the actual composition of *Lost in the Stars*, and may or may not have been originally intended for *Ulysses Africanus*; it seems to stand apart from either score, in a category by itself. In any case, it emerged as the latest in the significant chain of quasi-religious chorales that Weill had composed throughout his life—and the last, as it would turn out.

Jarvis has been greatly moved by this, and on the night Absalom is to be executed—as the chorus sings, "Four o'clock, it will soon be four"—he comes to Kumalo's house to offer consolation and friendship. This scene does not, of course, exist in the novel, since Alan Paton knew perfectly well that a white South African of Jarvis's generation, character, and status would never, under any circumstances, have visited a Black man's home. In the novel Kumalo goes off to meditate in the mountains on the night of his son's execution and happens to encounter Jarvis on the way; Jarvis is on horseback, and, though he manifests a certain growth of understanding and respect for Kumalo as a result of their intertwining tragic experiences, he makes a point of not getting off his horse during their brief conversation. Maxwell Anderson, on the other hand, has chosen to gratify the sensibilities of his audience by ending with a handshake and a pledge of friendship between these two men who have been brought together across racial barriers by their common bereavement as fathers. Indeed, tragedy has brought them to a point where color has no effect whatsoever on their respective abilities to make platitudes, as Jarvis urges Kumalo to stay in Ndotsheni and they ruminate together on good and evil. Then the clock strikes four and, as Stephen sits sadly and Jarvis puts an arm around his shoulders, the chorus sings a reprise of the most hopeful lines from "Thousands of Miles," ending the play.

Paton's novel ends with Kumalo alone in the mountains, realizing as dawn comes that his son is now dead. The last lines are:

> . . . For it is the dawn that has come, as it has come for a thousand centuries, never failing. But when that dawn will come, of our emancipation, from the fear of bondage and the bondage of fear, why, that is a secret.

But these words might have struck too close to home in America in 1949, and there is no hint of them in Anderson's play. *Lost in the Stars* was designed to make a liberal American theatergoer pensive but not too troubled, and satisfied in the end. The conclusion, from the perspective of another era, is curiously patronizing to Kumalo; for it suggests, however unintentionally, that everything suffered by him has now been made all right because he has gained a white friend. The 1949 white liberalism creaks; but the script nevertheless serves passably enough to uphold for all time a Kurt Weill score that will never lose its freshness and beauty.

A Bird of Passage

Lost in the Stars was received enthusiastically, and Olin Downes, for one, was struck by the virtually operatic power it attained in places through the use of mere song, a form he had once thought too humble for such possibilities. Weill immediately wrote him a letter saying that "you have hit here on one of the basic problems of our musical theatre. It must be somewhat surprising indeed to find a serious subject treated in a form which (in this country at least) has been used so far only for a lighter form of entertainment. But that was exactly the nature of my experiment—to do a 'musical tragedy' for the American theatre so that the typical American audience (not a specialized audience) can accept it; and the real success of the piece to me is the fact that the audience did accept it without hesitation, that they accepted a lot of very serious, tragic, quite un-Broadwayish music of operatic dimensions, together with some songs written in a more familiar style."

This, however, was for him just a prelude to the realization of larger aspirations. "Personally," he went on, "I don't feel that this represents a compromise because it seems to me that the American popular song, growing out of the American folk-music, is the basis of an American musical theatre (just as the Italian song was the basis of Italian opera), and that in this early stage of the development, and considering the audiences we are writing for, it is quite legitimate to use the form of the popular song and gradually fill it with new musical content. But I do agree with you

389

that this infiltration of song in the musical theatre will gradually become more refined and more removed from its origins."

There was much to do, in other words, and Weill wasted no time about getting to it. He and Arnold Sundgaard had already begun working on a full-length opera, "somewhat similar to *Down in the Valley*," according to Sundgaard, "and yet a departure from the form we had used in that one. Although [Weill] liked the form of *Down in the Valley*, he didn't want to repeat what had been done there." But Weill was eager to pursue the path that this folk opera had opened up, because since its premiere at the University of Indiana in July 1948, it had been enjoying great success: in the summer of 1949 it opened for a run at the Lemonade Opera in New York, and now, in its published form, it was a favorite of school singing groups throughout the country. This did not, however, turn the main focus of his aspirations away from Broadway, and shortly after the *Lost in the Stars* opening he was back in touch with Herman Wouk, now at work on *The Caine Mutiny*, to discuss their proposed musical play based on *Aurora Dawn*.

But one project arose in the immediate wake of *Lost in the Stars* to take precedence over all others. For Maxwell Anderson, pleased at the way everything had turned out this time, was ready to start immediately on another collaboration with Weill. They had already discussed over the past year various pieces of Americana that they might like to try. Walter Huston, for example, had interested them in the possibility of their doing a musical *Moby Dick* with himself in the role of Ahab; furthermore, his son, John Huston, had said that, if they wrote it, he would make a movie of it. They also had discussed doing a musical play about Major André, whose career as a spy during the American Revolution had been enacted not far from their homes in New City. But the project on which they went to work right after the *Lost in the Stars* opening was a musical play based on *Huckleberry Finn*. Rouben Mamoulian became interested enough in this idea that he was willing to turn down an invitation from the Metropolitan Opera to direct *Don Carlo* in the fall, in order to do the Anderson–Weill *Huckleberry Finn* instead.

For Weill, it was to be the great American folk epic of his dreams. He wrote a song about catfish and a raucous one about applejack that sounded as if it could have originated as something played on a harmonica around a nineteenth-century Midwestern campfire. And, best of all, he wrote a Mississippi "River Chanty" that was a miniature opera in itself, a piece of romantic scene-painting more evocative than any he had ever done.

Indeed, *River Chanty* was one of the titles he and Anderson now considered for their play.

But in the early weeks of 1950 the attention of Weill and Anderson was called away from their creative work by a sudden, alarming fact: *Lost in the Stars*, an apparent smash hit at the opening, was having financial problems. In general, this was a time when Broadway producers were becoming acutely aware of the effects the postwar inflation was having upon their field of activities. Costs had risen enormously, and the margin of profits had greatly diminished since the halcyon days of the Depression. The Playwrights Company had gone to great lengths to keep *Lost in the Stars* down to a production cost of $90,000, a large figure by prewar standards but a modest one for a musical in 1949. Indeed, a theater of only modest size for a musical—the Music Box—had been chosen to house the production, and this proved in the earliest returns to be the source of the problem. The weekly gross earnings then were about $26,000, whereas the weekly overhead was over $19,000. Even when things still seemed to be going well, this was considered a dangerously low profit margin; but Victor Samrock, general manager of the Playwrights Company, was hopeful at first that the initial investment would be paid off in about forty weeks from opening night.

By the end of January, however, the house was not filling up every night, and it became doubtful whether the play could run a long enough time to show a profit. Another financial disadvantage came from the fact that, through a technicality, the show could not count on a movie sale. Alan Paton had already sold the film rights for his novel to Alexander Korda in England, and Korda's exclusive claim to the property made *Lost in the Stars* ineligible for the movies. There was a sudden feeling of alarm at the Playwrights Company and among the authors of the play in particular. Weill had made a personal investment of $3,000 in it—and emotionally, a much greater one than that. Anderson, who, having accumulated a large debt to the Internal Revenue Service, was in permanent financial difficulties, had, along with his wife, invested $12,500. The irony was that the play was winning high honors: on February 2 Anderson was given the Brotherhood Award of the National Conference of Christians and Jews for his work on this play. At around the same time Weill was appointed chairman of a committee formed by the Playwrights to look into the general problem of production costs and how to reduce them.

Then, sometime in February, Victor Samrock learned that he could book *Lost in the Stars* for limited engagements at theaters in San Francisco and Los Angeles that summer. It seemed to him and other members of the Playwrights Company that these engagements could cause the show to achieve a profit at last; but taking them on would mean closing it in New York for the summer. Indeed, it could mean—depending on how the financial situation might look by then—that *Lost in the Stars* would not reopen at all after its California run. But if the other members looked upon this possibility with worldly resignation, Weill and Anderson were frantic about it. At first they opposed the California engagement altogether; then they reluctantly agreed to it, but only on condition that the play be guaranteed a New York reopening in the fall. According to John F. Wharton, the two authors sought to place the blame for the show's difficulties on the company's management. They began summoning Samrock and William Fields, the company's press agent, to meetings "where they demanded to know why Vic and Bill were permitting this to happen. I couldn't believe my ears when Vic and Bill described these meetings to me:—two veteran theatre men ordering a press agent and business manager to see that the house sold out! It was *Street Scene* all over again, only worse. Max became more and more irascible and Kurt more and more excitable. Bill said to me, 'I'm scared that Kurt is going to have a heart attack.'"

The tension was indeed getting the best of Weill. He had become extremely irritable, and was occasionally alienating old friends and colleagues. Some tensions had developed between him, Leah Salisbury, Ogden Nash, and S. J. Perelman over a proposed German production of *One Touch of Venus*, and in January he vetoed it entirely. Then at the end of February he came down with an attack of psoriasis: the rash, one of the worst he had ever had, covered his entire back. Most unusual for him, he stayed in bed a few days, although this did not stop him from conferring about *Huckleberry Finn* with Anderson, who was frequently by his bedside with whatever new pages he had written. On March 2, his fiftieth birthday, he was well enough to go downstairs and celebrate with the Andersons and their teen-age daughter, Hesper, who came for dinner. But in the next few days his condition worsened, and he had to miss an important meeting of the Playwrights on March 7. This was when the California invitation was finally accepted—except for Anderson and the absent Weill, the decision was unanimous—and Kurt felt impelled to write a long letter to Victor Samrock, of which carbons were sent to the other members, stating his views. Anderson seems to have been placated at the meeting, but as he wrote in his diary two days later, both Weill and Mamoulian were still "somewhat hysterical" about the California engagement.

In the next few days Kurt felt well enough to go for walks, but his state of mind was aggravated when Sam Zolotow, in his theater column in *The New York Times*, printed a rumor that *Lost in the Stars* was going to close after its California run. He and Anderson immediately called William Fields and persuaded him to run an ad to the effect that the show would reopen. He did so, and Kurt felt better. But on March 15 he had a relapse of the skin disease. This did not prevent him from getting back to work on the *Huckleberry Finn* score, but he was in acute discomfort.

The crisis came on the night of March 16, during which Kurt was kept awake by a sudden chest pain and a feeling of oppression around his heart. In the morning Lenya called a local doctor, who said that it could be a heart attack and gave Kurt something to make him sleep. She then called the Andersons, who found a specialist and summoned him to Brook House. He diagnosed a coronary thrombosis and arranged for day and night nurses to stay with the patient. "I saw him for a moment," Anderson wrote in his diary. "He looked ghastly."

That night Mab Anderson and Bunny Caniff kept vigil with Lenya, and the next day friends waited tensely for news. Kurt held on; but then on Sunday morning, March 19, he took a turn for the worse. The doctors recommended that he be brought to Flower-Fifth Avenue Hospital in New York, and an ambulance was summoned. On the one-hour drive to the hospital the ambulance was followed by Bunny Caniff's car, with her, Lenya, and the Andersons inside. At the hospital Weill was placed in an oxygen tent, and his condition was described as "precarious." After a tense dinner Mab Anderson settled in to spend the night with Lenya at the hospital, while her husband drove home with Bunny Caniff.

Then Weill's condition began to improve. The next day Lenya and Mab Anderson returned to New City for lunch and, after packing some clothes, drove back to New York and took a room at the Dorset Hotel. When they got back to the hospital and to Kurt's bedside, he waved at them from his oxygen tent. He was so much better the following day that when Anderson arrived, he said to his collaborator on *Huckleberry Finn*: "Finish the script. I'll be back to work on schedule." On Saturday the oxygen tent was removed and when Lenya came to see him after lunch he was listening to the Metropolitan Opera broadcast and reading *The New Yorker*. She checked out of the hotel and spent that night at home. On

Tuesday, March 28, she bought a small television set for Kurt in his hospital room, and he began planning new *Huckleberry Finn* songs in his head. There was a momentary alarm on Thursday when his skin rash broke out again, but it got better on Friday, and the doctor told him he could probably begin working again the following week. Meanwhile, the proofs of the piano score of *Lost in the Stars* were back from the printer, and Kurt began reading and correcting them in his bed.

Lehman Engel remembers calling Lenya at the hospital on Monday, April 3, to find out how Kurt was and ask if he might send him some flowers.

"No," she said, "Kurt is recovering nicely and he'd rather see you. Call tomorrow and if things are all right, come pay us a visit."

But this was not to be, after all. At ten minutes to five that afternoon, the Andersons, at home in New York City, were startled by a call from Lenya at the hospital, asking Mab to come at once.

Maxwell Anderson got on the phone. "Shall I come?"

"Yes," Lenya said, "I think so."

They arrived at the hospital at a quarter past six and went up in the elevator with a group of doctors who were in a commotion over something; they sensed it to be Kurt. Lenya was standing in the hallway outside his room.

"I think this is the end," she said.

And then at seven o'clock Kurt Weill died.

A modest funeral was held on Wednesday, April 5. The mourners gathered at Brook House that afternoon: they included friends and colleagues and even some family—Rita Weill, Hans's widow, was there, and so was Kurt's sister, Ruth, with her husband, Leon Sohn, having recently emigrated to the United States. But Kurt's parents, still in Israel, had to mourn from afar the second of their sons to die in their own lifetime. "It seemed a long, long day," Maxwell Anderson wrote in his diary. "At 3 Lenya looked at Kurt for the last time and the casket was closed and we started for the cemetery. Rain." The cortege drove to the nearby Mount Repose Cemetery in Haverstraw, to a plot from which one could see the Hudson. There Anderson read the eulogy he had prepared the night before.

"For a number of years," he said, "it has been my privilege to have a very great man as my friend and neighbor. I have loved him more than any other man I knew. And I think he had more to give to his age than any other man I knew.

"I wish, of course, that he had been lucky enough to have a little more time for his work. I could wish the times in which he lived had been less troubled. But these things were as they were—and Kurt managed to make thousands of beautiful things during the short and troubled time he had. He made so many beautiful things that he will be remembered and loved by many not yet born. . . .

"I remember that Kurt and I once talked of trying to write a funeral service for unbelievers. It was never written, but if he had written it, it might have contained eight lines that are sung by the chorus in *Lost in the Stars:*

> "A bird of passage out of night
> Flies in at a lighted door,
> Flies through and on in its darkened flight,
> And then is seen no more.
> This is the life of men on earth:
> Out of darkness we come at birth
> Into a lamplit room, and then—
> Go forward into dark again."

These lines, the last four of which were to be inscribed with their accompanying music on Kurt's gravestone, seemed just right for the modest creative man of whom Anderson spoke. But, as he finished his talk, some listeners wondered if it was right that the service remain so utterly secular. What second thoughts might the cantor's son have had about it all in his final moment? Then Leon Sohn stepped to the graveside and read the Kaddish, the Jewish prayer for the dead: "*Yisgadal v'yiskadash Sh'mey rabboh* . . ."—"Magnified and sanctified be His great Name . . ." The great questions were not settled, after all; and this, too, had been part of the music of Kurt Weill's life. After the final amen the coffin was lowered.

EPILOGUE
Since 1950:
The Legacy of Kurt Weill

Lost in the Stars closed on July 1, 1950, after 281 performances, with some $45,000 of the original investment still not paid off; during the summer it had its short runs in San Francisco and Los Angeles, but these did not make up the financial loss. It did not reopen in the fall.

As for *Huckleberry Finn*, Weill had written five songs, and Maxwell Anderson, who had done a complete draft of the text, hoped to find a composer who would finish the score and share the credits with Weill. After Rouben Mamoulian went on to other commitments, Joshua Logan expressed interest in directing the play; and he and Anderson got Irving Berlin—whose smash-hit show *Annie Get Your Gun* Logan had directed and who had been one of the investors in *Lost in the Stars*—to agree to do the remaining songs. But then a familiar pattern repeated itself, this time to the point of crisis: Logan made suggestions for revising the script that Anderson found intolerable, and the combination broke down. Logan and Berlin abandoned the project, and Anderson put it aside. He was to try every so often to get it going again; but the only public performance in any shape or form of *Raft on the River*, as it came to be called, was not to take place until 1964, six years after his own death—as a half-hour dramatization, with the Weill songs, on German television! Weill's final effort at a piece of definitive Americana had gone back to the country of his origins after all.

Indeed, the posthumous revival of the works of Kurt Weill had manifested a primarily German character by then. In Germany itself this was simply the spiritual recovery of another native artist whom Hitler had expelled. Almost as soon as the war had ended, *The Threepenny Opera* was back in the repertory of German theaters, and other Weill works followed suit. Even *Die Bürgschaft*, the least attractive of Weill's major compositions, was given a revival performance—drastically cut and with the libretto revised by Caspar Neher himself—at the Berlin Festival in 1957. In East Germany, even after Brecht's death in 1956, his Berliner Ensemble continued to do *The Threepenny Opera* and *The Little Mahagonny* as regular offerings in their repertory. Moreover, Germans got to see productions of *Street Scene* and *Lady in the Dark* in the few years following the death of their composer—but these were widely regarded as proof that, after his arrival on American soil in 1935, Weill had ceased to be an artist one could take seriously.

But the most significant revival of the German Weill took place in the United States. Within a year after the composer's death two important memorial concerts of his works were held in New York, the first in Lewisohn Stadium on July 10, 1950, the second in Town Hall on February 3, 1951. The first of these had largely been planned by Weill himself, and it continued, as he had done, to stress his American works. For Olin Downes, it was further demonstration of a point he had been making for several years. Weill, he wrote in an article occasioned by the stadium concert, had come to America and then had

> eschewed the highly intellectualized style of his early days in Germany, where he had been the very modern-minded and brilliant technician graduated from study with Humperdinck and Busoni. For practical as well as artistic reasons, he sought deliberately to find a medium of expression which should retain seriousness of purpose and at the same time reach the ears of the mass of his fellow beings. Whether this very purpose prevented Weill from attaining the highest position as a composer that he could have reached is a question for the speculative to answer. But one does not think so. One thinks of Weill as born to do exactly what he did, and to work steadily and successfully toward a modern art of the musical theater.

But the second concert, in Town Hall, featured Lotte Lenya singing, in their original language, a larger selection of her late husband's German songs than any New York audience had heard since the coolly received production of *The Threepenny Opera* in 1933. They made such a strong impression that the concert was scheduled twice more that spring.

Suddenly, after so many years during which the Broadway Weill had been a constantly recurring presence, an intriguingly different Weill, a voice from a departed era, was being heard.

Virgil Thomson, ever on the alert to what was happening in Weill's music, signaled the change of mood that the Town Hall concert helped bring about. In the week following Weill's death he had struck a careful balance in his *New York Herald Tribune* column concerning the late composer's German and American careers:

> Whether Weill's American works will carry as far as his German ones I cannot say. They lack the mordant and touching humanity of Brecht's poetry. They also lack a certain acidity in the musical characterization that gave cutting edge to Weill's musical style when he worked in the German language.
>
> Nevertheless, they are important to history. And his last musical play, *Lost in the Stars*, for all that it lacks the melodic appeal of *Mahagonny* and even of *Lady in the Dark*, is a masterpiece of musical application to dramatic narrative; and its score, composed for twelve players, is Weill's finest work of orchestral craft. His so-called "folk opera," *Down in the Valley*, is not without strength either. Easy to perform and dramatically perfect, it speaks an American musical dialect that Americans can accept. Its artfulness is so concealed that the whole comes off as naturally as a song by Stephen Foster, though it lasts a good half hour.

But upon hearing the Town Hall concert in February, Thomson was moved to revert unequivocally to an earlier position of his:

> It has long been the opinion of this reviewer that Kurt Weill's contributions to the German theater were more original than anything he wrote here. His American work was viable but not striking, thoroughly competent but essentially conformist. His German works, on the other hand, made musical history; and the most advanced movement in the European musical theater of today . . . stems directly from them. Consequently, it was sound program making that gave us on Saturday ample selections from *Mahagonny* and *Die Dreigroschenoper*, his masterpieces.
>
> The power of these works comes partly, of course, from the words, which are by a first-class poet, Bert Brecht. Partly also from their subjects, which belong to the literature of social protest. But their

musical setting and structure are also noble, grand, simple and plain. They are unique in their ability to plunge the listener into states of nostalgia and despair. They are intensely real and directly moving in a degree that very little music is. Add to their carefully chosen words and notes the very special charm and powerful artistry of Lotte Lenya, ever their perfect interpreter, and you have an experience few can forget.

And he concluded with these significant remarks:

After Weill came to live in America . . . he ceased to work as a modernist, renounced his intellectual position, along with his lovely satirical and tender European vein. He never worked with Brecht again either and never found again so authentic a poet for his purposes. His desire seems to have been to work correctly and successfully in the American commercial style. He succeeded. But he never wrote another *Mahagonny*. And he discouraged all attempts to produce it here. Now his commercial career is over; and his purer music, as we learned last Saturday night, can shine. It gives, I assure you, a lovely light. Surely his great contributions to the musical theater belong in our constantly available repertory.

These feelings now were spreading—in particular among a younger generation of Americans for whom the Broadway Weill was a bit before their time, but who were suddenly experiencing, in the years following World War II, a wave of nostalgia for the Central European culture that Hitler had destroyed. Indeed, for a moment, the task of bringing about a revival of the German Weill in America seemed to be taken on almost entirely by students and faculties. At the end of October 1949, just before the premiere of *Lost in the Stars*, the Juiliard School of Music had staged a Metropolitan Opera Studio production of *The Tsar Has His Picture Taken*—the "Tsar," however, was changed to a "Shah" to avoid cold war implications—with the young Frank Guarrera in the title role. Even before that, in November 1946 and in February 1948, productions of *The Threepenny Opera* had been done, respectively, at the University of Illinois and at Northwestern. They had scarcely been noticed; but when *The Threepenny Opera* was performed in a concert version at Brandeis University in June 1952, under the baton of Leonard Bernstein and with Lotte Lenya singing her original role, this became part of the revival that had been gaining momentum since the Town Hall concert of February 1951.

Part of the strength of the Brandeis production lay in the translation; for this was when the Marc Blitzstein version first presented itself to the public—indeed, Blitzstein himself served as narrator for this concert presentation. Blitzstein, as we have seen, had been a lover of *The Threepenny Opera* from the moment he saw it back in Berlin in 1928, when he was Arnold Schoenberg's pupil; and at least two of his works, *The Cradle Will Rock* and *No for an Answer*, had been strongly influenced by it. Long eager to see it win an audience in his own country, he had tried his hand a few years before at translating "Pirate Jenny" and other songs from the *Threepenny* score. Kurt Weill had seen the results and liked them; so had Maurice Abravanel, who had made a brief return from Utah to the Broadway theater at the end of 1949 to conduct Blitzstein's Broadway opera, *Regina*, based on Lillian Hellman's *The Little Foxes*. Abravanel and others persuaded Blitzstein to finish his *Threepenny* translation after Weill's death, and by 1952 it was ready to be aired at Brandeis. Less than two years later, on March 10, 1954, it was Blitzstein's version that opened, under Carmen Capalbo's direction and with Lotte Lenya in her old role as Jenny, for a scheduled run of three months, at the Theatre de Lys in New York's Greenwich Village; and the outcome was historic. Ultimately running for nearly seven years after its reopening in 1955, the production not only was the central event in a revival of Brecht and Weill in America, but it helped create styles in the arts for years to follow. The Blitzstein version was also well received in London when it opened there, at the Royal Court Theatre, on February 9, 1956.

A number of elements had converged to create this success. In a way, the time simply was ripe for another try at *The Threepenny Opera* in New York; in 1949, when Rex Harrison was starring as Henry VIII in *Anne of the Thousand Days*, a new English version of it with him in the role of Mackie was contemplated by Weill. This became all the more the case in the atmosphere of growing interest in the culture of pre-Hitler Germany that has already been mentioned. In particular, Brecht had become a principal focus for this revival of 1954, owing partly to the international fame he was achieving with the Berliner Ensemble, partly to a growing interest in European "experimental" theater in general, and partly to Brecht's aura as an artist of political radicalism—the arts being virtually the only outlet for the radical aspirations of young Americans at that time. Furthermore, there was an "Off-Broadway" renaissance taking place, a reaction on the part of a lively and idealistic theater culture downtown against a Broadway establishment going sour, and *The Threepenny Opera* became a major expression of the phenomenon—indeed, the success of

The Threepenny Opera down on Christopher Street was a kind of historic revenge for Broadway's rejection of it over twenty years before. But both the production and the translation had been rather indifferent in 1933, whereas both were outstanding in 1954 and major sources of the success.

Above all, however, the Theatre de Lys production was launched with the participation of Lotte Lenya, now singing in English the role she had created in German more than a quarter of a century before. Her well-deserved success in this performance was, furthermore, a new climax in one of the most remarkable stage careers of the twentieth century. We have seen her emerge into the light of a modest fame in Berlin in 1928, slip from it momentarily, then step back into a more brilliant light in 1931; only to plunge into virtual obscurity—an obscurity penetrated only once, and disastrously, with *The Firebrand of Florence* in 1945—from the time of her arrival in the United States. But now, the Theatre de Lys production of *The Threepenny Opera* catapulted her onto a new phase of her career that was to be more brilliant by far than anything before it. This new phase meant stardom even in her own right—in films, where she obtained an Academy Award nomination for her supporting role alongside Vivien Leigh in *The Roman Spring of Mrs. Stone*, and on Broadway in the hit musical *Cabaret*—but above all it meant, as in the previous successful phases, a special position as interpreter of her late husband's works.

Indeed, Lenya went directly from her success at the Theatre de Lys to become the chief instrument in a worldwide revival of the German Kurt Weill. Leaving the cast of the *Threepenny* revival in the fall of 1955, she made a return trip to Germany for the first time in more than twenty years and proceeded to do a series of recordings that still are classics: the *Berlin Theatre Songs by Kurt Weill* was soon followed by *The Seven Deadly Sins* (in which she sings her original role of Anna I), *Happy End* (in which she sings all the songs), and *The Rise and Fall of the City of Mahagonny* (in which she sings her role of Jenny as revised for the 1931–32 Berlin theater version). In the fall and winter of 1957–58 she was back in Berlin recording *The Threepenny Opera*, singing "Pirate Jenny" as part of her role just as she had done in the 1931 film and in the 1954 Theatre de Lys production.

These were exciting events, and in the course of them it was easy to forget that there had ever, either in Europe or in America, been a Weill of any interest whose music was not centered upon the voice of Lotte Lenya. Indeed, it became customary for journalists and copywriters to quote Weill as having used words to the effect that "my melodies always come to my inner ear in Lenya's voice." Alan Jay Lerner, who should know, attributes to him a statement something like this; but if he made it, then no one but Weill could possibly have understood what he meant by it. Outside Kurt Weill's inner ear, there is no audible connection between, say, Anna Maurrant's aria in *Street Scene*—to take at random one of dozens of possible examples—and Lenya's voice.

But, as if in an effort to prove a connection, Lenya even made recordings of herself singing some of her husband's American songs: in 1957, on an MGM recording of *Johnny Johnson*, she sang the role of the French nurse that she had been deprived of the first time around; and in 1959 she recorded a whole selection of Weill's Broadway songs that has more recently been marketed as a companion piece to her recording of the Berlin songs. The latter two recordings are indeed held together by a uniformity of vocal style, and the fact that Lenya is splendid—in some cases, definitive—on the Berlin songs recording could even lull a listener into not noticing that she is utterly inappropriate—in some cases, dreadful—in almost all the selections on the American songs recording.

The problem manifested here goes even a little further than meets the ear; for if a good listener can readily detect that the music of the American Weill does not lend itself to the position some have accorded Lenya as her husband's definitive interpreter in general, it is somewhat harder to notice the ways in which those European pieces of his generally taken to be her vehicles are not necessarily so, either. In the chapter on *The Rise and Fall of the City of Mahagonny*, we have seen that this work was originally composed as an opera and was only subsequently revived as a Berlin theater piece that starred Lenya. Parts of the role of Jenny were rewritten for her then; other parts of it were reworked to suit her particular vocal requirements in 1956, when the work was recorded. The 1956 recording is nonetheless unmistakably an opera; but Lenya's part in it, and her performance of selections from the score in her *Berlin Theatre Songs* recording, tend to create the illusion that this work is closer to *Threepenny* theater than to the grand opera stage. The belief that it could be performed by singing actors rather than trained operatic performers gave rise to a disastrous production of it, directed by Carmen Capalbo, at the Anderson Theatre in New York in 1970. Fortunately, New York has seen this situation corrected by a recent production of *The Rise and Fall of the City of Mahagonny* at the Metropolitan Opera House. What we now need is a recording of *The Seven Deadly Sins* sung in the range for which it was originally written, and not—this being the case with Gisela May's recording as well as Lenya's—as transposed for Lenya's Paris performance of it.

In other words, the remarkable Weill revival of the 1950s has left a legend that is in some ways restricting. The elements in that legend were Weill, Brecht, and Lenya—who in that order represented, in fact, an increasing particularization of the Weill canon. All three taken together form a legend that rests above all on *The Threepenny Opera*—certainly a notable foundation, being one of the most remarkable works of the musical theater in this century. But besides this work, Weill and Brecht together still stand on a foundation that includes not only the *Mahagonny* opera, to which Lenya's relationship is properly only marginal, but also so splendid a work as *Der Jasager*, to which she has no artistic relationship whatsoever. This work alone indicates that, even if we prefer the Weill of the Brecht collaboration to all others, that is still a broader Weill than the general public—in America, at least—has tended to see since the 1950s revival.

What we now need to do above all, however, is to view Weill in terms of all his works, those of Germany, France, England, and America combined. And this country should perhaps take greater note of the contribution he has made to its culture. There are signs of such a recognition: some of Weill's shows have been revived now and then, and *Lost in the Stars* and *Street Scene* have been done at the New York City Opera. Indeed, the new production of *Street Scene* introduced there in the fall of 1978 seems at last to have impressed many that this is an opera of permanent value. It led Andrew Porter, music critic for *The New Yorker*, to make this observation:

> In much the same way that Handel can be claimed as Britain's greatest opera composer, Kurt Weill might be claimed as America's: a master musician, master musical dramatist, and large soul who found song for the people of his adopted country, learned its idioms, joined them to his own, and composed music of international importance.

Weill had had the courage to embrace a whole new national idiom when he came to this country, and he was only just beginning to explore its possibilities in his own work when he was cut down at the age of fifty. We are left to long for what he might still have done in the course of a normal life-span; but this should not cause us to overlook the real achievements he nevertheless had time for. If it is now time to hear from yet other German Weills than the one stressed in the 1950s revival, it also is time to start hearing again from the American one.

Source Notes
and Bibliographies

Except for the handful of books and articles mentioned in the next two paragraphs, there is no general bibliography for this book. Instead, under the various chapters I have provided lists of the main works consulted for each topic. In the case of books for which I have used later editions but am aware of the first date of publication, I give both dates in the citation.

There are some works that require special mention here, as having either been particularly useful throughout the research, or as having at least provided helpful frameworks within which the research was begun. At this writing, only one volume has yet appeared anywhere that could be called a biography of Kurt Weill: Hellmut Kotschenreuther, *Kurt Weill* (Berlin-Halensee, 1962), is only 103 pages long, including supplements, and is hardly more than a long article; but it provided some helpful orientation at the beginning of the research. A better framework and richer observations are supplied in fewer pages by H. H. Stuckenschmidt in the chapter on Weill in his volume *Twentieth Century Composers, Volume II: Germany and Central Europe* (New York, 1971); in the source notes below, this will be referred to as Stuckenschmidt, "Weill." Another useful framework was in *Weill–Lenya* (New York, 1976), the catalogue of the exhibition of that name held at the Library and Museum of the Performing Arts, Lincoln Center, New York, from November 15, 1976, to March 12, 1977; the book, which unfortunately is not paginated, is particularly useful for its chronologies of the careers of Weill and Lenya—but these must be used with caution, for they are full of errors. Among the many biographical articles written by interviewers of Kurt Weill, the richest was "Up the Rungs from Opera," by Louis M. Simon, in *The New York Times* of April 13, 1941; in the source notes, this will be referred to as Simon, *The New York Times*. Weill's good friend and colleague Maurice Abravanel published an article entitled "Maurice Abravanel Remembers Kurt Weill" in *High Fidelity/Musical America*, July 1978, pp. 66–67; this will be referred to in the notes as Abravanel, "Weill."

Anyone who does research into the life and music of Kurt Weill must pay special tribute to the scholarship of the English music critic and musicologist David Drew. For a good many years Drew has been working on a monumental study of Weill that, at this writing, has yet to be completed; but in the meantime he has presented some vital contributions on the subject. These include articles, annotations, score editions, and an unpublished catalogue of Weill's works. Here I should single out two books, both edited by Drew and published in Frankfurt am Main in 1975, which were especially useful throughout the present study: *Kurt Weill, Ausgewählte Schriften*, a selection of the composer's articles and journalistic pieces (to be referred to in the source notes as Drew, *Schriften*); and *Über Kurt Weill*, a collection of articles and reviews about Weill and his works (to be referred to in the source notes as Drew, *Über KW*). Both have fine introductions by Drew, especially the latter.

In the following chapter-by-chapter source notes, the archives in which some of the cited materials are on deposit are designated by the following abbreviations: Lincoln Center's Library of the Performing Arts as LCL (the Rodgers and Hammerstein Archives of Recorded Sound will occasionally be singled out as RHA–LCL and the Theatre Arts Collection as TAC–LCL); the Library of Congress, Music Division, as LCM; the Maxwell Anderson Collection at the Humanities Research Center, University of Texas at Austin, as MAC; and the Paul Green Papers at the Southern Historical Collection, University of North Carolina, Chapel Hill, as PGP (except for some letters that Paul Green has retained in his personal possession, which will be designated PG–private). Full citations for printed scores and sheet music are given in the list of "Kurt Weill's Principal Compositions" that follows these source notes; full citations for recordings are given in the discography that follows thereafter. Except where indicated otherwise, all German sources have been translated by me.

Prologue—In Search of Kurt Weill

"September Song," by Kurt Weill and Maxwell Anderson, is from their *Knickerbocker Holiday* (see the list of compositions). The Stuckenschmidt quote is from his "Weill," p. 145. The quote on "serious" and "light" music is in a Kurt Weill interview with William G. King, *New York Sun*, February 3, 1940.

Chapter 1—Two Cornerstones

The principal sources used on the history of Dessau and of its Jewish community were: *Jahresbericht der Baronin von Cohn-Oppenheim-Stiftung der Israelitische Kultusgemeinde zu Dessau, für das Jahr 1907* (Dessau, 1907); Professor Dr. H. Wäschke, editor, *Geschichte der Stadt Dessau: Eine Festgabe zur Einweihung des neuerbauten Rathauses* (Dessau, 1901); *Die Haupt- und Residenzstadt Dessau* (Dessau, 1907); Alexander Altmann, *Moses Mendelssohn: A Biographical Study* (Philadelphia, 1973), especially pp. 5–8; and the articles "Anhalt" in the Jerusalem *Encyclopedia Judaica* and "Dessau" in the *Jewish Encyclopedia*. All the quotations on the synagogue and the dedication ceremony are from the *Jahresbericht*, pp. 33–40, including the material it reprints from a "local newspaper," the *Anhaltische Staatsanzeiger*.

On Cantor Albert Weill and his family history, the sources were interviews with Rita Weill, and two family genealogies: Alfred Sonder, *Ahnentafel der Kinder des Nathan Weill (Sohn des Löw Weill) in Kippenheim* (Mannheim, 1935); and Ernest B. Weill, *Weil–De Veil: A Genealogy, 1360–1956* (Scarsdale, New York, 1957). Albert Weill's *Kol Avraham: Synagogen-Gesänge für Cantor u. Männerchor* (Frankfurt am Main, 1893), can be found in the Music Division, LCL. On Aaron Ackermann, I consulted the articles "Kurt Weill" in the *Universal Jewish Encyclopedia* and "Aaron Ackermann" in the German *Encyclopedia Judaica*, as well as his long essay "Der Synag. Gesang in seiner historischen Entwicklung" in Winter and Wünsche, *Die Jüdische Literatur* (Berlin, 1896), vol. III, pp. 477–529. Indispensable works on the history of cantorial singing are: A. Z. Idelsohn, *Jewish Music in its Historical Development* (New York, 1929, 1967); and Eric Werner, *A Voice Still Heard . . . : The Sacred Songs of the Ashkenazic Jews* (University Park, Pa., and London, 1976). The description of Cantor Weill's songs as "orthodox and colorless" was made by Eric Werner in a letter to me of March 22, 1977. The dates of birth of the four children of Albert Weill are given in the Sonder *Ahnentafel*.

The history of the Dessau Court Theater comes mainly from: Moritz von Prosky, "Theater und Musik in Dessau," in the Wäschke *Geschichte der Stadt Dessau*, cited above, pp. 543–54; and Max Hasse, "Dessau, ein norddeutsches Bayreuth," in Ebeling and Stein, *Dessau (Monographien Deutscher Städte*, Oldenburg, 1914), pp. 34–46. Most of the quotations are from Prosky, except for "a North German Bayreuth" and "the Court Theater has remained a good Wagnerian one," which are from Hasse. Weill's recollection of the Duke "every morning between 10 and 11" is in Simon, *The New York Times*. His recollection of the programs as "overwhelmingly Wagner" is in Naomi Jolles, "Hitler Hates Weill's Songs," *New York Post*, October 20, 1943.

The material on the Weill household that follows is from Rita Weill and from Alice Bing (who is one of the Schwabe sisters mentioned in chapter 2 and the widow of Albert Bing's son, Peter). The closing anecdote about young Kurt at the palace is from Simon, *The New York Times*.

Chapter 2—In Times of Tumult and War

Prominent among the background works I used for this chapter were: Golo Mann, *The History of Germany Since 1789*, translated by Marian Jackson (Penguin Books, 1974); S. William Halperin, *Germany Tried Democracy: A Political History of the Reich from 1918 to 1933* (New York, 1946, 1965); Erich Eyck, *A History of the Weimar Republic*, translated by Harlan P. Hanson and Robert G. L. Waite (2 vols., Boston, 1962); and Jethro Bithell, *Modern German Literature, 1880–1938* (London, 1939). And the principal published primary sources were: Ernst Toller, *I Was a German* (New York, 1934); Erich Maria Remarque, *All Quiet on the Western Front*, translated by A. W. Wheen (New York, 1929, 1958); *In the Twenties: The Diaries of Harry Kessler*, translated by Charles Kessler (New York, 1971).

Young Weill's opera based "on an old German play" is mentioned in Robert Garland's column, "The Drama," in the *New York Journal American*, October 10, 1943. The song "*Im Volkston*" has not yet been published at this writing, but it was performed by Barry McDaniel at the Berlin Festival in 1975, and a tape of this is on deposit at RHA–LCL. The first page of the manuscript is reproduced in *Weill–Lenya*. The material on Albert Bing and the Schwabes is from Rita Weill, Alice Bing, and Fritz Bamberger (whose late wife, Käte, was another one of the Schwabe sisters). Bing is mentioned as a pupil of Pfitzner's in Walter Abendroth, *Hans Pfitzner* (Munich, 1935); there is also material about him in an article on music in Dessau in *Das Theater* (Berlin), March 1, 1926, p. 160. Weill's performance at a benefit concert on December 18, 1915, is advertised in a program flier in the possession of Rita Weill.

The Ernst Toller quotes are all from *I Was a German*, as follows: "All my friends," p. 42; "got up and wandered," p. 71; "The French soldiers scattered," p. 73; "And so it went on," p. 98; "brave words," etc., p. 99. I used the Fawcett Crest edition of the Remarque novel: the passages cited are on pp. 15, 153–58 and 102, respectively. Brecht's recollections of war service are in the interview, "Bert Brecht," by Sergey Tretiakov, originally published in the May 1937 issue of *International Literature* (Moscow) and reprinted in Peter Demetz, ed., *Brecht* (Englewood Cliffs, N.J., 1962), pp. 16–29.

The personal data on Kurt Weill and his family during and just after World War I are from Rita Weill, Alice Bing, Fritz Bamberger, and *Weill–Lenya;* as well as Simon, *The New York Times*. Simon is the source of "pretty nearly supporting his family" and the throwing out of "the old-fogey director" at the Hochschule. Information on the various members of the Hochschule faculty is in *Baker's Biographical Dictionary of Musicians* (New York and London, 1971); the quote on Friedrich E. Koch is in *Baker's*, p. 846. The Harry Kessler passages are in his *Diaries*, pp. 8–9 and 58, respectively. The information on Weill's Rilke symphonic poem, his scholarship, and his departure from the Hochschule is given in David Drew's insert notes to the Argo recording of Weill's First and Second symphonies (see discography).

Chapter 3—Ferruccio Busoni

The material on Weill as *répétiteur* in Dessau and conductor in Lüdenscheid is assembled from personal information provided by Rita Weill, Alice Bing, and

Fritz Bamberger; from the already cited articles by Simon in *The New York Times* and Naomi Jolles in the *New York Post;* and from *Weill–Lenya.* "He was always so small" is quoted by Jolles. (I have taken liberties with this. Jolles has: "Always he was so small. Now he's gone completely." This, unidiomatic English and all, is obviously too literal a rendering of what Weill told the interviewer; and since, after all, he was quoting something that had originally been said in German, a little editing of his English translation is not unwarranted.) The entire quoted passage on Lüdenscheid is from Simon. The Harry Kessler quote is on p. 117 of his *Diaries.* The remark about "everything I know about the stage" was quoted in an unsigned interview with Weill published in the *Brooklyn Daily Eagle,* December 11, 1938. The Lüdenscheid performance programs and Weill's letter of recommendation for an instrumentalist were on display at the "Weill–Lenya" exhibit at Lincoln Center, already cited. Weill's return to Leipzig is recalled by Rita Weill and confirmed by a handbill in the archive of the Leo Baeck Institute, New York: it advertises a concert in Leipzig on June 22, 1920, for which one of the performers on the piano is "Herr Kapellmeister Kurt Weill—Leipzig."

The basic information concerning the early Kurt Weill compositions described in this chapter is compiled from the following: *Weill–Lenya;* Heinrich Strobel, "Kurt Weill 1920–1927," *Melos,* 6, 1927, pp. 427 ff., reproduced in Drew, *Über KW;* and two pieces by David Drew—the Argo insert notes already cited and "The History of Mahagonny," *Musical Times* (London), January 1963, pp. 18 ff. The String Quartet in B minor and the Sonata for Cello and Piano, neither of which has been published, are on tapes on deposit at RHA–LCL (see list of compositions and discography). The editions I consulted of Weill's literary sources were: Ernst Hardt, *Ninon von Lenclos: Drama in einem Akt* (Berlin, 1967); and Hermann Sudermann, *The Song of Songs (Das Hohe Lied)*, translated by Thomas Seltzer (New York, 1909). Weill's application to the Busoni master class is in Drew, *Über KW,* in the chronology, p. 162.

There are two biographies of Busoni: E. J. Dent, *Ferruccio Busoni* (Oxford, 1932; London, 1974); and H. H. Stuckenschmidt, *Ferruccio Busoni,* translated by Sandra Morris (New York, 1970). Of Busoni's own prose writings, I used: *Sketch of a New Aesthetic of Music,* translated from the German by Dr. T. Baker, in *Three Classics in the Aesthetics of Music* (New York: Dover, 1962); and *The Essence of Music and Other Papers,* translated by Rosamond Ley (New York, 1957). Scores of all the Busoni works discussed have been published by Breitkopf and Härtel, Wiesbaden. Some are out of print, but piano scores of *Arlecchino* and *Doktor Faust* are available at present. Of the various recordings of Busoni works, I made special use of: the John Ogdon recording of the Piano Concerto, with the Royal Philharmonic Orchestra under the direction of Daniell Revenaugh (Angel SBL–3719); Martin Jones playing the Six Elegies for Piano (Argo ZRG 741); Paul Jacobs doing, among several piano pieces by various twentieth-century composers, the *Six Short Pieces for the Cultivation of Polyphonic Playing* (Nonesuch H–71334); the Glyndebourne Festival recording of *Arlecchino* (RCA Victor LM-1944); and the recording of *Doktor Faust* by the Chorus and Symphony Orchestra of Bavarian Radio, conducted by Ferdinand Leitner and starring Dietrich Fischer-Dieskau in the title role (three discs, Deutsche Grammophon 2709 032). Useful general background for the musical history of the early twentieth century is provided by William W. Austin, *Music in the Twentieth Century* (New York, 1966); and H. H. Stuckenschmidt, *Schönberg: Leben, Umwelt, Werk* (Zurich, 1974).

Busoni's view of *Madame Butterfly* as *unanständig* is in Dent, p. 160. His remark on the tendencies toward "anarchy" in Schoenberg's music is quoted in Austin, p. 114. Busoni's remarks about "a series of dissonances," about opera as "a series of short, concise pieces," and about love duets being "not only shameless but absolutely untrue," are in his essay "The Essence and Oneness of Music," in *The Essence of Music and Other Papers*, pp. 6, 14, and 10, respectively. The other quoted remarks of his are in *Sketch of a New Aesthetic of Music*, as follows: "there are 'obvious' psychic conditions," p. 83; the catalogue of permissible and impermissible moods, p. 82; "Measurably justified" to "decadence," p. 83. Kessler's remarks on Busoni are in *Diaries*, p. 118. The Weill paragraph on Busoni is from his article "Busoni und die neue Musik," in *Der neue Weg*, October 16, 1925, pp. 282 ff., reprinted in Drew, *Schriften*, pp. 19–21. "He called us disciples" is quoted in Stuckenschmidt, *Busoni*, p. 196.

Chapter 4—The Young Modernist

Some of the general background for this chapter and the following ones was obtained from: Walter Kiaulehn, *Berlin: Schicksal einer Weltstadt* (Munich and Berlin, 1958); Wolf Von Eckardt and Sander L. Gilman, *Bertolt Brecht's Berlin* (New York, 1975); Gerhard Masur, *Imperial Berlin* (London, 1971); Otto Friedrich, *Before the Deluge* (New York, 1972); Peter Gay, *Weimar Culture: The Outsider as Insider* (New York, 1968) and *Freud, Jews and Other Germans: Masters and Victims in Modernist Culture* (New York, 1978); Walter Laqueur, *Weimar: A Cultural History* (New York, 1974); and John Willett, *Art and Politics in the Weimar Period* (New York, 1979).

The opening description of Berlin in 1920 is quoted from Dent, *Busoni*, p. 251. The description of the Romanische Café is from Kiaulehn, *Berlin*, p. 233. The material on Weill's personal situation at the end of 1920 and the beginning of 1921 is from conversations with Rita Weill and Maurice Abravanel; and from a letter of March 21, 1978, from Wladimir Vogel, Weill's colleague in the Busoni master class, who refers to his *Bude* on Winterfeldplatz. Ernst Toller's *Transfiguration* is in his *Seven Plays* (New York, 1936), pp. 55–106, translated by Edward Crankshaw.

On Johannes R. Becher: Harry Kessler's comments are in his *Diaries*, p. 110. *Arbeiter Bauern Soldaten. Der Aufbruch eines Volks zu Gott. Ein Festspiel* is in Johannes R. Becher, *Um Gott* (Leipzig, 1921). Background information on Becher, Weill, and the First Symphony is in David Drew's Argo insert notes and in his introduction to the study score of the symphony (see list of compositions).

Neither Weill's Divertimento nor his *Recordare* has yet been published, but they have been performed, and these performances have been taped (see discography). "It was in Berlin" is from Abravanel, "Weill"; and the other data in the same paragraph are from Abravanel in a telephone interview.

The background information on *Die Zaubernacht* comes from *Weill–Lenya;* Abravanel, "Weill"; and the *Berliner Tageblatt*, November 17, 1922. All but a few fragments of the score has disappeared, but Weill's *Quodlibet*, Op. 9, is a suite from that score and provides some sense of its character (see list of compositions and discography). A surviving "Song of the Fairies" was performed at a concert in the auditorium of the Library and Museum of the Performing Arts, Lincoln Center, in March 1977 and has been preserved on a tape on deposit at RHA–LCL. A "Queen of the Toys" aria was performed by Barbara Martin, with the Greenwich Philharmonia under the direction of David Gilbert, at Avery Fisher Hall on October 25, 1978.

"In the summer of 1923" is from Eckardt and Gilman, *Brecht's Berlin*, p. 14. Background information on Weill's String Quartet, Op. 8, is given in the preface by "F.S." to the study score edition. *Frauentanz*, Op. 10, has been both published and taped. (See appropriate lists for both of the foregoing.) Stuckenschmidt's "Weill" is the source of the remark about affinities with Hindemith; "makes its way along the precipice" is from Rudolf Kastner, "Kurt Weill: Eine Skizze," *Musikblätter des Anbruch*, 7, 1925, pp. 753 ff., reprinted in Drew, *Über KW*, pp. 10–13.

Chapter 5—New Turnings

On Georg Kaiser, two books should be mentioned: Ernst Schürer, *Georg Kaiser* (New York, 1971); and Brian J. Kenworthy, *Georg Kaiser* (Oxford, 1957). There are various editions of Kaiser's plays, in English translation as well as in German. The account of Weill's meeting with Kaiser is based on: Simon, *The New York Times*; Howard Taubman, "From Long-hair to Short," *The New York Times*, January 28, 1949; Stuckenschmidt, "Weill"; and Weill's program notes for the original Dresden production of *Der Protagonist*, quoted by H. S. von Heister in *Der deutsche Rundfunk*, April 11, 1926, p. 1015, and reprinted in Drew, *Schriften*, pp. 52–53. Weill's description of the evolution from ballet to opera is quoted from his program notes.

Weill's trip to Italy in March 1924 is documented by a postcard from Rome sent at that time to Hans and Rita Weill and still in the latter's possession. The background information on the Violin Concerto is mainly from David Drew's insert notes for the Deutsche Grammophon recording. The score has been published. (See appropriate lists for information on the score and recordings.) Stuckenschmidt's remark about "dissonant expressionism" is in his "Weill," p. 138. The critic who hears a "tonal dialogue" is Irving Kolodin, in the jacket notes of the Westminster recording. Adorno's remarks are quoted in Drew's insert notes, already cited.

Vladimir Vogel's description of Weill in the master class and Busoni's perception of him is in his letter to me of March 21, 1978. "Don't be afraid of banality" is in the interview, already cited, with William G. King published in the *New York Sun* on February 3, 1940. Busoni's remark about "a Verdi of the poor" is quoted by Lotte Lenya in her foreword to the Grove Press paperback edition of *The Threepenny Opera* (New York, 1964), p. vii. Weill's remarks about Busoni, Liszt, and himself are in an interview with Ralph Winett published in the *Brooklyn Daily Eagle* on December 20, 1936.

On Lotte Lenya: this biographical sketch is put together from *Weill–Lenya;* "Lotte Lenya," an interview by Rex Reed printed in his collection, *Do You Sleep in the Nude?* (New York, 1969, pp. 87–99); and an interview by Neal Weaver published in *After Dark*, July 1969, pp. 32–40. "I came from Zurich to Berlin" to

"I never saw him at all" is from the Neal Weaver article, pp. 33–34. The statements about "four hungry children" and "the coal bin" are from Rex Reed, p. 89. It was Margot Asquith who said Lenya's voice was like that of "a disillusioned child, etc."; this is quoted in the insert notes of Lenya's recording of *Berlin Theatre Songs by Kurt Weill* (see discography). It is Stuckenschmidt, in "Weill," p. 139, who suggests that Lenya was doing household chores during her stay with the Kaisers.

The story of the actual meeting of Lenya and Weill has been put together from these sources: the Neal Weaver and Rex Reed interviews; the Naomi Jolles interview with Kurt Weill in the *New York Post*, already cited; and an interview with Lotte Lenya by Jay S. Harrison, published in the *New York Herald Tribune* on July 27, 1958.

The information on Nelly Frank was provided by a Weill family source, who also showed me a Kurt Weill letter to his mother of December 31, 1924, in which he announces his loss of faith. The performance of the *Frauentanz* is mentioned in *Weill–Lenya*, and that of the Violin Concerto in the Drew insert notes, Deutsche Grammophon recording. The closing description of Weill is by Hans W. Heinsheimer, *Best Regards to Aida* (New York, 1968), p. 109.

Chapter 6—Composing Opera

The remarks about listening to *Alessandro Stradella* and about "So revolutionary an institution as radio" are both from articles by Kurt Weill in *Der deutsche Rundfunk*, the first in the issue of April 12, 1925, p. 935, and the second in the issue of April 26, 1925, p. 1066; both are reproduced in Drew, *Schriften*, pp. 144 and 110. "Only when I observed" is from the program notes to the premiere of *Der Protagonist*, cited in the previous chapter. "The realization that there was nothing more to add" to "the clarified expression of a feeling, humanity," is from Kurt Weill, "Bekenntnis zur Oper," in *25 Jahre neue Musik*, the Yearbook for 1925 published by Universal Edition, Vienna; reprinted in Drew, *Schriften*, pp. 29–31.

On *Der Protagonist:* There is a translation, by H. R. Garten, of the original play in J. M. Ritchie, *Seven Expressionist Plays* (London, 1968). For the piano-vocal score, see list of compositions. There are several pictures of the opera as produced in this period in various issues of *Das Theater*. The first pantomime has been recorded by David Atherton and the London Sinfonietta (see discography). Maurice Abravanel's review of *Der Protagonist* was in *La Revue musicale*, 1926, p. 76, and has been reprinted in Drew, *Über KW*, pp. 16–18. Oskar Bie's review was in the *Berliner Börsen-Courier*, March 29, 1926, and has been reprinted in Drew, *Über KW*. The information on Fritz Busch and *Der Protagonist* is in Simon, *The New York Times*.

The information on the Violin Concerto is in Drew, insert notes to Deutsche Grammophon recording (see discography). The background on Weill's meeting and association with Yvan Goll is in Stuckenschmidt, "Weill," p. 140. A collection of Goll's German poems, *Gedichte 1924–1950*, including the text of "Der neue Orpheus," is in a paperback edition published in 1976 by the Deutscher Taschenbuch Verlag, Munich. The scores of *Der neue Orpheus* and of *Royal Palace* both were published by Universal Edition (see list of compositions).

The date of Weill's marriage is given in *Weill–Lenya*. The wedding photograph is reproduced in the insert notes of the original Columbia recording of *The*

Threepenny Opera in German (see discography). The description of the Weills' quarters in the Pension Hassforth is in the insert notes of the Columbia recording of the full-length *Mahagonny* (see discography), p. 6; and in Lenya's foreword to the Grove Press paperback edition of *The Threepenny Opera*, p. viii. This latter also is the source of "Kurt was always at his desk," p. viii. "I was not busy in the theater" to "music as his hobby" is from an interview with Lenya published in the *Philadelphia Inquirer*, April 28, 1976.

Rita Weill is the source of the anecdote about her daughter and the premiere of *Der Protagonist*. The rented tuxedo is mentioned by Lenya in an interview with Jay S. Harrison in the *New York Herald Tribune*, July 27, 1958. "After several drinks" is from Simon, *The New York Times;* the Simon article says Weill sat in the bar with Fritz Busch, but Busch was conducting and Simon obviously means Kaiser. The change in Weill's personality after *Der Protagonist* was described by Rita Weill. Other information about the production comes from the program flier and from two articles by Eugen Schmitz, one in *Die Musik*, 1926, pp. 617–19, the other in the *Allgemeine Musik-Zeitung*, 1926, pp. 310–11; in *Die Musik* Schmitz writes of Weill's lack of "creative individuality."

The information on the music for the Grabbe play is in the chronology of Drew, *Schriften*. The story of *Na und* is told by Hans W. Heinsheimer in his *Best Regards to Aida* (New York, 1968), pp. 114–19, and additional information is supplied in *Weill–Lenya*. A Weill family source recalls the small group performance of the work in Berlin. The piano-vocal score of *Der Zar lässt sich photographieren* was published, and the *"Tango Angèle"* is on a tape as performed by the London Sinfonietta (see appropriate lists).

Chapter 7—Enter Bertolt Brecht

There are three major biographies of Brecht: Martin Esslin, *Brecht: The Man and His Work* (New York, 1960); Frederic Ewen, *Bertolt Brecht: His Life, His Art, and His Times* (New York, 1967); and Klaus Völker, *Brecht: A Biography* (New York, 1978). Also very useful was Völker's *Brecht Chronicle*, translated by Fred Wieck (New York, 1975). Apart from score versions cited in the list of compositions, the editions of Brecht works used were, in German, various individual paperbacks published by Suhrkamp and by Rowohlt, and in English, the Vintage paperback series of the *Collected Plays*, edited by Ralph Manheim and John Willett. The main source of other writings by Brecht for this and ensuing chapters was John Willett, editor and translator, *Brecht on Theatre* (New York, 1964). Important material also is to be found in the collection edited by Peter Demetz, *Brecht*, already cited. Of various volumes of memoirs consulted for this and ensuing chapters, the most important was Ernst-Josef Aufricht, *Erzähle, damit du dein Recht erweist* (Berlin, 1966). Also useful were: Carl Zuckmayer, *A Part of Myself* (New York, 1970); Salka Viertel, *The Kindness of Strangers* (New York, 1969); and Arnolt Bronnen, *Tage mit Bertolt Brecht* (Vienna, 1960), as well as his *Arnolt Bronnen gibt zu Protokoll* (Hamburg, 1954). Mention should also be made of Hubert Witt, editor, *Brecht as They Knew Him* (New York, 1974). An interesting study is Gottfried Wagner, *Weill und Brecht: Das musikalische Zeittheater*, with a Foreword by Lotte Lenya (Munich, 1978).

On the first meeting of Weill and Brecht: the most likely sequence of events is formulated by Manheim and Willett in their Introduction to Volume 2 of Brecht's *Collected Plays*, p. xvii. Lenya's recollections about this are in her foreword to the Grove *Threepenny Opera*, p. vi, and in her conversation with Stephen Paul, printed in the insert to the Deutsche Grammophon recording of several Weill works made by the London Sinfonietta (see discography), p. 8. Nicolas Nabokov's recollection is described by Esslin in his *Brecht*, p. 36. Weill makes an ambiguous reference to his "first meeting with Brecht early in 1927"—it could mean simply his first meeting with him as a collaborator—in his "Anmerkungen zu meiner Oper *Mahagonny*," which appeared in *Die Musik* of March 1930, p. 29. Weill's two articles on Brecht's *Mann ist Mann* appeared in *Der deutsche Rundfunk* of March 13, 1927, p. 736, and March 27, 1927, p. 879. These two articles and the *Anmerkungen* are reprinted in Drew, *Schriften*.

Bronnen's remark on Brecht at the 1923 Hitler rally is from the Völker *Brecht Chronicle*, p. 37; Harry Kessler's remarks are in his *Diaries*, p. 353; and the story of Brecht and the poetry contest is in Esslin, pp. 31–32. Schlichter's "cold buffet" is described by Kiaulehn in his *Berlin*, p. 228. Lenya's "from that point on" is in her conversation with Stephen Paul, p. 8.

The principal sources on the Donaueschingen and Baden-Baden festivals are: Hans W. Heinsheimer, *Best Regards to Aida* (New York, 1968); Heinrich Strobel, *Paul Hindemith* (Mainz, 1948); Geoffrey Skelton, *Paul Hindemith* (New York, 1978); Darius Milhaud, *Notes Without Music* (New York, 1953); and John Willett, "Brecht: The Music," in Demetz, *Brecht*, pp. 157–70. Arnold Schoenberg's remarks on "this enterprise" are quoted in Skelton, p. 71. Accounts of the *Gebrauchsmusik* idea are to be found in the works just cited, as well as in Ian Kemp, *Hindemith* (London, 1970), especially pp. 22–26.

Weill's various ideas for a subject for the festival are given in Drew's insert text for the London Sinfonietta recording of Weill works. The edition I used of Brecht's *Die Hauspostille* or *Manual of Piety* was that of the Grove Press, a bilingual volume with English translations by Eric Bentley and Notes by Hugo Schmidt (New York, 1966). The *Mahagonny* poems are on pp. 186–205, and Brecht's original melodies for these are reproduced on pp. 263–70. Lenya's remarks about America are in the Rex Reed interview, pp. 91–92. The various theories about Brecht's word *Mahagonny*, including Arnolt Bronnen's on "masses of petit-bourgeois," are from Hugo Schmidt's notes to *Die Hauspostille*, pp. 305–6.

For the sources on Weill's music to the *Mahagonny Songspiel*, see the list of compositions and the discography. Brecht's "Up to that time" is from his "On the Use of Music in an Epic Theatre," in Willett, *Brecht on Theatre*, p. 86. Weill's remark about "the better type American popular song" is in his interview with "R.C.B." in the *New York World-Telegram*, December 21, 1935; this also is the source of the remarks on "Song" and "Songspiel," further on. The account of the German cabaret in that period comes primarily from Lisa Appignanesi, *The Cabaret* (New York, 1976). Carl Zuckmayer's description of Brecht's musicianship is in *A Part of Myself*, p. 263; and the passage on Brecht's music and *Misuk*, including Hanns Eisler's remark, is drawn from Esslin, p. 36.

The account of the preparation and performance of the *Songspiel* production, and of Lenya's part in it, is based on: Drew, "The History of Mahagonny"; Neal Weaver's interview with Lenya in *After Dark*; "Lotte Lenya Remembers

Mahagonny," in the insert notes, pp. 6–7, of the recording of the full-length *Mahagonny* opera (see discography); Stuckenschmidt, "Weill," pp. 141–42; and a personal interview with Ernst Wolff, who was the singing coach for the performance. "We're not giving anything" is in "Lotte Lenya Remembers *Mahagonny*," p. 6; and "with that deep courtesy and patience" is in Neal Weaver's *After Dark* interview, p. 34. Brecht's idea about bringing on the women naked, and, later, the image of Brecht blowing his whistle at the end of the performance, are from Ernst Wolff. The image of Lenya singing "in a hoarse voice" is in Stuckenschmidt, "Weill," pp. 141–42.

Lenya's recollections of the scene in the bar after the performance are in "Lotte Lenya Remembers *Mahagonny*," p. 7. The remark, "But that Alabama song," is in Simon, *The New York Times*. Aaron Copland's remarks are in *Modern Music*, November 1927, in a piece entitled "Forecast and Review: Baden-Baden, 1927," p. 32.

Chapter 8—The Birth of *The Threepenny Opera*
The opening quotations are from Kiaulehn, *Berlin*, p. 532; and Stefan Zweig, *The World of Yesterday* (New York, 1943; Lincoln, Nebraska, 1964), pp. 313–14. The principal sources on Berlin theater in the 1920s were: Walter Laqueur, *Weimar*, pp. 140–54; Peter Gay, *Weimar Culture*, passim; Frederic Ewen, *Brecht*, passim; Martin Esslin, *Brecht*, passim; Klaus Völker, *Brecht* and *Brecht Chronicle*, passim; Otto Friedrich, *Before the Deluge*, chapter 12 and passim; Walter Kiaulehn, *Berlin*, chapters 18 and 21; Salka Viertel, *The Kindness of Strangers*, primarily pp. 100–116; Helene Thimig-Reinhardt, *Wie Max Reinhardt lebte*, (Frankfurt am Main, 1975); Erwin Piscator, *Das politische Theater* (Berlin, 1929); and Maria Ley-Piscator, *The Piscator Experiment: The Political Theater* (New York, 1967). Ernst Toller's *Hoppla! Wir leben*, translated by Hermon Ould as "Hoppla! Such Is Life," is in Toller, *Seven Plays*, pp. 195–273. The edition I used of Jaroslav Hašek's *The Good Soldier Schweik* is that of Penguin Books, translated by Joseph Lada and published in 1942. Piscator's account of his production of it is in *Das politische Theater*, pp. 187–203. There also is a good account of it in Ewen, *Brecht*, pp. 153–54. The incident of the George Grosz drawing is described, with a reproduction of the drawing, in Hans Hess, *George Grosz* (New York, 1974), pp. 155–57.

The account of the inception of *The Threepenny Opera*, and the quotes, are from Aufricht, *Erzähle, damit du dein Recht erweist*, pp. 63–65. The point about Hindemith, his publishers, and *The Beggar's Opera* in 1925 comes from Skelton, *Hindemith*, p. 81. And the point that Brecht and Weill had already spoken to producers about this idea is in Simon, *The New York Times*.

The background on *Vom Tod im Wald* is given in Drew, insert notes to the Deutsche Grammophon recording (see discography). The background on the writing of *Konjunktur* is in Ewen, *Brecht*, pp. 154–55; on "Die Muschel von Margate," see both list of compositions and discography. Weill's meeting with the Gershwins in Berlin is mentioned in Robert Kimball and Alfred Simon, *The Gershwins* (New York, 1973), p. 96; additional details were supplied to me in a telephone conversation by Ira Gershwin's assistant. Harry Kessler's accounts of Josephine Baker and his planned ballet for her are in the *Diaries*, pp. 279–80 and 283–84; his meeting with Kurt Weill about the ballet project is on p. 335. The passage on the *sardanas*, not in the English translation, is reproduced in Drew, *Über KW*, pp. 21–22. On *Jonny Spielt auf*: the piano-vocal score was published by Universal Edition in 1926 (UE 8621); a recording of selections from the opera has been reissued by Mace Records (MXX 9094); and Kessler's comment about it is on p. 335 of his *Diaries*.

Most of the ensuing account of the production of *The Threepenny Opera*, including all quotations except those otherwise noted, comes from Aufricht, pp. 65–79. The trip to Le Lavandou is described in Manheim and Willett's Introduction to Volume 2 of Brecht's *Collected Plays*, p. xx; a major source is Lenya's foreword to the Grove Press *Threepenny Opera*, p. ii—except that the point about Brecht being "slightly water-shy" is in the slightly different version of this same foreword that appears in *Brecht as They Knew Him*, p. 58. This, and Weill's fondness for swimming, also were mentioned by Lenya in her interview with Schuyler Chapin shown on PBS-TV, as part of the "Skyline" series, on January 30, 1979.

Weill's remark to Stuckenschmidt about his work on *The Threepenny Opera* is in the latter's Preface to the "Philharmonia" study score edition of *Threepenny* (see list of compositions), p. v; the 1927 date given there is clearly an error. Weill's remark to Wladimir Vogel is in Vogel's letter to me of March 21, 1978. Different accounts of the origin of the *Moritat* melody: the Brecht version is widespread through the literature on him—see, for example, Eric Bentley in *Theatre of War* (New York, 1972), p. 109, who suggests that "some or all" of the tunes in *The Threepenny Opera* were contributed by Brecht; the American colleague who recalls the Weill version is Lehman Engel, who told it to me in a personal interview.

It is Lenya's foreword to the Grove Press *Threepenny Opera* that tells the story of Fritz Kortner, Caspar Neher, and the finale of the *Threepenny Opera*, as well as of Feuchtwanger's suggestion about the title, p. xii. This is also the source of "For the first and last time," to "from going on," p. xiii. "They'll know who I am tomorrow" is in Neal Weaver's *After Dark* interview, p. 38. Alfred Kerr's remarks were in the *Berliner Tageblatt* of September 1, 1928; Herbert Ihering's remarks are quoted in Frederic Ewen, *Brecht*, pp. 178–79. Schoenberg's remark about three-quarter time is quoted in Stuckenschmidt, *Schönberg*, p. 296; and Harry Kessler's comments are in the *Diaries*, p. 349.

Chapter 9—On *The Threepenny Opera*

The text editions of *The Threepenny Opera* that I used were: Bertolt Brecht, *Die Dreigroschenoper* (edition suhrkamp 229, Berlin, 1973); and the Manheim–Willett translation in their edition of Brecht's *Collected Plays*, Volume 2, pp. 145–226, as well as their very valuable notes, pp. 315–64. For score editions and recordings, see the appropriate lists below. The edition I consulted of John Gay, *The Beggar's Opera*, was that reprinted in the Modern Library volume *Twelve Famous Plays of the Restoration and 18th Century*, edited by Cecil A. Moore; this includes an appendix with the Johann Pepusch music. The quotations are from pp. 575 and 628 of that edition.

Weill's theoretical remarks: "Opera will be one of the essential factors" and, further on, "as it answers to the naïve attitude," are in his reply to a symposium question, "What do you think about the further development of opera today?"

which appeared in *Blätter der Staatsoper*, October 1927, p. 18; reprinted in Drew, *Schriften*, p. 36. The remarks about "splendid isolation," "what we wanted to create," "Here, for once," "the last Threepenny Finale," and "This return" are all in the article on *The Threepenny Opera* that he wrote for *Musikblätter des Anbruck*, January 1929, pp. 24 ff.; reprinted in Drew, *Schriften*, pp. 53–56. "How are the gestic elements of music shaped?" is from his essay, "Über den gestischen Charakter der Musik," in *Die Musik*, March 1929, pp. 419–25; reprinted in Drew, *Schriften*, pp. 40–45.

Brecht's "Hints for Actors" are in Manheim and Willett, Brecht's *Collected Plays*, Volume 2, p. 330. Schoenberg on Weill and Lehár is described in the introduction to Drew, *Über KW*, p. xxxi. Harry Kessler on Diaghilev is in the *Diaries*, p. 357.

Chapter 10—1929

The information on the Weill apartment in Bayernallee comes from Rita Weill. Hans W. Heinsheimer on Weill and his Graham-Page is in his *Best Regards to Aida*, p. 139. The description of Brecht's apartment is in Bernhard Reich, "Recollections of Brecht as a Young Man," in *Brecht as They Knew Him*, pp. 42–43. The description of Weill, "his face like a young seminarist's" is in Lenya's foreword to the Grove Press *Threepenny Opera*, p. ix.

The fact that Klemperer saw *The Threepenny Opera* "about ten times" is in Aufricht, p. 82. The background information on the *Kleine Dreigroschenmusik* is in Drew's insert notes to the Deutsche Grammophon recording (see discography). This also is the source for the background information on the *Berlin Requiem*, on the same recording. Weill's "it makes an attempt" is from *Der deutsche Rundfunk* of May 17, 1929, p. 613, as is "radio presents"; this is reprinted in Drew, *Schriften*, pp. 139–41.

That Hindemith's publishers had suggested a collaboration with Brecht back in 1925 is in Skelton, *Hindemith*, p. 81. For *The Lindbergh Flight*, see list of compositions. Brecht's text of *Das Badener Lehrstück vom Einverständnis* is in various editions of his works; I used the Rowohlt paperback edition of his *Lehrstücke*, which includes his own additional comments about Hindemith. The score of the Hindemith piece, called simply *Lehrstück*, was published by Schott in 1929. The Alfred Einstein quote is from his article, "Lindbergh Cantata," *The New York Times*, February 2, 1930.

The story of the *Happy End* production is told by Aufricht, pp. 96–101, and all the quotes are from him. Since Brecht banished *Happy End* from his collected works, a full text of the play is hard to come by. A typescript of it was produced and circulated in 1958 by Felix Bloch Erben of Berlin, owner of the production rights, and microfilms of this can be found in various archives, such as the Butler Library of Columbia University. My knowledge of it is based on this and Michael Feingold's English adaptation, produced in New Haven in the spring of 1972 and in New York in 1977. For the score and recordings, see the appropriate lists below; also for the "Berlin in Licht-Song" and "Das Lied von den Braunen Inseln." A translation of Lion Feuchtwanger's *The Oil Islands* is in his *Two Anglo-Saxon Plays* (New York, 1928). Harry Kessler on the death of Stresemann: *Diaries*, p. 368.

Chapter 11—The *Mahagonny* Opera

The most important texts for this chapter were: David Drew, "The History of Mahagonny," *Musical Times* (London), January 1963, pp. 18–24; Bertolt Brecht, *Aufstieg und Fall der Stadt Mahagonny* (Berlin: edition suhrkamp 21, 1970); *Rise and Fall of the City of Mahagonny*, translated by Michael Feingold, in Manheim and Willett, *Collected Plays* of Brecht, Volume 2, pp. 85–143 (also the notes, pp. 279–314); and the score edition cited in the list of compositions.

Weill's remark that "I am not sardonic" is in his interview with "N.S." in *The New York Times*, October 27, 1935. His "Any approximation of wild West" is in the frontispiece of the score edition. The story of his experience at the Brown Shirt rally is in Howard Taubman, "From Long-hair to Short," *The New York Times*, January 28, 1949. Alfred Polgar's descriptive piece, "Krach in Leipzig," first appeared in *Das Tagebuch*, 12, 1930, and was reprinted in his collection *Ja und Nein: Darstellungen von Darstellungen* (Hamburg, 1956), pp. 298 ff., as well as in Drew, *Über KW*, pp. 69–72. Both Esslin, pp. 49–50, and Ewen, pp. 191–92, translate portions of this piece, and I have made use of both of their translations in my own. "It was a scarlet occasion" is from Herbert F. Peyser, "Berlin Hears 'Mahagonny,' " *The New York Times*, January 10, 1932 (Peyser, on the occasion of the Berlin opening, is remembering the Leipzig experience). Lenya's "the riot had spread to the stage" is from "Lotte Lenya Remembers *Mahagonny*," in the insert notes to the *Mahagonny* recording, p. 8. Weill on "the Pope himself" is quoted in Drew, "History of Mahagonny," p. 20.

Stravinsky's remark about the *Mahagonny* score is in Robert Craft, *Stravinsky: Chronicle of a Friendship 1948–1971* (New York, 1973), p. 212. Theodor W. Adorno's essay, "Mahagonny," was in *Der Scheinwerfer*, 1930, pp. 111 ff., and was reprinted in Adorno, *Moments Musicaux* (Frankfurt am Main, 1964), pp. 131 ff., and in Drew, *Über KW*, pp. 58–66. Brecht's "Why is *Mahagonny* an opera?" is in the notes to Manheim and Willett's edition of his *Collected Plays*, Volume 2, pp. 279–81. Weill's "The content of this opera" is from his "Anmerkungen zu meiner Oper 'Mahagonny' " in *Die Musik*, March 1930, pp. 440–41; reprinted in Drew, *Schriften*, pp. 56–57. Kurt Tucholsky's "Life is not like that" is quoted in Esslin, pp. 50–51.

Chapter 12—School Opera: *Der Jasager*

The basic texts for this chapter were: Arthur Waley, *The Nō Plays of Japan* (London, 1921; New York, 1922); Bertolt Brecht, *Der Jasager und Der Neinsager: Vorlagen, Fassungen und Materialen*, edited by Peter Szondi (Frankfurt am Main: edition suhrkamp 171, 1966); and the score edition, listed among the compositions.

Weill's statement to a hypothetical audience of twelve-year-olds is on the jacket copy of the Telefunken reissue of the original cast recording of *The Threepenny Opera* (see discography). The article by the student about "The attitude toward the music of *Der Jasager*" is "Über den *Jasager*" by Günther Martens in *Anbruch*, 1930, p. 244; reprinted in Drew, *Über KW*, pp. 68–69. Frank Warschauer's "Nein dem Jasager!" was in *Die Weltbühne*, 1930, pp. 70–71, and is reprinted in the Szondi edition of *Der Jasager*, pp. 71–73; "Here it must be stated" is as translated by Fred Wieck in the English-language edition of Völker's *Brecht Chronicle*, p. 57. I read *Die Massnahme* in the Rowohlt edition of Brecht's *Lehrstücke;*

Hanns Eisler's "Die Musik zur 'Massnahme' " appears in that edition on pp. 46–47.
The student reactions in Neukölln to *Der Jasager* are given in the Szondi edition,
pp. 59–63, as are the alternate versions of the play that Brecht wrote.

Chapter 13—The *Threepenny* Trial and Film

The basic texts for this chapter were: Esslin, pp. 42–45; Manheim and Willett,
Collected Plays of Brecht, Volume 2, pp. xxv–xxvii; Brecht, "Die Beule. Ein
Dreigroschenfilm" and "Der Dreigroschenprozess," in *Bertolt Brechts Dreigroschen-
buch* (Frankfurt am Main, 1960), pp. 71–121; Brecht, *Threepenny Novel*, translated by Desmond I. Vesey, verses translated by Christopher Isherwood
(London, 1937; Penguin Books, 1976); Lotte H. Eisner, "The Dreigroschenoper
Lawsuit," in her book *The Haunted Screen*, translated by Roger Greaves (Berkeley,
1973), pp. 343–45; and the shooting script and revisions of the film of *The Threepenny Opera*, along with notes and supplementary material, as given in English
translation in *Masterworks of the German Cinema* (New York, 1973).

All the statements by John Oser, the film's editor, quoted here are from his
interview with Gideon Bachman, originally published in *Cinemages 3: Six Talks on
G. W. Pabst* (New York, 1955) and reprinted in *Masterworks of the German Cinema*,
pp. 298–300. Simone de Beauvoir's recollections of *The Threepenny Opera* are in *The
Prime of Life*, translated by Peter Green (New York, 1962), p. 45. All the
quotations about the trial by Lotte H. Eisner are from the source cited above.
Some of the material on Lenya in the concluding section of the chapter is from
Weill–Lenya and from the Neal Weaver interview in *After Dark*.

Chapter 14—Goodbye to Berlin

The account of the Berlin production of *Mahagonny* and the conflict between
Brecht and Weill comes from Aufricht, pp. 123–28.

The score edition of *Die Bürgschaft* is cited in the list of compositions below;
the Herder parable is given in the frontispiece. The 1957 Berlin Festival
performance has been taped (see discography). An important background study is:
David Drew, "Topicality and the Universal: The Strange Case of Weill's *Die
Bürgschaft*," *Music and Letters* (London), July 1958, pp. 242–55. Ernst Bloch's
remark about "a Jewish Verdi" is in his "Fragen in Weills *Bürgschaft*," *Anbruch*, 14,
1932, pp. 207 ff., reprinted in Drew, *Über KW*, 82–84. The remarks about
Avant-Gartenlaube and "the rough . . . Americanism" are in Stuckenschmidt,
"Weill," p. 144.

Harry Kessler's conversation with Heinz Simon is in his *Diaries*, p. 415.
Toller's plays are in his *Seven Plays*, already cited. For *The Captain of Köpenick*, I
read the translation by Carl Richard Mueller in *German Drama Between the Wars*,
edited by George E. Wellwarth, pp. 179–296. On the German cinema in this
period, the two basic works are: Siegfried Kracauer, *From Caligari to Hitler*
(Princeton, 1947), and Lotte H. Eisner, *The Haunted Screen* (Berkeley, 1973). The
information on *Wir sind ja sooo zufrieden . . .* comes from Wolfgang Roth, in a
personal interview; Roth, who designed sets for the production, has a flier on it in
his possession.

The information on Kaiser's career up to 1932 comes from Ernst Schürer,

Georg Kaiser. The text of *Der Silbersee: Ein Wintermärchen in drei Akten* was published by Gustav Kiepenheuer, Berlin, in 1933. For score editions, see compositions; for a recording, noncommercial and of limited distribution, see discography.

Harry Kessler's astonishment at Hitler's appointment is in his *Diaries,* pp. 443–44. The closing of *Der Silbersee* is described in Simon, *The New York Times,* and Howard Taubman, *The New York Times,* January 28, 1949, among other places. The *Völkischer Beobachter* remarks about Weill, by F. A. Hauptmann, appeared in the issue of February 24, 1933; they are reprinted in Drew, *Über KW,* pp. 110–11. The information on Berthold Viertel, Weill, and *Little Man, What Now?* is in Salka Viertel, *The Kindness of Strangers,* pp. 185–86.

An estrangement between Weill and Lenya beginning in about 1932 has been testified to by Maurice Abravanel and two family sources. The general nature of their relationship from this time on was characterized by a number of the people interviewed. Lenya's participation in the Piscator film and in the double-bill concert in Paris is in *Weill–Lenya.* The story of Weill's escape to France was told to me by both E. Y. Harburg and Morris Stonzek, who had heard it from him, but they cannot recall whether he described himself as having been alone or with Lenya. Various statements made by Lenya seem to be saying that she was with him, and she alone would know for sure; but Maurice Abravanel, who saw Weill in Paris at the end of this journey, thinks he was alone, as do the family sources, who were far from the scene.

Chapter 15—Paris Interlude

The material on the *Mahagonny Songspiel* production in Paris comes from: Darius Milhaud, *Notes Without Music,* p. 236; and Abravanel, "Weill," pp. 66–67. On Weill's life and personal circle in Paris, the sources are: interviews with Rita Weill and Maurice Abravanel; and the Kessler *Diaries,* p. 453.

The background on Les Ballets 1933 and the decision to ask Weill for a piece comes from Bernard Taper, *Balanchine* (New York, 1960, 1974), pp. 150–54; and from a telephone conversation with Barbara Horgan, who relayed to me some answers to questions I had posed to George Balanchine in a letter. The material on *The Seven Deadly Sins* itself comes from: a telephone interview with Maurice Abravanel; Esslin, pp. 66–67; the jacket copy by Heinrich Lindlar for the Gisela May recording (see discography); *Le Figaro,* June 7, 1933; Aufricht, p. 140. For data on the score and on recordings, see the appropriate lists below. The remarks about "The music of *The Seven Deadly Sins*" is in Völker, *Brecht,* pp. 181–82. The point about Tilly Losch and her husband both wanting Lenya for the role was made by George Balanchine through Barbara Horgan as cited above. Abravanel's remark that "Kurt was forgiving" was made to me in a telephone interview. Stuckenschmidt's remark that the production "enjoyed only literary success" is in his "Weill," p. 144. Brecht's remark about it is in Völker, *Brecht Chronicle,* p. 65. It is Taper, *Balanchine,* p. 154, who says that the audience found the work "disagreeable." Kessler gives Lifar's view and his own on the ballet in *Diaries,* pp. 458, 459. Weill's letter to his brother and sister-in-law mentioning the "great success" of the production was written from Positano, Italy, on July 23, 1933, and is still in the possession of Rita Weill. The quote from the *Dancing Times* is in Esslin, pp. 66–67.

Weill's attack of psoriasis and his trip to Italy are in the letter to Hans and Rita

Weill from Positano, cited above; the fact that he suffered from this skin disease all his life is from Rita Weill in personal conversation. The improvement in his relations with Lenya is from Rita Weill and Maurice Abravanel; Abravanel is the source of Weill's remark about "a good Jew." The story about renting the house in Louveciennes comes primarily from the Naomi Jolles interview in the *New York Post*, already cited.

Background information on the composition of the Second Symphony comes primarily from Ian Kemp's insert article for the Argo recording of Weill's two symphonies (see discography), and David Drew's preface to the score edition (see compositions). The long quote from Abravanel on the performance of the *Silbersee* suite is from his "Weill," p. 67. Bruno Walter's decision to conduct the symphony is from a telephone conversation with Maurice Abravanel. For the score and recordings of the symphony, see appropriate lists. Henri Monnet's remarks are from a typescript printed in Drew, *Über KW*, pp. 120–21.

The discussion of Weill and Offenbach is based primarily on information provided to me by Wladimir Vogel, and in Abravanel, "Weill," p. 67. The background on *Marie Galante* comes from articles and notices in *Le Figaro*, December 1934; and in *L'Illustration*, December 29, 1934. I read an edition of Jacques Deval's novel published by Éditions Mornay, Paris, in 1935. For the score and recordings of some of the songs, see discography.

The background on *A Kingdom for a Cow* comes from: Aufricht, p. 146; *The Times*, London, June 29, 1935; *Daily Telegraph*, London, July 8, 1935; *Variety*, New York, July 7, 1935; and the theater program for the production. No score was ever published, but individual songs were; see list of compositions.

Chapter 16—The Road to New York
Much of the narrative in the first half of this chapter is based on two accounts centering upon Meyer Weisgal: Meyer Weisgal, *So Far* (New York, 1971), his autobiography, especially pp. 107–40; and Michael Mok, "The Odyssey of an Optimist," the *New York Post*, February 8, 9, and 10, 1937. The Ludwig Lewisohn translation of Franz Werfel's text of *The Eternal Road* was published by the Viking Press, New York, 1936. For the score, see the list of compositions.

The main sources for Weill's part in the early evolution of *The Eternal Road* were, in addition to the above: "Score for 'The Eternal Road,' " an unsigned interview with Weill, *The New York Times*, December 27, 1936; "Eternal Road," an unsigned article in the *Brooklyn Daily Eagle*, January 3, 1937; and a press release on the production issued in 1935 by Reinhardt Stage Productions, New York. Weisgal's impression before meeting Weill that he was "some sort of Communist" is from a personal interview with him. Weill and the melody for Moses, as well as the confrontation with Werfel about it, is in the above-mentioned press release. The meeting in Venice is primarily from the *Brooklyn Daily Eagle* article. The account of the meeting at Schloss Leopoldskron in the summer of 1934 is almost entirely from Weisgal, *So Far*, pp. 120–21; except for "Weill cried," etc., which is from the Michael Mok article in the *New York Post*.

"With about 200 songs" is from the unsigned *New York Times* interview of December 27, 1936; and "it is Mr. Weill's conviction" is from the interview with "N.S." in *The New York Times* of October 27, 1935. The information about the emigration of Weill's sister and her family to Palestine is from Rita Weill. The events leading up to Weill's arrival in New York are from: Weisgal, *So Far*, pp. 122–26, as well as a personal interview with him; Michael Mok, especially the installment of February 9, 1937; "Reinhardt Is Here to Produce Play," unsigned news article in *The New York Times*, October 4, 1935; *Brooklyn Daily Eagle*, January 3, 1937. The observations on the relationship between Kurt and Lenya at this point come out of my personal conversations with people who knew them. The information about the additional song for the operetta in Zurich was provided by Wolfgang Roth, who worked on the production. The description of the Weill's first days in New York comes primarily from the Rex Reed interview with Lenya, already cited. Weisgal's anecdote about being "good-looking" was told to me by him in a personal interview. Gershwin's party and the remark about the *squitchadickeh* voice is in Edward Jablonski and Lawrence D. Stewart, *The Gershwin Years* (New York, 1973), p. 299. His later remark about Lenya's sounding like a hillbilly singer has often been repeated by her, including in my interview with her on May 27, 1976. The story of Weill at the *Porgy and Bess* rehearsal is told in an interview article about Ira Gershwin by Benjamin Welles, "Lyricist of 'The Saga of Jenny,' et al.," *The New York Times*, May 25, 1941.

Chapter 17—Taking on Broadway: *Johnny Johnson*

Some of the basic texts for the chapter were: Harold Clurman, *The Fervent Years* (New York, 1945, 1975); Cheryl Crawford, *One Naked Individual: My Fifty Years in the Theatre* (New York, 1977); Paul Green, *Five Plays of the South* (New York, 1963), as well as the Samuel French edition of *Johnny Johnson*, which has some textual variants upon the version printed in *Five Plays;* Lehman Engel, *This Bright Day* (New York, 1974); and Brooks Atkinson, *Broadway* (New York, 1970). For score and recording, see the appropriate lists below. I must also give special thanks again here to Paul Green for opening up his papers to me—both those at the Southern Historical Collection of the University of North Carolina Library (PGP) and those remaining in his private possession (PG–private).

The Kurt Weill interview with "R.C.B." was in the *New York World-Telegram* of December 20, 1935. The information on the concert for the League of Composers was provided by *Weill–Lenya* and by a personal interview with Ernst Wolff, who helped prepare the occasion. The story of Brecht and the New York production of *The Mother* comes from the two Klaus Völker books, *Brecht*, pp. 215–21, and *Brecht Chronicle*, pp. 74–76. The postponement of *The Eternal Road* is described in Michael Mok's *New York Post* series, in the installment of February 9, 1937. The fact that the Weills had moved to the Hotel Park Crescent is indicated by several of his letters to Paul Green at this time (PG–private).

The account of the gestation of *Johnny Johnson* is assembled from the books by Clurman, Crawford, and Engel, cited above; from interviews with Paul Green, Cheryl Crawford, Lee Strasberg, Harold Clurman, Lehman Engel, and Morris Stonzek; from the letters in the two Paul Green collections; from various contemporary newspaper accounts; and from "Kurt Weill in Hollywood—But not of it," a 1937 press release by Paul Davis of the J. Walter Thompson Company, New York. Cheryl Crawford's "bizarre trio" is on p. 52 of her book. Brooks Atkinson's description of the Group Theatre "kibbutz" is on p. 292 of *Broadway*.

The quote about the "two general themes" is from an undated, unsigned clipping from *The New York Times*, "Play Written to Order Foils Drama Famine," November or December 1936, on deposit at TAC–LCL. The next two quotes from Harold Clurman, about making contact with Paul Green, are in his *Fervent Years*, p. 184. The story of Kurt Weill's arrival in Chapel Hill was told to me by Paul Green in a personal interview. Cheryl Crawford's "In our search" and, further on, Kurt "worked at his piano," are on p. 94 of her book. Clurman's "As the script had only just begun" is on p. 187 of his book; Weill's remark to him that "*You*, of course" should direct is from a personal interview with Clurman. Lehman Engel's description of his first meeting with the Weills is in *This Bright Day*, p. 93; his recollection of Weill's calling out tempos behind him at rehearsals is from a personal interview, as is Morris Stonzek's story about the yawning pianist. The next three quotes from Clurman are on pp. 188–89 of *The Fervent Years*.

Lee Strasberg on the question of a musical or a play with music is from a personal interview with him. Clurman on "opening night" and "brought still another shock" is on p. 189 of his book; Cheryl Crawford's "The three huge cannons" is on pp. 96–97 of hers. Brooks Atkinson's review is in *The New York Times* of November 20, 1936, and Robert Benchley's is in *The New Yorker* of December 1, 1936. Weill's comment about "How many plays" is from a personal interview with Harold Clurman.

Chapter 18—The First Sally into Hollywood

On the opening of *The Eternal Road*: Weisgal, *So Far*, pp. 133–35; "Firemen on Guard at 'Eternal Road,' " *The New York Times*, January 8, 1937; Bosley Crowther, "Seen from a Signal Tower," *The New York Times*, January 10, 1937; Abravanel, "Weill," p. 67; Brooks Atkinson, *The New York Times*, January 8, 1937, and *Broadway*, p. 343.

The account of Kurt Weill in Hollywood is assembled from: Cheryl Crawford, *One Naked Individual*, pp. 94–99; Harold Clurman, *The Fervent Years*, pp. 196–201; "Kurt Weill in Hollywood—But not of it," the 1937 press release cited above; contemporary newspaper accounts; letters to Paul Green (both PGP and PG–private); a personal interview with Paul Green; a letter to Cheryl Crawford, February 14, 1937, in Cheryl Crawford Papers, LCL; a letter to Norman Bel Geddes, February 25, 1937, from Kurt Weill in Hollywood, in Bel Geddes Papers, Humanities Research Center, University of Texas at Austin; and a letter to Helen Deutsch, February 11, 1937, in the Helen Deutsch papers, Mugar Memorial Library, Boston University. A useful book for background was John Baxter, *The Hollywood Exiles* (New York, 1976). The story of the visits to the Gershwin home and the planned musical with Harburg and the Spewacks comes from a telephone interview with E. Y. Harburg. John Howard Lawson's remark about *Blockade* is in *Cinéaste*, vol. VIII, no. 2, p. 10. The Marc Connelly project is mentioned in the letter to Cheryl Crawford of February 14, 1937, cited above. Weill's *Liliom* idea is in *The New York Times* of May 9, 1937.

The Weills' trip to Canada at this time is mentioned in a letter from Weill to Paul Green dated August 19, 1937 (PGP). The purpose of this trip with respect to the establishment of immigrant status is given in the chronology of Drew, *Über KW*, and further attested to by a family source. The Weills' move to a duplex apartment on East Sixty-second Street: *The New York Times*, September 11, 1937. Death of George Gershwin: Jablonski and Stewart, *The Gershwin Years*, pp. 290–96. *The Common Glory*: letters from Weill to Paul Green; "a kind of Johnny Johnson of 1776" is in a letter of October 13, 1937 (PGP). Davy Crockett and *Heavenly Express*: letters from Weill to Paul Green, and *The New York Times*, December 5, 1937.

Weill's return to Hollywood is in various letters to Paul Green. On Fritz Lang and *You and Me*: Paul M. Jensen, *The Cinema of Fritz Lang* (New York, 1969), mainly pp. 124–28; Peter Bogdanovich, *Fritz Lang in America* (New York, 1969), mainly pp. 38–39; and Lotte H. Eisner, *Fritz Lang* (New York, 1977), mainly pp. 191–96.

Weill's two trips back to New York in early 1938: letters to Paul Green; three letters from Kurt Weill to Maxwell Anderson, April 17 and 28, and May 14, 1938, in MAC; a letter from Maxwell Anderson to John F. Wharton, May 18, 1938, printed in Laurence G. Avery, ed., *Dramatist in America: Letters of Maxwell Anderson, 1912–1958* (Chapel Hill, 1977), p. 73.

Chapter 19—Back to Old New York: *Knickerbocker Holiday*

The basic sources for this chapter were: Laurence G. Avery, ed., *Dramatist in America* (cited above) and *A Catalogue of the Maxwell Anderson Collection at the University of Texas* (Austin, 1968); Joshua Logan, *Josh: My Up and Down, In and Out Life* (New York, 1977); John F. Wharton, *Life Among the Playwrights: Being Mostly the Story of the Playwrights Producing Company* (New York, 1974); and the text of *Knickerbocker Holiday* (New York, 1958), and the score edition and recordings (see appropriate lists).

Harold Clurman's remark about *Winterset* is in *The Fervent Years*, p. 157. "I'd like to write a play with you," "Kurt, do you think," and "If the idea works out" are from the souvenir program of *Knickerbocker Holiday* (TAC–LCL). The current state of Weill's projects is gleaned from his letters to Paul Green and from contemporary newspaper clippings. Weill's letter about the three "fathers" is from "The Chief en route" to California, April 17, 1938 (MAC). Anderson's views on the New Deal and the point of his satire in *Knickerbocker Holiday* are spelled out in his essay, "A Preface to the Politics of *Knickerbocker Holiday*," which first appeared in *The New York Times* of November 13, 1938, and was subsequently published in his volume of essays, *The Essence of Tragedy and Other Footnotes and Papers* (New York, 1939). Elmer Rice's recollections about "the rest of us" are in his *Minority Report: An Autobiography* (New York, 1963), p. 380.

The rest of my account of the gestation of *Knickerbocker Holiday* is mainly from Joshua Logan, *Josh*, pp. 123–28. The information on Burgess Meredith is in *Dramatist in America*, p. 73, and Wharton, p. 40. The account of Logan's get-together with Walter Huston in California is mostly his own (pp. 124–25), but it also includes some material from Walter Huston's recollection of the scene in his article "There's No Place Like Broadway Be It Ever So Noisy," in *Stage*, October 1938, pp. 22–26. The account of the actual writing of "September Song" includes elements from the Naomi Jolles article in the *New York Post*, October 20, 1943. Wharton's "I still have a clear picture of Max" is on p. 42 of his book.

Chapter 20—Looking for a Niche

Some useful books in the preparation of this and subsequent chapters were: Stanley Green, *Ring Bells! Sing Songs! Broadway Musicals of the 1930's* (New Rochelle, N.Y., 1971), *The World of Musical Comedy* (3rd Edition, New York, 1974), and *Encyclopedia of the Musical Theatre* (New York, 1976); and John Russell Taylor and Arthur Jackson, *The Hollywood Musical* (New York, 1971).

Richard Watts, Jr.'s review is in the *New York Herald Tribune* of October 20, 1938. *Variety*'s remarks are in the issue of April 5, 1939. The judgment of the play as a "mild success" is in Wharton, p. 43. Lenya's engagement at Le Ruban Bleu is mentioned in letters from her and Kurt to Paul Green (PGP), as is their house in Suffern. The Florida vacation is mentioned in a letter of January 26, 1939, from Weill to a Musicians Committee to Aid Spanish Refugees, on deposit at the Butler Library, Columbia University.

Eneas Africanus: Harry Stillwell Edwards's book was published in several editions during the 1920s and early 1930s. Anderson's rough-draft manuscript—handwritten, except for a few of the song lyrics, which are typed—of *Eneas Africanus* (the *Eneas* is crossed out and replaced by *Ulysses*, in the title and throughout) is on deposit in MAC. Anderson's letter to Paul Robeson has been printed with useful annotations in Avery, *Dramatist in America*, pp. 84–86. Information about the decision to cast Bill Robinson in the role is in contemporary newspaper items and in a telegram from Weill in New York to Anderson in California, summer 1939 (MAC).

The New York World's Fair and *Railroads on Parade:* Stanley Applebaum, *The New York World's Fair 1939–1940* (New York, 1977); Souvenir Programs for *Railroads on Parade*, 1939 and 1940 (kindly lent to me by Michael Pender); Elliott Carter, "O Fair World of Music!" *Modern Music*, May–June 1939, reprinted in Else Stone and Kurt Stone, eds., *The Writings of Elliott Carter* (Bloomington, 1977), pp. 55–59; and contemporary newspaper accounts. Weisgal's remark, "fortunately for Bel Geddes," is in *So Far*, p. 133.

The information on the work on *Eneas Africanus* in California during the summer of 1939 is from: Avery, *Dramatist in America*, especially p. li; contemporary newspaper accounts; a letter from Weill in New York to Anderson in California just before he and Lenya were to depart for there, June 5, 1939 (MAC); a postcard to Victor Samrock from Kurt Weill in California, July 26, 1939, shown to me by Samrock; and a postcard to Erwin Piscator, in Douglaston, N.Y., from Weill in California, also July 26, 1939, in the Piscator papers, Morris Library, Southern Illinois University at Carbondale.

The information on Weill's relatives at this time was given to me by Rita Weill. The stories of Ossietzky, Tucholsky, and Toller are from various sources, especially Istvan Deak, *Weimar Germany's Left-wing Intellectuals: A Political History of the Weltbühne and Its Circle* (Berkeley, 1968); Toller's remark on "the twelfth hour" is in Harold Clurman, *All People Are Famous* (New York, 1974), p. 149. An account of the fate of Piscator, Carola Neher, and other friends of Brecht in the Soviet Union is in Völker, *Brecht*, pp. 201–5. The information on Hertzka is in *Baker's Biographical Dictionary of Musicians*, p. 703; and on Harry Kessler, in Otto Friedrich's introduction to his *Diaries*, p. xv.

The Ballad of Magna Carta: from *Weill–Lenya,* and William G. King, "Music and Musicians," in the *New York Sun,* February 3, 1940; all the ensuing quotes by Weill come from the latter. For score and a tape, see list of compositions and discography. Information about Norman Corwin's *Pursuit of Happiness* program and *Ballad for Americans* comes from Earl Robinson's jacket notes for the Vanguard (VSD–79193) recording of Paul Robeson's performance of the latter.

The information about Weill's other incidental music comes from *Weill– Lenya,* contemporary newspaper accounts, and a personal interview with Joseph Wiseman, who was in the cast of *Journey to Jerusalem.*

Chapter 21—Success on Broadway: *Lady in the Dark*
The basic materials for this chapter are: Ira Gershwin, *Lyrics on Several Occasions* (New York, 1959); the Ira Gershwin–Kurt Weill correspondence, on deposit at LCM; Moss Hart, "The Saga of Gertie," *The New York Times,* March 2, 1941; Benjamin Welles, "Lyricist of 'The Saga of Jenny,' et. al.," *The New York Times,* May 25, 1941; various other contemporary clippings and materials on deposit at TAC–LCL. The text of *Lady in the Dark* is reprinted in Stanley Richards, ed., *Great Musicals of the American Theatre,* Volume 2 (Radnor, Pa., 1976), pp. 55–123. For score and recordings, see the appropriate lists below.

The account of the meeting of Weill and Hart and the inception of their idea is assembled mainly from: Moss Hart's preface to the *Lady in the Dark* vocal score; "The How and Why of 'Lady in the Dark,' " in the show's souvenir program; and "It Happened This Way," unsigned article in the *Brooklyn Daily Eagle,* February 23, 1941. The information at the beginning about *The Common Glory* and the Davy Crockett project comes from letters to Paul Green (PGP).

The passages from Ira Gershwin, *Lyrics on Several Occasions,* are as follows: "The food was excellent," p. 201; "an enormous ranch," p. 208; "The third musical dream sequence," p. 207; "a six- or seven-minute . . . dissertation," pp. 207–8; his various remarks on the abandonment of the Minstrel Show and the "Zodiac Song," p. 208; his story of the "Tschaikowsky" song is on p. 187; the casting of Victor Mature, p. 144; Danny Kaye and Gertrude Lawrence performing the Circus sequence, pp. 208–9.

Weill's conception of the sequences as "little one-act operas" is in his jacket notes for the original cast recording of *Street Scene* (see discography). The meeting at Sam H. Harris's office and Weill's remark about "lunch at Child's" are in a letter from Weill to Ira Gershwin, September 2, 1940 (LCM); as is some of the material on the abandonment of the "Zodiac Song." The information on Gertrude Lawrence's activities after the New York closing of *Skylark* is from an article in the *New York Herald Tribune,* January 12, 1941. The contretemps with the Group Theatre over Victor Mature is in *The New York Times* of November 13, 14, and 15, 1940. Weill's view of the "Wedding Dream" as "a little slow, dragging and humorless" is in a letter from him to Ira Gershwin, September 14, 1940 (LCM). The information that Weill composed the melody of "My Ship" before the lyrics were written comes from Lotte Lenya, in my interview with her of May 27, 1976. George S. Kaufman's telegram is in *Weill–Lenya.*

Chapter 22—A Composer in Wartime

Virgil Thomson's earlier remarks, "Weill is not a Great Composer," are in "Most Melodious Tears," *Modern Music*, November–December 1933, pp. 13–17; his later remarks, from "monotonous, heavy" onward, are from "Plays with Music," the *New York Herald Tribune*, February 23, 1941. Weill's reaction to Thomson's criticism, as well as "it's lots of fun," are from his letter to Ira Gershwin of March 8, 1941 (LCM). The account of the success of *Lady in the Dark* also is derived from the Weill–Gershwin correspondence, as well as from contemporary newspaper accounts. The story about Lenya at Klein's and Kurt's new suit is told by Morris Stonzek, in a personal interview. Aufricht on Weill's prosperity is in his autobiography, pp. 238–39. The information on Brook House comes mainly from the Weill–Gershwin correspondence, from the *New York Herald Tribune*, April 13, 1941, and from various interviews.

Weill's continuing work with *Lady in the Dark* and his search for new projects are drawn from the Weill–Gershwin correspondence and from contemporary newspaper accounts. Georg Kaiser and *Billy Budd* is in Schürer, *Kaiser*, p. 139. Weill's remark about Gertrude Lawrence's voice sounding "a little shaky" is in a letter to Gershwin of March 8, 1941, and his statement that "it seems too silly just to write music" is in a letter to Gershwin of May 28, 1941 (both at LCM). Gershwin's "I felt then" is from a letter he wrote to Weill on January 15, 1942, a carbon copy of which is on deposit with the Weill–Gershwin correspondence, LCM.

It's Fun to Be Free is reprinted in *The Best One-Act Plays of 1941* (New York, 1942), pp. 233–54; and the background is supplied by Ben Hecht, *A Child of the Century* (New York, 1954), p. 518, and the Weill–Gershwin correspondence. The correspondence, along with *Weill–Lenya*, also supplies information on the various patriotic songs, as well as the Walt Whitman songs; also see list of compositions.

The account of *Lunch Time Follies* is derived from: Arlene Wolf, "Lunchtime Follies, S.R.O.," *The New York Times Magazine*, July 11, 1943; Kurt Weill, "A Coke, a Sandwich, and Us," a hitherto unpublished manuscript printed in Drew, *Schriften*, pp. 85–90 (this is the source of the quote about "the spontaneity, the unfeigned popular touch," p. 87, which I have translated back from the German); and a personal interview with Harold Rome.

The material on the renewed contact between Weill and Brecht in 1942 comes from: Völker, *Brecht*, pp. 282–305, and *Brecht Chronicle*, pp. 102–28; and Bertolt Brecht, *Arbeitsjournal* (2 volumes, Frankfurt am Main, 1973), Volume 1, p. 414.

We Will Never Die: Ben Hecht, *A Child of the Century*, pp. 550–57; Jerome Lawrence, *Actor: The Life & Times of Paul Muni* (New York, 1974), p. 276; the Weill–Gershwin correspondence; various contemporary newspaper accounts; and a privately published text of the play, on deposit at TAC–LCL. Aufricht's story about himself, Brecht, and Weill and the *Schweik* project is in his memoirs, pp. 250–51 and 256. Weill mentions his work on the army film in a letter to Ira Gershwin, May 15, 1944, in TAC–LCL. Weill's swearing-in as a citizen is from *The New York Times*, August 28, 1943, and Abravanel, "Weill," p. 67. Brecht's FBI file has been examined by Professor James K. Lyon of the University of California at San Diego, as reported by *The New York Times* on March 31, 1979. A copy of the

Department of Justice letter to Victor Samrock, along with an earlier letter by Samrock swearing to Weill's loyalty, is in the Playwrights Company papers, on deposit at the State Historical Society of Wisconsin. "It's strange" is from Jean Dalrymple's press release for *One Touch of Venus*, Fall 1943. Various people have recalled Weill's fondness for the drugstore in New City; the remark that "the Germans have arrived" is recalled by Rita Weill.

Chapter 23—Broadway Sophistication: *One Touch of Venus*

The basic materials for the chapter were: F. Anstey (Thomas Anstey Guthrie), *The Tinted Venus, A Farcical Romance* (New York, 1898); Cheryl Crawford, *One Naked Individual;* Mary Martin, *My Heart Belongs* (New York, 1976), pp. 122–32; the Leah Salisbury papers, on deposit at the Butler Library, Columbia University; and the text of *One Touch of Venus* as reprinted in Stanley Richards, ed., *Ten Great Musicals of the American Theatre.* For printed music and recordings, see the appropriate lists, below.

Weill's "first-rate idea" is in a letter to Ira Gershwin, November 13, 1941; his near-involvement with *La Belle Hélène* is also in the Weill–Gershwin correspondence (LCM). The ensuing account of the gestation of *Venus* is from Cheryl Crawford, *One Naked Individual*, pp. 116–25, and a personal interview with her; as well as from contemporary newspaper accounts. Mary Martin's story of "That's Him" and Mainbocher is in *My Heart Belongs*, pp. 122–23. The details about Irene Sharaff are in Kurt Weill's correspondence with Leah Salisbury, in her papers, cited above. In the ensuing description of the play the background information comes primarily from Cheryl Crawford, pp. 128–44, and a personal interview. Oscar Hammerstein's response to Mary Martin as "the innocent, eager little girl" is in *My Heart Belongs*, p. 130. Elliott Carter's remarks are from "Theatre and Films, 1943," *Modern Music*, November 1943, reprinted in his *Writings*, pp. 95–96.

Chapter 24—Last Efforts with Ira Gershwin

The general background was supplied by: Ira Gershwin, *Lyrics on Several Occasions;* the Weill–Gershwin correspondence, LCM; Edwin Justus Mayer, *The Firebrand* (New York: Samuel French, 1924). For printed music and recordings, see the appropriate lists below.

Ogden Nash's remarks are in his "Lines from a Lyricist at Bay," *The New York Times*, August 20, 1944. The details on sounds Weill liked to hear while composing come from various newspaper interviews and from Rita Weill. His remarks to *Life* magazine are in "Music of Kurt Weill Called Unusual," by Warren Storey Smith, the issue of October 25, 1943. The killing pace of orchestrating his own music was commented upon by Harold Rome, in a personal interview. Weill was called a "creative commuter" by Thornton Delehanty in his article, "Kurt Weill, a Commuter to Hollywood," in the *New York Herald Tribune*, June 3, 1945; this also is the source of Weill's subsequent quoted remarks about *Where Do We Go from Here?* Otis L. Guernsey, Jr.'s review of *Knickerbocker Holiday* was in the *New York Herald Tribune* of April 20, 1944. The background on Weill's relationship with Leah Salisbury, and his remarks to her about Hollywood, are in her papers, passim, and especially in his letter to her of February 15, 1944.

The background on *The Firebrand of Florence* comes from the Weill–Gershwin correspondence and from contemporary newspaper items. The contract for the Nell Gwynne musical is among the papers of Edwin Justus Mayer, TAC–LCL. Weill's being approached about *The Firebrand*, and his being "very unenthusiastic" are in a letter to Gershwin of February 27, 1944 (LCM). Gershwin's authorship of a song in the 1924 *Firebrand* is in *The Gershwin Years*, p. 354, and his statement on being able "to do a lot of things" is quoted by its authors, Edward Jablonski and Lawrence D. Stewart, in their jacket copy for the record *Ira Gershwin Loves to Rhyme* (see discography). Weill's "more as a light opera" is in a letter to Gershwin, May 15, 1944, a carbon of which is on deposit at TAC–LCL. The short history of various *Firebrand* musicals is based on the Weill–Gershwin correspondence, LCM, and accounts in *The New York Times* of June 22, 1944, and March 18, 1945. The "intelligent, intimate operetta" is in the May 15, 1944, letter to Gershwin.

The possibility of Ezio Pinza for the Cellini role comes from Morris Stonzek, in a personal interview. The change from Walter Slezak to Melville Cooper and its effect on Lenya: David Beams, "Lotte Lenya," *Theater Arts*, June 1962, p. 18. The information on Lenya's career in America is mainly from *Weill–Lenya*; the exchange about her between Abravanel and Weill is in Abravanel, "Weill," p. 67. Lenya's remark that "my style would never ever jell, etc.," is in the David Beams *Theater Arts* article, p. 18. The rumors of an antagonism between Lenya and Melville Cooper were conveyed to me by Morris Stonzek in a personal interview. "Unfortunately, one of the principals" is in an unsigned review in the *Boston Post*, March 4, 1945. Billy Rose's comments are in his syndicated "Pitching Horseshoes" column, sometime in the first third of 1947: from an undated clipping in the possession of Morris Stonzek. Ira Gershwin's story of the composing of "Sing Me Not a Ballad" is in *Lyrics on Several Occasions*, p. 106. George Jean Nathan's comments are in "When There Is Little Left for the Critic to Say," *New York Journal-American*, April 2, 1945.

Chapter 25—Broadway Opera: *Street Scene*

"Here in America" is from the Thornton Delehanty *Herald Tribune* article of June 3, 1945, already cited. The idea for a movie on Joseph Jefferson is dealt with in a letter from Maxwell Anderson to George Cukor in the fall of 1945, printed in Avery, *Dramatist in America*, pp. 199–200. The 1945 revision of *Ulysses Africanus* is dealt with in contemporary newspaper items, and in Maxwell Anderson's diary, particularly for July 1945 (MAC). Nash, Perelman, and the "very hot jazz composer" are in a letter from Weill to Leah Salisbury, April 19, 1945.

The account of the inception of *Down in the Valley* is assembled from: Olin Downes, *The New York Times*, July 11, 1948; Hans W. Heinsheimer, *The New York Times*, May 29, 1949; Kurt Weill, a letter to the editor of *The New York Times*, June 5, 1949; and a personal interview with Morris Stonzek. For score and recordings, see the appropriate lists.

The account of Weill's *Kiddush* is based on an exchange of letters and a telephone interview with Cantor David J. Putterman, who also was so kind as to make a copy of the music available to me. See also the discography.

The account of *A Flag Is Born* comes from: Jerome Lawrence, *Actor*, pp. 291–95; the souvenir program; and contemporary accounts and reviews. Howard Barnes's remark is in the *New York Herald Tribune* of September 15, 1946. Brooks

Atkinson's review is in *The New York Times* of September 7, 1946. Weill's election
to the Playwrights Company is from Wharton, *Life Among the Playwrights*, p. 51,
and a personal interview with Victor Samrock.

Weill's account of the inception of *Street Scene* is in his "Score for a Play," *The
New York Times*, January 5, 1947. The possibility of Anderson's participation in
the project is hinted at in his diary, especially for August 1945 (MAC). Weill's "I
address myself to Americans" is in "Broadway's First Real Opera," by Shana
Ager, in *PM*, February 9, 1947; this also is the source of "First we said." Much of
the account that follows is from Elmer Rice, *Minority Report*, pp. 411–13, and John
F. Wharton, *Life Among the Playwrights*, pp. 151–56. Wharton, pp. 153–54, and
Victor Samrock in a personal interview, are the sources on Elmer Rice's resistance
to changes in his text. Langston Hughes's recollections of Weill are in a brief
memoir published in Drew, *Über KW*, pp. 141–44. "First, I could see the country"
is from the Shana Ager interview. Wharton is the source of the following quotes:
"trouble began," p. 153; "One character in the play," p. 153; "Wiman," p. 151; "I
can reorchestrate," p. 153. Further information about the casting comes from the
New York Herald Tribune of December 31, 1946, and January 6, 1947. Abravanel's
"as though it were Bach" is from a telephone interview. Charles Friedman's
remark, which is quoted further on—"it was too much musical comedy"—is from
an undated newspaper clipping of the time (TAC–LCL). Rice's description of the
tryout as "cataclysmic" is in his *Minority Report*, p. 412.

The text of Elmer Rice's original *Street Scene* can be found in, among other
places, his *Three Plays* (New York, 1965); the text of the opera, including the
purely spoken passages, is complete in the piano-vocal score edition (see list of
compositions). For recordings, see discography. The remark about "a tired and
discouraged Puccini" is in *Variety*, December 18, 1946 (it was made with reference
to the Philadelphia production). Harold Rome's remark about "a good composer"
is from a personal interview. There is a recording of Hindemith himself
conducting the New York Philharmonic in *A Requiem for Those We Love*, with
Louise Parker, George London, and the Schola Cantorum of New York (Odyssey
Y–33821). Weill's remarks about the evolution of his approach to opera are on the
jacket of the original cast recording of *Street Scene* (see discography).

Chapter 26—Promised Lands

Olin Downes's remarks are in *The New York Times*, January 26, 1947. Weill's
feelings about Gian Carlo Menotti were conveyed to me by Morris Stonzek in a
personal interview. The dispute over the advertising of *Street Scene* is in Wharton,
Life Among the Playwrights, pp. 155–56. The material on Weill's brother, on Kurt's
own state of health at the time, on his parents, on his Jewish feelings, and on his
decision to go to Palestine comes from Rita Weill. The details of his trip are
gleaned primarily from memoranda among the Leah Salisbury papers and the
Playwrights Company papers, as well as from two letters Weill wrote to Maxwell
and Mab Anderson (MAC), one from Nahariya on May 30, 1947, the other from
New City (the Andersons were in California) on June 22, 1947, just after his
return. Meyer Weisgal's recollection of escorting Weill to Nahariya is from a
personal interview. The quote from the *Palestine Post* is in the issue of June 2, 1947.
Lenya's remarks to Mab Anderson are in a letter of May 23, 1947 (MAC).

The William Saroyan proposal is in a letter from him to Kurt Weill, dated February 21, 1947, on display at the *Weill–Lenya* exhibition at Lincoln Center, New York (cited above). The information on *Aurora Dawn* comes from a letter to me from Herman Wouk, April 30, 1978. The background on *Love Life* comes primarily from Cheryl Crawford, *One Naked Individual*, pp. 168–71, from a personal interview with her, and from contemporary newspaper items. A typescript of the play is on deposit at TAC–LCL. On sheet music and recordings, see the appropriate lists below.

"I do not consider myself a German composer": *Life*, March 10, 1947. Orchestration of *Hatikvah:* on the Chaim Weizmann testimonial dinner, *The New York Times*, November 26, 1947; on the Boston Symphony performance, letter to Kurt Weill from Serge Koussevitzky, December 1, 1947, displayed at *Weill–Lenya* exhibit, cited above. Weill's remark on "the drugstore in New City" is in "Talk of the Town," *The New Yorker*, June 10, 1944. Much of Brecht's testimony before the House Un-American Activities Committee is reprinted in Demetz, *Brecht*, pp. 30–32, among other places. It was recorded and has been offered for commercial distribution by Folkways Records.

The ensuing account of *Down in the Valley* comes from the *New York Times* items by Heinsheimer and Weill, already cited, and from Wolfgang Roth in a personal interview. Lenya's impressions of Bloomington and of the return trip are in a letter to Mab Anderson of July 27, 1948 (MAC). For score and recordings of *Down in the Valley*, see appropriate lists below.

Alan Jay Lerner's "the audience stood up" is in his memoir, *The Street Where I Live* (New York, 1978), p. 241. Brooks Atkinson's review is in *The New York Times*, October 8, 1948. Cheryl Crawford's remarks are on p. 171 of her book.

Chapter 27—Musical Tragedy: *Lost in the Stars*

Weill in Hollywood in the fall of 1948: the Leah Salisbury papers; a letter from Weill to Maxwell Anderson, undated, from Hollywood at this time (MAC). Social life on South Mountain Road: recollections of various persons interviewed; Maxwell Anderson diaries, passim (MAC); a letter from Lenya to Mab Anderson, July 6, 1948 (MAC), describes watching the Republican convention at the Caniffs'. The Weills and *Anne of the Thousand Days*: Anderson diaries, passim; the Kurt Weill letter from Hollywood, cited just above; Lenya's casting suggestion for Anne Boleyn is in her letter to Mab Anderson of July 6, 1948 (MAC). The incident of the "boom-boom-boom school" is in Joshua Logan, *Movie Stars, Real People, and Me* (New York, 1978), pp. 177–81. The idea for a spaceship musical is in the Anderson diary, especially March 10, 1947; and a letter from Kurt Weill to Maxwell Anderson, July 10, 1947, with a "Suggested Outline," apparently written by John F. Wharton, appended to it (MAC).

The story of the early genesis of *Lost in the Stars* aboard the S.S. *Mauretania* and just after is told by Anderson in his acceptance speech, given on February 2, 1950, of the Brotherhood Award of the National Conference of Christians and Jews; this is reprinted in Avery, *Dramatist in America*, pp. 298–301. Maxwell Anderson's remarks to Paton about "the form and the dialogue" are in a letter of March 15, 1948, reprinted in Avery, *Dramatist in America*, pp. 221–22. The early, less musical, conception of the play, and Daniel L. Haynes are from items in *The*

New York Times on May 7, 1948, and May 22, 1949. Most of the story about obtaining Rouben Mamoulian as director is from a telephone interview with Mamoulian; but, "on April 23 he said to us," is from Anderson's article "Assembling the Parts for a Musical Play," in the *New York Herald Tribune*, October 30, 1949; Anderson's remark that the subject "fitted exactly" into their old *Ulysses Africanus* scheme is from the Brotherhood Award speech. Weill's statement that they "had tried to do a musical play about racial problems" is in Harry Gilroy, "Written in the Stars," *The New York Times*, October 30, 1949, as is "a rare quality."

Anderson's letter to Paul Robeson of March 3, 1939, is in Avery, *Dramatist in America*, pp. 85–86. "There are a good many Negro actors" is in the article "Assembling the Parts for a Musical Play," cited above; this is the source of all the quotes down to "There's nobody else." The discussion of the matter of a conductor is mostly from Lehman Engel, *This Bright Day*, p. 96. The "Well, Rouben" story was told to me by Rouben Mamoulian in a telephone interview.

The text of *Lost in the Stars* is reprinted in Stanley Richards, ed., *Great Musicals of the American Theatre*, volume 2 (Radnor, Pa., 1976), pp. 125–76; from Alan Paton, *Cry, the Beloved Country* (New York, 1948). For the score and recordings, see the appropriate lists below. Weill's "It's not harmony and it's not melody" is in the Harry Gilroy article cited above. His observation that some six or eight of the numbers are songs is in Vernon Rice, "Mamoulian Has a Fan in Weill," the *New York Post*, October 26, 1949. "For it is the dawn" is on p. 273 of *Cry, the Beloved Country*.

Chapter 28—A Bird of Passage

Weill's letter to Olin Downes is quoted by Downes in "People's Composer," *The New York Times*, April 9, 1950. Arnold Sundgaard on the new opera being planned is from a press release, April 25, 1950, for the RCA Victor recording of *Down in the Valley*. The point about *Aurora Dawn* is in the Herman Wouk letter to me of April 30, 1978. The material on *Huckleberry Finn* comes from: contemporary newspaper accounts; the Maxwell Anderson diaries, especially December 1949 through March 1950 (this also is the source on the Hustons and *Moby Dick*, and on Major André); Anderson's handwritten rough draft of the play (this, and the diaries, in MAC); and a telephone interview with Rouben Mamoulian.

The story of the decline in the box office for *Lost in the Stars* and the dispute over the California engagement comes from: contemporary newspaper accounts; the Anderson diary, February–March 1950; letter from Weill to Victor Samrock, with carbons to the other members, of March 10, 1950 (carbon in MAC); Wharton, *Life Among the Playwrights*, p. 192; interviews with Victor Samrock and Rouben Mamoulian. Details about Weill's irritability come from the Leah Salisbury papers and from personal interviews.

With the exception of the quote from Lehman Engel, *This Bright Day*, p. 96, the account of Weill's final attack of psoriasis, heart attack, and death is entirely from Anderson's diary, February–April 1950 (MAC). The time of Weill's death is given in the *New York Times* obituary of April 4, 1950. Anderson's eulogy is in a typescript on deposit among his papers (MAC). Other details about the funeral are from his diary, April 5, 1950 (MAC), and from interviews with Rouben Mamoulian and Alan H. Anderson.

Epilogue—Since 1950: The Legacy of Kurt Weill

Closing of *Lost in the Stars: The New York Times*, June 21, 1950; and personal interview with Victor Samrock. The subsequent career of *Huckleberry Finn:* Avery, *Dramatist in America*, especially pp. lxiv–lxv; *Time*, August 21, l964, has an article on the German television production.

The information on the two early Weill memorial concerts is from contemporary newspaper items. Olin Downes's comments are in *The New York Times*, July 9, 1950. The two pieces of Virgil Thomson's which are quoted are from the *New York Herald Tribune* of April 9, 1950, and of February 5, 1951. The information on Weill revivals from 1949 to 1952 comes from contemporary newspaper items and Martin Esslin's list of Brecht productions in America at the end of his *Brecht*, pp. 352–63. Some of the information concerning Marc Blitzstein and *The Threepenny Opera* comes from a telephone interview with Maurice Abravanel. Some of the material on the Theatre de Lys production comes from *Weill–Lenya* and other printed sources, but most of the discussion here is based upon my own recollections of the production and the mood of the time. The discussion of Lenya's subsequent career is from *Weill–Lenya*; from several of her letters in MAC; and from the various recordings she has done, listed in the discography. Alan Jay Lerner's *The Street Where I Live* is the source of the fact that Weill was thinking of Rex Harrison for a *Threepenny Opera* revival, p. 49, and of a remark concerning Lenya's voice and Weill's melodies: "From that moment on [i.e., the time of *The Threepenny Opera*], he told me, he kept hearing her voice in every melody he wrote . . ." p. 80. The remark quoted in the text is from the insert to her recording of Weill's *Berlin Theatre Songs* (see discography).

Andrew Porter's remarks are from his "Musical Events" column in *The New Yorker* of November 13, 1978, p. 231.

Kurt Weill's
Principal Compositions

This list is complete as to works published by early 1979; although in the case of shows, operas, and other works containing songs, arias, or other component parts, only a few or none of the components are mentioned separately, for reasons of space. As to unpublished works, I have listed every one that has, to my knowledge, been publicly performed; and some others besides. Film adaptations of Weill scores are not mentioned, but his original film scores are. The arrangement of materials is year by year, according to the date of composition; under each year, they are arranged roughly in chronological order of composition so far as can be determined. Each entry is followed by information regarding publication or lack thereof; if it is fairly certain that a work has been entirely lost, this is mentioned. All information about tapes and recordings is reserved for the discography.

1910–11. First opera, based on "an old German play about knights and their ladies," possibly by Karl Theodor Körner. Unpublished and lost.

1914–18. Early songs. One of them, *"Im Volkston,"* is based on a poem by Arno Holz. Unpublished.

1919. *Die Weise von Liebe und Tod des Cornets Christoph Rilke* ("The Lay of the Love and Death of Cornet Christopher Rilke"), a symphonic poem based on the work of that title by Rainer Maria Rilke. Unpublished.

1919–20. String Quartet in B minor. Unpublished.
    Sonata for Cello and Piano. Unpublished.
    Ninon von Lenclos, one-act opera, based on a play of that title by Ernst Hardt. Unpublished and at least partly lost.

Das hohe Lied, one-act opera, based on the novel of that title (known in English as *The Song of Songs*) by Hermann Sudermann. Unpublished and at least partly lost.

Shulamith, oratorio, based on the biblical "Song of Songs." Unpublished.

"Maikatter Lied" ("May Tomcat Song"), based on a poem by Nathan Birnbaum. Unpublished and probably lost.

1921. Symphony no. 1. Study score, Edition Schott 5937 (Mainz: B. Schott's Söhne, 1968).

Arrangement of Symphony no. 1 for two pianos. Unpublished.

1922. Divertimento for Small Orchestra with Male Chorus. Unpublished.

Sinfonia Sacra (Fantasia, Passacaglia und Hymnus), Op. 6. Unpublished.

Busoni's Divertimento for Flute and Orchestra, Op. 52, arranged for flute and piano. Edition Breitkopf 5205 (Leipzig: Breitkopf & Härtel, no date).

Die Zaubernacht ("The Magic Night"), children's ballet. Unpublished and apparently lost.

1923. *Recordare (Lamentationes Jeremiae Prophetae)*. Unpublished.

String Quartet, Op. 8. Full score, UE 7699; parts score, UE 7700; study score, "Philharmonia" no. 474 (Vienna: Universal Edition, 1924).

Quodlibet, Op. 9. Orchestral score, UE 8348 (Vienna: Universal Edition, 1924).

Frauentanz: Sieben Gedichte des Mittelalters für Sopran, mit Flöte, Bratsche, Klarinette, Horn und Fagott ("Women's Dance: Seven Medieval Poems for Soprano, with Flute, Viola, Clarinet, Horn and Bassoon"), Op. 10. Full score, UE 7599N (Vienna: Universal Edition, 1924).

Stundenbuch ("Book of Hours") for Voice and Orchestra, based on poems of Rainer Maria Rilke. Unpublished; three of the five songs apparently are lost.

1924. Weill–Busoni, Arrangement for Piano of Dance no. 3 from *Frauentanz*. Unpublished.

Concerto for Violin and Wind Orchestra, Op. 12. Full score, UE 8340; violin and piano score, UE 8339 (Vienna: Universal Edition, 1924, 1965).

1925. *Der Protagonist*, one-act opera with libretto by Georg Kaiser, based on Kaiser's play of the same name. Piano-vocal score, UE 8387 (Vienna: Universal Edition, 1926).

Der neue Orpheus, Op. 15 ("The New Orpheus"), cantata for soprano, solo violin, and orchestra, based on the poem of the same name by Yvan Goll. Piano-vocal score, UE 8472 (Vienna: Universal Edition, 1926, 1954).

1926. *Royal Palace*, one-act opera with libretto by Yvan Goll. Piano-vocal score, UE 8690 (Vienna: Universal Edition, 1927). Weill's orchestration has been lost.

Music for radio production of Christian Dietrich Grabbe's *Herzog von Gothland*. Unpublished.

Na und, comic opera in three acts, libretto by Felix Joachimson (Felix Jackson). Unpublished and apparently lost.

1927. Incidental music for a production of August Strindberg's *Gustavus III*. Unpublished.

Der Zar lässt sich photographieren ("The Tsar Has His Picture Taken"), opera buffa in one act, libretto by Georg Kaiser. Piano-vocal score, UE 8964 (Vienna: Universal Edition, 1927).

Mahagonny Songspiel, with text by Bertolt Brecht. Piano-vocal score, UE 12889 (Vienna: Universal Edition, 1927). Includes "Alabama Song," "Benares Song," and "*Gott in Mahagonny.*"

"*Vom Tod im Wald*" ("Death in the Forest"), Op. 22, ballad for bass voice and ten wind instruments, based on a poem by Bertolt Brecht. Unpublished.

1928. "*Die Muschel von Margate*" ("The Mussel of Margate"), song with text by Felix Gasbarra, composed for the play *Konjunktur*, by Leo Lania. Published in the Kurt Weill *Song-Album*, UE 9787 (Vienna: Universal Edition, 1929).

Incidental music for the play *Katalaunische Schlacht*, by Arnolt Bronnen. Unpublished.

Die Dreigroschenoper ("The Threepenny Opera"), a play with music, text by Bertolt Brecht, after John Gay's *The Beggar's Opera*. Piano-vocal score, UE 8851; study score, "Philharmonia" no. 400 (Vienna: Universal Edition, 1928, 1956). Includes "Moritat of Mackie Messer," "Pirate Jenny," "Barbara Song," "Cannon Song," "On the Inadequacy of Human Striving," and the Tango Ballad.

Kleine Dreigroschenmusik, Suite for Wind Orchestra from *Die Dreigroschenoper*. Full score, UE 9712 (Vienna: Universal Edition, 1929).

Das Berliner Requiem ("Berlin Requiem"), small cantata for male voices and wind orchestra, after texts by Bertolt Brecht. Piano-vocal score, UE 9786 (Vienna: Universal Edition, 1929). Includes "*Marterl*" and "The Drowned Maiden."

1929. *Der Lindberghflug* ("The Lindbergh Flight"), radio cantata for soloists and orchestra. Full score, with English translation by George Antheil, UE 8838; piano-vocal score, UE 9938 (Vienna: Universal Edition, 1930). Later editions, with Brecht's altered text, are entitled *Ozeanflug*.

Aufstieg und Fall der Stadt Mahagonny ("The Rise and Fall of the City of Mahagonny"), opera in three acts, with libretto by Bertolt Brecht. Piano-vocal score, UE 9851 (Vienna: Universal Edition, 1930, 1969). Includes the *Songspiel* numbers, as well as the "Havana Song" and "*Wie man sich bettet.*" Universal Edition owns an unpublished promptbook for *Mahagonny* directors, written by Weill with Caspar Neher and perhaps Brecht.

Happy End, a comedy with music in three acts—adapted, according to the credits, by Elisabeth Hauptmann from a story by Dorothy Lane, with song texts by Bertolt Brecht. Piano-vocal score, UE 11685 (Vienna: Universal Edition, 1929, 1958). Includes "Surabaya Johnny," the "Bilbao Song," and the "Sailors' Song."

"*Berlin in Licht–Song*" ("Berlin in Lights Song"). Single sheet, for voice and piano, UE 8862 (Vienna: Universal Edition, 1929).

"*Das Lied von den braunen Inseln*" ("The Song of the Brown Islands"), with text by Lion Feuchtwanger, song for Feuchtwanger's play *Die Petroleuminseln*. Published in the Kurt Weill *Song-Album*, UE 9787 (Vienna: Universal Edition, 1929).

The Kurt Weill *Song-Album,* cited just above, includes not only *"Die Muschel von Margate"* and *"Das Lied von den braunen Inseln,"* both already cited, but also these four songs from other scores: *"Marterl"* ("Memorial Tablet") and *"Zu Potsdam unter den Eichen"* ("To Potsdam Under the Oaks") from *Das Berliner Requiem* (the latter, however, was subsequently removed by Weill from the *Berlin Requiem);* *"Ballade von der Sexuelle Hörigkeit"* ("Ballad of Sexual Need"), which had been dropped from the original production of *The Threepenny Opera;* and *"Vorstellung des Fliegers Lindbergh"* ("Presentation of the Flier Lindbergh") from *Der Lindberghflug.* Incidental music for *Das Lied von Hoboken.* Unpublished and apparently lost.

1930. *Der Jasager* ("He Who Says Yes"), school opera in two acts, with a libretto by Bertolt Brecht adapted from Arthur Waley's English translation of Zenchiku's *Taniko.* Piano-vocal score, UE 8206 (Vienna: Universal Edition, 1930, 1957).

Incidental music for Brecht's *Mann ist Mann,* produced in Berlin on February 6, 1931. Unpublished and apparently lost.

1931. *Die Bürgschaft* ("The Pledge"), opera in three acts, with libretto by Caspar Neher. Piano-vocal score, UE 1525 (Vienna: Universal Edition, 1931).

1932. *"Das Blinde Mädchen"* ("The Blind Girl"), song, with text by Günther Weisenborn, for the "Red Revue" *Wir sind ja sooo zufrieden . . . .* Unpublished.

Der Silbersee ("The Silver Lake"), a "winter's tale" in three acts, with libretto by Georg Kaiser. Piano-vocal score, UE 10464 (Vienna: Universal Edition, 1933). Includes *"Lied der Fennimore"* and "Caesar's Death."

1933. Possible sketches for score of film, *Kleine Mann, Was Nun?* The work was never completed, and whatever sketches may have been done are undoubtedly lost.

Die Sieben Todsünden der Kleinbürger ("The Seven Deadly Sins of the Petits Bourgeois"), *"Ballet chanté,"* with text by Bertolt Brecht. Piano-vocal score, Edition Schott 6005 (Mainz: B. Schott's Söhne, 1956).

1934. Symphony no. 2. Study Score, Edition Schott 5512 (Mainz: B. Schott's Söhne; and Paris: Heugel et Cie., 1966).

Suite from *Der Silbersee.* Unpublished.

Various single sheet songs: *"Youkali: Tango Habanera,"* lyrics by Roger Fernay (Paris: Heugel et Cie., 1946); *"Complainte de la Seine"* and *"Je ne t'aime pas,"* lyrics by Maurice Magre (Paris: Heugel et Cie., 1934); *"Der Abschiedsbrief"* ("The Farewell Letter"), lyrics by Erich Kästner, unpublished; other songs, possibly with Jean Cocteau and with Jacques Deval.

Marie Galante, a play in ten scenes with music, by Jacques Deval. Songs for voice and piano published in separate sheets (Paris: Heugel et Cie., 1934). Among the seven songs are: *"J'attends un navire," "Les Filles de Bordeaux,"* and *"Le Roi d'Aquitaine."*

1935. *A Kingdom for a Cow,* comic operetta, with an English libretto by Reginald Arkell and Desmond Carter, adapted from *Der Kuhhandel,* by Robert Vambery.

Two of its songs—"As Long as I Love" and "Two Hearts"—were published in separate sheets by Chappell & Co., Ltd., London, in 1935; in the United States the copyright was renewed and is owned by Chappell and TRO–Hampshire House Publishing Organization. "As Long as I Love" has been reprinted in *The Genius of Kurt Weill* (New York: Chappell & Co., no date).

"*Nanna's Lied*," song with text by Bertolt Brecht. It is not clear when this was written—very likely a year or two earlier; but it may have been the song that Weill gave Lotte Lenya to sing in an operetta in Zurich in the spring of 1935. In its present form, it is in an arrangement and a French translation by Boris Vian. Unpublished.

The Eternal Road, dramatic oratorio in four parts, with text by Franz Werfel, translated into English by Ludwig Lewisohn. Piano-vocal score, published only for rehearsal purposes (Paris: Heugel et Cie., 1935). Individual songs were published in sheets in the United States by Chappell & Co.—e.g., "Promise," "Song of Miriam," "The Dance of the Golden Calf," "Song of Ruth," and others—in 1937, and the copyright is now owned by Chappell and TRO–Hampshire House. The complete piano-vocal score is very rare; there is a copy on deposit in the Norman Bel Geddes Collection at the Humanities Research Center, University of Texas at Austin. "Song of Ruth" has been reprinted in *The Genius of Kurt Weill*.

1936. *Johnny Johnson*, a musical play, with text by Paul Green. Piano-vocal score (New York: Samuel French, Inc., 1941); this, too, is rare, having been withdrawn from circulation after Chappell claimed the copyright—the only copies I saw of it were in private hands. Three of the songs—"Johnny's Song," "Oh, Heart of Love," and "Mon Ami, My Friend"—have been reprinted in *Kurt Weill in America* (New York: Chappell & Co., 1975).

A High Wind in Jamaica, sketches for a film score, never completed. Autograph copies are on deposit at LCM.

1937. Probable sketches for the movie *The River Is Blue*. This eventually became *Blockade*, and Weill does not have a credit line for it; but even if none of his music was used for it, what he did write surely still exists in manuscript.

Sketches for an uncompleted musical, with book by Bella and Samuel Spewack, and lyrics by E. Y. Harburg. Unpublished.

"*Pauv' Madame Peachum*," additional song for the 1937 Paris production of *The Threepenny Opera*, sung by Yvette Guilbert as Madame Peachum. Unpublished.

Sketches for *The Ballad of Davy Crockett*, musical play with text by Hoffman R. Hays, never completed. Unpublished.

Sketches for *The Common Glory*, musical play with text by Paul Green, never completed. Unpublished.

1938. Two songs for the Fritz Lang movie *You and Me:* "You Can't Get Something for Nothing" and "The Right Guy for Me," both with lyrics by Sam Coslow. Unpublished.

Knickerbocker Holiday, a musical comedy, with book and lyrics by Maxwell Anderson. Piano-vocal score (New York: DeSylva, Brown & Henderson, 1938);

four of the songs—"It Never Was You," "September Song," "There's Nowhere to Go But Up," and "Will You Remember Me?"—are in *Kurt Weill in America*.

"Bring the Bricks" ("*Havu Lavanim*"), arrangement of Hebrew work song. Sheet music for voice and piano (New York: Hechalutz Organization of America, 1938).

1939. Songs for *Eneas Africanus* (later *Ulysses Africanus*), unpublished musical play with text by Maxwell Anderson, based on Harry Stillwell Edwards's novel of that title. The song "Lost in the Stars" and at least two others later used in the musical play of that name were written for *Eneas Africanus*. Most of the songs unpublished.

Railroads on Parade, dramatic pageant produced at the New York World's Fair, text by Edward Hungerford. Unpublished.

The Ballad of Magna Carta, cantata for solo voice, mixed chorus, and orchestra. Piano score, C-1035 (New York: Chappell & Co., 1940).

Incidental music for *Madam, Will You Walk*, a play by Sidney Howard; *Two on an Island*, a play by Elmer Rice; and an S. N. Behrman play that eventually (without the Weill music) became *The Pirate*. All unpublished.

1940. Revisions in score of *Railroads on Parade*.

Incidental music for *Journey to Jerusalem*, a play by Maxwell Anderson. Unpublished.

1941. *Lady in the Dark*, a musical play by Moss Hart, with lyrics by Ira Gershwin. Piano-vocal score (New York: Chappell & Co., 1941). Seven of the songs—"The Saga of Jenny," "My Ship," "Girl of the Moment," "One Life to Live," "The Princess of Pure Delight," "This Is New," and "Tschaikowsky"—are reprinted in *Kurt Weill in America*.

Incidental music for *It's Fun to Be Free*, pageant by Ben Hecht and Charles MacArthur. Unpublished.

1942. "Song of the Free," song with text by Archibald Macleish. Sheet music for voice and piano (New York: Chappell & Co., 1942).

Musical settings to recitations of patriotic texts by Helen Hayes. Unpublished.

Three Walt Whitman Songs: "Oh Captain! My Captain!" "Beat! Beat! Drums!" and "Dirge for Two Veterans," for voice and piano. The three songs in a single volume (New York: Chappell & Co., 1942).

"Inventory" and other songs for *Lunch Time Follies*. Unpublished.

1943. Music for *We Will Never Die*, a pageant by Ben Hecht. Unpublished.

"*Und Was bekam des Soldaten Weib?*", song to poem by Bertolt Brecht, and "*Wie lange noch?*", song to Walter Mehring poem, both unpublished.

One Touch of Venus, a musical comedy with book by S. J. Perelman and Ogden Nash, lyrics by Ogden Nash. No score edition; separate song sheets published (New York: Chappell & Co., 1943). Five of the songs—"Speak Low," "That's Him," "Foolish Heart," "The Trouble with Women," and "Westwind"—are reprinted in *Kurt Weill in America*.

1944. Music for one or more army training films.

Music for the film *Where Do We Go from Here?*, screenplay by Morrie Ryskind, lyrics by Ira Gershwin. Some of the songs published separately (New York: Chappell & Co., 1945). Four of them—"The Nina, the Pinta, the Santa Maria," "Song of the Rhineland," "All at Once," and "If Love Remains"—are reprinted in *Kurt Weill in America*.

1945. *The Firebrand of Florence*, a comic operetta, book by Edwin Justus Mayer and Ira Gershwin from Mayer's play *The Firebrand*, with lyrics by Ira Gershwin. No score edition; separate song sheets published (New York: Chappell & Co., 1945). Four of the songs—"Sing Me Not a Ballad," "There'll Be Life, Love and Laughter," "A Rhyme for Angela," and "You're Far Too Near Me"—are reprinted in *Kurt Weill in America*.

First version of *Down in the Valley* (see below, 1948).

1946. *Kiddush*, for cantor, mixed chorus, and organ. Printed in *Synagogue Music by Contemporary Composers* (New York: G. Schirmer, 1947).

A Flag Is Born, a dramatic pageant by Ben Hecht. Weill's incidental music is unpublished, but rehearsal blueprints of the manuscript are on deposit at LCM.

1947. *Street Scene*, an American opera, based on Elmer Rice's play of the same name, with book and some lyrics by Elmer Rice, and most lyrics by Langston Hughes. Piano-vocal score (New York: Chappell & Co., 1948). Five of the songs—"Lonely House," "We'll Go Away Together," "What Good Would the Moon Be?" "A Boy Like You," and "Moon-Faced, Starry-Eyed"—are reprinted in *Kurt Weill in America*; mention should also be made of Anna Maurrant's aria, "Somehow I Never Could Believe," and the duet, "Remember That I Care."

Symphonic suite from *Street Scene*. Unpublished.

More Walt Whitman songs. Unpublished.

Orchestration of "Hatikvah," Israel's national anthem. Unpublished.

1948. *Down in the Valley*, a folk opera, with libretto by Arnold Sundgaard. Piano-vocal score (New York: G. Schirmer, 1948).

Love Life, a vaudeville, with book and lyrics by Alan Jay Lerner. No score edition; separate song sheets published (New York: Chappell & Co., 1948). Seven of the songs—"Green-Up Time," "Here I'll Stay," "Susan's Dream," "Economics," "Love Song," "Mister Right," and "Is It Him or Is It Me?"—are reprinted in *Kurt Weill in America*.

1949. *Lost in the Stars*, a musical tragedy based on Alan Paton's novel *Cry, the Beloved Country*, with book and lyrics by Maxwell Anderson. Piano-vocal score (New York: Chappell & Co., 1950). Six of the songs—"Lost in the Stars," "Stay Well," "Trouble Man," "The Little Gray House," "Big Mole," and "Thousands of Miles"—are reprinted in *Kurt Weill in America*.

Other songs with Maxwell Anderson, for various possible projects. Unpublished.

1950. Songs for *Huckleberry Finn*, projected musical play based on Mark Twain's novel, with book and lyrics by Maxwell Anderson. The five songs Weill completed for this—"River Chanty," "Come In, Mornin'," "Catfish Song," "This Time Next Year," and "Apple Jack"—have been published in separate sheets (New York: Chappell & Co., 1952), and are reprinted in *Kurt Weill in America.*

A Kurt Weill Discography

No effort has been made here to list every recording ever produced of a piece of Kurt Weill music, down to the last individual song; the list would be endless. Even in the case of some of the larger works, not every record or tape is accounted for. What I have tried to do here above all is mention at least one reasonably accessible record or tape for as many Kurt Weill scores as have one or more. In the case of works for which several important recordings exist, the several are mentioned. Performance tapes of some works—such as *Der Protagonist* and *Der Zar lässt sich photographieren*—are on deposit with their publisher, but these are not accessible to the general public and therefore are not listed. For convenience of reference, the taped or recorded works are lined up in the order they follow in the list of compositions; this order has, of course, nothing to do with the date of the recording, which is only sometimes given.

Four of the early songs, including *"Im Volkston,"* were sung by Barry McDaniel, baritone, accompanied by Oliver Dreimann at the piano, during the 1975 Berlin Festival. A tape of this performance is on deposit at RHA–LCL.

String Quartet in B minor. This was performed by the Melos Quartet of Stuttgart at the 1975 Berlin Festival and is on a tape on deposit at RHA–LCL.

Sonata for Cello and Piano. Also performed at the 1975 Berlin Festival, by Siegfried Palm, cellist, and Aloys Kontarsky, pianist, it is also on a tape on deposit at RHA–LCL.

Symphony no. 1. There are two recordings, both with the Symphony no. 2 on the other side. Gary Bertini conducts the BBC Symphony Orchestra in no. 6 of the Calouste Gulbenkian Foundation Series (Argo ZRG 755); and Edo de Waart conducts the Leipzig Gewandhaus Orchestra (Philips 65006420).

The Divertimento for Small Orchestra and Male Chorus was conducted by Gary Bertini at the 1975 Berlin Festival and is on a tape owned by the Association of German Broadcasters.

Weill's transcription, for flute and piano, of Busoni's Op. 52 is performed by Severino Gazzeloni, flutist, along with works by Debussy, Varèse, and others, on Wergo WER 60029.

"The Song of the Fairies" from *Die Zaubernacht* was sung by Chrisseline Petropoulos, soprano, with the Chamber Orchestra of the Curtis Institute, on March 7, 1977, at the LCL auditorium. A tape of this performance is on deposit at RHA–LCL.

The *Recordare* (*Lamentationes Jeremiae Prophetae*) was performed at the Holland Festival, Utrecht, in 1973, by the Netherlands Radio Choir, conducted by Marinus Voorberg. Radio Nederland has produced a recording of this, though it is not for commercial distribution.

The *Quodlibet*, Op. 9, was recorded by Siegfried Landau conducting the Westphalian Symphony Orchestra (Candide QCE 31091).

There is more than one tape of the *Frauentanz*, Op. 10, but the one of special interest was made in 1957 by Margot Guillaume, soprano, with members of the North German Radio Symphony conducted by Busoni's old pupil and collaborator Philipp Jarnach. This can be heard at RHA–LCL.

There are at least three recordings of the Concerto for Violin and Wind Orchestra. The two earlier ones are: Robert Gerle, violin, with an orchestra conducted by Hermann Scherchen (Westminster WST–17087); and Anahid Ajemian, violin, with the MGM Wind Orchestra conducted by Izler Solomon (MGM E 3179). More recently, a performance by Nona Liddell, violin, with members of the London Sinfonietta conducted by David Atherton, has been included in a three-record album of Weill's earlier works that will be mentioned frequently below (Deutsche Grammophon 2709 064).

Der Protagonist has not yet been commercially recorded in full. The First Pantomime is performed by David Atherton with the London Sinfonietta in the Deutsche Grammophon album mentioned just above. The Second Pantomime has been taped by the RAI Rome Orchestra, but this tape is difficult to obtain.

Der neue Orpheus, Op. 15, is on a tape as performed by Anja Silja, soprano, and Hans Meier, violinist, with members of the Berlin Radio Symphony Orchestra under the direction of Gary Bertini at the 1975 Berlin Festival; on deposit at RHA–LCL.

Der Zar lässt sich photographieren. The *"Tango Angèle"* was performed at the 1978 Holland Festival by members of the London Sinfonietta, under the direction of David Atherton, and a tape of this performance is owned by Radio Nederland.

Two recordings of the *Mahagonny Songspiel* can be mentioned: one is part of the above-mentioned album made by David Atherton and the London Sinfonietta (Deutsche Grammophon 2709 064); the other is conducted by Lukas Foss, with the Jerusalem Symphony (Turnabout TV 34675).

"*Vom Tod im Wald*" is sung by Michael Rippon, bass, with Atherton and members of the London Sinfonietta in the three-record album already cited.

"*Die Muschel von Margate*" can be heard in a purely instrumental rendition, in an arrangement of questionable value, on the record of selections made by Peter Sandloff and his orchestra, *Kurt Weill in Berlin* (Angel 35727).

The definitive recording, in German, of *The Threepenny Opera* is the one made in Berlin in 1958 under the supervision of Lotte Lenya, with her in the role of Jenny, and with the orchestra and chorus conducted by Wilhelm Brückner-Rüggeberg. It contains both "The Ballad of Sexual Need" and "Lucy's Aria"; it also follows the later tradition of having the "Pirate Jenny" song performed by Spelunken-Jenny. Originally produced as Columbia 02S 201, it has been reissued as Odyssey Y2–32977, both in two-disc albums. As for the original Berlin recording of 1930, also starring Lotte Lenya, this has been reissued on LP several times; one of the most recent reissues is in the Telefunken *Dokumente* series (6.41911 AJ), also including three selections from the French film version. The Telefunken TH 97012 reissue, an earlier one, contains jacket copy that I quote in my text. Another recent recording in German was made by members of the Vienna State Opera, the orchestra conducted by F. Charles Adler (Vanguard SRV 2735D). Brecht's own renditions of two of the songs can be heard on Top Classic–Historia H 625, which also reproduces the 1930 Berlin recording of the score.

As for *The Threepenny Opera* in English, the Blitzstein version as performed by the original cast of the Theatre de Lys revival is still available (MGM S–31210C). The Ralph Manheim–John Willett translation, as performed by the cast of the 1976 revival at the Vivian Beaumont Theater, New York, is available on Columbia PS 34326.

There are innumerable recordings of individual numbers from *The Threepenny Opera*, but special mention should be made here of Lotte Lenya's performances, in German, of the "Moritat of Mackie Messer," the "Barbara Song," and the "Pirate Jenny" song on her classic recording of *Berlin Theatre Songs by Kurt Weill*, originally issued by Columbia as KL 5056, but now part of the two-record *Lotte Lenya Album* (Columbia MG 30087); also of Louis Armstrong's rendition of "Mack the Knife," which can be heard on various discs, such as *Louis Armstrong and Eddie Condon at Newport* (Columbia CL 931).

There are several recordings of the *Kleine Dreigroschenmusik*, including one performed by David Atherton with the London Sinfonietta in the three-record album, already cited, issued by Deutsche Grammophon. Of special interest is the one made in 1962 by Otto Klemperer, who had originally commissioned the piece and given it its first performance back in 1929; it is with the Philharmonia Orchestra of London.

The *Berlin Requiem* is performed by David Atherton and the London Sinfonietta in the three-record Deutsche Grammophon album. Lotte Lenya sings "The Drowned Maiden" on *Berlin Theatre Songs by Kurt Weill*, now part of *The Lotte Lenya Album*.

There is a recording of *The Lindbergh Flight* on the German Thorofon label (MTH 118, under the title *Ozeanflug*) which is hard to obtain. Three tapes are on deposit at RHA–LCL: RAI Orchestra, Rome, conducted by Michael Gielen; BBC Symphony Orchestra, conducted by Colin Davis; New York Choral Society, conducted by Robert De Cormier.

The only complete recording so far of the *Aufstieg und Fall der Stadt Mahagonny* is the one made in Berlin in 1956 under the supervision of Lotte Lenya, with her in the role of Jenny, and with the North German Radio Chorus and Orchestra under the direction of Wilhelm Brückner-Rüggeberg (Columbia K3L 243). For the most part, this is a good performance, but a few of the numbers suffer because of the limitations of Lenya's range as a singer. One should also mention her renditions of three of the songs on the *Berlin Theatre Songs by Kurt Weill*, cited above; and her 1931 recordings of the "Alabama Song" and "*Wie man sich bettet*" reproduced on the above-mentioned Telefunken *Dokumente* disc and others.

Neither of the two *Happy End* recordings is completely satisfactory. On one of them (Columbia Special Products COS–2032), with Wilhelm Brückner-Rüggeberg conducting, Lotte Lenya does all of the songs: this is a nice star turn, but it does not give a proper sense of the score. In the performance by David Atherton with soloists, chorus, and the London Sinfonietta that forms another portion of the three-record Deutsche Grammophon album, the numbers are properly performed, but there are two major flaws: the order of the numbers has been changed in accordance with an unconvincing notion of a suitable concert sequence, and, on the same principle, the "Bilbao Song" has been eliminated entirely. Lotte Lenya also performs three of the songs on her *Berlin Theatre Songs by Kurt Weill*.

"*Das Lied von den braunen Inseln*" and "*Zu Potsdam unter den Eichen*" can be heard in purely instrumental arrangements, again of questionable value, as performed by Peter Sandloff and his orchestra on *Kurt Weill in Berlin*.

A fine recording of *Der Jasager* has been made by Siegfried Kohler conducting the Düsseldorf Children's Chorus and Chamber Orchestra, with Josef Protschka as the young boy, Lys Bert as the mother, and Willibald Vohla as the teacher (Heliodor H/HS 25025).

A tape was made of the 1957 Berlin Festival performance of *Die Bürgschaft*, conducted by Hermann Scherchen. The libretto for this performance was somewhat revised by Caspar Neher himself, and some severe cuts were made in the score, particularly in the second act. The tape, a copy of which is on deposit at RHA–LCL, is cut off just before the opera's finale.

Der Silbersee was recorded in a performance at the 1971 Holland Festival, with Gary Bertini conducting the Concertgebouw Orchestra, and with Lotte Lenya in the role of Frau von Luber; but it was never commercially distributed. Copies of it (Unique Opera Records UORC 261) are on deposit at LCM and at RHA–LCL, among other places. A concert performance of most of the *Silbersee* musical numbers, with their order somewhat changed, was given at the 1975 Berlin Festival by the Berlin Radio Symphony Orchestra under the direction of Gary Bertini; this is on tape, copies of which are owned by RHA–LCL and the Association of German Broadcasters, among others. Two of the songs from this score, *"Lied der Fennimore"* and the *"Ballade von Cäsars Tod,"* are performed by Lotte Lenya on *Berlin Theatre Songs by Kurt Weill*.

Lotte Lenya recorded *The Seven Deadly Sins* in Berlin in 1956, with male quartet and orchestra under the direction of Wilhelm Brückner-Rüggeberg (Columbia Special Products, CKL 5175). It has also been recorded by Gisela May, a former member of the Berliner Ensemble, with the Radio Symphony Orchestra of Leipzig, under the direction of Herbert Kegel (Deutsche Grammophon SLPM 139 308). May sings in the same lower key as that which Weill had provided for Lenya as an alternative to what he first had written; the piece has yet to be recorded in the original higher key.

Symphony no. 2. See the entry for Symphony no. 1.

"Complainte de la Seine" is sung by Lotte Lenya in the three-disc 78 rpm album issued by Decca in 1943, *Six Songs of Kurt Weill* (Decca 5017–9), in which she performs all the songs with piano accompaniment. Other songs in this album are: "Lost in the Stars," "Lover Man" (the earlier version of "Trouble Man"), *"J'attends un navire,"* "Surabaya Johnny," and *"Wie man sich bettet."*

Marie Galante has never been recorded as a whole, but four of the seven numbers can be found on various recordings. *"J'attends un navire"* is sung very well by the Italian singer Laura Betti on *Kurt Weill 1933–1950* (Orrizonte ORL 8028), with an orchestra conducted by Bruno Maderna; by Lotte Lenya on the above-mentioned *Six Songs of Kurt Weill;* and by Margery Cohen on *Berlin to Broadway with Kurt Weill* (Paramount Records, PAS 4000), a recording of the 1972 Theatre de Lys production of that name. *"Les Filles de Bordeaux"* and *"Le Roi d'Aquitaine"* are sung by Florelle, the original Marie Galante, on Polydor 524012. *"Le Roi d'Aquitaine"* also is sung by Catherine Sauvage on *Songs of Kurt Weill* (Epic LC 3489), which also includes Les Quatre Barbus singing *"Le Grand Lustucru,"* a fourth song from *Marie Galante; "Le Grand Lustucru"* also is sung by Laura Betti in her recording mentioned above. Martha Schlamme sings *"Le Roi d'Aquitaine"* on two of her recordings, *The World of Kurt Weill in Song* (MGM E 4052) and *A Kurt Weill Cabaret* (MGM E 4180).

"Nanna's Lied" is performed, in the French version, by Catherine Sauvage on the above-mentioned *Songs of Kurt Weill* (Epic LC 3489).

A recording of most of the musical numbers of *Johnny Johnson* was made in 1957, with Burgess Meredith as Johnny, Evelyn Lear as Minny Belle, and Lotte Lenya in the role of the French nurse; the orchestra is conducted by Samuel Matlowsky (formerly MGM E 3447, it is now Heliodor H/HS 25024).

A condensed version of *Knickerbocker Holiday*, starring Walter Huston in his Stuyvesant role, was produced for radio in 1939 by the Theatre Guild on the Air; this was recorded, and a limited number of copies has long been in existence. In about 1976 a producer called Joey Discs in Lawton, Maryland, issued a simulated stereo edition of this recording (Joey–7243), which could be found in record stores for a brief time. This, of course, is one of several discs that reproduce Huston's splendid rendition of "September Song"; it includes six of the show's other numbers besides. Three of the show's songs not included on this recording—"The One Indispensable Man," "Our Ancient Liberties," and "Dirge for a Soldier"— were sung by Barry McDaniel, accompanied by Oliver Dreimann at the piano, at the Berlin Festival in 1975, and a tape of this performance is on deposit at RHA–LCL. One should also mention Bing Crosby's 78 rpm recording of the "September Song" (Decca 23754, 10"), which helped make it famous.

The Ballad of Magna Carta was performed in the United States Capitol on June 3, 1976, by the United States Air Force Symphony Orchestra. A tape of this performance was made available to me by the kind efforts of Col. Roger L. Williams, USAF; it is an Official United States Air Force Symphony Orchestra Recording.

A nearly complete recording of the musical sequences of *Lady in the Dark*, excluding a few brief sections and the "Dance of the Tumblers," was made under the direction of Lehman Engel, with Risë Stevens as Liza Elliott, Adolph Green as Russell Paxton, and John Reardon as Randy Curtis (Columbia Special Products COS–2390). Gertrude Lawrence's old 78 rpm album of selections has been reproduced on LP, with Weill's *Down in the Valley* on the other side, as part of the RCA Victor Vintage Series (LPV–503). The "Dance of the Tumblers," a purely instrumental piece, is performed by Arthur Winograd and the MGM Chamber Orchestra on a recording of Weill selections made in the 1950s (MGM E 3334). Danny Kaye sings "Tschaikowsky" on various recordings, such as *Danny Kaye Entertains* (Columbia CL 931).

Helen Hayes's album of patriotic texts, recited to musical settings by Kurt Weill, was made for RCA Victor in 1942 and was called *Mine Eyes Have Seen the Glory*.

A 78 rpm recording of the *Three Walt Whitman Songs* was issued in the 1940s by Concert Hall Records, in two discs, with William Horne, tenor, and Adam Garner, piano. Alan Titus sang them at the LCL auditorium on March 7, 1977, and this performance is on a tape at RHA–LCL.

Lotte Lenya's performances, accompanied by Kurt Weill at the piano, of *"Und Was bekam des Soldaten Weib?"*, text by Bertolt Brecht, and *"Wie lange noch?"*, text by Walter Mehring, are on a tape on deposit at RHA–LCL. This is the only record or tape in existence on which Lenya and Weill perform together.

An album of selections from *One Touch of Venus*, sung by Mary Martin and Kenny Baker and performed by the orchestra under the direction of Maurice Abravanel, was issued on 78 rpm at the time of the show, and was subsequently reissued in the 1960s on LP (Decca Stereo DL 79122). This includes the two ballets, but several important numbers are left out; and one of those included —"Westwind"—is misleadingly sung on the record by Kenny Baker, whereas it was John Boles's song in the show. Two other songs from the show that are not on this recording—"Very, Very, Very" and "The Jersey Block" (dropped from the score)—along with some that are, can be heard sung by Kurt Weill himself on *Tryout* (Heritage LP–H 0051), an LP made in 1953 from rehearsal records cut by Weill when the show was being created. The title song, "One Touch of Venus," is sung by Greta Keller on *Greta Keller Sings Kurt Weill* (Atlantic ALS 405 10"); this is not included in the Decca show recording. Another *Venus* number not included on the Decca recording, "The New Art," was included in the condensed version of the show produced on radio for *The Railroad Hour* on April 16, 1951, a tape of which is on deposit at RHA–LCL.

The sound track of *Where Do We Go from Here?* has yet to be recorded commercially, but Ira Gershwin, accompanied by Kurt Weill at the piano and sometimes vocally, sang much of the score for a series of rehearsal recordings. Some of these were reproduced on the *Tryout* record mentioned just above, but more recently they have been assembled in their entirety in the two-record LP album, *Ira Gershwin Loves to Rhyme*, issued by Mark56 Records (no. 721), Anaheim, California. The performance of the Christopher Columbus sequence in particular, in which Weill frequently joins in on the singing, belongs in a prominent place among the curiosities of recorded music.

No show recording of *The Firebrand of Florence* ever was made, but in this case, too, a large part of the score was done on rehearsal records by Gershwin and Weill, and these also have been reproduced on the above-mentioned *Ira Gershwin Loves to Rhyme*. The duet "Love is My Enemy," not on the Mark56 recording, was performed by Chrisseline Petropoulos and Alan Titus at the LCL auditorium on March 7, 1977, and this is on a tape on deposit at RHA–LCL.

A tape of the *Kiddush*, as performed by Cantor Murray E. Simon of Temple Israel, Boston, is on deposit at RHA–LCL.

A recording of selections from *Street Scene* was made at the time of the original run, performed by the original cast, and this has been reissued as an LP record (Columbia Special Products COL 4139). A commercial recording of the complete opera has yet to be made, but the performance of it given at the Manhattan School of Music on February 29, 1976, under the direction of Anton Coppola, is on tape; copies of it are at the school and at RHA–LCL, among other places.

Two recordings of *Down in the Valley* were made under Weill's supervision shortly before his death, and both are now on LP. Both have minor cuts in the score. The RCA Victor recording, now in the Vintage Series with Gertrude Lawrence's *Lady in the Dark* selections on the other side (LPV–503), is conducted by Peter Herman Adler, and features Marion Bell, soprano, as Jennie, and William McGraw, baritone, as Brack. Jane Wilson and Alfred Drake sing these roles on the Decca recording (DL 74239), conducted by Maurice Levine.

No show recording of *Love Life* ever was made, but seven of its songs, sung by Alan Jay Lerner, by Kaye Ballard, and by accompanists, can be heard on the Heritage Record *Alan Jay Lerner Sings His Own Songs* (LP–H 0060). "Susan's Dream," sung on this record by Kaye Ballard, also can be heard sung by Martha Schlamme on her MGM record mentioned above, *The World of Kurt Weill in Song*. "Green-Up Time," sung by Kaye Ballard on the Heritage record, is performed by Lotte Lenya on her recording *September Song and Other American Theatre Songs of Kurt Weill* (Columbia KL 5229), which has been reissued, with the old *Berlin Theatre Songs by Kurt Weill*, as part of a two-record set, *The Lotte Lenya Album* (Columbia MG 30087).

Most of the score of *Lost in the Stars* is on the original cast recording issued by Decca (DL 79120). An instrumental version of the song "Gold," which was dropped from the score, is performed by Arthur Winograd and the MGM Chamber Orchestra on MGM E 3334.

A tape of the 1964 German television production of *Raft on the River* (*Huckleberry Finn*) is on deposit at RHA–LCL.

Acknowledgments

This has been what is often called an "unauthorized" biography. That is to say, Lotte Lenya, who is Kurt Weill's widow and the owner of his estate, has not given me her cooperation in my research on the book—except for a single interview, which she granted on May 27, 1976. But there has been abundant material for a biography all the same, since Weill published many works, gave many interviews, wrote many letters that I have been able to see, and had many friends and collaborators, some of whom I have been in touch with, others of whom have had their experiences recorded either by themselves or by others. In the paragraphs that follow and the pages that immediately precede, the reader will perceive that this life study has been amply documented.

I am grateful to a number of people who knew Kurt Weill and one or another of his worlds at first hand and who gave me the benefit of their recollections either in personal conversation, by telephone, by letter, or through intermediaries. In alphabetical order, they are: Maurice Abravanel, Alan H. Anderson, George Balanchine, Fritz Bamberger, Alice Bing, Harold Clurman, Aaron Copland, Cheryl Crawford, Lehman Engel, Ira Gershwin, Paul Green, E. Y. Harburg, Hans W. Heinsheimer, Pearl Lang, Rouben Mamoulian, Cantor David J. Putterman, Harold Rome, Wolfgang Roth, Victor Samrock, Julie Sonder, Morris Stonzek, Lee Strasberg, H. H. Stuckenschmidt, Wladimir Vogel, Rita Weill, Meyer Weisgal, Eric Werner, Joseph Wiseman, Ernst Wolff, and Herman Wouk. I also am especially grateful to Fritz Bamberger for having read and criticized portions of the manuscript of this book, and to Paul Green for having made his papers available to me.

I also want to thank the following institutions, organizations, and archives, and in some cases the persons at those places who were particularly helpful: The Association of German Broadcasters, especially their U.S. Representative, David Berger, and his assistant, Mrs. Marlis Nast; the Leo Baeck Institute, especially Sybil Milton; the Brüder-Busch-Gesellschaft, especially Wolfgang Burbach; the manuscript division of the Butler Library, Columbia University; Chappell Music Company, especially Daphne Beck; the Dutch Consulate in New York, and Radio Nederland, especially J. H. Scheltema; European American Music, Inc.; Goethe House; the Humanities Research Center of the University of Texas at Austin, especially Ellen S. Dunlap; the Library of Congress, Music Division, especially Wayne Shirley; the Library and Museum of Performing Arts, Lincoln Center, especially the staffs of the Music Division, the Theatre Arts Collection, and the Rodgers and Hammerstein Archives of Recorded Sound; the Morris Library, Southern Illinois University at Carbondale, especially Kenneth W. Ducket; the Mugar Memorial Library, Boston University, especially Dr. H. B. Gotlieb; the Museum of the City of New York, especially Mary Henderson; the Museum of Modern Art Film Study Center; the Richmond Organization, especially Jay Mark; the Southern Historical Collection, University of North Carolina Library, Chapel Hill; the State Historical Society of Wisconsin, Archives Division, especially Dr. Josephine L. Harper; the United States Air Force Office of Information, especially Colonel Roger L. Williams.

In addition, I received valuable help or advice from Jervis Anderson, Gabrielle Bamberger, Edgar Carter, Dominic Garvey, Leon Gersten, Judith Gingold, Barbara Horgan, Michael Pender, and Ian Strasfogel. I am especially grateful to Mr. Strasfogel for reading portions of the manuscript.

From my editor, Marian Wood, and my literary agent, Georges Borchardt, I received encouragement and moral support beyond the call of duty.

But it is especially gratifying, at this point, to be able to replace the usual "last but not least" with an emphatic "above all": for my wife, Beverly Sanders, did far more than provide advice, criticism, and moral support. She shared the tasks of research with me equally, played the piano to my singing as we made our way through the entire Kurt Weill canon, typed the manuscript, and single-handedly gathered the photographs that appear on these pages. This, then, is only the beginning of the thanks that I shall always give to her.

INDEX

453